John Dowson

The History of India as Told by Its Own Historians the Muhammadan Period

John Dowson

The History of India as Told by Its Own Historians the Muhammadan Period

ISBN/EAN: 9783741176753

Manufactured in Europe, USA, Canada, Australia, Japa

Cover: Foto ©Thomas Meinert / pixelio.de

Manufactured and distributed by brebook publishing software (www.brebook.com)

John Dowson

The History of India as Told by Its Own Historians the Muhammadan Period

THE HISTORY OF INDIA.

THE

HISTORY OF INDIA,

AS TOLD

BY ITS OWN HISTORIANS.

THE MUHAMMADAN PERIOD.

EDITED FROM THE POSTHUMOUS PAPERS
OF THE LATE
SIR H. M. ELLIOT, K.C.B.,
EAST INDIA COMPANY'S BENGAL CIVIL SERVICE,

BY

PROFESSOR JOHN DOWSON, M.R.A.S.,
STAFF COLLEGE, SANDHURST.

VOL. II.

LONDON:
TRÜBNER AND CO., 60, PATERNOSTER ROW.
1869.
[*All rights reserved.*]

STEPHEN AUSTIN

PRINTER, HERTFORD.

PREFACE.

In this volume the history of Muhammadan rule in India is commenced. The first volume was, from the nature of the materials, introductory in its character; this opens with the accounts of the earliest inroads of the Ghaznivide conquerors. The copious extracts which it brings together from the oldest and most approved of the native historians supply ample means for tracing the rise and progress of that power which was destined to bring the whole peninsula under its sway, and to stand for seven centuries a conspicuous and brilliant example of the strength and weakness, the crimes, vices, and occasional virtues of Musulmán despotism.

The history is here carried down to the year 1260 A.D., embracing the consecutive annals of the Ghaznivides, the Ghorians, and the Slave Kings, as far as the end of the reign of Násiru-d dín. The lives of the other Slave Kings will be drawn from the *Táríkh-i Fíroz Sháhí* of Zíáu-d dín Barní, which, as its name implies, is a work more particularly devoted to the reign of Fíroz

Sháh, and must, from the date of its composition, occupy a place in the next volume.

The portion of history over which this volume extends may be considered as nearly complete, though some scattered notices of the period embraced will be drawn occasionally from later writers, and Khondamír's account of the Ghaznivides will appear hereafter as the principal extract from the *Habíbu-s Siyar*.

Since the publication of the first volume of this edition, some animadversions have appeared in print upon the absence of any recognition of the assistance rendered to Sir H. M. Elliot in the preparation of the materials for this work; and one or two special claims have been made for acknowledgments of aid contributed and work done. The Editor is informed, by those best acquainted with the circumstances, that Sir H. M. Elliot was especially anxious to acquit himself of all obligation for assistance so rendered to him; but still, care has been and will be taken to acknowledge fully every contribution deserving of notice. It so happened, however, that the whole of the matter in the first volume, with the exception of two anonymous translations, was the work of Sir H. M. Elliot himself, his munshis, or the present Editor.

Sir H. M. Elliot was assisted by many friends, both English and native, in his search for rare works, and notably by Dr. Sprenger; but at this distance of time it is impossible to do more than make a general acknowledgment of the fact. The notices, bibliographical and biographical, all appear to have been written by Sir H. M. Elliot himself, with the exception of those of the geographers and a few distinguished by brackets, which are the work of the Editor. There remain the translations, and it is in these that the greatest aid was received. Many of the contributed translations are by English officers, both civil and military; and many more by munshis. They differ greatly in merit; some are valuable, others require the Editor's incessant attention from beginning to end,[1] and in two instances it has been found necessary to entirely reject the work done. Under these circumstances, the Editor has resolved to make no general acknowledgment, but to give the translator's name whenever that name carries with it sufficient assurance, or when a translation proves to be accurate, and in want of little or no editorial revision. By this arrangement, the translator will bear the responsibility of his own work; and the extent and value of the aid rendered will be fully understood and appreciated by the reader. In cases of translations which require to be

[1] In pages 70 and 88 will be found two short passages showing the quality of one of these translations—a fair specimen of many others.

checked and amended throughout, no name has been or will be given. The original translator cannot lay claim to the revised work, and there are few who would like their names to appear as the authors of translations obnoxious to correction.

To set this question entirely at rest, the Editor here gives a complete list of the translations which appear in the first and in the present volume, with the names of those who are responsible for them. From this it will be seen that no one has any real ground of complaint. The list is confined to the translations, because all else is the work of Sir H. M. Elliot or the Editor, except a few contributions specially and scrupulously recognized where they appear.

VOL. I.
GEOGRAPHERS.

The bibliographical notices are by the Editor, excepting the notice of the Ashkálu-l Bilád, No. V., which is chiefly by Sir H. M. Elliot.

    I.—Salsilatu-t Tawárikh—Translated from Reinaud's French version by the Editor.

    II. III.—Ibn Khurdádba and Mas'údi—Translations printed in the old volume revised by Editor.

    IV.—Istakhrí—Editor.

    V.—Ashkálu-l Bilád—Partially revised by Editor.

    VI.—Súru-l Duldán—None.

    VII.—Jámi'u-t Tawárikh—The old translation revised after a collation of the various MSS. by the Editor.

    VIII.—Idrisi—Translated from Jaubert's French version by the Editor.

    IX.—Kazwíní—Editor.

PREFACE.

HISTORIANS.

I.—Mujmalu-t Tawáríkh—Sir H. M. E. and the Editor.
II.—Biládurí—Sir H. M. E. and the Editor.
III.—Chach-náma—A munshi, revised by the Editor.
IV.—Ma'súmí—Page 237 to 240 by Sir H. M. E., all the rest by Editor.
V.—Táríkh-i Táhirí—Lt. Perkins.[1]
VI.—Beg-Lár-náma }
VII.—Tarkhán-náma } A munshi, revised by the Editor.
VIII.—Tuhfatu-l Kirám—Anonymous, but revised by the Editor and found to be accurate.
Appendix.—Sir H. M. E., excepting where brackets show the Editor's work.

VOL. II.

I.—Táríkhu-l Hind }
II.—'Utbí } Sir H. M. E.
III.—Baihakí—From page 61 to 129 by a munshi, and although said to have been revised, it required very extensive correction by the Editor; page 129 to 154 by Sir H. M. E.
IV.—Jámi'u-l Hikáyát—A munshi, whose style had been improved by an Englishman, but the translation needed a thorough revision by the Editor.
V.—Nizámu-t Tawáríkh—Sir H. M. E.
VI.—Kámilu-t Tawáríkh—Editor.
VII.—Táju-l Ma-ásir—Sir H. M. E.
VIII.—Tabakát-i Násirí—Page 266 to 359, a munshi, revised and sundry long gaps filled up by the Editor; page 360 to 383* by the Editor.
IX.—Jahán-Kushá—Sir H. M. E.

---

[1] This translation bore no name, but the Editor has reason for believing it to be the work of Lt. Perkins. It was checked by the Editor and found to be very correct.

[2] Translations of this and of sundry other portions of the Tabakát-i Násirí had been made by an English officer; but the Editor, with every desire to make use of them and save himself labour, was obliged to reject them. Prefixed to the translations were the following notes, the later one written after Sir H. M. Elliot's death. These of themselves will show that no harsh judgment has been exercised:—

"This translation is imperfect. By allowing myself great latitude in guessing at the author's meaning, supplying words, sometimes whole passages, I have succeeded in making it appear a somewhat connected narrative. Had I marked in the margin

APPENDIX.

The various Notes are the work of Sir H. M. Elliot, excepting where the brackets show the Editor's additions, or special references are made to the sources of information, as in Notes D. and E.

Note C.—The translations of the extracts were made by munshis, and have been revised by the Editor.

Note F.—Majma'l Wasáyá—A munshi, unrevised.

Nigáristán,
Zínatu-l Majális. } A munshi, revised by the Editor.

Note G.—Mir-át-i Mas'údí—Translated by R. D. Chapman, Esq., B.C.S.
Note II.—Extracts translated by Sir H. M. E.

all the passages which were doubtful, I find I should have to mark the whole translation almost ; I have therefore only marked those which are more especially obscure, and when the meaning appeared to be of more than usual importance.

" N. B.—This translation was done and the remarks in the margin made under the impression that it would be looked over by Sir H. M. Elliot."

PORTRAIT.

The Portrait prefixed to this volume has been copied from a sketch made by an amateur on the occasion of one of Lord Dalhousie's official receptions. As chance would have it, this is the only likeness of Sir Henry Elliot extant, otherwise, neither the formal costume nor the profile face would have recommended themselves as best calculated to convey an effective representation of the author.

CONTENTS.

I. *Táríkhu-l Hind* of Birúní
II. *Táríkh Yamíní* of 'Utbí
III. *Táríkhu-s Subuktigín* of Baihakí
IV. *Jámi'u-l Hikáyát* of Muhammad 'Úfí
V. *Táju-l Ma-ásir* of Hasan Nizámí
VI. *Kámilu-t Tawáríkh* of Ibn Asír
VII. *Nizámu-t Tawáríkh* of Baizáwí
VIII. *Tabakát-i Násirí* of Minháju-s Siráj
IX. *Jahán Kushá* of Juwainí

APPENDIX.

NOTE A.—The Hindu Kings of Kábul
B.—Extract from Thomas' Prinsep
C.—The Historians of the Ghaznivides
D.—Mahmud's Expeditions to India
E.—Coins of the Ghaznivides and Ghorians
F.—Extracts from Story-books:—
    1. *Majma'-i Wasáyá*
    2. *Nigáristán*
    3. *Zínatu-l Majális*
G.—Extracts from the *Mir-át-i Mas'údí*
H.—Jalálu-d dín on the Indus
I.—The Karmatians
J.—Geographical Notes

ERRATA.

Page 76, line 3 from the bottom, substitute "Manjurán" for "the wine-drinkers (mai-khurán)."—A subsequent passage shows the true reading.

Page 129.—For "July, 1033" read "July, 1034."

" 157.—For "(This last contains only) *the first two kisms,*" substitute "— part of the first kism as far as Chapter 23, where it ends abruptly."

" 204.—For No. "IV." read "V."

" 249.—To note add, "See Vol. I. p. 445."

" 276.—In note 2, for "words" read "word."

" 485.—For Appendix "E" read "F."

HISTORIANS OF INDIA.

I.

TÁRÍKHU-L HIND

OF

ABU' RÍHÁN AL BÍRÚNÍ.

ABÚ RÍHÁN[1] MUHAMMAD BIN AHMAD AL BÍRÚNÍ AL KHWÁR-IZMÍ, was born[2] about A.H. 360, A.D. 970-1. He was an astronomer, geometrician, historian, and logician. He was so

---

[1] Raihán would be more correct, according to the Kámús. In Drigg's *Firishta* (p. 113), the name is strangely perverted into "Asrury Khán."

[2] The place of his birth is disputed. His earliest biographer is Shahrazúrí, who, in his *Tawárikh-i Hukamá*, written shortly after Bírúní's death, says that he was born at Birún, in Sind, "a beautiful city full of excellent and marvellous things." He has been followed by Hájí Khalfa, by Ibn Abú Usaibiah, and by Abú-l Fidá, on the authority of Ibn Sa'íd. M. Reinaud also states that he was a Sindian. Yet, where is this city of Birún in Sind? There is a Nírún, or Nírún Kot, near the site of the present city of Haidarábád, corresponding in position with the Birún indicated by Abú-l Fidá, which probably has had its first letter altered by a transposition of the vowel point. But M. Reinaud (p. 195) is distinct in condemning Capt. McMurdo and other English writers who, following Idrísí, read Nírún for Birún. Abú-l Fidá's reading cannot be disputed, for he not only gives, but describes the nature of, the diacritical point, and all that can be said against him is that he never was in India, and that he derived his information from others. (See Vol. I. Appx. p. 396.) In the *Kitábu-l Ansáb* by Sam'ání, a book of very great authority, written A.H. 562, A.D. 1166, Bírúní is derived from the Persian, and made to apply to any one born out of Khwárizm. Some authorities distinctly assert that he was born at Birún, a town of Khwárizm, but I know not if the existence of such a town has been established. Bírúní in his Indian Geography takes little notice of Sind, and says nothing of his birthplace. [The passage quoted from the "Quarterly Review," (*infra* p. 3) seems to decide the question, for Bírúní is there said to be a native of Khwárizm, and the whole tenor of the article confirms the statement.]

VOL. II. 1

studious that Shamsu-d dín Muhammad Shahrazúrí, his earliest biographer, tells us "he never had a pen out of his hand, nor his eye ever off a book, and his thoughts were always directed to his studies, with the exception of two days in the year, namely Nauroz [New Year's day at the vernal equinox], and Mihrján [the autumnal equinox], when he was occupied, according to the command of the Prophet, in procuring the necessaries of life on such a moderate scale as to afford him bare sustenance and clothing." [As a logician he obtained the sobriquet of "*Muhakkik*" or "the exact," on account of the rigorous precision of his deductions].[1]

[Abú-l Fazl Baihakí who lived about half a century after Al Bírúní, says, "Bú Ríhán was beyond comparison, superior to every man of his time in the art of composition, in scholarlike accomplishments, and in knowledge of geometry and philosophy. He had, moreover, a most rigid regard for truth;" and Rashídu-d dín, in referring to the great writer from whom he has borrowed so much, says "The Master Abú Ríhán al Bírúní excelled all his cotemporaries in the sciences of philosophy, mathematics, and geometry. He entered the service of Mahmúd bin Subuktigín, and in the course of his service he spent a long time in Hindustán and learned the language of the country. Several of the provinces of India were visited by him. He was on friendly terms with many of the great and noble of that country, and so acquired an intimate knowledge of their books of philosophy, religion, and belief. The best and most excellent of all their books upon the arts and sciences is one resembling the work of Shaikh Rais Abú 'Alí ibn Siná (Avicenna). It is called Bátakal, or in Arabic Bátajal; this book he translated into Arabic. From this work also he extracted a great deal which he made use of in his Kánún Mas'údi, a work upon mathematics and geometry, named after the Sultán Mas'úd. All that the sages of India have said about numbers, ages, and eras (*tawáríkh*), has been exactly given by Abú Ríhán in his translation of the Bátakal."]

[1] *Mémoire sur l'Inde*, p. 29.

He was indebted to the Sultán of Khwárizm for the opportunity of visiting India, for he was appointed by him to accompany the embassies which he sent to Mahmúd of Ghazní. Al Farábí and Abú-l Khair joined one of these embassies, but the famous Avicenna, who was invited to accompany them, refused to go, being, as it is hinted, averse to enter into controversy with Abú Ríhán, with whom he differed on many points of science, and whose logical powers he feared to encounter. [On the invitation of Mahmúd, Abú Ríhán entered into his service, an invitation which Avicenna declined. It was in the suite of Mahmúd and of his son Mas'úd that] Abú Ríhán travelled into India, and he is reported to have staid forty years there; but if we may judge from some errors that he has committed in his geographical description of the country, such as placing Thánesar in the Doáb, it would appear that he never travelled to the east of Lahore.[1] Abú Ríhán died in A.H. 430, A.D. 1038-9.

He wrote many works, and is said to have executed several translations from the Greek, and to have epitomised the Almagest of Ptolemy. His works are stated to have exceeded a camel-load, insomuch that it was supposed by devout Muhammadans that he received divine aid in his compositions. Those most spoken of are astronomical tables, a treatise on precious stones, one on Materia Medica, an introduction to astrology, a treatise on chronology, and the famous Kánúnu-l Mas'údí, an astronomical and geographical work frequently cited by Abú-l Fidá, especially in his tables of Lat. and Long. For this last work he received from the Emperor Mas'úd an elephant-load of silver, which, however, he returned to the Royal Treasury, "a proceeding contrary to human nature," according to the testimony of Shahrazúrí.

[An accomplished writer in a late number of the "Quarterly Review," observes: "Abú Ríhán a native of the country (of Khwárizm) was the only early Arab writer who investigated the antiquities of the East in a true spirit of historical criticism," and he proceeds to give some examples of his knowledge of ancient

[1] See note Vol. I. p. 353.

technical chronology which are of the highest importance in establishing the early civilization of the Arian race. According to this reviewer, Abú Ríhán says, "the solar calendar of Khwárizm, was the most perfect scheme for measuring time with which he was acquainted, and it was maintained by the astronomers of that country, that both the solar and the lunar zodiacs had originated with them; the divisions of the signs in their systems being far more regular than those adopted by the Greeks or Arabs. * * * Another statement of Abú Ríhán's asserts that the Khwárizmians dated originally from an epoch anterior by 980 years to the era of the Seleucidæ (equal to B.C. 1304), a date which agrees pretty accurately with the period assigned by our best scholars to the invention of the Jyotisha or Indian calendar."[1] This most curious and interesting information, for which we are indebted to the writer in the "Quarterly," raises higher than ever the reputation of Abú Ríhán, and must intensify the desire so long felt for a complete translation of his extant works.]

The names of his writings are given in full by Reiske in the Supplement to the *Bibl. Or.* on the authority of Abú Usaibiah. The work by which he is best known, and which to the cultivator of Indian history is the most important, of all his works is the Tárikhu-l Hind in Arabic. A manuscript of this work, or of a portion of it, is in the Imperial Library, Paris (*Fonds Ducaurroy*, No. 22), and from this MS. M. Reinaud extracted two chapters which he published in the *Journal Asiatique*, and separately in his "*Fragments Arabes et Persans inédits relatifs a l' Inde antérieurement au* xi. *siècle de l'ère Chrétienne.*" [The work, according to M. Reinaud, was written in India in 1031 A.D., and he observes upon it—"Cet écrit est un tableau de l'état littéraire et scientifique de la presqu'île, au moment ou les armées musulmanes y pénétrèrent pour la première fois. On y voit successivement apparaitre les principaux travaux littéraires, philosophiques et astronomiques des Indious, le tableau de leurs ères, la manière

[1] "Quarterly Review," No. 240, p. 490.

dont ils comptaient les jours, les mois, les années et les cycles."[1] Sir H. Rawlinson possesses a MS. of a part of Al Birúni's works,][2] and there is a manuscript of some portions thereof mentioned by M. Hœnel as existing in the Library of the Arsenal at Paris. This MS. appears to be the one noticed by D'Herbelot in the article *Athar*, [and to be the same as that "which was formerly much referred to by M. Quatremère under the title 'Athár el Bákieh.'"[3]] The *Táríkhu-l Hind* is not known at all in India, and M. Reinaud states that it is not mentioned in any of the bibliographical works in Arabic which have come under his observation. It will be seen hereafter that Abú-l Fazl Baihakí attributes to him another work, "A History of Khwárizm," which is noticed by M. Froehn in his catalogue.[4]

The *Táríkhu-l Hind* treats of the literature and science of the Indians at the commencement of the eleventh century. It does not bear the name of the author, but we learn from it, that he accompanied Mahmúd of Ghazní; that he resided many years in India, chiefly, in all probability, in the Panjáb, studied the Sanskrit language, translated into it some works from the Arabic, and translated from it two treatises into Arabic. This statement is confirmed by Abú-l Faraj, in his "Catalogue of Ancient and Modern Authors." Birúni says, towards the end of his preface, "I have translated into Arabic two Indian works, one discusses the origin and quality of things which exist, and is entitled Sankhya, the other is known under the title of Patanjali,[5] which treats of the deliverance of the soul from the trammels of the body. These two works contain the chief principles of the Indian creed."[6]

Neither the original nor the translation of this work [presumed

---

[1] [*Mém. sur l'Inde* p. 30.]
[2] [This fact, and the general character of the article in the "Review," which probably no one else in Europe could have written, afford sufficient indication of the writer, Sir H. Rawlinson.]
[3] ["Quarterly Review," No. 240, p. 490, note; *Mém. sur l'Inde*, p. 30.]
[4] *Indications Bibl.* p. 28.
[5] [See Note, next page.]   [6] Reinaud's *Fragments*, p. xlii.

to be that] of Patanjali has descended to us; but as M. Reinaud
observes, the declaration quoted in the preceding paragraph serves
to indicate the author of the *Tárikhu-l Hind*, which other circumstances would have rendered extremely probable. Rashidu-d dín,
in his history, quotes as one of the works to which he is indebted
for his information, an Arabic version of "the Bátakal," made
by Al-Bírúní.[1] Binákiti also mentions this translation of the

---

[1] [The Sanskrit work translated by Abú Ríhán has, upon this identification
made by Reinaud, been unhesitatingly believed to have been the production
of the sage Patanjali, a well-known philosopher and Vedic commentator and
grammarian (Müller's Sanskrit Lit. p. 236.) The description given of that work
by Abú Ríhán accords very well with the sage's writings; but the specimens
which we have of the work in the published fragments of Al Bírúní, and in
their reproduction by Rashidu-d dín are of a very different character. The latter
writer says it was a book upon the arts and sciences, containing all that the sages
of India have written about numbers, ages, and eras, and accordingly we find the
book cited upon questions of chronology and geography. In the Extract printed
by M. Reinaud, the word is given distinctly as "Bátanjali," but I have not found
it so written in any of the MSS. of the Jámi'u-t Tawáríkh or of Binákití. The MS.
of the E. L. Library says "the name of the book is باتنكل which in Arabic they
write باسجل In the passage translated and printed in Vol. I. p. 44, it is written
باتجل and in another باسجل The Lucknow MS. has باتكل and
The Arabic MS. is equally explicit and says—

و لفظه باتنجل معرّبة و اصلها باتكل

"The word Bátajal is the Arabic form of what in the original is Bátakal."
(Judging from analogy there is but one letter between the *alif* and the *jím*, for the
t is so found written in words about which there can be no doubt, as تفرير) Here
we have the remarkable fact that the Arabic form of the name (Bátajal or Bátanjal)
is more like the presumed Sanskrit original (Patanjali) than the word Bátakal or
Bátankal, which is given as the exact or nearest transcription of that original word.
Mr. Morley found the word written Bánatakal or Bátanakal in two manuscripts
of Binákití (Jour. R. A. S. VI. 26). In the R. As. Soc.'s copy of Binákití it is
written باتنكل A Persian note prefixed to the MS. No. 16 of the R. As. Society,
and translated by Dr. Duncan Forbes, says, "After Abú Ríhán had made thorough
proficiency in the sciences of the Indian philosophers, he translated from the Indian
language into the Arabic tongue, the book of Pátankal, or Pátanjal [پاتنكل]
which is a collection of all the sciences, and one of the most valuable works of the
sages of Hind. * * * To this work he gave the name of Pátanjal, [پاتنجل]
a copy of which he carried away with him."—(Forbes, Jour. R.A.S. VI. p. 38.)
This note would seem to have been drawn from Rashidu-d dín's notice of Abú
Ríhán above quoted—and the spelling of the name of the book is identically the

work, and says that Bírúní included the translation in the Kánúnu-l Mas'údí,¹ but a close examination of the Kánún does not confirm this, for there is nothing special about India in the work.

The two chapters of his work, edited by M. Reinaud, relate to the eras and geography of India. Like the Chinese travels of Fa-hian and Hwen Tsang, they establish another fixed epoch to which we can refer for the determination of several points relating to the chronology of this country. We learn from them that the Harivansa Purána, which the most accomplished orientalists have hitherto ascribed to a period not anterior to the eleventh century, was already quoted in Birúní's time as a standard authority, and that the epoch of the composition of the five Siddhántas no longer admits of question, and thus the theories of Anquetil du Perron and Bentley are demolished for ever.³

The extract from the Táríkhu-l Hind given below is of great historical interest. The succession of the last princes of Kábul

same as in the MS. of the R. I. Library. It thus appears very questionable whether the sage Patanjali is really the author referred to, but at any rate it is certain that no Sanskrit work bearing his name has yet been discovered which at all corresponds to the book used by Abú Ríhán. If a guess may be ventured on, the final syllable *kal* is possibly the Sanskrit *kala*, "time."]

¹ M. Reinaud (p. 97) says of this work that "unfortunately it has not come down to us." It appears to have escaped him that nearly the entire first volume exists in the Bodleian Library, collated with the autograph of the author, and dated as far back as A.D. 1083. The contents of that volume are given in Dr. Nicoll's and Pusey's Catalogue. In the notes to that article the learned Doctors have surely taken very unnecessary trouble to write elaborate remarks upon Arín ارین, which can be no other place than Ujain, in Malwa, which by Bílídurí (Vol. I. p. 126), and the early Arabic authors was written زین as being more in conformity with Ptolemy, who calls it by the name of Ὀζήνη. [There is a copy of the *Kánúnu-l Mas'údí* among Sir H. Elliot's MSS.]

² Compare Reinaud's *Fragments, Mém. sur l'Inde*, p. 29-239, and *Abou-l Feda*, I. xcv.; Sprenger's *Mas'údí*, p. 151; Casiri, *Biblioth. Arabico-Hispana*, Tom. I. p. 322; D'Herbelot, *Bibl. Or.* Tom. i. pp. 45, 407, 496, and Tom. iv. pp. 697, 732. Greg. Abulfaragii *Hist. Dynast.* p. 229; Wüstenfeld, *Abulfedae Tab. Geogr.* p. 77; *Biographia Univ.* s. v. De Rossi, *Dizionario Storico degli Autori Arabi*, s. v. Nicoll and Pusey, *Bodl. Cod. MSS. Or. Cat. Arab.* pp. 263, 360-363, 552; Flügel, *De Interpretibus*, No. 76. Wüstenfeld, *Arabische Aerzte*, No. 139; *As. Res.* vi. 537, ix. 195; *Rampoldi*, v. 510, vi. 535; *Grunälde-saal*, iv. 160; *Mod. Univ. Hist.* II. 487.

given there, though not in accordance with the statements of Mirkhond and other Persian historians, yet, being dependent on the contemporary testimony of Birúni, is of course more trustworthy than that of subsequent compilers, and is moreover confirmed by the *Jámi'u-t Tawáríkh*. With respect to this table of succession, the ingenuity of the French editor induced him to surmise that it probably represented a series of Bráhman princes who succeeded in subverting a Buddhist dynasty of Turks, and to whom should be attributed certain coins of a peculiar type which numismatists had previously some difficulty in assigning to their true masters. M. A. Longpérier has confirmed this opinion by certain arguments, which have been printed as an appendix to M. Reinaud's work, and he has been ably followed by Mr. E. Thomas, B.C.S., who has published a paper in the "Journal of the Royal Asiatic Society,"[1] respecting the proper attribution of this series. The result is that we are able to trace Bráhman kings of Kábul to the beginning of the tenth century, about A.D. 920, and thus clear up the mist which enveloped a whole century of the Indian annals previous to Mahmúd's invasion.[2]

In the same paper Mr. Thomas observes that the word Hamíra, so long supposed to be a proper name, and so eagerly sought for among the Hindú kings of India, proves to be an abbreviation of the full title of the Khalif of Baghdád,—*Amiru-l Múminín*,—continued by the Muhammadans in this curtailed form from the Arabic reverses of their own Ghazní money, when they adopted the style of coin found current in the countries they had subdued. "The abbreviation of the full titles of the Khalif into Śrí Hamíra will be seen," says Mr. Thomas, "to be necessary, as the space occupied by the device did not admit of the introduction of many more Hindí letters of the size it was the custom to employ." But this supposed abbreviation is disproved by examining the gold coins of Muhammad Ghori, on one of

---

[1] Vol. ix. p. 194; [see also his *Prinsep*, I. 321.]
[2] See note in Appendix on "The Hindu Kings of Kábul."

which, in the possession of General Cunningham, Srí Hamír is ascribed as the title of the king, not of the Khalif. The legend on one side only (not on two sides) is *Sri Hamir Muḥammad Sámí.* On the copper coins Srí Hamír is on the reverse, but the purport of the expression is fully shown by the position it occupies on the gold coins. Amír is used by Baihakí as equivalent to Sultán, and that is no doubt the use of it in all these places. The legend of Srí Samant Deo on many of this series of coins, upon which so much stress is laid, as indicative of Samant's power as one of the chief founders of the dynasty, does not seem to have reference to that prince, but to be an honorary title assumed by the reigning prince, meaning the "fortunate warrior;" otherwise it certainly would not have been stamped on the coins of Prithí Ráj, who lived 250 years later, and was not, like Samant, a Bráhman, but a Chaubán Rájpút, and proud of his lineage.[1]

EXTRACT.[2]

Kábul was formerly governed by princes of the Turkish race. It is said that they were originally from Tibet. The first of them, who was named Barhtigín, dwelt, when he arrived at Kábul, in a cave, in which no one could enter except by crawling on all fours. The cave contained a spring, and he provided himself therein with food for some days. This cave is now well known by the name of Bakar, and is entered by those persons who wish to obtain the blessing which a visit to it is supposed to confer, and bring out some of the water, not without much difficulty. Groups of peasants used to labour near the entrance of the cave. Such a thing (as remaining in the cave without food)

---

[1] [See Mr. Thomas' reply to this, *Prinsep* I. 331, and "Jour. B. A. S." xvii. 170; extracts from which will be found in the Appendix to this volume.

[2] [Sir H. Elliot himself prepared this Extract for the press from M. Reinaud's French version, comparing that as he went on with the Arabic text. The Editor has made no alteration in the translation, except the substitution of "Barhtigín" for "Barhatzôr," as the name appeared in the first edition. In Sir H. Elliot's draft translation the word is written "Barhatgín," but the copyist or printer read "Barkatzôr," as an ignorant person might well do.]

could not be practised without the connivance of some one. The
people who were in league with Barhtigín engaged the peasants
to labour without ceasing, relieving each other night and day, by
which it happened that the place was constantly surrounded.
After some days, Barhtigín came all of a sudden out of the cave,[1]
and the men who were near the entrance saw him appear as one
just born, clothed as a Turk, with a tunic, cap, boots, and armed
from head to foot. He was looked upon as a wondrous person,
and destined for empire. So he rendered himself master of the
kingdom of Kábul, which continued in his family for sixty
generations.

The Indians attach little importance to the sequence of events,
and neglect to record the dates of the reigns of their kings.
When they are embarrassed, they are silent. I will here mention what I have heard some people of the country say. It is
true, according to what I have heard, that the succession of
these reigns was written on a piece of silk, which was found in
the fortress of Nagarkot. I vehemently desired to read this
writing, but different circumstances prevented me.

Among the number of these kings was Kanak,[2] who founded
the Vihár at Peshawar, which bears his name. It is said that
the Rái of Kanauj offered to this prince, among other presents,
a piece of cloth of excellent texture, and of a new kind, of which
Kanak wished to make a dress. But the tailor refused to make
up the garment, saying, "I see the figure of a human foot, and
notwithstanding all my endeavours, still the foot will come be-

---

[1] He seems to have imposed upon the credulous people by the same means which
are even now practised in the west of India. Lieut. Boileau in his "Personal Narrative of a Tour in Rajwarra," and Capt. Osborne in his "Court and Camp of Runjeet
Sing," gives an account of a man who allowed himself to be interred for a month.
The former is circumstantial in his account, and seems to yield faith to the statement
of his narrators. It is not improbable that the ancients alluded to this practice
when they spoke of Indians who lived without food, and in caves. Aulus Gellius
speaks of them as "gentem, apud extrema Indiæ nullo cibatu vesentium." Noct.
Att. ix. 4. See also Philostratus, Vit. Apoll. iii. 46; Ctesias, Indic. Excerpt. xxiii.;
Grote's Greece, III. 113.

[2] [See Reinaud, Mém. sur l'Inde, p. 73; Thomas' Prinsep, Index, Kanishka; see
Cunningham, "Jour. Ben. As. Soc. Vol. xxiii.]

tween the shoulders." This bears a relation to the story which
I have elsewhere narrated in the legend of Bal.

Kanak understood that the Rái of Kanauj intended to insult
him, and to evince the small estimation in which he held him, so
Kanak departed quickly with his army towards Kanauj. At
this news the Rái of Kanauj was greatly embarrassed, not finding himself in a position to contend with the king of Kábul. He
consulted with his minister, who said, "You have roused a man
who was peaceably disposed, and an untoward act has been
committed. Now cut off my nose and lips, and mutilate me,
that I may search out a way of practising some artifice, since
there are no means of open resistance."

The Rái did as his minister advised, and allowed him to
depart to the frontier. When the army of Kábul met the
minister, he made himself known, and was conducted to the
presence of Kanak, who demanded of him how he was reduced
to that (pitiable) condition. He replied, "I endeavoured to dis-
suade the Rái from contending with you, and recommended him
to make his submission, but, charging me with collusion, he
mutilated me. If you march by the road which lies before you,
you will find it long. You will more easily arrive at your destination by encountering the difficulties of the desert between him
and us, provided you can carry with you a supply of water for a
few days." Kanak said, "This is easy." So he took with him
water, as recommended, and was guided on his way by the
minister, who preceded him when he entered the boundless
desert. When some days had elapsed, and the king knew not
his way, he enquired of the minister, who replied, "No rebuke
can attach to me for seeking to secure the safety of my master,
and the destruction of his enemy. The nearest way to escape
from the desert is that by which you entered it. Do to me as
you wish, but none of you can escape alive from this desert."
At these words Kanak mounted his horse, and urged it towards
some low ground, in the midst of which he dug his spear, and
water gushed out from it, which sufficed for the present and

future wants of the whole army. Then the minister said to the king. "I did not intend to practice deceit upon powerful angels, but only upon weak men; and since things have so turned out, accept my intercession, and pardon my gracious master. Kanak replied, "I now retrace my way, and grant your solicitation. Your master has already received the punishment due to him." Upon this the king returned to his country, and the minister to his master the Rái. But on his arrival he found that the Rái had been deprived of the use of his feet and hands on the self-same day that Kanak had planted his spear in the ground.[1]

The last of these kings was Laktúzamán, and his minister was Kalar, a Bráhman. * * * Laktúzamún's thoughts and actions were evil, so that many complaints reached the minister, who loaded him with chains and imprisoned him for his correction. * * * So the minister established himself on the throne, and was succeeded by the Bráhman Sámand, whose successor was Kamalava, whose successor was Bhím, whose successor was Jaipál, whose successor was Ánand Pál, whose successor was Nardajanpál,[2] who ascended the throne A.H. 412. His son, Dhím Pál, succeeded him after the lapse of five years, and under him the sovereignty of India became extinct, and no descendant remained to light a fire on the hearth. These princes, notwithstanding the extent of their dominions, were endowed with excellent qualities, were faithful to their engagements, and gracious towards their inferiors. The letter which Ánand Pál wrote to Amír Mahmúd, at the time enmity existed between them, is much to be admired. "I have heard that the Turks have invaded your dominions, and have spread over Khurásán: if you desire it, I will join you with 5,000 Cavalry, 10,000 Infantry, and 100 Elephants; but if you prefer it, I will send my son with twice the number. In making this proposal, I

---

[1] The story is told in the *Jámi'u-l Hikáyát*, I. xii. 18, with some variations, [see *post*, the article on the Jámi'u-l Hikáyát]. Kanak's name is not mentioned, but the hero is Sháh-i Zábulistán, *i.e.* King of Zábul, Sístán, Ghazní, etc.

[2] [Reinaud says the MS. will admit of this same being read Tardajanpál, Tarvajanpál, or Narvajanpál.]

do not wish to ingratiate myself with you. Though I have vanquished you, I do not desire that any one else but myself should obtain the ascendancy."[1] This prince was a determined enemy of the Musulmáns from the time that his son Nardajanpál was taken prisoner, but his son was, on the contrary, well disposed towards them.[2]

[1] This is translated somewhat differently by M. Reinaud, but the version here given seems more in conformity with the original Arabic.

[2] [Mr. Thomas has brought forward strong evidence against the accuracy of this passage. He quotes the counterpart passage in the Persian and Arabic versions of the Jámi'u-t Tawáríkh which says "And Kank returned to his country and was the last of the Katúrmán kings." So that the name of Laktúzamán would appear to be nothing more than an incorrect rendering of the designation of the tribe of Katúr.—"Jour. R. A. S." ix. 177; Prinsep, Vol. I. p. 315. It may be added that Reinaud's text gives the name as "Laktúzamán" in the first, but "Laktúrzamán" in the second instance.]

II.

TÁRÍKH YAMÍNÍ
OR
KITÁBU-L YAMÍNÍ
OF
AL 'UTBÍ.

[1] [THE author of this celebrated work was named Abú Nasr Muhammad ibn Muhammad al Jabbáru-l 'Utbí. He was a member of the family of 'Utba, which held important offices under the Sámánís, and he himself was Secretary to Sultán Mahmúd, so that he enjoyed excellent opportunities of becoming fully acquainted with the operations of that conqueror. His work comprises the whole of the reign of Násiru-d dín Subuktigín, and part of that of Mahmúd, down to the year 410 Hijra (1020 A.D.) The author would appear to have lived a few years later than this, as he records an event as happening in 420 Hijra,[2] but the interest of his work ceases with the year 410.]

[Though holding an appointment near the person of Mahmúd, he does not seem to have accompanied him in his expeditions, for he evidently had no knowledge of the topography of India, and his statements in respect of localities are of little authority. He never mentions Lahore or Dehli, and with the exception of

---

[1] [This article has been compiled, for the most part, from Sir H. Elliot's rough notes and memoranda.]   [2] [Reynolds Translation, 474.]

the title *Rái*, no Hindí word is found in his pages. In dates he is deficient, and far from precise.]

[There are several Persian translations of this work, which bear the title of Tarjuma-i Yamíní. The most ancient of these is that of Abú-l Sharaf Jarbádkání, or Jarbázkání, which was made in 582 Hijrí, or 1186 A.D. This version is very rarely met with in India, but it has been rendered into English by the Rev. J. Reynolds, and published under the auspices of the Oriental Translation Fund (London, 1858). Another version is the modern one made by Muhammad Karámat 'Alí of Dehli. This is known as the *Táríkh-i Amíní* or *Tarjuma-i Yamíní*, and although it is not common, it can easily be procured. Karámat 'Alí's translation is very literal, the order of the words even following that of the original Arabic, and it is in general very correct and free from errors. He interposes *fáidas* or notes containing explanations of meaning and surmises about identifications of places, but these are common place, and of little value.]

[A knowledge of the work of 'Utbí was at one time considered a great desideratum in Europe, but it is now found to contain but little which is not accessible through other channels. Firishta and other historians have, by means of the Persian versions, extracted from it all that is of value and interest. But for all this it must continue a work of authority and an object of curiosity, as the original source from which later writers have drawn much of their information respecting Mahmúd's campaigns.]

[The style of the original has generally been considered difficult and inflated, and Karámat 'Alí describes it as "very difficult, but at the same time good and elegant." Sir H. Elliot, who himself translated the extracts which follow from the original Arabic, observes that he "was alarmed at first at the declared difficulty of the text, but found it to vanish after a little examination." "All passages relating to India have been extracted, and the translations are literal, except that some of the useless illustrations have been omitted."]

[The Bibliothèque Imperiale possesses three copies of the

Arabic, and one of the Persian version. From the latter, Silvestre de Sacy published in "Notices et Extraits," Tome iv. 1799, an almost complete translation into French.][1] Copies of the *Táríkh Yamíní* are not uncommon in India. One of the best is in the Library of Nawwáb Siráju-l Mulk, of Haidarábád; and Sir H. Rawlinson has a very good copy. The edition lithographed at Dehli in the year 1847, is a very clear one, and contains some useful marginal notes, explanatory of the difficulties of the text. It was edited by Maulaví Ashraf 'Alí and Dr. Sprenger: size, large 8vo. 423 (497) pages each containing 16 lines. Professor Fleischer has remarked on the errors of its pagination.[2] Silvestre de Sacy notices a copy of one of the commentaries in a Library at Constantinople.[3] I only know one copy from which I have made the Extracts given hereafter. This belongs to a pertinacious old lady at Belgrám, who, without knowing what it is, scrupulously guards it from leaving her house, ever since my enquiries respecting the work have led her to look upon it as of exceeding value.

SHARH-I TÁRÍKH-I YAMÍNÍ.

There are several commentaries upon 'Utbí's history bearing this title. Their object is the explanation of the difficult passages, and the settling the right orthography of names. They are thus enumerated by Hájí Khalfa:[4]—

"The commentators are Majda-d dín Kirmání; Kassam bin Husain Khwárizmi, who died A.H. 555; Táju-d dín 'Ísa bin Mahmúd; Haibatu-d dín Abú 'Abdu-llah; Mahmúd bin 'Umar Manjání Naishápurí, who has entitled his work "Gardens of the excellent and odoriferous herbs of the learned." Another is Abú-l Márin Aitánia, who tells us that having consulted five

---
[1] *Mém. sur l'Inde*, p. 24.
[2] Zeitschrift, D. M. Gesellschaft, Vol. III. p. 389.
[3] Hist. priorum regum Pers. ex Mirkhond, Pers. et Lat. Vienna 1784, p. 168; Litteratura Turchesca dell 'Abbate Toderini, Tom. II.
[4] *Lexicon Bibliographicum*, v. "Yemini;" and Vol. II. p. 50; *Notices des Manuscripts*, Tom. iv. p. 326.

other commentaries, he extracted from them all that was useful, and made to them many important additions of his own. When it was complete, he presented his work to his master, the celebrated Kutbu-d dín Shírází, who honoured it with his approval. In the end, Kutbu-d dín desired him to join the text to the commentary, an arrangement of which the author did not approve; but having extracted from the text the most important words in it, he joined to them the necessary explanation in such a manner that one could not distinguish the text from the commentary, which together form one well-combined whole. He completed his labours on the entire work of 'Utbí at Tabríz, in the year 721 H. (1321 A.D.)

It is difficult to conceive the nature of the work thus spoken of. A combination of text and commentary so as to represent an harmonious unity, seems an impossibility.

The only commentary I know in India is by 'Alí bin Muslihu-s Sama'ání-al Kirmání. The year of composition does not appear, but the copy which I have seen cannot be less than three hundred years old. It is not a commentary upon the complete text, but only the most difficult words are selected for explanation. The portion thus selected for exegetical notes amounts to about one-tenth of the text. The extravagances of which the author is guilty, in the following short extract (p. 51), where he endeavours to show the correct way of writing Indian names, proves that the work can be of no real value, and that it is an impudent attempt of ignorance to appear learned. Yet his notions of the value of what he was engaged upon are correct enough, though it must be confessed they are very original. He says :—" Books of history operate as a warning to the wise, and their perusal inspires even the negligent with subjects of reflection, and especially those who have occasion to travel. Moderns derive benefit from the instructions of the ancients, those who are present learn from those that are absent, and posterity becomes acquainted with the occupations of its ancestors." It is for these solemn truisms that the author considered a commentary upon a work which treats of such exalted subjects as history treats of, a most useful labour to undertake.

The Conquest of Kusdár.

The ruler of Kusdár, which was near the territory of Ghazna, rebelled against Amír Subuktigín.[1] His fort was itself strong, naturally as well as in its approaches, and he thought that the difficulties of the road, as well as the distance, would prevent the Amír from attacking him; but he was afraid lest his territory might be plundered, while his city was invested by the Amír's cavalry. Amír Subuktigín marched that long distance over lofty and difficult hills, with his troops in close columns, one after the other, and with such expedition, that his body knew no rest, nor his eyes sleep, and his army had but little repose.

So Subuktigín and his followers attacked the city of the ruler of Kusdár, and seized him suddenly, like as a sheep is seized, when its limbs are torn to be roasted and placed before a guest; and the faces of the inhabitants were so changed through alarm, that the very dogs barked at them, and mothers in their fright deserted their children. The Amír thought it expedient to show kindness to the ruler of Kusdár, and to restore to him his possession all that he had taken from him. He made peace with him on condition that he should immediately pay a contribution in money and hereafter promise to send an annual tribute. The Khutba also was read in that territory in the name of Amír Subuktigín, and comers and goers, and the far and near became acquainted with these circumstances.[2]

Amír Subuktigín's First Incasion of Hind.

o   o   o   o   o

After this victory he made frequent expeditions into Hind, in

---

[1] This name was not uncommon about this period. The famous Amíru-l Umará, of Baghdád, the Turk Subuktigín died in A.H. 364. Hammer-Purgstall, on the authority of Sha'dri, says the name is Sebuktigín; but Ibn Khallikán says it should be Subuktigín.

[2] We find the ruler of Kusdár subsequently refusing to pay his tribute, in consequence of which the Sultán was again compelled to attack him.—*Dehli edition,* p. 316.

the prosecution of holy wars, and there he conquered forts upon lofty hills, in order to seize the treasures they contained, and expel their garrisons. He took all the property they contained into his own possession, and captured cities in Hind, which had up to that time been tenanted only by infidels, and not trodden by the camels and horses of Musulmáns.

When Jaipál[1] had ascertained the calamity which had befallen him from the reports of the people who travelled in his country, and how Subuktigín was taking different parts of the territory into his own possession, and injuring everybody who opposed him in his projects of ambition, the deepest grief seized him and made him restless, and his lands became narrow under his feet, though their expanse was broad. Then he arose with his relations and the generals of his army, and his vassals, and hastened with his huge elephants to wreak his revenge upon Subuktigín, by treading the field of Islám under his feet, and doing dishonour to that which should be treated with respect. In this disposition he marched on until he passed Lamghán, and approached the territory of Subuktigín, trusting to his own resources and power, for Satan had laid an egg in Jaipál's brain and hatched it; so that he waxed proud, entertaining absurd thoughts, and anticipating an immediate accomplishment of his wishes, impracticable as they were.

When the Amír heard of Jaipál's approach towards his territory, and of his great power, he girt up his loins to fight, and collecting his vassals and the Muhammadan forces whose duty it was to oppose infidels, he advanced from Gharna against Jaipál, who was encamped between that place and Lamghán, with soldiers as black as night, and as impetuous as a torrent. Yamínu-d daula Mahmúd accom-

---

[1] S. de Sacy reads "Halbal," and says some manuscripts have it "Hainal" and "Djibal." He observes also that Dow has "Jerpal;" and "Abistagi" for "Alptaghín," "Subuktagi" for "Sábekteghín," "Tighi" for "Togan," and "Bab Toer" for "Baitour." Firishta has "Jaipál, the son of Ishtpál;" in Briggs, "Hutpal." See Mém. sur l'Inde, p. 252.

panied Amír Subuktigín, like a lion of the forest or a destructive eagle, and they attempted no difficult undertaking which they did not easily accomplish.

The armies fought several days successively against each other, and cups filled to the brim with blood, drawn from wounds inflicted by sword and spear, circulated amongst them till they were drunken. In the field of this battle there was a very lofty mountain near the infidels, which was very difficult to ascend, called the 'Ukba Ghúzak.[1] In one of its ravines there was a clear fountain of water of the dimensions required by the Hanafí law for purification,[2] in which there were no impurities, or even watermoss. If any filth were thrown into it, black clouds collected, whirlwinds arose, the summits of the mountains became black, rain fell, and the neighbourhood was filled with cold blasts, until red death supervened. The Amír ordered that some dirty substance should be thrown into it, and immediately upon doing so the horrors of the day of resurrection rose up before the wicked infidels, and fire fell from heaven on them, and hailstones accompanied by loud claps of thunder; and a blast, calculated to shake trees from their roots, blew upon them, and thick black vapours formed around them, as that they could not see the road by which they could fly, and their food and water were filled with dust.[3]

In consequence of the great fear which fell upon Jaipál, who confessed he had seen death before the appointed time, he sent a deputation to the Amír soliciting peace, on the promise of his paying down a sum of money, and offering to obey any order he might receive respecting his elephants and his country. The Amír Subuktigín consented on account of the mercy he felt towards those who were his vassals, or for some other reason which

---

[1] Ghdask or Ghúrak is mentioned by Al Birúní as one of the mountains under which the Kabul river flows.—Vol I. p. 47.

[2] That is, a cube of ten spans.

[3] This passage is omitted from S. de Sacy's translation. [Muhammad 'Ufí gives this story in his Jámi'u-l Hikáyát at greater length and with some variations, though he professes to have taken it from this work, see post.]

seemed expedient to him. But the Sultán Yamínu-d daula
Mahmúd addressed the messengers in a harsh voice, and refused
to abstain from battle, until he should obtain a complete victory
suited to his zeal for the honour of Islám and of Musulmáns,
and one which he was confident God would grant to his arms.
So they returned, and Jaipál being in great alarm, again sent
most humble supplications that the battle might cease, observing,
" You have seen the impetuosity of the Hindus and their indifference to death, whenever any calamity befalls them, as at
this moment. If, therefore, you refuse to grant peace in the
hope of obtaining plunder, tribute, elephants and prisoners, then
there is no alternative for us but to mount the horse of stern
determination, destroy our property, take out the eyes of our
elephants, cast our children into the fire, and rush on each other
with sword and spear, so that all that will be left to you, is
stones and dirt, dead bodies, and scattered bones."

When the Amír heard these words and knew what Jaipál
would do in his despair, he thought that religion and the views
of the faithful would best be consulted by peace, and the acquisition of tribute. So the Amír Mahmúd agreed with Subuktigín
as to the propriety of withdrawing the hand of vengeance, on the
condition of receiving at that time 1,000,000 dirhams of royal
stamp, and fifty elephants, and some cities and forts in the
middle of his country. Jaipál was to deliver these forts to the
officers nominated by the Amír, and was to send hostages from
among his relatives and friends to remain with the Amír until
these conditions of cession were fulfilled. The Amír sent two
deputies with Jaipál to see that he did not swerve from his engagements, and they were accompanied by confidential officers
who were to receive charge of the ceded places.

When Jaipál had marched to a great distance, and thought
that the demand upon him had relaxed, and that the rope round
his throat was loosened, his bad disposition suggested to him to
break his engagements, and his folly made him beget enmity,
insomuch that he imprisoned those who accompanied him on

the part of the Amír, in reprisal for those of his relations whom the Amír had taken as hostages.

Amír Subuktigín's Second Invasion of Hind.

When this intelligence reached the Amír, he considered it false, as being opposed to the usual habits of Jaipál; until repeated accounts to the same effect were brought, when the curtain which obscured the truth was withdrawn, and he knew that God had set his seal upon Jaipál's heart, so that he might obtain the reward of his evil deeds, and had placed a veil between it and rectitude, so that he might obtain punishment for his wickedness and infidelity. The Sultán therefore sharpened the sword of intention in order to make an incursion upon his kingdom, and cleanse it from impurity and from his rejection of Islám. So he departed with his valiant servants and allies, relying upon the one God, and trusting in the fulfilment of the promise of victory; and he went on till he arrived with his troops in the country of Hind, and he killed every one who, on the part of Jaipál, came out to oppose him.

The Amír marched out towards Lamghán, which is a city celebrated for its great strength and abounding in wealth. He conquered it and set fire to the places in its vicinity which were inhabited by infidels, and demolishing the idol-temples, he established Islám in them, He marched and captured other cities and killed the polluted wretches, destroying the idolatrous and gratifying the Musulmáns. After wounding and killing beyond all measure, his hands and those of his friends became cold in counting the value of the plundered property. On the completion of his conquest he returned and promulgated accounts of the victories obtained for Islám, and every one, great and small, concurred in rejoicing over this result and thanking God.

When Jaipál saw what had occurred to him on account of the infraction of his engagements, that his chiefs had become the food of vultures and hyenas, and that weakness had fallen on his

arm, he became greatly agitated, and knew not whether to retire
or advance. He at last determined to fight once more, and satisfy
his revenge. He thought, resolved, gave orders, and collected
troops to the number of more than one hundred thousand. When
Amír Subuktigín heard this intelligence, he again advanced to
fight him, and ascended a lofty hill from which he could see the
whole army of the infidels, which resembled scattered ants and
locusts, and he felt like a wolf about to attack a flock of sheep.
He urged the Musulmáns upon the uncircumcised infidels, and
they willingly obeyed his orders. He made bodies of five hundred attack the enemy with their maces in hand, and relieve
each other when one party became tired, so that fresh men and
horses were constantly engaged, till the accursed enemy complained of the heat which arose from that iron oven. These
detached parties then made one united charge, in order to exterminate their numerous opponents. Men and officers mingled in
close conflict, and all other arms were useless except the sword.
The dust which arose prevented the eyes from seeing; swords
could not be distinguished from spears, men from elephants, the
valiants from cowards. It was only when the dust was allayed
that it was found that the impure infidels were defeated, and
had fled, leaving behind them their property, utensils, arms,
provisions, elephants, and horses. The jungles were filled with
the carcases of the infidels, some wounded by the sword, and
others fallen dead through fright. "It is the order of God respecting those who have passed away, that infidels should be put
to death; and the order of God is not changed respecting your
execution of the same precept."

The Hindús turned their tails towards their heads like frightened dogs, and the Rájá was contented to offer the best things
in his most distant provinces to the conqueror, on condition that
the hair on the crowns of their heads should not be shaven off.
So the country in that neighbourhood was clear and open before
Amír Subuktigín, and he seized all the wealth which was found
in it. He levied tribute and obtained immense booty, besides

two hundred elephants of war. He increased his army, and the Afgháns and Khiljís having submitted to him, he admitted thousands of them[1] whenever he wished into the ranks of his army, and thereafter expended their lives in his service.

* * * * *

Receipt by Mahmúd of a Khila't from the Khalífa.

Kádir bi-llah Amíru-l-múminín, the Khalífa of Daghdád, sent a Khila't, such as had never before been heard of, for the use of Sultán Saifu-d doula, and he entitled Mahmúd in his imperial rescript, "Yamínu-d daula Amínu-l millat, the friend of the Amír-l múmiuín," which had not yet been bestowed upon any prince, either far or near, notwithstanding their intense desire to receive such an honour. The Sultán sat on his throne and robed himself in his new Khila't, professing his allegiance to the successor of the prophet of God. The Amírs of Khurásán stood before him in order, with respectful demeanour, and did not take their seats till they were directed. He then bestowed upon the nobles, his slaves, his confidential servants, and his chief friends, valuable robes and choice presents, beyond all calculation, * * * and vowed that every year he would undertake a holy war against Hind.

* * * * *

Defeat of Jaipál by Mahmúd.

Sultán Mahmúd at first designed in his heart to go to Sijistán, but subsequently preferred engaging previously in a holy war against Hind, and he distributed arms prior to convening a council on the subject,[1] in order to secure a blessing on his designs, of exalting the standard of religion, of widening the plain of right, of illuminating the words of truth, and of strength-

---

[1] M. de Sacy says "they agreed to furnish 100,000 men whenever he wished."
[1] Alluding to a passage in the Kurán, which it is unnecessary to explain here more particularly.

ening the power of justice. He departed towards the country of Hind, in full reliance on the aid of God, who guiding by his light and by his power, bestowed dignity upon him, and gave him victory in all his expeditions. On his reaching Purshaur (Peshāwar), he pitched his tent outside the city. There he received intelligence of the bold resolve of Jaipál, the enemy of God, and the King (*malik*) of Hind, to offer opposition, and of his rapid advance towards meeting his fate in the field of battle. He then took a muster of his horses, and of all his warriors and their vassals from those in whose records it was entered, and then selected from among his troops 15,000 cavalry, men and officers, all bold, and strictly prohibited those who were rejected and not fit or disposed for war, from joining those who had been chosen, and who were like dragons of the desert and lions of the forest. With them he advanced against the wicked and accursed enemy, whose hearts were firm as hills, and were as twigs of patience on the boughs of affection. The villanous infidel came forward, proud in his numbers and strength of head and arm, with 12,000 horsemen, 30,000 foot soldiers, and 300 elephants, at the ponderous weight of which the lighter earth groaned, little reflecting that, under God's dispensation, a small army can overturn a host, as the ignorant man would have learnt, could he have read the word of God,—"Oftentimes a small army overcomes a large one by the order of God."

That infidel remained where he was, avoiding the action for a long time, and awaiting craftily the arrival of reinforcements and other vagabond families and tribes which were on their way; but the Sultán would not allow him to postpone the conflict, and the friends of God commenced the action, setting upon the enemy with sword, arrow, and spear,—plundering, seizing, and destroying; at all which the Hindús, being greatly alarmed, began to kindle the flame of fight. The Hindú set his cavalry in and beat his drums. The elephants moved on from their posts, and line advanced against line, shooting their arrows at one another like boys escaped from school, who, at eventime, shoot at a target for a wager. Swords flashed like lightning amid the blackness of clouds, and fountains of blood flowed like the fall of setting stars. The friends of God defeated their obstinate opponents, and quickly put them to a complete rout. Noon had not arrived when the Musulmáns had wreaked their vengeance on the infidel enemies of God, killing 15,000 of them, spreading them like a carpet over the ground, and making them food for beasts and birds of prey. Fifteen elephants fell on the field of battle, as their legs, being pierced with arrows, became as motionless as if they had been in a quagmire, and their trunks were cut with the swords of the valiant heroes.

The enemy of God, Jaipál, and his children and grandchildren, and nephews, and the chief men of his tribe, and his relatives, were taken prisoners, and being strongly bound with ropes, were carried before the Sultán, like as evildoers, on whose faces the fumes of infidelity are evident, who are covered with the vapours of misfortune, will be bound and carried to Hell. Some had their arms forcibly tied behind their backs, some were seized by the cheek, some were driven by blows on the neck. The necklace was taken off the neck of Jaipál,—composed of large pearls and shining gems and rubies set in gold, of which the value was two hundred thousand dínárs; and twice that value was obtained from the necks of those of his relatives who were taken prisoners, or slain, and had become the food of the mouths of hyenas and vultures. God also bestowed upon his friends such an amount of booty as was beyond all bounds and all calculation; including five hundred thousand slaves, beautiful men and women. The Sultán returned with his followers to his camp, having plundered immensely, by God's aid, having obtained the victory, and thankful to God, the lord of the universe. For the Almighty had given them victory over a province of the country of Hind, broader and longer and more fertile than Khurásán. This splendid and celebrated action took place on Thursday, the 8th of Muharram, 392 H. (27th November, 1001, A.D.)

After the victory, the Sultán directed that the polluted infidel,

Jaipál, should be paraded about, so that his sons and chieftains might see him in that condition of shame, bonds, and disgrace; and that the fear of Islám might fly abroad through the country of the infidels. He then entered into conditions of peace with him, after demanding fifty elephants, and took from him as hostages his son and grandson, till he should fulfil the conditions imposed upon him.

The infidel returned to his own country and remained there, and wrote to his son, Andpál, whose territory, on which he prided himself, was on the other side of the Sihún (Indus), explaining the dreadful calamity which had befallen him, and beseeching him with many entreaties to send the elephants which were according to agreement to be given to the Sultán. Upon this Andpál sent the elephants to Jaipál, after dismissing the courier who had brought the letter, and the elephants were sent on to the Sultán. The Sultán, therefore, ordered the release of the hostages, and his myrmidons gave them a smack on the buttocks, telling them to return to their country.

Andpál reflected that his father, Jaipál, had put on the sheaf of old age, and had fallen under the influence of Lyra and other unlucky constellations, and it was time he should contemplate his death and devote himself to religious exercises. There is a custom among these men that if any one is taken prisoner by an enemy, as in this case Jaipál was by the Musulmáns, it is not lawful for him to continue to reign. When Jaipál, therefore, saw that he was captive in the prison of old age and degradation, he thought death by cremation preferable to shame and dishonour. So he commenced with shaving his hair off, and then threw himself upon the fire till he was burnt.[1]

[1] In the version of *Jerbádkání* it is said that, after the self sacrifice of Jaipál, the Sultán again sent forth his army into Hindustan, and that after having exterminated all those who had taken part in this rebellion, he returned in triumph to Ghazní. There is no authority for this in the original. The transactions at Waihind are not noticed in *Jerbádkání*.—Reynolds, 282—Notices et Extraits, iv. 350.

Battle of Waihind.

When the Sultán had accomplished all his wishes and reduced all his enemies; in his happiness, he resolved on another holy expedition. He ornamented the entrance to his tent as well as his standards, and marching towards Waihind, he encamped there in state, until he had established himself in that country, and had relieved himself from the toils of the campaign. News reached him of the Hindús taking refuge in the passes of the neighbouring hills, and concealing themselves in the forests and jungles, consulting amongst themselves about the means of attacking the Musulmáns. He therefore despatched an army against them, to conquer their country, and disperse them. The army fell upon them, and committed such slaughter that their swords were covered with blood. Those who escaped death fled away like mountain goats, having seen the swords flashing as bright as stars at noonday, and dealing black and red death around them. Thus did the infidels meet with the punishment and loss due to their deserts. The standards of the Sultán then returned happy and victorious to Ghazní, the face of Islám was made resplendent by his exertions, the teeth of the true faith displayed themselves in their laughter, the breasts of religion expanded, and the back of idolatry was broken.

* * * * *

The Conquest of Bhátia.

When Sultán Mahmúd had settled the affairs of Sijistán, and the action of his beating pulse had subsided, and the clouds had dispersed, he determined upon invading Bhátia. So he collected armies with trustworthy guides and valiant standard bearers, and crossing the Indus in the neighbourhood[1] of Múltán, he marched towards the city of Bhátia, the walls of which the

---

[1] Literally, "behind," or "beyond," [and Ibn Aṣír uses the same expression,] but the position of Múltán is such as to render the author's meaning very doubtful.

wings of the eagle could not surmount, and which was surrounded as by the ocean with a ditch of exceeding depth and breadth. The city was as wealthy as imagination can conceive in property, armies, and military weapons. There were elephants as headstrong as Satan. The ruler at that time was Diji Ráí,[1] and the pride which he felt in the state of his preparations, induced him to leave the walls of his fort and come forth to oppose the Musulmáns, in order to frighten them with his warriors and elephants and great prowess.

The Sultán fought against him for three days and nights, and the lightnings of his swords and the meteors of his spears fell on the enemy. On the fourth morning a most furious onslaught was made with swords and arrows, which lasted till noon, when the Sultán ordered a general charge to be made upon the infidels. The friends of God advancing against the masters of lies and idolatry with cries of "God is exceeding great!" broke their ranks, and rubbed their noses upon the ground of disgrace. The Sultán himself, like a stallion, went on dealing hard blows around him on the right hand and on the left, and cut those who were clothed in mail right in twain, making the thirsty infidels drink the cup of death. In this single charge he took several elephants, which Diji Ráí regarded as the chief support of his centre. At last God granted victory to the standards of Islám, and the infidels retreated behind the walls of their city for protection. The Musulmáns obtained possession of the gates of the city, and employed themselves in filling up the ditch and destroying the scarp and counterscarp, widening the narrow roads, and opening the closed entrances.

When Diji Ráí saw the desperate state to which he was reduced, he escaped by stealth and on foot into the forest with a few attendants, and sought refuge on the top of some hills. The Sultán despatched a select body of his troops in pursuit of them, and surrounded them as a collar does the neck; and when Diji

[1] Dow says "Bachera;" S. de Sacy "Bohaira;" Wilken "Bahiru;" Briggs "Berjy Ray." [Ibn Asír has "Bahírá."]

Rái saw that there was no chance of escape, he drew his dagger, struck it into his breast, and went to the fire which God has lighted for infidels and those who deny a resurrection, for those who say no prayers, hold no fasts, and tell no beads.—Amen.

The army of the Sultán kept moving on, and committing slaughter and pillage. One hundred and twenty elephants[1] fell to the share of the Sultán, besides the usual share of property and arms. He also obtained an accession of territory without any solicitation. He remained at Bhátia till he had cleansed it from pollution, and appointed a person there to teach those who had embraced Islám, and lead them in the right way. He then returned to Ghazna in triumph and glory, and his fortune was in the equator (ascendant); but as his return was during the rains, when the rivers were full and foaming, and as the mountains were lofty, and he had to fight with enemies, he lost the greater part of his baggage in the rivers, and many of his valiant warriors were dispersed. God, nevertheless, preserved his person from those calamities which beset his road, for God is the friend of the virtuous. * * *

The Capture of Múltán.

Intelligence reached the Sultán of the acts committed by the ruler of Múltán, Abí-l futúh, namely, respecting the impurity of his religion, the seditious designs of his heart, and the evidence of his evil doings, and his endeavours to make proselytes of the inhabitants of his country. The Sultán zealous for the Muhammadan religion, thought it a shame to allow him to retain his government while he practised such wickedness and disobedience, and he besought the assistance of a gracious God in bringing him to repentance, and attacking him with that design in view.

He then issued orders for the assembling of armies from among the Musulmáns for the purpose of joining him in this

[1] Firishta says 280, and Mirkhond 170, but does not notice that this was the personal share of the Sultán.

holy expedition,—those on whom God had set his seal and selected for the performance of good deeds, and obtaining either victory or martyrdom. He departed with them towards Múltán in the spring, when the rivers were swollen with the rain, and the Indus and other rivers prevented the passage of the cavalry, and offered difficulties to his companions. The Sultán desired of Andpál,[1] the chief of Hind, that he would allow him to march through his territory, but Andpál would not consent, and offered opposition, which resulted in his discomfiture. The Sultán, consequently, thought it expedient to attack Rái Andpál first, notwithstanding his power, in his jungles, to bow down his broad neck, to cut down the trees of his jungles, to destroy every single thing he possessed, and thus to obtain the fruit of two paradises by this double conquest.

So he stretched out upon him the hand of slaughter, imprisonment, pillage, depopulation, and fire, and hunted him from ambush to ambush, into which he was followed by his subjects, like "merchants of Hazramaut, who are never without their sheets."[2] The spears were tired of penetrating the rings of the coats of mail, the swords became blunt by the blows on the sides, and the Sultán pursued the Rái over hill and dale, over the soft and hard ground of his territory, and his followers either became a feast to the rapacious wild beasts of the passes and plains, or fled in distraction to the neighbourhood of Kashmir.

When Abí-l futúh, the ruler of Múltán, heard what had happened to the chief of Hind, notwithstanding all his power and the lofty walls of his fort, and his shining sword, and when he began to measure their relative strength, and considered how Andpál, a much greater potentate than himself, had been subdued, he looked upon himself, as compared with the Sultán, as a ravine in comparison with the top of a mountain. He, therefore, determined with all expedition to load all his property on

---

[1] No doubt Anand-pál, as in Firishta; Mirkhond calls him Jalpál, as in the *Tárikh-i Alfi*.
[2] This verse is quoted by the author from a poet named Jariru-l-Khadfi.

elephants, and carry it off to Sarandíp, and he left Múltán empty for the Sultán to do with it as he chose.

The Sultán marched towards Múltán, beseeching God's aid against those who had introduced their neologies into religion and had disparaged it. The inhabitants of the place were blind in their errors, and desirous of extinguishing the light of God with their breath, so the Sultán invested Múltán, took it by assault, treated the people with severity, and levied from them twenty thousand thousand dirams with which to respite their sins. Then the reports of the Sultán's conquests spread over distant countries, and over the salt sea as far even as Egypt; Sind and her sister (Hind) trembled at his power and vongeance; his celebrity exceeded that of Alexander the Great, and heresy (*ilhád*), rebellion, and enmity, were suppressed.

* * * * * * *

Indians in Mahmud's Army.

When the Sultán heard of Ílak Khán crossing the Jihún with 50,000 men or more, he went in haste from Tukhiristán to Balkh, and remained there in order to anticipate Ílak Khán, who wished to obtain supplies from that province. The Sultán advanced ready for action with an army composed of Turks, Indians, Khiljís, Afgháns, and Ghaznivides.[1]

* * * * * * *

Nawása Sháh.

After this victory over Ílak Khán, the Sultán resolved upon going to Hind for the purpose of making a sudden attack upon the person known as Nawása Sháh, one of the rulers of Hind, who had been established as governor over some of the territories in that country conquered by the Sultán, for the purpose of protecting their borders. Satan had got the better of Nawása Sháh,

[1] De Sacy reads Ghozz, perhaps more correctly.

for he was again apostatizing towards the pit of plural worship, had thrown off the slough of Islám, and held conversation with the chiefs of idolatry respecting the casting off the firm rope of religion from his neck. So the Sultán went swifter than the wind in that direction, and made the sword reek with the blood of his enemies. He turned Nawása Sháh out of his government, took possession of all the treasures which he had accumulated, re-assumed the government, and then cut down the harvest of idolatry with the sickle of his sword and spear. After God had granted him this and the previous victory, which were tried witnesses as to his exalted state and proselytism, he returned without difficulty to Ghazna.

Victory near Waihind.[1]

The Sultán, contrary to the disposition of man, which induces him to prefer a soft to a hard couch, and the splendour of the cheeks of pomegranate-bosomed girls to well-tempered sword blades, was so offended at the standard which Satan had raised in Hind, that he determined on another holy expedition to that land. On the last day of Rabí'u-l-ákhir of the same year,[2] the Sultán prayed God for the accomplishment of his wishes. When he had reached as far as the river of Waihind, he was met by Brahmanpál, the son of Andpál, at the head of a valiant army, with white swords, blue spears, yellow coats of mail, and ash-coloured elephants. Fight opened its crooked teeth, attacks were frequent like flaming meteors, arrows fell like rain from bows, and the grinding-stone of slaughter revolved, crushing the bold and the powerful. The battle lasted from morning till evening, and the infidels were near gaining the victory, had not

---

[1] This is left out by all the other chroniclers.
[2] The year is not mentioned, but that the Sultán should have gained his victory near Balkh, expelled Nawása Sháh, that he should have returned to Ghazna and rested, and then have commenced another expedition, all within four months of the same year, is to suppose almost an impossibility, unless Nawása Sháh was on the Peshawar frontier.

God aided by sending the slaves of the household to attack the enemy in rear, and put them to flight. The victors obtained thirty large elephants, and slew the vanquished wherever they were found in jungles, passes, plains, and hills.

Capture of Bhimnagar.

The Sultán himself joined in the pursuit, and went after them as far as the fort called Dhímnagar,[1] which is very strong, situated on the promontory of a lofty hill, in the midst of impassable waters. The kings of Hind, the chiefs of that country, and rich devotees, used to amass their treasures and precious jewels, and send them time after time to be presented to the large idol that they might receive a reward for their good deeds and draw near to their God. So the Sultán advanced near to this crow's fruit,[2] and this accumulation of years, which had attained such an amount that the backs of camels would not carry it, nor vessels contain it, nor writers' hands record it, nor the imagination of an arithmetician conceive it.

The Sultán brought his forces under the fort and surrounded it, and prepared to attack the garrison vigorously, boldly, and wisely. When the defenders saw the hills covered with the armies of plunderers, and the arrows ascending towards them like flaming sparks of fire, great fear came upon them, and, calling out for mercy, they opened the gates, and fell on the earth, like sparrows before a hawk, or rain before lightning. Thus did God grant an easy conquest of this fort to the Sultán, and bestowed on him as plunder the products of mines and seas, the ornaments of heads and breasts, to his heart's content. The

---

[1] Dow calls it "Bimé;" S. de Sacy "Bebim-bagra;" 'Utbí has "Bhím-naghar;" and Rashídu-d dín "Dhínbaghra;" Wilken "Behim Bagea;" Briggs "Bheem;" D'Herbelot and Hampoldi, "Bchesim;" Tárikh-i Alfí, "Bhím." [There can be no question that the lithographed edition is right in declaring the name to be Bhímnagar. Firishta uses the names of Nagarkot, or Fort of Bhím (Briggs I. 48). It is the modern Kángra which is still called Nagarkot.]

[2] That is, the best; and probably there is an allusion in the expression to the blackness of the Hindús, the early Muhammadans being fond of designating them as "crows," as will be seen from the Táju-l Ma-ásir.

Sultán entered the fort with Abú Nasr Ahmad bin Muhammad Faríghuní, the ruler of Júzján, and all his own private attendants, and appointed his two chief chamberlains, Altúntásh and Asightigín,[1] to take charge of the treasures of gold and silver and all the valuable property, while he himself took charge of the jewels. The treasures were laden on the backs of as many camels as they could procure, and the officers carried away the rest. The stamped coin amounted to seventy thousand thousand royal dirhams, and the gold and silver ingots amounted to seven hundred thousand four hundred *mans* in weight, besides wearing apparel and fine cloths of Sús, respecting which old men said they never remembered to have seen any so fine, soft, and embroidered. Among the booty was a house of white silver, like to the houses of rich men, the length of which was thirty yards and the breadth fifteen.[2] It could be taken to pieces and put together again. And there was a canopy, made of the fine linen of Rúm, forty yards long and twenty broad, supported on two golden and two silver poles, which had been cast in moulds.

The Sultán appointed one of his most confidential servants to the charge of the fort and the property in it. After this he returned to Ghazna in triumph; and, on his arrival there, he ordered the court-yard of his palace to be covered with a carpet, on which he displayed jewels and unbored pearls and rubies, shining like sparks, or like wine congealed with ice, and emeralds like fresh sprigs of myrtle, and diamonds in size and weight like pomegranates. Then ambassadors from foreign countries, including the envoy from Taghán Khún, king of Turkistán, assembled to see the wealth which they had never yet even read of in books of the ancients, and which had never been accumulated by kings of Persia or of Rúm, or even by Kárún, who had only to express a wish and God granted it.

* * * * *

[1] [Reynolds gives this name as "Istargín."]
[2] [Jurbádkání, according to Reynolds, makes the measurement "sixty cubits long and fifty wide."]

Capture of Nárdín.[1]

The Sultán again resolved on an expedition to Hind, and marched towards Náráin, urging his horses and moving over ground, hard and soft, until he came to the middle of Hind, where he reduced chiefs, who, up to that time obeyed no master, overturned their idols, put to the sword the vagabonds of that country, and with delay and circumspection proceeded to accomplish his design. He fought a battle with the chiefs of the infidels, in which God bestowed upon him much booty in property, horses, and elephants, and the friends of God committed slaughter in every hill and valley. The Sultán returned to Ghazna with all the plunder he had obtained.

Embassy from India to Ghazna.

When the ruler (malik) of Hind had witnessed the calamities which had inflicted ruin on his country and his subjects, in consequence of his contests with the Sultán, and had seen their effects far and near, he became satisfied that he could not contend with him. So he sent some of his relatives and chiefs to the Sultán, supplicating him not to invade India again, and offering him money to abstain from that purpose, and their best wishes for his future prosperity. They were told to offer a tribute of fifty elephants, each equal to two ordinary ones in size and strength, laden with the products and rarities of his country. He promised to send this tribute every year, accompanied by two thousand men, for service at the Court of the Sultán.

The Sultán accepted his proposal, as Islám was promoted by the humility of his submission and the payment of tribute. He sent an envoy to see that these conditions were carried into effect. The ruler of Hind strictly fulfilled them and despatched one of his vassals with the elephants to see that they were duly presented to the Sultán. So peace was established, and tribute was paid, and caravans travelled in full security between Khurásán and Hind.

* * * *

[1] [This is called "Nardin" in Reynolds' translation, p. 360.]

Conquest of Nárdin.[1]

After the Sultán had purified Hind from idolatry, and raised mosques thereiu, he determined to invade the capital of Hind, to punish those who kept idols and would not acknowledge the unity of God. He collected his warriors and distributed money amongst them. He marched with a large army in the year 404 H. 1013 A.D. during a dark night, and at the close of autumn, on account of the purity of the southern breezes at that season. When the Sultán had arrrived near the frontier of Hind, snow fell, such as had never been seen before, insomuch that the passes of the hills were closed, and mountains and valleys became of one level. The feet of the horses and camels were affected by the cold, so it may be conceived what the faces, hands, and feet of men suffered. The well-known roads were concealed, and the right could not be distinguished from the left, or what was behind from that which was before, and they were unable to return until God should give the order. The Sultán employed himself, in the meantime, in collecting supplies, and sent for his generals from the different provinces. After having thus accumulated the means of warfare, and having been joined by his soldiers, who had come from different directions, in number equal to the drops of an autumnal rain, he left these winter quarters in the spring, and, had the earth been endowed with feeling, it would have groaned under the weight of the iron, the warriors, the horses, and the beasts of burden. The guides marched on in front over hill and dale, before the sun arose, and even before the light of the stars was extinguished. He urged on his horses[2] for two months, among broad and deep rivers, and among jungles in which wild cattle even might lose their way.

When the Sultán arrived near the end of his destination, he set his cavalry in array, and formed them into different bodies,

---

[1] [Reynolds, in his translation of Jarbádkání's version, gives the name as "Nazin," and the date "400," page 388.]
[2] This may also be rendered "boats."

appointing his brother, Amír Nasr, son of Násiru-d dín, to
command the right wing, consisting of valiant heroes; Aralánu-l
Jázib to the left wing, consisting of powerful young men; and
Abú 'Abdu-lla Muhammad bin Ibráhímu-t Táí to the advance-
guard, consisting of fiery Arab cavaliers. To the centre he
appointed Altúntásh, the chamberlain, with the Sultán's personal
slaves and attendants, as firm as mountains.

Nidar Bhím, the enemy of God and the chief of Hind, alarmed
at this sudden invasion, summoned his vassals and generals, and
took refuge within a pass, which was narrow, precipitous, and
inaccessible. They entrenched themselves behind stones, and
closed the entrance to the pass by their elephants, which looked
like so many hills from their lofty stature. Here he remained in
great security, being persuaded that the place was impervious to
attack, but he did not know that God is the protector of the
faithful, and the annihilator of infidels!

When the Sultán learnt the intention of Nidar Bhím, with
respect to the protraction of the war, and his confidence in his
security, he advanced against them with his Dailamite warriors,
and Satanic Afghán spearmen, and they penetrated the pass like
gimlets into wood, ascending the hills like mountain goats, and
descending them like torrents of water. The action lasted for
several days without intermission, till at last some of the Hindús
were drawn out into the plain to fight, like oil sucked up into
the wick of a candle, or like iron attracted by a magnet, and
there they were assaulted and killed by the cavalry, just as the
knight on the chess-board demolishes pawns.

When his vassals had joined Nidar Bhím with reinforcements,
he consented to leave his entrenchments and come out himself
into the plain, having the hills behind him, and elephants drawn
up on each wing. The battle raged furiously, and when the
elephants of the Hindús moved on, with the object of destroying their opponents, they were assailed by showers of arrows upon
their trunks and eyes. When Abú 'Abdu-llu-t Táí had through
his bravery advanced into the midst of the infidels, he was

wounded in his head and different parts of his body; but the Sultán seeing the extreme danger to which his general was exposed, despatched part of his own guards to his assistance, who brought him out of the conflict to the Sultán, severely wounded in many places. The Sultán ordered him to be placed on an elephant, in order to relieve him from the pain of his wounds, and thus he was exalted like a king above all the leaders of the army.

The conflict continued as before until God blew the gale of victory on his friends, and the enemy were slain on the tops of the hills, and in the valleys, ravines, and beds of torrents. A large number of elephants, which the enemy had looked upon as strongholds to protect them, fell into the hands of the victors, as well as much other booty. So God granted the Sultán the victory of Nárdín, such as added to the decoration of the mantle of Islám, which had not before that period extended to that place.

A stone was found there in the temple of the great Budda,[1] on which an inscription was written purporting that the temple had been founded fifty thousand years ago. The Sultán was surprised at the ignorance of these people, because those who believe in the true faith represent that only seven thousand years have elapsed since the creation of the world, and the signs of resurrection are even now approaching. The Sultán asked his wise men the meaning of this inscription, and they all concurred in saying that it was false, and that no faith was to be put in the evidence of a stone.

The Sultán returned, marching in the rear of this immense booty, and slaves were so plentiful that they became very cheap; and men of respectability in their native land, were degraded by becoming slaves of common shopkeepers. But this is the goodness of God, who bestows honours on his own religion and degrades infidelity.

[1] It is plainly so written in the Arabic original, and cannot be meant for *But*, "an idol," as that word is Persian. [See Vol. I. p. 307.]

Conquest of Tánesar.

The Sultán learnt that in the country of Tánesar there were large elephants of the Sailamán (Ceylon) breed, celebrated for military purposes. The chief of Tánesar was on this account obstinate in his infidelity and denial of God. So the Sultán marched against him with his valiant warriors, for the purpose of planting the standards of Islám and extirpating idolatry. He marched through a desert which no one had yet crossed, except birds and wild beasts, for the foot of man and the shoe of horse had not traversed it. There was no water in it, much less any other kind of food. The Sultán was the first to whom God had granted a passage over this desert, in order that he might arrive at the accomplishment of his wishes.

Beneath it (Tánesar!) flowed a pure stream; the bottom was covered with large stones, and its banks were precipitous and sharp as the points of arrows. The Sultán had reached this river where it takes its course through a hill-pass, behind which the infidels had posted themselves, in the rear of their elephants, with a large number of infantry and cavalry. The Sultán adopted the stratagem of ordering some of his troops to cross the river by two different fords, and to attack the enemy on both sides; and when they were all engaged in close conflict, he ordered another body of men to go up the bank of the stream, which was flowing through the pass with fearful impetuosity, and attack the enemy amongst the ravines, where they were posted in the greatest number. The battle raged fiercely, and about evening, after a vigorous attack on the part of the Musulmáns, the enemy fled, leaving their elephants, which were all driven into the camp of the Sultán, except one, which ran off and could not be found. The largest were reserved for the Sultán.

The blood of the infidels flowed so copiously, that the stream was discoloured, notwithstanding its purity, and people were unable to drink it. Had not night come on and concealed the traces of their flight, many more of the enemy would have been slain. The victory was gained by God's grace, who has established Islám for ever as the best of religions, notwithstanding that idolaters revolt against it. The Sultán returned with plunder which it is impossible to recount.—Praise be to God, the protector of the world, for the honour he bestows upon Islám and Musulmáns!

* * * * *

Passage of the Panjáb and the Jamna.

On the Sultán's return to Ghazna from Khwárizm, he appointed spies to go to the frontier of Hind and communicate all particulars respecting that country, and he resolved upon employing the close of the year in resting his horses and troopers, and in contemplating schemes of future religious conquests.

* * * * *

As no part of Hind remained unconquered, except Kashmír, he resolved on an expedition to that country. Between it and Ghazna there were forests resounding with the notes of birds and other animals, and the winds even lose their way in it. It happened that 20,000 men from Máwaráu-n nahr and its neighbourhood, who were with the Sultán, were anxious to be employed on some holy expedition, in which they might obtain martyrdom. The Sultán determined to march with them towards Kanauj, which no other king but the all-powerful Gushtasp had been able to take, as has been related in the histories of the Magians.

Between Ghazna and Kanauj the journey occupies three months, even for camels and horses. So the Sultán bade farewell to sleep and ease, and praying God for success, he departed accompanied by his valiant warriors. He crossed in safety the Síhún (Indus), Jelam, Chandráha, Ubrá (Rávi), Bah (Biyáh), and Sataldur (Sutlej). These are all rivers, deep beyond description; even elephants' bodies are concealed in them, so it may easily be conceived what is the case with horses. They bear along with them large stones, so camels and horses are of course in danger of being carried down the stream. Whatever countries the Sultán traversed, ambassadors were sent to him proffering submission, inasmuch that Sabli, son of Shahí,[1] son of Bamhí,[2] who held the passes leading into Kashmír, looking upon the Sultán as one sent by God, also came forward, offering his allegiance, and his services as a guide. He led the way, crossing forest after forest. At midnight the drum sounded for the march, and the friends of God mounted their horses, ready to bear the inconvenience of the journey, and they marched on until the sun began to decline from the meridian. They placed behind their backs the river Jún (Jamna), crossing it on the 20th of Rajab, 409 H., 2nd December, 1018 A.D.

Capture of Baran.

The Sultán took all the lofty hill forts which he met on the road, so lofty indeed were they, that beholders sprained the back of their necks in looking up at them. At length he arrived at the fort of Darba (Baran[3]), in the country of Hardat,[4] who was one of the Ráís, that is "kings," in the Hindi language. When Hardat heard of this invasion by the protected warriors of God, who advanced like the waves of the sea, with the angels around them on all sides, he became greatly agitated, his steps trembled, and he feared for his life, which was forfeited under the law of God. So he reflected that his safety would best be secured by conforming to the religion of Islám, since God's sword was drawn from

---

[1] ["Janki," marginal note in Dehli Edn.]

[2] S. de Sacy calls him "Khabli-ben-Schaml." Firishta says, "When Mahmúd reached the confines of Kashmir, the ruler sent presents, which were graciously accepted, and he accompanied the advance guard." Briggs, without authority, adds that Mahmúd had established this prince in Kashmir. [Reynolds gives the names Habali-'bn-Shámí.]

[3] 'Alí bin Muslih says, in his commentary, that the name is Barhah, but that some copies read Barna. S. de Sacy reads "Barma," so does [Jarbádkání, Reynolds, 451] Kartmat 'Ali and Rashidu-d dín. The original copies read "Barba," and "Bardur." I make it "Baran," the old name of Bolandshahr.

[4] S. de Sacy gives "Haroun" and "Harout." 'Ali bin Muslih says it is either "Hardis," or "Hardit." [Jarbádkání, according to Reynolds, reads "Hardís," p. 451].

the scabbard, and the whip of punishment was uplifted. He came forth, therefore, with ten thousand men, who all proclaimed their anxiety for conversion, and their rejection of idols. God confirmed the promises he had made, and rendered assistance to the Sultán.

Capture of Kulchand's Fort.

After some delay, the Sultán marched against the fort of Kulchand, who was one of the leaders of the accursed Satans, who assumed superiority over other rulers, and was inflated with pride, and who employed his whole life in infidelity, and was confident in the strength of his dominions. Whoever fought with him sustained defeat and flight, and he possessed much power, great wealth, many brave soldiers, large elephants, and strong forts, which were secure from attack and capture. When he saw that the Sultán advanced against him in the endeavour to engage in a holy war, he drew up his army and elephants within a deep forest ready for action.

The Sultán sent his advance guard to attack Kulchand, which, penetrating through the forest like a comb through a head of hair, enabled the Sultán to discover the road which led to the fort.[1] The Musulmáns exclaim, "God is exceeding great," and those of the enemy, who were anxious for death, stood their ground. Swords and spears were used in close conflict. * * * The infidels, when they found all their attempts fail, deserted the fort, and tried to cross the foaming river which flowed on the other side of the fort, thinking that beyond it they would be in security; but many of them were slain, taken, or drowned in the attempt, and went to the fire of hell. Nearly fifty[2] thousand men were killed and drowned, and became the prey of beasts and crocodiles. Kulchand, taking his dagger, slew his wife, and then drove it into his own body. The Sultán obtained by this victory one hundred and eighty-five powerful elephants, besides other booty.

[1] The *Táríkh-i Alfí* calls the fort by the name of "Mand."
[2] Jarbádkání reduces the number to "five thousand," according to Reynolds, p. 464.]

Capture of Mathurá.

The Sultán then departed from the environs of the city,[1] in which was a temple of the Hindús. The name of this place was Maharatu'-l Hind. He saw there a building of exquisite structure, which the inhabitants said had been built, not by men, but by Genii, and there he witnessed practices contrary to the nature of man, and which could not be believed but from evidence of actual sight. The wall of the city was constructed of hard stone, and two gates opened upon the river flowing under the city, which were erected upon strong and lofty foundations, to protect them against the floods of the river and rains. On both sides of the city there were a thousand houses, to which idol temples were attached, all strengthened from top to bottom by rivets of iron, and all made of masonry work; and opposite to them were other buildings, supported on broad wooden pillars, to give them strength.

In the middle of the city there was a temple larger and firmer than the rest, which can neither be described nor painted. The Sultán thus wrote respecting it:—"If any should wish to construct a building equal to this, he would not be able to do it without expending an hundred thousand thousand red dínárs, and it would occupy two hundred years, even though the most experienced and able workmen were employed." Among the idols there were five made of red gold, each five yards high, fixed in the air without support. In the eyes of one of these idols there were two rubies, of such value, that if any one wore to sell

---

[1] S. de Sacy has "bâtie sur une éminence." I see no authority for this in the original.

[2] Authors who have succeeded 'Utbí call this Mathura, but there is no other authority for it, but that which is in the text. It is probable that it may be here called "Maharat," because in speaking below of the Great Temple, it is said to have been built by خُمْر *i.e.*, experienced men, the plural of ماهر. Its resemblance to Mathura may have induced the pun. 'Alí bin Muslih Sam'ání, in his Commentary, derives the word from مَهْر "a dog's whine," because it resembles the casting sound uttered by Hindús in worship. This is nonsense.

such as are like them, he would obtain fifty thousand dinárs.. On another, there was a sapphire purer than water, and more sparkling than crystal; the weight was four hundred and fifty miskáls. The two feet of another idol weighed four thousand four hundred miskáls, and the entire quantity of gold yielded by the bodies of these idols, was ninety-eight thousand three hundred miskáls. The idols of silver amounted to two hundred, but they could not be weighed without breaking them to pieces and putting them into scales. The Sultán gave orders that all the temples should be burnt with naphtha and fire, and levelled with the ground.

The Conquest of Kanauj.

After this, the Sultán went on with the intention of proceeding to Kanauj, and he derived a favourable omen, when he opened the Kurán, from finding the resemblance of "Kanauj" to "victories."[1] He left the greater part of his army behind, and took only a small body of troops with him aginst Rái Jaipál, who had also but a few men with him, and was preparing to fly for safety to some of his dependant vassals.

The Sultán levelled to the ground every fort which he had in this country, and the inhabitants of them either accepted Islám, or took up arms against him. He collected so much booty, prisoners and wealth, that the fingers of those who counted them would have been tired.

He arrived on the 8th of Sha'bán, at Kanauj, which was deserted by Jaipál[2] on hearing of his approach, for he fled across the Ganges, which the Hindús regard as of exceeding sanctity, and consider that its source is in the paradise of heaven. When they burn their dead, they throw the ashes into this river, as

---

[1] "Kanauj" and "fatúh" when spelt without discritical points, assume the same form: a good illustration of the difficulty of reading accurately oriental names, —here two words of the same form, have not a letter in common.
[2] De Sacy reads "Hébul," Don calls the Rájá "Karrah." Reinaud reads "Rájá Pal," and "Rajaipál." It may be presumed he is the same as the "Parú Jaipál," subsequently mentioned. [Jurbádkání has "Haipal," Reynolds, 456.]

they consider that the waters purify them from sins. Devotees come to it from a distance, and drown themselves in its stream, in the hope of obtaining eternal salvation, but in the end it will only carry them to hell, so that it will neither kill them nor make them alive.

The Sultán advanced to the fortifications of Kanauj, which consisted of seven distinct forts, washed by the Ganges, which flowed under them like the ocean. In Kanauj there were nearly ten thousand temples, which the idolaters falsely and absurdly represented to have been founded by their ancestors two or three hundred thousand years ago. They worshipped and offered their vows and supplications to them, in consequence of their great antiquity. Many of the inhabitants of the place fled and were scattered abroad like so many wretched widows and orphans, from the fear which oppressed them, in consequence of witnessing the fate of their deaf and dumb idols. Many of them thus effected their escape, and those who did not fly were put to death. The Sultán took all seven forts in one day, and gave his soldiers leave to plunder them and take prisoners.

Capture of Munj.

He then went to Munj,[1] known as the fort of Bráhmans, the inhabitants of which were independent as headstrong camels. They prepared to offer opposition, like evil demons and obstinate Satans, and when they found they could not withstand the Musulmáns, and that their blood would be shed, they took to flight, throwing themselves down from the apertures and the lofty and broad battlements, but most of them were killed in this attempt.

Capture of Asi.

After this, the Sultán advanced against the fort of Asi,[2] the

---

[1] [Jarbádkání has "Manaj," Reynolds, 457.] The Rauzatu-s safá has "Mih," and "Bhij;" Haidar Rází, "Mahaj." Briggs says "the fort of Munj, full of Rájpúts." The Táríkh-i Alfí says "Manj." Firishta says it held out fifteen days.

[2] S. de Sacy calls it "Aster," and "Amír." [Reynolds has "Aster, held by Jandbúl the violent."]

ruler of which was Chandál Dhor, one of the chief men and generals of the Hindús. He was always engaged in a career of victory, and at one time he was at war with the Rái of Kanauj, when the campaign lasted a long time, but in the end the Rái was compelled to retreat, after having put to some trouble the friends of the ruler of Ásí. Around his fort there was an impenetrable and dense jungle, full of snakes which no enchanters could tame, and so dark that even the rays of the full moon could not be discerned in it. There were broad and deep ditches all around.

When Chandál heard of the advance of the Sultán, he lost his heart from excess of fright, and as he saw death with his mouth open towards him, there was no resource to him but flight. The Sultán ordered therefore that his five forts should be demolished from their foundations, the inhabitants buried in their ruins, and the demoniacal soldiers of the garrison plundered, slain, and imprisoned.

* * * * * *

Defeat of Chand Rái.

The Sultán, when he heard of the flight of Chandál, was sorely afflicted, and turned his horse's head towards Chand Rái, one of the greatest men in Hind, who resided in the fort of Sharwa,[1] and in his pride and self-sufficiency thought the following verse applicable to himself:

"I sneeze with expanded nostrils, and hold the Pleiades in my hand even while sitting."

Between him and Purú Jaipál,[2] there had been constant fights, in which many men and warriors had fallen in the field, and at last they consented to peace, in order to save further bloodshed and invasion of their respective borders. Purú Jaipál sought his old enemy's daughter, that he might give her in marriage to his son, Dhímpál, thus cementing the peace between them for ever,

---

[1] [Sirsáwa, to the east of the Jumna near Sahárampur.—*Cunningham*.]
[2] S. de Sacy reads "Péron Hebal," and considers him the same as the Bájá of Kanauj, previously called "Hebal." [See Thomas' *Prinsep*, I. 292.]

and preserving their swords within their sheaths. He sent his son to obtain the bride from Chand Rái, who imprisoned the son and demanded retribution for the losses which had been inflicted by the father. Jaipál was thus compelled to refrain from proceeding against Chand Rái's fort and country, being unable to release his son; but constant skirmishes occurred between them, until the arrival of Sultán Mahmúd in those parts, who, through the kindness of God, had wish after wish gratified in a succession of conquests.

Purú Jaipál in order to save his life, entered into a friendly engagement with Bhoj Chand,[1] who was proud in the strength of his forts and their difficulty of access, and there he considered himself secure against pursuit in his inaccessible retreat. But Chand Rái, on the contrary, took up arms, trusting in the strength of his fort; but had he remained in it he would infallibly have had it destroyed, and had he trusted to his army, it would have been of no avail. Under these circumstances, Dhímpál[2] wrote him a letter to this effect:—"Sultán Mahmúd is not like the rulers of Hind, and is not the leader of black men. It is obviously advisable to seek safety from such a person, for armies flee away before the very name of him and his father. I regard his bridle as much stronger than yours, for he never contents himself with one blow of the sword, nor does his army content itself with one hill out of a whole range. If therefore you design to contend with him, you will suffer, but do as you like—you know best. If you wish for your own safety, you will remain in concealment."

Chand Rái considered that Dhímpál had given him sound advice, and that danger was to be incurred by acting contrary to his suggestions. So he departed secretly with his property, elephants, and treasure, to the hill country, which was exceed-

---

[1] Apparently the same as Chandál Bhor, the governor of Aú. Some copies read Bhoj-deo, whom M. Reinaud supposes to be the same as Bhoj-deva, who is mentioned by Al Birúni as the king of Málwa.—See *M/m. sur l' Inde*, p. 261.

[2] S. de Sacy calls him "Behimal," and thinks he was probably the son of Parm-Hóbal, whom Chand Rái retained as a prisoner.

ingly lofty, hiding himself in the jungles which the sun could not penetrate, and concealing even the direction of his flight, so that there was no knowing whither he was gone, or whether he had sped by night or day. The object of Bhímpál in recommending the flight of Chand Rái was, that the Rái should not fall into the net of the Sultán, and thus be made a Musulmán, as had happened to Bhímpál's uncle and relations, when they demanded quarter in their distress.

The Sultán invested and captured the fort, notwithstanding its strength and height. Here he got plenty of supplies and booty, but he did not obtain the real object of his desire, which was to seize Chand Rái, and which he now determined to effect by proceeding in pursuit of him. Accordingly, after marching fifteen parasangs through the forest, which was so thorny that the faces of his men were scarified and bloody, and through stony tracts which battered and injured the horses' shoes, he at last came up to his enemy, shortly before midnight on the 25th of Sha'bán (6th January, 1019 A.D). They had travelled over high and low ground without any marked road, not like merchants of Hazramaut travelling at ease with their mantles around them.

The Sultán summoned the most religiously disposed of his followers, and ordered them to attack the enemy immediately. Many infidels were consequently slain or taken prisoners in this sudden attack, and the Musulmáns paid no regard to the booty till they had satiated themselves with the slaughter of the infidels and worshippers of the sun and fire. The friends of God searched the bodies of the slain for three whole days, in order to obtain booty. The elephants were carried off, some by force, some were driven, and some went without any compulsion towards Mahmúd, upon whom God bestows, out of his great kindness, not only ordinary plunder, but drives elephants towards him. Therefore they were called "God-brought,"[1] in gratitude to the

[1] This word is represented by the Persian "Khudá-áward," in the middle of the Arabic text.

Almighty for sending elephants to the Sultán, which are only driven by iron goads, and are not usually captured without stratagem and deceit; whereas, in this instance, they came of their own accord, leaving idols, preferring the service of the religion of Islám.   *   *   *

The booty amounted in gold and silver, rubies and pearls, nearly to three thousand thousand dirhams, and the number of prisoners may be conceived from the fact, that each was sold for from two to ten dirhams.[1] These were afterwards taken to Ghazna, and merchants came from distant cities to purchase them, so that the countries of Máwaráu-n nahr, 'Irák, and Khurásán were filled with them, and the fair and the dark, the rich and the poor, were commingled in one common slavery.

*   *   *   *   *

Battle of the Ráhib.

After the expedition against the Afgháns, the Sultán turned again towards Hind with his bold warriors, whose greatest pleasure was to be in the saddle, which they regarded as if it were a throne; and hot winds they looked on as refreshing breezes, and the drinking of dirty water as so much pure wine, being prepared to undergo every kind of privation and annoyance. When he arrived in that country, he granted quarter to all those who submitted, but slew those who opposed him. He obtained a large amount of booty before he reached the river, known by the name of Ráhib.[2] It was very deep, and its bottom was muddy like tar used for anointing scabby animals, and into it the feet of horses and camels sank deeply, so the men took off their coats of mail and made themselves naked before crossing it.

Purú Jaipál was encamped on the other side of the river, as a measure of security, in consequence of this sudden attack, with

---

[1] The *Tárikh-i Alfí* adds that the fifth share due to the Saiyids was 150,000 slaves.
[2] M. Reinaud observes that 'Utbí does not name the river, but the place where the Rájá had taken up his position was called "Ráhib," which means in Arabic "a monk." I translate 'Utbí differently.—See *Mém. sur l'Inde*, p. 267.

his warriors dusky as night, and his elephants all caparisoned. He showed a determination to resist the passage of the Sultán, but at night he was making preparations to escape down the river. When the Sultán learnt this, from which the weakness of his enemy was apparent, he ordered inflated skins to be prepared, and directed some of his men to swim over on them. Jaipál seeing eight men swimming over to that distant bank, ordered a detachment of his army, accompanied by five elephants, to oppose their landing, but the eight men plied their arrows so vigorously, that the detachment was not able to effect that purpose. When the Sultán witnessed the full success of these men, he ordered all his soldiers who could swim to pass over at once, and promised them henceforward a life of repose after that day of trouble. First his own personal guards crossed this difficult stream, and they were followed by the whole army. Some swam over on skins, some were nearly drowned, but eventually all landed safely; and praised be God! not even a hair of their horses tails was hurt,[1] nor was any of their property injured.

When they had all reached the opposite bank, the Sultán ordered his men to mount their horses, and charge in such a manner as to put the enemy to flight. Some of the infidels asked for mercy after being wounded, some were taken prisoners, some were killed, and the rest took to flight, and two hundred and seventy gigantic elephants fell into the hands of the Musulmáns.[2]

Extract from the Sharh-i Tárikhi Yamíní.
The Conquest of Mathura and Kanauj.

Mathurá : The proper way of pronouncing this word is "Mah-

---

[1] Literally, "Praise be to God! their horses tails were not distant." S. de Sacy translates "Les autres en se tenant aux crines de leurs chevaux," The Jámi' says, "Some swam over near their horses." I have adopted Karámat 'Alí's as being more appropriate to the introduction of the pious ejaculation "Praised be God!"
[2] The *Jámi'u-l Tawárikh* leaves out two hundred. That work and the *Yamíní* are the only two which mention the victory on the Ráhib.

arrah." Some people say this is the fifth conjugation of "harīr,"[1] on account of the Hindús chanting their prayers in that city. In some copies it is written "Mahrah," and in others "Mahharah."

Kanauj: The proper way of pronouncing this word is "Kinnauj," with the last letter but slightly enunciated.

* * * * * * *

Sihún and Jelam: The last name is spelt "Jailam," it is a city in Hind.

Chindb: The proper way of spelling the word is "Chandurúhá." It is the name of a place in the country of Hind.

Rárí: The correct mode of writing this word is "Airán," but in some copies it is written "Iráya."

Biyás: The correct mode of spelling this name is "Yiyat."

Sutlej: This should be written "Shataludr." It is the name of a province in Hind. But I have ascertained from well-informed people that it should be "Sataludr," not "Shataludr."

* * * * *

Janki: This should be written "Chanki," one of the names current in Hind.

Bamhi: This should be written "Sammhi," another name current in Hind.

* * * * *

Jamnd: This should be written "Jaun," the name of a river in Hind.

* * * * *

Baran: The mode of writing this name is "Barbah;" but in some copies it is "Barnah." It is a city among the cities of Hind.

Hardat: This is written "Hurdiz;" but in some copies it is represented as "Hurdib."

* * * * *

[1] The real meaning of "*harīr*," is a "a dog's whine." The derivation of an Indian name from an Arabic root shows the absurd ignorance of the commentator.

III.

TÁRÍKHU-S SUBUKTIGÍN

OF

ABU-L FAZL AL BAIHAKÍ.

[THE author[1] himself gives his name at full length as Khwája Abú-l Fazl bin al Hasan al Baihakí. According to his own account he was sixteen years of age in 402 Hijra (1011 A.D.) and he writes of a period as late as 451 H. (A.D. 1059), being then as he says an old man, or, as would appear, approaching 70 years of age. Kháki Shírází states that he died in 470 (1077 A.D.)

The title of the work is sometimes read "*Tárikh-i Ál-i Subuktigín*,"[2] and it is also known as the "*Tárikh-i Baihakí*." Its voluminous extent has also obtained for it the name of the "*Mujalladát-i Baihakí*; Volumes of Baihakí." The work would also seem to have been known under the name of the "*Tárikh-i Násirí*," for a passage in the *Tárikh-i Wassáf* attributes a history of this name to Abú-l Fazl Baihakí. It therefore seems to be a title of this work, or at least of some of its earlier volumes devoted to the history of Násiru-d dín Subuktigín, in the same way as the later volumes containing the reign of Mas'úd are entitled *Tárikh-i Mas'udí*.[3] The portion relating to Mahmúd's history was called *Tájn-l Futúh* as is evident from Unsúrí's Kasáid.

Hájí Khalfa, in his Lexicon, describes this work as a comprehensive history of the Ghaznivides in several volumes. Mírkhond quotes it among Persian histories, and in his preface to the *Rauzatu-s safá*, he says that it consists of thirty volumes.

---

[1] [The first part of this article has been re-written by the Editor, partly from notes added by Sir H. Elliot to his original sketch, and partly from letters relating to the various extant MSS. addressed to Sir H. Elliot by Mr. Morley.]

[2] [Morley's edition of the text.]   [3] [*Mém. sur l'Inde*, p. 27.]

Firishta evidently refers to this author, when he speaks of the Mujalladát of Abú-l Fazl, at the beginning of Mahmúd's reign, but it may be doubted if he ever saw the work. He does not notice it in his list of works, and he certainly did not use it for Mas'úd's reign, as he omits many important events recorded in it. The Mujalladát are also referred to for the same reign by the *Táríkh-i Guzída*. The author is mentioned by Haidar Rází, by Ziáu-d dín Barní, by Abú-l Fazl in the *Ayín-i Akbarí*, and by Jahángír in his Memoirs.

Though the work was thus well-known to historians, a large portion of it seems to be irrecoverably lost, and the extant portions are of rare occurrence in India. After some research, Sir H. Elliot discovered a portion of the work in the possession of Ziáu-d dín Khán, of Lohárú near Dehli, and he subsequently procured three other copies, one from Dr. Sprenger (Lucknow), another from Agra, and a third from Lahore. The Dehli MS. was forwarded to the late Mr. Morley, in England, who was previously in possession of a copy.[1] Another MS. was found in the Bodleian Library, and the libraries of Paris and St. Petersburg also possess one copy each. The last two were lent to Mr. Morley,[2] who, after a collation of six MSS., produced a revised text, which some years after his death was printed in the Bibliotheca Indica under the supervision of Major N. Lees and his staff of munshis. This comprises part of vol. 6, the whole of vols. 7, 8, 9, and part of vol. 10 of the original work. There is some confusion in the numbering of the volumes; for instance, the indices of the Dehli and Agra MSS. call that portion of the work, vol. 5, which Mr. Morley calls vol. 6, but there is ample evidence among Sir H. Elliot's papers, that Mr. Morley took great pains to ascertain the correct division of the work, and his decision must be accepted.

All, or at any rate, six of the MSS. contain exactly the same matter, beginning and ending with the same words, and they

[1] [Purchased at a London book-stall for a few shillings.]
[2] [A contrast to the retentive practices of our great libraries.]

further agree in showing a lacuna after the account of the raid to Benares (page 408 of Morley's edition), where about a page and a half of matter seems to be missing. Mr. Morley remarks that one copy had a marginal note of *Sic in orig.*

Thus it is apparent that all these copies must have been taken immediately or intermediately from the same original. The dates of the various MSS. are not all known, but that of the Paris copy is 1019 Hijra (1610 A.D.) The inference to be drawn from these facts is, that the voluminous work of Baihakí was reduced to the remnant which we still possess by the end of the sixteenth century, and the chance of recovering the remainder though not impossible, is beyond hope.]

Baihakí has laid down the requisites for a good historian at the beginning of his tenth volume, and he has professed to conform to the model he has there laid down. He says:—" Man can be read by the heart of man. The heart is strengthened or weakened by what it hears and sees, and until it hears or sees the bad and the good, it knows neither sorrow nor joy in this world. Be it therefore known that the eyes and ears are the watchmen and spies of the heart, which report to it what they see and hear, that it may take advantage of the same, and represent it to Wisdom, who is a just judge, and can separate the true from the false, and can avail itself of that which is useful, and reject that which is otherwise. It is for this reason that man wishes to learn that which is concealed, that which is neither known nor heard of; that which has occurred in past times, and that which has not. But this historical knowledge can only be obtained with difficulty, either by travelling round the world and undergoing trouble, or searching in trustworthy books, and ascertaining the real occurrences from them. * * * There are two kinds of past history, and no third is known; either that which one hears from others, or that which one reads in books. It is a necessary condition that your informant should be trustworthy and true, and that wisdom should testify to the probability of the story, to give independent sanction to the statements, and that the book should be such that the reader or hearer should not reject but readily adopt its assertions. Most people are so constituted that they love silly stories more than truth, such as those about fairies, hills, and the demons of the deserts and seas, which fools make so much fuss about: as where a narrator says that in a certain sea I saw an island, on which five hundred people landed, and we baked our bread and boiled our pots, and when the fire began to burn briskly, the heat descended into the earth, and it then moved away, when we saw that it was merely a fish. Also, I saw such and such things moving on a certain hill. Also, how an old woman turned a man into an ass by witchcraft, and how another old woman by the same means, after rubbing oil in his ear, turned him into a man again, and other fables like to these which bring sleep, when they are repeated at night-time to people who are ignorant, for so they are considered by those who search for truth that they may believe it. Of these the number is exceedingly small, who can accept the true and reject the false. I, who have undertaken the history, have endeavoured so to manage, that whatever I write may be from my own observation, or from the accounts I have received from credible informants."

The *Táríkhu-s Subuktigín* wears more the appearance of a gossiping memoir than an elaborate history. The author perpetually alludes to himself, his own intimacies, his own proceedings, and his own experiences. He gives us a graphic account of most of the contemporary nobles; the pursuits of the emperor Mas'úd bin Mahmúd ; his dictations to his secretaries ; his addiction to wine ; and his repentance on the occasion of one of his visits to Hindústán, when he forswore liquor and threw the wine and drinking vessels into the river Jailam; which strongly reminds us of a later but identical freak of Bábar's. We have a vivid representation of the court ; the mode of transacting business, the agents by whom it was transacted, and the nature of the subjects which came under discussion before the council at Ghazní. [All related with such detail and verbosity as to be open to the

charge of prolixity which the author apprehended. But although
tedious, the work is eminently original, and it presents such a
reflex of the doings and manners of the time that its minutiæ
and trifles frequently constitute its chief merit. The writer may
not inaptly be described as an oriental Mr. Pepys.]

The book is very discursive, and by no means adheres to a
chronological succession of events. At one time the author
mentions his personal interviews with the famous Emperor Mahmúd; at another we are favoured with a view of the court of
Ibráhím or Mas'úd, then we are suddenly transported back again
to that of Mahmúd. He states in one part that he has written
the events of fifty years in several thousand pages, and that if
any one complains of his prolixity, it must be remembered that
he has written of several princes and illustrious persons, and that
the matter, therefore, was too important to be compressed in a
small space, especially when it concerned the great Emperors
whose servant and subject he was.

The style of the work is a most singular kind of colloquial
Persian, written down without any attempt at order and the due
arrangement of the sentences; the construction is consequently
often very perplexed and the meaning obscure. Had I not heard
men from the neighbourhood of Ghazní speak Persian very much
in the style of our author, I should have conceived the work to be
a literal translation from the Arabic, the sequence of words according to that language being very frequently observed. In
speaking of his tenth volume, the author says he intends to
devote it to an account of the Emperor Mas'úd's last invasion of
Hindustán, and to the history of Khwárizm. To enable him to
accomplish the latter purpose, he confesses that he will be indebted
to the history written by Bú Ríhán, which he had seen some years
before. This is, no doubt, the famous Abú Ríhán al Dírúní,
mentioned in a former article, who was a native of Khwárizm,
and a member of the learned society which was in his time congregated at the capital under the auspices of the king.

Besides this voluminous work, he quotes, as one of the

historica written by him, "the *Makámát-i Mahmúdí*," though, perhaps, this may mean merely passages in which he has written of the affairs of Mahmúd in some of the previous volumes. He also distinctly mentions that he is the author of "*Táríkh-i Yamíní*." This cannot possibly allude to the famous work of 'Utbí just noticed, who, under the name of 'Abdu-l Jabbár, is frequently noticed in this fragment; Baihakí, therefore, by this expression probably means that part of his work in which he has written of Mahmúd, entitled Yamínu-d daula.

The Extracts from this work are more than usually copious, as they are calculated to attract particular attention.

In one of the passages we find mention of the capture of Benares as early as A.H. 424 (A.D. 1033), only three years after Mahmúd's death. In other authors we have mention of an expedition to Kashmír during that year by Mas'úd himself, but no mention of Ahmad Niáltigín's capture of Benares. All we have hitherto known of the Indian transactions of that year is that the king resolved on making an expedition into India. He took the route of Sarsutí, situated among the hills of Kashmír, the garrison of which fort being intimidated, sent messengers to the king, promising valuable presents, and an annual tribute, if he would desist from his enterprise. Mas'úd felt disposed to listen to the proposals, until he understood that some Muhammadan merchants, having been seen by the garrison, were then captives in the place. He accordingly broke up the conference and besieged the fort, ordering the ditch to be filled up with sugar canes from the adjacent plantations. This being done, he caused scaling-ladders to be applied to the walls; and the fort, after a bloody contest, was taken. The garrison, without distinction, was put to the sword, except the women and children, who were carried off by the soldiers as slaves. The king, moreover, commanded that a part of the spoil should be given to the Muhammadans who had been prisoners in Sarsutí, and who had formerly lost their effects. This year is also recorded by Indian historians as remarkable for a great drought and famine in many parts of the world, especially in Persia and India, in which entire provinces were depopulated. The famine was succeeded by a pestilence, which swept many thousands from the face of the earth; for in less than one month forty thousand persons died in Ispahán alone.

The more celebrated Abú-l Fazl, the minister of Akbar, mentions in his Ayín-i Akbarí, that Sultán Mahmúd twice visited Benares: once in A.H. 410, and again in A.H. 413. I have in another work,[1] printed by direction of Government, pointed out the extreme improbability of these visits; and here the doubts are confirmed by a contemporary, who distinctly says that the Muhammadans had not yet penetrated so far before the time of Ahmad Niáltigín. Unfortunately, in the original a lacuna occurs at the very place where the extract closes, or we might have gained more information about this remote and interesting expedition.

The old form of spelling Lahore is also worthy of observation. Lahúr is very unusual. Ziáu-dín Barní always spells it Lohúr, and the Farhang-i Jahángírí says it is spelt Lánhaur, Loháwnr, and Laháwar, as well as Lohúr. It is only of late years that the uniform practice has been observed of spelling it Láhore.[2]

In another passage we have an account of an expedition to India in A.H. 420. In Firishta and Mirkhond, we have no intelligence under that year, but as they mention that Hánsí was taken in A.H. 427, and as the extract mentions that it was commonly called a "virgin fort," because it had never yet been taken, no doubt, though the details are different, the same event is referred to.

Another extract is pregnant with information respecting the early credit assigned to Hindú soldiers, by their victorious enemies. Had we not other instances of the consideration in which the military qualities of Hindús were held, we might have hesitated to yield our belief that such sentiments could have been entertained by a chief of Ghazní. But we learn from other

[1] [The "Glossary."]
[2] [See Vol. I., p. 46. On coins of this dynasty it is clearly engraved لوهور].

histories that even only fifty days after the death of Mahmúd, his son dispatched Sewand Rái, a Hindú chief, with a numerous body of Hindú cavalry, in pursuit of the nobles who had espoused the cause of his brother. In a few days a conflict took place, in which Sewand Rái, and the greatest part of his troops were killed; but not till after they had inflicted a heavy loss upon their opponents.[1]

Five years afterwards we read of Tilak, son of Jai Sen, commander of all the Indian troops in the service of the Ghaznivide monarch, being employed to attack the rebel chief, Ahmad Niáltigín. He pursued the enemy so closely that many thousands fell into his hands. Ahmad himself was slain while attempting to escape across a river, by a force of Hindú Jats, whom Tilak had raised against him. This is the same Tilak whose name is written in the *Tabakát-i Akbarí*, as Malik bin Jai Sen, which, if correct, would convey the opinion of the author of that work, that this chief was a Hindú convert.

Five years after that event we find that Mas'úd, unable to withstand the power of the Seljúk Turkománs, retreated to India, and remained there for the purpose of raising a body of troops sufficient to make another effort to retrieve his affairs. It is reasonable therefore to presume that the greater part of these troops consisted of Hindús.

In the reign of his successor, when Abú 'Alí, Kotwál of Ghazní, was deputed to command the army in India, and maintain the Ghaznivide conquests in that country, we read of his sending a letter to Dijí Rái, a general of the Hindús, who had done much service even in the time of Mahmúd, inviting him to return to Ghazní, whence he had fled on account of some political dissensions, and had taken up his abode in the mountains of Kashmír.

These few instances will confirm the impressions which the extract is calculated to convey.

[1] Wilken, 164.

Events of the Year 422 H. *Investiture of Khwája Ahmad Hasan.*[1]

The first of Muharram of this year fell on a Tuesday. Amír Mas'úd, may God be pleased with him! went during the day to the garden-palace, with the intention of spending some time there. The public court rooms were arranged in it, and many other buildings were added. One year when I went there, the court-yard of the palace and the shops were all reconstructed in a different manner, under the orders of the king, who was a very clever architect, and not excelled by any mathematician. And this new sarái which is still to be seen in Ghaznín, is a sufficient proof of this. There was at Shádiákh, in Naishápúr, no palace or parade ground; yet he designed both with his own hands, and built a sarái there, which now excites admiration, besides numerous smaller saráís and enclosures. At Bust he so increased the cantonments of the Amír, his father, that some of them exist to this day. This king was singularly excellent in everything. May the Almighty God, whose name should be respected, be merciful to him!

From Hirát an order was despatched through the agents of Khwája Bú Suhal Zauzaní, summoning Khwája Ahmad Hasan to the court, for Jangí,[2] the governor of the fort, had liberated him from prison, and he (the Khwája) had said to Hájib Ariyáruk, commander of the army of Hindustán. "Your reputation at present stands rather bad; it is advisable that you should come with me and see his majesty, I will speak in your favour, and you shall return with a robe of honour and a good name. Affairs are now carefully settled, and such a generous and kind prince as Amír Mas'úd has mounted the throne." Ariyáruk was moved by his soft words, and the spells of the venerable man took effect upon him; so he accompanied the Khwája on the way, and served him exceedingly well; for, indeed, amongst the civil officers of those days, no one possessed greater dignity and excellence than the Khwája.

[1] [Morley's Text, page 168 to 198.]
[2] [So in MS., Morley's edition has "Japhí," or "Chapkí."]

The great Khwája 'Abdu-r Razzák, the eldest son of Khwája Ahmad Hasan, who was detained in the fort of Nandna, was liberated, upon his own demand, by Sárugh, the cup-bearer, who brought him to his father. The son expressed his great obligation to Sárugh, before the father. The Khwája said, I am under greater obligation to him than you are. He ordered him (Sárugh) to go back to Nandna, because it was not such a place that it should be left empty, and told him that on his reaching the court he would report his case and possibly gain him promotion. Sárugh immediately went back. The great Khwája was very happy to come to Balkh. He went to see the Amír, and to pay his respects and duty. The Amír questioned him very warmly, gave him advice, and conversed with him kindly. He made obeisance and returned. He lodged in a house which was prepared for him, and took three days rest, and then came again to court. When this great man (says Abú-l Fazl Baihakí) had rested himself, a message was sent to him regarding the post of Wazír. Of course he did not accept it. Bú Suhal Zauzaní was connected with him (the Amír), and had the arrangement of all his affairs; the amercing and approving of men, the buying and selling, was all done by him. The Amír was constantly closeted with him and 'Abdús. These two persons were his chosen councillors, but they were both inimical to each other. The people of his father Mahmúd's time had selected them that things might go peaceably. I never saw Bú Nasr, my instructor, more busy and perplexed at any time than he was now. When the messages were passing between the king and Khwája Ahmad Hasan, the latter said to Bú Suhal, "I am become old and can not do the duties. Bú Suhal Hamadání is a qualified and experienced man, he might be appointed 'Áriz (general). The office of Wazír should be conferred on you, I will look on from a distance and assist you with any necessary advice." Bú Suhal said, "I did not expect this from my lord. What man am I? I am a worthless and useless person." The Khwája said, "Holy God! since the time you came back from Dámaghán to the Amír, have you not performed all the duties, even when the affairs of the country were unsettled, and now that our lord has occupied the throne, and the whole business is reduced to a system, you can do the duty more easily and better." Bú Suhal observed, for a long time there was no one to act under the king, but now that such an eminent personage as you are come, I and those like me have no courage and ability to do anything. How shall a mere atom prevail against the sun. We are all insignificant persons. The true master has appeared, and every hand is restrained. He said, very good, I will consider over it. He went home, and in two or three days about fifty or sixty messages were sent to him upon this business; but still he did not accept the offer. One day he came to see the Amír, and when the conversation began, the Amír directed him to sit down. He then dismissed the attendants and said, Khwája, why don't you undertake this duty, you know you are to me as a father. I have many important matters before me, and it is not proper that you should deprive me of your ability. The Khwája replied, I am your obedient servant, and next to the Almighty, I owe my life to your majesty. But I am become old and unfit for work. Besides, I have vowed and have taken a solemn oath, that I will never more engage in business, for much trouble has come upon me. The Amír said, I will have thee absolved from thine oaths; you must not refuse me. He said, if there is no help, and I must accept the appointment, I will, if your majesty sees fit, sit in the court room, and if there is anything to ask about, I will send a message to you by a confidential person, and act according to your reply. The Amír said very good, but whom will you make your confidant. He replied, Bú Suhal Zauzaní is concerned in the business, and perhaps it would be better if Bú Nasr Mishkán were also made a medium between us, for he is a honest man, and in days gone by he has been my confidential mouthpiece. The Amír said it was very proper. The Khwája departed, and went to the Díwán's office, which they cleared out. I heard Bú Nasr Mishkán say that when he was about to leave, the Khwája made him sit down, and told him not to depart, for it was now his duty to carry messages to the king's court. He said, the king will not leave me in retirement, although it is time for me to sue for forgiveness of the Almighty, and not to be acting as minister. Bú Nasr observed, may my lord live long! the Amir thinks what he has proposed advisable, and it also seems good to his servants; but you, my lord, will fall into trouble, for there are many important matters which nothing but great foresight and enlightened wisdom can settle. The Khwája observed, what you say is true, but I see that there are many ministers here; and I know that this is not concealed from you. Bú Nasr acknowledged that there were such persons, but that they were only fit to obey orders, and he then asked of what use he was in the business? Bú Suhal was sufficient, and as he (Bú Nasr) had been much troubled by that person, he wished by some device to keep aloof from him. The Khwája told him not to be afraid, for he had confidence in him. Bú Nasr bowed his acknowledgments. Bú Suhal now came and brought a message from our lord the Sultán, saying, In the time of my father the Khwája endured great troubles and hardships, and he was treated with ignominy. It is very surprising that his life was spared, but he was left to adorn my reign. He must consent to serve me, because dignity like his is needed. He has numerous followers and friends like himself, who will all work according to his instructions, so that business will be managed upon a regular system.

The Khwája said, I have made a vow never to serve the Sultán: but as his Majesty commands me and says that he will absolve me from my oath, I yield to his wishes. But there are duties attached to this office which if I try to carry out and obey my lord's orders, all the servants will rise with one accord against me and become my enemies. They will play the same tricks now as they did in the last reign. I shall thus throw myself into great difficulty. But now I have no enemy and live in peace. If I do not discharge the duties, but act dishonestly, I shall be charged with weakness, and I shall find no excuse either before the Almighty or my master. If there is no help for it, and I must perforce take the office, I must be fully informed of its duties, and I must be allowed and have authority to offer such advice and counsel as may be necessary.

We two (Bú Nasr and Bú Suhal) went to say this to the Amír I asked Bú Suhal, as he was to be the intermediun, what work I should have to do? He replied, the Khwája has chosen you; perhaps he has no confidence in me. He was much displeased with my intervention. When I went into the presence I observed a respectful silence, for I wished Bú Suhal to speak. When he opened the business, the Amír turned towards me and wanted me to speak. Bú Suhal discreetly moved away, and I delivered all the messages. The Amír said I will entrust him (the Khwája) with all the duties, excepting such as respect conviviality, wine-drinking, fighting, the game of *chaugán* and *chaukkabak*. All other duties he must discharge, and no objection shall be urged against his sentiments and views. I returned and brought the answer. Bú Suhal had quitted his place, although I left everything to him. But what could I do, the Amír did not leave me alone, neither did the Khwája. He (the Khwája) said, I am obedient. I will think and write down some points which must be taken to-morrow to his Majesty. May the Almighty increase his dignity! Answers to them must be written under the king's own hand and attested by his seal. This business must be conducted in the same manner as in the time of the late Amír; and you know how it was managed in those days. Well we went and spake (as we had been desired). The Amír said, Bú Nasr! Welcome! To morrow you must finish this business, that on the following day he may put on the robe (of office). We said we will tell him, and we were departing, when he called to me, Bú Nasr, and said—When the Khwája returns do you come back for I have something to say to you. I said, I will do so; and repaired to the Khwája and related the whole to him. Bú Suhal went away and I and the Khwája remained. I said, May my lord live long! I said to Bú Suhal, as we were going along—This is the first time that we have carried a message together, and since you have the management what am I to do? He replied, The Khwája has selected you because he, perhaps, has no confidence in me. The Khwája said—I chose you because I wished to have a Musulmán in the business, who would not tell a lie or pervert words, and who would, moreover, know what ought to be done. This sorry cuckold and others think that if I take this office, they will really perform the duties of minister. The first thing to do is to overload him so with business that all life and spirit shall be taken out of him, and that he withdraw from ministerial duties. The others will then do the same. I know he will not be content, and will withdraw reluctantly. The king has given many low fellows access to his throne, and has made them presumptuous. I will do what I think right in the way of counsel and kindness, and we shall see what will come to pass. He went back, and I repaired to the Amír, who asked me what the Khwája would write, I replied,—the rule has been that when the post of Wazír is conferred on a person of distinction he writes his terms[1] and enquiries about the responsibilities of his position. The Sovereign then writes with his own hand an answer and attests it with his seal. After this, God is called to witness it. The Wazír then examines it, and it becomes a solemn compact with stringent provisions, which the minister must repeat with his tongue and attest with his signature, adding thereto witnesses to his promise of acting in conformity therewith. The Amír directed that a draft of the reply to his proposals should be drawn up, and that a copy of the oath also should be prepared so that the business might be concluded on the morrow, and the minister might assume his robe of office, for business was at a standstill. I said, I will do so and returned. The The papers were written out, and at the time of afternoon prayer, another private interview was granted. The Amír then apprized himself of their contents and approved them. Next day the Khwája came (to the palace) and when the *lerée* was

[1] ["مضایف"]

over he came into the public court (*táram*), ordered it to be cleared, and then seated himself. Bú Suhal and Bú Nasr brought forward the conditions. The Amír called for ink and paper, wrote answers to each of them with his own hand, attested them with his seal and signature, and confirmed the whole by an oath written at the bottom. The paper was brought to the Khwája, and when he had read the answers, he stood up, kissed the ground, went to the throne and kissed the hand of the Amír, and then returned to his place and sat down. Bú Nasr and Bú Suhal placed the solemn oath before him. The Khwája pronounced the words of it with his tongue and then affixed his signature to the paper. Bú Nasr and Bú Suhal were the witnesses. On the oath being taken, the Amír praised the Khwája and congratulated him heartily. The Khwája kissed the ground. On this he was ordered to retire, and next day to assume the robe of office, because all business was in arrear and many important matters had to be settled. The Khwája said, I am your obedient servant, kissed the ground, and retired to his house taking the articles of agreement with him. The oath was deposited in the secretary's office (*dawdt-khána*). I have inserted a copy of the oath and of the articles in another book which I have written, and called "Makámát-i Mahmúdí." Not to be prolix, I have avoided to repeat them here. Every one knew that the post of Wazír was filled, and fear fell upon every heart, for it was no common person who had been appointed. Those from whom the Khwája had received an injury were much alarmed.

Bú Suhal Zauzaní began to boast in the most dreadful manner. He told the people that the office of Wazír had been offered to him, but he did not accept it, and that he had brought forward the Khwája. Those who had any sense knew that it was not so. Sultán Mas'úd, May God approve him! was too intelligent, wise, and well-informed, to bestow the post of Wazír on any other person, so long as Khwája Ahmad was alive, because he knew the rank and qualifications of every one, and what they were fit for. There is an evident proof of what I have said.

When Khwája Ahmad had gone to Hirát, the Amír passing his various officers in review (*in kaumrá mí-díd*) remembered Khwája Ahmad 'Abdu-l Samad, and said,—There is none fitter than he for this office. When I arrive at the proper period in my history, I will give a full account of this incident. I have not said this because I received injuries from Bú Suhal, for he and all these people are dead, and it is clear also that I have but a little time to live. But I speak the truth. I know that wise and experienced men who now read this will find no fault with me for what I have written. What I have mentioned in this matter is correct, and I can answer for it. May God, whose name is glorious, keep me and all Muhammadans from fault and error, through his grace and wisdom, power and mercy.

The following day, which was Sunday, the 9th of the month of Safar, the Khwája entered the court. The great men and the elders, the generals and the other military officers, all waited upon him, and observed the ceremonials of respect. The Amír turned his face towards the Khwája, and said, you must now put on the robe of office, because we have many important things to attend to. He then said, let it be known that the Khwája is my representative (*khalífa*) in all matters requiring consideration. His orders and directions must be executed and observed in all things. Whatever he deems proper, no one must oppose. The Khwája kissed the ground, and professed his allegiance.

The Amír made a signal to Hájib Bilkátigín, who was chief of the guards, to take the Khwája to the state wardrobe. He came forward and took the Khwája by the arm. The Khwája stood up and went to the place, and remained there till about 12 o'clock, because the astrologer had fixed on that time as auspicious for his putting on the dress. All the chief men and military officers attended the court, some sitting and others standing. The Khwája then invested himself with his official robes. I stood and saw what passed. What I say is from ocular observation, and according to the list I possess. There was a garment of scarlet cloth of Baghdád, embroidered with small

flowers; a long turban of the finest muslin, with a delicate lace
border; a large chain, and a girdle of one thousand miskáls,
studded with turquoises. Hájib Dilkátigín was sitting at the
door of the wardrobe, and when the Khwája came out, he stood
up and offered his congratulations, and presented one dinár, one
small turban, and two very large turquoises, set in a ring. He
wished to walk before him (in procession), but the Khwája said,
upon the life and head of the Sultán, you must walk by my side;
tell the other guards to go before. Dilkátigín answered, O great
Khwája, say not so, because you know my friendship, and besides,
you are now dressed in the robe of my lord the Sultán, to which
we, his slaves, must show respect. So he walked before the
Khwája and two other men of the guards with him, beside many
officers. A slave of the Khwája was also appointed a guard, and
a coloured vestment was given to him, because it was not customary in the army for the guards of Khwájas to go before them.
When he reached the palace, other guards came to receive him,
and they conducted him to the Amír, and there seated him. The
Amír offered his congratulations to the Khwája, who stood up,
kissed the ground, approached the throne, and presented a bunch
of pearls to the king, which was said to be valued at ten thousand
dinárs. The Amír Mas'úd gave to the Khwája a ring set with a
turquoise, on which his majesty's name was engraved, and said,
this is the seal of state, and I give it to you that people may
know that the Khwája's authority is next to mine. The Khwája
took the ring, kissed the Amír's hand and the ground, and returned
to his house. He was attended by such an escort as nobody
recollected to have seen before, so that, except the musicians (who
play at fixed times every day), nobody remained at the royal
palace. He alighted at the gate of 'Abdu-l 'Ala, and went into
his house. The great men and ministers of the state began
to pour in. So many slaves, presents, and clothes were brought,
that the like of them no minister had ever received. Some
brought them with pleasure, and others from fear. A list of all
the things brought was kept, so that all might be taken to the king.

He did not keep back even a thread for himself. Such things were learnt from him, for he was the most honest and the greatest man of the age. He sat till the time of midday prayer, and only left his place for that duty. The whole day he spent busily among the people. On the following day he went to court, but had not the robe on him. He had got a garment made after the old fashion, and a turban of Naishápúr or Káín, and in these people always saw this great man dressed. May God approve him! I have heard from his companions, such as Bú Ibráhím Káíni, that he had his reception dress and twenty or thirty other garments all made of the same colour, and these he used to wear for a year, so that people thought that he had only one dress, and used to express their surprise that the garment did not wear or fade. There were no bounds to his manliness, industry, and magnanimity. I shall make some mention of them hereafter in their appropriate place. When the year had passed, he had twenty or thirty more garments made, and put them in the wardrobe.

This day, when he came to see the king, the court broke up, and Sultán Mas'úd held a private conference with the minister, which lasted till the time of mid-day prayer. There were many who withered with fear, and a muttering arose as of a drum beaten under a blanket. Afterwards he (the Khwája) came out and kept silence. Neither I nor any one else could know aught of what had passed in the council, still some of the effects became manifest. One party had offices and robes bestowed upon them, others were dismissed, and their robes were torn off; these and other transactions were perceived by intelligent men to be the results of that private conference.[1] When the drum was beat at

[1] [The original translation of this passage, made by a munshí, and revised by an Englishman, ran as follows. It is by no means an unfair specimen of many of the translations, and it is inserted to show the quality of much of the assistance received by Sir M. Elliot. Another passage is given in page 89. "Some of the councillors quarrelled among themselves. There was a drum which was beat under a blanket, and a noise issued from it. The councillors and others like me became acquainted with what had happened in that council. But as some signs of the deed were becoming public, offices were conferred on one party, and robes of honour granted, while another party was expelled and degraded, and affairs became smooth. The wise men knew that all this was the result of one council."]

the time of noon-day prayer, the Khwája came out. His horse was sent for and he returned home. All day long, until evening, those persons who had been alarmed, came and made presents to him.

Bú Muhammad Káíní, who was his old private secretary, and in the days of his misfortune had, by the Amír Mahmúd's order, served under Khwája Abú-l Kásim and afterwards under Díwán Hasnak in the same capacity, and secretary Ibráhím Bailhakí, who attended the minister's office; these two persons were called by the Khwája who said to them—"Secretaries must needs be attentive to orders. I place my confidence in you. To morrow you must attend the office and engage in writing; bring also with you scholars and assistants." They said we are obedient. Bú Nasr, of Bust, a clerk, who is still alive, was an intelligent and good man and a fine caligrapher. He had rendered many services to the Khwája in Hindustán, and had been warmly devoted to him when he was in need. When the Khwája got over his troubles, he (Bú Nasr) came with him to Balkh, and the Khwája now patronized him, and bestowed a high office on him. His distress vanished, and he obtained an ample competence. Bú Muhammad and Ibráhím are departed. May God forgive them! Bú Nasr is yet alive at Ghazní, and in honor in the service of this family. In the time when Khwája 'Abdu-r Razzák was minister, he was controller (*hájib*) of the Secretary's office. He patronized Bú 'Abdu-lla Pársí, who also served under the Khwája. This Bú 'Abdu-lla, in the time of the ministry of the Khwája, was chief of the royal messengers at Balkh, and lived in great splendour, but he had endured great hardships during the Khwája's adversity. At his removal from office, Amírak Baihaki hastened from Ghazní, as I have before mentioned, and they took immense riches from him.

The next day, which was Tuesday, the Khwája attended the Court and visited the Amír, and then came to his office. A fine cloth of brocado set with turquoises had been spread near his seat for him to kneel on. He went through two forms of prayer, and then sitting down, but not in his official seat, he asked for an inkstand. It was brought to him with a quire of paper, and a box of sand, such as are used by ministers. These he took and there sat and wrote a thanksgiving in Arabic.[1]

He then ordered the complainants and suitors to be called. Several were brought before him. He heard their statements, dispensed justice, and sent them away happy. He said, This is the minister's Court; its gates are open, there is no hindrance, whoever has business may come in. People heartily prayed for him and were inspired with hope. The military and civil officers came in with strict decorum and sat down, some on his right hand, some on his left. He turned, looked at them, and said, To-morrow come so prepared that you may be able to give a ready answer to whatsoever I may ask you, make no reservation. Up to this time business has been carried on very improperly. Every one has been occupied with his own concerns, and the king's business has been neglected. Ahmad Hasan knows you well, and will not allow things to go on as heretofore. You must now put on a new appearance, every one must attend to his duty. No one dared to speak, all were alarmed, and cowered. The Khwája arose and went home; all that day also presents were brought till nightfall. At the time of afternoon prayer he asked for the lists and examined them. Those things which the treasurers of the Sultán and accountants of the Court had written down were all brought one by one before the Amír. There were numberless articles of gold, silver, entire pieces of cloth, Turkish slaves of high price, valuable horses and camels, and everything most suitable for royal pomp and splendour. The king was highly pleased. He said, the Khwája is empty handed, why did he not take them? So he ordered ten thousand dínárs, five hundred thousand dirhams, ten Turkish slaves of great price, five horses from the royal stable, and ten 'Abdús camels to be taken to him. When the camels brought these presents before

[1] [Given at full length in the text.]

the Khwája, he rose up, kissed the ground, and gave many blessings. The camels then returned.

The next day, which was Wednesday, 7th of Safar, the Khwája attended the Court. The Amír was very severe,[1] and the day passed in great pomp and splendour. When the Court broke up, the Khwája came to his office, engaged in business, and arranged matters to the best of his judgment. At breakfast time (*chásht-gáh*) he called Bú Nasr Mishkán, and when he came he (the Khwája) gave him a secret message to be delivered to the Amír that, as he had before stated, the business of reporting matters was not properly conducted, adding that Bú Suhal Zauzuní was an honourable and respectable man, and that if his Majesty thought proper, he might be summoned and the robe of the appointment conferred on him, in order that he might conduct this most important of all duties. The Khwája himself was rendering all the guidance and assistance possible, in order that discipline might be preserved in the army.

Bú Nasr went and delivered the message. The Amír made a signal to Bú Suhal, who was sitting in the court with other courtiers. He went forward, and his majesty spoke one or two words to him. Bú Suhal bowed and retired. He was conducted to the wardrobe by two guards, one of whom served outside, and the other inside the palace. A rich khil'at was bestowed on him, and a girdle, with seven hundred pieces of gold, which had all been prepared overnight. He came back and paid his respects to the Amír, who offered him his congratulations, and ordered him to go to the Khwája, under whose directions he was to act; he also desired him to give special attention to the important matter of military administration. Bú Suhal expressed his obedience, kissed the ground, and retired. He came directly into the Khwája's office. The Khwája made him sit by his side, and spoke very kindly to him. He then went home. All the great men, elders, and servants, went to his house and paid him great respect, and presented him with

[امیر مظالم کرد] [1]

many valuables. He also ordered that a list should be made of all that they had brought, and he sent it to the treasury.

The day afterwards a very rich robe was conferred on Bú Suhal Hamadúní, who had been removed from the post of Wazír, and appointed to the duty of controlling the financial affairs[1] of the kingdom. The four persons who had before discharged this duty, with all the other accountants of the court, were to act as his assistants. He came before the Amír and paid his respects. The Amír said, You are an old servant, and a friend who has performed great deeds in favour of the State. You must now efficiently execute these (new) duties. He consented, and taking leave, he went into the office of the Khwája, who made him sit on his left hand according to established custom, and spoke very kindly to him. Presents were also given to him, and what people brought he sent to the treasury. The whole business of administration was arranged, and the dignity of minister was such as nobody remembered to have seen before. The Amír had conferred great honour on the minister. The Khwája began, even from the first, with vengeance and threats. He related the story of Khwája Bú-l Kásim Kasír, who was removed from the office of paymaster ('áriz) as well as of Abú Bakr Hasírí and Bú-l Hasan 'Ukailí, who were courtiers, and who had formed a design which I have before mentioned in this history. Hasírí was a violent man, and in the time of the Amír Mahmúd he quarrelled with the king at a drinking party, and twice received blows. Bú-l Kásim Kasír, had himself been minister, and Abú-l Hasan was his purchased slave. I will mention, hereafter, what happened to each of them.

On Sunday, the 11th of Safar, a very magnificent and costly robe was prepared for the great chamberlain (hájib), besides fine drums and flags, and flag-staffs, slaves, purses of dirhams, uncut pieces of cloth, according to the list of things which had been given to Hájib 'Alí Karíb, at the gate of Gurgán.

When the court broke up the Amír ordered Hájib Bilkátigin

[1] [شغل إشراف]

to be conducted to the wardrobe, and a robe was put on him. The kettle-drums were placed on camels, and banners were raised at the palace-gate. The flags, purses of silver, and pieces of cloth were placed in the garden. He came forward dressed in a black garment, with a two horned cap and a golden girdle. Advancing he paid homage. The Amír spoke kindly to him, and he returned and came into the Khwája's office. The Khwája spoke very affably to him. He went home, and the grandees and chief men all paid him due respect. Thus he obtained distinction and honour. A man more liberal, open, and brave, was seldom seen. But levity was predominant in him, and his frivolity was very disagreeable. However, no man is without blemish. Perfection belongs only to God the great and glorious.

An extraordinary occurrence happened in these days to the lawyer Bú Bakr Hasírí. A fault was committed by him in a state of intoxication, through which the Khwája got the upper hand of him, and revenged himself to his heart's content. Although the Amír, like a just sovereign, inquired about the case, the man had disgraced himself. I must perforce give an account of this matter for the information of my readers. The destiny of God, great and glorious, is unavoidable. It so happened that Hasírí, with his son Bú-l Kásim, had gone to the garden of Khwája 'Alí Míkáíl, which was near, and had drunk to excess. They passed the night there and the next morning they again drank, and it is bad to drink in the morning. Wise men seldom do this. They drank till half the interval between the times of the first and second prayers, and then mounting, and still continually drinking, they passed through the lane of 'Ubbád. As they approached the 'Áshikán Bázár, the father, who was riding a camel and had a cavalcade of thirty horse and an escort of thirty slaves, by chance met with a servant of the Khwája, who was also riding. The road was narrow, and there was a crowd of people. Hasírí, as drunkards will, got a whim into his head, because the servant did not dismount and pay his respects. He grossly abused the man, who said, O king! why do you abuse me! I have a master who is greater than you, and the like of you. That lord is the great Khwája. Hasírí began to abuse the Khwája, and said, Seize this dog. Who is there so bold as to listen to his complaint? He then used stronger language against the Khwája. The slaves of Hasírí flew upon the man, beat him severely on the back, and tore his garment. Bú-l Kásim, his (Hasírí's) son, called out loud to the slaves, because he was discreet, far-seeing, and intelligent. (He has passed through life so happily that he has performed the pilgrimage to Mecca, and has retired from service, devoting himself in seclusion to worship and virtuous acts. May this great man and worthy friend long survive!) He (Bú-l Kásim) made many apologies to the man, and besought him not to tell the occurrence to his master, lest next day he should demand an apology. For the garment that had been torn three should be given in return. (After this) they all went away. The man arose, but did not find himself capable of forbearance, because menial servants are accustomed to carry such matters too far, and do not consider the result.

This event took place on Thursday, the 15th of Safar. He went running to Khwája Ahmad and repeated the matter, making it ten or fifteen times worse to him. He displayed his bruised head and face, and showed the garment which was torn. The Khwája had eagerly wished for such a chance, and was seeking for a pretext against Hasírí, by which he might crush him, so he deemed this a fitting opportunity. For the Amír was in every way inclined towards him, and as he had given the minister's robe to him yesterday, he would not to-day give it to Hasírí. He had found dirt and he knew how to wallow in it.[1]

Next day the Amír was about to go out hunting in the direction of the wine drinkers;[2] and the tents, cooking utensils, wines, and other necessaries, were all taken out. Next day the Khwája sat down and wrote a petition under his own hand and

[و چون خالك يافت مراغت دانست كرد] [1]
[برجانب ميخواران] [2]

seal, and sent it to Dilkátigín with a message directing him, if the king asked him why Ahmad did not come, to hand the petition to him; or even if he did not enquire, the letter was still to be delivered to him, for it was important and ought not to be delayed. Dilkátigín promised to obey, as there was great friendship between them. The Amír did not hold a court, for he wished to go out riding, and the insignia and the umbrella had been brought out, and many slaves were ready mounted. The call was raised for the female elephant with the canopy, and the Amír mounted and sat in the howda. The Amír's elephant was driven on and all the servants were standing to pay their respects. But when his Majesty came to the court gate, and did not see Khwája Ahmad, he said, The Khwája is not come. Bú Nasr Mishkán replied, This is Friday, and he knows that your majesty intends to go hunting, for this reason probably he has not come. Dilkátigín then presented the paper, saying that it had been sent the previous night, with an intimation that whether his Majesty asked for him or not this was to be submitted. The elephant was stopped and the Amír took the paper and read it. It was thus written—"May my lord's life be prolonged! Your slave protested that he was not fit to be minister, and begged to be excused. Every one has got some vain thoughts in his mind; and in his old age, your slave has not vigour enough to contend against hardship and struggle with mankind, making the world his enemy. But as your Majesty by your royal words inspired him with great hopes and agreed to conditions worthy of a prince, he, next to the grace of Almighty God, received a new life from your Majesty and felt compelled to submit himself to the Imperial orders. Ten days have not yet passed, but Hasírí has disgraced your faithful servant. Hasírí was coming in a litter from the garden, after draining the cup to the dregs, and in the Sa'idí Bázár, not in a solitary place, but in the presence of many men, he ordered his slaves to beat one of my trustworthy servants. They sorely beat him and tore his garment to pieces. When the man said he was my servant, Hasírí uttered a hundred thousand opprobrious names against me before the crowd. Your servant can on no account come to court and conduct the ministerial duties, because it is hard to endure the insults of such people. If your Majesty sees fit to be merciful to him, then let him abide in some building or fort which your high wisdom may point out. But if he is not excused, then let him receive due chastisement, so that he may suffer both in property and person. He now aspires too high. His immense riches raise him and his son above themselves. Your servant will pay for the father and the son three hundred thousand dinárs into the treasury, and this letter, in the handwriting of your slave, shall stand as a bond. Peace be to you!"

When the Amír had read the letter, he wrote on it, and giving it to one of his personal attendants who carried the inkstand, he ordered him to take care of it. The elephant then moved on. Every one said, Let us see what will happen. In the open country he ordered the Commander-in-Chief of the army, and Ariyáruk general of Hindustán, and all the soldiers to return, for they were not allowed to accompany the royal hunt. He was followed only by some of his personal attendants. Then he called the High Chamberlain, Bilkátigín, and spoke a few words to him in the Turkish language. The Chamberlain retired and the Amír called for Bú Nasr Mishkán. A messenger hastened to him in the ministers' office, and told him that his Majesty was calling for him. He mounted and hastened to the Amír. He went on a little way with the Amír, and a few words passed; the Amír then sent him back. He did not return to the office, but went to the house of the great Khwája Ahmad, and sent Bú Mansúr, the keeper of the minister's offices, with orders for the secretaries to return. We did so. I followed the steps of my tutor (*ustád*) to the house of the Khwája, where I saw such a mob of spectators that no estimate of them could be made. I asked one person what the matter was? He replied, the Khalífa (governor) in armour and boots,[1] has brought Hasírí and his son to the Khwája's house,

---

[1] [باجبه و موزه]

and has set them up there and chastised them. Nobody knows what is the matter. And a large force is come on duty, and horsemen are posted, for this is Friday, and nobody is allowed to enter except Khwája Bú Nasr Mishkán, who came and went in. I, Bú-l Fazl was confounded when I heard this, because I had been much benefited by that nobleman and his son. I dismounted and went into the court-yard, where I remained till near breakfast time (*chásht-gáh*). Now, an inkstand and some paper were brought, and I heard 'Abdu-llah Pársí loudly proclaim that the great Khwája says, " though the Sultán had sentenced you and your son to receive one thousand blows each, yet I compassionate you and remit the strokes, but you must pay five hundred thousand dínars and purchase the stick, otherwise the sentence will be enforced. Beware, lest you receive the blows and have to pay the money also." The father and the son said, we are ready to obey whatever order is given, but we beg that some reduction be made, because it is known that we cannot afford to pay even the tenth part of it. Abú 'Abdu-llah went and returned several times, until three hundred thousand dínárs were agreed to be paid, and a bond for that amount was given. An order was then issued that they were to be kept in custody. The Khalífa (governor) of the town put them both under guard and detained them. The people then retired. Bú Nasr, my *ustád*, remained there to take wine, and I returned to my home. After an hour Sankúí Wakíl came to me and said that Khwája Bú Nasr had sent him with a message that I, Bú-l Fazl, was to go to the Sultán and report that he (Bú Nasr) had according to the royal orders gone to the Khwája, and agreeably to his instructions had poured water upon fire, so that Hasírí and his son had not been flogged. A bond for three hundred thousand dínars had been taken from them, and they were kept in custody. The great Khwája was greatly delighted at the order which your Majesty gave, and with the new favour bestowed upon him, and he had therefore detained him (Bú Nasr) to drink wine. It would have been churlish to refuse the favour, and this was the cause why he had not come himself. He had sent Abú-l Fazl in order that he might not be charged with disrespect and conceit.

I (Abú-l Fazl) instantly went, and found the Amír at the outskirts of the city, in a garden, engaged in conviviality and drinking. His companions were sitting round, and the musicians were playing. I said to myself, if I cannot gain access to speak to him, I must send him the message in writing, that it may come to his notice. I wrote down an explicit statement and went forward. The Amír asked loudly what it was? I replied, your slave Bú Nasr has sent a message, and I showed him the petition. He ordered his ink-bearer to take it, which he did and gave it to the Amír, who having read it, called me before the throne and returning the letter to me, and speaking aside, said, "Go back to Bú Nasr and tell him that all has gone on well, and that I am much pleased with what he has done. To-morrow I will take such further steps as may be necessary—tell him also it is good that he has not come himself, and that he stayed to be entertained by the Khwája."

I returned and reached the city at the time of the afternoon prayer. I called Sankúí, and wrote the message on a paper, thus completing my commission. Sankúí took it and gave it to my *walid*. He read it and became acquainted with its contents. He remained with the Khwája till the time of the night prayer, and returned home very drunk. The next evening he called me and I went. He was sitting alone, and he asked me what I had done. I related all that had passed, and he said it was all well, and added, the Khwája is about his work. He will exact a fine revenge, and will devour up these people. But the king is a kind protector and a lover of justice. Yesterday, as he read the letter of the minister, he was obliged to control himself by saying that it was not right to give him that post, and then within a week to overlook such contemptuous treatment of him. So the king determined to inflict punishment, and ordered the chief chamberlain *(hájib)* to go to the palace and direct the governor to take Hasírí and his son to the Khwája's house. "Let him also," said he, "take the executioner and whips, and let one thousand stripes be inflicted on each of these persons, so that henceforth nobody may dare to mention the Khwája's name except with respect." Although he gave such an order, and Hasírí had committed a very great fault, yet he did not wish that he should all at once lose his character and station. A man soon came to me (Bú Nasr) and called me. When I went to the Sultán he said to me openly, "You did not want to come with me to the feast." I answered, "It is the good fortune of your slave to be always before his master. But your majesty had ordered me to write some important letters to Re and other places in that direction, and told me not to come, but to send a secretary at once to him." He smiled, and was very gracious in all respects. He said, " I remember, but I only joked." There are some other points," continued he, "which must be inserted in those letters, and I did not wish to send them to you as a message, but to tell them myself to you." He then ordered the elephant to be stopped. The driver and his assistant descended from the neck of the animal. The personal attendant of the Sultán left the howda, and all people kept aloof; I stood before him. First he told me the subject of the Khwája's letter, and then said "the chamberlain was good to pacify the mind of the Khwája. I have ordered suitable punishment for the fault which Hasírí committed, with the view of giving satisfaction to the Khwája. But of all the courtiers of my father, Hasírí has the greatest claims upon me, and in his attachment to me he has suffered much hardship. At all events I will not give such power to the Khwája as that he may crush such servants for his own revenge. I have told you my views, and you must keep secret what I have said. Observe these words, and either by using my order or by your own contrivance, provide that neither he nor his son be hurt. I have directed the chamberlain, in the Turkish language, to frighten them, but to procrastinate. You must step in and extinguish the fire." I said "I quite understand that you have done what was proper in the matter," and I quickly returned. What was the case you have seen. I told the chamberlain to defer executing the royal order till I could see the great Khwája. I said to Hasíri, "Shame on you; you are an old man, and yet for a single thing you have brought this disgrace upon yourself, and have troubled the hearts of your friends." He answered, "This is no time for reproach; destiny has done its work; you should rather think of some remedy." I was called back, and immediately admitted into the court. On the road I saw Abú-l Fath of Bust dressed in an old garment, and having a small water bottle hanging from his neck. He stopped me on the road, and said "it is about twenty days since I have been set to carry water to the stable—please to exert your interest for me. I know the great Khwája is much pleased (with you) and nothing can be done without your recommendation." I told him I was going on some very important business, and when it was finished I would exert myself for him, and hoped that he would be successful. Upon reaching the Khwája I found him in great indignation and wrath. I paid my respects, and he eagerly spoke to me and said he was told that I had been with the Amír, and asked why I had returned. I answered that "he sent me back to attend to the Ito business, which was no secret to him (the Khwája). But these letters must be written to-morrow, because at present nothing can be done. I have come to take a little wine with you on the occasion of this new favour which has been shown to you by the Sultán in the matter of Hasíri." He said, "You have done quite right, and I am much obliged. But nevertheless I do not want you to intercede for him and be disappointed, because I will not relent on any account. These rascals[1] have entirely forgotten Ahmad Hasan, and have had the field empty for a while; they have made the great hand of the minister powerless, and have degraded him; but let them now look to the breadth of their blanket and awake from slumber." He then turned towards 'Abdu-llah Pársí, and asked if the stripes had been

[1] [كشخانان] "willing cuckolds," apparently a favourite term of abuse of the Khwája's.]

inflicted. I said, "They will inflict them and execute the great lord's command, but I requested the chief chamberlain (*Ádjíb*) to stop a little, till I had seen you." He said, "You have seen me, but I will not listen to your intercession—they must inevitably be beaten that their eyes may be opened. Go 'Abdullah, and give orders to beat them both (Hasírí and his son)." I said, "If there is no alternative let me speak a few words to you in private, and meanwhile let their punishment be delayed—after that let your commands be executed." He called 'Abdu-llah back, and then had the room cleared, so that we were alone together. I said, "May my lord's life be prolonged; it is wrong to push matters to extremes in any thing. Great men have said, 'Mercy attends His power,' and mercy is considered most worthy, even when we have power to take revenge. The Almighty God has shown you His might and also His mercy. He has delivered you from suffering and imprisonment. It is, therefore, right to do good to them who have done ill to us, so that shame and remorse may come upon them. The story of Mámún and Ibráhím is well known to you. It is foolish for me to speak of such a thing to you. It is like carrying dates to Basra. The king has bestowed on you this distinction, and is mindful of your feelings and position; he has sent this old man here, and has sentenced him to such punishment; but you must know how much it must have afflicted him, because he esteems the man his friend in consequence of the hardships suffered on his account at the hands of the late king, his father. He firmly believes that the Khwája also will act like nobles and great men, and not torture him. It seems much preferable to your humble servant that you should consider the feelings of the Sultán, and direct these men to be detained and not to be beaten. You can take from him and his son an agreement for paying (money) into the public treasury, and then inform the Sultán of it, and see what he directs. I think most probably he will forgive him. And if the Khwája recommend the measure it will be still better, because the obligation will be all from his part.

The Lord knows I have no interest in these matters. I only desire that peace may be preserved on both sides. I have spoken to the best of my judgment. It is for you to order, for you know best what is the result of such matters."

When the Khwája heard these words from me, he hung his head down and remained thoughtful for a while. He knew that there was reason in what I had said, for he was not a man of that kind from whom such things could be concealed. He said, "I remit the beating for your sake; but whatever wealth the father and son possess they must give to the Sultán." I bowed, and he sent 'Abdu-llah Pársí to settle the matter. A bond of three hundred thousand dínárs was taken under the hand of Hasírí, and father and son were taken to the guard.

After this the Khwája called for bread and wine and singers, and we began our banquet. When I had drunk some cups of wine, I exclaimed, "May the Khwája live long! This day is propitious, I have another request to make." He said, "Tell me, and you shall find a ready compliance." I said, "I saw Abú-l Fath carrying a leather water-bag, but he is a shocking bad stable-man; although he deserves punishment, still he has many and strong claims for services rendered. The Sultán knows him, and acts upon the principles of Amir Mahmúd. If he sees him he will pardon him also." He said, "Very good; do so, let him be called." So he was brought, and he came forward dressed in the same threadbare garment. He kissed the ground and arose. The Khwája asked him, "Do you repent speaking indecently?" He replied, "O lord! the water-bag and the stable have forced me to repent." The Khwája laughed and ordered him to be conducted to the warm bath and newly clad. When he came back he kissed the ground again; he was told to sit down, and dinner was ordered to be brought for him, of which he partook. After this, he was asked to take some wine, and was comforted and sent home. This being done, we drank deeply, and I then returned. "O Bú-l Fazl! (continued Bú Nasr) this Ahmad is a great noble, but he is fond of revenge; and I am in great distress

about the course he has taken, for it is impossible that it should
be approved. The Sultán will not allow him to swallow up his
servants. I do not know what will be the end of these proceedings. Keep these words secret: go back and do your work, for
you have to go to the Amír."

I came back and prepared to go. Then I went to him again
and he gave me a sealed letter, which I took and set out for the
hunting-place. I reached there about the time of evening prayer.
I found that the Sultán had been drinking all day, and had now
gone to his private tent. I took the letter to Agháchí, the king's
attendant, and having given it to him, I went and stood by the
curtain at the entrance of the tent. In the morning a *Farrásh*
having come to call me, I went, and Agháchí took me before
the Amír, who was sitting in a sedan in his royal tent. I
saluted him. He said, "tell Dú Nasr that what he has done in
behalf of Hasiri was quite right. But I am coming to the city
directly and I will do what is necessary." He threw the letter
to me, and I took it up and returned. The Amír said the morning prayer and set out towards the city. I arrived sooner, and
I saw near the city, my *ustád* and the great Khwája standing
with all the officers and ministers of the court to receive the
Sultán. Dú Nasr saw me, but said nothing; I kept in my place.
The insignia and the umbrella of the Sultán advanced. The
Amír was on horseback; the people went forward. My *ustád*
came to me and made a signal, so I approached him. He
covertly asked me what I had done and what had passed. I
told him all, and he said, "I understand." The Amír then
arrived, and all mounted and marched on. The Khwája was on
the right of the Amír and Bú Nasr just before his majesty; the
other officers and grandees were in front, so that there should be no
crowding. The Amír kept conversing with the Khwája till they
approached the garden. The Amír asked what was to be done
in respect of that reckless man. The Khwája said, "Let his
Majesty deign to alight and then what has passed and what is
proper to be done his humble servant will report through Dú

Nasr." He said, "Very good," and moved on. The Amír went to the Khizrá,[1] and the Khwája sat down on the ministerial bench; he called my *ustád* and gave him this message, "My lord, in his magnanimous pleasure, has secured what he considered due to me in this case of Hasírí, and I shall be under obligation to him for this favour as long as I live. Although Hasírí is a vain, boasting fellow, yet he is an old man, and has claims for his long service. He has always been a dutiful and faithful friend, and because of his loyalty he has, like myself, endured many hardships. His son is wiser and more prudent than himself, and is fit for any duty. Two proper men like these will not soon be found again, and now my lord stands in need of many able servants. How then can I allow two such devoted followers to be overthrown. My object was only this, that all men, great and small, might know how far his majesty was favourably disposed towards me. I have succeeded in that object, and all men have learned that they must keep within their respective bounds. I was fully aware that they ought not to be beaten. But I sent them to be confined so that they may awake a little. They have given a bond of their own free will, promising to pay three hundred thousand dínárs into the royal treasury, but they cannot pay this without being reduced to beggary, and a servant should not be destitute. If his majesty pleases, my recommendation in their behalf should not be rejected. Let them be excused from paying the money, and send them both home honourably."

Bú Nasr went and delivered this noble message. The Amír was highly pleased, and answered, "I accept the Khwája's plea for them. The matter is entirely in his hands. If he thinks proper let him dismiss them, and give back the bond." Bú Nasr returned and informed the Khwája of this. The Amír left the public hall and went into his palace. The Khwája also returned to his house. He ordered two of his own horses to be taken to the gate of the prison. The father and the son were both

[1] [كذا]

mounted on them, and conducted respectfully to the Khwája. When they came before him they kissed the ground and sat down. The Khwája for a little while admonished Hasírí in firm but kind words, till he made his apologies. It was a good thing that he was old. The Khwája treated him kindly, took him in his arms, and made apologies and comforted him. He also kissed his face, and told him to go in the same dress to his house. He said, I do not like to change your clothes, for to-morrow the Sultán will grant you khil'ats. Hasírí kissed the Khwája's hand and the ground. His son did the same. They then returned home riding on the Khwája's horses. In their passage both father and son were greeted by the people with loud acclamations and congratulations. I, Bú-l Fazl, was their neighbour. I hastened to go to them sooner than the other visitors. Hasírí privately told me that as long as he lived he should not be able to make a return of Khwája Bú Nasr's kindness, but that he would thank him and pray for him. I, however, did not speak a word to him about what had passed, lest he should be ashamed, but I gave him my blessing and retired. I told my *nafdd* what had happened, and he mounted to go and congratulate him. I also accompanied him. Hasírí with his son came forward to receive him. They sat down, and both expressed their thanks. Bú Nasr said, "My efforts in the matter are well known to you, but you must thank the Sultán and the Khwája." He said this and took his leave.

One or two weeks after I heard Bú Nasr say that the Amír, while drinking wine in a private party, spoke to Hasírí about what had passed. That day Hasírí was dressed in a yellow coat, and his son in a *Pandárí* coat, very magnificent and highly ornamented. Next day they were again brought before the Sultán, and he showed them attention. The Khwája requested that they might be taken to the wardrobe, when, according to the king's order, a dress was bestowed on each. They came from thence to the Khwája, and then with great honour they were both conducted from the Khwája's presence to their house. The citizens showed them due honour.

They are all now gone except his (Hasírí's) son Abú-l Kásim, who still survives. May the mercy of God be upon them all. Every one who reads this passage must examine it with intelligence, and draw lessons from it, and not consider it a mere story. They will thus learn what great men there were in days gone by.

I have read in the chronicles of the Khalifs, of the reign of Mu'tasim, a story very similar to this which I have just related, only much more terrible. I deemed it the more necessary to record this, that my book of the notabilities of the day might with such matters be made more acceptable. Words blossom into words, that the pleasures of readers may be enhanced, and that reading may increase.

Execution[1] of Amír Hannak, the Minister.[2]

I intend to write a chapter on this subject, and it thus begins: I begin to write this narrative to-day, in the month of Zí-l Hijja, A.H. 450 (January, 1059, A.D.), in the prosperous reign of the great Sultán, Abú-l Shujá' Farrukh-zád bin Násir-i dín: May the Almighty God ever preserve him. Of the people (kaum) of whom I am now about to speak, only one or two individuals survive in obscure circumstances. It is some years since Khwája Bú Suhal Zauzaní passed away, and was placed in prison for the answer which he gave.[3] But we have nothing to do with that business, although I was ill-treated by him in every way. I have now arrived at the age of sixty-five, and I must act as becomes my years. In the history which I am writing I will allow no partiality or prejudice to mingle, so that the readers of my work should say, Shame on this old man; but I will speak so that they may agree with me on the subject, and censure me not.[4]

---

[1] [*Bardár-kardan*, "lifting up" by hanging, impalement or crucifixion.]
[2] [Page 207 to 221 of Text.]
[3] [و بپاسخ آنانك ازوي رفت گرفتار]
[4] [Original translation (see note, page 70).—"I have arrived at the age of sixty-

This Bú Suhal was the son of an Imám, and a powerful, clever, and accomplished man; but malignity *(shararat)* and ill-temper were predominant in his nature. "And there is no changing what God has made." On account of his malignity he had no friend. He was always on the alert, and if the great and glorious king was angry with a servant, and directed him to be beaten or bastinadoed, this man would jump up from a corner, seize the opportunity, add to the beating, and aggravate the pain of the unhappy man. Then he would boast that he had paid out such a one. When he did (anything of this sort) he looked on and enjoyed it.[1] Wise men knew that he was not what he professed to be; they shook their heads and secretly laughed, and said he was not such a man. But he could not humble my *ustád*, notwithstanding all the arts he used against him. He was never successful against him, because the destiny of God did not accord with his schemes. Besides, Bú Nasr had been a man of great discretion during the reign of Amír Mahmúd, and he had never acted dishonestly towards his master, but he was careful to please the Sultán Mas'úd in all things, because he knew that he would succeed his father on the throne. It was just the reverse with Hasnak, who was wholly devoted to Mahmúd, and always obliged and pleased him, but often offended the prince; and did and said things which his equals would not endure; how then could a king? The same was the case with Ja'far Barmakí, whose family held the post of Wazír in the time of Hárúnu-r Rashíd, and the result of their conduct was the same as befel this minister. Servants and officers should keep control over their tongues when speaking to their masters, because it is impossible for foxes to face lions.

Bú Suhal, in rank, wealth, and manliness, was like a mere

five, and I should act as behoves me now. In the narration which I am now going to give, I shall mention a topic on which I may be prejudiced, and the readers of this compilation will say,; Shame on this old man, say, I fear they may censure and reproach me for it.]

[و اگر کرد دید و چشید] [1]

drop by the side of Amír Hasnak, and in point of ability he held a very different rank. He was guilty of many tyrannical actions as I have before mentioned in this history, and the following is an instance. He said to 'Abdús, "Tell your lord that all that I do is in obedience to my master's order; if hereafter the throne devolves upon him he must cause Hasnak to be executed."

When the Sultán became king, Hasnak mounted the scaffold. But who was Bú Suhal, and the like of Bú Suhal that Hasnak should at last feel the effects of his malevolence and injustice. A king should never shut his eyes against three things, viz., disturbances in the country, divulging of secrets, and opposition. God save us from wickedness!

When Hasnak was brought from Bust to Hirát, Bú Suhal Zauzaní placed him in charge of his servant, 'Alí Ráíz. Hasnak suffered all kinds of indignities, which could not be avenged, and for which no satisfaction could be made. On this account all people uttered reproaches against Bú Suhal, saying, A man does not strike one who is beaten and fallen; the man is is he who acts according to the words—"Mercy accompanies power." The Almighty, whose name is glorious, says, "Those who restrain their anger, and who are merciful towards men; and God will reward the beneficent."

When Amír Mas'úd marched from Hirát towards Balkh, 'Alí Ráíz carried Hasnak there as a prisoner, and treated him with great rigour and indignity; yet I privately heard from 'Alí's own lips that it would have been much worse for Hasnak if he ('Alí) had carried out a tenth part of what Bú Suhal had ordered, but much had been omitted. He (Bú Suhal) stopped in Balkh, and instigated the Amír to put Hasnak to death. The Amír was very gentle and generous, and he told this to his trusty 'Abdús,—One day after the death of Hasnak I heard from my *ustád* that the Amír told Bú Suhal he must have some reason and justification for destroying this man. Bú Suhal said, "What greater reason can there be than this,—that he is a Karmatian, and that he received a khil'at from the Egyptians, which displeased Kádir Bi-llah, the commander of the faithful, and induced him to reject the letter of Amír Mahmúd. He still speaks continually about this. Your Majesty must remember that at Naishápúr an ambassador came from the Khalif and brought a flag and a khil'at. But what was the mandate about this matter? The injunctions of the Khalif in this behalf must be observed." The Amír said, "I will not hesitate in this case." After this, 'Abdús who was much against Bú Suhal, told my tutor that when Bú Suhal importuned him much in the matter, the Amír one day desired Khwája Ahmad Hasan, as he was departing from the palace, to remain alone in his court because he had a message to send him through 'Abdús. The Khwája obeyed, and the Amír called 'Abdús and said—"Tell Khwája Ahmad that he knows the history of Hasnak, how in the time of the late king, my father, he (Hasnak) had given me several causes of offence, and when the Sultán departed this life, what great efforts he made in behalf of my brother. Still he did not go to him. As the Almighty has given me the throne and country with such ease, it is right that I should accept the excuses of the guilty and not trouble myself with the past. But with respect to this man they say that he received a robe from the Egyptians to the annoyance of the Khalif, the commander of the faithful, who was displeased and tore the letter of my father. It is also said that the ambassador who came to Naishápúr bringing a letter, a flag and robe, was charged with the message that Hasnak was a Karmatian, and should be put to death. I heard this in Naishápúr, but do not remember well. What does the Khwája think and say about this matter." When this message was delivered the Khwája reflected for a long time and then asked, "What has been done to Bú Suhal Zauzaní by Hasnak, that he makes such efforts to shed his blood." I ('Abdús) replied, "I do not know well, but I have heard this much—that one day he went on foot wearing a coarse garment to the house of Hasnak while the latter was minister. A porter insulted him and threw him down." The Khwája said, "O holy God! why should he cherish such hatred in his mind." He then directed me to speak thus to his Majesty—"At the time I was detained in the fort of Kálinjar an attempt was made to destroy my life, but the Almighty preserved me. I then vowed and swore never to speak a word, right or wrong, in the matter of shedding any one's blood. At the time Hasnak came to Balkh, after his pilgrimage to Mecca, we marched towards Máwaráu-n Nahr, and visited it with Kadar Khán. After our return I was left in Ghazní. I do (not) know what happened to Hasnak, nor what the late king said to the Khalif. Bú Nasr Mishkán knows the facts, and he should be asked. The Amír our lord is sovereign, and it is for him to order. If it be proved that Hasnak is a Karmatian, I will not say a word as to his death, although he has had his own designs in this troublesome matter which now engages me. I have told you my thoughts, that he may not have anything to speak against me. I am averse to shedding the blood of any man; but still I must not withhold my counsel from the king, for I should act dishonestly (in advising) that neither his nor any one else's blood should be shed, although the spilling of blood is assuredly no child's play." When I took this reply, the king remained thinking for a long while; and then said, "Tell the Khwája to issue such orders as may be proper." The Khwája rose up and went towards the office. On the way he said to me, "'Abdús, do what you can to induce his Majesty not to shed Hasnak's blood, because it will bring infamy on him." I said, "Very good," and returned and communicated the same to the Sultán. But fate was on the watch and accomplished its object.

After this (the Sultán) consulted with my ustád, who told me what passed in the conference. The Amír asked about Hasnak and then about the matter of the Khalif, and wanted to know what was his opinion about the religion and belief of this man, and of his receiving a robe from the Egyptians. Bú Nasr stood up and related before him the whole account of Hasnak, his going on pilgrimage to Mecca, his returning viá Medina and Wádia-l

Kara on the way to Syria, his receiving the khil'at from the Egyptians and the necessity of the act; his changing his route to Músal and not going back to Baghdád; and the Khalif's thinking that perhaps he had been ordered to do so by the Amír Mahmúd. All this was stated in full detail. The Amír asked how Hasnak was in fault in the matter. Had he come through the desert he would have caused the death of many people. Bú Nasr replied, "It would have been so. But such representations were made to the Khalif as made him very angry and disturbed, so that he called Hasnak a Karmatian. Much correspondence passed about the matter, and the late king being greatly annoyed and vexed, said, one day, 'Write to this doting old Khalif, that out of regard to the 'Abbásides I have meddled with all the world. I am hunting for the Karmatians, and whenever one is found who is proved to be so, he is impaled. If it were established that Hasnak is a Karmatian, the commander of the faithful would soon learn what had happened to him. But I have brought him up and he stands on an equality with my sons and my brothers. If he is a Karmatian, so am I also.' (He said this though) it was not becoming in a king. I (Bú Nasr) came into the minister's office and wrote a letter in the style in which servants address their masters. After much consideration it was determined that the robe which Hasnak had received, and the presents which the Egyptians had sent to Amír Mahmúd, should be sent with a messenger to Baghdád to be burnt there. When the messenger returned, the Amír asked in what place the robe and the presents were consumed, because he was sorry that Hasnak had been called a Karmatian by the Khalif. Notwithstanding this, the suspicion and bigotry of the Khalif increased more and more, but secretly not openly, until at length Amír Mahmúd received the Farmán. I have related the whole of what had passed" (said my ustád). The Amír answered, "Yes, I understand it." Even after this Bú Sahal did not desist from his object.

On Tuesday, the 7th of Safar, when the Court broke up, the king ordered the Khwája to sit in his Court (*táram*) because

Hasnak was to be brought there, with the judges and assessors,[1] that a bond in favour of the Amír might be taken from him for all things he had purchased and brought with him. The Khwája obeyed and went into the Court. All the Khwájas, the principal men, and ministers of the State, Khwája Bú-l Kásim Kasír (though he had been dismissed), Bú Suhal Zauzaní, and Bú Suhal Hamadúní came there. The wise Amír also sent there the commander-in-chief of the army, and Nasr Khalaf, the Kázís of Balkh, nobles, learned men, lawyers, just men, religious men, and all who were renowned and famous were present, and took notes. When this assembly was convened, I Bú-l Fazl and other people sat out of the court-hall, in shops, expecting to see Hasnak; and after a while he appeared unshackled. He wore a coat of some blackish colour, a vest, an upper garment, an exceedingly white shirt, a Naishápúr turban, and a new pair of Mikáili boots on his feet, and his hair was smoothed down and hidden under the turban, except a few locks which were visible. The governor of the prison was with him, and 'Alí Ráíz and many soldiers from every band (*dastí*), and they took him into the Court. He was there till near the time of mid-day prayer; and then he was brought out and taken again to the prison. He was followed by the Kázís, and the lawyers. I heard two persons conversing and asking each other what could have brought Khwája Bú Suhal to this act, for it would bring disgrace upon himself. Afterwards, Khwája Ahmad came out with the chief men, and went to his house. Nasr Khalaf was my friend; I asked him what passed there. He said: When Hasnak came in, the Khwája rose up, and when he showed him this respect, all the others, whether they liked it or not, did the same. Bú Suhal Zauzaní could not control his anger, albeit he stood up, though not quite straight, and kept muttering to himself in his rage. Khwája Ahmad said, "In all things there is imperfection; he is greatly

[مزكيان] [1]

fallen"[1] (?) Although Khwája Amír Hasnak desired to sit before the Khwája, yet he did not allow him. He made me and Khwája Bú-l Kásim Kasír and Bú Nasr Mishkán sit on his right hand; for although Bú-l Kásim Kasír had been dismissed from his office yet his reputation was very great. Bú Suhal sat on the left of the Khwája, and this offended him still more deeply. The great Khwája turned his face towards Hasnak and asked him how he was, and how he passed his time! He replied, "I have reason to be thankful." The Khwája said, "Do not be broken-hearted. Such accidents often befall mankind; you must submit to whatever his Majesty commands, for while life remains in the body, there are a hundred thousand hopes of happiness and comfort."

Bú Suhal now recovered himself, and exclaimed, "Who shall reconcile our lord to this dog of a Karmatian, who must be gibbeted as ordered by the commander of the faithful." The Khwája looked angrily at Bú Suhal, and Hasnak exclaimed, "Who this dog is I do not know; but all the world knows to what family I belong, and what state, grandeur, and luxury have been mine. I have enjoyed this world, I have directed its affairs, but the end of man is death; and if the destroying angel has now approached me, no one can withstand him—whether the gibbet or any other be the appointed means. I am not greater than Imám Husain 'Alí. The Khwája who tells me this, and has called me a dog[2] once stood at my door. The charge of being a Karmatian is more applicable to him than to me—for it is well known that I do not understand such things." Bú Suhal's bile was stirred; he called out and was about to abuse him, but the Khwája restrained him, and said, "Is no respect due to this assembly of the Sultán in which we are sitting? We are called to settle the question, and shall soon finish it. This man has been five or six months in your hands; do what you like." Bú Suhal was silent, and spoke not a word till the assembly broke up.

[شغر] [1]   [در همه کارها نا تمامي وي نیك از جاي بشد] [1]

Two bonds were written out on behalf of the king, which contained an inventory of all the chattels and estates of Hasnak. The name of each estate was read out to him, and he agreed to sell them of his own pleasure and free will at the prices set upon them, and accept the money. All the people affixed their signatures as witnesses. The Chief Judge affixed his seal to them, and so did the other Kázís one after the other in their turns. When this was done, Hasnak was told to retire. He looked at the Khwája, and exclaimed, "May the life of the great Khwája be prolonged! In the time of Sultán Mahmúd and by his instructions I ridiculed the Khwája; it was a fault, but I had no help but to obey. The post of Wazír was given to me, though it was no place for me. Still I formed no design against the Khwája, and I always favoured his people. I committed a fault, continued he, and deserve whatever punishment my Lord may order. But the all-merciful master will not reject me. I am weary of life. Some care ought to be taken of my family and children, and the Khwája must forgive me." He burst into tears, and all those who were present pitied him. The Khwája's eyes filled with tears, and he said, "You are forgiven, but you must not be so dejected, for happiness is still possible. I have considered and I accept it of the Almighty, that if he is doomed I I will take care of his family."

After this Hasnak rose up, and the Khwája and the other people also rose. When all had gone away, the Khwája greatly censured Bú Suhal, who earnestly begged to be excused, saying that he could not suppress his anger. An account of this assembly was given to the Amír by the governor of the city and the lawyers. The Amír sent for Bú Suhal and reprimanded him sharply, saying, "Granting that you thirst for this man's blood, still respect and honour is due to the assembly of my minister." Bú Suhal said, "I remembered the impudence which he exhibited to my Lord at Hirát, in the reign of Amír Mahmúd, and so I could not restrain myself and deal tenderly with him."

And I learnt from 'Amíd 'Abdu-r Razzák that on the night

preceding the day on which Hasnak was executed, Bú Suhal went to 'Abdu-r Razzák's father at the time of the night prayer, and when he was asked why he had come, he replied, I will not leave you until you go to sleep, lest you should write to the Sultán interceding for Hasnak. He was told that a letter had already been written, but that he had effected Hasnak's ruin, and had acted very badly.

That day and night preparations were made for Hasnak's public execution. Two men were dressed up as messengers coming from Baghdád, bearing a letter from the Khalif to the effect that Hasnak, the Karmatian, should be executed and stoned, so that no one else in contempt of the Khalif might dare to wear the khil'at of the Egyptian and lead pilgrims to Egypt. When everything was ready, the next morning, on Wednesday, two days before the last day of Safar, Amír Mas'úd mounted his horse, intending to go out hunting for three days, with his courtiers, attendants, and singers. He ordered the governor of the town to put up a scaffold by the side of the mosque of Balkh, below the city. People repaired to the place. Bú Suhal Zauzaní rode to the gibbet and there stood overlooking it. Horsemen and foot soldiers were sent to bring Hasnak. When he was carried through the 'Ashikán Bázár and had reached the centre of the city, Mikáíl, who was riding, pushed his horse in front of him, called him names and abused him. Hasnak did not look at him, nor give him any reply. But all people cursed him for this disgraceful act, and for the abuse he had uttered. The respectable people could not, however, say what ought to be done to this Mikáíl. But after Hasnak's death he took the sister of Ayáz for his wife, and he suffered great misfortunes and endured many hardships. He still lives, engaged in devotion and in reading the Kurán. When a friend misbehaves what is the good of dilating about it?

Hasnak was brought to the foot of the scaffold. May God save us from a disgraceful death! The two messengers who were declared to have come from Baghdád were stationed there, and they whose business it was were reading the Kurán. Hasnak was ordered to put off his clothes. He fastened the string of his trowsers and tied up his drawers. He took off his coat and shirt and threw them away, and there he stood naked with only his turban and trousers on, and his hands clasped together. His body was as white as silver, and his face like hundreds of thousands of pictures. All men were crying with grief. An iron helmet and visor was brought, which had been purposely made small, so that it did not cover his face and head. Men cried aloud for his head and face to be covered, that they might not be battered by the stones, because his head was to be sent to the Khalif at Baghdád. Hasnak was held in this state, and his lips kept moving, repeating something, until a larger helmet was brought. At this juncture, Ahmad, the keeper of the wardrobe, came riding and, looking at Hasnak, delivered this message, His Majesty says, "This is your own wish, for you desired me to bring you to the scaffold whenever I became king. I wished to have mercy on you, but the Commander of the Faithful has written, that you have become a Karmatian, and by his order you are led to the scaffold." Hasnak made no reply whatever. After this his head and face were covered with the large helmet that was just brought. They then spoke to him, but he gave no reply, and did not heed them. Every one exclaimed, Are you not ashamed to slay such a man upon the scaffold? A great uproar was just about to commence, when the horsemen moved hastily towards the populace, and repressed the noise. Hasnak was then taken to the gibbet and led to the spot, and placed on that stool on which he had never sat before. The executioner fastened him tight, and the robes hung down. It was proclaimed that he was to be stoned, but nobody touched a stone. All were bitterly crying, particularly the Naishápúrians. At last a parcel of vagabonds were hired with money to throw stones; but the man was already dead, for the executioner had cast the rope round his neck and had suffocated him. This was the end of Hasnak, his life and story. May God be merciful to him! He used to say, Let the prayers of the Naishápúrians be made for me, but they were not made.[1] If he did take the land and water of the Muhammadans by violence, neither land nor water remained with him, and all the slaves, the estates, and goods, and silver and gold, and valuables were of no use to him. He departed, and those people who laid this plot have also pursued the same path. May God's mercy be upon them all! This story affords a striking warning, that the causes of disputes and quarrels on account of the vanities of this world should be set aside. Foolish is the man who sets his heart on this world, for it bestoweth a gift and taketh it away again harshly.

When all was done, Bú Suhal and the others retired from the scaffold, and Hasnak was left alone as he came alone from the womb of his mother. Afterwards I heard from Bú-l Hasan Jazílí, who was a friend of mine, and one of the associates of Bú Suhal, that he was in Bú Suhal's society one day when he was drinking wine. It was a goodly assembly, and many servants were waiting, and melodious singers were present. By his order the head of Hasnak was brought in unknown to the guests, placed in a dish with a cover over it. He then said, Some fresh wine has been brought in; let us partake of it. All cried, Let us have some. He ordered it to be brought forward, and at a little distance the cover was removed from the vessel. All were shocked when they saw the head of Hasnak. The narrator of the story fainted, but Dú Suhal Zauzmní laughed, and threw away some wine which he happened to have in his hand. The head was then removed. Another day, my informant continued, when there was nobody else present, I reproached him seriously; but he said, O Abú-l Hasan! you are a chicken-hearted fellow—this is the right way of dealing with the heads of our enemies. These facts became generally known, and all men condemned and cursed him.

The day on which Hasnak was led to the scaffold, my ustád

[مرا دعای نیشابوریان بازد و ساخت] [1]

Bú Nasr did not break his fast, and was exceedingly sorrowful and pensive; I had never seen him before in such a state. He exclaimed, What hope is left? The same was the case with Khwája Ahmad, who did not go to his office that day. Hasnak remained seven years on the gibbet. His feet dropped off and his corpse entirely dried up, so that not a remnant of him was left to be taken down and buried in the usual way—no one knew where his head was or where his body. His mother was a woman of great courage. I was told that his death was concealed from her for two or three months, and when she did hear of it she did not weep as women usually do; but she cried aloud with such anguish that those who were present shed tears of blood. She then exclaimed, What a fortune was my son's! a king like Mahmúd gave him this world, and one like Mas'úd the next! She made great mourning for her son, and every wise man who heard of it approved, and it was all proper.

One of the poets of Naishápúr composed an elegy upon his death, which I call to memory:—

"They cut off the head of him who was the head of heads,
The ornament of his country, the crown of the age.
Whether he was Karmatian, Jew, or infidel,
'Twas hard to pass from the throne to the scaffold."

Capture of 'Ali Ariyáruk, the Hájib and Commander-in-Chief of the Army of India, and the circumstances which befel him from this time till his Execution at Ghor. May God be merciful to him![1]

I have already given an account of Ariyáruk, commander of the army of Hindustán, how presumptuous he grew, even in the time of Amír Mahmúd, and how, when he was arraigned[2] in the reign of Muhammad, he did not submit. In these days the great Khwája, Ahmad Hasan, with great cleverness allured him

[1] [Page 261 to 286 of the Text.]   [2] [نيم عاصي كرفتند اورا]

from Hindustán, and when he saw him he told the Amír that if he valued Hindustán, Ariyáruk ought not to be there. The coming of Ariyáruk every day into the court with so many retainers and arrogant followers along with Ghází, the commander-in-chief of the army, was offensive to the Amír. The officers of his father Mahmúd's time looked with disgust upon their arrogance and superciliousness. And as this was the case with every one, there was no person to give one word of advice to these two grandees, Ariyáruk and Ghází.[1] It was observed that these two generals had two clever, wise, and experienced men to conduct their household affairs, and it was clear that little could be done by Sa'íd, a mere money changer, and others like him—mere servants of little worth, and no position. These Turks did just as these men prescribed, without considering the result or the possibility of evil befalling them. They had no experience, and although personally they were daring and ready, and their goods and effects ample, yet they had no knowledge of household management, and made no distinction between to-day and to-morrow. What defence had they against mishaps?

When the Mahmúdians perceived this, and found an opening by which they might assail them, they conspired together to ruin the generals, and to involve them in trouble and danger. This was one of their plans. 'Abdús, by direction of the Amír, inveigled the stewards of the two generals to come secretly to the Amír's council. The Amír was very gracious to them, held out prospects of promotion, and directed them to reckon the very breaths of their masters, and to tell every thing that passed to 'Abdús, who was to report it to him. These two despicable base persons were gained over by the favour shown to them, the like of which they had never dreamed of. They did not know that when their masters should be cast down they would be

[1] [The whole of this passage is confused and ambiguous, and there are omissions in Morley's edition of the text, which make it more so. In Sir H. Elliot's MS. the words "He said to his wazír in private," have been crossed out; but these words, or others equivalent, are necessary, as the passage is clearly conversational, not narrative.]

"viler than the dust—lower than the ground." How were they to know this? they were not scholars, and had never read books. They set about their business; and whatever passed, right or wrong, they observed and reported to 'Abdús. From what the Amír heard, his heart and mind became disgusted with Ariyáruk; Ghází also was somewhat depreciated in his eyes. The Mahmúdians became bolder in their statements; and as the king listened and attended to all they had to say on the matter, they persevered in their conspiracy, and determined first to effect the downfall of Ariyáruk, for when he had fallen, and Ghází remained alone, it would be possible to overthrow him also. The Mahmúdians once got information that these two servants, while in their cups, had boasted that they were servants of the king, and that they had been corrupted. So they began to flatter them and to make them presents, and they held out to them the prospect of being employed in some important duties by the Sultán, if their masters were disgraced. Another difficulty was that Ghází, the general of the army, was a very cunning fellow,[1] so that Iblís himself (may the curse of God be upon him!) could not weave his toils over him. He had never drunk wine, but when all his work was finished and his object gained he took to drinking. When the Amír was told of this, he gave wine to both the generals. Wine is a great evil, and when drinking is carried to excess, one can do as one pleases with the winebibber and excessive drinker. Ghází being commander of the army also began to lavish favours upon the soldiers, and kept every day one division of it at his house, to which he gave wine and presents. Ariyáruk and Ghází were frequently the guests of each other. In their parties, when wine had taken effect, the chief men used to praise them in the Turkish language, and used to call the great Hájib Bilkátigín an eunuch; 'Alí Dáya an old woman; Bagtaghdí, the commander of the guards (*ghulám*) of the palace, blind and lame; and similarly they derided and reviled everybody.

[1] (*Kurbuze*, "a great cucumber."]

I heard from 'Abdu-llah, who after the downfall of the two generals, was manager of the affairs of Bagtaghdí, that one day the king did not hold his court, but drank wine. Ghází returned home with Ariyáruk and they took many persons with them, and all sat down to drink. The commander, Bagtaghdí, secretly sent me to Bilkátigín and 'Alí, with this message, "These two conceited persons exceed all bounds; if you deem it expedient, ride out with twenty guardsmen on pretence of going a hunting." This was done, that he, with Abú 'Abdu-llah and some guards, might meet him and consult about the plans to be adopted. He (Bilkátigín) approved and said he would go on towards Manjúrán until the commander should arrive. They all mounted and rode on. Bagtaghdí also mounted and took me with him. He also took hawks, panthers, and every requisite with him. When we had gone two parasangs, these three persons stood on a rising ground with their three stewards, viz., myself, Bú Ahmad Takalki, who was steward to the great Hájib, and Amírak, deputy of 'Alí; and they sent away the guards with the falconers hunting, and we six persons remained there. The chiefs conversed with each other, and for a while expressed their disappointment at the Amír, on account of the ascendancy of these two generals. Bagtaghdí observed, "It is very surprising, for in the palace of Mahmúd there was no one of less repute than these two persons, thousands of times they have kissed the ground before me; still they have both turned out hardy and bravo. Ghází is the most artful of the artful (*Kurbuze az kurbuzán*), but Ariyáruk is an ass of asses. Amír Mahmúd promoted them and placed them in a high position, so that they are become nobles. Ghází rendered a very meritorious service to our Sultán in Naishapúr, and thus he obtained this high rank. Although the Sultán dislikes Ariyáruk and likes Ghází, yet when they drink wine and carouse familiarly we may divert his mind from the latter also. But it will be no use to attempt anything against Ghází until Ariyáruk falls. They are held together by a single tie, and both will fall together: we shall then be delivered from their annoyance."

The great Hájib and 'Alí said, "Some drink must be concocted, or some one must be sent openly to kill Ariyáruk." General Bagtaghdí said, "Both these plans are worthless, and will not succeed. We shall be disgraced and they will acquire greater stability. The best plan is for us to abstain from such schemes, and to make a show of friendship to them; we may then employ certain persons to tell tales of them, and to exaggerate what the Turks and these two generals say, and to spread it abroad. We shall then see how far matters will go." They so determined. The guards and falconers returned, bringing much game, and as the day was far advanced, the hunting-boxes were opened and they partook of food—servants, guards, inferiors and all. They then returned, and, in accordance with their resolution, they busied themselves about those two persons.

Some days passed. The king was incensed with Ariyáruk, and secretly designed to arrest him. He complained of him to the minister, saying, that matters had reached such a pitch that Ghází was getting spoilt by him. No king could endure such things. It was not right for generals of the army to be disobedient, and for children to exhibit such boldness. It was indispensably necessary to arrest him, because Ghází would then come to a right understanding. What had the Khwája to say to this?

The Khwája considered awhile, and then said, "May my lord's life be prolonged. I have taken an oath not to fail of my duty in any case concerning the prosperity of the country. The duty of commanding an army is very difficult and delicate, and it is entrusted to the king. May it please His Majesty to excuse his slave from pronouncing an opinion in this particular matter, and to do what may seem to him right, for if I should say anything about this affair, it might seem inappropriate to his Majesty, and cause him to be displeased with me."

The Amír answered, "Khwája, you are my khalífa, and the most trusted of all my servants. I must of necessity consult you in such affairs, and you must give me your advice according to your knowledge. I will listen to it, and after pondering over it to myself, whatever seems to be reasonable, I will direct to be done." The Khwája replied, "Now I cannot say anything. What I expressed with respect to Ariyáruk on a former occasion was advice applicable to Hindustán. This man had there acted tyrannically and rashly. He had acquired a great name in that country, but spoiled it. The late king summoned him, but he was tardy and remiss in obeying, and made frivolous excuses. Neither did he attend when Amír Muhammad called him, for he answered that Amír Mas'úd was heir-apparent of his father, but that if Mas'úd would acquiesce in the succession of his brother and not march from 'Irák to Ghazní, then he would come to pay his allegiance. When he heard your name and I told him what I had to say, he came with me hither. Up to this time I have never heard that he has been guilty of any presumption or disobedience worthy of notice. It is a very simple matter to make a great display with boundless means, and to drink wine without permission with Ghází and the Turks. In one interview I will set him right, so that you need not speak one word about the matter. Your Majesty's dominions have been extended, and useful men are required. It will be long before you find one like Ariyáruk. I have said what occurs to me, but it is for you to command."

The Amír said, "I understand. It is just as you say. But you must keep this matter secret, and we will consider it more carefully." The Khwája expressed his obedience and retired.

The Mahmúdians did not desist from their representations, but went so far as to insinuate to the Amír that Ariyáruk had grown suspicious,—he had proposed to Ghází that they should raise a disturbance, and if they did not meet with support to take their departure. More than this the greater part of the army was willing to obey Ariyáruk.

The Amír one day held a Court, and all men assembled. When the Court broke up, he said, "Do not go away, but stay and we will take some wine." The great Khwája, the *'Áriz*, and the *Diwán* also sat down, and the dishes were brought in:

one was placed before the Amír on his throne, one before Amír Ghází and Ariyáruk, one before the 'Áriz Bú Suhal Zauzaní and Bú Nasr Mishkán, and one before the officers of these two persons (Ariyáruk and Ghází). Abú-l Kásim Kasír was sitting there like the courtiers. Various dishes were ordered and were brought in. When these great men had dined, they arose and came back into the court-hall (*táram*), and there sat and washed their hands. The great Khwája praised both the generals and spoke very graciously. They said "Our lord is always kind and gracious, and we are ready to sacrifice our lives in his service; but people have produced anxiety in our minds, and we do not know what to do." The Khwája observed, "This is absurd, and is a vain fancy which you must banish from your minds. Wait a little till I am at leisure; I will then call for you." So he went in alone, and seeking a private interview with the king, he brought up this matter, and begged that they might again receive the royal regard, but it was for his Majesty to decide. The Amír answered, "I understand:" and then he called all the party back again. The minstrels came and began to play. Pleasure was at its height, and everything went on merrily. When the time of the first prayer arrived, the Amír made a sign to the singers and they kept silence. He then turned towards the minister and said, "I have hitherto observed, as I ought, the obligations I owe to these two generals. As to Ghází, he rendered me a service at Naishapúr which no man of the army I had with me did, and he came from Ghaznín. And when Ariyáruk heard that I had reached Balkh, he hastened thither with the Khwája and tendered his services. I hear that some people are jealous of them, and speak ill of them and make their minds perplexed. They must not be alarmed, but must place full reliance in my words, for I will not listen to what anyone may say against them." The Khwája observed, "Nothing now remains to be said, for what greater favour can there be than that which has been expressed by His Majesty's words." Both the generals kissed the ground and the throne also, and returning to their places sat down very happy. The Amír ordered two fine garments to be brought, both wrought with gold, with two sword-belts set with jewels, said to be of the value of fifty thousand dínárs each. He again called them both forward, and ordered them to put on the garments and fasten them. The Amír placed the sword-belt round their necks with his own hands. They then kissed his hand, the throne, and the ground, and having returned to their places they sat down, and afterwards departed. All the dignitaries of the Court went away with them to their own abodes. To-day, it was my, Bú Fazl's, turn of service, and all this I witnessed and noted down in the calendar of the year.

After they had gone away the Amír ordered two golden cups with bottles of wine, plates of sweetmeats, and vases of flowers to be prepared. He directed one of his courtiers, Bú-l Hasan Karkhi, to go to Gházi, saying that these things should be carried after him, and that three singers should accompany him. He also instructed him to tell Ghází that he had left the Court too early, and that he must now drink wine with his companions and listen to the minstrels. Three singers accordingly went with Bú-l Hasan, and the porters carried the things. Muzaffar, a courtier, was ordered to go with the three singers, and with the same kind of presents to Ariyáruk. The Khwája made many remarks, and said what he deemed right on the subject. About the time of afternoon prayer he returned home, the others also took their leave. The Amír was there till about evening, and then he rose up and went into the palace.

The Mahmúdians were much grieved by what had just passed. Neither they nor any one else knew what the future would bring forth. Time spake with an eloquent tongue, but no one regarded.

The two courtiers went to the generals with those things and the singers. The generals expressed their obligations, and when the message of the Sultán was delivered to them they drank the wine with pleasure and rejoiced greatly. When they became elated with wine, they gave to (each of) the royal messengers a horse, a saddle inlaid with gold, a robe, some silver, and a Turkish slave, and sent them away delighted. In the same manner they rewarded the singers with garments and silver, and sent them away. Ghází then went to sleep, but Ariyáruk had the habit that when he once sat down to drink he would continue boozing for three or four entire days. This time he drank for two days, rejoicing over the favour which had been shown to them. The king held his Court again the next morning, and the commander of the army, Ghází, came with a different air and great display. When he sat down the Amír asked him why Ariyáruk had not also come. Ghází replied, " It is his habit to drink successively for three or four days, and he will especially do so now in his delight and gratification." The king smiled and said, We must also drink to-day, so we will send some one for Ariyáruk. Ghází kissed the ground and wished to retire, but he bade him remain, and they began to drink. The Amír commanded the attendance of Amírak Sipáh-dár Khummárchi, who also used to drink, and for whom Ariyáruk had great friendship. Amír Mahmúd had sent this man to Ariyáruk in Hind with a message for him to come to Court, and he returned in the month in which (Mahmúd) died as I have before stated. Amírak came before the Amír, who said to him " Take fifty flagons of wine to Hájib Ariyáruk and stay with him, as he is a great friend of yours, until he gets drunk and goes to sleep; tell him also that I excuse his attendance at Court, and that he is to drink according to his wont." Amírak went and found that Ariyáruk had become like a ball.[1] He was rambling about in the garden and drinking wine and the singers were singing. The message was delivered to him, on which he kissed the ground and wept much. He gave much wealth to Amírak and the porters. The latter returned, but Amírak remained with him. The General Ghází remained in the same place with the king till the next morning, when he

---

[1] [چون گوی شدہ *Gui-shudan*, according to the dictionaries, signifies "to place the head on the knees, to watch narrowly," the text would rather seem to mean "Restless as a ball that is tossed about."]

returned home taking several military officers and Hájibs, and there sat down to drink. That day he gave away immense riches in dinárs and dirams in cash, horses, clothes, and slaves. Ariyáruk, as he was wont, continued dozing and rousing up, sipping soup[1] and again drinking wine, without knowing in the least what he was doing. That day and night, and the day after it, he never ceased. The king did not hold his Court next morning, but was prepared to arrest Ariyáruk. He came out and sat on a green (*khazrá*) close to the minister's office. We were in the office. Somebody secretly went and brought accounts of Ariyáruk. When noon arrived, 'Abdús came and whispered something in the ear of Bú Nasr Mishkán, who rose up and ordered the writers to leave, because the garden was to be cleared. With the exception of myself all rose up and went away. Me he privately told to send his horse back to his house and to seat myself at the portico of the office, for there was something important to be done. I was to carefully ascertain all that passed, and then come to him. I undertook to do so, and he went away. The minister, the 'Áriz, and all the other people also left. Daktagín Hájib, son-in-law of 'Alí Dáya came into the portico and went to the king. He was there only for a minute (*sá'at*) and returned. The king called Muhtáj, chief of the guards, and said something to him privately. He went away, and returned with five hundred soldiers completely armed from every division, and sent them into the garden where they were to sit concealed. The Hindu officers also came, bringing with them three hundred soldiers, and they also were posted in the garden. One of the chamberlains and a general went to Ariyáruk and told him that the Sultán was enjoying his wine, and invited him to join him. Some people had also been sent to invite General Gházi. He (Ariyáruk) was in such a state of drunkenness that he could not use his hands and feet. He said, "How can I go in this condition, and what shall I be able to do?" Amírak, *sipáh-dár*, whom the king

[رشته می اشامید] [1]

had trusted said, "May the general's life be prolonged, the king's order must be obeyed, and you must attend the Court. When he sees you in this state, he will excuse you and send you back. But it will be very bad for you if you don't go; and remarks will be made upon you." He also made Ariyáruk's *hájib*, Altútigín[1] second him, and say that the general must of course go. So Ariyáruk called for garment, stockings, and cap, put them on, and summoned a large number of guards *(ghulám)* and two hundred soldiers. Amírak said to his *hájib*, "This is bad; he is going to drink wine. Ten guards *(ghulám)* with shields and a hundred soldiers are sufficient." So he sent the other soldiers back, and Ariyáruk himself knew nothing of what was passing in the world. When he reached the court, Hájib Baktigín advanced, and the captain of the guards made him alight, and they walked before him to the court-house, where they made him sit down. Ariyáruk, after a moment, stood up and said, "I am drunk, and can do nothing, I must go back." Baktagín told him it was improper to go away without permission, and that they were going to inform the king. So he sat down in the portico, and I, Bú-l Fazl, was looking at him. He called Hájí, water carrier, who came and put a pitcher of water before him. He put his hand in, took out the ice and ate it. Baktagín said, "Brother, this is wrong. You are a general, and yet you are eating ice here in the portico; go into the court and do there what you like." So he went in. If he had not been drunk, and they had wanted to take him, they would have found it a difficult matter. While he was seated in the inner apartment, fifty brave soldiers, on hearing the signal, suddenly rushed in. Baktagín also entered and took Ariyáruk in his arms. The soldiers came up on both sides and held him so that he could not move in the least. He cried out to Baktagín, "O brother, you coward! Was it for this purpose that you brought me here?" Other slaves came and pulled off the boots from his feet. In each boot there were

[1] [Variously written "Altarniyátigín" and "Altúbatigín."]

two daggers.[1] Muhtáj also came, and heavy chains were brought which were put round his legs. His coat was also taken off, and in it some poison was found, and also some charms. They were all taken away, and he was carried out. Fifty soldiers surrounded him, and other men rushed and seized his horse and trappings and his guards. The head of his escort with three guards escaped. The other guards seized their arms and got upon a roof, and a great tumult arose. The Amír was engaged with Baktagín in securing Ariyáruk, and people had run to Bagtaghdí, the chief Hájib Bilkátigín, and the officers of the army, to tell them what was going on, and to summon them. They were all mounted ready. The guards and attendants of Ariyáruk, seeing him thus bound, made a great outcry, and, collecting together, went towards his house. Numerous other horsemen of all classes also joined them, and a great and obstinate strife arose. Amír 'Abdús was sent to Ariyáruk's party to say, "Ariyáruk was a self-conceited man and a hard master. To-day it has been deemed expedient to suppress him. We are your masters, do not act like children; give up the strife, for it is clear you are too few to resist. You will all be slain in an instant, and Ariyáruk will gain nothing by it. If you restrain yourselves you shall be suitably rewarded." To the commander of these people a friendly and comforting message was sent. When 'Abdús delivered the message, it acted like water thrown on fire—the leader and the guards kissed the ground and the tumult instantly subsided. The house was attached and seals were affixed to the doors; night fell, and no one would have said he had ever been there. I returned and related to my preceptor all that I had seen. Then I said my night prayers. Ariyáruk was taken from the Court to Khunduz, and after ten days he was sent to Ghazní, and given into the charge of Bú 'Alí Kotwál, who according to orders kept him some time in the fort, so secretly that nobody knew that he had been dismissed. Afterwards he was sent to Bú-l Hasan Khalaf in Ghor, who kept him in some place there. Here ends his story.

[1] Worn as Highlanders wear their knives.

I will now relate according to my own information what was his end and how he was slain. He was captured in Balkh, on Wednesday, the 19th of Rabi'u-l Awwal A.H. 422 (March 1031). On the day after his arrest, the Amír sent to his house, Píroz Wazírí Khádim, Bú Sa'íd Mushrif, who still survives and lives at the Kandí inn, who had not then obtained the rank of a Mushrif, but was one of the grandees of the Court, and was known by the name of Kází Khusrú Hasan; Bú-l Hasan 'Abdu-l Jalíl, and Bú Nasr Mustaufí (commander of a detachment). They also brought with them the Mustaufí and steward of Ariyáruk (whom they had caught), and opened the doors. They appropriated immense wealth, and reported that there was much property in Hindustán. Three days were occupied in the work of completing an inventory of all that belonged to Ariyáruk, and it was taken to the court. His best slaves were made captives, those of the second order were given to Ghází, the commander, and the king's attendants. Bú-l Hasan 'Abdu-l Jalíl, and Bú Sa'íd Mushrif were ordered to go to Hindustán to fetch the property of Ariyáruk. They proceeded with great speed, but before Ariyáruk was captured, officers had been hastily despatched thither with letters directing that Ariyáruk's party should be carefully watched.

Ghází came to the Court the day after the seizure of Ariyáruk, greatly troubled and alarmed. He was admitted, and when the court broke up, the Amír privately observed to the minister and Ghází that "the conduct of this man (Ariyáruk) was very different from that of my other servants. He had grown disobedient and had become so arrogant in the time of my father, that he shed much innocent blood. The reporters of the news dared not expose his conduct, they were afraid of their lives, because he had taken possession of the roads and nobody could pass without his permission. He did not come from Hindustán when he was summoned by my father, and would never come. If coercive measures were taken against him he used to create a great disturbance. The Khwája showed great adroitness in contriving to bring him here. Such a servant is of no use. I have spoken thus that the commander-in-chief may not entertain any fear in his mind from what has just passed. His case is quite different. Different also was the service he rendered me at the time I was in Ispahán when I started from thence to Khurásán." He kissed the ground and said, "I am your slave, and I should even consider it an honour if the king were to make me keeper of his stable. The power of command is his and he well knows every one's worth." The Khwája also spoke a few appropriate words to the same effect about Ariyáruk, and for the comfort of Ghází. He said what he thought suitable, and then they retired. Both the Khwájas¹ sat with him in the court-room, and he called my preceptor, Bú Nasr, who told them all the acts of hardship and injustice which were committed by Ariyáruk as they had been reported by his enemies. Ghází was surprised and said, "Of course it is on no account proper to set him free." Bú Nasr went in and reported this to the king and brought satisfactory answers from him. Both these nobles spoke pleasant things to each other; so Ghází was much gratified and retired. I heard Bú Nasr state that Khwája Ahmad said "This Turk is very suspicious, for he is very cunning and sly (*kurbus o dáhí*), and these things will be all stored up in his memory. But alas! for a man like Ariyáruk who might conquer another region besides Hindustán, and for whom I would be surety. The king has heard enough about him and will not release him. He (the king) will ruin everything. Ghází also will fall; Mark my words." He then arose and went into his office, very disturbed in mind. And this old wolf said,² There is a conspiracy of the men of Mahmúd's and Mas'ud's time, and they are prosecuting their designs. God grant it may end well.

[هردو خواجه با وي بطارم بنشست و استادم نو نصرا بخواند] ¹
[وابن کرک پیر گفت] ²

Account of an Inundation at Ghazní.—Mahmúd Warrák and his Sons.[1]

On Saturday, the 9th of Rajab, between the morning and afternoon prayers, there were some slight showers which sufficed to wet the ground. Some herdsmen were encamped in the dry bed of the Ghazní river with their droves of cattle. Although they were told to decamp, as in the event of a flood they would be in danger, they would not listen, till at last, when the rain fell heavier, they began to take their departure, but slowly, and removed toward the wall near the suburb of the ironmongers, where they sought shelter and rest, but were again at fault. In another direction, where the stream flows by Afghánshála, there were several of the Royal mules stabled. Trees extended from the stream as far as the walls, and the stable keepers raised mounds of dung and other refuse to protect themselves against the flood, but without any effect, for they were direct in the path of the flood. Our prophet Muhammad says, (God's mercy be on him!) "Defend us from the two dumb and the two deaf," meaning thereby water and fire.

The bridge which stood at that time was a massive structure, supported by strong buttresses. The top was securely covered, and on each side of the roadway, there was a row of shops, just as there is now. When, in consequence of the flood, the bridge was so destroyed that no one could pass over it, that holy personage (Amír Mas'úd) God's mercy on him! constructed the present bridge, of one arch, of such excellence and beauty, that may he be long remembered for his goodness and humanity!

At the time of afternoon prayers the bridge was in such a state as no one ever remembered, and when about one watch of the night had passed, such a flood came, that the oldest inhabitants agreed that they had never seen the like. Many trees, torn up by the roots, came rushing down towards the bridge. The cattle and the mules endeavoured to save their lives, but the flood

[1] [This extract was translated by Sir H. Elliot. Pages 315 to 318 of the Text.]

carried many of them down; and as the waterway of the bridge was narrow, it was impossible that trees and animals together could pass through it at the same time. They filled up the arches, so that even the water could not escape through them. Then the water rose over the roadway, and carried away everything, like a dispersed army, and entering the Bazar reached as far as the Bankers' quarters, and did a great deal of injury. What showed the great force of the water more than anything else was, that it carried away the bridge from its foundations, with all its shops. It carried away many caravansorais in its way, destroyed the bazars, and came rushing in a flood against the old fort, which stood then as it stood before the time of Ya'kúb Lais, whose brother, 'Umrú, built this city and fort of Ghaznín.

All these matters the learned Mahmúd Warrák has described most excellently in the history which he wrote in the year 450 H. He composed a history of several thousand years, ending with 409 H. As he ended there, I determined to continue his history from that period. This Mahmúd Warrák is a true and faithful historian. I have seen ten or fifteen of his excellent compositions on every subject, and I intended to write something in his praise, but when his sons heard of it, they exclaimed and said, "are not we, his sons, able to write an account of him, that you should undertake it, as you have declared your intention of doing?" Let it alone." Being helpless, I abandoned my intention.

This inundation did so much injury that there is no computing it. The next day, men stood on each side of the river looking on. About twelve o'clock the flood began to abate. But for several days there was no bridge, and men found it difficult to pass from this side to that and from that side to this, until the bridge was again mended. I have heard from several Záwalí[1] narrators that, after the subsidence of the flood, many wretched sufferers found gold, silver, and garments that the water had swept away, and

[1] Of Zábulistán, or the country about Ghazni.

God Almighty knows what the destitute did not meet with from his goodness.

The Amír returned from his hunting ground to the Sadhazár[1] garden, on Saturday the 16th of Rajab, and remained there seven days, pleasuring and drinking.

* * * * * * *

Ahmad Niáltigín appointed Governor of Hindustan.[2]

The Amír, addressing the Khwája, said, "Hindustán must not be left without a governor, but who is to be sent there?" He answered, "You, my lord, know all the servants and you must have thought about the person to be appointed. The office is very important and honourable. When Ariyáruk was there he kept up great state, and now a man ought to be sent of the same dignity. Although under the authority of your Majesty matters may go on well, still a trained and experienced general is required." The Amír said, "I have fixed my heart upon Ahmad Niáltigín, though he has not been trained under generals; he was treasurer to my father, and accompanied him in all his journeys. He studied and knew the ways and habits of the late king." The Khwája remained thinking for a while.[3] He had an ill feeling towards this man, because he had formed many designs when he, the Khwája, was discharging the fine imposed upon him.[4] Ahmad had also purchased his goods at the very lowest prices. But the Khwája had been restrained, and had never taken revenge, until the present time when he had directed that a reckoning should be held with him. His excesses were searched out and close calculations were made so that money might be exacted from him. But the king had now selected him, and so the Khwája wished to cure the wound of his heart. The Khwája

---

[1] Literally 100,000—from its containing as many shrubs or flowers.
[2] [Page 323 to 329 of the Text.]
[3] [The whole of the following passage is very obscure and doubtful.]
[4] [Morley's edition says خواجه مرافعه مي داد but Elliot's MS. has the words مال مصادره before the verb.]

also was very inimical to Kazí Shíráz Bú-l Hasan 'Alí, because Amír Mahmúd had often said in his usual way, "How long shall I bear with the airs of this Ahmad, he is not so indispensable, for there are other persons fit for the office of Wazír. For example, there is one, Kází Shíráz." Now this Kází Shíráz did not possess even one-tenth part of the abilities of that great man (the Khwája). But kings say what they like, and no one can argue with them. At all events in this counsel the Khwája deemed it allowable to set a great man like Ahmad Niáltigín against Kází Shíráz, as the latter might thus be disgraced. He replied, "May my lord's life be prolonged, it is a very good selection, and there is no one so fit as Ahmad. But promises must be taken from him on oath, and his son must be left here with other sureties." The Amír coincided, and directed the Khwája to send for Ahmad to tell him all that was proper and to do what was needful. The Khwája came into the minister's office and called for Ahmad, who was terribly afraid he might have to suffer another punishment. However, he came. The Khwája made him sit down and said to him, "Don't you know that you have to render several years' account, and that I am bound by oath to do my utmost in the king's business. Your demeanour must not be such as to aggrieve me, and I must not take such proceedings as to irritate you. When a king has determined upon a matter, nothing remains for his servants but to give counsel and show kindness (to each other)." Ahmad kissed the ground and said, "I can in nowise consider this as difficult, for I have not seen the king to-day, nor have I seen him for years. We servants must agree with what the king orders, and with what you, the great Khwája, considers best." The minister observed, "The Sultán consulted with me in private to-day on different topics, of which the most important was that of Hindustán. He said, 'There is a man there like Kází Shíráz, who wears a soldier's garment, but who is no commander. A general is needed there, one of renown and dignity to lead the forces and to exact tribute. It is the Kází's business to carry on civil affairs and collect the revenue, but the general at his convenience makes war, takes tribute, seizes upon elephants, and chastises the refractory Hindús.'" The Khwája continued—"When I said to him 'Your Majesty knows the merits of all your servants, whom do you choose for the duty?' he replied, 'I have fixed my mind upon Ahmad Niáltigín,' and I saw he had a very high opinion of you. I also spoke what I knew regarding your bravery and experience. He directed me to send for you to acquaint you with his majesty's will and to arrange matters. What have you to say about it?" Ahmad kissed the ground, rose up and said, "I have no words to express my thanks for this favour, nor do I think myself deserving of it; but I will perform the duty which may be assigned to me to the best of my power." So all was settled, and neither kindness nor counsel was wanting. The Khwája gladdened him and praised him, and sent him away. He then called Muzaffar, chief of the royal attendants, told him all that, had passed, and directed him to request the Amír to order a khil'at to be prepared, more magnificent than that which was granted to Ariyáruk, the late governor of Hindustán, and that Bú Nasr Mishkán should write out the royal diploma for him, and get it impressed with the royal signet, so that at the time of granting the robe all the necessary orders might be given to him to enable him to assume his command at once, and enter on his expedition in time. Muzaffar went and delivered the message. The king gave the order, and a robe of honour was prepared for Ahmad, together with kettle-drums, flags, and all things usually given to generals of the army.

On Sunday, the second of Sha'bán, of this year, the Amír ordered Ahmad Niáltigín to be taken to the wardrobe and he was invested with the khil'at. It was very splendid: first came the golden girdle, which was of the value of one thousand kánís, and with it was also given a cap with two points, which was also prepared at the expense of the same sum. He observed the ceremonials of respect, and the Amír received him graciously;

he then returned home with great honour. People offered him presents according to custom. The next day he again came to the Court. The Amír held a private consultation with the great Khwája and Khwája Bú Nasr, Secretary of State; Ahmad was also called, and he received orders from the king's own tongue. From thence they came into the court-hall, and all three sat there alone. The Royal diploma and the articles and agreement[1] were written out, and both the papers were duly sealed. They were taken to Ahmad, and the writings and a solemn oath were put before him. He took the oath according to custom, and put his signature to it. Then the papers were shown to the king, and given into the charge of the record keeper.

The Khwája said to Ahmad, "that self-sufficient fellow of Shíráz wishes the generals to be under his command, and when he had to deal with such a weak man as 'Abdu-llah Karátigín, he governed all. On hearing the name of Ariyáruk he knew that a man who had teeth was coming; he wished to have a revenue-collector and and an accountant-general sent there, so Abú-l Fath and Daniaghání were sent with Abú-l Faraj Kirmání, but they could not cope with Ariyáruk. However, what happened to Ariyáruk happened in consequence of his conducting matters for his own benefit; but you who are a general, must act according to the articles and your agreement. You must not say anything to any person respecting the political or revenue matters, so that no one's word may be heard against you, but you must perform all the duties of a commander, so that that follow may not be able to put his hand upon your sinews and drag you down. Bú-l Kásim Bú-l Hakam, the superintendent of the news carriers, a most confidential officer, reports in due time all that occurs, and the imperial and ministerial orders are regularly sent to him. You two persons must not give trouble to the Court. What you have to write to me you must state in full detail, that a distinct reply may be sent. His majesty deems it advisable to send

[1] [موافعه و جواب and below منشور و موافعة جوابها]

with you some of the Dailamí chiefs, such as Bú Nasr Taifúr and others, in order that they may be at a distance from the Court, because they are strangers; he also sends some others of whom apprehensions are entertained, such as Bú Nasr Dámítní, brother of the Prince of Balkh and nephew of the chief of Sarkhas; also some refractory slaves who have committed many disloyal actions, which have been proved against them. They are to be set at liberty and some assistance is to be given to them, so that it may appear that they belong to your army. You must take them all with you and treat them very kindly and well. But, of course, none of them must be allowed to go beyond the river Chandráha,[1] without the king's order, or without your knowledge and permission. Whenever you march on an expedition you must take these people with you, and you must be careful not to let them mingle with the army of Lahore and not allow them to drink wine or play at *chaugán*. You must keep spies and observers to watch them, and this is a duty which must in no case be neglected. Injunctions also will be sent to Bú-l Kásim Bú-l Hakam to give you a helping hand, and to do everything that may be necessary in this matter. In other affairs he is to act under the orders of the Court, and in accordance with the royal mandate and the conditions of his appointment. What you have just heard are the secret orders of the king, and you must not divulge them. When you reach the station you must report all circumstances which occur, also what reliance is to be placed on each individual, and whether he acts upon the royal orders which he has received."

Ahmad Niáltigín said, "I will do all this, so that no harm may be done." Then he retired. Close at his heels the Khwája sent him a message by Hasan, his Hájib, to say that his Majesty had directed that his (Niáltigín's) son was to remain behind, though he would no doubt take with him his wife and children who lived in privacy. The son was to be left at home under the care of a tutor, a friend and a confidential person, in order that

[1] [The Chináb, see Vol. I. p. 63.]

the father might feel himself more at liberty. This was an arrangement made by his Majesty out of regard to Ahmad, for he did not wish to see his son associating with the body guards. The Khwája added, "I was ashamed to tell you this, for it is not right to require a pledge from you; but although the Sultán has not given a distinct order about it, yet the conditions and the customs must not be departed from. I have no option, but to look after all the affairs of the country, great and small, and to protect the interest of you and the like of you." Ahmad answered, "I am obedient and think it best both now and henceforth to do that which the great Khwája approves and directs." He gave a handsome present to the Hájib and dismissed him. He also made proper arrangements for his son. His equipment as a general, retinue, arms, guards, and everything else he carefully prepared in the manner which he had seen and had learnt to be the rule in such cases. When all was done he got leave to set out.

On Saturday, five days before the end of Sha'bán, the king rode and came to the desert of Shábahár with many attendants and riding under a canopy on an elephant. He stopped there, and Ahmad Niáltigín came before him, dressed in a red garment, and paid his respects. A very fine calvacade, many armed men, military officers, the Dailamís, and others, who were placed under his command, passed by. They were followed by one hundred and thirty royal slaves whom the Amír had set free, who carried their letters of freedom, and delivered them to him. These were under three of the king's own officers, and had with them three flags, bearing the device of a lion and spears, according to the fashion of royal slaves. After them came kettle drums, and the banners of Ahmad of red cloth and with gilded balls on their tops, accompanied by seventy-five slaves, richly caparisoned camels and dromedaries. The king said, "Ahmad, rejoice, and be happy; be careful to understand the value of this favour. Keep my image ever before your eyes and do good service, so that you may attain to greater honour." He promised to do all that could be required of a servant, and saluted. The horse of the commander of the army of Hindustán was called for; and he mounted and rode away.

In the end, this Ahmad Niáltigín was ruined; he turned away from the the path of rectitude, and took a crooked course, as I shall have to relate in the proper place.

Ahmad Niáltigín at Benares.[1]

In this summer [424 H., 1033 A.D.] another event took place in which Ahmad Niáltigín, the commander of Hindustán, was concerned. A certain man was driven to rebellion by tyranny, and this was the cause of the rise of disturbances in Khurásán, and of the Turkománs and Saljúkians becoming powerful, according to the decree of God, whose name is glorious. There is a cause for everything. The great Khwája, Ahmad Hasan, was badly disposed towards this Ahmad, for the reason we have before stated, that is, he had formed designs against the Khwája's goods and effects, at the time when he was involved in law troubles. The Khwája was also at variance with Kází Shíráz, because Amír Mahmúd had often declared him to be fit for the office of Wazír. Ahmad Hasan, at the time of dispatching Ahmad Niáltigín on the command to Hindustán, had instructed him to be watchful against Kází Shíráz, saying, you are by the Sultán's order appointed generalissimo in Hindustán, and the Kází has no control over you. Let him not cast his spell over you and bring you under his control. Ahmad Niáltigín went boldly and proudly; he did not heed the Kází in the least in his duties of commander. This Ahmad was a bold man. He was called the *alter ego*[2] of Amír Mahmúd, and well knew the distinction between right and wrong. People used to tell stories about his mother, his birth, and Amír Mahmúd. There was certainly a friendly relation between that king and his mother,—but God knows the truth. This man thoroughly understood the affairs

[1] [Page 495 to 497 of the Text.]
[2] ['*Atsat*, lit. "the sneeze," or as we have it in the vulgar tongue, "the spit."]

and habits of Amír Mahmúd, by association and converse with him. When he reached Hindustán, he kept several sturdy slaves, and had a fine equipage and retinue. A difference took place between him and Kází Shíráz with respect to the command of the army. The Kází said, "The command ought to be given to 'Abdu-llah Karátigín, as was expressed in his farmán." Ahmad protested he would not agree to anything of the kind, saying, "The Sultán conferred this office on me, and I am in all respects better and greater than 'Abdu-llah; he and others must march under my banners." The matter went very far. The army of Lahore and the warriors sided with Ahmad; and he with his followers irritated the Kází, and formed a plan of going to some distant place. The Kází sent messengers complaining of him, who reached Bust just as we were about to go toward Hirát and Naishapúr. Amír Mas'úd asked the great Khwája, Ahmad Hasan, what he thought most advisable, and he replied, "Ahmad Niáltigín is a fitter person to be general than anyone else. An answer must be written to the Kází that his business is to manage the revenue, and that he has nothing to do with the command or with the army. Ahmad must himself do what he ought to do, and take the revenue and the tribute from the Thákurs, go on expeditions and bring large sums into the treasury. There is a proverb—'There must be no contention between the door and the house.'"

The Amír approved of this, and an answer was written to the above effect. Ahmad Niáltigín was much encouraged, because the Khwája wrote to inform him of what Kází Shíráz had written, and what reply had been sent. He marched out with his warriors and the army of Lahore, and exacted ample tribute from the Thákurs. He crossed the river Ganges and went down the left bank. Unexpectedly (*ná-gáh*) he arrived at a city which is called Banáras, and which belonged to the territory of Gang. Never had a Muhammadan army reached this place. The city was two parasangs square, and contained plenty of water. The army could only remain there from morning to mid-day prayer, because of the peril. The markets of the drapers, perfumers, and jewellers, were plundered, but it was impossible to do more. The people of the army became rich, for they all carried off gold, silver, perfumes, and jewels, and got back in safety.

The Kází, on the achievement of this great success, was likely to go mad. He speedily sent messengers, who reached us in Naishápúr and represented that Ahmad Niáltigín had taken immense riches from the Thákurs and tributaries. Enormous wealth had been obtained, but Ahmad had concealed the greater portion of it, and had sent only a little to the Court. The Kází went on to say that "his confidential agents had secretly accompanied Ahmad, who knew not of their presence. Some accountants and the chief of the couriers were also there, and these had kept an account of all that he had exacted. This account he had now sent for the information of his Majesty, without the knowledge of that base dishonest man. Ahmad had also clandestinely sent men to Turkistan *vid* Banjhír (Panjshír?) to procure Turkish slaves for him. That up to this time about seventy slaves (*háftad o and*) had been brought and others were expected. That he had made all the Turkománs who were there his friends, and they were disaffected; what his intentions are nobody knows, but ho calls himself son of Mahmúd. Your slaves have dutifully given the information. Your Majesty's will is supreme."

These letters took effect on the Amír's heart, and produced a deep impression. He ordered my instructor, Bú Nasr, to keep tho matter secret, and let no one be informed of it. Bearers of good tidings also soon arrived, and brought letters from Ahmad Niáltigín, Governor of Hindustán and general of the army, reporting the news of the conquest of Benares, which was a very great achievement, and by which the army had become rich. Immense wealth had been obtained, and tribute had been exacted from the Thákurs. Several elephants had also been taken. His Majesty's servants wrote these letters from Indar-dar-bandi,[1]

---

[1] [This is the reading of Morley's edition. Sir H. Elliot's MSS. have Indar-bodi.]

and were returning towards Lahore very happy: what had passed they had reported.[1]

Tilak the Hindú appointed General.[2]

One day the Amír went to the garden of Sadhazára with the intention of staying there a week, and all necessary furniture was taken. In this interval letters were constantly arriving with the information of Ahmad Nísltigín having reached Lahore with the Turkománs, and that numerous turbulent fellows of Lahore, from all classes of people, had flocked around him, and that if his proceedings were not soon taken notice of, the affair would reach an awkward length, for his power and dignity were increasing every day. The Amír, in the garden of Sadhazára, convened a private council of the commander-in-chief and the generals and officers of the army,[3] and asked their opinions as to what ought to be done in order to extinguish the fire of this rebellious general so that their hearts might be relieved of all concern on his account. The commander-in-chief said, "When one runs away from Ahmad there cannot be much honour left, but whatever general is sent against him, he will have enough to do, for there is a strong force at Lahore. If my lord orders me to go, I can set out in a week, although the weather is very hot." The Amír observed, "It is wrong and impossible for you to go on such an insignificant duty, because there are disturbances in Khurásán, and insurrections have also broken out in Khatlán and Tukháristán. Our minister has gone there and he is sufficient, yet as the autumn has passed, it is expedient for me to march to Bust or Balkh, and you must accompany my standard. We will send a general, to Sind it may be." The commander-in-chief said, "It is for my lord to order, the generals and officers are present here in your council, and others are at the court; whom do you order to go." Tilak Hindú said, "May my lord's life

[1] [Here occurs the lacuna mentioned in the Bibliographical notice at page 64.]
[2] [Page 500 to 505 of the Text.]
[3] [Khwája Ahmad, the wazír, was absent on a journey.]

be prolonged! Be pleased to let me go and perform this service that I may make some return for favours received and obligations incurred. Besides, I am a native of Hindustán, the weather is hot, and I can travel in that country with greater ease. If your high wisdom deems me fit for this service, I will not fail." The Amír admired him for the readiness he thus showed; and asked those who were present for their opinions. They replied, he was a famous man and was fit for any duty, for he had a sword, equipments, and men, and as he had received the royal favour he might accomplish the object. The Amír told his councillors to retire and leave him to consider about it. So they left. The Amír said to his private councillors, "None of these officers have their hearts in the business, and in fact they have not exhibited their wonted devotion. So Tilak, perhaps, felt ashamed and stepped forward." The Amír sent a Persian secretary to Tilak, secretly, with many kind messages, saying, "I am fully alive to what you have said and have promised to perform, but the people around me did not at all like it. You have shamed them all, and your words shall be proved true, for to-morrow you shall be named for the service. I will do whatever is possible in this matter, and I will give you much money, a strong force, and everything necessary, so that the work may be accomplished by your hands, and the insurrection may be put down without any thanks or obligations to these people. You shall be raised to higher rank; for these people do not at all like that I should exalt a man, but wish me to remain always dependent on them, though they do nothing. They have been greatly annoyed at your exaltation, Now you must be resolute in doing what you have said. The fault has been committed: it was manifest in their talk and observations; and what is passed cannot be recalled." Tilak kissed the ground, and said, "If this undertaking were beyond the powers of your slave, he would not have ventured to speak with such boldness before your majesty and the assembly; what I have sought for in this matter I will accomplish. I will draw up a plan for the approval of his

Majesty; and I will soon set forth and overthrow that rebel." The Persian came back and related all this. The Amír highly approved it, and ordered the writing to be sent in. The secretary devoted himself with all his heart to the execution of this mission, and laid before his Majesty the detailed statement which Tilak had drawn up of his designs. The Amír then gave power to Tilak to do whatever he deemed proper, after passing Bazghúrak[1] for securing the allegiance of the Hindús. He also sent a message by the Persian to the Secretary of State, directing him to draw up a farman and letters in behalf of Tilak. It was customary with Bú Nasr to write in very hyperbolical language[2] on all matters that he was directed to pen by the Amír himself, because he was afraid that the responsibility might fall upon him. What was to be written was drafted. The ministers of the Court considered it a foolish proceeding—or as the Arab proverb says "A shot without a shooter."

This man (Tilak) was the cause of the death of Ahmad Niáltigín, as I will mention in its proper place. But first I must recount the history of this Tilak, showing what his origin was and how he attained to this rank. Many advantages attend the writing of such matters.

Account of Tilak of Hind.[3]

This Tilak was the son of a barber, but he was handsome in face and appearance, and had an eloquent tongue. He wrote an excellent hand, both in Hindí and Persian. He had lived a long time in Kashmír, where he studied and acquired some proficiency in dissimulation, amours, and witchcraft. From thence he came to Kází Shíráz Bú-l Hasan, who was captivated by him, for every great man who saw him was enamoured of him. * * * * The Kází restrained him from going anywhere else; but Tilak contrived by stratagem to have his

[1] [See Vol. I. p. 49.]
[2] [مبالغتی سخت تمام کردی]
[3] [Page 603 to 606.]

case, and the iniquity of which the Kází was capable, reported to the great Khwája Ahmad Hasan (May God be pleased with him). There was ill-feeling between the Khwája and the Kází. The Khwája sent royal orders with three peons, and to the great disgust of the Kází they brought Tilak to the court. Khwája Ahmad Hasan heard what he had to say, saw the way clear before him, and took measures to have the matter brought to the notice of Amír Mahmúd in such a manner that he did not know the Khwája had contrived the means. The Amír ordered the Khwája to hear Tilak's complaint, and the Kází fell into great difficulty.

After this event Tilak became one of the great confidants of the Khwája. He was made his secretary and interpreter between him and the Hindús.[1] Thus he acquired great influence in the minister's court, where I, says Bú-l Fazl, used to see him standing before the Khwája, doing the duties of a secretary and interpreter, and carrying and bringing messages, and managing difficult affairs. When that trouble fell on the Khwája, which I have before mentioned, Amír Mahmúd called together his servants and secretaries, in order that he might appoint the most clever to offices in his court. Tilak met with his approval, and was associated as interpreter with Bahrám. He was a young man and a clever speaker. Amír Mahmúd wanted such persons. His fortune thus improved. Secretly he rendered valuable services to Sultán Mas'úd, that is, he brought all the Hindú Kators and many outsiders under his rule,[2] and he obtained honour from such a great king as Mahmúd.

When Sháh Mas'úd arrived in Balkh from Hirát and the affairs of the country were settled, Sundar, the general of the Hindús, was not in his place. He therefore promoted Tilak,

[1] [The text has the words *hamchunán Birbal, badiwán-i má*, "like Birbal is our Court." These words, unless they will bear some other interpretation, would seem to apply to Akbar's officer Birbal, and if so they must be an interpolation of a later date.]

[2] See Thomas' Prinsep, Vol. I. p. 317.] همه هندران کتور و بعضی را از بیرونیان در عهد وی

and granted him a gold embroidered robe, hung a jewelled necklace of gold round his neck, and placed an army under him. Thus he obtained the name of man. A tent and an umbrella were also given to him. Kettle drums were beaten at his quarters, according to the custom of the Hindú chiefs, and banners with gilded tops were granted. Fortune befriended him; he was elevated to such a degree as to sit among the nobles in the privy councils, and, as I have said, he was employed in important duties, until at length he undertook the command against Ahmad Niáltigín. His luck and fortune aided him, and carried him through. The Arabs say, "There is a cause for everything, and men must seek it." Wise men do not wonder at such facts, because nobody is born great—men become such. But it is important that they should leave a good name behind. This Tilak soon became a man, and had excellent qualities. All the time he lived he sustained no injury on account of being the son of a barber. But if with such a character, wisdom, and spirit, he had been of good extraction, he would have been better, for nobility and talents are both very agreeable. But nobility is good for nothing, if learning, propriety and spirit are wanting.

o   o   o   o   o

The rebellion of Ahmad Niáltigín in Hindústán.[1]

In the middle of this month (Ramazán II. 425; July, 1033) letters were received from Lahore (Lahúr), stating that Ahmad Niáltigín had arrived there with several men ; that Kází Shíráz, with all his counsellors, had entered the fort of Mandkákúr;[2] that there was perpetual fighting, and that the whole neighbourhood was in a state of turmoil and agitation. The Amír became exceedingly thoughtful, because his mind was troubled from three

---

[1] [Pages 523, 524. This and all the following Extracts from Baihakí were translated by Sir H. Elliot himself.]
[2] Two copies concur in this reading; a third omits the first syllable. [See Vol. I. pp. 62 and 530.]

different sources, viz. the Turkománs of 'Irák, Khwárizm, and Lahore, as I have already described. * * * On Tuesday, the 'Íd was celebrated, when the Amír (God be satisfied with him!) directed that great preparations should be made, and ordered trays of food to be set down, with wine, in order that the officers and men might regale themselves, which they did, and departed drunk.

The Amír also sat down to drink wine with his companions, when, in the middle of his happiness, while he was fully occupied with every kind of pleasure, a very important despatch was received from Lahore, stating that Ahmad Niáltigín had taken the fort; but it was reported that Tilak Hindú had collected a powerful army from every detachment and quarter, and was advancing in that direction; that the heart of that vile rebel was quaking within him, and that there was a space of only two kos between the two armies. The Amír read this despatch even while he was drinking, and ordered a letter to be written to Tilak Hindú, and placed in its case. He directed Tilak to proceed against Ahmad with all speed. The Amír sealed the letter, and added a postscript with his own hand, written with all the force which characterized his style, imperious, and at the same time appropriate to the person addressed. This was concealed from his confidential Díwán, and sent off with all haste.

On Thursday, the 18th of Shawwál, a despatch arrived from Gurdez,[1] stating that General Ghází, who was stationed in that quarter, had died.

* * * * * *

The Cowardice of the Hindús at Kirmán, and their Disgrace.[2]

Ahmad 'Alí Noshtigín made every kind of exertion, but the Hindús would not advance, and turned their backs in flight. The panic spread to the rest of the troops, and Ahmad was obliged to fly from the field. He, with his own troops and the royal army, returned, by way of Káín, to Naishápúr. Part of

[1] [A town fifty miles east of Ghazní.] [2] [Page 533.]

the army fell back to Makrán. The Hindús fled to Sístán, and thence to Ghaznín.¹ I, who am Abú-l Fazl, had gone on duty to the Amír, at the Sad-hazára Garden, and I saw the officers of the Hindús who had come there. The Amír ordered that they should be kept in the large house, which is used as the despatch office. Bú Sa'íd, the accountant, brought several severe orders to them from the Amír, and matters went so far, that a message came to tell them they were dismissed. Six of their officers committed suicide with their daggers, so that blood was flowing in the office. I, Bú Sa'íd, and others, left the place, and came and told the Amír what had happened. He said they should have used these daggers at Kirmán. He treated them severely, but in the end forgave them.² After this, all went wrong, and it was not possible to send any one else to Kirmán. Ahmad 'Alí Noshtigín also came to Ghaznín, and as he was ashamed and deeply grieved, no long time elapsed before he died.

* * * * * *

The Death of the Rebel Ahmad Niáltigín and the Sultán's Rejoicings.³

Amír Mas'úd wrote orders to Tilak to expedite matters against Ahmad Niáltigín, who should be driven from Lahore, and the Kází and his army should leave the fort. The Kází also was ordered to exert himself to the utmost in order that the Amír's mind might be at once relieved from anxiety on account of this rebellion. * * * * The Amír arrived at

---

¹ This was at the battle of Kirmán, where they formed one-half of the cavalry force, there being 2000 Hindús, 1000 Turks, and 1000 Kurds and Arabs.

² The Hindus, about 100 pages after this, are represented as incurring similar disgrace near Merv, when they fled before the Turkomans; but there they were not a bit more culpable than the rest of the army, and the reasons assigned was sufficient. "The Amír also summoned the Hindús and reprimanded them, when their leaders said —We are ashamed to speak before our Lord, but the fact is our men are hungry, and our horses weak, for it is now four months since any of us have eaten barley-bread. Notwithstanding what has happened, as long as we live we shall not be found deficient." ³ [Pages 635 to 638.]

Takínábád[1] on the 7th of Zí-l ka'da [A.H. 425, Sept. 1034 A.D.], and remained there seven days, on one of which he drank wine, for he was troubled on many accounts. After that, he went to Bust for three days, and on Thursday, the 17th of this month, he arrived at the palace of Dasht-langán, where he laid out much money in gardens, buildings, and *sardís*.

* * * * * *

On Wednesday, the last day of this month, he left Bust, and while on the road messengers arrived from Tilak, bringing intelligence of his having slain the proud rebel Ahmad Niáltigín, of having taken his son prisoner, and of his having subdued the Turkománs who were with Ahmad. The Amír was exceedingly rejoiced at this news, for it relieved the anxiety of his heart. He ordered the drums to be beaten, and the clarions to be sounded; he invested the messengers with robes of honour upon their introduction, gave them plenty of money, and directed that they should be paraded through the camp.

The letters of Tilak, Kází Shíráz, and the intelligencers were to this effect:—When Tilak arrived at Lahore, he took several Musulmáns prisoners, who were the friends of Ahmad, and ordered their right hands to be cut off; that the men who were with Ahmad were so terrified at this punishment and display of power, that they sued for mercy and deserted him; that the proper arrangements were then made for the conduct of affairs of Revenue and Police; that Tilak, in full confidence and power, pursued Ahmad with a large body of men, chiefly Hindús; that in the pursuit several skirmishes and actions took place; that Ahmad, the forsaken of God, kept flying before him; that Tilak had persuaded Ahmad's men to desert; that a severe engagement ensued, when Ahmad, not able to stand his ground, was defeated and took to flight; that the Turkománs left him in a body, and asked for quarter, which was given to them; that Ahmad escaped with his personal attendants, and others, amounting to three hundred horsemen in all; that Tilak did not abate his

[1] [The largest town in Garmsír. See *Tabakát-i Násirí, post*.]

pursuit, and had written letters to the Hindú Jat rebels to desert the cause of that godless man, and to remember that whoever should bring him or his head should receive a reward of 500,000 dirhams. On this account the span of Ahmad's life was narrowed, his men deserted, and at last matters reached so far, that the Jats and every kind of infidel joined in the pursuit of him.

One day, the despatches continued, he arrived at a river on his elephant, and wished to cross it, when two or three thousand mounted Jats were close upon him, whereas he had less than two hundred horsemen with him. He plunged into the water, while the Jats were attacking him on two or three sides, chiefly for the purpose of seizing his property and money. When they reached him, he attempted to kill his son with his own hand, but the Jats prevented him, and carried off the son, who was on an elephant, and then fell upon Ahmad himself, with arrow, spear, and sword. He defended himself most gallantly, but they at last killed him and cut off his head. They killed or took captive all who were with him, and immense wealth fell into the hands of those Jats. Their Chief sent some messengers from the spot to Tilak, who was not far off, to convey intelligence of what had happened. Tilak was greatly delighted, and despatched some men to demand the son and the head of Ahmad; but the Jats asked for the reward of 500,000 dirhams. Tilak replied, that the immense wealth which belonged to Ahmad had fallen into their hands, and they ought to forego their demand. Twice messengers went backwards and forwards upon this errand, and at last it was agreed that they should receive 100,000 dirhams. When this sum was sent to them they brought the head and the son of Ahmad to Tilak, who having obtained his object returned to Lahore to complete his arrangements for the management of the country, and then to hasten to Court with all expedition, God willing.

The Amír ordered congratulatory answers to be written, expressed his obligations to Tilak and the others, and praised them for their conduct. He sent the couriers back, and ordered Tilak to come to Court with the head and the son of Ahmad Niáltigín. Such is the end of the perfidious and disobedient! From the time of Adam (peace be with him!) to this day, it has so happened that no servant has rebelled against his master who has not lost his head; and since it is written in books, there is no occasion to make a long story about it.

The Amír wrote letters on this subject to his nobles and officers, and despatched messengers to different parts of the country to proclaim this very great victory.[1]

The Amír arrived at Hirát on Thursday, the middle of Zí-l hijja.

* * * * *

Prince Majdúd appointed Governor of Hindustán.[2]

On Saturday, the 6th of Zí-l ka'da, the Prince Amír Majdúd, who was appointed Governor (Amír) of Hindustán, received a khil'at before his departure for Lahore. It was such a one as befitted a governor, especially one who was son of such a king. Three chamberlains were appointed, with their attendants; Mansúr, son of Bú-l Kasam 'Alí Noki of our office, was appointed to be his secretary, Sa'd Salmán to be accountant and treasurer, and Sarhang Muhammad to be paymaster of the troops. A drum, a standard, and a kettle-drum, an elephant and seat were bestowed on the Prince, and the next day he went by appointment to visit his father in the Fírozí garden. The Sultan embraced him, and gave him a dress upon taking his leave. So he went on his way, and took with him Rashíd, the son of Khwárizm Sháh, that he might be kept under surveillance in the city of Lahore.

* * * * *

[1] A few pages after this we find the minister Khwája-buzurg Ahmad 'Abdu-s Samad stating at a council, that, notwithstanding the death of Ahmad Niáltigín, Hindustán was still in so disaffected a state that he considered it imprudent that the Sultán should enter upon an expedition against the Turkománs.

[2] [Page 622.]

Prince Maudúd appointed Governor of Balkh.[1]

Trays of food were put down in abundance, and they drank wine. On the next day, a khil'at was given to Amír Maudúd, such as he had not received before, for it comprised a kettle-drum, standards, a tymbal, and a tabor, and the Sultán made over to him the country of Balkh, and issued a patent to that effect; so the Prince returned with all these honours to his residence, which was the sarái of Aralán Jázib, and the Sultán ordered all the nobles and officers to pay him their visits there, and they accordingly showed him such honour as had never been shown before.

The Sultán determines to take the Fort of Hánsi—His Consultation with the Nobles.[2]

On another day of the 'Íd, the public audience being dissolved, the minister, the Commander-in-Chief, the 'Áriz, my preceptor, and the chamberlains Bagtaghdí and Bú-l Nasr, were told to remain, and the conversation turned upon the direction in which the Sultán ought to march. These counsellors observed, "Let our lord explain to his servants what his own reflections are, for his opinion is probably the soundest; then will we speak what we know on the subject."

The Amír replied, "At the time that I was attacked by my illness at Bust, I made a vow that, if Almighty God would restore me to health, I would go to Hindustán, and take the fort of Hánsi; for, from the time that I returned from that place without accomplishing my object, my heart has been filled with vexation, and so it still remains. The distance is not very great, and I have determined to go there, for I have sent my son Maudúd to Balkh, and the Khwája, and the Commander-in-Chief will accompany him with large armies. The Chamberlain Sabáshí is at Merv with a powerful army, so that the Turkománs dare not make inroads upon the inhabited tracts. Súrí also is at

[1] [Page 660].   [2] [Page 660 to 661.]

Naishápúr with an army. Tús, Kohistán, Hirát, Ghurjistán, and other places are well garrisoned, so that there can be no disturbance, rebellion, or other obstacle from Khurásán; and if there should, you all of you, one with the other, are at hand, and can arrive at the spot immediately. The sons of 'Alí Tigín and the Kotwál are quiet in their several places; 'Abdu-s Salám is near them and has bound them by strong engagements, as Bú Suhal Hamadúní has written. The son of Kákú is possessed of no power, and his men can do nothing, and the Turkománs place no reliance in his promises, so that on that side also there can be no obstacle. I will at once relieve my neck of the burden of this vow, for until I have taken the fort of Hánsí, I can undertake no other expedition. I can come back in time to be at Ghaznín by New Year's Day. I have thought well over the business, and I must of necessity carry my plans into effect. Now do you tell me without fear what you think on the matter."

The minister looked round the assembly and asked what they had to say on the subject on which their master had addressed them. The Commander-in-chief replied, "I and those who are like me wield the sword and obey the orders of the Sultán. We are ready to go to wherever we are ordered, and lay down our lives for his sake. The evil and the good of these matters the great Khwája knows, for they are included amongst the difficult questions of Government, and we cannot tell what he wishes, hears, knows, and sees. This is the business of the minister, not ours." Then he turned his face towards the chamberlains and said, "You are doubtless of my opinion," to which they replied, "We are."

The minister then said to the 'Áriz and Bú Nasr. "The Commander-in-chief and the Chamberlains have laid the responsibility on my neck and freed themselves from it. What say you." The 'Áriz, who was a man of few words, said, "I am not able to say anything better than what has been advanced. My own business is difficult enough to occupy all my time." Bú Nasr Mishkán said, "It appears that this matter is devolved upon the responsibility of the great Khwája. It is necessary to speak with great deliberation, for our lord calls upon us to do so." The minister said, "He has been graciously pleased to tell us to speak out without hypocrisy. Therefore I give it as my opinion, that he should on no account go to Hindustán. It is not expedient that he should stay even at Balkh, but proceed to Merv, and after the Sultán has subdued Re, Khurásán, and the Jabbál (hills), he should then fulfil his vow. If his intention is to conquer Hánsi, the chief of the Gházis, the army of Lahore, and a chamberlain deputed by the Court might undertake the business, and thus the intention might be fulfilled, and Khurásán be secured at the same time. If my lord should not go to Khurásán, if the Turkománs should conquer a province, or if they should conquer even a village, and do that which they are acustomed to do, namely, mutilate, slaughter, and burn, then ten holy wars at Hánsi would not compensate. These evils have actually occurred, for they are already at Ámul,[1] and still it is considered more expedient to go to Hindustán! I have now said what seemed to me best, and have relieved myself from all responsibility. The Sultan can do as he pleases."

My preceptor said, "I agree entirely, and may add this to aid the argument. If my lord sees proper, let him send some persons secretly about the camp amongst the people and amongst the nobles, and let them ascertain the general opinion, let them mention the present perturbed state of Khurásán, Khwárizm, Re, and the Jabbál, and let them say that the Sultán is going to Hánsi, and then let them ask whether this is proper or not proper. Your slave feels confident that they will all say it is not proper. The people will give their opinions freely, when they are told that it is the desire of the Sultán that they should do so without reserve."

The Amír replied, "Your friendship and good advice are unquestionable. The vow is upon my neck, and accomplish it I will, in my own person. If any great disturbance should

[1] [A town on the Oxus. The river is also known by the name of Ámol or Ámu.]

arise in Khurásán, I rely upon Almighty God to set it all to rights." The minister replied, "As it is so we must do whatever men can do. I only trust that during this absence no difficulty may arise." He then went away, and the rest also went away after making their obeisances. When they had gone out, they went aside to a private spot, and exclaimed, "This lord of ours is very obstinate, beyond all bounds and degrees. No one could have spoken more openly than we have done, and one could not have done more so without being disrespectful; and as for what he said about Almighty God! we shall see;" and then they separated.

On Thursday, the middle of Zí-l hijja, the Commander-in-chief, 'Alí, was invested with a very superb robe of honour, for which he came forward and paid his respects. The Amír praised and flattered him, and said, "The confidence of my son, my minister, and my army, reposes upon you. The Khwája will remain with you as my vicegerent. To give good advice and find pay for the army, is his business; discipline and fighting is yours. You must attend to his orders, and all of you should have but one hand, one heart, one opinion; so that no interruption to business may arise during my absence." The Commander of the forces kissed the earth and said, "Your slave will obey your orders implicitly," and departed.

On Saturday, the 17th of this month, a very handsome khil'at was bestowed upon the minister, according to the usual value, and even much more than that, because the Sultán was anxious in every respect to maintain a good understanding with him, seeing that he was to conduct the affairs of State during his absence. When he came forward the Amír said, "May this robe be auspicious, as also this confidence which I repose in you during my expedition to Hindustán. May the grace of God rest with the Khwája. I have made a vow, and that vow I must needs fulfil. To him I have made over, first, my son, then, the commander, and the whole army which remains here, and all should be obedient to his orders." The minister replied, "Your slave is ready to discharge all obligations of his service." He then retired, after having been treated with very great distinction.

The Sultán leaves Ghazní—Falls ill, and Forswears Drinking.[1]

On Monday, the 19th of Zí-l hijja, the Amír rose early, and went to the Fírozí garden, that he might see the different detachments of his army pass by in review; and afterwards, about mid-day prayers, those three precious individuals, his son, the minister, and the commander, came on foot, and paid him their respects and then went away. He appointed Khwája Bú Nasr Nokí, my preceptor, to be in attendance on him, and an order went to the minister to this effect.

At last, on Thursday, when eight days of Zí-l hijja remained, the Amír, (God be satisfied with him!) departed from Ghazní on his way to Hindustán, by the road of Kábul, to prosecute his holy war against Hánsí. He remained ten days at Kábul. The first day of Muharram, A.H. 429 (14 Oct., 1037), fell on a Saturday.

On Thursday, the 6th of Muharram, he left Kábul, and on Saturday the 8th despatches arrived from Khurásán and Re, all of them important; but the Amír cared nothing for them, and told my preceptor to write a letter to the minister and enclose these despatches in the same case, for that the minister knew all about the matter, and would do all that was necessary in every respect; adding, "I myself am not well acquainted with the subject."

On Tuesday, when five days of Muharram remained, the Amír arrived at the Jailam, and encamped on the banks of that river near Dínárkotah. Here he fell ill, and remained sick for fourteen days, and got no better. So in a fit of repentance he forswore wine, and ordered his servants to throw all his supply of it, which they had in store, into the Jailam, and to destroy all his other instruments of frivolity. No one dared to drink wine openly, for the officers and censors who were appointed to superintend this matter carried their orders strictly into effect.

[1] [Page 664.]

Dú Sa'íd Mushrif was sent on an expedition against Chakkí[1] Hindu, to a fort about which no one knew anything. We were still on the Jailam, when news arrived of the great Rái and the state of the roads to Kashmír, and we were still there when intelligence reached us of the death of the Rái of Kashmír.

The Sultán takes the fort of Hánsí.[2]

On Saturday, the 14th of Safar, the Amír had recovered, and held a darbar, and on Tuesday, the 17th, he left the Jailam, and arrived at the fort of Hánsí on Wednesday the 0th of Rabí'u-l awwal, and pitched his camp under the fort, which he invested. Fights were constantly taking place in a manner that could not be exceeded for their severity. The garrison made desperate attempts at defence, and relaxed no effort. In the victorious army the slaves of the household behaved very gallantly, and such a virgin fort was worthy of their valour. At last, mines were sprung in five places, and the wall was brought down, and the fort was stormed by the sword on Monday, ten days before the close of Rabí'u-l awwal. The Brahmans and other higher men were slain, and their women and children were carried away captive, and all the treasure which was found was divided amongst the army. The fort was known in Hindustán as "The Virgin," as no one yet had been able to take it.

The Sultán Returns to Ghazní.[3]

On Saturday, when five days remained of this month, he left Hánsí, and returned to Ghaznín on Sunday, the 3rd of Jumáda-l awwal. He came through the pass of Sakáwand, where so much snow had fallen, that it was beyond all calculation. Letters had been sent to to Bú 'Alí, the Kotwál, to send out some men to clear the road, and if they had not done so, it would have been impossible to pass it. It is all one ravine, like a street, from the caravanserai of Muhammad Salmán to the city.

---

[1] In allusion to one of the Chak tribe apparently once so powerful in Kashmír.
[2] [Page 665] [3] [Page 666.]

For the three last days before entering the city, snow fell uninterruptedly. Amír Sa'íd, the Kotwál, the principal inhabitants, and others, came out two or three stages to meet him. The Amír alighted at the old palace of Mahmúd and stayed there one week, until the carpets were laid down in the new palace, and the decorations for his reception[1] were prepared, when he went and remained there. The commanders and officers of the garrison of the five forts returned also to Ghaznín. Ever since I have served this great family, I have never seen such a winter as there was this year at Ghaznín. I am now worn out, for it is twenty years that I have been here, but please God! through the munificence of the exalted Sultán Ibráhím, Defender of the Faith, (may his dominion last for ever!) I shall again be restored to what I was then.

On Tuesday, the 3rd of Jumáda-l awwal, the Amír celebrated the festival of New Year's Day, when the lower classes presented their offerings, and were received kindly by the Amír. A drinking bout was also held, in which he repaid himself for his past abstinence, for, from the time of his repentance on the Jailam to this day, he had drunk nothing.

Misfortunes in Khurásán and Re.[2]

On Tuesday, the 3rd of Jumáda-l Ákhir, very important despatches arrived from Khurásán and Ro, stating that during his absence the Turkománs, at the beginning of the winter, had come down and plundered Tálikán and Fáriyáb,[3] and misfortunes had fallen on other places which it was impossible for the victorious armies to reach at such a season. All this had befallen on account of the Sultán's expedition to Hánsí. It was beyond endurance. Re itself was in a state of siege. The Amír was

---

[1] The word used is آڙ, signifying "a temporary arch or structure, on which boughs and flowers are arranged, to celebrate the entry of a Prince into a city."

[2] [Page 656.]

[3] [According to Ibn Haukal, who is followed by Abú-l Fidá and the Marásidu-l Ittilá', Tálikán is between Merv and Balkh at three days' journey from Merv.— Fáriyáb is a city west of the Oxus in Júsján six days' journey from Balkh. There is a Tálikhán in the maps east of Kundux, but this is not the place intended.]

ashamed of his having gone to Hindustán, from which he had derived no advantage, for no one can oppose the desires of God. He ordered answers to be written, telling his officers to keep up their courage, for as soon as ever the weather was fair, the royal standards would advance.

On Saturday, the middle of this month, Amír Maudúd and 'Alí the Commander of the forces, came to Ghaznín from Balkh, where the minister remained according to order, for he had many important matters there to occupy his attention.

'Abdu-r Razzák appointed Governor of Peshawar.[1]

On Wednesday, the 23rd of Rajab, 'Abdu-r Razzák was invested with a robe of honour on his appointment to the government of Pershaur[2] and received his orders, and ten military[3] slaves of the household were appointed as his chamberlains. The office of preceptor and a khil'at was bestowed on Suhal 'Abdu-l Malík, a man admirably adapted for the situation; he was born in the household of Ahmad Mikáíl, and was a long time in the service also of Bú Suhal Hamadúní. The governor departed for Pershaur, on Tuesday the 9th of this month, in great state, and took with him two hundred slaves.

Punishment of Hindu Elephant Riders.[4]

The Amír celebrated the festival of the new year, on Wednesday, the 8th of Jumáda-l ákhir (430 H., March 1039 A.D.) On Friday, the 10th of this month, news arrived that Dáúd had reached Tálikán with a powerful and well equipped army. On Thursday the 16th of this month, further news was received, that he had reached Fáriyáb, and from that had been summoned in haste to Sabúrkán,[5] and that plunder and massacre had attended him wherever he went. On Saturday, the 18th of this month, ten Turkomán horsemen came during the night near the garden of the Sultán for the purpose of plunder, and killed four Hindu foot soldiers,

[Page 666.] [2] Peshawar. [3] One copy says "black." [Page 708.]
[5] ("Shibberghán" of Thornton's Map, west of Balkh. Ibn Haukal's reading seems to be "Shabúrkán."—*Jour. As. Soc. Bengal*, xxii. p. 168.]

and retreated to the neighbourhood of Kunduz, where the elephants were stabled, and after looking about them intently, they found a boy asleep on the neck of an elephant. The Turkománs came up and began to drive the elephant away, the boy sleeping all the while. When they had gone as far as a parasang beyond the city, they awoke the boy, and threatened to kill him if he would not drive the elephant quickly, which he agreed to do. The horsemen rode behind the elephant, brandished their spears, and goaded the animal on. By the morning, they had travelled a good distance, and reached Sabúrkán, where Dáúd rewarded the horsemen, and told them to take the animal to Naishápúr. Great discredit was incurred by this affair, for it was said—"Is there so much neglect amongst these men that they allow an elephant to be driven off?" Next day, it was reported to the Amír, who was exceedingly vexed, and severely rebuked the drivers, and ordered one hundred thousand dirams, the price of the animal, to be recovered from them. Some of the Hindu[1] elephant-riders were chastised.

On Monday, the 20th of this month, Álti Salmán, the chamberlain of Dáúd, arrived with two thousand horsemen at the gates of Balkh, encamping at the place, which is called "the Infidels' embankment," and plundered two villages, at which the Amír was greatly annoyed.

* * * * *

The Author out of Employ.[2]

Just now, in the year 451 H. (1059 A.D.) I am residing in my own house by command of my exalted master, the most puissant Sultán Abú-l Muzaffar Ibráhím, (may God lengthen his life and protect his friends!) waiting for the period when I may again be called before the throne. It is said that a service subject to the fluctuations of rising and falling will probably be permanent,

[1] A curious change has occurred in this respect. There are no Hindu elephant-riders in the Muhammadan parts of India. They are now almost invariably Saiyids, or if not Saiyids, are addressed as "Mír Sáhib," for their position is one of honour, being seated in front, with their backs to potentates and grandees. [2] [Page 823.]

but that which smoothly jogs on is liable on a sudden to incur the whims or rancour of one's master. God preserve us from fickleness and vicissitude!

Prince Maudúd proceeds to his Government.[1]

The Amír (God's satisfaction rest on him!) held an audience, and when the minister and nobles had taken their places, Khwája Mas'ud was introduced, and after paying his respects, stood before the Amír, who said,—"I have appointed you tutor to my son Maudúd. Be on the alert and obey the orders which the Khwája gives you." Mas'úd replied,—"Your slave obeys." He then kissed the ground and departed, after being received with distinguished honour. He lost not a moment in going to Amír Maudúd, to whom he was introduced by the same parties who presented him at Court. Amír Maudúd treated him with great kindness, and then Mas'úd went to the house of the minister, who received his son-in-law very graciously.

On Sunday, the tenth of Muharram [432 H. Sept. 1040 A.D.], Amír Maudúd, the minister, the chamberlains Hadar and Irtigín, received each a very valuable khil'at, such as were never remembered to have been given before at any time. They came forward, and retired after paying their respects, Amír Maudúd received two elephants, male and female, a drum and tymbal, and other things suited to his rank, and very much more, and the others in like manner, and thus their business was brought to a close.

On Tuesday, the 12th of the month, the Amír went to the Fírozí Garden, and sat in the green pavilion, on the Golden Plain. That edifice was not then as it is now. A sumptuous feast was ordered to be prepared, and messes of pottage were placed round. The Amír Maudúd and the minister came and sat down, and the army passed in review before them. First passed the star of Amír Maudúd, the canopy, flaunting standards, and two hundred slaves of the household, with jackets of

[1] [Page 823.]

mail and spears, and many led horses and camels, and infantry with their banners displayed, and a hundred and seventy slaves fully armed and equipped, with all their stars borne before them. After them came Irtigín the chamberlain, and his slaves, amounting to eighty. After them followed the military slaves of the household, amounting to fifty, preceded by twenty officers beautifully accoutred, with many led horses and camels. After them came some other officers gaily decorated, until all had passed.

It was now near mid-day prayer, when the Amír ordered his son, the minister, the chief chamberlain Irtigín, and the officers to sit down to the feast. He himself sat down, and ate bread, and then they all took their leave, and departed. "It was the last time they looked on that king (God's mercy on him!)"

The Sultán has a Drinking Party.[1]

After their departure, the Amír said to 'Abdu-r Razzák:— "What say you, shall we drink a little wine?" He replied:— "When can we better drink than on such a day as this, when my lord is happy, and my lord's son has attained his wish, and departed with the minister and officers: especially after eating such a dinner as this?" The Amír said,—"Let us commence without ceremony, for we have come into the country, and we will drink in the Fírozí Garden." Accordingly much wine was brought immediately from the Pavilion into the garden, and fifty goblets and flagons were placed in the middle of a small tent. The goblets were sent round and the Amír said:—"Let us keep fair measure, and fill the cups evenly, in order that there may be no unfairness." Each goblet contained half a *man*. They began to get jolly, and the minstrels sang. Bú-l Hasan drank five goblets, his head was affected at the sixth, he lost his senses at the seventh, and began to vomit at the eighth, when the servants carried him off. Bú-l 'Alá, the physician, dropped his head at the fifth cup, and he also was carried off. Khalíl Dáúd drank ten; Siyábírúz nine; and both were borne away to the

[1] [Page 825.]

Hill of Dailamán. Bú Na'ím drank twelve, and ran off. Dáúd Maimandí fell down drunk, and the singers and buffoons all rolled off tipsy, when the Sultán and Khwája 'Abdu-r Razzák alone remained. When the Khwája had drunk eighteen cups, he made his obeisance and prepared to go, saying to the Amír,—"If you give your slave any more, he will lose his respect for your majesty, as well as his own wits." The Amír laughed and gave him leave to go; when he got up and departed in a most respectful manner. After this, the Amír kept on drinking and enjoying himself. He drank twenty-seven full goblets of half a *man* each. He then arose, called for a basin of water and his praying carpet, washed his face, and read the mid-day prayers as well as the afternoon ones, and so acquitted himself, that you would have said he had not drunk a single cup. He then got on an elephant and returned to the palace. I witnessed the whole of this scene with mine own eyes—I, Abú-l Fazl.

On the 19th, Bú 'Alí Kotwal left Ghaznín with a strong army on an expedition against the Khilj, who had been very turbulent during the Amír's absence, and he was ordered to bring them to terms, or attack them.

Bú Suhal Hamadúní.[1]

After the departure of the minister, all State business was referred to Bú Suhal Hamadúní, who had an exceeding aversion to the work, and avoided giving his own opinion by referring everything to the minister. He called on me at every private audience and consultation, to testify what the objections of the minister were, for I was present at all of them. He carried his dislike to the administrative business so far, and he was so hesitating in his opinion, that one day, at a private audience, when I was present standing, the Amír said,—"The country of Balkh and Tukháristán should be given to Portigín, that he may go there with the army of Máwaráu-n Nahr and fight against the Turkománs." Bú Suhal replied:—"It would be proper to

[1] [Page 326.]

address the minister on this subject." The Amír said: "You throw off everything upon him, and his sentiments are well known on the subject." He then directed me on the spot to write the orders and letters, and sealed them, saying: "You must give them to a horseman to deliver." I said, "I obey." Bú Suhal then said: "It certainly would be right to send the horseman to the minister first, and to hold back the order so that he may send it off." I agreed, and went away. It was then written to the great Khwája, that the Sultán had given such and such foolish commands, and that the Khwája knew best what orders to issue. Bú Suhal told me that his intention was to relieve himself of responsibility, as he could not participate in such injudicious counsels and sentiments. I wrote in cypher to the minister, and told him all that had happened, and the horseman was despatched. When he reached the Khwája, the Khwája detained him as well as the order, since he considered it injudicious, and he sent me a sealed answer by the hands of the Sikkadar, or seal-bearer.

Reception of Prince Muhammad and his Sons.[1]

On Monday, the 1st of Safar, Prince Yazdyár came from Naghar[2] to Ghaznín, had an interview with the Amír, and returned. During the night Amír Muhammad was brought from the fort of Naghar, accompanied by this prince, and was carried to the fort of Ghaznín, and Sankoí, the chief jailer, was appointed to guard him. The four sons of Muhammad, who also were brought away with him, namely, Ahmad, 'Abdu-r Rahmán, 'Umar, and 'Usmán, were placed in the Green Pavilion in the Fírozí garden.

Next day, the Amír drank wine from early morning, and about breakfast time sent for me and said: "Go quietly to the

[1] [Page 826.]
[2] [Sir H. Elliot read the name "Naghz" and the *Mardídu-l Ittilá'* gives this as the name of a city in Sind; but the printed text has "Naghar," which probably means the fort of Nugarkot.]

sons of Muhammad, and engage them by strong oaths to remain faithful to me, and to offer no opposition. Take great care in this business, and after you have accomplished this, affect their hearts warmly in my favour, and order robes of honour to be put on them. Do you then return to me, when I will send the son of Sankof to bring them to the apartments prepared for them in the Sháristán."[1]

I went to the Green Pavilion in the Fírozí Garden, where they were. Each of them had on a coarse old cotton garment, and was in low spirits. When I delivered my message, they fell on the ground and were extravagantly delighted. I wrote out the oaths binding them to allegiance, which they read out aloud, and after subscribing their names, they delivered the document to me. The robes were then brought, consisting of valuable frocks of Saklátún[2] of various colours, and turbans of fine linen, which they put on within their apartment, and then they came out with red boots on, and sat down. Valuable horses were also brought forward with golden caparisons.

I returned to the Amír, and told him what had transpired. He said: "Write a letter to my brother, and tell him I have done such and such things respecting his sons. I have enlisted them in my service, and mean to keep them near me, that they may come into my views, and that I may marry them to my children who have their heads covered (daughters), in order that our reconciliation may be evident." He addressed him as "the Amír, my illustrious Brother." When the letter was written, he put his seal to it, and gave it to Sankof, saying: "Send it to your son," which he promised to do.

Next day, the nephews of the Sultán came with their turbans on, and paid their respects, when the Amír sent them to the wardrobe chamber, that they might be clothed with golden frocks, caps with four feathers, and golden waistbands. Valuable horses, one thousand dinárs, and twenty pieces of cloth, were presented

[1] A suburban villa.
[2] Usually translated as "scarlet cloth," being the origin of our word "scarlet;" but this cannot be correct here, as the Saklátún is described as of various colours.

to each, and they returned to their apartments. An agent was
appointed to attend them, and pensions were assigned to them.
They came twice every day, and once at night, to pay their
respects. Hurra-i Gauhar was at once betrothed to Amír Ahmad,
preparatory to the betrothal of the others; but the nuptials
were not then celebrated.

*The Sultán determines to go to Hindustán.—His Perverseness.—
The Consultation of the Nobles.—The Author's Concern in these
transactions.*[1]

Orders were despatched with the utmost secrecy to the confidential servants of the Amír, to pack up everything he had at
Ghaznín—gold, and dirhams, and robes, and jewels, and other
property, and the work was commenced on. He sent a message
to his mother, sisters, daughters, aunts, and freed slaves, to prepare themselves for a journey to Hindustán, and to leave nothing
behind at Ghaznín on which they might set their hearts. They
had to set all in order for that purpose, whether they would or
no. They asked Hurra Khutalí, the mother of the Sultán, to
interpose in the matter, but she replied, that any one who wished
to fall into the hands of the enemy might remain behind at
Ghaznín; so no one dared to say a word. The Amír began to
distribute the camels, and passed the greater part of the day in
private audience with Mansúr Mustaufí on the subject of pro-
viding camels for his great treasures, his officers, and his army.
They asked me privately—"What is all this about?" but no
one dared say a word.

One day, Bú Suhal Hamadúní and Bú-l Kásim Kasír said,—
"The minister should be consulted on this matter, and some one
should be deputed to call him back;" but no one would take the
initiative in writing to him, so long as he was absent from the
Amír. It so happened, that, next day, the Amír ordered a letter
to be despatched to the minister, telling him "I have deter-

[1] [Page 825.]

mined to go to Hindustán, and pass the winter in Waihind, and Marminára, and Barshúr (Peshāwar) and Kírí, and to take up my quarters in those parts away from the capital. It is proper that you should remain where you are, till I arrive at Darshúr and a letter reaches you, when you must go to Tukháristán, and remain there during the winter, or even go to Ilalkh if you can, to overthrow my enemies." This letter was written and despatched. I wrote at the same time, in cypher, a full explanation how my master was alarmed at the mere anticipation of danger, and would not draw rein till he reached Lahore, for that letters had privately been despatched there to prepare everything for his reception, and that it appeared to me that he would not rest even at Lahore; that none of the ladies of the household were left at Ghaznín, nor any of the treasure, and that the officers and army which were left had neither hand nor foot to use, and were in great alarm; that the hopes of all rested on him, the great Khwája; that he should take every care to oppose this dangerous resolution, and that he should write distinctly, as he could act with very much greater effect than we could to prevent the mischief. To the officers also I wrote in cypher such and such things, and I said—"We are all here of the very same opinion. Please God! that sage old adviser, the minister, will write a reply at length, and rouse our king from his lethargy."

I received an answer to this letter, and, praised be God! it was written in terms awfully plain,¹ and the minister discharged every arrow from his quiver. He said distinctly,—"If my lord departs from the capital, the enemy will fight at the very gates of Balkh, and your majesty will not be able to enter the city, for the people are already so ill-disposed, that they are leaving the city and fighting against us. If your majesty gives orders, your slave will go and drive the enemy from those parts. Why should my lord go towards Hindustán? He should remain this winter at Ghaznín, for, God be praised! there is no cause for

¹ [" *Sukhanháe Aowl*"—a curious anticipation of the English school-boy's use of the word " awful."]

alarm, as your slave has despatched Portigín against this people, and he will arrive shortly. Know of a surety, that if my lord goes to Hindustán with the ladies of the household and treasure, when the news gets abroad amongst friends and enemies, calamity will befal him, for every one is desirous of increasing his own power. Besides, I have no such confidence in the Hindus, as to trust my lord's ladies and treasures to their land. I have no very high opinion of the fidelity of the Hindus, and what confidence has my lord in his other servants, that he should show his treasure to them in the desert? My lord has already seen the result of his excessive obstinacy, and this opinion of his obstinate disposition is entertained by all. But if, which God forbid! he should depart, the hearts of his subjects will be broken. His slave has given this advice, and discharged the obligations of gratitude and relieved himself of further responsibility. My lord can do as he sees best."

When the Amír had read this address, he immediately said to me,—"This man has become a dotard, and does not know what he says. Write an answer and say, 'that is right which I have determined on. I am ready to acknowledge that you have written according to the dictates of affection for me, but you must wait for further orders, which will explain my resolution; for that which I see you cannot see.'"

The answer was written, and when all knew it, they sorrowed without hope, and began to prepare for their departure. Bú 'Alí Kotwál returned from the Khilj[1] expedition, having adjusted matters. On Monday, the 1st of Rabí'u-l Awwal he had an interview with the Amír, was kindly received, and returned.

Next day, he had a private audience with the Amír; they read mid-day prayers, and it was soon learnt that the Amír had made over to him the city, fort, and environs of Ghaznín. He said: "I will return by the spring. Take great care that no evil

---

[1] The original says "Balkh," but "Khilj" must be meant, as it was before represented that the Kotwál was sent against that people. The Amír as well as the minister have already spoken about sending Portigín to Balkh.

befals the city, for my son Maudúd, the minister, and a large army, will be away. Whatever may happen during the winter, in the spring I will settle the matter in another fashion. The astrologers have declared that my star is not propitious during this winter." The Kotwál replied, "To secure the ladies and treasure in strong forts is preferable to carrying them into the plains of Hindustán." The Amír rejoined,—"I have determined that they shall remain with me, and may Almighty God grant us all peace, welfare, and success during this journey!" He then went away.

At the time of afternoon prayers, the officers of the army went and sat with the Kotwál, and held a long conversation, but it was of no avail. God only knew the secret of what was to happen. They said,—"To-morrow we will throw the stone again, and see what will come of it." The Kotwál observed, "Although there is no use in it, and it is very vexatious to the Amír, yet it will be proper to make another attempt."

Next day, the Amír held a private audience after the Darbár with Mansúr Mustaufí, and said he still wanted several camels to enable him to go, but they were not procurable, and he was much vexed at it. The chiefs came to the Darbár, and 'Abdu-l Jalíl the son of Khwája 'Abdu-r Razzák sat amongst them and said,—"I cannot stay to hear any ridiculous suggestions," and went away.

They then came down to the Iron Gate and sat in the room with four projecting windows, and sent to me to say, they had a message for the Sultán, which I was to deliver quickly. I went and found the Amír sitting in his winter apartment, alone with Mansúr Mustaufí, and Ághájí at the door. I sent in to announce my arrival, and the Amír said, "I know he has brought a formidable remonstrance; let him come in and tell me." I came back to them, and said, "A holy man tells no lies to his lord, yet, though he never heard my message, he said you have brought a handful of nonsense." They said, "We must at any rate cast this responsibility from our own shoulders." So they stood and dictated a long message to me, to the same effect as the minister had written, and even plainer. I said, "I have not ability sufficient to remember every particular in the order in which you dictate; it is better that you should write, for when it is written, he must necessarily read the whole." They said, "You have spoken well." So I took a pen, and wrote most fully, while they stood by suggesting improvements. They then wrote their signatures at the bottom, attesting that this was their message.

I took it to the Amír and stood while he read it over twice, deliberately. He then said,—" Should the enemy make their appearance here, let Bú-l Kásim Kasír give up to them the wealth he has, and he may obtain from them the appointment of 'Aríz. Let Dú Suhal Hamadúní, who also has wealth, do likewise, and he may be appointed minister. Tahir Bú-l Hasan, in like manner. I am doing what is right in my own estimation. You may return and deliver this short reply."

So I came, and repeated all that I heard, when all were thrown into despair and distraction. The Kotwál said:—" What did he say about me?" I replied, " I declare to God that he said nothing about you." So they arose, saying: " We have done all that we were bound to do, we have nothing further to advance," and departed. Four days subsequent, the Amír commenced his march.

Now this volume has been brought to a conclusion. Up to this I have written the history of the king's going towards Hindustán, and there I have stopped, in order that I might commence the tenth volume with an account of Khwárizm and the Jabbál, complete up to this date, and in the mode in which history requires. After I have completed that, I will return to the account of the king's journey to Hindustán down to the end of his life: please God!

Beginning of the Tenth Volume.[1]

At the end of the ninth volume I brought the history of

[1] [Page 232.]

Amír Mas'úd down to that period when he had completed his arrangements for proceeding to Hindustán four days after the interview, and there I ended the volume. I begin the tenth with an account of Khwárizm, Re and the Jabbál, and Dd Suhal Hamadúní, and the period of his family's residence here, and their departure, and of my being appointed to the Government of Khwárizm, and of my losing it and going to Re, and of Altúntásh. All this I will mention, to make my history complete. After I have performed this task, I will revert to the history of this king, giving an account of those four days down to the end of his life, of which but little then remained.

I will now commence these two chapters replete with wonders and marvels. Let wise men reflect upon this, and be well assured that man by mere labour and exertion, notwithstanding that he has property, armies, and military stores, can succeed in nothing without the aid of Almighty God. In what was Amír Mas'úd deficient in all the appurtenances of a king?—Pomp, servants, officers of State, lords of the sword and pen, countless armies, elephants and camels in abundance, an overflowing treasury, were all his, but destiny decided that he should live a reign of pain and vexation, and that Khurásán, Khwárizm, Re, and the Jabbál should depart from his hands. What could he do but be patient and resigned to the decree, that "man has no power to strive against fate." This prince made every exertion and collected large armies. Notwithstanding that he was exceedingly independent of the opinion of others, and passed sleepless nights in contemplating his schemes, yet his affairs were ruined, because the Mighty God had decreed from all eternity that Khurásán should be inevitably lost to him, as I have already described, and Khwárizm, Re and the Jabbál in like manner, as I shall shortly relate, in order that this truth may be fully established. God knows what is best!

* * * * *

IV.

JÁMI'U-L HIKÁYÁT.

OF

MUHAMMAD 'UFÍ.

[The full title of this work is Jawámi'u-l Hikáyát wa Lawámi'u-l Riwáyát, "Collections of Stories and Illustrations of Histories," but it is commonly known by the shorter title prefixed to this article. The author was Mauláná Núru-d dín Muhammad 'Ufí, who lived during the reign of Shamsu-d dín Altamsh, to whose minister, Nizámu-l Mulk Muhammad, son of Abu Sa'íd Junaidí, the book is dedicated. In one of his stories he states that his tutor was Ruknu-d dín Imám, and that he attended the Madrasa in Bukhárá, from which it may be inferred that he was born in or near that city. It would appear also that he was a traveller, for he speaks in different places of the time when he was in Cambay, and of when he was in Khwárizm.

In the Preface of the work he relates in very inflated language the defeat of Násiru-d dín Kubácha by Nizámu-l Mulk Junaidí and his subsequent suicide. It does not exactly appear what part the author took in this transaction, but he distinctly says that he was besieged in the fort of Bhakkar with Násiru-d dín, and he was evidently well acquainted with all the details. A short abstract of this account will be given at the end of the historical extracts.

The work may shortly be described as a Romance of History. It bears much the same relation to the history of India and Central Asia as the "Memorabilia of Valerius Maximus" bear to the History of Rome. Gen. Briggs (Firishta I. 23 and 212) describes it as "a collection of historical stories and anecdotes illustrative of the virtues, vices, and calamities of mankind, but more useful in commemorating the prevailing opinions of contemporaries than as a source of authenticity." This estimate of the work is somewhat tempered by the remarks of Mr. Thomas (Prinsep I. 37,) who says, "the compiler of a succession of tales does not ordinarily carry the weight that belongs to the writer of history; and favourite oriental legends, as is well known, are suited from time to time with many and various heroes, but the author of the Jámi'u-l Hikáyát is something better than a mere story-teller and his residence at Dehli under Altamsh (A.H. 607, A.D. 1211) gave him advantages in sifting Indian legends of no mean order." Many of the stories which are here recorded of historical persons have no doubt a foundation of fact, but some of them have certainly been amplified and embellished to make them more agreeable reading. Thus the story about the miraculous spring of water which is said to be quoted from 'Utbi enters into details which are not to be found in the original relation (*supra* p. 20.)

The work is divided into four Kisms or parts, each containing twenty-five chapters, but the first part is the longest and comprises about half the work. The first five chapters are devoted respectively to (1) Attributes of the Creator, (2) Miracles of the Prophets, (3) Marvellous Stories of the Saints, (4) Anecdotes of the Kings of Persia, and (5) Anecdotes of the Khalifas. The next chapter is upon Justice, and all the rest are similarly devoted to the illustration of some moral or intellectual quality. This arrangement, however well adapted to accomplish the object of the author, is particularly perplexing to those who are seeking for historical or biographical notices, and a long and laborious search is necessary to find any anecdote which has not been carefully noted down. The extracts which follow have therefore been arranged in something like chronological sequence, but the chapters from which they are taken are always specified so as to make easy a reference to the original.

A great number of different books are mentioned as the sources from which the stories have been derived. Among them are the Tárikh Yamíní, Táríkh-i Násirí, Táríkh-i Mulúk-i 'Ajam, Taríkhu-l 'Abbás, Majmaʻu-l Ansál, 'Aínu-l Akhbár, Sharfu-n Nabí, Faraj b'ada-l Shiddat, Khalku-l Insán, Fawáid-i Kutb-i Hikáyátí, Miftáhu-l Hajj, Sarru-l Darí, Shajratu-l 'Akl, Akhbár-i Dorámika, etc.

The work has been a popular one, and has served as a mine from which many subsequent writers have drawn largely. Hájí Khalfa notices three different Turkish versions, and one of these has been described by Hammer-Purgstall.

Besides the Jámi'u-l Hikáyát the author produced a Persian Tazkira, bearing the title "Lubábu-l Albáb," which is, however, more of an Anthology than a Biography.

Copies of the Jámi'u-l Hikáyát are not uncommon. Sir H. Elliot used in India two large folio MSS., one containing 850, and the other 1000 pages. There is a fine copy in the East India Library. The Editor has had three large MSS. for use and reference. One fine perfect copy in Naskh characters belonging to Mr. H. T. Prinsep, size, 16 × 11 inches; another in folio belonging to the late Raja Ratan Sing, of Bareilly, in which the third Kism is deficient, and lastly, a MS. which formerly belonged to Ranjít Singh and is now the property of Mr. Thomas. This last contains only the first two Kisms, but as far as it goes it is fuller and more accurate than the others. The different copies vary considerably in the number of stories.[1]

Stratagem of the Minister of King Fúr of Hind.
[Kism I. Báb xiii. Hikáyat 46.]

It is related in the books of the people of Hind that when Fúr the Hindu succeeded to the throne of Hindustán, he brought the country under his rule, and the Ráís made submission to him.

[1] See Hájí Khalfa II. 510; Rampoldi VI. 495, 514, XI. 186; Grassldossal II, 244 et passim; Assemins, 221, Goldsna Horde XXVII; Firishta I. 23, 212, IV. 420; Jahrbücher, No. 70.

He had a minister exceedingly clever and intelligent, unequalled in ability and unsurpassed in ingenuity. This minister maintained a firm government and made himself most valuable to his master. Under him the power of the Brahmans was curtailed and their mummeries unheeded; hence they hated him, and conspired to overthrow him. They at length resolved to write a letter to Fúr in the name of the deceased Rái to this effect:—
"I am very happy where I am, and the affairs of my State are well administered, still I am distressed for the want of my minister, for I have no one like him to confer with,—you must send him to me." They sealed this with the royal signet, and gave it to one of the king's personal attendants, with directions to place it on his pillow while he was asleep. When the king awoke, he saw the letter, and having read it he sent for his minister and showed it to him, telling him that he must prepare for a journey to the next world. The minister evinced no repugnance, but expressed his willingness to go. He knew full well that the dead cannot write, and that they have no power to send letters and messengers, so he felt assured that this was a plot of the Brahmans. He said to the King, "Grant me one month that I may make preparation for my departure—to satisfy my enemies, redress some injuries, and bestow a few gifts and offerings on the meritorious, so that I may depart in peace." The King granted the respite. The minister then had a large hole dug in the open ground, and all around it he had quantities of firewood placed. He then had a tunnel dug from his house to this hole, and made its outlet immediately under the firewood. When all things were ready, the minister took leave of his master, who gave him a letter addressed to his father saying, "According to your command, I have sent my minister, and I am now awaiting further directions from you, for I will do whatever you desire." The King proceeded to the appointed place, the minister placed himself under the firewood, and the Brahmans set fire to it. The minister then went through the tunnel to his home, and remained closely concealed there for four months. At

the end of that time, he one night sent information to the King that his minister had returned from the other world. The King was amazed, but the minister waited upon him, and kissing the ground, presented a letter written in the language of the King's father, which said, "You sent me the minister in compliance with my direction, and I am greatly obliged; still I know that your kingdom is going to ruin without him, and that all the affairs of State are in confusion, so I send him back to you, and make this request, that you will despatch the Brahmans to me, so that I may be at peace and your throne may receive no injury from them." When the King had read this, he called the Brahmans before him and made known to them the communication he had received. They were greatly alarmed, and saw that it was all a trick of the minister's, but as they were unable to expose it, they were all burnt.

Rái Shankal and Bahrám Gúr.
[I. iv. 16.]

When Bahrám resumed the government, and again exercised a beneficial influence over his subjects, he desired to examine the country of Hindustán, and bring it under subjection. So he placed his army and country in charge of his brother Zarí, and clothing himself in the garb of a merchant he went to Hindustán. At that time the Rái of Hind was named Shankal, who in dignity and prosperity, in territories, treasures, and armies, excelled all the other Ráis.

Bahrám arrived in his territory, and made himself acquainted with all its affairs. It happened that at this time a huge elephant made its appearance in the forest without the city, and so distressed the people that all traffic on the road was put a stop to. The King's men were unable to prevent this, but Bahrám went out against it, and, single-handed, killed it. This exploit being reported to the Rái, he called Bahrám before him, and asked him who he was, whence he had come, and for what reason he had hitherto kept aloof from him. These questions Bahrám answered by saying that he was a native of Írán, that he had fled thence to save his life, which had been attempted by the king of that country, who for some reason had become inimical to him. On hearing this, Shankal treated him with great kindness and received him into his especial favour. Bahrám remained in attendance upon Shankal, until shortly after a powerful enemy rose up against and threatened the Rái, who, deeming himself not sufficiently strong to hold his own, wished to submit to, and become a tributary of his invader. This, however, Bahrám would not hear of, but, putting himself at the head of an army, expelled the enemy. This feat made his courage famous throughout Hindustán, and Rái Shankal, having witnessed his valour, and how by his aid the enemy had been overthrown, loaded him with honours. One day, Bahrám was drinking wine in the company of the Rái, and having become intoxicated, blurted out the following Persian verses:—

"I am that ferocious lion; I am that huge elephant;
My name is Bahrám Gúr, and my patronymic Bújabala."[1]

Shankal heard this, and becoming aware that his friend was Bahrám, he rose up, and leading him into the presence chamber, and kissing the ground before him, excused himself for his apparent neglect, saying, "though greatness is depicted in your countenance, yet I, through my blind folly, have hitherto been wanting in the respect due to so exalted a character. I stand before you stupified, and shall ever bless my fate, if you will but condescend to take up your abode at my residence, and grace my poor house with your august presence. I am altogether and devotedly at your service. Your orders shall be my law, even should you command me to leave my kingdom and become an exile."

Bahrám answered, "You have nothing to reproach yourself for; you have invariably treated me with the greatest kindness and hospitality, and have done all, nay, more than all, that could

[1] The *Hadíka-l Balághat* and the *Majma'u-i Sanáyi* say that this was the first verse composed in the Persian language.

be expected. One request I would make of you. You have in your harem a daughter, whose beauty outshines the sun, and whose figure shames the cypress. Give her to me, by so doing our friendship will be more strongly cemented, and you will have laid me under the deepest obligation to you."

Shankal promptly complied, and gave him his daughter in marriage, and many gifts and presents. He also made such magnificent preparations for the ceremony, that they became the topic of conversation amongst all people. Bahrám, protected by the prestige of his name, returned to Írán. His army and subjects came forth to meet him, and celebrated the joyous occasion by sacrificial offerings, almsgiving, and every sort of festivity. Bahrám, gratified by the delight his subjects showed on his return, gave orders that the taxes of seven years should be refunded to them, and that for the ensuing seven years, all business should be set aside, and the people should give themselves up to complete ease and pleasure.

Accordingly, all devoted themselves to the pursuit of pleasure, and neglected their professions, and trade, and farming; in consequence of which, an utter stagnation of all commerce ensued. No grain was grown—a dearth followed, and the condition of the people was altogether changed. On seeing this, Bahrám directed that the people should divide the day into two portions,—the first half was to be spent in work and business, and the other half in ease and enjoyment. This arrangement being carried out, the time flew by with lightning speed.

The Solts of Persia.
[L iv. 17.]

Bahrám Gúr, while out hunting, observed a party of shopkeepers diverting themselves in the evening with drinking in a boat without musicians. He asked them why they had no minstrels, and they replied that his Majesty's reign was a happy one for musicians, who were in great demand, and could not be obtained even for a high price. They themselves had offered

100 dirhams, but could not get one. Bahrám said he would consider the matter and provide for their pleasure, so when he got home he wrote off to Shankal requesting him to send a supply of them. Shankal accordingly sent 1000 sweet-voiced minstrels to Persia, there to dwell and multiply. The present Solís are descended from the colony which came over upon this invitation.[1]

Anecdote of Kisrá.[2]
[IV. x. 8.]

It is related that when Kisrá (Naushírwán) became king and inherited vast possessions, he sent an officer to Hindustán,[3] entrusting him with the government of that country, and told him that he should rule with equity over the subjects and not distress them by tyranny and injustice, for until the people were made happy, the country could not be populated and his fame would never spread itself over the world. The first object in becoming a king is to obtain a good name. The officer promised to observe these precepts, and accordingly marched towards Hindustán. He had no sooner reached its borders, than he taxed the subjects and demanded one year's revenue from them. He exacted from them one-tenth of their property, and the people finding it too heavy for them to pay, objected, saying that the former kings had exempted them from such a payment, and they could not submit to such a rule. They therefore consulted with each other, and addressed a petition to Kisrá, containing a full representation of the case. Kisrá consequently ordered that it was but proper for them to follow the customs and rules of their forefathers, and any others ought not to be introduced.

Rái Jai Sing of Nahrwála.
[I. vi. 2.]

Muhammad 'U'fí, the compiler of this work, observes that he never heard a story to be compared with this. He had once been

---
[1] The same assertion is made in the Tabakát-i Násiri.
[2] [I have not found this story in either of the MSS. that I have used.—ED.]
[3] Another copy reads Tabaristán.

in Kambáyat (Cambay), a city situated on the sea-shore, in which, a number of Sunnís, who were religious, faithful, and charitable, resided. In this city, which belonged to the chiefs of Guzerát and Nahrwála, was a body of Fire-worshippers as well as the congregation of Musulmáns. In the reign of a king named Jai Singh, there was a mosque, and a minaret from which the summons to prayer was cried. The Fire-worshippers instigated the infidels to attack the Musulmáns, and the minaret was destroyed, the mosque burnt, and eighty Musulmáns were killed. A certain Muhammadan, a khatíb, or reader of the khutba, by name Khatíb 'Alí, escaped, and fled to Nahrwála. None of the courtiers of the Rái paid any attention to him, or rendered him any assistance, each one being desirous to screen those of his own persuasion. At last, having learnt that the Rái was going out to hunt, Khatíb 'Alí sat down behind a tree in the forest and awaited the Rái's coming. When the Rái had reached the spot, Khatíb 'Alí stood up, and implored him to stop the elephant and listen to his complaint. He then placed in his hand a kasída, which he had composed in Hindí verse, stating the whole case. The Rái having heard the complaint, placed Khatíb 'Alí under charge of a servant, ordering him to take the greatest care of him, and to produce him in Court when required to do so. The Rái then returned, and having called his minister, made over temporary charge of the Government to him, stating that he intended to seclude himself for three days from public business in his harem, during which seclusion he desired to be left unmolested. That night Rái Jai Sing, having mounted a dromedary, started from Nahrwála for Kambáyat, and accomplished the distance, forty parasangs, in one night and one day. Having disguised himself by putting on a tradesman's dress, he entered the city, and stayed a short time in different places in the market place, making enquiries as to the truth of Khatíb 'Alí's complaint. He then learnt that the Muhammadans were oppressed and slain without any grounds for such tyranny. Having thus learnt the truth of the case, he filled a vessel with sea water, and returned to Nahrwála, which he entered on the third night from his departure. The next day he held a court, and summoning all complainants he directed the Khatíb to relate his grievance. When he had stated his case, a body of the infidels wished to intimidate him and falsify his statement. On this the Rái ordered his water carrier to give the water pot to them that they might drink from it. Each one on tasting found that the vessel contained sea water, and could not drink it. The Rái then told them that he had felt unable to put implicit confidence in any one, because a difference of religion was involved in the case; he had himself therefore gone to Kambáyat, and having made personal enquiries as to the truth, had learnt that the Muhammadans were the victims of tyranny and oppression. He said that it was his duty to see that all his subjects were afforded such protection as would enable them to live in peace. He then gave orders that two leading men from each class of Infidels, Brahmans, Fire-Worshippers,[1] and others, should be punished. He gave a lac of Bálotras[2] to enable them to rebuild the mosque and minarets. He also granted to Khatíb four articles of dress.[3] These are preserved to this day, but are only exposed to view on high festival days. The mosque and minaret were standing until a few years ago. But when the army of Bálá[4] invaded Nahrwála, they were destroyed. Sa'íd Sharaf Tamín rebuilt them at his own expense, and having erected four towers, made golden cupolas for them. He left this monument of The Faith in the land of Infidels, and it remains to this day.

Rái Jai Sing of Nahrwála.

[T. xiii. 15.]

In the city of Nahrwála there was a Rái who was called Jai Sing. He was one of the greatest and wisest princes of the time.

---

[1] [*Tarsá*. This name is used for Christians and for Fire-worshippers. It would also sometimes seem to be applied to Buddhists.]

[2] These Bálotras appears to derive their name from the Bálás.

[3] [چهار چیز بداد از جامه طیفور طرقوا]

[4] [One MS. writes this name " Balwá," another " Málá."—Málwá ?]

Before his time there was no Rái in Guzerát and Nahrwála. He was the first man who possessed dominion and claimed sovereignty there. He ruled over the country with great gentleness, and controlled the other chiefs. When his fame had reached all quarters of the world, the Rái of Daur,[1] who was the head of all the Ráis of Hindustán, heard of him and sent ambassadors to ascertain upon what grounds he had assumed royalty; for in former times there was no Rái in Nahrwála, which had only been a den of thieves, and threatening that if he did not relinquish his pretensions he would lead an army against him, and hurl the very earth of Guzerát into the air with the hoofs of his horses. When the ambassadors arrived and delivered the message, the Rái showed them the greatest civility and hospitality. One night the Rái changed his clothes, putting on such as were worn by soldiers, and having buckled a sword round his waist, he went out and proceeded to the house of a courtezan, and having bargained with her, he stayed in her house that night, but kept himself under control. When the woman was fast asleep, the Rái took away all the clothes and property he could find, and buried them in a certain place. He then turned homewards, but as he was going along he saw a weaver, who was engaged in weaving cotton. He called him and said, "If to-morrow you are brought before the Rái, and are charged with having committed a theft in the night preceding, you first deny it, but afterwards confess and say that you buried the property in such and such a place. Rest assured that you shall receive no harm, but shall be made happy by my reward." Next morning, the Rái mounted an elephant, and the ambassadors of the Rái of Hind rode out with him, intending to go to the forest. When they had gone a little way, the Rái saw the courtezan worrying the chief police officer of the city, and saying, " Last night my clothes were stolen; find out who the thieves

---

[1] Perhaps meant for Dravida, or the country of Coramandel; on which name see M. Reinaud, *Mémoire sur l'Inde*, p. 234, and *Fragments Arabes*, pp. 104 and 121. Mr. Thomas's MS. reads " Kaur."]

were, or make good the loss." The Rái asked what the woman was saying, and what she was complaining about. He replied that she complained of a man who came to her house in the previous night, and consorted with her, and when she was asleep stole her clothes. I want time to find the thief or the clothes, but she will not hear of any delay. The Rái said, "She is right. She had only those clothes, and it is your duty to be vigilant, and as you have been negligent you must pay the penalty." The police officer replied, "It is as the king says; still if a man goes at night to the house of a prostitute and carries off her clothes, how am I to blame? I promise, however, that if I do not find the thief within a week I will pay the value of the things." The Rái replied, "You must find the thief instantly, or I will punish you as a warning to others." The police officer said it was not in his power to produce him. The Rái asked him, "Would you like me to find him?" and the poor man replied, "Yes." There was an idol of stone in Nahrwála resembling a negro. The Rái told the ambassadors that this idol was obedient to him. He then made a signal to it, and waited a moment, then turning his face towards the ambassadors he said, "Do you see this negro?" They said, "We see nothing." The Rái then addressed it, saying: "A theft was committed last night, and the clothes of a prostitute were stolen; tell me where they are." After a short time he exclaimed, "They are buried in such and such a place." People proceeded to the spot, and there found the things which had been stolen. The police officer said, "If the Rái would be pleased to give the necessary directions the thief also might be caught and punished." The Rái answered: "The idol says you have recovered the stolen goods, what more do you want?" The police officer still pressed the point, and the king replied, "The idol says he will direct you to the thief if you will promise to pardon him." The officer gave the required promise, and the king then said, "The idol says that a weaver who dwells in such and such a place was the thief." The weaver was brought forward. At first he denied the theft, but at length confessed, and told them where he had buried the clothes. The ambassadors were surprised at this. Some days after, Jai Sing Deo said to the ambassadors, "Go and tell your master that I have a slave who, if I give him the order would bring your master's head to me in a moment; but as he is a great king, and his territory is a long distance off, I will not molest him. If, however, he again shows hostility, he shall get the punishment he deserves." The ambassadors returned and related all the circumstances to their master. The Rái of Daur was much alarmed, and sent him great presents. By this artifice the Rái of Nahrwála gained his purpose, without shedding the blood of a single man.

A Hindú Merchant of Nahrwála.

[1. vi. 12.]

In the city of Nahrwála there lived a Hindú merchant who having deposited nine lacs of Bálotras in the hands of a certain person, after some time died. The trustee then sent for the merchant's son and said,—Your father left with me nine lacs of Bálotras. The son replied that he knew nothing about it, but that there would probably be mention made of the transaction in his father's accounts. These he sent for but could find nothing about nine lacs! on this he observed: "Had my father entrusted anybody with so large a sum, surely mention would have been made of it in his account book; this not being the case, I cannot feel myself justified in taking possession of the money." The trustee urged the youth to take the money, but he still refused, and the contention grew hot between them. At last they agreed to refer the matter to the arbitration of Rái Jai Sing Deo, who gave it as his opinion, that since the two could not agree as to the disposal of the money, it was advisable that it should be expended on some work of lasting utility, so that the real owner would reap the reward of virtue and charity. Accordingly, the 'nine-lac reservoir," the finest in the world, hitherto unsurpassed by all that the cleverest and wisest have executed or imagined, was built; and remains to be seen to this day.

The Biter Bit.
[I. vi. 19.]

A certain Rái of Hind conferred on his brother the chieftainship of Nahrwála. This brother was of an exceeding cruel and wicked disposition. He made counterfeit dirhams and circulated them in different parts of the country. After the lapse of some time, a certain person became acquainted with this dishonest act, and reported it to the Rái, who, on hearing it, sent a powerful force which captured and sent this brother to him.

It happened curiously enough, that this brother had given one of his servants some poison with instructions to go and seek employment in the Rái's kitchen, and, when opportunity offered, to administer some of the poison to the Rái, in order to procure his death, so that he himself might succeed to the vacant throne. On his employer's capture and imprisonment, it occurred to this servant that, as things had so fallen out, it was advisable that he should inform the Rái of the circumstance. So he went to the king and having showed him the poison, told him of the plot his brother had laid against his life. On hearing this, the Rái returned thanks to Almighty God for his great escape, and punished his brother for his intended crime. Thus by this act of royal justice was he saved from assassination, and the fame of his goodness spread abroad through all nations.

Rái Gúrpál of Nahrwála.
[I. vi. 33.]

The following is one of the most interesting stories relating to the people of India. There was a Rái of Nahrwála named Gúrpál,[1] who surpassed all the other rulers in Hindustán in good

---
[1] [This name is so given in the draft translation made in India, and it is written "Gúrbál" in Rája Balan Singh's MS.; but in the other MSS. that I have used it is "Aldrbár," and "Alódbal."]

qualities and amiable disposition. Before he had been raised to the throne he had passed many of his years in beggary, during which period he had experienced all the vicissitudes of fortune, having shared both its smiles and frowns, and endured all the miseries of travel. When he obtained power he exercised it with a right appreciation of the duties of a ruler, remembering his own days of adversity he afforded full protection and justice to his subjects, ruling with impartiality and equity.

It is said that one day having left the city, he rode into the surrounding country on an elephant. While looking about him, his eye suddenly fell on the wife of a washerman who was going to the jungle to wash clothes. She was dressed in red, and of surpassing beauty; all who beheld her became passionately in love with her and lost all control over themselves.

The Rái overcome by the feelings her beauty excited in his heart, turned his elephant towards her and was tempted to let his passion get the mastery over his better feelings. Suddenly he came to himself, and, restraining his wrongful desires, said, "O passions you are doing wrong, beware. Good never comes to him who does ill." He then turned back filled with remorse, and assembling all the Brahmans, he ordered them to prepare fuel, declaring his intention of burning himself alive. The Brahmans asked him what sin he had committed. He then told them of the wicked desires he had entertained in his heart. The Brahmans having heard his relation, said that they undoubtedly must burn him, and that even then the expiation would be incomplete. For he was king, and his power supreme; if he could not restrain his passions, then in a short time all the female inhabitants of the city would become degraded and all the offspring illegitimate. It was right, therefore, that he should immolate himself, and by so doing, obtain forgiveness for his sins, and enter into eternal life. Wood was then brought, and a funeral pile having been made, it was lighted. When it was thoroughly on fire and the flames mounted high, then the Rái made preparations to throw himself into the midst, but the Brahmans prevented him, saying:

"The work of expiation is complete, inasmuch as the fault was of the mind and not of the body. The innocent should not be punished for the guilty, had your body been a participator in the crime, then indeed it had been necessary to have burnt it also. Your mind has already been punished and purified by fire." They then removed the Rái from the pyre, and he in celebration of this sacrifice, gave as a thank-offering one lac of Bálotras, and bestowed large sums in charity.

> "If a king be just, although he be an infidel,
> His country will be secure from all injury and loss."

March of the King of Zábulistán upon Kanauj.[1]
[T. xii. 15.]

In the early part of their career there was friendship between the King of Zábulistán[1] and the Rái of Kanauj, but it ended in animosity and war. The King of Zábulistán marched against Kanauj with a large army. The Rái called together his advisers and asked their opinions, when each one spoke to the best of his ability. One of them said that he had a decided opinion on the matter, but he could only speak it in private. The Rái ordered the council chamber to be cleared, when the minister said: "War is attended with great dangers, and the result is doubtful; the best thing the Rái can do is to inflict punishment upon me and to drive me forth in disgrace to the highway, so that when the enemy shall approach, I may be taken to act as his guide. I will then lead them into the desert so that all may perish with thirst, and you will thus be relieved from all apprehension. The Rái praised him for the proposition he had made, and a few days after he put it in execution, giving orders for him to be expelled the country. The Hindú then went and placed himself in the way of the King of Zábulistán, and when the king drew near with his army, the Hindú made his case known. The king said "How can a minister who has been thus treated have any kind

[1] [This is another version of the story told by Abú Ríhán at page 11, supra; and a similar one is given with Mahmúd for the hero, at page 191, infra.]

feeling towards his persecutor!" The Hindú said, "All this was done on the absurd suspicion of my being friendly to you." He then added, "From this place where you now are to that where the Rái is, the distance is eleven days' journey by the desert, but no one besides me knows the road, and the Rái feels secure that your army cannot make the passage; if, however, you will assure my life and will hold out promises and hopes of reward, I will lead you by that way and enable you to take the Rái by surprise." The king gave orders for his army to provide eleven days' provision of grain and water, and plunged into the desert. After marching twelve days their water was exhausted, and they nowhere found a trace of any. The king called for the Hindú, and asked how it was that they had not come to any water. He replied: "I have accomplished my object in bringing you here, and have discharged my duty to my master. You are now in the middle of the desert, and no water is to be found within eleven days march—my work is done, do with me as you please." A cry arose from the bystanders, and a commotion broke out in the army. The king in the extremity of his despair mounted his horse and galloped in all directions. He perceived a hillock crowned with verdure, and joyfully directed his men to dig a well there. When they had sunk about ten yards they came upon some excellent water, at the sight of which the king and all his army gave thanks to God. Each man dug a well in front of his tent, and gained new life. The king then called together his elders, and asked what ought to be done to the man who had misled them. They all declared that he ought to be put to death with the most cruel tortures, and each one specified some particular mode of torture. But the king said, "My judgment is that you should give him a little water and let him go. What he has done has been out of pure devotion to his lord and master; to save him he has risked his own life. He has done what he intended, but our good fortune has rendered his scheme abortive." So they gave him water and permission to depart. The story of this incident spread, and through it the whole country of Kanauj was secured to him, and the people bowed their heads in obedience.

Rái Kamlú and the Governor of Zábulistán.[1]
[l. xii. 18.]

It is related that 'Amrú Lais conferred the governorship of Zábulistán on Fardaghán and sent him there at the head of four thousand horse. There was a large Hindú place of worship in that country, which was called Sakáwand,[2] and people used to come on pilgrimage from the most remote parts of Hindustán to the idols of that place. When Fardaghán arrived in Zábulistán he led his army against it, took the temple, broke the idols in pieces, and overthrew the idolators. Some of the plunder he distributed among the troops, the rest he sent to 'Amrú Lais, informing him of the conquest, and asking for reinforcements.

When the news of the fall of Sakáwand reached Kamlú,[3] who was Rái of Hindustán, he collected an innumerable army and marched towards Zábulistán. Upon hearing of this march Fardaghán secured several Hindús and sent them to Hindustán. These men entered the camp of Kamlú and reported to him that when Fardaghán had conquered Sakáwand, he immediately despatched people to different quarters of the country, calling for additional forces, knowing that the Hindú would certainly endeavour to take revenge. The result was that an army of Muhammadans had been collected around him, such as would coerce the very ends of the earth. Behind him also the army of 'Amrú Lais was advancing, with the design of leading their antagonists into the defiles and there slaughtering them all. When Rái Kamlú heard this intelligence, he halted where he was, and was very cautious in his movements. In the meantime, Fardaghán received reinforcements from Khurásán, such that the enemy had not the power to cope with. By this ingenious device he succeeded in his object.

---

[1] [The text of this story is printed in Thomas' Prinsep, Vol. I. 317.]
[2] "Iláhawand" in another place. [See supra p. 140.]
[3] [Mr. Prinsep's MS. reads "Kalmó."]

Discovery of Treasure.
[I. vi. 11.]

There is a story to be found in some Hindú works, that a man having bought a house from another, began to make alterations in it. While prosecuting these he happened to light upon a concealed treasure. He took the money to the former owner, and said, " I have discovered this treasure under the wall of the house I purchased from you." The man replied—" I sold the house just as I bought it, and know nothing about the money. I cannot take it, as I do not believe myself to be entitled to it." On this they both agreed to go to the king and deliver the treasure up to him, that he might expend it on some work of public utility. Accordingly they went, and having represented the whole case, made the money over to the king. On this the king exclaimed—" You are people of the middle class, and meddle with what does not become you. I am entrusted with the responsible duty of managing and adjusting the affairs of my subjects, and to me God has entrusted the reins of government. How can I take this charitable money?" The men replied, " You are the king, and we come before you in this difficult case, in order that it might be settled by your justice and equity." The king then told them to make some marriage arrangement between their families. It happened that the seller of the house had a daughter, and the purchaser a son, so the daughter of the former, with the money in question as dowry, was given in marriage to the son of the latter. The king from an innate sense of justice, would not suffer the skirt of his robes of equity and righteousness to be soiled by the dirt of oppression and dishonesty.

The Herb which produces Longevity.
[I. vi. 14.]

I have read in a book that certain chiefs of Turkistán sent ambassadors with letters to the kings of India on the following mission, viz.: that they, the chiefs, had been informed that in India drugs were procurable which possessed the property of prolonging human life, by the use of which the kings of India attained to a very great age. The Ráís were careful in the preservation of their health, and the chiefs of Turkistán begged that some of this medicine might be sent to them, and also information as to the method by which the Ráís preserved their health so long.[1] The ambassadors having reached Hindustán, delivered the letters entrusted to them. The Rái of Hind having read them, ordered the ambassadors be taken to the top of an excessively lofty mountain, and then he told them that, when the hill on which they then were should be rent asunder and thrown down, then he would give them their answers, and permission to return to their own country. The ambassadors on hearing this became greatly alarmed, and despaired of living to revisit their home, relations, and friends. They pitched their tents in the valleys, and fervently prayed to Almighty God for deliverance from their troubles. They spent their whole time in offering up prayers to heaven. In this manner a long time passed. At last having one day offered up their prayers to God most earnestly, they observed the mountain shaking. The sorrow of their hearts had moved the heart of the mountain. It began to totter, and presently its lofty summit toppled over and fell to the ground. Having lifted up their voices in praise and thanksgiving to God, they informed the Rái of what had occurred. The Rái said "this is my reply to your mission. Though you are few in number, having given up your minds to prayer, by the force of your devotions you have caused the mountain to fall down. Your kings rule tyrannically, so that the people pray earnestly for their destruction, and by means of their prayers they at last blast the prosperity and annihilate the power of their oppressors. It is the paramount duty of all those in whose hands authority and power are placed, to walk in the path of justice and benevolence, in order that those who are weak should be

[1] This was a favourite persuasion of the Orientals. In the fourth Book and fifteenth chapter of this work, the third story relates to a chief of Jálandhar, who had attained the age of 250 years.

strengthened and protected by the law, and that those who are wealthy should enjoy their riches in peace and security. Wealth is but a faithless friend, and life but an uncertain companion; neither one nor the other is enduring and permanent."

Self-possession of an Indian Minister.
[I. xiv. 17.]

A certain Indian prince had in his employ a minister remarkable for his learning and wisdom. The prince had also some slave girls, who were most elegant and beautiful, and possessed of every imaginable charm. One day the minister went before the king while these slaves happened to be in attendance, for the transaction of certain business. The minister cast an eye of love on one of them, and then perceived that the prince was observing him. He therefore still kept his eye fixed in the same direction. For twenty years he continued in the prince's service, and every time he went into the presence he kept his eye fixed in that direction. By this means he allayed the royal jealousy, as the prince thought that the glance he had observed was not intentional, but merely the effect of a natural squint.

The Arming of Ya'kúb Lais.
[I. xiii. 35.]

At the commencement of the career of Ya'kúb Lais, a body of his friends bound themselves to raise him to the dignity of chief. When Sálih Nasr had taken Sistán, and become powerful, they observed to Ya'kúb that Sálih had grown strong, and that if he did not take heed at once, he would not be able to do much afterwards. Ya'kúb consulted with an old and wise man in this matter, who said, "It is as your friends have told you, something must be done instantly." Ya'kúb then asked him what steps he should take, and the old man replied that there were two divisions of Sálih's army—one the Sanjarís, the other the Dustís, and the best thing he could do was to irritate the Sanjarís by telling them that though battles were won by their hard fighting, the plunder obtained by the conquests was carried off by the Bustís. "By your persuading them of this," said the old man, "hostility will be created between them. They will separate from each other; and in all probability the Sanjarís will come over to you, because they are fully aware of your skill and address, and of the courage you have shown in battle; they are also conscious of your having saved them from the Khárijís." Ya'kúb acted upon this advice, and so worked upon the Sanjarís, that enmity sprung up between them and the Bustís, and Sálih Nasr found himself in a very precarious situation. The Sanjarí troops went over to Ya'kúb, and when Sálih Nasr saw that affairs were come to extremities, he proceeded with his army of Bustís towards the enemy. Ya'kúb, Ibráhím and Hafz came forward and encamped at the pass of Ghanjara. Ya'kúb resolved to make a night attack, and Sálih being apprised of it, fled in alarm towards Bust. Thus did Ya'kúb, by a clever stratagem, obtain the victory over his enemy.

Ya'kúb Lais and Rúsal.
[L. xiii. 21.]

Almighty God endowed Ya'kúb Lais with a very lofty mind so that he rose from the most abject position to the highest pitch of glory and prosperity. He encountered many dangers and passed through great difficulties, till at length he aspired to the acquisition of dominion. When Sálih Nasr[1] fled from before him, he went and joined Rúsal,[2] and excited him to collect his troops and march against Ya'kúb Lais. Rúsal assembled his armies, and placed Sálih Nasr at the head of the foremost division. Ya'kúb Lais on receiving the intelligence, called together some old and experienced men and asked their advice as to the

[1] In one of the stories of the next chapter Ya'kúb is said to have been the darwín, or doorkeeper of Sálih Nasr.

[2] In most of the passages where the name recurs in this story it is spelt as "Rúsal," but in one as "Raibal," and in another as "Rathil." (Mr. Prinsep's MS. has "Rasal" and "Rútsal," but Mr. Thomas' "Zambíl." See Vol. I. pp. 167, 168.]

means of repelling the invasion of Rúsal. They advised him to oppose the enemy, and represented that although he had a small force, yet he ought to trust in the help of God, and resort to every wile and stratagem to harass his opponent, but not to engage in a pitched battle. When Ya'kúb reviewed his army, it was found not to consist of more than three thousand horse. However, he proceeded to oppose Rúsal, and when he reached Bust, people derided him, saying, "How can he fight against Rúsal with this small number of horse." Ya'kúb Lais now had recourse to stratagem and deception. He sent one of his confidential servants to Rúsal with a message to say that, he wished to come and meet him, and render him homage; he knew he was not able to cope with such a potentate, but that if he should tell his people that he was going to meet Rúsal, they would not obey him, and might possibly kill both him and his dependants. He had consequently told them he was proceeding to give battle to his enemy, in order to induce them to accompany him; but that when he should join Rúsal and make his submission, they must perforce follow his example. When the ambassadors of Ya'kúb came to Rúsal and delivered the message to him, it was very agreeable to him, because he was greatly harassed by Ya'kúb, who continually made incursions into his country, and attacked it in different directions. He made the ambassadors welcome, and sent messages to Ya'kúb, giving him many kind promises and holding out hopes of preferment. Ya'kúb despatched his messengers one after the other, and to prevent his followers from being disheartened he told them that he had sent the messengers to reconnoitre the enemy's army.

When both the armies came in front of each other, Rúsal called Sálih Nasr and told him that as the enemy had come to proffer his submission, there must be no fighting. A day was fixed for a parley between the parties. It was not the habit of Rúsal to ride a horse, but he used to sit on a throne which a party of his servants carried on their shoulders. When both the armies were drawn up in array, Rúsal seated himself upon his throne and ordered his troops to stand in line on each side of it. Ya'kúb with his three thousand brave horsemen advanced between these two lines, and his men carried their lances concealed behind their horses and wearing coats of mail under their garments. The Almighty made the army of Rúsal blind, so that they did not see the lances. When Ya'kúb drew near Rúsal, he bowed his head as if to do homage, but he raised the lance and thrust it into the back of Rúsal, so that he died on the spot. His people also fell like lightning upon the enemy, cutting them down with their swords, and staining the earth with the blood of the enemies of religion. The infidels, when they saw the head of Rúsal upon the point of a spear, took to flight, and great bloodshed ensued. The bride of victory drew aside her veil and Ya'kúb returned victorious. Next day six thousand horsemen of the infidels were sent prisoners to Sistán. He also placed sixty of their officers on asses, and having hung the ears of the slain upon the necks of these officers, he sent them in this manner to Bust. In this conquest he obtained such immense treasure and property that conjecture cannot make an estimate of them.

Sálih Nasr fled from the field and went to the king of Zábulistán. His troops deserted him and joined Ya'kúb, who, after he had secured peace to the country, sent a messenger to the ruler of Zábulistán requesting him to surrender Sálih Nasr. His request was complied with; and when Sálih came, Ya'kúb put him in prison, where he died. The hostility which the people of Bust had shown to Ya'kúb, he now retaliated upon them. He fixed the same poll-tax upon them as was levied from the Jews, and this was collected with severity. This victory which he achieved was the result of treachery and deception, such as no one had ever committed.

Surrender of Ghazna to Alptigín.
[l. vi. 25.]

When Alptigín, the master of Subuktigín, deserted the Sámánians and went to Ghazaín, they were by his departure reduced to great destitution, and serious disturbances broke out in the country. We will make mention in the proper place of this occurrence, as well as of his reasons for separating himself from them. On his reaching Ghaznín, the garrison shut themselves up in the fort and refused to surrender to him. He, therefore, pitched his camp without, and speedily possessed himself of the suburbs and surrounding country.

There he exercised his power with such impartiality and regard for justice, that the people around were in the enjoyment of perfect peace. One day he was going along the road when he perceived a party of his servants coming from a village, with poultry slung from their saddle-straps. Having stopped them, he enquired how the fowls came into their possession. They pretended that they had purchased them in a neighbouring village. On this Alptigín sent a horseman to the village with instructions to bring the head man of it into his presence. When he was brought, Alptigín asked him whether the men had bought the fowls or seized them by force. The man appeared desirous of hiding the truth, so Alptigín told him to tell the truth on pain of punishment. The man then said, "When a Turk comes into a village he does not buy fowls but always takes them by force." On hearing this, Alptigín gave orders that the culprits should be punished with death. Those around implored mercy, and entreated that some lesser punishment than death might be inflicted on the thieves. He complied with this request, and ordered the offender's ears to be bored and the birds to be suspended from them by a string tied to their legs. This having been done, the birds, in struggling to escape, so flapped and beat with their wings the men's heads and faces that blood flowed copiously from the wounds inflicted. In this condition they were paraded through the army. The news of this act of justice having reached the ears of the people, they all assembled together, and agreed that a man so upright and just was worthy to be their ruler. That very evening they went to him and agreed upon the terms of capitulation. The following day the city was surrendered. So, by this one act of judicious impartiality he became possessed of the city of Ghaznín, which rose to be the shrine of prosperity and abode of wealth.

Bravery of Amír Subuktigín.
[I. xiii. 24.]

When Bilkátigín[1] went towards Ghaznín, the Sámánians were informed that the Turks were coming from Khurásán. He (the king) sent his minister, Abú Is'hák, with a large body of men, and another force also to stop the advance of the enemy. When information of this design reached Bilkátigín, he despatched Subuktigín with his followers to frustrate it. Subuktigín observed that the passes were narrow and difficult, and that his enemies were acquainted with them, while he was a stranger. He therefore considered it advisable to employ stratagem in resisting them. So he proceeded to the head of one of the passes and there formed three ambuscades, in which he placed some of his men, while he with another party advanced into the pass. When the enemy saw the smallness of his force they came out and attacked him. Subuktigín pretending to fly from before them, induced them to leave the passes in which they were posted, and they were thus drawn out into the open plain. Amír Subuktigín then made such an attack on them that the earth shook, and the enemy fled with precipitation to seek safety among the passes.

Subuktigín then let loose his three ambuscades, and these falling on the foe ere they reached the defiles, not one of them escaped. Subuktigín then cleared the passes of the enemy's men, and he (Bilkátigín) having witnessed the dauntless courage of Subuktigín, spoke of him in terms of admiration. He went through the passes in safety, so that not a single camel was missing; and this was solely attributable to the judgment of Subuktigín.

[1] [See a coin of this chief and some observations on the time of his reign by Mr. Thomas in Jour. R. A. S. Vol. xvii. p. 140. See also Tabakát-i Násirí, infra.]

The Vigilance of Subuktigín.

[II. xv. 6.]

When Dilkátigín[1] came from Khurásán to Ghaznín and took possession of the country, the chief of it, Abú 'Alí Kúbak,[2] abandoned it.[3] Dilkátigín soon gave himself up to debauchery, and entrusted Subuktigín with the management of the city. In this high post, Subuktigín discharged the duties with great efficiency and courage, and with all vigilance and care. One day, Amír Dilkátigín took wine, and held a great carouse, and from early dawn to midnight was engaged in drinking. He also endeavoured to persuade Subuktigín to drink, but without success. When the curtain of darkness was drawn over the face of the sun, Amír Dilkátigín fell into a sound sleep, but Subuktigín was very watchful and his eyes were open like the stars. Suddenly he heard a noise which proceeded from some corner, and immediately after it was followed by an uproar. With lamps and torches he went in that direction, and then he saw a body of armed men standing in the street, ready to raise a tumult. He demanded, in a loud voice, who they were? They gave an incoherent reply. Subuktigín threatened to attack them, when they were constrained to confess that a body of malcontents had conspired to make a rising that very night, and, as a sign of their success, to light a fire upon the roof of the fort. At this signal, Abú 'Alí was to bring up his force, capture Bilkátigín and his adherents, and drive all his troops out of the country. Subuktigín, on hearing these words, killed four men upon the spot and rushed out of the fort. He found a large

---

[1] [The munshí's translation had the name "Alptigín," on which Sir H. Elliot made a note that another copy (Ratan Singh's) read "Badkátigín." The name is Bilkátigín in Mr. Prinsep's MS., and consequently I have substituted that name in the translation.]

[2] [Mr. Prinsep's MS. has "Amír Alí *Kibed*, and, when the name next occurs, *Kúbak*. Sir H. Elliot read the name as "Uvek." The *Tabakát-i Násirí* (*post*) reads the name Amír Audk. See *Journal R. A. S.*, xvii. p. 141.]

[3] M. Reinaud observes that Ibn Haukal, who, in consequence of his personal acquaintance with Abú Is'hák Ibráhím, might be supposed to be well acquainted with the affairs of the Ghaznivides, does not mention to whom Ghaznín belonged when it was taken by Alptigín.—*Mémoires sur l'Inde*, p. 244.

number of men assembled in arms, who were waiting for Abú 'Alí Kúbak. He put them all to the sword, and then advanced against Abú 'Alí. He took his brother prisoner, and then returned to the city. When morning dawned, Amír Subuktigín brought some of the insurgents, with the heads of some of those he had killed, to Bilkátigín, and related the whole story of the transactions of that night. The Amír expressed admiration of his conduct, and considered him worthy of great favours; and because he was very cautious and never negligent of his enemy, he appointed him his deputy and elevated his rank above that of all his equals. He also rewarded his companions with five hundred thousand dirhams. All this was the fruit of watchfulness. Wise men know that vigilance is necessary in all circumstances.

Mahmúd's Youthful Strategy.
[IV. II. 6.]

It is related by Abú-n Nasr 'Utbí in his work called *Táríkh Yamíní*[1] that the King of Kábul made war upon the Muhammadans at the beginning of the career of Násiru-d daula Subuktigín. When intelligence of this war was brought to the Amír Násiru-d dín, he called out his forces from Khurásán to oppose him. Sultán Mahmúd was then about fourteen years of age. Amír Násiru-d dín summoned his officers and consulted with them upon the plan to be pursued. Amír Mahmúd gave it as his opinion that the best course was to go in advance of the army and seek a strong place in the mountains, where they might make themselves secure, and from whence they might make nocturnal and unexpected assaults upon the enemy. They would thus prevent the foe from advancing against them, and distress him with incessant raids. The counsel was approved by all, and Amír Násiru-d dín advanced and occupied a position near Baghrú.[2] The King of Kábul marched thither with a countless army, and for some time the opposing forces encamped there.

[1] [Mr. Prinsep's MS. reads "Táríkh-i Daulat-i Yamíní.]
[2] [The first letter has no point.]

One day a woman of the neighbourhood came to Amír Násiru-d dín and told him that there was a spring not far off in the mountains which had this property, that if filth was cast into it the sky became overcast, snow and storms followed, and the weather became so cold that no one in these parts could endure it. This cold and foul weather would last as long as the filth remained in the fountain. He sent and had some dirt thrown into the spring. Cold and stormy weather followed. The army of Hind was reduced to extremities, and the Musulmáns were completely victorious.[1]

Sultán Mahmúd and the Sister of Ayáz.
[II. axl. 8.]

It is said that Sultán Yámínu-d daula Mahmúd Subuktigín had been long enamoured of the sister of Ayáz—he was sincerely attached to her, and anxious to espouse her. But it occurred to him that he might by this act incur the reproaches of the neighbouring kings and princes, and forfeit the respect and esteem of his own servants. This apprehension he entertained for a long time.

Abú Nasr Mishkání says—"I was one night in attendance on the king, and when all the assembly was gone, he stretched out his legs and ordered me to "shampoo" them. I knew that he certainly intended to tell me some secret. At last he said, "It is a maxim with wise men that there are three people from whom a secret should not be concealed, viz.: a skilful physician, a kind preceptor, and a wise servant. I have been long greatly perplexed, but I will this night unburden my mind and learn your opinion on the matter." I observed, "I am not worthy of the high honour done me by the king, but as he, in his high wisdom has determined it, I will to the best of my ability represent what may appear to me as good or evil in the matter." The king said, "It has long been a secret within me, that I am desirous of espousing the sister of Ayáz. But will not the neighbouring

[1] [See page 20, supra.]

kings call me a fool and low-minded, and will not you also, my servants and slaves, speak ill of me in respectable society. I ask your advice in this matter; have you ever heard or read, in any history, of kings wedding the children of their slaves?" I made obeisance and said—"Many cases similar to this have occurred. Several kings of the Sámánian dynasty married their own slave girls. This act will not seem to the world as derogatory to the king's honour and rectitude. Perhaps your Majesty is unaware that Kubád, at the time he went to Turkistán, took as his wife the daughter of a villager, from whom was born Naushírwán. In Persian history, I have also read that Bahrám Gúr married a washerman's daughter. The Sultán asked me the particulars of the story, so I said, "I have heard that one day Bahrám Gúr went out hunting, and having started a stag, followed it so far that he became separated from his train. He felt thirsty and went towards a village. He there saw a washerman sitting on the edge of a pond washing clothes; his wife and daughter were sitting by him with a heap of clothes ready to be washed. Bahrám approached them, and said, 'O washerman, give me some water to drink.' The washerman stood up, and having paid him the usual marks of respect, ordered his wife to fetch some water for the king. She took the cup, and having washed it several times in clean water, said to her daughter, 'I am not a virgin, man's hand has touched me, but you, who are an unbored pearl, should give the water to the king.' The girl took the cup and brought it to the king, who, looking at her, perceived that she was incomparably beautiful and charming, and possessed of excellent disposition and manners. He then asked the washerman if he would admit him as a guest for that day, who replied, that if the king could be contented with dry bread he would spare nothing in his power; saying this, he spread a clean cloth on the bank, and Bahrám sat down. The washerman then took his horse and fastened it to a tree, and gave his daughter a fine cloth with which she fanned the king, and protected him from flies. He himself hastened to the village and procured food, wine, meat, in short, everything on which he could lay his hand, he brought. He gave his daughter the wine and cup, and ordered her to act as cup-bearer to the king. On which she cleansed the cup, and having filled it with wine, brought it to the king, who took her hand within his—she kissed them. Bahrám said, 'O girl, the lips are the place to kiss and not the hand.' The girl paid her respects, and said that the time had not yet come for that. The king was surprised at the elegance of her appearance and the eloquence of her speech. They were thus engaged when the train of Bahrám appeared in sight. He told the girl to conceal her face, on which she pulled her veil over it. He then on that spot having performed the nuptial ceremony, placed her on an elephant under a canopy, and made her father ride away with them; her mother also accompanied them."

When the Emperor heard this story, he was much pleased, and bestowed presents upon me: saying, " You have relieved me of this care." After two days he espoused the sister of Ayáz.

Anecdote of Sultán Mahmúd.
[I. xii. 9.]

When Khwája Ahmad acted as minister to Sultán Mahmúd (may God be merciful to him!) all the principal officers of State were inimical to him and traduced him to the Emperor, who thus contracted a great dislike to him, and was desirous of removing him from office. On this subject Abú Nasr Mishkán says that Arslán wrote him a letter, saying that "The king is displeased with Khwája Ahmad, and we, his Majesty's servants, must beware of resisting his will. But in common charity we are bound to declare what we know or have heard. Khwája Ahmad is undoubtedly the most able minister of the time, and has been very useful to our sovereign. He has long been in government employ and has experienced great changes of fortune. It is now some time since he was appointed Minister of State, and now all men of influence, rank, and dignity are his enemies. The cause of their hatred to him is his devotion to his master, and his disregard of their wishes and pleasure. His associates in office are also inimical to him for the same reason. You would do right to communicate this letter to his Majesty, although I know that his mind has been so perverted by them that my counsel will be useless. Still the time may come when his Majesty may feel some regret, when he will not check but excuse our representations."

Abú Nasr Mishkán continues: I read the letter and for a long time I was watching for an opportunity to lay it before the king. I also received constant messages from the minister imploring my support and assistance. I replied that it would not do to be precipitate, but that I must wait till a suitable occasion offered itself.

The Sultán Mahmúd also knew that I was watching my opportunity, but he kept strict silence on this matter, till at length it happened one day that the Sultán went out on a hunting excursion, and though it was not customary with me to attend him, yet on this occasion I did so. The Sultán asked me why I, who never went out hunting, had now come with him. I replied that it was always the duty of a servant to attend on his master. The Sultán then said, "I know that you have come in order that you might speak to me about Ahmad, but matters like these ought not to be forced upon me." I replied, "May your Majesty's judgment be always right." He then became silent and spoke not another word. That day and that night passed by. On the next night the Sultán was drinking wine and enjoying himself, when he made me sit down with him, and he talked upon all sorts of topics. At length he asked me if I had ever heard or had ever read in any book that ministers were their king's enemies. I said, "No; but I have read that the man is foolish and stupid who seeks to be a minister." He asked wherefore, and I replied, "Kings cannot endure that any one should share their authority, nor will they allow any one but themselves to give orders. If the office of minister is given to one who is looked upon as the dearest of friends, before a week has passed he is deemed an enemy and is despised." Nothing farther passed at this meeting. After his return to Ghazním, he was sitting one night alone, and calling for me, bade me be seated, and said, "Hitherto I have kept silence with you regarding Ahmad. Now be mindful that you tell me the truth without equivocation or reservation." I replied that I would obey his Majesty. He observed that Ahmad was an experienced and well qualified minister, who had been in the service from his youth, and had conferred lustre on his office, but he held his master in slight esteem, and he was at the same time covetous of the wealth of the Musulmáns, which he extorted from them, and opposed the king's orders. He said that he had been informed of many oppressive acts towards the slaves (*ghulám*) and such people. That he had resolved on his dismissal, and that all with whom he had consulted on this business had concurred with him. He then asked me what I had to say on the subject. I replied, that "What your Majesty in your wisdom deems most advisable is certainly best,—who can gainsay it?" The king then insisted on my expressing an opinion,—I said, "Arslán Jázib[1] had sent me a letter," and having it with me, I shewed it to him, and begged his permission to give him my views on the case to the best of my ability. The king consenting, ordered me to speak. I then said,—"If the charges of oppression and opposition which have been brought against the Khwája are proved to your Majesty's satisfaction, they must not be passed over, but punishment must be meted out to the minister, so that no injury may come to the country. But if, on the other hand, merely suspicions have been excited in the king's mind, then search and enquiry must be patiently made throughout the country for a man competent to fill Ahmad's place. On such a man being found, then his Majesty may follow his own will and pleasure. If one cannot be found, the greatest precautions must be taken." Having finished, the king said he would consider of it, and gave

[1] [One MS. calls him "Jázib," another "Kháris." Baihakí uses the former name, p. 136, *supra*.]

me permission to depart. At last, the Khwája was deprived of his situation and imprisoned, but the king soon regretted it, for the affairs of the State and country fell into great confusion.

Depreciation of Coin.
[1. xii. 14.]

When Yamínu-d daula Mahmúd came to the throne, and the effects of his greatness spread through all countries, and his rule swept away the idol temples and scattered the worshippers, some sharp men of India formed a plan (for enriching themselves). They brought out a dirham of great purity and placed a suitable price upon it. Time passed on and the coin obtained currency. Merchants coming from Muhammadan countries used to purchase these dirhams and carry them to Khurásán. When the people had grown accustomed to the value of the coin, the Indians began by degrees to debase the standard. The merchants were unaware of this depreciation, and finding a profit upon silver, they brought that metal and gold from all parts of the world, and sold it for (debased coins of) copper and brass, so that by this trick the wealth of the Muhammadans was drawn to Hindustán.

When 'Aláu-d daula[1] ascended the throne, this grievance had become intolerable, and he determined to remedy it, and consulted with the merchants as to the measures most proper to be taken to effect this purpose. They advised that the debased coinage should be exchanged for good from the royal treasury. Accordingly 'Aláu-d daula gave the necessary orders, and 100,000,000 dirhams were issued from the treasury to the mint, and thence distributed to the servants of the Almighty as redress and compensation. The fame of this act spread the lustre of Aláu-d daula's glory throughout the world.[2]

[1] "'Aláu-d daula" is not the title of the Mas'úd who succeeded Mahmúd, but of Mas'úd III.
[2] [A translation of this story is given by Mr. Thomas in *Jour. R. A. S.*, Vol. xvii. p. 181.]

Anecdote of Khwája Hasan Maimandí.

[III. sl. 1.]

In the reign of Sultán Yamínu-d daula Mahmúd, and in the days when Khwája Hasan Maimandí was his minister, there was a man called Abú Ahmad Suhal Barár. He was a great spendthrift, a peculator and a wine-bibber. At one time twenty thousand *mans* of indigo, which belonged to the Sultán, fell into the hands of the son of Ahmad.[1] Some of this he sold and spent the proceeds. One day, Abú Suhal Barár came to the minister to pay his respects. The minister said, "I have heard that your son has embezzled government property, when you saw him doing so why did you connive at it? Do you think that I will pass it over? Should he who possesses such a name as Ahmad ('most laudable') be such a fool and commit such follies!" In short, he expressed himself in unmeasured terms. Abú Suhal exclaimed, "May your life, my lord, be increased! pardon my son; his name is Ahmad, and he should be forgiven." The Khwája was extremely annoyed, but laughed at his ignorance and folly. He said to Abú Suhal, "You are worse than your son. Curses be upon you, thoughtless fool." Abú Suhal, on hearing this abuse, did not even then perceive that what he had said (was improper), nor did he consider that his name was Ahmad, and that it did not become him to utter such words. He commenced to retort in disrespectful language, and said, "Perhaps somebody has excited you against me, and consequently you are thus angry with me." The Khwája replied, "No, I have heard it from your own tongue." He then dismissed him ignominiously from his service.

It is proper for those who have access to kings and great men, that they should take heed to their actions and speech, and neither do or say anything boldly and rashly, to bring shame

---

[1] It appears from a statement of Ibn Haukal, that the Sultáns used to reserve a large portion of indigo to themselves as a sort of royalty.—See M. Reinaud, *Mémoire sur l'Inde*, p. 244.

and destruction upon themselves. They should behave respectfully towards their master, so that they may reap the benefit of their services.

Anecdote of Mahmúd.

[I. xi. 46.]

One night Sultán Mahmúd was drinking wine, while his sons, Muhammad and Mas'úd, were present. Abú Nasr Mishkán says that, when some time had passed in this manner, the conversation happened to turn upon Amír Subuktigín, when the Sultán offered up prayers for his father, and his eyes were filled with tears. He said, " My father (may God's mercy be on him!) had established very good rules for the management of the country, and took great pains in enforcing them. I thought that when he should be no more, I should enjoy the exercise of my power in peace and security, and eat and enjoy myself. I also considered that after his demise I should become a great king. But the truth was revealed to me when he died and his shadow was removed from my head, for since his departure I have not had one day's happiness. You think I drink this wine for pleasure, but this is a great mistake. I take it merely as a device to gain a few days' peace, and relieve the people from all annoyance from me. These my sons entertain similar ideas to those which I did in my youth; but when the kingdom devolves upon them, they will find out the truth."

His sons made their obeisances and said, "May such thoughts never enter our minds. We both desire to sacrifice our lives at your Majesty's feet." The king commended them and bade them to sit down, which they did, but they soon afterwards departed. He then (says Abú Nasr) called me to him, and making me sit down, he stretched his legs towards my lap, and I shampooed them for a short time. He asked me what I thought of his sons, I kissed the ground and answered, " What can I say, how can tongue describe the excellencies of those two suns of grandeur, and those two moons of the heaven of prosperity! Thank God,

they possess such qualities as are beyond all expression." He
said, "The excellence you ascribe to them does not mean much."¹
(I said) "Fathers know best the character of their sons." He
then enquired whether I had a son. I replied, " Yes, I have
one, his Majesty's slave." He said, " Tell me by my soul and
head, is he like you, and as worthy as you ?" I anwered, "My
lord, you know all, but my son is young, and not old enough
to have shown what his real disposition is." On this the king
observed, "Let him grow up and then you will see that he will
not be worth your finger; if he is he will be one of the marvels
and wonders of the time. Mas'úd," he continued, "is a proud
fellow and thinks there is nobody better than himself. Muhammad is stout of heart, generous, and fearless, and if Mas'úd indulges in pleasure, wine, and the like, Muhammad outdoes him.
He has no control over himself, has no apprehension of Mas'úd,
and is heedless of the important concerns of life. I fear I find
but little satisfaction in the thought of Muhammad succeeding
me; for woe to him at the hands of Mas'úd, who will devour
him, and woe also to the generals of my army, for Mas'úd is a
very covetous man and has great love of money. If he should
hear of any officer possessing a little property, he will be sure to
destroy him in a few days, and appoint some worthless fellow in
his place. It will thus come to pass that in this great kingdom
every one will strive to benefit himself, and you may imagine the
pass to which matters will come." I replied, "My lord, may
you ever enjoy sovereignty! dominion in this kingdom will for
ever remain in this family!" The conversation was continued
for some time in this strain, and when the Sultan went to sleep,
I returned. Eventually what the king had said came to pass
in every particular. The history of Muhammad and Mas'úd is
well known, and will be related in this book in its proper place.

¹ [The MSS. differ slightly here, but the sense appears to be as translated.]

strength to walk, perhaps he might find it out. On this the Sultán ordered him to be placed on horseback, and the old man led them to a certain spot on the bank of the river, when he said, I think this was the place where the passage was made. The Sultán sent some men into the river, but nowhere did they find it fordable. The Sultan, casting himself upon the protection of Providence, regardless of himself and fearless of the consequences, with the name of God upon his tongue, urged his horse into the stream. His whole army and all his attendants followed his example, and, with the assistance of God, crossed the water in safety. This was one of the many marvellous deeds of the Sultán, in which also the treachery of the infidels became evident to all men.

Destruction of Robbers by Sultán Mas'úd.
I. xiii. 47.

When Sultán Mahmúd sent costly presents to the ruler of Kirmán, the ambassador who took them proceeded *vid* Tabbas. In the desert of Khabís[1] there was a body of Kafaj[2] and Balúchís who robbed on the highway. They were eighty in number, and had built a stronghold upon an eminence, and had sunk a well. They had committed many robberies, but their conduct had never yet reached the ears of the Sultán. When the ambassador came to this place these people came out and carried off all the presents and rarities in his possession. Some of the men attached to the embassy were slain, but others who escaped returned to Tabbas, and there reported the circumstance to the Sultán, who was proceeding from Ghaznín to Khwárizm by way of Bust. When he arrived at Bust, Sultán Mas'úd came from Hirát and met him. On his arrival, the Sultán would not look at him or give him his hand, but appeared evidently displeased with him. Mas'úd was greatly alarmed, and kissing the

---
[1] [Khabís in Kirmán. Variously written in the MSS. as Habes, Hasar, Hasir, Habis, and Khabis.]

[2] [So in Mr. Thomas' MS. The word representing *Kafaj* is illegible in Mr Prinsep's MS., and is omitted in Ratan Singh's.]

ground, he asked what fault he had committed! The Sultán replied, "How can I be pleased with you, and why should I look at you. You are my son, and yet robberies are committed under your nose without your knowing anything about them?" He replied, "Oh king, I was staying in Hirát, and if robberies are committed in the desert of Khabís, what fault is it of mine!" The king replied, "I care not what you say, but I will not look at you unless you bring all the thieves to me, either alive or dead." Sultán Mas'úd, after his interview with the Sultán, returned to Hirát, and there having chosen a party of two hundred men he started in search of the robbers, making continual enquiries about them. On approaching their fort, it occurred to him that they would probably have spies about, and that on hearing of the approach of so large a body of horse, they would take to flight. He therefore ordered fifty horsemen to fasten on their turbans, give their horses their heads, hide their arms under their saddles, so that no one could see them, and to ride forward and keep the enemy engaged until he should come up. He himself slowly followed with 150 horse. The robbers fought strenuously, seeing only a few horsemen before them, but suddenly the Sultan Mas'úd came up in the rear and captured them all. Not one of them escaped, forty were slain, and forty were sent prisoners to the Sultán. Large booty also was taken. The Sultán ordered them to be punished, and they were executed in a most ignominious way. The fame of his vigilance and justice thus spread far and wide.

Poisoning a Band of Robbers.
I. xiii. 48.

A band of robbers had collected in the desert of Kirmán, and whenever the king sent a force against them they saved themselves by flight. Sultán Mas'úd was informed of this when he was king in 'Irák, and after some consideration he hit upon a plan for getting rid of them. Some poison was taken out of the store-house, and a quantity of apples were brought from Isfáhán.

He then directed a trusty servant to make holes in the apples with a bodkin and to introduce the poison. When the apples were all poisoned, they were given in charge of a caravan that was passing through the desert. A party of the king's men was also sent with the caravan, and directed to lag behind when they approached the haunt of the robbers. The caravan would no doubt be attacked and taken, and the robbers would eat up the apples and all of them would die. The king's men were then to advance and liberate the caravan. This scheme was effectually carried out. The thieves, delighted with their prize, devoured the apples, and no one that ate thereof ever rose again. Sultán Mas'úd's men then came up, released the merchants, and restored them their goods without any loss. By this ingenious scheme[1] the robbers were destroyed without giving any trouble to the soldiers. The wise may thus learn that stratagem will accomplish that which a thousand horsemen cannot effect.

Conquest of Ghor by Sultán Mas'úd.
III. xii. 9.

An injured man came to Sultán Mas'úd and complained that as he was proceeding to Ghor, the chief of the country seized and forcibly took from him all his property. A letter was consequently written to the chief directing the restoration of the man's property. The man got the letter and took it to the chief of Ghor. The chief was vexed, and ordered him to be punished. The man returned to Ghaznín and complained once more against the Ghorians. The Sultán directed that another letter should be written in threatening terms, that if the chief did not in every way satisfy the man, he would march against him and humble his pride. The man said, "O king, direct that the letter be written in as small a compass as possible, because I shall be forced to swallow it, and if there is but a small quantity of paper it will be the easier to get down." Sultán Mas'úd was extremely incensed at this, and on the same day pitched his

[1] ["*Hilah-i latíf*," a clever or pleasant trick.]

tents, and marched against Ghor. He took possession of the country, and chastised the chief, returning to the poor man more than had been taken from him. The Amír of Ghor was thus punished for his tyranny.

The Punishment of Túmán.[1]
III. xix. 7.

It is related in the Táríkh-i Násirí that during the time Amír 'Abdu-r Rashíd reigned at Ghaznín, he had a young slave named Túmán, a man of bad disposition, base and low minded. 'Abdu-r Rashíd was, however, favourably disposed towards him, and conferred on him a high rank. The slave began to interfere in the affairs of government, and being a mean and worthless fellow he did all in his power to ruin and extirpate the nobles and great men. He showed favour to Abú Suhail Rázihí, and they both joined cause and conspired against the great Khwája, the minister of the throne, 'Abdu-r Razzák. He quarrelled with Ahmad Maimaní and had him suspended and called to account. He elevated his own brother, called Mubárak Marde, to high rank, and at last entrusted him with several offices at I'arsháwar. He encouraged tale-bearers and back-biters, and these people obtained great influence at court. They gave false reports, representing that the assignments were in excess of the authorised amount, and this brought destruction upon the kingdom, for the government servants and the orphans were subjected to reductions in a manner which had not been resorted to by any one before.

Amongst the other slaves who were notorious for their wickedness and bad character, was one whose name was Khatíb Lút. This man was exalted by him and made accountant of the state, an office which had been held by Khwája Abú Táhir Husain with great credit and to the satisfaction of the government. When three months had elapsed after the Khwája's appoint-

---
[1] [I have not found this story in the MSS. that I have used.—ED.]

ment, he was ordered to go to Hindústán, and after collecting the revenues of that country, to return to the capital.

Khwája Abú Táhir proceeded to Hindústán, and in every place that he visited he found an agent of Túmán oppressing the people and exercising authority; and thus great embarassment had arisen in the affairs of the state. The Khwája reported all the circumstances to the Secretary of State, which office was then held by Abú-l Fazl Baihakí. When numerous reports had been received from Husain, Sultán 'Abdu-r Rashíd threatened Túmán with condign punishment. Túmán now became an enemy of Abú-l Fazl, and secretly circulated false reports against him. The Sultán, without investigation, ordered Túmán to seize and imprison Abú-l Fazl, and plunder his house and property.

When Abú-l Fazl was removed, Túmán had an unbounded field for the exercise of his power. He conferred a khil'at of investiture on Khatíb Lút, and sent him to Parsháwar. This officer lighted the fire of oppression, and exalted the standard of bloodshed. He made all kinds of demands upon the people. When Khwája Husain reached Parsháwar to examine and report upon the affairs of that province, people complained to him against the Khatíb. The Khwája admonished him, but it was all in vain. The Khatíb gave him disrespectful replies and uttered abusive words against him to his very face. Husain could not restrain his indignation, and ordered him to be taken away from his presence. The matter was reported to Túmán, who told 'Abdu-r Rashíd that as Khatíb Lút was aware that Husain had unlawfully exacted money from the people, the latter had thrown the Khatíb into prison with the view that he might retain in safety the money which Husain had extorted.

When Túmán had made these representations, Amír 'Abdu-r Rashíd ordered him to go and bring Husain a prisoner to the court. Túmán marched the same night to Parsháwar with three hundred thousand[1] horse, and when he arrived there he showed

[1] "Thousand" is omitted in the *Zínatu-l majális*, which gives us the same anecdote.

the royal mandate to the governor of the place. He seized Khwája Husain, and took Khatíb out of prison. He dishonoured and disgraced many good Musulmáns, and then returned to the court.

Khwája Husain was put in heavy chains, and when they had reached the pass at Búdri some horsemen came and reported that Amír 'Abdu-r Rashíd had himself been murdered, and that the ingrate Tughril had usurped the government. On receiving this intelligence, the soldiers, horse and foot, all came forward to Khwája Husain and said unto him, " circumstances have now taken altogether a different turn: he who had triumphed has been vanquished, and now we are all ready to obey your command. What orders may you be pleased to address to us?" The Khwája replied, "Your first duty is to remove the chains from off my feet, and put them on those of Túmán." Upon this the soldiers seized Túmán, pulled him down with great ignominy, and put the chains on his feet. They placed the Khwája on a horse, and Túmán, Khatíb Lút, and his other slaves were seated on camels, and in this manner they took them to Ghaznín. God the most glorious and powerful thus punished Túmán for his wickedness. The moral of this story is to show the consequences of tale-bearing, and to teach that great and wealthy men should not encourage base characters, or take wicked men into their favour, and thus bring disgrace and shame upon themselves.

Anecdote of Sultán Ibráhím.
II. xxiv. 6.

One day when Sultán Razí Ibráhím (God's mercy on him!) was in Ghaznín, he saw a labourer carrying a heavy stone on his head to some building which was then in course of erection, and that he staggered under the load. The Sultán, observing his suffering, ordered him to put down the stone. The labourer obeyed his orders, and after that time the stone remained on that identical spot. One day, some of the royal attendants represented to the king that the stone was still lying in the plain, that it frightened the horses and prevented them passing on quietly, and that it would be well if the king gave the order to have it removed. The king said, I have once ordered it to be placed where it is, and there would be an incongruity in my now ordering it to be removed. So the stone remained lying in the plain of Ghaznín, and in order to maintain the words of the Sultán, his sons also would not, any of them, suffer it to be taken away.[1]

Death of Malik Arslán.
I. v. 147.

It is narrated that after the demise of Sultán Mas'úd bin Ibráhím, Malik Arslán, his son, mounted the throne, and determined to overthrow Sultán Bahrám Sháh. This prince fled from his brother, accompanied by only one of his attendants, and they took the precaution of having their horses shod backwards. He proceeded first to Sístán, from thence to Kirmán, and at last he threw himself on the protection of Sultán Sanjar, who, espousing his cause, marched to Ghaznín against Malik Arslán, and defeated him there, on Wednesday, the fourteenth of Shawwál, A.H. 511 (Feb. 1118, A.D.). Sultán Sanjar appointed Sultán Bahrám Sháh his deputy in Ghaznín and Hindustán, and having seated him on the throne, he himself went to Balkh. When Sultán Sanjar had returned, Malik Arslán again advanced to recover his kingdom, and Bahrám Sháh retired towards Balkh, from whence Sultán Sanjar sent out a force to meet him. He thereupon returned to Ghaznín. Malik Arslán fled before him, and being pursued, was captured in the Shakrán[2] hills, and despatched to the next world. The army then returned to Balkh.

[1] [This story is told in the Akhlák-i Muhsini, but is there attributed to Mahmúd.]
[2] These are the hills spoken of in the account of Sultán Jalálu-d dín's retreat to Hindustán. [The name is written "Sanán" in Mr. Prinsep's MS.]

Muhammad Sám's Victory over Kola [Pithaurá].[1]
[l. xiii. 43.]

It is related that when the martyr Mu'izzu-d dunya wau-d dín Muhammad Sám (May God illumine his tomb,) was about to fight the second time against Kola, between Hanjar[2] and Tabarhindh,[3] it became known to him that (the enemy) kept their elephants drawn up in a separate array when preparing for action. The horses were afraid of them, and this was an element of disaster. When the opposing forces approached each other and the camp fires were visible on either side, the Sultán gave directions that every man should collect plenty of wood before his tent. At night he directed a party of soldiers to remain in the camp, and to keep fires burning all the night, so that the enemy might suppose it to be their camping ground. The Sultán then marched off in another direction with the main body of his army. The infidels saw the fires and felt assured of their adversaries being there encamped. The Sultán marched all night and got in the rear of Kola. At dawn he made his onslaught upon the camp followers[4] and killed many men. When the rear pressed back on the main army Kola sought to retreat, but he could not get his forces in order, nor the elephants under control. The battle became general, the enemy was signally defeated, and Kola was taken prisoner. The Musulmáns obtained a complete victory and the Sultán returned triumphant.

Equity of Muhammad Sám.
[l. vi. 37.]

When the heroic Sultán Muhammad Sám, the honour of the world and of religion, who by his sword had darkened the pros-

---

[1] [The *Táju-l Ma-ásir* and *Tabakát-i Násirí* (*infrá*) use the same term "*Kola.*" The word signifies "bastard" in Persian, and Firishta so explains it.—Briggs. *Ferishta* I. 170.]

[2] [The orthography is doubtful. In two MS. it is جمر Mr. Thomas' MS. has جمر *Anjiz*.]

[3] [Mr. Thomas' MS. gives the name so distinctly. The other two MSS. are defective, and simply give ردنذر. See note on the name in the *Tabakát-i Násirí*, *infra*.]

[4] [*Busa*, baggage.]

perity of the infidels, marched upon Nahrwála, he sustained a defeat, and returned without having effected his object. He then made preparations to retrieve his disasters and avenge his loss of fame and treasure. One of his well-wishers represented to him that in Nahrwála there resided a certain person, by name Wasa Abhir,[1] who was one of the head men of the city. This man always sent consignments of his merchandize to his agents for sale, and at that time there was property belonging to him in Ghaznín, to the amount of ten lacs of rupees. It was suggested to the king, that were he to confiscate this money to his own use, he might by means of it be enabled to raise an army and replenish the exhausted treasury. The king wrote his answer on the back of the petition, to the effect that, if Nahrwála falls into my hands, then the appropriation of Wásá Abhis' wealth would be lawful, but to seize his property in Ghaznín would be contrary to the dictates of justice. So he did not touch the money; and his virtue met its reward, for it happened that, two years afterwards, the most generous king, the staff of the world and supporter of religion (may the Almighty be merciful to him and pardon him!), marched at the head of his army from Dehli, and conquered the territory, and punished the people for their previous misconduct. So the whole world received proofs that the injury which the cause had once received was but as a black spot on the face of The Faith to guard it from the effects of an evil eye.

Preface.—Death of Násiru-d dín Kubácha.

In the beginning of Rabi'u-l awwal, 625 H. (Jan. 1228), the king of kings, Shamsu-d dunya wau-d dín sent an army to repress the inroads of Násiru-d dín Kubácha. Unable to oppose this force, Násiru-d dín sent his forces in boats to the fort of Bhakkar. The royal forces reached Bhakkar on the 10th, and under the directions of Nizámu-l Mulk, made preparations for assaulting the fort. The attack was made on the 1st Jumáda-l awwal, and

---

[1] ["Rúsá Aims" in one MS., "Askd Abhir," in another.]

was so successful that Násiru-d dín was driven from the fortifications (*hisár*) and compelled to take refuge in the inner fort (*kil'ah*) without the assailants losing a single man. A proclamaof amnesty to all Musulmáns was then issued, which was joyfully accepted. Násiru-d dín, with his few remaining adherents offered to capitulate, on condition of being allowed to send away his sons and his treasure, but was told that he must hasten to make an unconditional surrender. He had no faith in his conqueror, and preferred death to submission; so on the night of Thursday, the 19th Jumáda-l A'khir he went to the bank of the river and cast himself into the water. The good fortune of Nizámu-l Mulk thus gained a complete victory.

A Rare Animal.

IV. xxiii. 4.

Abú Ríhán[1] mentions in his writings that within the boundaries of Hindustán, to the east of the Ganges, in the forests of Oudh, there exists an animal called Sharú. It is larger than a rhinoceros,[2] and has two long horns and a small trunk. On the back it has four protuberances resembling four feet. It is so powerful that it will attack an elephant and tear him asunder. No animal has strength enough to contend against it, nor does man venture to hunt it, in fact nothing has power over it except death. Besides natural death, one cause of its destruction is that it often takes up an animal on its horns and tosses it in the air. The flesh adhering to the horns creates worms, which falling on its back, eat into the flesh till it becomes very sore; they then attack its stomach and destroy it. Or, if there be a

---

[1] [Sir H. Elliot omitted this passage from the version given by Rashídu-d dín (Vol. i. p. 61). Reinaud's translation says the animal is to be found in the Konkan (*Fragments*, p. 109), and Rashídu-d dín confirms this (Lucknow MS.). The page is introduced in speaking of the Konkan, so that there can be little doubt of the Konkan being there intended. In the passage before us, the locality is distinctly given as "east of the Ganges," and the name of it is no doubt Oudh, though Mr. Prinsep's MS. gives only "Ou." Konkan and Gangos (Gang) present only a difference of one letter in the original characters.]

[2] [The word in the text may be read *kary*, "rhinoceros," or *gary*, "wolf."]

high mountain near, when it thunders, it will rush as if to attack (some unseen foe) and falling from the mountain destroy itself. People go out to pick up its horns. Its specific peculiarities (*khássiyat*) are not known.

A Description of the Rukh.
IV. xxiii. 5.

This animal resembles a camel. It has two protuberances on the back and it generally has teeth, the limbs and organs of the body are venomous, and no other animal can escape it. Its spittle, dung, etc., are all deadly poison. Whatever meets its eye becomes its prey, for it runs as swift as the wind, and overtakes all creatures. It kills every animal that it may encounter. If anyone takes refuge from it in the top of a high tree which it cannot get up, it stands at the foot, and curling its tail into a sort of ladle, it tosses its water up—this in a very few moments brings its victim down. If any one to avoid it gets into a well, it will stand at the brink and cast its dung and urine down, and if one drop of this falls upon a man he will die.

IV.

TÁJU-L MA-ÁSIR,

OF

HASAN NIZÁMÍ.

This celebrated work is devoted chiefly to the history of Kutbu-d dín Aibak, but it also contains portions of the history of his predecessor Muhammad Ghází, and his successor, Shamsu-d dín Altamsh, but without any notice of Árám, the son and immediate successor of Kutbu-d dín. The name of Táju-l Ma-ásir is nowhere given to the work by the author himself, but it has never been known by any other name from the earliest period. It means "The Crown of Exploits." Titles similar to this are common in Asiatic literature, the most celebrated being the *Táju-t Tawáríkh* of the Turkish historian Sa'du-d dín Muhammad, better known as Khwája Effendi, "the Prince of Ottoman Historians."[1] Considering that the historical portion of this work is devoted exclusively to India, it enjoys a wide reputation throughout the Eastern Muhammadan world; which is ascribable less to the subject of the history than to the peculiar mode of its treatment. This has already been brought to the knowledge of European scholars by a very good account which has been given of the work by Hammer, in his life of Kutbu-d dín Aibak, contained in the *Gemäldesaal der Lebensbeschreibungen grosser Moslemischer Herrscher*, (Vol. iv. pp. 172-182). He re-

[1] A. L. David's *Grammar of the Turkish Language*, p. 1, where there is a long extract given from the work. More may be found respecting the author and the work in the *Biographie Univ.* Vol. xxxix. p. 399; the *Penny Cyclopædia*, Vol. xx. p. 292, and the *Geschichte d. Ottom.* Other works with the title of "Táj" are noticed, but with some omissions, by Hájí Khalfa; *Lexicon Biblio.* Vol. ii. pp. 91-4.

marks that Kutbu-d dín would probably have been enrolled among other conquerors of whom history is silent, had not Hasan Nizámí of Lahore, the writer of the *Táju-l Ma-ásir*, entered into competition with Sábí the historian of Kábus, and 'Utbí the historian of Subuktigín and Mahmúd. This is paying too great a compliment to the historical value of the work, for the simple style of the *Tabakát-i Násirí*, a work nearly contemporaneous, was much better adapted to rescue from oblivion the exploits of Kutbu-d dín, who receives his due share of notice in that history.

The *Táju-l Ma-ásir* is in fact exceedingly poor in historical details, though the period of which it treats is one of the most interesting in the history of Asia,—that of the first permanent establishment of the Muhammadan power in India. It contains, according to Hammer's enumeration, twelve thousand lines, of which no less than seven thousand consist of verse, both Arabic and Persian. It is swelled out to this unnecessary magnitude by the introduction of tedious and meaningless descriptions and digressions, which amount to not less than an hundred in the first half of the work. M. Hammer considers that there are fewer in the second, as the descriptive faculty seems to have been exhausted; but this apparent barrenness is occasioned more by the omission of the marginal notes indicating their recurrence, than by any exhaustion of the author's power, which flows on to the end in an even strain of eloquence, which is perfectly marvellous for its abundance, continuity, and fantasticness. It is produced apparently with but little effort, leaving us to regret that the author should have admitted into an historical work so much rhapsodical and tropological stuff, which is of little use except to show his powers of fancy and invention. It is, however, this which constitutes its value in the estimation of oriental writers, who to this day are fond of attempting imitations, without any of the richly exuberant vein of Hasan Nizámí.

Towards the close, indeed, there is a new variety of illustration, which makes it appear that the descriptions are fewer. But though fewer, they are much longer, for here the author occasionally introduces a subordinate series of descriptions, or *sifats*, within one leading subject. For instance, in the second half we have images derived from mirrors, pens, and chess, each running on for many pages, but all containing several minor descriptions referrible, as it were, to those chief subjects. Here also we are introduced to new conceits, where whole sentences and pages are made to consist of nothing but sibilants and labials. Even the death of Muhammad Ghází is not sufficient to repress the gaiety of his imagination, for we are told that, "*one* or *two* men out of the *three* or *four* conspirators, inflicted *five* or *six* wounds upon the lord of the *seven* climes, and his spirit flew above the *eight* paradises and the *nine* heavens, and joined those of the *ten* Evangelists."

Some of the passages where these descriptions are introduced are noticed in the following abstract, showing that they are derived from anything in heaven or earth, as the prolific fancy of the author may suggest. The *Gemäldensaal* has given the following classified distribution of them:—Of nature, its elements and phenomena,—fire, water, heat, cold, lightning, thunder, rain, snow, the sea, the desert, fields, woods, meadows, and gardens. Of seasons,—day, morning, evening, night, spring, summer, autumn, and winter. Of flowers,—the rose, the tulip, the basilicon, the jasmin, the lily, the narcissus, the violet, the lotus, the hyacinth, the anemone. Of fruits,—the pomegranate, the apple, the orange, the citron. Of beasts,—the lion, the serpent, the elephant, the horse, the camel, the lynx, the falcon, the peacock, the dog. Of war and its appurtenances,—the contending armies, arrows, bows, clubs, lances, spears, daggers, and spoils. Of musical instruments,—kettle-drums, viols, tymbals, and barbytons. Of beautiful women,—cheeks, hair, curls, eyes, and moles. Of festivals and their appurtenances, — cup-bearers, singers, bowls, wines, and fire-pans; and lastly, pens, physicians, and learned men. Most of these have been given in the following abstract in the order in which they occur, and they by no means include the whole series introduced by the author.

The reader may satisfy himself of the nature of these descriptions by reading the commencement of one devoted to the sword, which he will find in the abstract under "The Conquest of Gwáliár." If he should be desirous of seeing the conclusion of it, he will find it in the *Gemäldesaal*, pp. 178, 179.

There is but little related of the author by biographers, and all we know of him is to be ascertained only from his own account in the preface of the *Táju-l Ma-ásir*. He gives his own name as Hasan Nizámí simply. Mirkhond in his preface, and Háji Khalfa (No. 2051), call him Sadru-d dín Muhammad bin Hasan Nizámí, and so he is styled by Abú-l Fazl, in an untranslated chapter of the *Ayín-i Akbarí*. Hammer calls him Hasan Nizámí of Lahore, but that was neither his birthplace nor chief residence.

Hasan Nizámí was born at Naishápúr, and he tells us that he never dreamt of travelling abroad, until the troubles of his native country of Khurásán induced him to seek a residence elsewhere. Another cause was that no regard was paid to learning, in consequence of these distractions, and that ignorant and envious men were seeking to injure him, for it is a matter of common observation that "the wise are rarely regarded in their own country."[1]

He for a long time entertained the thought of leaving his country before he could put it into execution, and at last, when the disorders of which he complains had reached their climax, and he himself was reduced to the greatest distress, "in the very prime of manhood, and before his hair began to turn gray," he left his native city, notwithstanding the continued remonstrances of his friends, to which he had yielded for some time. He set out for Ghazni, at the suggestion of Shaikh Muhammad Káfi, and on his arrival at that capital, after being delayed by a severe

[1] This resembles the Hindí proverb, *Apne gáṅw ká jogí, an gáṅw ká sidh*. "The jogí of his own village is a deity in another," and our Saviour when he says, "A prophet is not without honour save in his own country, and in his own house," is merely repeating a common Asiatic proverb.

attack of fever on the road, he made several agreeable acquaintances amongst the learned, and after a short time departed in company with some of his new friends for Dehli, "the country of mercy and the altar of wealth.—The reins of choice were given to his horse, the traverser of deserts and the passer of hills.—The heat of the fiery blast opened the very gates of hell, and the wild beasts of the mountain and deserts sought for the shade of trees.—The boughs of the jungle were so closely interlaced, that the wind in the midst of them was confined like a bird in a cage.—A tiger was seen in every forest.—In every ravine and plain poisonous serpents were met with.—It came into his thoughts, will the boat of his life ever reach the shore of safety?—The crow-like Hindús had intercepted the roads, and in the rapidity of their movements exceeded the wild ass and the deer, you might say they were demons in human form, and covered with blackness."

Having escaped from all these dangers, he arrived at Dehli, and paid his respects to the Chief Judge, Sharfu-l Mulk, and was received with great kindness. After he had resided for some time in this city, his friends recommended him to write something in the shape of contemporary history, "for the purpose of ascertaining the powers of his style;" and as the king had about that time issued orders that an account of his victories should be recorded, Hasan Nizámí determined to engage himself upon that particular subject.

With regard to the dedication of his work, Hammer informs us (*Gemäld.*, iv. 174), that "this history of Kutbu-d dín Aibak, was composed by Nizámí, his contemporary, as early as twelve years after his death, for Muhammad bin Sám bin Husain, the ruler of Lahore, who styled himself 'Násir-i Amíru-l Muminín, helper of the prince of the believers.' Nizámí of Lahore, a slave of Muhammad bin Sám, wrote this history for his master, who being an admirer of the great achievements of Aibak, took them for the model and rule of his reign."

There is evidently a great misapprehension here respecting

Muhammad bin Sám, who is no other than the famous Muhammad Ghorí, the master of Kutbu-d dín Aibak. Muhammad Ghorí died before Kutbu-d dín reigned, and he could not therefore have taken his own slave for his great exemplar. What the author really says regarding this potentate is this: After dwelling on the advantage and necessity of holy wars, without which the fold of Muhammad's flock could never be filled, he says that such a hero as these obligations of religion require has been found, "during the reign of the lord of the world Mu'izzu-d dunyá wau-d dín, the Sultán of Sultáns, Abú-l Muzaffar Muhammad bin Sám bin Husain, in the person of the puissant Sultán, the lord of the fortunate conjunction of the planets, the pole of the world and religion, the pillar of Islám and Musulmáns, the asylum of princes and sultáns, the destroyer of infidels and plural-worshippers, etc., the Khusrú of Hindustan, Abú-l húris Aibak the Sultán," and that "Almighty God had selected him from amongst the kings and emperors of the time," for he had employed himself in extirpating the enemies of religion and the state, and had deluged the land of Hind with the blood of their hearts, so that to the very day of resurrection travellers would have to pass over pools of gore in boats,—had taken every fort and stronghold which he attacked, and ground its foundations and pillars to powder under the feet of fierce and gigantic elephants,—had made the heads of crowned Ráís crown the top of impaling posts,—had sent the whole world of idolatry to the fire of hell, by the well-watered blade of his Hindí sword,—had founded mosques and colleges in the places of images and idols,—and had made the names of Naushírwán, Rustam, and Hátim Táí to be forgotten." Such was the hero to the record of whose achievements the work was principally dedicated.

The *Táju-l Ma-ásir* was commenced in the year 602 H. (1205 A.D.), in the eighth month of which (Sha'bán) Muhammad Ghorí died, and it is evident that it was begun before his death, because the preface, which, however unusual, was really composed at the beginning, and not the conclusion of the work, contains a prayer for the prolongation of his life and the prosperity of his kingdom.

The history opens with the transactions of the year 587 H. (1191 A.D.), when Muhammad Ghori undertook his expedition to India to retrieve the dreadful disaster he had a short time before experienced on the field of Náráin, near Thánesar, to which, however the courtly historian makes no allusion. The copies ordinarily to be met with carry the history down to the year 614 H. (1217 A.D.), or seven years after the death of Kutbu-d dín, and at the close of that portion the author indulges in a panegyric on his own work, in which he invites the reigning monarch Shamsu-d dín, the second Alexander, to compare his work with those of other celebrated historians, and he will see that it is "superior to anything written by ancients or moderns," and he concludes by saying, that if his life is spared, he will continue the work in the same manner. That he did so continue it is evident from a very valuable copy in the possession of Nawwáb Ziáu-d dín of Dehli, written as early as the ear 779 H. (1377-8 A.D.) in the *Naskh* character styled *Hijází*. In this, though itself imperfect at the end, we have the history carried down even twelve years later, or to 626 H. (1228-9 A.D.), and it is not improbable that it might have been prolonged to the close of Shamsu-d dín's reign, or seven years later than this period. From the general meagreness of historical details, it cannot be said that this deficient portion is worth much enquiry.

Beyond the praise which the author bestows upon his heroes, there is nothing to indicate that he was contemporary with the events which he describes, and the absence of all particulars, as well as a certain confusion and indistinctness about some of the dates, show that he was no active participator in any of his patrons' campaigns. It is singularly strange that he says nothing of the transactions of Kutbu-d dín's actual reign, for the same short chapter records his accession and his death.

The following abstract contains all that is of the remotest historical interest in the work, no name or event being omitted.

The passages between inverted commas imply that the words of the original have been translated, but even in these many intermediate words, such as synonyms and reduplications of the same expression, have been omitted, and it has been considered sufficient to group together words and phrases, which, though actually to be found in the *Táju-l Ma-ásir* do not in the translation preserve the exact order of the original. The passages in the first chapter, which are printed in italics indicate that they are written in Arabic, and nearly the same proportion of Arabic occurs throughout the work, showing that, without a knowledge of that language, it would be impossible to understand thoroughly the *Táju-l Ma-ásir*.

The *Táju-l Ma-ásir* is rare in Europe. Hammer[1] says that the only copy to be found is in the royal library of Vienna, but there is one also in the British Museum. In India it is by no means uncommon, much less so than the difficulty of understanding the work would lead one to suppose. The copy in the library of the Asiatic Society of Bengal is a very clean one, but abounds with errors, and many chapters are recopied towards the close. There is a beautiful copy in the Dehli College, and there is one of surpassing excellence belonging to Maulaví Sadru-d din, the Sadru-s sudúr of Dehli, written in the Naskh character, apparently about three hundred years ago, by Muhammad bin Muhammad, who professes to have copied it from the author's autograph. The transcriber imitates successfully the style of the work in a chapter at the end, devoted to its praise.

There are also two good copies of the *Táju-l Ma-ásir* in the library of Nawwáb Siráju-l mulk, but so little known and appreciated as to be lettered, one the *Tárikh-i Mahmúd Ghaznirí*, the other *Jahán-kushá*; but all must yield the palm to Nawwáb Ziáu-d dín's copy noticed above, on account of its containing the additional matter, but it must be confessed that the character

---

[1] *Gemäldesaal der Lebensbeschreibungen*, vol. iv. p. 175.

is not easy to read, and the manuscript is unfortunately damaged by water and worms.

The copy noticed above, which shows the verses in separate lines detached from the prose, contains 570 pages of twenty lines each; the additional matter being comprised in thirty pages.

[The following Abstract was prepared entirely by Sir H. Elliot himself.]

ABSTRACT.

Invasion of Hindustán.

"In the year 587 H. (1191 A.D.), the Lord of *the World, the Sultán of Sultáns, Mu'izzu-d dunyá wau-d dín* (Muhammad Ghorí) *in a happy moment*, and under a fortunate star, departed from Ghazna, *may God protect it from calamities!*

Had he not imparted *movement* to his hands and *reins*,
The feet of his *stirrups* would have *stopped the air* in its course.
If his horse be so wearied that it cannot carry him,
His courage would urge him against his enemies.

Having equipped and set in order the army of Islám, and unfurled the *standards of victory* and *the flags of power*, trusting in the *aid of the Almighty*, he proceeded *towards* Hindústán.

His standards proclaim victory,
Indeed, they are almost prepared to write the book of victory,
His ensigns and black umbrella are full of adornment,
How beautiful on the face of time are the curls and *freckles* of the *state!*

When the tent of *eternal prosperity, encompassed by splendour, arrived near* Lohúr, and when the *air of that country* became *perfumed and crescented* by the dust of *the armies and the shoes of the horses*, the great Sadr *Kiwámu-l mulk Rúhu-d dín Hamza*, who was among *the chiefs of the country and the renowned of the state*, and had obtained *distinction by the customs of embassage and the proprieties of missions*, and his *position* in the *service* of the *sublime* Court (*may God surround it with increased glory*)! had met with approval, *and in the beauty of his moral character and the excellence* of his endowments, *the above mentioned person, in whose* merits all concurred, and from *the flame of whose wisdom and the light of whose penetration abundant delight and perfect good fortune* arose.

Indeed all kinds of excellences united in his person,
And he was singularly endowed in the practice of all virtues,
He was such a *Sadr* that *the substance of greatness* found in him *a soul,*
He was a *sea* in which the eyes of *meaning* found *vision.*

Such was the man who was sent on an *embassy* to Ajmír, in order that the Rái (Pitháurá) of that *country* might see the right way without the *intervention* of the sword, and that he might incline from *the track of opposition into the path of propriety,* leaving his *airy* follies for the *institute* of the knowledge of God, and acknowledging the *expediency of uttering the words of martyrdom and repeating the precepts of the law,* and might abstain from *infidelity and darkness,* which entails *the loss of this world and that to come,* and might place in his ear *the ring* of slavery to the *sublime* Court, (*may God exalt it!*) which is *the centre of justice and mercy, and the pivot of the Sultáns of the world, and* by these means and modes might *cleanse the fords of a good life* from *the sins of impurity.*

When the ambassador arrived in *the country* of Ajmír, and *in accordance with* his orders brought *forward the conditions of his mission,* and in *uttering his speech* presented *the usual inducements of fixing the mind,* and adorned *the selection of his words with the excellence of their significations,* and *strung well the pearls of exhortations and admonitions* upon *the thread of style.*

They were such words that if the world were to hear them,
On account of their beauty the people would incline to become ears.

Your *words* are right and your *meaning correct,*
Your *opinion* is the soul and your *greatness the body.*
Your words are the product of the bough of *rhetoric,*
And your *clemency* is the fruit of the seed of eloquence.
In no *respect* did *the words of threats, or promises* become

established in the *heart* of that man of dark *understanding*, nor did *advantages or menaces* addressed to the heart (*and indeed he who menaces offers* the alternative of *advantages*) have place in the *hearing* of that *obstinate*, for from his *large army and grandeur* the *desire of something like* the conquest of the world had raised a *phantom* in his *imagination;* and he remained *neglectful of the subtle principle that armies do not profit when the time has passed*, and he had placed on *the shelf of forgetfulness* the good maxim that "*when fate comes the field of opportunity is narrowed*," and had not read *the divine order that* "*it is a duty imposed on me to give aid to the faithful;*" and in *the sight* of his idolatry *the commands of the law* were *the dreams of oppression, and the light of instruction* showed *the darkness of his perdition*, and since in *the sublime understanding* of the sovereign which *derived aid and support from the world of holiness, and the light of his wisdom exceeds and surmounts that splendour* of the sun and moon.

> *If his light were to contend with the dawn,*
> *Even his night would exceed the brilliancy of the day.*
> Gold would not be produced from earth by *the power* of the sun,
> Unless his wisdom had *power* over the sun.

When these *circumstances* were *represented*, and the *intelligence of the declarations of* that *God-forsaken* reached the *blessed hearing, which was filled with gladness, the signs of disturbance* overspread his *auspicious countenance*.

Conquest of Ajmír.

He accordingly prepared for an expedition against the Rái, and mounted his steed, of which there is a poetical description. "The victorious army on the right and on the left departed towards Ajmír." "When the Kola (natural son) of the Rái of Ajmír, the vaunts of whose courage had reached the ears of far and near, heard of the approach of the auspicious standards and the victorious armies, he advanced for the purpose of fighting, and having adjusted the robe of slaughter and the arms of battle, marched on over hills and deserts with a well-equipped army, the number which cannot be conceived in the picture-gallery of the imagination."

"When the crow-faced Hindús began to sound their white shells[1] on the backs of the elephants, you would have said that a river of pitch was flowing impetuously down the face of a mountain of blue."

Description and attributes of elephants, spears, and arrows.— The army of Islám was completely victorious, and "an hundred thousand grovelling Hindús swiftly departed to the fire of hell." The Rái of Ajmír was taken prisoner during the action, but his life was spared. After this great victory, the army of Islám marched forward to Ajmír, where it arrived at a fortunate moment and under an auspicious bird, and obtained so much booty and wealth, that you might have said that the secret depositories of the seas and hills had been revealed."

Poetical description of fountains, gardens, birds, and flowers.— While the Sultán remained at Ajmír, "he destroyed the pillars and foundations of the idol temples, and built in their stead mosques and colleges, and the precepts of Islám, and the customs of the law were divulged and established." The Rái of Ajmír, who had managed to obtain his release, or at least, immunity from punishment, and whose "ancient hatred against the Musulmáns was deeply rooted and concealed in the bottom of his heart," appears to have been detected in some intrigue, which is only very obscurely indicated, so that orders were issued for his death, and "the diamond-like sword severed the head of that abandoned wretch from his body."

[1] سحاب سفيد in the original, to which, as no meaning is attached in the dictionaries, I have thought myself warranted in translating thus; but a few pages after this (the fourth instance of their being used), these words cannot bear this meaning, because the instruments in that case were sounded by the Muhammadans, to whom shells are an abomination. In that passage I have called this instrument a kettle-drum, as it resembles a shell in shape.

The Government of Ajmír conferred on the son of Rái Pithaurá.[1]

"The son of Rái Pithaurá, in whose qualities and habits the proof of courage and the indexes of wisdom were apparent, and who, both abroad and at home, exhibited familiarity with rectitude, and prognostications of goodness, was appointed to the government of Ajmír.

*   *   *   *   *   *

The Conquest of Dehli.

After settling the affairs of Ajmír, the conqueror marched "towards Dehli (may God preserve its prosperity and perpetuate its splendour!) which is among the chief (mother) cities of Hind." When he arrived at Dehli, he saw "a fortress which in height and strength had not its equal nor second throughout the length and breadth of the seven climes." The army encamped around the fort. "A torrent of blood flowed on the field of battle, and it became evident to the chiefs that if they did not seek for safety from the sword of the king of the earth, and if they should deliver into the hands of Satan the time of option and the reins of good counsel, the condition of Dehli would be like that of Ajmír; so from the dread of kingly punishment, the Rái and mukaddams of that country placed their heads upon the line of slavery, and their feet within the circle of obedience, and made firm the conditions of tribute (*málguzárí*) and the usages of service."

The Sultán then returned "towards the capital of Ghazna (may God preserve it in prosperity!)" but "the army remained encamped within the boundary of Dehli, at the *mauza* of Indarpat (Indraprastha)."

The Government of Kohrám and Sámána.

The Government of the fort of Kohrám and of Sámána were made over by the Sultán to "Kutbu-d dín, on whose fortunate

[1] This is the heading in the original, but in the preceding chapter the name of the Rái is not given. In this it is spelt Pitaurá. There is mention of the son (پسر) not natural son (گلد) as in the preceding chapter.

forehead the light of world-conquest shone conspicuous," "and who by his lofty courage and pure faith without doubt was worthy of the kingdom and suitable for the throne of sovereignty; and by the aid of his sword of Yemen and dagger of India became established in independent power over the countries of Hind and Sind." "He purged by his sword the land of Hind from the filth of infidelity and vice, and freed the whole of that country from the thorn of God-plurality, and the impurity of idol-worship, and by his royal vigour and intrepidity, left not one temple standing." "He extinguished the flame of discord by the splendour of the light of justice, and the smoke of the darkness of oppression vanished from the face of the earth."

The chiefs of the country around Kohrám came to pay their respects and acknowledge fealty, and he was so just and generous "that the name of Naushirwán and the tale of Hátim Táí were in course of oblivion."

An assembly is commenced, a feast is held, and the sumptuous preparations described.—The merits of cup-bearers, wine, goblets, companions, flowers, hunting, horses, falcons, panthers, dogs, and huntsmen are poetically eulogized.

The flight of Jatwán and his[1] Death in Battle.

"When the honoured month of Ramazán, 588 H., the season of mercy and pardon, arrived, fresh intelligence was received at the auspicious Court, that the accursed Jatwán, having admitted the pride of Satan into his brain, and placed the cup of chieftainship and obstinacy upon his head, had raised his hand in fight against Nusratu-d dín, the Commander, under the fort of Hánsí, with an army animated by one spirit."

Digressions upon spears, the heat of the season, night, the new moon, morning, and the sun.—Kutbu-d dín mounted his horse, and "marched during one night twelve parasangs." "The accursed Jatwán, when he heard the news of the arrival of the

---

[1] The singular prevails throughout. He was probably a mere leader of the Ját tribe, which still maintains its position in the neighbourhood of this scene of action.

victorious armies, felt himself compelled to depart from under the fort," and fled. "The soldiers of Islám came up to the army of Hind on the borders of Bágar; and although Jatwán saw there was no chance of successful opposition in battle, yet as he saw destruction impending on him from the throat of the dragon, and the road for flight was blocked up, and the standards of the State and royal victory were unfurled, yielding to the necessity of the case, and not at his own option," he prepared for fight, and "the noise of the hautbois and shells confounded the world, the thunder of the drums ascended to heaven, and the blast of the brazen clarions resembled the sounding trump (of resurrection.)"

The armies attacked each other "like two hills of steel, and the field of battle became tulip-dyed with the blood of the warriors."—Poetical digression on swords, daggers, spears, and maces.—The Hindús were completely defeated, and their leader slain. "Jatwán, who was the essence of vice and turbulence, and the rod of infidelity and perverseness, the friend of grief, and the companion of shame, had his standards of God-plurality and ensigns of perdition lowered by the hand of power;" "and the dust of the field of battle was commingled with the blood of that God-abandoned wretch, and the whole country was washed from the filth of his idolatry."—Praise of Kutbu-d dín's justice, encouragement of the learned, and his civil administration. Mention of the booty taken by the Musulmáns.—He marched to Hánsí, "and encamped there a few days, in order to repair the fort, and after that returned towards Kohrám, which acquired fresh beauty from his blessed feet."

"The intelligence of this happy victory and these important incidents was divulged over the face of the world, and the noise of it spread to the countries of Hind and Sind, far and near, and proclamations announcing the victory of the chiefs of the State, and the defeat of the enemies of the kingdom were written and despatched to the capital of Ghazna, (may the Almighty preserve it in wealth and prosperity!)" and in them was added "that the foundation of all this success was the lofty courage and pure faith of his Majesty."

The Capture of Mírat.

"When the chief luminary threw its shade in the sign of Libra, and temperate breezes began to blow, after putting to flight the army of heat," Kutbu-d dín marched from Kohrám, "and when he arrived at Mírat—which is one of the celebrated forts of the country of Hind, for the strength of its foundations and superstructure, and its ditch, which was as broad as the ocean and fathomless—an army joined him, sent by the dependent chiefs of the country." The fort was captured, and a Kotwál appointed to take up his station in the fort, and all the idol temples were converted into mosques.

Capture of Dehli.

He then marched and encamped under the fort of Dehli, which was also captured, "and the standards of the State were also carried into the neighbouring tracts. The conqueror entered the city of Dehli, which is the source of wealth and the foundation of blessedness." The city and its vicinity was freed from idols and idol-worship, and in the sanctuaries of the images of the Gods, mosques were raised by the worshippers of one God."

The Rebellion of Hiraj, Brother of the Rái of Ajmír.

After Kutbu-d dín had settled affairs in this quarter, the chief Sadr, Kiwám-u-l mulk Rúhu-d-dín Hamza, sent him intelligence from Rantanbor, that Hiráj,[1] the brother of the Rái of Ajmír, had gone into rebellion, and "had turned his face towards the siege of the fort of Rautanbor," and that the son of Pitaurá, who had been advanced under the protection of the sublime Court, was in a state of extreme danger. On receiving this intelligence, Kutbu-d dín appointed the Amír Sábiku-l

---

[1] Firishta calls him Hemrâj, which is a common Indian name. "Hiráj" is not; but it is plainly so written in all the copies. It is probably an abbreviation of the Sanskrit "Dhírāj," a potentate, which is still used on the seals of Hindú Rájás.

mulk Nasru-d dín" to take charge of the affairs of State during his absence, "a man who in knowledge of the rules and customs of government was superior to his contemporaries, and in resolution and courage was celebrated throughout Hind, far and near," and himself departed for Rantanbor, "passing over hill and desert like a wild ass or an antelope."

"When Hiráj heard of the arrival of the auspicious standards, knowing he could not contend with the army of Islám, and impelled by necessity, he placed the hands of weakness in the skirts of flight, and for fear of the blade of the scimetar fled like the wind with his resurrectionless army." The conqueror then engaged himself in administering "the ways of justice, and received both high and low under the shadow of his benignity," and the people were happy. "At this time the son of Rái Pitaurá was favoured with a robe of honour and other kindnesses; and in return for this friendship, he sent abundant treasure for the service of the State, together with three golden melons, which with extreme ingenuity had been cast in moulds like the full moon."

"About this time they wrote to the heavenly throne, that the Rái who had fled from Dehlí had raised an army of idolatrous, turbulent, and rebellious tribes, the vapour of pride and conquest having entered his thoughtless brain." Kutbu-d dín pursued him, "and when the wretch was taken, his head was severed from his body and sent to Dehlí, which had been his residence and capital." Kutbu-d dín then himself returned to Dehlí, and sent "written accounts of his capture of forts and strongholds, and his victories and holy wars" to Ghazna, to which capital he was invited to receive thanks in person from Mu'izzu-d dín Sám Ghorí. The invitation arrived when the sun was in Cancer, and the heat was so great as to prevent travelling, but he set out on his journey at the commencement of the rainy season.

Kutbu-d dín proceeds to Ghazna.

"When the fortunate stirrups reached the capital of Ghazna

(may God shed splendour on it!), he enjoyed the happiness of kissing hands, and received other marks of special favour before the great throne, and in the degree of his rank was raised above all the other chiefs of the world." A festival was held in celebration of his arrival, "and splendid jewels, and valuable clothes, and costly arms, and slaves of great price" were presented to the king.

Kutbu-d din was accommodated in the garden of the minister Ziáu-l mulk.—Here follow poetical descriptions, of horses, ice, apples, citrons, oranges, cold, wind, and fire.—On the return of the hot season he was taken ill, and "removed from the residence of the minister to the palace of the sovereign, which is the seat of prosperity; but on account of his illness and want of strength, he could not rejoice in his heart with the festivities." On his recovery, he took his leave of the king, and received a patent conferring upon him the government (of Hindustán) "and every one of the principal officers of his army was rejoiced exceedingly, at receiving from his Majesty suitable presents and promotion of rank."

On his arrival at Karmán[1] from the great capital, Táju-d dín Yalduz received him with great kindness and honour, and gave him his daughter in marriage, and a fête was held on the occasion.—Poetical descriptions follow, of stars, female beauty, cupbearers, curls, cheeks, eyes, lips, mouths, stature, elegance, cups, wine, singers, guitars, barbats, trumpets, flutes, drums, on the morning, and the sun.

Kutbu-d din returns to Dehli.

When he arrived at Dehli, "which is the capital of the kingdom, and the centre of God's aid and victory, the crown and throne of sovereignty received honour and adornment in his kingly person," "and the lords of the sword and pen hastened to pay their respects at the magnificent Court, and observed the usages of benediction and praise; while the city and its vicinity

[1] This Karmán is in the Bangash country, between Kábul and Banu.

rejoiced and was decorated like the garden of Iram, and the gates and walls were adorned with the gold tissues of Chín and the brocades of Rúm," "and triumphal arches were raised, beautiful to look at, tho top of which a strong-winged bird could not surmount, and the glittering of the lightning of the swords and the splendour of the arms, which were suspended on all sides of them, inspired terror in the spirit of the beholder."

Rhapsody upon spring and birds.—Kutbu-d dín built the Jámi' Masjid at Dehli, and "adorned it with the stones and gold obtained from the temples which had been demolished by elephants," and covered it with "inscriptions in Toghra, containing the divine commands."

Kutbu-d dín advances to Kol.

After staying sometime at Dehli, he marched in the year 590 H. (1194 A.D.), towards Kol and Benares, passing the Jún (Jumna) "which, from its exceeding purity, resembled a mirror." He took Kol, "which is one of the most celebrated fortresses of Hind." Those of the garrison "who were wise and acute were converted to Islám," but those who stood by their ancient faith were slain with the sword. "The nobles and chiefs of the State entered the fort, and carried off much treasure and countless plunder, including one thousand horses."

There intelligence was received of the march of Muhammad Ghorí from Ghazna; Kutbu-d dín advanced to meet him, "and had the honor of kissing hands, which is the highest of glories, and the essence of miracles, and presented an elephant laden with white silver and red gold," "and an hundred horses," "and sundry kinds of perfumes."

Fight with the Rái of Benares and Capture of Asni.

When the army was mustered, it was found to amount to "fifty thousand mounted men clad in armour and coats of mail," with which they advanced to fight against the Rái of Benares. The king ordered Kutbu-d dín to proceed with the vanguard, consisting of one thousand cavalry, which fell upon "the army of the enemies of religion," and completely defeated it. On its return to the king, the officers were presented with robes of honour.

"The Rái of Benares, Jai Chand, the chief of idolatry and perdition, advanced to oppose the royal troops with an army, countless as the particles of sand," "and the noise of the war-drum proclaimed to the ears of the worshippers of one God, aid comes from the Almighty, and the sound of the silver kettle-drum and the blast of the brazen trumpets resounded to heaven." Rhapsodical description of swords, spears, war-nouses, and archers. "The Rái of Benares, who prided himself on the number of his forces and war elephants," seated on a lofty howdah, received a deadly wound from an arrow, and "fell from his exalted seat to the earth." His head was carried on the point of a spear to the commander, and "his body was thrown to the dust of contempt." "The impurities of idolatry were purged by the water of the sword from that land, and the country of Hind was freed from vice and superstition."

"Immense booty was obtained, such as the eye of the beholder would be weary to look at," including one (some copies say three) hundred elephants. The royal army then took possession "of the fort of Asní where the treasure of the Rái was deposited," and there much more precious spoil of all kinds rewarded the victors.

The Capture of Benares.

From that place the royal army proceeded towards Benares, "which is the centre of the country of Hind," and here they destroyed nearly one thousand temples, and raised mosques on their foundations; and the knowledge of the law became promulgated, and the foundations of religion were established;" "and the face of the dinár and the diram was adorned with the name and blessed titles" of the king. The Ráis and chiefs of Hind came forward to proffer their allegiance. "The government of that country was then bestowed on one of the most celebrated and exalted servants of the State," in order that he might distribute justice and repress idolatry.

When the king had settled all the affairs of the city and its vicinity, and "the record of his celebrated holy wars had been written in histories and circulated throughout the breadth of the fourth inhabited quarter of the world," he returned to Ghazna. "The standards of the Khusrú, victorious in battle,[1] were planted for some days on the fort of Asní, and the chiefs and elders all around hastened to his service with various kinds of rarities and presents, and his noble Court became the scene where the princes and generals of the world came to bow their heads in reverence."

Kutbu-d dín returns to Kol, and entrusts its Government to Hisámu-d dín 'Ulbak.

There was a certain tribe in the neighbourhood of Kol, which "after the manner of fox playing with lions" had occasioned much trouble by their deceits and stratagems, therefore "by the edge of the sword they were despatched to the fire of hell." "Three bastions were raised as high as heaven with their heads, and their carcases became the food of beasts of prey." "That tract was freed from idols and idol worship, and the foundations of infidelity were destroyed," and all those who were oppressed found protection under the shadow of royal clemency." "The keys of command and prohibition in the kasba of Kol were given to Maliku-l Umará Hisámu-d dín 'Ulbak, one of the chief pillars of the State." Here follows a didactic passage on what he was expected to do as a good governor.

He returns to Dehli.

"When he was at complete leisure from the important concerns of Kol, and the affairs of that neighbourhood had been adjusted by the aid of the kindness of his heart, he turned his face towards the abodes of Dehli, the altar of the prosperity of the worlds," and when he arrived there he administered justice

---

[1] Kutbu-d dín is usually styled throughout the work خسرو پیروز جنگ

with so much impartiality, that among other results "the wolf and sheep drank water out of the same pond," "and the very mention of thieves and theft, which had before been current on the tongues of every one, fell to the dust."

The Second Visit to Ajmír.

"In the year 589 H. (1193 A.D.) they represented to the Court that Hiráj, the Rái of Ajmír, having raised the standards of perdition, and fanned the flame of idolatry in his heart, had opened the road of rebellion which he had hitherto closed by his deceit, and that from being exceedingly forsaken by God, he had delivered the reins of vanity into the hands of Satan, and having conceived the ladders of grandeur in his brain, had become proud." "Jíhtar,[1] supported by an army, hastened to the borders of Dehli, and the people were suddenly caught in the darkness of his oppression and turbulence, and the blood and property of the Musulmáns fell into danger and destruction. When the mention of these circumstances was made to the blessed ear of the Khusrú, in a moment of courage and royal determination, he employed himself in the punishment and extinction of the rebel." "He ordered that a portion of his victorious army should be set apart and equipped for his personal service, and that the rest of his army should be detached to the frontiers for the subjection of the accursed, and the destruction of the enemies of the state and religion." Kutbu-d dín marched towards Ajmír in the middle of the hot season, "when the armour on the bodies of the valiant was inflamed by the heat of the sun, and the sword in the scabbard melted like wax," so that he was compelled to make night marches.

"When Jíhtar heard of the approach of the victorious standards, the blackness of sorrow was fixed in his breast," and "knowing that he had not power to oppose them on the field of battle, he tightened the girths of the horse of flight, and sped like the wind out of the net of danger, and arrived at the shore

[1] The name is written "Jíhtar" in one MS. and "Jhítar" in another.

of safety from the whirlpool of destruction, and from fear of the Khusrú's sword drew his head within the four walls of that strong fortress of Ajmír, like a tortoise," where, in despair, he sacrificed himself in the flames of a pyre, after which the fort, "which was one of the most celebrated in Hind," was easily taken. "The country of Ajmír was restored to the honours of the ancient time and the dignities of its past days, for the circumstances of that province had altogether departed from their former course to which they now reverted," "religion was re-established," "the road of rebellion was closed," "infidelity was cut off, and the foundations of idol-worship were utterly destroyed." The roads were freed from the fear and danger of robbers, and the oppressed subjects were delivered from their distresses." "The blessed lamp was visited by Ráís and Ránas, and the earth was rubbed by the foreheads of the chiefs and celebrated men of Hind." After settling the affairs of Ajmír, Kutbu-d dín returned to Dehli.

Arrival of Sultán Muhammad Ghori in Hindustán.

When Kutbu-d dín heard of the Sultán's march from Ghazna, he was much rejoiced, and advanced as far as Hánsí to meet him, and "had the honour of kissing hands, and being distinguished above all the princes of the earth by the endless favours which were lavished on him." In the year 592, H. (1196 A.D.), they marched towards Thangar,[1] and the centre of idolatry and perdition became the abode of glory and splendour, and when the ropes of the royal tent were raised to heaven, the neighbourhood was tinged with an hundred hues by the varied coloured tents which were erected round that fortress, which resembled a hill of iron." "By the aid of God, and by the means of courage and the daily increasing prosperity of the king, that strong castle was taken, which had hitherto remained closed to all the sovereigns and princes of the world."

[1] The text of Firishta says "Thangar, which is now called Biána."

"Kuwar Pál,[1] the Rái of Thangar, who had prided himself on the numbers of his army and the strength of his castle, when he saw the power of the army opposed to him, fear invaded his breast, and he begged for safety for his life, and, like a slave, kissed the face of the earth with the very roots of his teeth." Upon which he was pardoned and admitted into favour, and, though with the loss of his kingdom, was content that his life was left to him." "The Musulmáns, and *harbís*, and *zimmís* entered into conditions for paying revenue. The country was purified from the defilement of infidelity, and no opportunity remained for opposition and rebellion."

"The government of Thangar was conferred on Bahá-u-d dín Tughril," "who was acquainted with matters of administration, and the customs of setting soldiers in array," and who received advice and instruction from his majesty how to comport himself properly in his new appointment.

The Capture of Gwáliár.

When the affairs of this tract was settled, the royal army marched, in the year 592 H., (1196 A.D.) "towards Gálewár (Gwáliár), and invested that fort, which is the pearl of the necklace of the castles of Hind, the summit of which the nimble-footed wind from below cannot reach, and on the bastion of which the rapid clouds have never cast their shade, and which the swift imagination has never surmounted, and at the height of which the celestial sphere is dazzled."—Description of swords and other military weapons.—"In compliance with the divine injunction of holy war, they drew out the bloodthirsty sword before the faces of the enemies of religion. That sword was coloured of cœrulean blue, which from its blazing lustre resembled a hundred thousand Venuses and Pleiades, and it was a well-tempered horse-shoe of fire, which with its wound exhibited the peculiarity of lightning and thunder; and in the perfect weapon the extreme of sharpness lay hid, like (poison in)

[1] [Sir H. Elliot writes the name thus, but his MS. has only "Kú Púl."]

the fangs of a serpent; and (the water of the blade) looked like ants creeping on the surface of a diamond;" and so forth.

"Rái Solankh Pál who had raised the standard of infidelity, and perdition, and prided himself on his countless army and elephants, and who expanded the fist[1] of oppression from the hiding place of deceit, and who had lighted the flame of turbulence and rebellion, and who had fixed the root of sedition and enmity firm in his heart, and in the courtyard of whose breast the shrub of tyranny and commotion had shot forth its branches, when he saw the power and majesty of the army of Islám," he became alarmed and dispirited. "Wherever he looked, he saw the road of flight blocked up." He therefore "sued for pardon, and placed the ring of servitude in his ear," and agreed to pay tribute, and sent ten elephants as a peace offering, in which he was graciously admitted to protection, and was allowed to retain his fort. "When the neighbouring country was freed from the enemies of religion, and the Rái of Hind became enrolled amongst the number of servants and friends," the Sultán prepared to return to Ghazna, and Kutbu-d dín, after his departure, returned to Dehli, where festivities were celebrated on his arrival.—Praise of wine-bibbing and cup-bearers.

The Conquest of Nahrwála, and the Flight of the Rái.

In the year 591 H. (1195 A.D.), when Kutbu-d dín was again at Ajmír, intelligence was brought him that a party of seditious Mhers, "who were always shooting the arrow of deceit from the bow of refractoriness," had sent spies and messengers towards Nahrwála, representing that a detachment of the army of the Turks had arrived at Ajmír, of no great strength and numbers, and that if from that quarter a force could be immediately sent to join them, before the enemy could find the opportunity of putting themselves in a state of preparation, they could make a sudden night attack upon them, and might rid the country of

[1] Hammer (*Gemäld.*, iv. 181,) translates "den Spannring des Bogens der Umbill zum Dämmring gemacht;" for which I see no authority in the original.

them, and if anyone of the Turkish army were to escape from the talons of the eagle of death, he must necessarily take the road of flight, and with his two horses would make three stages into one, until he reached Dehli in a state of distraction."

When this treacherous plan was revealed, Kutbu-d dín determined to anticipate it, and during the height of the hot season "before the sun arose, fell upon the advance guard of the black infidels, and like lions attacked them right and left." The action lasted during the whole day, and next morning that immense army of Nahrwála came to the assistance of the vanguard, slew many of the Musulmáns, wounded their commander, pursued them to Ajmír, and encamped within one parasang of that place.

In this predicament, a confidential messenger was sent to Ghazna[1] "to explain before the sublime throne the position of the army of the infidels, and to ask for orders as to future proceedings." "A royal edict was issued conferring all kinds of honours and kindnesses upon the Khusrú, and leaving to his entire discretion the subjection and extirpation of the turbulent." A very large army was despatched to reinforce him, under the command of Jahán Pahlawán, Asadu-d dín Arslán Kalij, Nasíru-d dín Husain, 'Izzu-d dín son of Muwaiyidu-d dín Balkh, and Sharfu-d dín Muhammad Jarah." These reinforcements arrived at the beginning of the cold season, when "the vanguard of the army of winter began to draw its sword from the scabbard, and the season of collecting armies and the time of making raids had returned."

"In the middle of the month of Safar, 593 H. (Jan., 1197), the world-conquering Khusrú departed from Ajmír, and with every description of force turned his face towards the annihilation of the Rái of Nahrwála." When he reached the lofty forts of Páli and Nandúl,[2] he found them abandoned, and the abode of

---

[1] In the latter half of the work the spelling is usually Ghaznín.

[2] Hammer (*Gemäld.* iv. 184,) following Briggs (*Ferishta* I. 196) reads "Bali and Nadole." They assume various forms in different manuscripts,—"Rahi and Bartaki, Nadól and Nanól." There are places between Ajmír and Mount Ábú, which correspond to the names given in the the text. The lithographed edition of Ferishta (I. 109) reads "Dhútali and Banól."

owls, for the people had fled at the approach of the Musulmáns, and had collected under their leaders Rái Karan and Dárábara, in great numbers "at the foot of Mount Ábú, and at the mouth of a pass stood ready for fight and slaughter." The Musulmáns did not dare to attack them in that strong position, especially as in that very place Sultán Muhammad Sám Ghori had been wounded, and it was considered of bad omen to bring on another action there, lest a similar accident might occur to the commander. The Hindús seeing this hesitation, and misconstruing it into cowardice and alarm, abandoning the pass, "turned their faces towards the field of battle and the plain of honour and renown;" for "they were persuaded that fear had established itself in the hearts of the protectors of the sacred enclosure of religion." "The two armies stood face to face for some time, engaged in preparations for fight, and on the night preceding Sunday, the 19th of Rabi'u-l awwal, in a fortunate moment the army of Islám advanced from its camp, and at morn reached the position of the infidels." A severe action ensued from dawn to mid-day, when "the army of idolatry and damnation turned its back in flight from the line of battle. Most of their leaders were taken prisoners, and nearly fifty thousand infidels were despatched to hell by the sword, and from the heaps of the slain, the hills and the plains became of one level." Rái Karan effected his escape from the field. "More than twenty thousand slaves, and twenty elephants, and cattle and arms beyond all calculation, fell into the hands of the victors." "You would have thought that the treasures of the kings of all the inhabited world had come into their possession."

"The city of Nahrwála, which is the most celebrated in that country, full of rivers," and the kingdom of Gujarát, which is "a separate region of the world," came under the dominion of the Musulmáns, "and high and low were treated with royal benignity and justice." "The chief nobles and pillars of the State were favoured with handsome robes of honour, and received abundant proofs of royal kindness," then "the standards of the

Khusrú, victorious in battle, returned to Ajmír," whence they were moved towards Dehli, where they arrived at an auspicious moment. As an earnest of his regard and respect, Kutbu-d dín sent to Ghazna treasures and various rarities, which were received by his majesty with suitable acknowledgments of the value and splendour of his general's services.

Capture of the Fort of Kálinjar.

In the year 599 H. (1202 A.D.), Kutbu-d dín proceeded to the investment of Kálinjar, on which expedition he was accompanied by the Sáhib-Kirán, Shamsu-d dín Altamsh. Encomiums on both warriors follow through several pages. "The accursed Parmár," the Rái of Kálinjar, fled into the fort after a desperate resistance in the field, and afterwards surrendered himself, and "placed the collar of subjection" round his neck, and, on his promise of allegiance, was admitted to the same favours as his ancestor had experienced from Mahmúd Subuktigín, and engaged to make a payment of tribute and elephants, but he died a natural death before he could execute any of his engagements. His Díwán, or Mahtca, by name Aj Deo, was not disposed to surrender so easily as his master, and gave his enemies much trouble, until he was compelled to capitulate, in consequence of severe drought having dried up all the reservoirs of water in the forts. "On Monday, the 20th of Rajab, the garrison, in an extreme state of weakness and distraction, came out of the fort, and by compulsion left their native place empty," "and the fort of Kálinjar which was celebrated throughout the world for being as strong as the wall of Alexander" was taken. "The temples were converted into mosques and abodes of goodness, and the ejaculations of the bead-counters and the voices of the summoners to prayer ascended to the highest heaven, and the very name of idolatry was annihilated." "Fifty thousand men came under the collar of slavery, and the plain became black as pitch with Hindús." Elephants and cattle, and countless arms also, became the spoil of the victors.

"The reins of victory were then directed towards Mahobá, and the government of Kálinjar was conferred on Hazabbaru-d dín Hasan Arnal. When Kutbu-d dín was satisfied with all the arrangements made in that quarter, he went towards Badáún,[1] "which is one of the mothers of cities, and one of the chiefest of the country of Hind."

The Visit of Muhammad Bakhtiyár Khiljí and the Return of of Kutbu-d dín to Dehli.

Shortly afterwards, "Ikhtiyáru-d dín Muhammad Bakhtiyár, one of the chief supports of the State, the splendour of Islám, and celebrated throughout Hind for his religious wars, joined the auspicious stirrups and came to pay his respects from the direction of Oudh and Behár." "He presented twenty elephants and various kinds of jewels and moneys." "He was received with royal kindness and beneficence, and he was exalted above the leaders of the time;" and when he took his audience of leave, the blessed commands, investing him with authority, were renewed and augmented, and a tent, a *naubat*, a drum, a standard, and magnificent robe of honour, a horse and trappings, a waistband, sword, and a vest from the private wardrobe were conferred upon him."

"In a fortunate moment, and under an auspicious bird, the blessed standards were waved, and directed towards Dehli, the capital of prosperity and the altar of excellence."—Rhapsody on Kutbu-d dín's justice.

The Return of Muhammad Ghori from Khwárizm and his War against the Gakkhurs.

When the sublime standards were returning in the year 600 H. (1203 A.D.) from the capital of Khwárizm, the army of Khitá (God's curse on it!) made an attack upon them, while on their

[1] Hammer (*Gemäld.* iv. 185) following Briggs (*Frishta* I. 198) places Badáún between the Ganges and the Jamna, for which there is no authority in the original It is in Rohilkhand, to the east of the Ganges.

march within the borders of Andkhúd, in numbers exceeding the stars of heaven and the particles of the earth, and the great king, wounded and defeated, fled from the field of hatred towards Ghazna."

"Aibak Bák, one of the most confidential servants of the State, an officer of high rank in the army, who had been brought up in the royal court, fled from the field of battle, and carried away the impression that by heavenly visitation, the blessed person of the king had met with a misfortune and been slain. He fled with the speed of the wind to Multán, and, on his arrival, went immediately to Amír Dád Hasan, the lord of a standard, and deceitfully persuaded him that he had come for the purpose of imparting to him a royal command, which could only be communicated to him in private, and should not be publicly divulged." When the private conference was accorded to him, he took the opportunity of assassinating the governor, and so got possession of the fort of Multán. "For a long time the truth of the matter was not revealed, and a report was spread to the effect that the governor had been imprisoned by the royal commands. After some delay, the various servants and officers of the Province became aware of what had really happened, and the intelligence of the true circumstances was spread throughout the far and near countries of Hind and Sind. Upon this, the tribe of Kokars (Gakkhurs) (God annihilate them!) said that from any one who had the least knowledge and sense, it could not be concealed that if the sacred person of the Sultán had been alive, the like of these transactions could never have been done by Aibak Bák, and that therefore the great king had exchanged his throne of empire for one of dust, and had departed from the house of mortality to the world of holiness. In consequence of these impressions, seditious thoughts entered the brains of the Hindús, and the madness of independence and dominion affected the heads of Bakan and Sarkí, the chiefs of the Kokars, who thrust their heads out of the collar of obedience, and opened their hands for the destruction of villages and the plunder of cattle, and kindled the flames of turbulence and sedition between the waters of the Sodra¹ and the Jelam, by the aid of a crowd of the dependants of Satan." "When their ravages had exceeded all bounds, Bahá-u-d dín Muhammad, governor of Sangwán, with his brothers, who held lands (*aktá'*) within the borders of Multán, accompanied by many of the chief people of the city, marched out against them, determined to repress the violence of those accursed rebels and enemies of the State and religion ; but many of them were captured or slain by the exertions of the army of the infidels, in number like the drops of rain or leaves of the forest. Their power consequently increased day by day, and a general named Sulaimán was obliged to fly before the superior numbers of the enemy." When these circumstances were reported to Muhammad Ghorí, he determined on proceeding to the scene of action, and sent on the Amír Hájib, Siráju-d dín Abú Bakr, one of his confidential servants, to inform Kutbu-d dín of his intentions. In consequence of which, Kutbu-d dín advanced to meet his Majesty, at the opening of the cold season. "At every stage intelligence reached him from the royal camp, urging his advance, and informing him that the blood-thirsty sword would be sheathed, and the camp would halt, and that no measures would be taken to exterminate the infidels, until he had passed the river (Chináb) which intervened between him and the royal camp."

"Near the river of Sodra, Kutbu-d dín killed four fierce tigers, at the roaring of which the heart was appalled," and on the day after crossing that river, he joined the camp of the king on the bank of the Jelam, and was received with royal kindness. "They mounted their horses and swam them like fish across the Jelam," "and on the bank of the river entered on their plans for the approaching action, and arranged all the preparations for fight, after joining together in consultation." Kutbu-d dín suggested

¹ Hammer (*Gemäld.* iv. 183) says, "the river of Sodra, which, flowing by Siálkot, Sodra, and Wazírábád, discharges itself into the Chináb." But there is no such stream. The Sodra is the Chináb itself, so called from the old town of that name on its eastern bank.

that it was not right for the king to expose his person against such enemies, and suggested that the command of the Musulmán army should be entrusted to himself alone; but the persuasion of his general seem to have had no effect upon the resolution of the Sultán.—Description of the battle near the ford of the Jelam, the waves of which were filled with blood, and in which "the armies of infidelity and true faith commingled together like waves of the sea, and contended with each other like night and day, or light and darkness." Shamsu-d dín was also engaged in this fight.—Extravaganzas upon spears and other weapons, and upon war-horses.

The Kokars were completely defeated, and, "in that country there remained not an inhabitant to light a fire." "Much spoil in slaves and weapons, beyond all enumeration, fell into the possession of the victors." One of the sons of the Kokar Rái, the chief instigator of these hostilities, rushed into the river with "a detachment of his Satanical followers, and fled with one horse from the field of battle to a fort on the hill of Júd, and having escaped the sword, threw into it the last breathings of a dying man." The next day, Muhammad Sám advanced towards the hill of Júd, when the action was renewed, which ended in the capture of the fortress, "and the Hindús like a torrent descended from the top of the hill to the bottom." "The Rái of the hill of Júd, putting on the robes of a Brahman, presented himself like a slave, and kissed the face of the earth before the Sultán," by whom he was admitted to pardon. Immense booty was taken in the fort.

The Sultán then advanced to Lahore, accompanied by Kutbu-d dín and the chief officers of State, and on Kutbu-d dín's taking his audience of leave, before his return to Dehlí, he received a dress of honour and an affectionate farewell.

Death of the Sultán of Sultáns, Muhammad Sám.

On the king's return from Lahore towards Ghazní, he had fixed his camp "within the borders of Dhamek, and his tent was pitched on the bank of a pure stream in a garden filled with lilies, jasmine," and other flowers. Here while he was engaged in his evening prayer, "some impious men (God's curse and destruction on them!) came running like the wind towards his majesty, the king of the world, and on the spot killed three armed attendants and two chamber-sweepers. They then surrounded the king's own tent, and one or two men out of these three or four conspirators, ran up towards the king, and inflicted five or six desperate wounds upon the lord of the seven climes, and his spirit flew above the eight paradises and the battlements of the nine heavens, and joined those of the ten evangelists."

A long elegy follows upon his death. His body was carried to Ghazna. "When this dreadful intelligence was conveyed to the lion-hearted Khusrú," he was deeply distressed, and, "when he was alone, streams of blood coursed down the face of his cheeks."

Allegiance of the Nobles to Kutbu-d dín, and his Confirmation in the Kingdoms of Hind and Sind.

"For the consolation and satisfaction of the distant provinces, the auspicious mandates were issued to the different quarters of both sea and land," and the nobles and dependants of the Court came forward to offer their allegiance, and "the carpet of his audience-chamber was kissed by the Ráís of Hind and the Khusrús of Chín." "The keys of direction and prohibition in the capital of Ghazna fell into the hands of his officers, after the flight of Táju-d dín Yalduz, and the whole country of Hind, from Pershaur to the shores of the ocean, and in the other direction, from Siwistán to the borders of the hills of Chín, came into the power of his servants and under the dominion of the executors of his orders." "The public prayers and coinage of dínárs and dirhams thoughout the whole country, full of rivers, received honour and embellishment from his name and royal titles," and Lohúr, where the throne of Sultáns had been established, and which was the altar of the good and pious, became the capital." "By his orders, the precepts of Islám received great promulgation, and the sun of righteousness cast its shadow on the countries of Hind from the heaven of God's assistance."—Happy results of the king's mercy and justice.

Death of the Sultán of Sultáns " by a fall from his horse while playing the game of chaugán, and his burial at Lahore," like a treasure in the bowels of the earth.—An elegy upon his death.

Accession of Shamsu-d dín.

"In the year 607 H. (1210 A.D.), the throne of the kingdoms of Hindustán received honour and embellishment from Shamsu-d dín wau-d dunyá the Emperor of Turk and 'Ajam, Abú-l Muzaffar Altamish."

Revolt of the Turks in the City of Dehlí.

"Sirjándár Turkí, who was the leader of all sedition, and who opened his hand to shed the blood of Musulmáns, with an army of bloodthirsty Turks broke out into open rebellion. Although the Sultán was frequently requested to repress their violence, he "refrained for several days" from doing so. At last, he determined to oppose them with a large army, headed "by the chiefs of the time, such as 'Izzu-d dín Bakhtiyár, Nasíru-d dín Mardán Sháh, Hazabbaru-d dín Ahmad Súr, and Iftikháru-d dín Muhammad 'Umar, all valiant warriors."

"This army, assaulting like fire and moving like the wind, was drawn out in battle array like a hill of iron, near the Bágh-i Jún (the Jamna Garden)."—Hyperboles on battle, arms, and slaughter.

Aksankar Kitta and Táju-d dín Farrukh Sháh were slain in battle, but Sirjándár Turkí "threw himself into the waters of the Jún, took to flight like a fox in fear of a lion, and departed by the way of river and hill like a crocodile and a leopard, and, starting and trembling, concealed himself in the jungles and forests, like a sword in a scabbard, or a pen in a writing-box," and all their followers were either killed or dispersed.

Capture of Jálor.

After some time, they represented to his Majesty that the inhabitants of the fort of Jálewar (Jálor) had determined to revenge the blood which had been shed, "and once or twice mention of the evil deeds and improprieties of that people was made before the sublime throne. Shamsu-d dín accordingly assembled a large army, and headed by "a number of the pillars of the State, such as Ruknu-d dín Hamza, 'Izzu-d dín Bakhtiyár Nasíru-d dín Mardán Sháh, Nasíru-d dín 'Alí and Badru-d dín Saukartigín," valiant men and skilful archers, "who could in a dark night hit with their arrows the mirror[1] on the forehead of an elephant." "The king took his way towards Jálewar by the aid of God," "and by reason of the scantiness of water and food it was a matter of danger to traverse that desert, where one might have thought that nothing but the face of demons and sprites could be seen, and the means of escape from it were not even written on the tablet of providential design."

"Udí Sah, the accursed, took to the four walls of Jálewar, an exceedingly strong fortress, the gates of which had never been opened by any conqueror." When the place was invested by Shamsu-d dín, Udí Sah requested some of the chiefs of the royal army to intercede for his forgiveness. While the terms of his surrender were under consideration, two or three of the bastions of his fort were demolished. He came, "with his head and feet naked, and placed his forehead on the earth" and was received with favour. The Sultán granted him his life, and restored his fortress, and in return the Rái presented respectfully an hundred camels and twenty horses, in the name of tribute and after the custom of service." The Sultán then returned to Dehli, "which is the capital of prosperity and the palace of glory," and after his arrival, "not a vestige or name remained of the idol temples which had reared their heads on high; and the light of faith

[1] This was probably made of burnished steel, and must have been placed as a protection over the most vulnerable part of the elephant. Shortly afterwards, the author styles this plate "a Chinese mirror."

shone out from the darkness of infidelity, like the sun from a curtain of sorrow, or after its emerging from an eclipse,[1] and threw its shade over the provinces of Hind and Sind, the far and near countries of idolatry; and the moon of religion and the State became resplendent from the heaven of prosperity and glory."—Praise of Islám, justice and courage.

Defeat of the army of Ghazna, and seizure of Táju-d dín Yalduz.

"When the beautiful Canopus arose, and the vanguard of winter put the centre of the army of summer to flight," it entered into the royal determination "to destroy some tribe of the accursed infidels, or to move the auspicious standards for the purpose of capturing some city in the land of Hind." "In the midst of these reflections, messengers arrived frequently from Táju-d dín, who had admitted into his brain the wind of pride and the arrogance of dominion," charged with the delivery of ridiculous propositions, which the Sultán was incensed to listen to. Shamsu-d dín resolved to oppose his pretensions by force, and advanced with a large army to Sámánd, which he reached on Monday, the 3rd of Shawwál, 612 H. (Jan., 1216), and on his arrival was attacked by the advanced guard of Malik Táju-d dín. During the action, the enemy suddenly came up towards the left wing of the auxiliaries of the faith, and desired to raise up a disturbance with their "watered blades, and to practice their deceits after the manner of of foxes playing with lions, and with the absurd idea that they could thus take the countries of Hind and Sind."—Then follows a description of the battle, which is described in terms peculiar to chess, with the introduction of hyperboles upon swords, dirks, maces, war-nooses, horsemen, horse-archers, arrows, spears, elements, justice, and stars.—Táju-d dín was wounded by an arrow shot by Muwaiyidu-l Mulk, and was subsequently taken prisoner and brought before Shamsu-d dín.

---

[1] This implies a temporary revival of the Hindú power, which may have occurred under the unconverted rebel Turks who are represented as having shed the blood of Musulmáns.

The Flight of Násiru-d dín and Conquest of Lahore.

"After some time, the great lord Muwaiyidu-l Mulk Muhammad Junnidí was appointed Wazír."—Encomium on his merits.—It was represented to his Majesty, that Malik Násiru-d dín "had placed his former engagements under the water of forgetfulness," "and that in the receipts and disbursements of the account of his tribute he had incurred debt and balance," "and that all the excellent advice that was offered to him was valued as so much dirt." His Majesty accordingly, in a fortunate moment, marched in the beginning of Jumáda-l ákhir from Dehlí, "may God protect it! (for its water and soil have always been mild and favourable to various temperaments, and its fire and wind have at all times been suitable and agreeable to the disposition of everybody.") He marched with a large army towards the country of Lohúr, of which when the enemy became aware "they began to be greatly agitated like fish upon dry land, and like water-fowl sought protection from the waters of the Biyáh," "on the banks of which stream they encamped with an army innumerable as ants and locusts."

"On the fourteenth of the month of Shawwál, the victorious standards advanced with the whole army in battle array, from the borders of Lorúh to the ford at the village of Chamba." "Wind-footed they swam across the river, in comparison of which the Oxus and Jaxartes looked like a fountain."

When Násiru-d dín "saw the victorious army cross that foaming stream without the aid and means of boats," he fled in alarm, "turning his face from the battle and slaughter" towards Lohúr, whither he was pursued by the victorious army" which could not see a trace of the dust raised by their swift-flying horses."—His standards, drums, and camp equipage, besides immense booty, fell into the hands of the Royalists. The defeated general afterwards continued his flight "by the road of Uch."

Shamsu-d dín arrived at Lohúr, "which is among the mothers of the countries of religion, and among the chiefs of the provinces of Islám, and the abode and repose of the excellent and pious, and which for some days, on account of a number of calamities, and changes of governors, and the sedition of rebels, had been distracted by the flames of turbulence and opposition, and was now again reduced to order by the breath of the zephyr of his justice." The captives who were taken in battle were pardoned, and after writing accounts of the victory and despatching them in various directions, Shamsu-d dín returned to Dehli.

Prince Násiru-d dín appointed Governor of Lahore.

In the beginning of 614 H. (1217 A.D.), the government of Lohúr was committed to the king's son, Násiru-d dín Mahmúd, and the advice which was given to him as to the mode of conducting his administration is given at length.—Description of festivities, with a repetition of rhetorical flourishes about beauties, cups, goblets, stars, locks, mouths, singers, companions, horses, hawks, dogs, tigers, horses, arrows, forts, and the game of chaugán, at which the king recreates himself.

The Capture of Bhakkar.

This portion of the work opens with praise of God and king, upon whom Almighty favours are showered, as is testified by his conquest of Kálewar (Gwalior), Rantanbhor, and Mandúr,[1] Kanauj, Behár, and Bárah, and his subjection of powerful Ráís, and by his spreading the knowledge of Islám as far as the ocean; and amongst other arrangements made by which good government was secured, "an account of the proceedings of the king was written according to dates so as to form a model for the kings and Sultáns." The forts of Uch Multán "which were stronger than the wall of Alexander" were also taken "in a manner which astonished the world," and while he was engaged in these conquests, it was reported to the king that Malik Násiru-d dín Kubácha, who was proud and arrogant, and "who regarded in his cruelty and unkindness the people of God as less than rubbish,"

[1] [Or Mandawar, in the Siwálik hills. See infra, Tabakát-i Násirí.

"and out of his own pleasure and drunkenness would roast even hearts and draw tears of blood from the eyes," had fortified himself within the strong fort of Bhakkar, "the eye of the forts and the face of the kingdom of Hind," "and which had not been taken by any Khusrú," and in which were deposited immense treasures.

Upon receiving this information, Shamsu-d dín despatched his minister Khwája-i Jahán Nizámu-l Mulk Muhammad Junaidí with a large army to Bhakkar, in the very height of the hot weather. Part of the army marched by land "a difficult road through the jungles," and part went by water. After the fort was invested, and the enemy was reduced to extremities, Násiru-d dín despatched his son 'Aláu-d dín Muhammad to Shamsu-d dín with an hundred lacs of Dehliwáls,[1] and thousands of suits of clothes. The Sultán received him kindly, but would not allow him to return, in consequence of which, Násiru-d dín became much alarmed and ill, "and his head was bowed down to his knees like a violet, with his eyes of expectation open like a narcissus," and he "wailed like Jacob for the absence of Joseph."

Násiru-d dín shortly after died of grief, "and the boat of his life was drowned in the whirlpool of death," "though he left behind him nearly a thousand boats" which could render no service to him.[2] The result of his death was that "more than five hundred lacs of Dehliwáls, various kinds of inlaid articles and jewels, and pearls exceeding white, and costly garments were deposited in the royal treasury of Shamsu-d dín," and possession was also taken of "twelve celebrated forts, which had never been before captured," "and Siwistán and Lúk (Lakkí) as far as the shores of the sea;" "and the coinage was struck, and the prayers read in his auspicious name throughout all the countries of Hindústán and the provinces of Kusdár and Makrán." He returned to Dehli on the 14th of Rabí'u-l awwal, 624 H.

---

[1] Coins of the period struck at Dehli, composed of a mixture of silver and copper. See E. Thomas, *Coins of Patán Sultáns of Hindustán*, pp. 10, 11; and Jour. R. A. S. N. S. II. p. 149.   [2] [See supra, page 201.]

Arrival of a dress of investiture from the 'Abbási Khalifa.

After some time a dress of honour was received from the Imám Mustansirbi-llah by the Sultán at Dehli, accompanied by a diploma confirming him in the kingdom of Hindústán, with the title of the great Sultán. He received the diploma with deep respect, and appointed the following day, namely the 23rd Rabí'u-l awwal, 626 H. (Feb. 1229 A.D.) for a general assembly, in which the farmán was read out in the presence of the King, the princes, and nobles. It declared that he was confirmed in the possession "of all the land and sea which he had conquered." Robes were bestowed upon the ambassadors, the chiefs, and nobles, in honour of the event, and great joy prevailed upon the occasion throughout the capital.

VI.

KÁMILU-T TAWÁBÍKH

or

IBN ASÍR.

[Called also by the author *Kámil fi-t Táríkh*. It is also known to Persian writers as *Táríkh-i Kámil*. The author of this celebrated general history was Shaikh Abú-l Hasan 'Alí Ibn Abú-l Karam Muhammad ibn Muhammad ibn 'Abdu-l Karím ibn 'Abdu-l Wáhid as Shaibání. He was surnamed "'Izzu-d dín; majesty of religion," but he is commonly known as Ibn Asír (or Athír according to Arabic pronunciation). He was born in the year 555 H. (1160) in the Jazírat ibn 'Umar, an island of the Tigris above Mosul, and hence the epithet "al Jazarí, the islander," is frequently added to his name. Ibn Khallikán, who was personally acquainted with him, says that he studied first at Mosul and afterwards at Baghdad, in Syria, and at Jerusalem. Returning to Mosul he devoted himself most assiduously to literary pursuits, and his house became the resort of all the learned men who inhabited or visited that town. Ibn Khallikán met him at Aleppo in 626 H., 1229 A.D., and describes him as "a man of the highest accomplishments and most excellent qualities, but extremely modest." He speaks of him fondly in another place as "Our *Shaikh*, Ibn Asír," and of his accomplishments he says "His knowledge of the traditions and his acquaintance with that science in its various branches placed him in the first rank, and his learning as an historian of the ancients and moderns was not less extensive; he was perfectly familiar with the genealogy of the Arabs, their adventures, combats, and history; whilst his great work, the *Kámil* or complete, embracing the history of the world from the earliest period to the year 628 of the Hijra (1230 A.D.), merits its reputation as one of the best productions of the kind."

The Kámilu-t Tawáríkh enjoys a very high reputation, and has been much used and quoted both in Asia and Europe. Ibn Khaldún borrowed largely from it, and it has been drawn upon by Ockley for his History of the Saracens, by Malcolm for the History of Persia, and by Weil for his *Geschichte der Chalifen*. The narrative is very clear and succinct, but the work, from its great range, is very voluminous. It contains a few brief notices of the Jats in the second and third centuries of the Hijra, and it also gives some interesting details of the Arab occupation of Sind, but so far as India is concerned it is chiefly valuable for its notices of the Ghaznivides and the Ghorians. The work closes soon after the decline of the latter dynasty.

The author of the *Hablbu-s Siyar* relates that "the *Táríkh-i Kámil*, one of the two histories written by Ibn Asír" was translated into Persian under the orders of Mírán Sháh, son of Tímúr, by Najmu-d dín, surnamed Nizárí, one of that prince's secretaries.

Besides the work before us, Ibn Asír wrote an abridgement, containing many corrections and improvements of Abú Sa'du-s Samáuí's *Ansáb*, upon *Patronymics*, etc. Another of his works was the "*Akhbáru-s Sahába*; history of the companions of the Prophet." He had two brothers, who also engaged in literary pursuits, and one of them, Majdu-d dín, wrote a work on the traditions, entitled "*Jámi'u-l Usúl min Hadísu-r Rasúl*," which has been erroneously attributed to our author.

There are MSS. of several portions of the *Kámilu-t Tawáríkh* in the British Museum and in the Bodleian Library; and in Sir H. Elliott's Library there is a borrowed MS. of part of the work, in bad condition and much worm-eaten. A complete edition of the whole work will soon be available, as it is passing through the press at Leyden, under the careful and able editorship of Professor Tornberg, who bases his text upon the MSS. of Berlin,

Paris, and the British Museum. Seven volumes have already been published, and the whole work will be comprised in twelve.[1]

EXTRACTS.

Hijra 151. A.D. 768.

In this year the Kurks made an attack upon Jidda.

Hijra 153. A.D. 770.

In this year Al Mansúr returned from Mecca to Basra, and embarked forces in ships against the Kurks who, as before related, had made an incursion upon Jidda.

Hijra 160. A.D. 776.—*Conquest of the town of Barada.*[2]

In the year 159, Al Mahdí sent an army by sea under 'Abdu-l Malik bin Shahábu-l Musamma'í to India. The force consisted of a large number of troops and volunteers, among whom was Al Rabí' bin Subaih. They proceeded on their way and at length disembarked at Barada. When they reached the place they laid siege to it. The people of the neighbourhood fought with them frequently. The town was reduced to extremities, and God prevailed over it in the same year. The people were forbidden to worship the Budd, which the Muhammadans burned. Some of the people were burned, the rest were slain, and twenty Musulmáns perished in testimony of their faith. God came to them, and raised the sea against them, so they waited until the weather should be favourable. Disease then fell upon them, and about a thousand of them died, among whom was Rabi' bin Subaih. They then returned homewards and reached the coast of Persia, in what is called the Bahru-l Hamrán. There the wind rose in the night time and wrecked their vessels. Some were drowned, and some escaped.

---

[1] De Slane's Ibn Khallikán, Introd. xii. II. 289.— See D'Herbelot, "Gezeri;" De Rossi, "Atir;" Bodleian Cat. 693, 696, 784; Hamaker, 164; Fraehn, 41; Wüstenfeld, 81; Rampoldi, viii. 517, ix. 291, xi. 57; Gemäldesaal Pref. xi. and vi. 2; Jenisch Reg. Pers. 123; Wilken, Samankhanum, 191-2; D'Ohsson, Mongols. Pref. x.; Weil, II. ix; Reinaud's Abool Feda, 9; Sprenger, on Mahomedanism, 73; Bush, Life of Mahomet, 255; Nouv. Mel. As. I. 433, 434; Col. Or. 1. 208; Not. et Ext. I. 542; Jour. As. 4 Ser. iv. 188; Not. des MSS. II.; Hammer, Gold. Horde, xv. xxv.; Univ. Hist. III. 239, 263. [2] برده in the MS. of the B. Mus.

Hijra 219. A.D. 834.—*War against the Jats.*

In the month of Jumáda-l ákhir, Al M'utasim sent 'Ajíf bin 'Isa to fight against the Jats, who had seized upon the roads of Hajar, and had plundered the corn which was in the stacks of Kaskar, and in the stores of the towns. They spread terror over the roads, and planted posts in all directions towards the desert. At the news of the approach of Ajíf they retired. Ajíf marched to below Wásit and there took post on the river Bardád and Anhárá. Then they retreated and entered another place, but the roads baffled them. Ajíf then forced 1,500 of them to fight, and killed on the field of battle 300 men. Their leaders he made prisoners, and sent the chief to the gate of M'utasim. Ajíf was engaged against the Jats twenty-five days, and vanquished a great many of them. The chief of the Jats was Muhammad bin 'Usmán, and the commander was Samlú. Ajíf then took up a position, and remained opposed to them seven months. Mansúr bin Dassám was at Músal.

Hijra 220. A.D. 835.—*Defeat of the Jats by Ajíf.*

In this year Ajíf came to Baghdad from his expedition against the Jats, after having defeated and killed many of them. The remnant was compelled to ask quarter, which was conceded to them. They then marched away with him in Zi'l hijja, 219 (834 A.D.) and their number, including women and children, was twenty-seven thousand. The fighting men among them were twelve thousand. Ajíf placed his conquered foes in boats, and sent them dressed as they had appeared in battle, with their trumpets, to Baghdad. They reached that city on the tenth Muharram, 220. They proceeded in boats to the Shammásiya (suburb of Baghdad). The Jats were accontred as for battle, and were blowing their horns. And Azíf gave to each of his men two dinárs (as a present). The Jats stayed on board their ships three days, and were then handed over to Bishr ibnu-s Samaida', who conveyed them to Khánikin. Thence they were removed to the (northern) frontier to 'Ain-zarba, and the Byzantines made a raid upon them and not one of them escaped.[1]

Conquest of Bhátía.

In the year 396 Hijra (1006 A.D.) Yamínu-d daula fought against Bhátía, one of the dependencies of Hind, which is situated beyond Multán. The chief of the place was named Bahírá. It is a fine city, enclosed with high walls, and a deep ditch. The chief marched out to meet his enemy, and fought for three days with the Musulmáns. On the fourth he fled, and sought to get back into the city; but the Musulmáns reached the gate before the fugitives, overpowered them, and disarmed them. A dreadful slaughter ensued, the women were dishonoured, and the property seized. When Bahírá saw this destruction, he fled with some trusty followers to the tops of the mountains. Mahmúd sent a force in pursuit, which overtook and surrounded the party, and put all the chiefs to the sword. Bahírá saw that no hope was left, so he drew a dagger and killed himself. Mahmúd remained in Bhátía until he had settled its affairs, and drawn up rules for its governance. He then returned towards Ghazna, having appointed a representative at Bhátía to instruct the people who had become Muhammadans. On his journey home he encountered great difficulties from heavy rains and swollen rivers, and great quantities of things belonging to him and his army were carried away by the waters.

Conquest of Multán.

In the year 396 Hijra (1006, A.D.) Sultán Yamínu-d daula fought against Multán. The cause of this was that the ruler of the place, Abú-l Futúh was disaffected, false to his faith, and inclined to heresy (*ilhád*). He had also required the people of his country to follow his opinions, and they had consented. Yamínu-d daula resolved to attack him and marched against him, but the rivers on the road were very large and broad,

[1] [There are some doubtful words in this extract, but the sense appears to be as translated.]

especially the Sihún (Indus), and the enemy was ready to oppose the passage. So Mahmúd sent to Andbál[1] and asked permission to pass through his country to Multán, but the request was refused. Mahmúd resolved therefore to deal with him first, and afterwards to prosecute his original intention. So he entered into his country and overran it; and he killed many of the people, plundered their property, and fired their houses. Andbál fled and Mahmúd followed his traces, like fire in the tracks of Satan, from pass to pass until he reached Kashmír. When Abú-l Futúh heard of this victory, he saw the futility of his rebellion, and sending his property to Sarandíp, he evacuated Multán. Yamínu-d daula then went to Multán, and finding the people infatuated in their heresy, he besieged the place closely, and carried on the fight until he took it by storm. He fined the inhabitants 20,000 dirhams for their rebellion.

Conquest of Mansúra.

After the capture of Somnát, Mahmúd received intelligence that Bhím the chief of Anhalwára had gone to the fort of Kandahat, which is situated about forty parasangs from Somnát between that place and the desert. He marched thither, and when he came in front of the place he questioned some men who were hunting, as to the tide. From them he learned that there was a practicable ford, but that if the wind blew a little, he might be submerged. Mahmúd prayed to the Almighty and then entered the water. He and his forces passed over safely, and drove the enemy out of the place. From thence he returned, intending to proceed against Mansúra, the ruler of which was an apostate Muhammadan. When the news of Mahmúd's approach reached this chief, he fled into the date-palm forests. Mahmúd proceeded against him, and surrounding him and his adherents, many of them were slain, many drowned, and but few escaped. Mahmúd then went to Bhátía, and after reducing the inhabitants to obedience, he returned to Ghazní, where he arrived on the 10th Safar 417 H.

[1] [Anand-pál.]

Revolt and Death of Ahmad Niáltigín.

In the year (4)25 (1034 A.D.), Mas'úd, son of Mahmúd, returned to Hind to destroy the Turks (*al ghuzz*); and Ahmad Niáltigín again exerting himself to excite rebellion in the provinces of Hind, proceeded with all his assembled forces to the territories (*bilád*) of Bálází. Mas'úd sent a numerous army against him, and the chiefs of Hind being averse to his entering into their territories, closed the roads against him. Before the army reached the passage he attacked it, and retreated fighting towards Multán. Several of the Indian chiefs proceeded to Dhátía. He had with him a considerable unbroken force, and the chief of the place not having strength to arrest his progress, Ahmad demanded boats to enable him to cross the river Indus, and these were supplied. In the midst of the stream there was an island, which Ahmad and his adherents perceived, and close by in another direction lay the desert. They did not know that the water was deep there. The Indian chief directed the owners of the boats to transport the fugitives to the island and to return. Ahmad and his adherents remained there, and they had no food but what they had brought with them. They stayed there nine days, and their provisions were consumed. Having even devoured their animals they were reduced to extremity, and resolved to pass through the water; but they had no sooner entered it than they discovered its depth, and, besides this, a great impediment in the mud. The Indian sent over his soldiers against them in boats, who attacked them while they were in that plight, and killed many of them. The sons of Ahmad were taken prisoners, and when Ahmad himself fell into their hands they killed him. His companions also were all either slain, taken prisoners, or drowned.

War between Shahábu-d dín and the King of Benares.

Shahábu-d dín Ghorí, king of Ghazní, sent his slave, Kutbu-d dín, to make war against the provinces of Hind, and this general made an incursion in which he killed many, and returned home with prisoners and booty. The king of Benares was the greatest king in India, and possessed the largest territory, extending lengthwise from the borders of China to the province of Maláwa (Málwá), and in breadth from the sea to within ten days' journey of Lahore. When he was informed of this inroad, he collected his forces, and in the year 590 (1194 A.D.), he entered the territories of the Muhammadans. Shahábu-d dín Ghorí marched forth to oppose him, and the two armies met on the river Jumna,[1] which is a river about as large as the Tigris at Músal. The Hindu prince had seven hundred elephants, and his men were said to amount to a million. There were many nobles in his army. There were Mussulmáns in that country since the days of Mahmúd bin Subuktigín, who continued faithful to the law of Islám, and constant in prayer and good works. When the two armies met there was great carnage; the infidels were sustained by their numbers, the Musulmáns by their courage, but in the end the infidels fled, and the faithful were victorious. The slaughter of the Hindus was immense; none were spared except women and children, and the carnage of the men went on until the earth was weary. Ninety elephants were captured, and of the rest some were killed, and some escaped. The Hindu king was slain, and no one would have recognized his corpse but for the fact of his teeth, which were weak at their roots, being fastened in with golden wire. After the flight of the Hindus Shahábu-d dín entered Benares, and carried off its treasures upon fourteen hundred camels. He then returned to Ghazní. Among the elephants which were captured there was a white one. A person who saw it told me that when the elephants were brought before Shahábu-d dín, and were ordered to salute, they all saluted except the white one. No one should be surprised at what I have said about the elephants, for they understand what is said to them. I myself saw one at Músal with his keeper, which did whatever his keeper told him.

[1] [Tornberg reads ما خون but ما جون "the river Jumna" must be meant. The battle was fought near that river.]

VII.

NIZÁMU-T TAWÁRÍKH

OF

SA'ÍD 'ABDU-LLAH, BAIZÁWÍ.

This "Arrangement or String of Histories" is a small work devoted to general history, well known in Europe, but in too compendious a form to be of any great use, for in some of the dynasties treated of we have little beyond the names of the kings and the dates of their decease. Its value is chiefly attributable to the early period at which it was written.

The author was Abú Sa'íd 'Abdu-llah bin Abú-l Hasan 'Alí Baizáwí.[1] His father was, as well as himself, a "Káziu-l kuzzát," or chief kází, and his grandfather exercised the functions of Imám. He was born at Daizá, a town at a short distance from Shíráz, and was kází, first at Shíráz and afterwards at Tabríz, where he died in the year 685 H., 1280, A.D. Háji Khalfa says he died either in that year or 692 H.[2] This author has obtained great celebrity from his commentary upon the Kurán, entitled *Anwáru-t Tanzíl wa asráru-t Táwíl*—"the lights of revelation and mysteries of allegorical interpretation," which has itself been commented on by many succeeding authors, of which a list is given by Háji Khalfa, in his *Lexicon*, Vol. I.

---

[1] This is what he calls himself in the Preface to the *Nizámu-t Tawárikh*, but Háji Khalfa styles him Nasiru-d dín Abú Sa'íd 'Abdu-llah bin 'Umar Baizáwí. S. de Sacy also calls him Abú-l Kasim, 'Umar his father, and Abú-l Hasan 'Alí his grandfather. In one biography in my possession, he is named Kází Nasiru-d dín Abú-l Khair' Abdu-llah bin 'Umar bin Muhammad bin 'Alí Shírází Baizáwí. The *Haft Iklím* calls him Kází Nasiru-d dín bin Kází Imám Badru-d dín 'Umar bin Fakhru-d dín bin 'Alí.

[2] The two first dates are given by most of the European authorities who follow Háji Khalfa. Rampoldi gives his death in 1286 A.D. or 685 A.H. The *Fakhru-l Wásitta* has a chronogram which gives 691. Abú-l Mahásin and the MS. quoted by Casiri gives 685, and Yáfi'í mentions his death under the annals of 692.

pp, 469-81. This is considered generally the best commentary, and has been largely used by Sale and others. There are several copies of it in Europe, enumerated by De Rossi. It has lately been printed at Leipsig by Professor Fleischer. Baizáwí was the author of other works on law, theology, logic, and grammar, all written in Arabic, but the *Nizámu-t Tawáríkh* is in Persian, in order, as he says, "that it might be of more general use."

A full account of the *Nizámu-t Tawáríkh* has been given by Silvestre de Sacy, in the *Notices des Manuscripts*, Tom. iv. pp. 672-690, from the Appendix of which article it appears that there is another work of the same name, composed by Kází Jalálu-d dín, wazír of Mahmúd the Ghaznivide, in which I am disposed to apprehend some error of name or designation. Amongst other extracts given by him he has translated the brief histories of the Assassins and Atábaks.

There is some doubt about the exact date of the composition of this work. It is generally supposed that it was written about 674 H., but there are dates mentioned in it subsequent to that period. For instance, in the history of the Atábaks, there is one of 686, and towards the close of the Moghal history, there are 684 and 690; and 694 is repeated four times. There appears nothing like interpolation in these passages, and there would therefore appear some reason to suppose that 694 was the real date of composition, or at least of final revision, and that the latest date mentioned by Hájí Khalfa, namely, 699 (A.D. 1299-1300), is the most probable one of the author's death. Still this is opposed to all other authorities. M. Silvestre de Sacy examined two copies of the work in the Bibliothèque Nationale, in one of which he found dates later than 674. He mentions particularly the date of 689 (in my copy 686) in the history of the Atábaks, and he observes, what is very true, that at the beginning of that history their power is said to have commenced in 543, and to have lasted up to the time of composition, 130 years (131 in mine), which fixes the date in 674. It is easy, however, to read 650 for 630. M. de

Sacy does not notice the additions to the Moghal history in either of the copies in the Bibliothéque Nationale. My own copy, which is taken from a very excellent one written in 1108 H., has distinctly in the preface, as well as the conclusion, the year of 694 H. It is to be observed, that in Arabic 90 and 70 are written almost in the same form, when without diacritical marks. I have seen one copy in which the Perso-Moghal history is carried down to 739 H., but that evidently contained additions by the copyist. Altogether, if so many authorities were not arrayed against me, I should prefer fixing the date at 694, instead of 674. The question, however, is not of the least consequence. The work is divided into four books.

CONTENTS.

Book I.—Prophets and Patriarchs from Adam to Núh, pp. 6-12.

Book II.—Kings of Persia to the time of the Musulmáns. 1. Peshdádí; 2. Kaiání; 3. Ashgání; 4. Sassání. Pp. 13-77.

Book III.—Muhammad and his successors, including the Ummayides and 'Abbásides. Pp. 78-119.

Book IV.—Dynasties established in Írán during the time of the 'Abbásides. 1. Saffárí; 2. Sámání; 3. Ghaznivides; Dailime; 5. Saljúkí; 6. Maláhida; 7. Salgharí; 8. Khwárizmí; 9. Moghal. Pp. 119-200.

Size.—Small 8vo. containing 200 pages, each of 11 lines.

The *Nizámu-t tawárikh* is better known in Europe than in India. Besides the copies noticed by S. de Sacy, there is one in the British Museum, No. 16708. Sir W. Ouseley quotes another. Yet it is mentioned by M. Frœhn amongst his Desiderata.[1]

---

[1] Compare *Biographie Universelle*, Tom. iv. p. 67; De Rossi, *Dizionario degli Autori Arabi*, p. 49; Ahmad Rází's *Haft Iklím*, p. 190; D'Herbelot's *Bibliothèque Orientale*, Tom. v. p. 721; M. Frœhn's *Indications Bibliographiques*, No. 161; Rampoldi's *Annali Musulmani*, Tom. i. p. 339, Tom. ix. p. 445; T. W. Beale's *Miftáhu-t tawárikh*, p. 104; Ouseley's *Jehánárá*, p. xvi.; Casiri's *Bibliotheca Arab.*, Tom. i. p. 491; S. de Sacy's *Anthol.*, p. 37.

Extracts.

The Kings of Ghazní.

Their number amounts to twelve, and their rule endured for one hundred and sixty-one years. The origin of this family dates from the middle of the days of the Dailamites, but as its members were great men under the Sámánís, I am desirous that my accounts of these two dynasties should not be separated. The following are the names of these kings, viz.:—1. Sultán Yamínu-d daula Abú-l kásim Mahmúd, son of Násiru-d dín Subuktigín; 2. Mas'úd, son of Mahmúd; 3. Muhammad Makhúl (the blind), son of Mahmúd; 4. Maudúd, son of Mas'úd; 5. Mas'úd, son of Maudúd; 6. 'Alí, son of Mas'úd; 7. 'Abdu-r Rashíd, son of Mahmúd; 8. Ibráhím, son of Mas'úd; 9. Mas'úd, son of Ibráhím; 10. Arslán Sháh, son of Mas'úd; 11. Bahrám Sháh, son of Mas'úd; 12. Khusrú Sháh, son of Bahrám Sháh. Násiru-d dín died in the year 387 H. (997 A.D.) and the command of his troops descended to Mahmúd by inheritance, and by confirmation of Núh, son of Mansúr. His victory over 'Abdu-l Malik, when that chieftain was put to flight, added much to his power, and he was confirmed in the government of Khurásán and Sijistán, and he received a robe of honour with the title of Sultán from the Khalif, who also made a treaty with him. In consequence of the complaints of the oppression practised by the descendants of Fakhru-d dín Dailamí, he marched towards Júrján and 'Irák, and took the country from them. Afterwards he turned his arms towards Hind, and conquered many of its cities and forts. He demolished the Hindú temples[1] and gave prevalence to the Muhammadan faith. He ruled with great justice, and he stands unparalleled among all the Muhammadan kings. He summoned Isráíl son of Sulaimán, the Saljúk, from Máwaráu-n Nahr, and apprehending danger from the immense number of that tribe, he sent him to the fort of Kálinjar in Hind, where he remained till he died. The capture of this Saljúk chief

---

[1] [The two following lines are not in Sir H. Elliott's MS.]

was the cause of the weakness of his descendants. Mahmúd Subuktigín died in A.H. 420 (1029 A.D.).

Sultán Mas'úd.

According to the will of Mahmúd, his son Mas'úd was to have the government of Khurásán, 'Irák, and Persia, and his second son, Muhammad, the kingdom of Ghazní and the country of Hind. Mas'úd requested his brother to have his name read along with his own in the Khutba, but this was not complied with, therefore Mas'úd marched to invade Ghazní. Before he reached there, Muhammad was taken prisoner by Yúsuf, son of Subuktigín, and sent to the fort of Bulbad.[1] Mas'úd, after his arrival at Ghazní, sent Yúsuf to prison, and became master of all the dominions of his father. In his time the Saljúks crossed the Jíhún and invaded Khurásán. He fought with them and made peace with them several times, but being defeated in A.H. 432 (1040 A.D.) he returned to Ghazní where his brother Muhammad had regained power in his absence. On his arrival he was consigned to a fort, and Ahmad, son of Muhammad went direct from his father to the fort and there slew him, A.H. 433 (1041 A.D.)

Sultán Muhammad, Makhúl.

Sultán Muhammad Makhúl bin Mahmúd ruled for nearly four years over the dominions of Ghazní, after the death of his father. When his brother was slain, Maudúd, son of the deceased, armed against him, and proving victorious, put him and his sons to death.

Sultán Maudúd.

Maudúd, having taken revenge for his father's death, sat on the throne for nearly seven years, and brought the country of his uncle under his dominion. He died in A.H. 441 (1049 A.D.).

Sultán Mas'úd II.

Mas'úd, son of Maudúd, was quite a boy at the death of his

---
[1] Another copy reads "Manpúl."

father. The Government was carried on for a few days in his name, but the ministers and nobles then conspired to place the royal crown on the head of his uncle.

Sultán 'Alí.

When Sultán 'Alí, son of Mas'úd, obtained the throne, 'Abdu-r Rashíd, son of Mahmúd, who for many years had been in prison, contrived to escape, and having collected an army, 'Alí fled before him, and was discomfited.

Sultán 'Abdu-r Rashíd.

He reigned nearly seven years, and died A.H. 445 (1053 A.D.).

Sultán Ibráhím.[1]

Sultán Ibráhím, son of Mas'úd, ruled for a period extending from A.H. 450 to 492 (1058 to 1098). He raised no palaces for himself, but only mosques and colleges for the great and glorious God.

Sultán Mas'úd III.

Mas'úd, son of Ibráhím, occupied the throne for sixteen years, and expired in A.H. 508 (1114 A.D.).

Sultán Arslán Sháh.

Sultán Arslán Sháh, by his wisdom and prudence, obtained the succession to his father Mas'úd. His brother Bahrám then fled in alarm, and sought refuge with his maternal uncle, Sultán Sanjar, the Saljúk, whom he brought against Ghazní. A battle ensued, in which Arslán Sháh was defeated, and Sanjar having placed Bahrám on the throne, returned to Khurásán. Soon after his departure, Arslán Sháh attacked Bahrám, who was again obliged to fly, but being once more assisted by Sanjar, with a large army, he went up against Ghazní, gained a victory, and put Arslán Sháh to death, in A.H. 512 (1118 A.D.).

[1] [The author passes unnoticed the interval of five years which he has left between the reigns of 'Abdu-r Rashíd and Ibráhím, and makes no mention of the reign of Farrukh-zád.]

Sultán Bahrám Sháh.

Bahrám Sháh, son of Mas'úd, had reigned some days, when he was attacked in Ghazní by 'Aláu-d dín Husain, son of Hasan, the first of the kings of Ghor. Bahrám Sháh fled before him from Ghazní, in which place 'Aláu-d dín established his own brother, Saifu-d dín, and then returned. Afterwards Bahrám Sháh came back to Ghazní, and ordered Saifu-d dín to be seated on a cow, and paraded round the city. When 'Aláu-d dín heard of this he became greatly infuriated, and marched with a large army towards Ghazní, but Bahrám died before his arrival. He was succeeded by his son, Khusrú Sháh.

Sultán Khusrú Sháh.

A few days after his accession 'Aláu-d dín arrived, and Khusrú fled to the country of Hind. 'Aláu-d dín then plundered Ghazní, and massacred a great number of its inhabitants. He left there his nephews, Ghiyásu-d dín Abu'l Fath Muhammad, and Shahábu-d dín Abú-l Muzaffar, sons of Sám, son of Hasan. They having succeeded in the capture of Khusrú Sháh, by various expedients through which he was lulled into security, kept him prisoner in a fort. They subjugated all the countries which had been under the rule of the kings of Ghazní, and and chose Dehlí for their residence. Khusrú Sháh died in A.H. 555 (1160 A.D.), and with him ended the Ghaznivide dynasty.

After some time Ghiyásu-d dín died, and the country remained in the sole and absolute possession of Shahábu-d dín to the time of Sultán Muhammad Takash, when he was assassinated by the *Malahida* (Isma'íleans) in Hirát. He was succeeded in the kingdom of Hind by Sultán Shamsu-d dín Altamsh, one of his slaves (*mawáli*), with whose descendants it remains to this day. The only names which the compiler knows of the Ghorian dynasty who ruled in Hind are these three:—'Aláu-d dín Husain Jahán-soz, Ghiyásu-d dín Muhammad, Shahábu-d dín Muhammad,

VIII.

TABAKÁT-I NÁSIRÍ

OF

MINHÁJU-S SIRÁJ.

[This is a general history from the earliest times up to 658 Hijra (A.D. 1259). The author was Abú 'Umar Minháju-d dín, 'Usmán ibn Siráju-d dín al Júzjání. In the course of his work he mentions many interesting facts concerning himself and his family. He tells us that his ancestor in the third degree, Imám 'Abdu-l Khálik, came from Júzján[1] to Ghazní to seek a wife, in compliance with a command which he several times received in dreams. Here he gained the good graces of the reigning monarch, Ibráhím, and received in marriage one of his forty daughters, all of whom were "married to illustrious nobles or learned men of repute." They had a son named Ibráhím, who was father of Mauláná Minháju-d dín 'Usmán, who was father of Mauláná Siráju-d dín, who was father of our author, Minháju-s Siráj. Siráju-d dín was a man of some distinction. He was appointed Kázi of the army of Hindustán by Muhammad Ghori in A.H. 582 (1186 A.D.), and his son refers to him by his titles of "*Ajúbatu-z Zamán afsahu-l 'Ajam*—the wonder of the time and the most eloquent man of Persia."

The author of this work, Minháju-s Siráj, came from Ghor to Sind, U'ch and Multán in 624 A.H. (A.D. 1227), and his character for learning must then have been already established, as he tells us that the Firozí College at U'ch was placed under his charge. In the year following, Sultán Shamsu-d dín Altamsh led his armies from Dehli to suppress Násiru-d dín Kubácha, who

[1] [The country between Merv and Balkh.]

had succeeded in gaining sovereign authority in those quarters, and after the defeat and death of Kubácha, Minháju-s Siráj was admitted to an interview with Altamsh, and returned in his train to Dehli, where he arrived in Rámazán, 625 (August, 1229). In 629 A.H. he followed Altamsh to the siege of Gwalior, where he was appointed one of the court preachers, and soon afterwards was made "law-officer, and director of the preaching, and of all religious, moral, and judicial affairs." He abandoned this position in 635, when the forces of Sultán Raziya marched there. After the death of this able but unfortunate queen, we find him at Dehli, writing congratulatory verses upon the accession of her successor, Bahrám Sháh, and when a panic fell upon the city at the threatened incursion of the Moghals, he was called upon to preach and conciliate the minds of the people. Soon after this, in A.H. 639 (1211 A.D.) Bahrám Sháh made him Kázi of the capital and of all his territories. But he did not hold this office long. Bahrám Sháh was deposed, and slain at the end of 639 H., and Minháju-s Siráj immediately afterwards tendered his resignation.

In Hijra 640, he started for Lakhnauti, and stayed there until the end of 642. This residence in the capital of Bengal afforded him opportunities for acquiring accurate information respecting that outlying Musulmán territory, and makes all that he says upon that subject of especial value.

At the end of 642, he returned to Dehli and arrived there early in the following year. He was immediately appointed Principal of the Násiriya College, and superintendent of its endowments. He was also made Kází of Gwalior, and preacher in the metropolitan mosque. At the beginning of 644 H. (1246 A.D.) Násiru-d dín Mahmúd ascended the throne, and our author received a prize for his congratulatory ode on the occasion, specimens of which he inserts in his history. The full tide of prosperity had now set in upon him; he received many honours from the Sultán Násiru-d dín, and from the distinguished noble whom he calls Ulúgh Khán-i Mu'azzam, who succeeded Násiru-d dín on the throne, and is better known as Ghiyásu-d dín Balban. The author records the grant of a village which he received in *in'ám*, and mentions with great complacency the many favours of which he was the recipient. Finally he was honoured with the title of *Sadr-i Jahán*, and was again made Kází of the state and magistrate of the capital.

In honour of his patron, Núsiru-d dín, he named his work *Tabakát-i Násiri*, and he breaks off his history rather abruptly in the fifteenth year of that monarch's reign, intending, as he said, to resume his pen if life and opportunity were afforded him. The date of his death is not known, but he probably survived Násiru-d dín, as the period of that monarch's reign is stated in this work as extending to twenty-two years, which, however, is an error, as it lasted only twenty years. The eulogistic way in which he always speaks of the successor of Násiru-d dín would induce the belief that the work appeared in the reign of that Sultán, and the fact is proved by his more than once offering up an ejaculatory prayer for the continuance of his reign.

The following careful analysis of the contents of the history has been borrowed from Mr. Morley's catalogue of the MSS. of the Royal Asiatic Society:—

"The Tabakát-i Násiri is divided into twenty-three books, and contains as follows:—

"Author's Preface, in which he dedicates his work to Abú-l Muzaffar Núsiru-d dín Mahmúd Ibnu-s Sultán Altamsh, king of Dehli.

"Book I.—Account of the Prophets and Patriarchs; of Jesus Christ; of Ishmael and the ancestors of Muhammad; and a history of Muhammad himself to the day of his death.

"Book II.—History of the first four Khalífas; of the descendants of 'Ali, and of the ten Mubashshir.

"Book III.—The Khalífas of the Bani Umnayya.

"Book IV.—The Khalífas of the Bani 'Abbás, to the extinction of the Khálifat in A.H. 656 (A.D. 1258).

"Book V.—The history of the early kings of Persia, comprising the Peshdádians, the Kaiánians, the Ashkánians, the Sásánians, and the Akásira from Naushirwán to Yazdajird.

"Book VI.—History of the kings of Yaman, from Hárisu-r Ráísh to Bádán, who was converted to the Islám.

"Book VII.—History of the Táhirides from the Táhir Zúu-l Yumnain to that of Muhammad bin Táhir, the last king of the dynasty, who was conquered by Ya'kúb Lais, in A.H. 259 (A.D. 872).

"Book VIII.—History of the Saffárides from Ya'kúb Lais to the death of 'Amrú Lais in A.H. 289 (A.D. 901).

"Book IX.—History of the Sámánides from their origin to A.H. 389 (A.D. 998) when 'Abdu-l Malik bin Núh was sent as a captive to Uzjand.

"Book X.—History of the Buwaihides from their origin to the time of Abú-l Fawáris Sharafu-d Daula.

"Book XI.—History of the Ghaznivides from Subuktigín to the death of Khusrú Malik in A.H. 598 (A.D. 1201).

"Book XII.—History of the Saljúks of Persia from their origin to the death of Sultán Sanjar in A.H. 552 (A.D. 1157); of the Saljúks of Rúm and 'Irák, from their origin to the time of Ruknu-d dín Kilij Arslán; and an account of Tughril bin Tughril, to his death, and the conquest of 'Irák by Takash, King of Khwárizm.

"Book XIII.—History of the Sanjáriya kings, viz., 1. The Atábaks of 'Irák and Azarbáiján from the time of the Atábak Alptigín to that of the Atábak Abú Bakr bin Muhammad. 2. The Atábaks of Fárs, from Sankar to the time of the Atábak Abú Bakr bin Sa'd bin Zangí A.H. 658 (A.D. 1259) when the author wrote. 3. The Kings of Naishápúr from Maliku-l Muaiyidu-s Sanjarí to the defeat and capture of Sanjar Sháh bin Tughán Sháh, by Takash, king of Khwárizm.

"Book XIV.—History of the kings of Nimrúz and Sijistán from Táhir bin Muhammad to Táju-d dín Niáltigín Khwárizmí who was slain by the Mongols in A.H. 625 (A.D. 1227).

"Book XV.—History of the Kurdíya kings, viz: The Atábaks

of Syria, Núru-d dín Zangí and Maliku-s Sálih; and the Ayyúbites of Egypt, from the time of Ayyúb to the death of Maliku-s Sálih bin Maliku-l Kámil.

"Book XVI.—History of the Khwárizmians, from their origin to the death of Jalálu-d dín Mankbarní, in A.H. 629 (A.D. 1231).

"Book XVII.—History of the Shansabániya Sultáns of Ghor, from the origin of the family to the time of 'Aláu-d dín Muhammad bin Abú 'Alí, the twenty-second and last king, who surrendered the city of Fíroz-Koh to Muhammad Khwárizm Sháh in A.H. 612 (A.D. 1215).

"Book XVIII.—The Shansabániya Kings of Bámián and Tukháristán, from Fakhru-d dín Mas'úd, the first king, to the time of the fifth monarch, 'Aláu-d dín Mas'úd, who was slain by his nephew Jalálu-d dín 'Alí.

"Book XIX.—History of the Shansabániya Sultáns of Ghaznín, from the time of Saifu-d dín Súrí, who conquered Bahrám Sháh Ghaznawí, to that of Kutbu-d dín Aibak, who expelled Táju-d dín Yaldúz, in A.H. 603 (A.D. 1206).

"Book XX.—The Múizziya Sultans of Hindustán, comprising the history of Kutbu-d dín Aibak, and of his son Árám Sháh, whose capital was Dehlí; of Násiru-d dín Kubácha al Mu'izzí and Baháu-d dín Tughril al Mu'izzí; and of the first four Khiljí princes who reigned at Lakhnautí or Gaur, ending with Husámu-d dín Ghiyásu-d dín, who was defeated and slain by Násiru-d dín Mahmúd bin Shamsu-d dín Altamsh, governor of Behár, in A.H. 634 (A.D. 1226).

"Book XXI.—History of the Shamsiya Sultáns of Hindustan, whose capital was Dehlí, from the time of Shamsu-d dín Altamsh, who expelled Árám Sháh from the throne in A.H. 607 (A.D. 1210) to A.H. 658 (A.D. 1259), when Násiru-d dín Mahmúd, the seventh king of the dynasty, reigned in Dehlí, and the author completed the present history.

"Book XXII.—Account of the most eminent nobles, viceroys, governors, etc., who flourished under the Shamsiya dynasty, from A.H. 625 (A.D. 1227) to the author's own time, ending with a life of Ikhú-d dín Alú Khán Ilalban who was the wazír of Násiru-d dín Mahmúd, and who afterwards, on the death of that monarch, ascended the throne of Dehlí without opposition.

"Book XXIII.—On the incursions of the infidels; comprising an account of the war between Sultán Sanjar Saljúkí and the tribes of Kará Khitá; of the conquest of Turkistán by Muhammad Khwárizm Sháh, and the defeat and death of Gúr Khán, the Kará Khitáian, in A.H. 607 (A.D. 1210); and of Changíz Khán and his descendants, viz:—Jújí Khán, Uktái Khán, Chaghatái Khán, Kuyúk Khán, Bátu Khán, Mangú Khán, Hulákú Khán, and Barakah Khán, to A.H. 658 (A.D. 1259)."

The Tabakát-i Násirí is held in very high esteem both in India and Europe. Firishta and others refer to it as an excellent work of high authority; Anquetil du Perron calls it a "precious work," and Elphinstone mentions it as a work of the highest celebrity. Stewart in his History of Bengal, follows it very closely, and considers it "a very valuable book." These encomiums are not altogether undeserved; it is written in a plain, unaffected style, and the language is considered very correct. The author but rarely indulges in high-flown eulogy, but narrates his facts in a plain, straightforward manner, which induces a confidence in the sincerity of his statements, and the accuracy of his knowledge. He appears to have been industrious in collecting information from trustworthy persons, and he often mentions his authority for the facts he records. Still he is very meagre in his details, and Mr. Morley justly observes, "many portions of the history are too concise to be of much use." He is also particularly disappointing occasionally in the brevity with which he records important matters about which he might have obtained full information, such, for instance, as the irruption of the "infidels of Changíz Khán" into Bengal, as far as the walls of Lakhnautí, in 642 H. (1245 A.D.)

Another defect of the work arises from its plan, which necessitates repetition, and requires events to be related in more than one place. Thus, the record of the reign of Násiru-d dín and the memoir of Ulugh Khán (Ghiyásu-d dín) go over the same ground, and record many of the same facts but with considerable variety of detail.]

It is strange (says Sir Henry Elliot) that the Tabakát-i Nasiri should be so scarce in India. I know of only one copy besides my own, although there is no work for which I have searched so much.[1] It is in one of the royal libraries of Lucknow, and though several of my correspondents had declared that it was not to be found there, I discovered it at last by making a man ascend a ladder, and read out the title of every work in the library. After the lapse of almost three hours the name was read out. The work is by no means uncommon in Europe. Scarcely any one is so much quoted by Orientalists. It is possible that the reason of its being so scarce in India is that it vituperates the Mughals, and shows the consternation which they occasioned at the time of their first conquests, inasmuch as the author represents them as manifest signs of the approach of the day of judgment.[2]

[The portions of the Tabakát-i Násiri which relate to India have been printed in the Bibliotheca Indica, under the superintendance of Major Lees, in a volume of 450 pages. This contains the 11th and the 17th to the 22d Tabakats or books. Major Lees' preface to this volume states the reasons for thus limiting the publication, and contains some critical observations upon the

[1] [Stewart describes a copy belonging to Tippu's Library said to have been copied by the author himself.]

[2] It was the terror arising from the same cause which induced European writers to give these hordes the name of Tartars. The correct word is Tatars, which signifies a tributary people, and though improperly applied to the Mongols themselves, yet represented the great majority of the races which swelled their ranks. Superstitious monks supposed them to have come from the infernal regions, and hence called them Tartars. St. Louis writes to his queen Blanche, "This divine consolation will always exalt our souls, that in the present danger of the Tartars, either we shall push them back into the Tartarus whence they are come, or they will bring us all into Heaven." Klaproth, *Asia Polyglotta*, p. 202. See also Schmidt, *Forschungen im Gebiete der Völker mittel Asiens*, p. 52; and Pallas, *Sammlung Historischer Nachrichten über die Mongolischen Volkerschaften*, vol. ii. p. 429; De la Croix *Histoire d' Genghiscan*, p. 63.

value of this work, and of others which furnish the materials for the history of the early Muhammadan rulers of India.[1]

Size of Sir H. Elliot's MS.—Small folio, 12 by 8 inches. Seventeen lines in each page.]

EXTRACTS.

TABAKAT XI.

HISTORY OF THE GHAZNIVIDE SOVEREIGNS.

[Page 6 to 27 of the Printed Text.]

Imám Abú-l Fazl al Hasan Baihakí relates in the Tárikh-i Násirí, that Sultán Sa'íd Mahmúd heard from his father, Amír Subuktigín,[2] that his (Subuktigín's) father was called Kará-bahkam. His name was Jauk (troop), and in Turkí they call a troop bahkam; so that the meaning of the name Kará-bahkam is "black troop." Whenever the Turks in Turkistán heard his name they fled before him on account of his activity and courage.

Imám Muhammad 'Alí Abu-l Kásim Hamádí says in his Tárikh-i Majdúl, that Amír Subuktigín was a descendant of King Yazdajird. When this monarch was slain in a mill in the country of Merv, in the reign of the commander of the faithful 'Usmán, his followers and dependants (atbá' wa ashyá'), came to Turkistán, and entering into intermarriages with the people of that country after two or three generations (their descendants) became Turks. Their palaces in this country are still standing. The following is a genealogical table of this race:—Amír Subuk-

---

[1] See Elphinstone's History; Stewart's History of Bengal, and his Catalogue of Tippoo's Library; Jour. R. As. Soc. xvii. 138; Jour. des Savants, 1840, p. 221; Jour. Asiatique, IV. serie, vol. iii.; Collection Orient. I. 198; Hammer, Goldene Horde, I. xv. xliii.; Haji Khalfa, iv. 163; Ouseley, Jehánárá, s. 7.

[2] Hammer Purgstall (Gemaldesaal, iv. 102) says, on the authority of the Farhang-i Shu'úrí, that the only correct spelling of this name is "Sabuktigín," or, according to the system adopted in this work, Síbuktigín, but Ibn Khallikán distinctly says the word should be spelt Subuktigín. [A carefully written MS. of 'Utbí in the British Museum writes it "Sabuktikín." The orthography of all these Turkí names is very variable and unsettled. Historians differ from each other and are often at variance with themselves.—Jour. R. A. S. ix. 268.]

tigín, son of Jauk Kará-balíkam, who was the son of Kará Arslán, the son of Kará-malat, son of Kará Nu'mán, son of Fíroz, son of Yazdajird, who was the sovereign of Persia,[1]—but God knows the truth.

I.—*Amíru-l Ghází Násiru-d dín Subuktigín.*

Imám Abú-l Fazl Baihakí writes that Nasr Hájí was a trader in the reign of 'Abdu-l Malik Núh Sámání. He bought Subuktigín, and took him to Dukhárá as a slave. The marks of wisdom and activity were stamped upon his forehead, and he was purchased by the Lord Chamberlain (*Amír hájib*), Alptigín. In the service of this nobleman he went to Tukháristán, and when Alptigín was appointed governor of that place he continued to serve him. In the course of events Alptigín came afterwards to Ghaznín, when he conquered the country of Záwulistán, and wrested Ghaznín from the hands of Amír Anúk.[2]

Eight years afterwards Alptigín died,[3] and was succeeded by his son Is'hák. This chief fought with Anúk, and being defeated he went to Dukhárá, where he succeeded in obtaining assistance from Amír Mansúr Núh. Thus strengthened, he returned and retook Ghazní. One year later he expired, and Bilkátigín,[4] the

---

[1] A long account of the parentage of Subuktigín is given in the Jámi'u-t Tawáríkh, in which his descent is traced from Toghril, king of Merv. Firishta follows the genealogy here given. The Raumtu-s Safá does not notice either. Briggs, Ferishta I. 13; Osmáldemal, IV. p. 103.

[2] [Mr. Thomas published a translation of this passage in the Jour. R. As. Society, vol. xvii. p. 141. In his translation, and in the Munshi's original translation from the MS., the word "amír" does not appear, but the editors of the printed text must have had authority for it. The word is important, because Mr. Thomas takes "Anúk" to be a local, not a personal or tribal appellation, and proposes to change the orthography so as to make the word to be "Lambak," *i.e.* "Lamghán." If the name is a local one we must here read "Amír of Anúk." I have my doubts upon this, and I cannot acquiesce in the change of "Anúk" to "Lambak." The printed text gives "Anúk," and the MSS. of the India Library, of the R. A. Society, and of Paris, agree in this orthography. Sir H. Elliot's MS. has "Ahúk." In a previous page (181) we have had it as "Edhak," and Mr. Thomas says it is also written "Láyak." The change of any of these forms to "Lambak" is a bold one, and I prefer adhering to the best authorized form, although we are unable to identify it with any known name.]

[3] [There are coins, one of them at least undisputed, dated a. 317, bearing the name of "Albtigín."—See Note in the Appendix on the Coins.]

[4] [The printed text here gives the name "Milkátigín," but Sir H. Elliot's MS.

chief of the Turks, was raised to his place. This chief was a very just and religious man, and was one of the greatest warriors in the world. He died after a reign of two years. Amír Subuktigín was in his service. Bilkátigín was succeeded by Amír Pari,[1] who was a very depraved man. A party of the inhabitants of Ghazní opened communications with Abú 'Alí Anúk, and invited him back. Abú 'Alí obtained the aid of the son of the king of Kábul,[2] but when they came into the vicinity (*hadd*) of Charkh,[3] Subuktigín with five hundred Turks fell upon them, and defeated them. He put a great number to the sword, and took many prisoners. He also captured two elephants, and carried them to Ghazní. After the achievement of this victory the people, who were disgusted with Pari on account of his wickedness (*fasád*), raised Sabuktigín with unanimous consent to the chieftainship of Ghazní. On the twenty-seventh of Sha'bán, A.H. 366 (April, 977), on Friday, he came out of the fort with the umbrella, jewels, and banners, and proceeded to the Jámi' Masjid, where he was confirmed in the government and sovereignty of the country. He carried his arms from Ghaznín to different countries, and brought Zamín-dáwar,[4] Kusdár, Bámián, the whole of Tukháristán and Ghor into his possession. On the side of India he defeated Jaipál at the head of a large army and numerous elephants. He also drove back Dughrá Khán, of Káshghar, (from his attacks upon) the Sámánian dynasty. He then went to Balkh, and restored the chief of Bukhárá to his throne. In his time great exploits were performed, and all the sources of internal dissensions in Khurásán were eradicated.

has "Bilkátigín," which is correct. The elevation of Bilkátigín is a fact unnoticed by every other known historian, but it supported by the evidence of the Jámi'u-l Hikáyát, and it is incontestibly proved by a unique coin bearing his name, and dated A.H. 359 (A.D. 969). See *Jour. R. A. S.* xvii. 142.]

[1] ["Mari" in Sir H. E.'s MS., and "Pirí" in Mr. Thomas' translation of this passage.]   [2] [The Munshí's translation had "Mír Sháh of Kabúl."]

[3] [Var. "Kharj."—Charkh has been identified with a village of that name in Lohgar. —See Jour. R. A. S. xvii. 141. Ayín-i Akbarí II. p. 181. Erskine's Babr. p. 48.]

[4] [Dáwar or Zamín-dáwar is the country on the Helmand, between Sijistán and Ghor.]

In the month of Shawwál, A.H. 384 (November, 994), the command of Khurásán was conferred on Amír Mahmúd, under the title of Saifu-d daula, and Amír Subuktigín received the title of Násiru-d dín. He expelled Abú-l hasan Saimjúr, and Khurásán was cleared of its enemies. Amír Subuktigín was a wise, just, brave, and religious man, faithful to his agreements, truthful in his words, and not avaricious for wealth. He was kind and just to his subjects, and the Almighty God had bestowed upon him all the great qualities which are admirable in nobles and princes. The length of his reign was twenty years, and of his life fifty-six years. He died in the vicinity of Balkh, at the village of Barmal Madrúí, A.H. 386 (996 A.D.).[1]

II.—*Reign of the great King Yamínu-d daula Mahmúd Nizámu-d dín Abú-l Kásim Mahmúd, son of Subuktigín.*

Sultán Mahmúd was a great monarch. He was the first Muhammadan king who received the title of Sultán from the Khalíf. He was born on the night of Thursday, the tenth of Muharram, A.H. 361[1] (2nd October, 971), in the seventh year after the time of Bilkátigín. A moment (*sá'at*) before his birth, Amír Subuktigín saw in a dream that a tree sprang up from the fire-place in the midst of his house, and grew so high that it covered the whole world with its shadow. Waking in alarm from his dream, he began to reflect upon the import of it. At that very moment a messenger came, bringing the tidings that the Almighty had given him a son. Subuktigín greatly rejoiced, and said, I name the child Mahmúd. On the same night that he was born, an idol temple in India, in the vicinity of Parsháwar, on the banks of the Sind, fell down.

* * * * *

Mahmúd was a man of great abilities, and is renowned as one of the greatest champions of Islám. He ascended the throne in

---

[1] [The coins of Subuktigín in some variety are extant.—See Note in the Appendix.]
[2] [Firishta gives the date as 9th Muharram, 357 H., and he has been followed by Elphinstone.—Briggs' *Firishta*, I. 33; Elphinstone, 323.]

Balkh, in the year 387 H. (997 A.D.), and received investiture by the Khalífa Al Kádir bi-llah. His influence upon Islám soon became widely known, for he converted as many as a thousand idol-temples into mosques, subdued the cities of Hindustán, and vanquished the Ráís of that country. He captured Jaipál, who was the greatest of them, kept him at Yazd (!), in Khurásán, and gave orders so that he was bought for eighty dirams.[1] He led his armies to Nahrwála and Gujarát, carried off the idol (*mandí*) from Somnát, and broke it into four parts. One part he deposited in the Jámi' Masjid of Ghazní, one he placed at the entrance of the royal palace, the third he sent to Mecca, and the fourth to Medina. 'Unsurí composed a long *Kasída* on this victory. [*The story of his return from Somnát through the desert of Sind follows* (see supra, p. 191), *and an account is given of the state and pomp of his Court.*] He died in the year 421 H. (1030 A.D.), in the thirty-sixth year of his reign, and at sixty-one years of age.

III.—*Muhammad bin Mahmúd Jalálu-d daula.*[2]

Jalálu-d daula Muhammad was a good amiable man. Many curious poems are attributed to him. When his father Mahmúd died, his brother Mas'úd was in 'Irák, and the nobles of the court of Mahmúd resolved upon placing Muhammad on the throne, which they did in the year 421 H. (1030 A.D.). He was a man of gentle temper, and had not the energy necessary for governing a kingdom. A party of the friends of Mas'úd wrote to him in 'Irák, and that prince gathered a force, with which he marched upon Ghazní. When intelligence of his design reached Ghazní, Muhammad prepared an army and went out to meet his brother. 'Alí Karíb was Hájib and commander-in-chief. When

[1] The meaning of this passage is obscure. The text runs thus :—

جیپال را .... بگرفت و در من یزید بخراسان بداشت و بفرمود تا بهشتاد درم اورا بخریدند

[2] [Note in the Text.—" Names of the sons of Muhammad, Mayidu-d daula Ahmad, 'Abdu-r Rahmán, 'Abdu-r Rahím."]

they reached Takínábád[1] they heard of Mas'úd's approach, so they seized upon Muhammad, blinded him, and put him in prison. 'Alí Kuríb then led his army on to Hirát to meet Mas'úd. When he came within a stage of that place, he went to wait upon the Sultán, but Mas'úd ordered him to be made prisoner, and his whole force to destroyed. On this occasion Muhammad reigned for seven months. When Mas'úd was killed at Márikala, Sultán Muhammad was brought out of prison, and although he was blind he was once more placed upon the throne. He then marched at the head of his army towards Ghazní, but Maudúd, son of Mas'úd, came forth to avenge his father, met his uncle in battle, defeated him, and slew him and his children. The second time he reigned four months. His age was forty-five years when his death occurred, in the year 432 H.

IV.—*Násiru-d dín Allah Mas'údu-sh Shahíd (the Martyr).*[2]

Násiru-d dín Allah was the appellation of this prince, but his family name was Abú Mas'úd. He and his brother Sultán Muhammad were born on the same day. Sultán Mas'úd, the martyr, ascended the throne in A.H. 422 (1031 A.D.). He was so exceedingly generous that people used to call him "the second 'Alí," and for his bravery they named him "the second Rustam." No man could lift his battle-axe from the ground with one hand, and even an elephant could not stand before him. His father envied his strength, and used to keep him under control. He (Mahmúd) kept Muhammad at Ghazní, and at length he obtained authority from the Khalíf to place the name and titles of Muhammad in the Khutba before those of Mas'úd. Khwája Abú Nasr Mishkán says: "When the letters (of the Khalíf) were read in Mahmúd's court, it was felt by us, and by all the princes and great men, to be a heavy blow, for marks of intelligence and courage were apparent on the brow of Mas'úd. When

---

[1] [The largest town in Garmsir.—See *infra.*]
[2] [Note in one MS.—" Names of the children of Sultán Mas'úd:—Muhammad, Maujúd, Maudúd, Ibráhím, Faid-yár, Farrukh-zád, Shujá', Murád Sháh, 'Alí."

the prince came forth from the presence of his father, I, Abú Nasr Mishkán went after him and said to him, "O prince, this postponement of your name in the letter of the Khalíf is very offensive to your servants." The prince said, "Don't grieve about it, the sword is a truer prophet than the pen." He then told me to return. I had no sooner got back than the informers told the Sultán Mahmúd of my devotion to Mas'úd. He sent for me, and I waited upon him. He asked me why I went after Mas'úd, and what I had said to him. I related exactly all that had passed, without reserve, for by concealment my life would have been imperilled. The Sultán then said, "I know that Mas'úd excels Muhammad in every respect, and after my death the kingdom will devolve upon him, but I take this trouble now on behalf of Muhammad, that the poor fellow may enjoy some honour and gratification during my lifetime, for after my death it will not be so safe for him. May God have mercy on him."

Abú Nasr Mishkán goes on to say:—"In this incident two things surprised me very much. The first was the answer which Mas'úd so kindly and discreetly gave me. The second was the quickness and strict control of Mahmúd, from whom this little attention of mine could not be concealed." When Sultán Mahmúd took 'Irák he placed Mas'úd on the throne of that country, and before that period Hirát and Khurásán had been ruled in his name. After he ascended the throne of Spáhán (Ispahán) he took the countries of Re, Kazwín, Hamadán, and Táram,[1] and he overcame the Dailamites. Several times he received robes of honour from the Khalifate. After the death of Mahmúd he came to Ghazní, and took possession of his father's kingdom. Several times he led his armies to India, and waged religious war. Twice he went to Tabaristán and Mázandarán. Towards the end of his reign the Saljúks made inroads, and three times he scattered their forces in the neighbourhood of Marv and Sarakhs. But as it was the will of God that the

[1] [Here written with *ee*. The Marásidu-l Ittilá' writes it with *u*, and says the place is situated in the hills between Kazwin and Jílán.]

kingdom of Khurásán should come into the hands of the Saljúks, he eventually fought a bloody battle with them for three days at Tálikán.[1] On the third day, which was a Friday, the Sultán was defeated, and retreated by way of Gharjistán to Ghazní. In panic he collected his treasures and went towards India, but in Márikala[2] his Turkí and Hindí slaves revolted, took him prisoner, and raised Muhammad to the throne. They sent Mas'úd to the fort of Kírí,[3] and there he was slain in the year 432 H. (1040 A.D.). His age was forty-five years, and he had reigned nine years.

V.—*Maudúd, son of Mas'úd, son of Mahmúd*.[4]

Shahábu-d daula Abú Sa'd Maudúd, son of Násiru-d dín Allah Mas'úd, upon receiving the news of his father's assassination, ascended the throne. When his father, Mas'úd, started for Hindustán, he was appointed to act as vicegerent over Ghazní and its dependencies, and it was in the year 432 H. (1040 A.D.), that he mounted the throne. To avenge his father he collected an army, and set out towards Hindustán, against his uncle Muhammad. The opposite party had taken Muhammad out of prison, and had seated him on the throne. The nobles of

---

[1] [A city between Merv and Balkh. Istakhri and Ibn Haukal call it the largest city in Khurásán, and say it was three days' journey from Merv. Firishta states that the battle was fought at Dandánkán, a town ten parasangs from Merv, on the road to Sarakhs.]

[2] Sir H. Elliot reads " Márgala," and says, " according to Firishta he was taken at the Saráí of Márgala, near the Sind, or, according to others, on the Jhailam. Briggs reads the name Mariáls, and Wilken, Marietla. The noted pass of Márgala is meant, near which there is a place of note called Saráí. The Tabakát-i Akbarí and the Tárikh-i Badáúní concur in reading Márgala."

[3] Abú-l Fidá, according to Reinke (III. 669), gives the name as Kendí and Kaidí. Haidar Rází bin Bakar. The extract of the Rauzata-s Safá, printed by Sir H. Elliot, gives " Kírí," but Wilken's printed edition, and the Bombay lithographed edition of that work, have Kabri or Kabra, this being in all probability intended for Kírí, as one dot only makes the difference (كبرى - كبرى). Firishta also has Kírí, though Briggs reads the name " Kurry."—See Abbot's Map, Jour. As. Soc. Ben. Dec. 1848.

[4] [Note in the Orig.—" Names of the children of Sultán Maudúd: Mansúr, Muhammad, Sulaimán, Mahmúd."]

Hindustán submitted to him, and the Mahmúdí and the Mas'udí Turks who had revolted against Mas'úd rallied round him and supported him. For four months they upheld him as ruler, but Maudúd defeated him at Takarhárúd,[1] and took him prisoner, with all his children and dependants. Maudúd avenged his father's blood upon him, and the Turks and Tájiks and every one else who had taken part in his father's assassination he put to death. He thus obtained honour and renown. Afterwards he returned to Ghazní, and brought his father's territories under his power. He reigned nine years, and died in the year 441 H. (1049 A.D.), at the age of thirty-nine years.

VI.—'Alí, son of Mas'úd, and Muhammad, son of Maudúd.

These two princes, uncle and nephew, were raised jointly to the throne by the Turks and nobles. Every man took matters into his own hands, and when it was seen that they had no wisdom or power, and that ruin was coming upon the army and the people, they were dethroned after two months' reign, and sent back to a fort. 'Abdu-r Rashíd was raised to the throne in their stead.

VII.—'Abdu-r Rashíd, son of Mahmúd.

Sultán Baháu-d daula 'Abdu-r Rashíd, son of Mahmúd, ascended the throne in the year 441 H. (1049 A.D.) He was a learned and clever man, and used to listen to chronicles and write history; but he had no firmness or courage, and so changes and reverses came upon the state. The Saljúks, on the side of Khurásán, coveted the throne of Ghazní. Dáúd obtained the throne of Khurásán. Alp Arslán, son of Dáúd, was a good general, and they resolved to attack Ghazní. Alp Arslán advanced from Tukháristán with a large force, and his father, Dáúd, marched by way of Sístán to Bust. 'Abdu-r Rashíd collected an army, and placed at the head of it Tughril, who

---

[1] Or "Bakarhá," perhaps Bakhrála. [Firishta's text says "Dupás," not "Dustoor," as in Briggs' translation.]

had been one of the slaves of Mahmúd, and was a very energetic man. He marched against Alp Arslán, and routed him in front of the valley of Khamár. From thence he returned speedily to Dust, and Dáúd retreated before him to Sístán. He defeated Beghú, the uncle of Dáúd, and when he had achieved two or three such victories he returned to Ghazní, where he killed 'Abdu-r Rashíd and placed himself on the throne. 'Abdu-r Rashíd reigned two years and-a half.¹ His age was thirty.

VIII.—*Tughril, the accursed.*

Tughril had been a slave of Mahmúd, and was a man of great energy and courage. In the reign of Sultán Maudúd he went from Ghazní to Khurásán, and entered the service of the Saljúks. For some time he remained there, and learnt their method of war. In the time of 'Abdu-r Rashíd he returned to Ghazní, where he took 'Abdu-r Rashíd and slew him, together with eleven other princes. He then ascended the throne of Ghazní, and reigned for forty days with great tyranny and injustice. Some one asked him how the desire of sovereignty had entered into his mind, and he replied, "When 'Abdu-r Rashíd sent me against Alp Arslán he made some promises to me, and confirmed them by giving me his hand. He was then so overpowered by fear that the sound of the tremor which had seized upon his bones came to my ears, and I knew that such a coward could never rule and govern. It was then that the desire of sovereignty fell upon me." Forty days after his usurpation, a Turk, by name Noshtigín, who was a soldier, turned against Tughril, and conspiring with some of his friends, they killed him on the throne. His head was then brought out, placed upon a pole, and carried round the city, so that the people might have assurance of security.

IX.—*Farrukh-zád, son of Mas'úd.*

When the Almighty God had recompensed Tughril for his atrocious deeds, and the people were delivered from him and his

¹ [Two MSS. say "two years" only.]

unbounded tyranny, there were left surviving in the fort of Barghand,¹ two princes who were sons of Mas'úd. One of these was named Ibráhím, and the other Farrukh-zád. Tughril, the accursed, had sent a party of men to the fort of Barghand to put them to death. The commandant of the fort pondered over the matter for a day, and kept these emissaries at the gate of the fort upon the understanding that they were to come in on the following day, and execute their orders. Suddenly some fleet messengers arrived with the intelligence that the accursed Tughril had been killed. When that wretched man fell in Ghazní by the hand of Noshtigín, the grandees, princes, and generals set about searching for a king. It was then discovered that two persons (of the royal family) were left surviving in the fort of Barghand. Accordingly they all repaired to that place. At first they wished to raise Ibráhím to the throne, but he was very feeble in body, and as no delay could be admitted, Farrukh-zád was brought out, and proclaimed king on Saturday, the ninth of Zilka'da, A.H. 443 (March, 1052 A.D.).

Farrukh-zád was very mild and just. When he ascended the throne the country of Záwulistán was in a state of desolation from disease and murrain,² so he remitted the revenue that it might again become prosperous. He secured the territories of the kingdom, and reigned seven years. He died of colic in the year 451 (1059 A.D.), at the age of thirty-four years.

X.—*Sultán Ibráhím.*³

Sultán Zahíru-d daula wa Nasíru-l Millat Razíu-d dín Ibráhím, son of Mas'úd, was a great king,—wise, just, good, God-fearing, and kind, a patron of letters, a supporter of religion, and a pious man. When Farrukh-zád became king, Ibráhím was

¹ [The printed text has Barghand, but Sir H. Elliot reads Barghand, and says Barghand lies between Ták and Ghazní.]

² ['*Awáris-e mássu.*—The former words mean literally diseases, but it is also used for those diseases of the body politic, extraordinary imposts.]

³ [A note gives the names of his thirty-six sons, which are said to differ slightly in the three MSS. used.]

taken out of the fort of Barghand, and brought to that of Nai, and on the death of Farrukh-zád all men concurred in recognizing his succession. An officer named Hasan went to wait upon him, and with the approbation of the people of the kingdom he was brought out from the fort, and on Monday he auspiciously ascended the throne. The next day he spent in mourning for his late brother, and paid a visit to his tomb, and to the tombs of his ancestors. All the nobles and great men walked on foot in attendance upon him. He bestowed no favours upon any one, and hence apprehensions about his rule took possession of the hearts of the people. When the intelligence of his accession reached Dáúd, the Saljúkí, he sent some nobles into Khurásán, and made peace with him. After the death of Dáúd, his son, Alp Arslán, confirmed this treaty of peace. Ibráhím strengthened himself in the possession of his ancestors; the disorders which had arisen in the country from the late extraordinary events he rectified, and the Mahmúdí kingdom began once again to flourish. Ruined places were built afresh, and several fortified places and towns were founded, as Khairábád, Ímánábád, and other places. Many wonders and marvels appeared in his reign, and Dáúd, the Saljúkí, died, who in havoc, war, slaughter, and conquest, passed like a flash of lightning. Ibráhím was born at Hirát, in the year of the conquest of Gurgán, 424 H. (1033 A.D.) He had thirty-six sons and forty daughters. All the daughters he married to illustrious nobles or learned men of repute. One of these princesses was ancestress in the third degree of Minháj Siráj. The cause of the emigration of the author's ancestors from Júzján, was that Imám 'Abdu-l Khálik, who is buried at Tábírábád, in Ghazní, saw in a dream while he lived in Júzján, an angel who told him to rise, go to Ghazní, and take a wife. Upon his awaking it struck him that this might be some work of the devil, but as he dreamed the same thing three times successively, he acted in compliance with his dream, and came to Ghazní. There he married one of the daughters of Ibráhím, and by that princess he had a son named Ibráhím. This Ibráhím was father of Mauláná Minháju-d dín 'Usman, who was father of Mauláná Siráju-d dín, the wonder of his time, and father of Minháju-s Siráj. Sultán Ibráhím reigned happily for forty-two years, and died in the year 492 H. (1098 A.D.), at the age of sixty.

XI.—*'Aláu-d dín Mas'úd, the Generous, son of Ibráhím.*[1]

Sultán Mas'úd, the generous, was a virtuous prince, who had a prosperous reign. He possessed many excellent qualities, and was adorned with justice and equity. He ascended the throne in the days of Al Mustazhar bi-llah Ahmad, commander of the faithful, son of Muktadar. He was very modest and liberal. He abolished all the tyrannical practices which had been introduced in former reigns, and cancelled the newly-established imposts throughout the dominions of Mahmúd, and the country of Záwulistán. Taxes and imposts were remitted in all his dominions. He restored to the princes, nobles, and grandees their possessions as they had held them in the reign of Sultán Ibráhím, and he adopted whatever seemed best for the welfare of the state. Amír 'Azdu-d daula was confirmed in the governorship of Hindustán. In the days of this prince the great Hájib died; but Hájib Taghátigín crossed the river Ganges, and made an incursion into Hindustán, carrying his arms farther than any army had reached since the days of Sultán Mahmúd. All the affairs of state were reduced to a system in his reign, and there was nothing to disturb the minds of any one in any quarter. He was born in Ghazní in A.H. 453 (1061 A.D), and after reigning seventeen years, he died in the year 509 (1115 A.D.), at the age of fifty-seven. He married the sister of Sultán Sanjar, who was called Mahd-i 'Irák (Cradle of 'Irák).

XII.—*Malik Arslán, son of Sultán Mas'úd.*

Malik Arslán Abú-l malik ascended the throne A.H. 509 (A.D. 1115), and brought Garmsír and the kingdom of Ghazní under

[1] [A note gives the names of his seventeen sons.]

his rule. Bahrám Sháh, his uncle, fled to Sultán Sanjar, in Khurásán. Several wonderful phenomena occurred in the reign of this prince. One was that fire and lightning fell from the sky, and burnt the markets of Ghazní. Other distressing calamities and events occurred during his reign, making it hateful to the people. Arslán was famous for his magnanimity and energy, courage, and bravery. After he had ascended the throne he treated his mother, Mahd-i 'Irák, with contempt, and this incensed Sanjar, who gave his aid to Bahrám Sháh, and marched to Ghazní. Malik Arslán gave him battle, but being defeated, he fled to Hindustán, and fell into great distress. He expired in A.H. 511 (1117 A.D.), after a reign of two years, in the thirty-fifth year of his age.

XIII.—*Bahrám Sháh*.[1]

Mu'izzu-d daula Bahrám Sháh, was handsome and manly, liberal, just, and a friend of his people. In the early part of his career, when Malik Arslán succeeded his father, Sultán Mas'úd the generous, he went to Khurásán, the throne of which country was occupied in those days by the great Sultán Sa'íd Sanjar. Bahrám Sháh remained for some time at his Court. But at length Sultán Sanjar marched against Ghazní, and defeated Malik Arslán in battle. Bahrám Sháh then mounted the throne, and was supported by Sultán Sanjar. Saiyid Hasan composed an ode, which he recited at Court in the presence of Sanjar. Sanjar went back to Khurásán, and Bahrám took possession of the country. He made some expeditions to Hindustán, and on the twenty-seventh of Ramazán, A.H. 512, he captured Muhammad Báhalim, and kept him a prisoner; but he afterwards liberated him, and assigned the whole country of Hindustán to him. This officer again revolted and built the fort of Nágor, in the Siwálik hills, in the vicinity of Dera.[2] He had many sons and dependants. Bahrám Sháh proceeded to Hindustán to subdue the fort, and Muhammad Báhalim marched

[1] [A note gives the names of his nine sons.]   [2] ["Sabra" in one MS.]

towards Multán to meet him, and gave battle, but God punished him for his ingratitude, and he, with his ten[1] sons, their horses and arms, fell on the day of battle into a quagmire,[2] so that no trace of him was left. Bahrám Sháh returned to Ghazní, and had to fight against the kings of Ghor. In the war his son Daulat Sháh was slain, and in one campaign he was defeated three times by Sultán 'Aláu-d dín. Ghazní fell into the hands of the Ghorians, who set it on fire and destroyed it. Bahrám Sháh went to Hindustán, but when the Ghorians had retired, he again came to Ghazní, and there expired. His reign lasted forty-one years.

XIV.—*Khusrú Sháh, Son of Bahrám Sháh*.[3]

Sultán Yaminu-d daula Khusrú Sháh ascended the throne in A.H. 552 (1157 A.D.) The kings and princes of Ghor had shaken the throne of the descendants of Mahmúd, and had wrested from them and desolated the countries of Ghazní, Bust, Zamín-dáwar, and Takínábád. Weakness had thus fallen on the kingdom and its splendour was departed. When Khusrú Sháh ascended the throne he was weak and unable to bring the country under his rule.

A body of Ghuzz (Turks) also arose and attacked Khurásán[4] where the reign of Sultán Sa'íd Sanjar had come to an end. An army likewise came against Ghazní, and Khusrú Sháh being unable to resist them went to India. He thus lost Ghazní which fell into the hands of the Ghuzz, and so remained for twelve years. But at length Sultán Sa'íd Ghiyásu-d dín Muhammad Sám led an army from Ghor, expelled the Ghuzz, took possession of Ghazní, and mounted the throne. Khusrú Sháh

---

[1] [The printed text says "two," but "ten" seems to be the correct number.—See Firishta I. 161.]

[2] [The text has some unintelligible words which vary in the different MSS. Briggs says "a quagmire," and something like that must be intended.]

[3] [Note in the Text.—"Sons of Khusrú Sháh—Khusrú Malik, Mahmúd Sháh, Kai Khusrú."]

[4] [The printed text omits the word "Khurásán," but it is necessary to the sense and true to the fact.]

had gone to Láhore in Hindustán, where he died. He reigned seven years.

XV.—*Khusrú Malik Son of Khusrú Sháh, the last King of the Ghazniride Dynasty.*

Khusrú Malik Táju-d daula Sultán Jahán, the gentle king, mounted the throne at Lahore. This prince was exceedingly gentle, liberal, and modest, but fond of pleasure. He possessed many excellent qualities, but as he lived when the rule of his family came to an end, he was held in small esteem. With him closed the power of his house, and anarchy reigned in the country. All the nobles and officers of the State, both Turks and freemen, (*atrák o ahrár*), deserted him. The slaves and servants of the throne took the government into their own hands, while he in-indulged in luxury and pleasure.

Sultán Sa'íd Mu'izzu-d daula Muhammad Sám came every year from Ghazní, continually increasing his hold upon Hind and Sind, till at length in A.H. 577 (1181 A.D.), he advanced to the gates of Lahore, where he took the elephant and the son of Khusrú Sháh and carried them off with him.

In A.H. 583 (1187 A.D.) he again advanced on Lahore and took it. He then dethroned Khusrú Malik, sent him to Ghazní from whence he was subsequently sent to Fíroz-Koh, which was the capital of the great king Sultán Ghiyásu-d dín Muhammad Sám. By order of this monarch, Khusrú Malik was kept a prisoner in the fort of Balrawán, in Gharjistán. When the war (*hádisa*) of Sultán Sháh (of Khwárizm) broke out in Khurásán, the kings of Ghor[1] were obliged to throw themselves into it, and they then put Sultán Khusrú Malik to death in the year 598 H. (A.D. 1201). His son Bahrám Sháh who was a captive in the fort of Saifrúd in Ghor, was also slain. Thus ended the house of Násiru-d dín Subuktigín. The kingdom of Írán, the throne of Hindustán, and the country of Khurásán all fell into the possession of the Shansabániya Kings.

[1] [Ghiyásu-d dín and Muhammad Shaháb-d dín were brothers, and held a sort of joint rule.]

TABAKAT XVII.

THE SHANSABÁNIYA SULTÁNS AND THE KINGS OF GHOR.[1]

[Page 34 to 48 of the printed Text.]

1.—*Amír Fúlád Ghorí Shansabí*.[2]

Amír Fúlád Ghorí was one of the sons of Malik Shansab, son of Harnak. The mountains of Ghor came into his possession, and he gave new life to the names of his forefathers. When the founder of the house of 'Abbás, Abú Muslim Marwazí, revolted, and resolved upon expelling the officers of the Ummayides from Khurásán, Amír Fúlád led the forces of Ghor to his assistance, and took an active part in the victories of the race of 'Abbás, and of the people of the house of the prophet. The fortress of Mandesh[3] was in his possession, and he ruled for some time over the Jabbál and Ghor. Upon his death he was succeeded by the sons of his brother, but after these nothing is known of the rulers of Ghor until the time of Amír Banjí Nahárán.

2.—*Amír Banjí, son of Nahárán*.

Amír Banjí Nahárán was a great chief, and his history is well known in Ghor. He is considered one of the greatest kings of that territory, and all its kings are descended from him. His pedigree is thus given.

* * * * *

Amír Banjí was a handsome and excellent man, possessing good qualities, and of very estimable character. When the power of the family of 'Abbás was established, and the territories of the Muhammadans came under the rule of the Khalífs of that house, the first person of the Ghorí family who went to the seat

---

[1] [The opening of this book is occupied with genealogies by which the pedigree of the kings of Ghor is carried through Zahák up to Noah.]

[2] Briggs in Firishta writes this name "Shiuty." See Mr. Thomas' Paper on the Coins of the Ghorí Dynasty.—Jour. R. As. Soc. xvii. 190.]

[3] [A fortress in Khurásán.]

of the Khiláfat, and obtained the title of sovereignty and a royal banner was Amír Banjí Nahárán. The cause of his going to the presence of Hárúnu-r Rashíd, the commander of the faithful, was as follows:—There was a tribe in Ghor called Shishání, who asserted that their ancestors were first converted to Muhammadanism, and then the Shansabánís. Muhammad is called in the Ghorí language Hamd, and when they espoused the faith they were designated Hamdís, or Muhammadans. In the time of Amír Banjí there was a man of the Shishání tribe whose name was Sís, or in the Ghorí language Shísh. A dispute arose between this Amír Shísh and Amír Banjí, for the chiefship of Ghor, and contention broke out among the people. It was agreed by both parties that Amír Banjí and Shísh should both repair to the Khalíf, and whoever brought back a patent of sovereignty and royal ensign should be the chief.

[*Account of the interview which the two chiefs had with the Khalif, when Amir Banji, through the instruction in court etiquette which he had received from a Jew, was named chief, and Shish was made general.*]

From that time the title of the Shansabání kings, according to the gracious words of Hárúnu-r Rashíd, commander of the faithful, became Kasím-i Amíru-l Múminín. The two chiefs returned to Ghor, and assumed their respective offices of ruler of Ghor and commander of the army. These two offices are held to this day by the different parties, according to this arrangement. The kings of Ghor were all Shansabáníaus, and the commanders of the army are called Shisháníyins, such as Múadu-d dín, Abú-l 'Abbás Shísh, and Sulaimán Shísh.

3.—*Amír Súrí.*

The writer of this work has not been able to obtain the annals of the kings of Ghor from the reign of Amír Banjí down to the present reign, so as to enable him to write their history in detail. The author resides in Dehli, and through the disorders which the inroads of the infidel Mughals have caused in the territories of

Islám, there has been no possibility of his copying from the histories which he had seen in Ghor. He has written what he found in the Táríkh-i Násiri and the Táríkh-i Haizam Nábí, as well as what he was able to gleam from old men of Ghor, but his readers must pardon imperfections.

It is said that Amír Súrí was a great king, and most of the territories of Ghor were in his possession. But as many of the inhabitants of Ghor, of high and low degree, had not yet embraced Muhammadanism, there was constant strife among them. The Saffárians came from Nímroz to Bust and Dáwar, and Yákúb Lais overpowered Lak-lak, who was chief of Takín-ábád, in the country of Rukhaj.[1] The Ghorians sought safety in Sarhá-sang,[2] and dwelt there in security, but even among them hostilities constantly prevailed between the Muhammadans and the infidels. One castle was at war with another castle, and their feuds were unceasing; but owing to the inaccessibility of the mountains of Rásiát, which are in Ghor, no foreigner was able to overcome them, and Shansabání Amír Súrí was the head of all the Mandeshís. In Ghor there are five great and lofty mountains, which the people of Ghor agree in considering as higher than the Rásiát mountains. One of these is Zár Murgh, in Mandesh, and the capital and palace of the Shansabání kings are at the foot of this mountain. It is said that Zál Zar, father of Rustam, was here nourished by a Símurgh, and some of the inhabitants of the foot of the mountain say that between the fifth and sixth centuries a loud voice of cry and lamentation was heard to proceed from it, announcing the death of Zál. The second mountain is called Sar Khizr; it is also in the territory of Mandesh, in the vicinity of Takhbar. The third is Ashak, in the country of Timrán, which is the greatest and highest of the whole territory of Ghor. The country of Timrán lies in the valleys and environs of this mountain. The fourth is Wazní, and the territories of Dáwar and Wálasht, and the fort of Kahwarán,

---
[1] [A division of Sijistán; Arachosia.]
[2] ["Sarhtosang," or "Sarhá wa Sang," in some copies.]

are within its ramifications and valleys. And the fifth mountain is Fáj Hanisár,[1] in the country of Ghor. It is very inaccessible and secure. It is said that the length, breadth, and height of of this mountain are beyond the limits of guess, and the power of understanding. In the year 590 (1194 A.D.), a piece of the trunk of an ebony tree was found on this mountain, which exceeded two hundred mans in weight, and no one could tell how large and high the tree must have been.

4.—*Malik Muhammad Súrí.*

Abú-l Hasan al Haizam, son of Muhammad-n Nábí author of the Tárikhu-l Haizam, says that when the government of Khurásán and Záwulistán departed from the Sámánians and Saffárians, and fell to Amír Subuktigín, he led his army several times towards the hills of Ghor, and carried on many wars. When Amír Mahmúd Subuktigín succeeded to the throne, the kingdom of Ghor had devolved upon Amír Muhammad Súrí, and he had brought all the territories of Ghor under his sway. Sometimes he made submission to Sultán Mahmúd, and at others he revolted, and withheld the payment of the fixed tribute, and the contingent of arms which he had agreed to supply. Relying on the strength of his forts, and the numbers and power of his army, he was continually engaging in hostilities. Sultán Mahmúd was consequently always on the watch, and his mind was much disturbed by Súrí's power, his large army, and the security afforded to him by the height and inaccessibility of the hills of Ghor. At last he marched to Ghor with a considerable army. Muhammad Súrí was besieged in the fort of A'hangarán, and held out for a long time. He fought desperately, but was at last compelled to evacuate the fort, upon conditions, and made his submission to Sultán Mahmúd.

The Sultán took him and his younger son, whose name was Shísh, to Ghazní, because the lad was very dear to his father. When they reached the neighbourhood of Gílán, Amír Mu-

[1] [Or "Hanár."]

hammad Súrí died. Some say that he was taken prisoner, and and as he had a very high spirit he could not brook the disgrace. He had a ring, under the stone of which was concealed some poison, which he took and then died. The Sultán immediately sent his son Shísh back to Ghor, and gave the chieftainship of Ghor to the eldest son, Amír Abú 'Alí bin Súrí, an account of whom follows.

5. *Amír Abú 'Alí bin Muhammad bin Súrí.*
6. *Amír Abbás bin Shísh bin Muhammad bin Súrí.*
7. *Amír Muhammad bin 'Abbás.*
8. *Malik Kutbu-d dín al Hasan bin Muhammad bin 'Abbás.*
9. *Malik 'Izzu-d dín al Husain bin Hasan Abu-s Salátín.*
10. *Malik Kutbu-d dín Muhammad bin Husain, King of the Jabbál.*
11. *Sultán Bahául-d dín Sám bin Husain.*
12. *Malik Shahábu-d dín Muhammad bin Husain, King of Mádín, by Ghor.*
13. *Malik Shujá'u-d dín 'Alí bin Husain.*
14. *Sultán 'Aláu-d dín Husain bin Husain bin Sám.*

[Page 54 to 63 of the Printed Text.]

Sultán Bahául-d dín Sám, son of Husain, died in Kidán, whilst he was leading his army to Ghazní in order to exact revenge for the death of Sultán Súrí, King of the Jabbál. Sultán 'Aláu-d dín then ascended the throne of Ghor and Fíroz Koh. He assembled the forces of Ghor and Gharjistán, firmly resolved upon attacking Ghazní. Sultán Yamínu-d daula Bahrám Sháh, when he heard of these preparations, assembled the troops of Ghazní and Hindustán and passing through Garmsír by way of Rukhaj and Takínábád, he came to Zamíu-dáwar. When 'Aláu-d dín came up with his army, Bahrám Sháh sent messengers to him, saying, "Go back to Ghor, and stay in the states of your forefathers; you have not the strength to resist my army, for I have brought elephants with me." When the envoys delivered this message,

'Aláu-d dín replied, "If you have brought elephants (*píl*) I have brought the Kharmíls,—besides, you mistake, for you have slain my brothers, whilst I have killed no one belonging to you. Have you not heard what the Almighty says? 'Whosoever is slain unjustly we have given his heir power (to demand satisfaction); and let him not exceed bounds in putting to death, for he is protected.'" When the messengers returned, both armies made ready for battle, Sultán 'Aláu-d dín called for his two champions,[1] named Kharmíl, who were the heads of the army and the renowned heroes of Ghor. One of these was Kharmíl Sám Husain, father of Malik Násiru-d dín Husain; the other was Kharmíl Sám Banjí. Both of these men were famous for courage. 'Aláu-d dín sent for them and said, "Bahrám Sháh has sent to say that he has brought elephants, and I have answered that I have brought the Kharmíls. You must each take care to bring an elephant to the ground to-day." They bowed and retired. The two armies were drawn up at a place called Kotah-báz-báb. The two champions were on foot, and throwing off their coats of mail, they advanced to battle. When the elephants of Bahrám Sháh charged, the two champions each singled out one; and creeping under the armour, they ripped open the bellies of the animals with their knives. Kharmíl Sháh Banjí fell under the feet of the elephant, and the animal rolling upon him, they both perished together. Kharmíl Sám Husain brought down his elephant, extricated himself, and mounted a horse.

When 'Aláu-d dín had cased himself in armour ready for the fight, he called for an overcoat of red satin, which he put on over his armour. His attendants enquired why he did so, and he said, it was to prevent his men seeing his blood and feeling discouraged, in the event of his being wounded with a lance or arrow.

It is the practice in the armies of Ghor for the infantry to protect themselves in battle with a covering made of a raw hide covered thickly on both sides with wool or cotton. This defen-

[1] ["*Pahlawán*."—Briggs in his *Firishta* says "two gigantic brothers."]

sive covering is like a board, and is called *károh*. When the men put it on they are covered from head to foot, and their ranks look like walls. The wool is so thick that no weapon can pierce it.

Daulat Sháh, son of Bahrám Sháh, advanced to the assault, mounted on an elephant at the head of his cavalry, and 'Aláu-d dín directed his *károh*-wearers to make an opening in their line, and allow the prince and his followers to pass through. When all had gone through the *károh*-wearers closed up the gap in their line, and the prince with his elephant and all his cavalry were slain.

When the armies of Bahrám Sháh saw this manœuvre and its bloody result, they broke and fled. 'Aláu-d dín pursued them from stage to stage until they reached a place called Josh-áb-garm (hot wells) near Takínábád. Here Bahrám Shah made a stand, but was again defeated. 'Aláu-d dín followed in hot pursuit, and Bahrám Sháh having drawn together some of his scattered forces, and some reinforcements from Ghazní, he a third time gave battle, and once more was routed.

The victor then entered Ghazní, and for seven nights and days he gave it to the flames. Writers record how that during these seven days the clouds of smoke so darkened the air that day seemed to be night, and the flames so lighted the sky at night that night looked like day. For these seven days plunder, devastation, and slaughter, were continuous. Every man that was found was slain, and all the women and children were made prisoners. Under the orders of the conqueror, all the Mahmúdí kings, with the exception of Mahmúd, Mas'úd, and Ibráhím, were dragged from their graves and burnt. All this time, 'Aláu-d dín sat in the palace of Ghazní occupied with drinking and debauchery. He had directed that the tomb of Saifú-d dín Súrí and of the King of the Jabbál should be sought out. Coffins were made for their bodies, and all the army was ordered to prepare for mourning. When the seven days were over, the city burnt and destroyed, and its inhabitants slain or scattered, on that very night, 'Aláu-d dín composed some verses in his own praise, which he gave to the minstrels to set to music and sing before him. (Verses.)

He then ordered that the remnant of the people of Ghazní should be spared. Breaking up his court, he went to the bath, and on the morning of the eighth day he led the nobles and followers of Ghor to the tombs of his brothers, where he put on garments of mourning, and with all his army he remained there seven days and nights, mourning, making offerings, and having the Kurán read. He then placed the coffins of his brothers in cradles, and marched with them towards Dáwar and Bust: he destroyed all the palaces and edifices of the Mahmúdí kings, which had no equals in the world, and devastated all the territory which had belonged to that dynasty. After that he returned to Ghor, and interred the remains of his brothers in the tombs of their ancestors.

While at Ghazní he had given directions that several of the Saiyids of that town should be taken in retaliation of Saiyid Majdu-d dín, wazír of Sultán Súrí, who was hanged with him from the bridge of Ghazní. These captives were brought into his presence, and bags filled with the dirt of Ghazní were fastened round their necks. They were thus led to Fíroz-koh, and there they were slain. Their blood was mixed with the earth they had carried from Ghazní, and with that mixture 'Aláu-d dín built some towers on the hills of Fíroz-koh, which are standing to this day. May God forgive him!

Having thus exacted vengeance, he devoted himself to pleasure and wine, and he composed some more verses for minstrels to sing in his praise.

When he ascended the throne of Fíroz-koh he imprisoned his two nephews, Ghiyásu-d dín Muhammad Sám and Mu'izzu-d dín Muhammad Sám, sons of Sultán Baháu-d dín Sám, in a fort of Wahíristán, and settled an allowance for their maintenance.

[*Transactions with Sultán Sanjar Saljúkí.*]

Towards the end of his life some emissaries of the Muláhidatu-l maut came to him, and he paid great honour to these heretics, inviting them into all parts of his kingdom. They on their part were desirous of establishing their sway over the people of Ghor. This remains a stain upon the fame of 'Aláu-d dín.

15. *Malik Násiru-d dín al Husain bin Muhammad al Madaini.*
16. *Sultán Saifu-d dín Muhammad bin Sultán 'Aláu-d dín Husain.*
17. *Sultánu-l 'azam Ghiyásu-d dunyá wau-d dín Abú-l Fath Muhammad Sám Kasím Amíru-l muminín.*
18. *Máliku-l Hájí 'Aláu-d dín Muhammad bin Abú 'Ali bin Husain ash Shansabí.*
19. *Sultán Ghiyásu-d dín Mahmúd bin Muhammad Sám Shansabí.*
20. *Sultán Baháu-d dín Sám bin Mahmúd bin Muhammad Sám.*
21. *Sultán 'Aláu-d dín Atsar bin Husain.*
22. *Sultán 'Aláu-d dín Muhammad bin Abú 'Alí,* the last of these kings.

TABAKAT XIX.

THE SHANSABÁNIYA SULTÁNS OF GHAZNÍ.

[Printed Text, p. 111.]

This book contains an abridged account of the Shansabání Sultáns, whose glory added lustre to the throne of Ghazní, and elevated the kingdoms of Hind and Khurásán. The first of them was Sultán Saifu-d dín Súrí. After him came Sultán 'Aláu-d dín Husain, who took Ghazní, but did not reign there. The throne was next taken by Sultán Mu'izzu-d dín Muhammad Sám. When he was killed the crown was confided to his slave, Sultán Táju-d dín Yalduz, and so the line ended.

I.—*Sultán Saifu-d dín Súrí.*

Saifu-d dín was a great king, of handsome appearance and noble carriage, and distinguished for courage, energy, humanity, justice, and liberality. He was the first individual of this family who received the title of Sultán. When the news reached him of the destruction which had fallen upon his elder brother the king of the Jabbál (Kutbu-d dín), he resolved upon taking vengeance upon Bahrám Sháh. He gathered a great force in the states of Ghor and marched to Ghazní, where he routed Bahrám and took the city. Bahrám fled to Hindustán, and Saifu-d dín ascended the throne of Ghazní, when he placed the territories of Ghor under his brother, Sultán Baháu-d dín Súrí, father of Ghiyásu-d dín and Mu'izzu-d dín. After he had secured Ghazní the chiefs of the army and the nobles of the city and environs submitted to him, and he conferred many favours upon them, so that the army and the subjects of Bahrám Sháh were overwhelmed by his bounteous care. When winter came on he sent his own forces back to Ghor, and kept with him only the troops and officers of Bahrám Sháh in whom he placed full confidence. His wazír, Saiyid Majdu-d dín Musawí, and a few of his old servants remained with him, all the rest of his officers both at Court and in the country had been in the service of the old government.

In the depth of the winter, when the roads to Ghor were closed by heavy falls of snow, the people of Ghazní saw that no army or assistance could come to Saifu-d dín from that quarter, so they wrote to Bahrám Sháh explaining how matters stood, and pressing upon him the necessity of seizing this favourable opportunity for the recovery of his dominions. The deposed king acted upon these advices, and marched suddenly to Ghazní and attacked his foe. Súrí, with his wazír and his old servants, abandoned the city and took the road to Ghor, but the horsemen of Bahrám Sháh pursued them and overtook them in the neighbourhood of Sang-i Surákh.[1] They fought desperately until they were unhorsed,

[1] [Or Sang-i Surkh, a strong fort in Ghor, probably near the Harí river.]

and then retreated into the hills, where they kept up such a shower of arrows that the foe could not approach them. When the last arrow had been shot the horsemen captured them, bound them hand and foot, and conducted them to Ghazní. At the gate of the city Sultán Súrí was placed upon a camel, and his wazír, Majdu-d dín, upon another. They were then led ignominiously round the city, and from the tops of the houses, ashes, dirt, and filth were thrown upon their venerable heads. When they reached the one-arched bridge of Ghazní, the Sultán and his wazír were both gibbeted over the bridge. Such was the disgraceful cruelty practised upon this handsome, excellent, just, and brave king. The Almighty, however, prospered the arms of Sultán 'Aláu-d dín Jahán-soz, brother of Sultán Súrí, who exacted full retribution for this horrible deed, as we have already related in another place.

2. *Sultánu-l Ghází Mu'izzu-d dunyá wau-d dín Abú-l Muzaffar Muhammad bin Sám.*[1]

Historians relate that Sultán 'Aláu-d-dín was succeeded by his son Sultán Saifu-d dín. This king released the two princes Ghiyásu-d dín and Mu'izzu-d dín (his cousins) who were confined in a fort of Wahíristán, as has been already narrated in the history of Sultán Ghiyásu-d dín. Prince Ghiyásu-d dín dwelt peacefully at Fíroz-koh in the service of Sultán Saifu-d dín, and Prince Mu'izzu-d dín went to Bámián into the service of his uncle Fakhru-d dín Mas'úd.

When Ghiyásu-d dín succeeded to the throne of Ghor after the tragical death of Saifu-d dín, and the intelligence thereof came to Bámián, Fakhru-d dín addressed his nephew Mu'izzu-d dín saying, "Your brother is acting, what do you mean to do? You must bestir yourself." Mu'izzu-d dín bowed respectfully to

[1] This king is commonly called "Mahammad Ghorí," or "Muhammad Sám." Ibn Asír and Firishta, followed by Elphinstone, call him "Shahábu-d dín Ghorí." The superscription on his coins is "Sultánu-l 'azam Mu'izzu-d dunyá wau-d dín Abú-l Muzaffar Mahammad bin Sám." See Note on the Coins, in the Appendix. In the text of this work he is generally designated Sultán-i Ghází, the victorious king.]

his uncle, left the Court, and started just as he was for Firozkoh. When he arrived there he waited upon his brother and paid his respects, as has been already related. One year he served his brother, but having taken some offence he went to Sijistán to Malik Shamsu-d dín Sijistání and staid there one winter. His brother sent messengers to bring him back, and when he arrived he assigned to him the countries of Kasr-kajúrán and Istiya.[1] When he had established his authority over the whole of Garmsír he made over to his brother the city of Takínábád, which was the largest town in Garmsír. This Takínábád is the place which was the cause of the quarrel with the house of Mahmúd Subuktigín, and it passed into the hands of the kings of Ghor. Sultán-i Ghází 'Aláu-d dín sent the following quatrain to Khusrú Sháh bin Bahrám Sháh:

"Thy father first laid the foundation of this place
"Before the people of the world had all fallen under injustice.
"Beware lest for one Takínábád thou shouldest bring
"The empire of the house of Mahmúd to utter ruin."

When Sultán Mu'izzu-d dín became master of Takínábád the armies and leaders of the Ghuzz had fled before the forces of Khitá towards Ghazní, where they remained for twelve years, having wrested the country from the hands of Khusrú Sháh and Khusrú Malik. Sultán Mu'izzu-d dín kept continually assailing them from Takínábád, and troubling the country. At length in the year 569 H. (1173 A.D.) Sultán Ghiyásu-dín conquered Ghazní, and returned to Ghor, after placing his brother Mu'izzu-d dín upon the throne, as has been before related. This prince secured the territories of Ghazní, and two years afterwards in 570 H. (1174 A.D.) he conquered Gurdez.

In the third year he led his forces to Multán and delivered that place from the hands of the Karmatians. In the same year 571 H. (1175 A.D.) the people of Sankarán[2] revolted and made great confusion, so he marched against them and put most of them to the sword. It has been written by some that these

[1] [Or "Istiyá," a city of Ghor, in the hills between Hirát and Ghazní.]
[2] [Written also "Shankarán" and "Sankarán."]

Sankaraniáns have been called martyrs, in agreement with the declaration of the Kurán, but as they stirred up strife and revolted they were made examples of, and were put to death from political necessity.

In the year after this victory he conducted his army by way of Uch and Multán towards Nahrwála. The Rúl of Nahrwála, Bhím-deo,[1] was a minor, but he had a large army and many elephants. In the day of battle the Muhammadans were defeated and the Sultán was compelled to retreat. This happened in the year 574 H. (1178 A.D.).

In 575 H. (1179 A.D.) he attacked and conquered Farsháwar (Pesháwar), and two years afterwards he advanced to Lohor (Lahore). The power of the Ghaznivides was now drawing to its close and their glory was departed, so Khusrú Malik sent his son as a hostage, and an elephant as a present to the Sultán. This was in the year 577 H. (1181 A.D.) Next year the Sultán marched to Dewal, subdued all that country to the sea shore, and returned with great spoil. In 580 H. (1184 A.D.) he went to Lahore, ravaged all the territories of that kingdom, and returned after building the fort of Siálkot, in which he placed Husain Kharmíl as governor. When the Sultán was gone, Khusrú Malik assembled the forces of Hindustán, and having also obtained a body of Kokhars (Gakkars) he laid siege to Siálkot, but, after some interval, was obliged to withdraw. The Sultán returned to Lahore in 581 H. (1185 A.D.).

The house of Mahmúd had now come to its end; the sun of its glory was set, and the registrar of fate had written the mandate of its destruction. Khrusrú Malik could offer no resistance; he came forth peacefully to meet the Sultán, and was made prisoner. Lahore fell completely into the power of the Ghori prince, and he secured all its dominions in Hindustán.

'Alí Karmúkh, chief of Multán, was appointed commander at Lahore, and the father of the writer of this book, Mauláná

---

[1] [The text has "Bhasu-deo," but some copies give the name correctly "Bhim deo." See post, page 300; Firishta I. 179.]

A'júbatu-z Zamán Afssbu-l 'Ajam Sirája-d din Minháj, was appointed Kází of the army of Hindustan, and received the honour of investiture from Mu'izzu-d din. He held his Court at the head quarters of the army, and twelve camels were assigned for moving from place to place his Bench of Justice.

The Sultán returned to Ghazní carrying Khusrú Malik with him, and on arriving there he sent him on to Firoz-koh, to the Court of the great king Ghiyásu-d din. This monarch sent him prisoner to the fort of Bahrawán, and confined his son Bahrám Sháh in the fort of Saifrúd.[1] When the war with Khwárizm Sháh broke out in the year 587 H. (1191 A.D.) Khusrú Malik and his son were put to death.[2]

The victorious Sultán then prepared another army, with which he attacked and conquered the fort of Sarhind. This fort he placed under the command of Ziáu-d din Kází Tolak, (son of) Muhammad 'Abdu-s Salám Nasáwí Tolakí. This Kází Ziáú-d din was cousin (son of the uncle) of the author's maternal grandfather. At the request of the Kází, Majdu-d din Tolakí selected 1200 men of the tribe of Tolakí, and placed them all under his command in the fort so as to enable him to hold it until the return of the Sultán from Ghazní.

Rái Kolah Pithaurá came up against the fort, and the Sultán returned and faced him at Narúin.[3] All the Ráís of Hindustán were with the Rái Kolah. The battle was formed and the Sultán, seizing a lance, made a rush upon the elephant which carried Gobind Rái of Dehli. The latter advanced to meet him in front of the battle, and then the Sultán, who was a second Rustam, and the Lion of the Age, drove his lance into the mouth of the Rái and knocked two of the accursed wretch's teeth down

---

[1] ["Sankarán," in some copies.]   [2] [The text does not say by whom.]

[3] [The text has "Tarāin," but Firishta gives the name as Nārāin and says it was afterwards called Tirauri. He places it on the banks of the Sarsuti, 14 miles from Thánesar and 80 from Dehli, but according to Gen. Cunningham the battlefield of Nārāin is on the banks of the Rākshi river four miles south west of Tirauri and ten miles to the north of Karnál. Tirauri is also called Azímábád. See Elphinstone, p. 363.]

his throat. The Rái, on the other hand, returned the blow and inflicted a severe wound on the arm of his adversary. The Sultán reined back his horse and turned aside, and the pain of the wound was so insufferable that he could not support himself on horseback. The Musulman army gave way and could not be controlled. The Sultán was just falling when a sharp and brave young Khiljí recognized him, jumped upon the horse behind him, and clasping him round the bosom, spurred on the horse and bore him from the midst of the fight.

When the Musulmans lost sight of the Sultán, a panic fell upon them; they fled and halted not until they were safe from the pursuit of the victors. A party of nobles and youths of Ghor had seen and recognized their leader with that lion-hearted Khiljí, and when he came up they drew together, and, forming a kind of litter with broken lances, they bore him to the halting-place. The hearts of the troops were consoled by his appearance, and the Muhammadan faith gathered new strength in his life. He collected the scattered forces and retreated to the territories of Islám, leaving Kází Tolak in the fort of Sarhind. Rái Pithaurá advanced and invested the fort, which he besieged for thirteen months.

Next year the Sultán assembled another army, and advanced to Hindustán to avenge his defeat. A trustworthy person named Mu'ínu-d dín, one of the principal men of the hills of Tolak, informed me that he was in this army, and that its force amounted to one hundred and twenty thousand horsemen bearing armour. Before the Sultán could arrive the fort of Sarhind had capitulated, and the enemy were encamped in the vicinity of Náráin. The Sultán drew up his battle array, leaving his main body in the rear, with the banners, canopies, and elephants, to the number of several divisions. His plan of attack being formed, he advanced quietly. The light unarmoured horsemen were made into four divisions of 10,000, and were directed to advance and harass the enemy on all sides, on the right and on the left, in the front and in the rear, with their arrows. When the enemy collected his forces to attack, they were to support each other, and to charge at full speed. By these tactics the infidels were worsted, the Almighty gave us the victory over them, and they fled.

Pithaurá alighted from his elephant, mounted a horse, and galloped off, but he was captured near Sarsutí,[1] and sent to hell. Gobind Rái, of Dehli, was killed in the battle, and the Sultán recognized his head by the two teeth which he had broken. The capital, Ajmír, and all the Siwálik hills, Hánsí, Sarsutí, and other districts were the results of this victory, which was gained in the year 588 H. (1192 A.D.)

On his return homewards the Sultán placed Kutbu-d dín in command of the fort of Kahrám, and in the same year this chief advancing to Mírat conquered that town, and took possession of Dehli. In the following year he captured the fort of Kol. The Sultán came back from Ghazní in the year 590 (1193 A.D.), by way of Benares and Kanauj,[2] defeated Rái Jai Chandar, in the neighbourhood of Chandawáh, and captured over 300 elephants in the battle.

Under the rule of this just king victory followed the standards of his slave Kutbu-d dín Aibak, so that the countries of Nahrwála and Bhangar, the forts of Gwalior and Badáún, and other parts of Hindustán were conquered. But these victories will be related more in detail hereafter, in describing the victories of Kutbu-d dín.

Sultán Sa'íd Ghiyásu-d dín died at Hirát, when his brother Sultán Mu'izzu-d dín was between Tús and Sarakhs in Khurásán, but the latter returned and secured his succession to the throne.

[*Proceedings west of the Indus.*]

A rebellion had broken out among the Kokhars (Gakkars), and the tribes of the hills of Júd, and in the winter the Sultán went to Hindustán to put down the revolt. He defeated the rebels,

[1] [The text has "Sarsd" in which it is followed by Núru-l Hakk and others. Firishta says "Sarsutí." Briggs I. 177.]
[2] [The author's knowledge of geography is evidently at fault. Firishta says the battle was fought "between Chandwar and Etawa."]

and made their blood to flow in streams, but as he was returning home to Ghazní he fell into the hands of these infidels, and was put to death in the year 602 H. (1206 A.D. The period of his reign was thirty-two years. [*Detailed lists are given of his judges, relations, generals, victories, and of his*] Slaves who attained royalty:—Sultán Táju-d dín Yalduz, Sultán Násiru-d dín Kubácha, Sultán Shamsu-d dín Altamsh, Sultán Kutbu-d dín Aibak.

TABAKAT XX.

THE MU'IZZIYA SULTÁNS OF HIND.

[Page 137 to 165 of the Printed Text.]

This chapter is devoted to the history of those kings who were the slaves and servants of the Sultán Ghází Mu'izzu-d dín Muhammad Sám, and sat upon the throne of royalty in the country of Hindustán. The throne of that king descended to them, as he had designed and as is mentioned above. They adorned their heads with the crown of royalty which had belonged to that king, and the influence of the light of Muhammadanism was preserved through their power over the different parts and provinces of Hindustán.

1. *Sultán Kutbu-d dín Aibak.*[1]

Sultán Kutbu-d dín, the second Hátim, was a brave and liberal king. The Almighty had bestowed on him such courage and generosity that in his time there was no king like him from the east to the west. When the Almighty God wishes to exhibit to his people an example of greatness and majesty he endows one of his slaves with the qualities of courage and generosity, and then friends and enemies are influenced by his bounteous generosity and warlike prowess. So this king was generous

---

[1] [This name is written آی بک in the inscriptions of the Kutb-minár at Dehli. Mr. Thomas reads it "Ai-beg."—Thomas' Prinsep I. 327. The *Kutub-i Mahál* says "Ípak." See Note *supra*, p. 266.]

and brave, and all the regions of Hindustán were filled with friends and cleared of foes. His bounty was continuous and his slaughter was continuous.

When Sultán Kutbu-d dín was first brought from Turkistán, his lot fell in the city of Naishápúr, where he was bought by the chief Kází, Fakhru-d dín 'Abdu-l 'Azíz of Kúfa, who was one of the descendants of the great Imám Abú Hanífa of Kúfa. This Kází was governor of Naishápúr and its dependencies. Kutbu-d dín grew up in the service and society of his master's sons, and with them he learned to read the Kurán, and also acquired the arts of riding and archery. In a short time he became remarkable for his manly qualities. When he had nearly arrived at the age of manhood, merchants brought him to Ghaznín, and the Sultán Gházi Mu'izzu-d dín Muhammad Sám purchased him from them. He was possessed of every quality and virtue, but he was not comely in appearance. His little finger[1] was broken from his hand, and he was therefore called Aibak, "maimed in the hand."[2]

Sultán Mu'izzu-d dín used occasionally to indulge in music and conviviality, and one night he had a party, and in the course of the banquet he graciously bestowed gifts of money and of uncoined gold and silver upon his servants. Kutbu-d dín received his share among the rest, but whatever he got, either gold or silver, coined or uncoined, he gave it all, when he went out of the assembly, to the Turki soldiers, guards, faráshes and other servants. He kept nothing, either small or great, for himself. Next day when this was reported to the king, he was looked upon with great favour and condescension, and was appointed to some important duties about the Court. He thus became a great officer, and his rank grew higher every day, until by the king's favour he was appointed Master of the Horse. While he held

---

[1] ["*Khinsar*," little or middle finger.]

[2] ["*Shal*" is the Persian word used as the explanation of *aibak*. But the statement of the text cannot be correct, as the name Aibak frequently occurs, and must be the name of a tribe, not a nickname.]

this station, the kings of Ghor, Ghaznín, and Bámián went towards Khurásán. Kutbu-d dín showed great activity in repelling the attacks of Sultán Sháh. He held the command of the foragers, and one day while in quest of forage, he was unexpectedly attacked by the cavalry of the enemy. Kutbu-d dín showed great bravery in the fight which ensued, but his party was small, so he was overpowered, made prisoner, and carried to Sultán Sháh. This prince ordered him into confinement, but when the battle was fought, and Sultán Sháh was defeated, the victors released Kutbu-d dín and brought him in his iron fetters, riding on a camel, to his master Sultán Mu'izzu-d dín. The Sultán received him kindly, and on his arrival at his capital Ghaznín, he conferred on him the districts of Kahrám. From thence he went to Mírat, of which he took possession in A.H. 587 (1191 A.D.) In the same year he marched from Mírat and captured Dehli.

In A.H. 590 (1194 A.D.) he and 'Izzu-d dín Husain Kharmil, both being generals of the army, accompanied the Sultán and defeated Rái Jai Chand of Benáres in the neighbourhood of Chandawál. In the year 591 H. (1195 A.D.) Thankar was conquered; and in 593 H. (1197 A.D.) he went towards Nahrwála, defeated Rái Bhím-deo, and took revenge on the part of the Sultán. He also took other countries of Hindustán as far as the outskirts of the dominions of China on the east. Malik 'Izzu-d dín Muhammad Bakhtiyár Khiljí had subdued the districts of Bihár and Núdiya[1] in those quarters, as will be related hereafter in the history of that general.

When Sultán-i Gházi Muhammad Sám died, Sultán Ghiyásu-d dín Mahmúd Muhammad Sám, his nephew, gave Kutbu-d dín the royal canopy, and the title of Sultán. In A.H. 602 (1205 A.D.) the new monarch marched from Dehli to attack Lohor, and on Tuesday, the 18th of the month of Zi-l Ka'da, in the same year (June 1206), he mounted the throne in that city. After some time a dispute arose between him and Sultán Táju-d

[1] [نودیه—Nuddea.]

dín Yalduz respecting Lohor, and it ended in a battle, in which the victory was gained by Sultán Kutbu-d dín. Táju-d dín fled. Sultán Kutbu-d dín then proceeded towards Ghaznín, which he captured, and for forty days he sat upon the throne of that city, at the end of which time he returned to Dehli, as has been before mentioned. Death now claimed his own, and in the year 607 H. the Sultán fell from his horse in the field while he was playing chaugán, and the horse came down upon him, so that the pommel of the saddle entered his chest, and killed him. The period of his government, from his first conquest of Dehli up to this time, was twenty years, and the time of his reign, during which he wore the crown, and had the Khutba read and coin struck in his name, was something more than four years.

2. *Arám Sháh, son of Sultán Kutbu-d dín Aibak.*

On the death of Sultán Kutbu-d dín, the nobles and princes of Hindustán deemed it advisable for the satisfaction of the army, the peace of the people, and the tranquillity of the country, to place Arám Sháh upon the throne. Sultán Kutbu-d dín had three daughters, of whom the two eldest were, one after the death of the other, married to Malik Násiru-d dín Kubácha, and the third to Sultán Shamsu-d dín. Now that Kutbu-d dín was dead, and Arám Sháh was raised to the throne, Malik Násiru-d dín Kubácha marched towards Uch and Multán. Kutbu-d dín had regarded Sultán Shamsu-d dín as well suited for empire, had called him his son, and had given him Badáún in Júgír. The chief men of Dehli now invited him from Badáún and raised him to the throne. He espoused the daughter of Sultán Kutbu-d dín.

When Arám Sháh expired, Hindustán was divided into four principalities. The province of Sind was possessed by Násiru-d dín Kubácha; Dehli and its environs belonged to Sultán Sa'íd Shamsu-d dín; the districts of Lakhnautí were held by the Khiljí chiefs and Sultáns, and the province of Lohor was held sometimes by Malik Táju-d dín, sometimes by Malik Násiru-d dín Kubácha, and sometimes by Sultán Shamsu-d dín. An account of each will be given hereafter.

3. *Násiru-d dín Kubácha.*

Malik Násiru-d dín was an excellent monarch, and was a slave of Sultán Mu'izzu-d dín. He was a man of the highest intelligence, cleverness, experience, discretion, and acumen. He had served Sultán-i Ghází Mu'izzu-d dín for many years in all kinds of offices and positions, and he was well acquainted with all matters, small and great, concerning courts, and military and and civil affairs. He obtained Uch and Multán, which were ruled by Malik Násiru-d dín Aitamur.¹ In the battle of Andkhod,² which Sultán Mu'izzu-d dín fought with the armies of Khitá and the princes of Turkistán, Násiru-d dín had displayed great valour by the stirrups of the Sultán, where he fought desperately, and sent many of the infidels to hell. The warriors of the army of Khitá were distressed by the slaughter which he dealt around, so they all at once came upon him and thus he was overpowered.³ The Sultán Ghází, through this event, came safely to the throne of Ghaznín, and the town of Uch was assigned to Malik Násiru-d dín Kubácha. He married two daughters of Sultán Kutbu-d dín; by the first he had a son, Malik 'Aláu-d dín Bahrám Sháh, who was handsome and of amiable character, but he was addicted to pleasure, and gave way to his youthful passions. When Malik Násiru-d dín Kubácha, after the death of Sultán Kutbu-d dín, went to Uch, he took the city of Multán; and Hindustán, Dewal, and all as far as the sea shore, fell into his power. He also took the forts, towns, and cities of the territory of Sind, and assumed regal dignity. He extended his rule to Tabar-hindh,⁴ Kahrám, and Sarsutí. He

---

¹ [This sentence is defective and ambiguous.]

² [The name is written correctly "Andkhod," not "Andkho" as in the translation of Firishta, which is followed by Elphinstone and the maps. The text of Firishta has "Andkhod," and this is the spelling of Ibn Haukal, Yákut, and the geographers generally. Yákut says the "ethnic name is Ankhudí," and Gen. Cunningham presumes to identify it with the "Alikodra" of Ptolemy.]

³ ["*Shahídat yáft*," lit. "he obtained martyrdom" or, "was slain."]

⁴ [There can be little, if any, doubt that this place is the same as Sarhindh, but from this point onwards the name is most persistently written "Tabarhindh," although the name "Sarhindh," has been used previously (pp. 295, 296). It may be a

took Lohor several times, and fought a battle with the army of Ghaznín which had come there on the part of Sultán Táju-d dín Yalduz; but he was defeated by Khwájá Muwaidu-l Mulk Sanjarí, who was minister of the king of Ghaznín. He still maintained possession of the territory of Sind. During the struggles with the infidels of Chín, many chiefs of Khurásán, Ghor, and Ghaznín joined him, and upon all his associates he bestowed great favours and honours. There was continual variance between him and Sultán Sa'íd Shams.

When the battle between Jalálu-d dín Khwárizm Sháh and Changíz Khán was fought on the banks of the Indus, Jalálu-d dín came into Sind and went towards Dewal and Makrán. After the victory of Nandua-tari the Moghal prince came with a large army to the walls of the city of Multán and besieged that strong fort for forty days. During this war and invasion Malik Násiru-d dín opened his treasures and lavished them munificently among the people. He gave such proofs of resolution, energy, wisdom, and personal bravery, that it will remain on record to the day of resurrection. This Moghal invasion took place in the year 621 H. (1224 A.D.) One year and six months after, the chiefs of Ghor through this irruption of the infidels, joined Násiru-d dín. Towards the end of the year 623 H. (1226 A.D.), the army of Khilj, consisting of all the forces of Khwárizm, under the command of Malik Khán Khilj, invaded the lands of Mansúra, one of the cities of Siwistán. Malik Násiru-d dín marched to expel them, and a battle ensued, in which the army of Khilj was defeated and the Khán of Khilj was slain. Malik Násiru-d dín then returned to Multán and Uch.

In this same year, the compiler of these leaves, Siráj Minháj, came from the country of Khurásán, via Ghaznín and Mithán, and thence reached Uch by boat, on Tuesday, the 26th of the month of Jumáda-l awwal A.H. 624 (April, 1227 A.D.). In the month

blunder of the copyist, but on the other hand, it may be another and older form of the name. The etymology of the word Sarhindh is doubtful, and has been a subject of speculation.—See Thornton.]

of Zí-l hijja of the same year, the Firozí college at Uch
was consigned to the care of the author. On the provocation of the army of 'Aláu-d dín Bahrám Sháh, in the month
of Rabí'u-l awwal, A.H. 624, Sultán Sa'íd Shamsu-d dín en-
encamped in sight of Uch. Malik Násiru-d dín fled by water
towards Bhakkar, and the army of the Sultán, under the command of the Minister of State, Nizámu-l Mulk, pursued him and
besieged him in that fort. The Sultán remained two months
and twenty-seven days before Uch, and on Tuesday the 27th
of Jumáda-l awwal the fort was taken. When the news of
this conquest reached Malik Násiru-d dín, he sent his son,
'Aláu-d dín Bahrám Sháh to wait upon the Sultán; but as he
reached the camp on the 22nd of Jumáda-l ákhir, the news of
the conquest of Bhakkar arrived. Malik Násiru-d dín drowned
himself in the river Sind and thus ended his life. He reigned in
the territory of Sind, Uch, and Multán for twenty-two years.

4. Sultán Bahdu-d dín Tughril.

Malik Baháu-d dín Tughril was a man of kindly disposition,
just, charitable, and polite. He was one of the oldest servants
of Sultán Gházi Mu'izzu-d dín, who with his favour had made
him a great man. When the Sultán conquered the fort of
Thankar[1] in the country of Bhayána[2] after fighting with the Rái,
he consigned it to Baháu-d dín, and he so improved the condition of the country that merchants and men of credit came
thither from all parts of Hindustán and Khurásán. He gave all
of them houses and goods, and also made them masters of landed
property, so that they settled there. As he and his army did
not like to reside in the fort of Thankar, he founded the city of
Sultán-kot,[3] in the territory of Bhayána and made it the place of
his residence. From this place he constantly sent his horsemen
towards Gwalior. When Sultán Gházi retired from that fort

---

[1] ["Bhankar" or "Bhangar" in other places, see p. 296. A note in the text gives the preference to "Thankar," but no reason is assigned.]

[2] [Bayána or Biana, fifty miles S.W. of Agra.]

[3] [See Firishta I. 196. A note in the text says "Bílkot," but this is impossible.]

he told Daháu-d dín that he ought to secure it for himself. Upon this hint Daháu-d dín, posted a division of his army at the foot of the fort of Gwalior, and at two parasangs distance he constructed a fortification, where his cavalry might picket at night and return in the morning to the base of the rock. A year passed and the garrison being reduced to extremities sent messengers to Kutbu-d dín and surrendered the fort to him. There was a little misunderstanding between Daháu-d dín and Sultán Kutbu-d dín. Malik Daháu-d dín Tughril was a man of excellent qualities, and he has left many marks of his goodness in the territory of Bhoyáná.

5. *Malik Ghází Ikhtiyáru-d dín Mahammad Bakhtiyár Khiljí, of Lakhnautí.*

It is related that this Muhammad Bakhtiyár was a Khiljí, of Ghor, of the province of Garmsír. He was a very smart, enterprising, bold, courageous, wise, and experienced man. He left his tribe and came to the Court of Sultán Mu'izzu-d dín, at Ghaznín, and was placed in the *díwán-i 'arz* (office for petitions), but as the chief of that department was not satisfied with him he was dismissed, and proceeded from Ghaznín to Hindustán. When he reached the Court of Dehli, he was again rejected by the chief of the *díwán-i 'arz* of that city,[1] and so he went on to Badáún, into the service of Hizbaru-d dín Hasan, commander-in-chief, where he obtained a suitable position. After some time he went to Oudh in the service of Malik Hisámu-d dín Ughlabak. He had good horses and arms, and he had showed much activity and valour at many places, so he obtained Sahlat and Sahlí[2] in Jagír. Being a bold and enterprising man, he used to make incursions into the districts of Munír (Monghír), and Behár, and bring away much plunder, until in this manner he obtained plenty of horses, arms,

[1] [Here there is a variation in the text for four or five lines, but the reading adopted seems the most intelligible and consistent. See printed text p. 146.]
[2] [Var. "Salmat," "Sahlast."]

and men. The fame of his bravery and of his plundering raids spread abroad, and a body of Khiljís joined him from Hindustán. His exploits were reported to Sultán Kutbu-d dín, and he sent him a dress and showed him great honour. Being thus encouraged, he led his army to Behár and ravaged it. In this manner he continued for a year or two to plunder the neighbourhood, and at last prepared to invade the country.

It is said by credible persons that he went to the gate of the fort of Behár with only two hundred horse, and began the war by taking the enemy unawares. In the service of Bakhtiyár there were two brothers of great intelligence. One of them was named Nizámu-d dín and the other Samsámu-d dín. The compiler of this book met Samsámu-d dín at Lakhnautí in the year 641 H. (1243 A.D.), and heard the following story from him. When Bakhtiyár reached the gate of the fort, and the fighting began, these two wise brothers were active in that army of heroes. Muhammad Bakhtiyár with great vigour and audacity rushed in at the gate of the fort and gained possession of the place. Great plunder fell into the hands of the victors. Most of the inhabitants of the place were Brahmans with shaven heads. They were put to death. Large numbers of books were found there, and when the Muhammadans saw them, they called for some persons to explain their contents, but all the men had been killed. It was discovered that the whole fort and city was a place of study (*madrasa*). In the Hindí language the word Behár (*vihár*) means a college.

When this conquest was achieved, Bakhtiyár returned laden with plunder, and came to Kutbu-d dín, who paid him much honour and respect. A body of the nobles of the Court looked upon the favours which Sultán Kutbu-d dín bestowed upon him, with jealousy. In their convivial parties they used to sneer at him, and to cast jibes and ironical observations at him. Their animosity reached to such a pitch that he was ordered to combat with an elephant at the White Palace. He struck it such a blow with his battle-axe on the trunk that it ran away, and he pursued it. On achieving this triumph, Sultán Kutbu-d dín bestowed rich gifts upon him from his own royal treasure, and he also ordered his nobles to present to him such ample offerings as can scarcely be detailed. Muhammad Bakhtiyár in that very meeting scattered all those gifts and gave them away to the people. After receiving a robe from the Sultán he returned to Behár. Great fear of him prevailed in the minds of the infidels of the territories of Lakhnautí, Behár, Bang (Bengal), and Kámrúp.

It is related by credible authorities that mention of the brave deeds and conquests of Malik Muhammad Bakhtiyár was made before Rái Lakhmaniya, whose capital was the city of Núdiya. He was a great Rái, and had sat upon the throne for a period of eighty years. A story about that Rái may be here related:—

When the father of the Rái departed this world, he was in the womb of his mother, so the crown was placed upon her belly, and all the great men expressed their loyalty before her. His family was respected by all the Ráis or chiefs of Hindustán, and was considered to hold the rank of Khalíf, or sovereign. When the time of the birth of Lakhmaniya drew near, and symptoms of delivery appeared, his mother assembled the astrologers and Jímhmana, in order that they might see if the aspect of the time was auspicious. They all unanimously said that if the child were born at that moment it would be exceedingly unlucky, for he would not become a sovereign. But that if the birth occurred two hours later the child would reign for eighty years. When his mother heard this opinion of the astrologers, she ordered her legs to be tied together, and caused herself to be hung with her head downwards. She also directed the astrologers to watch for the auspicious time. When they all agreed that the time for delivery was come, she ordered herself to be taken down, and Lakhmaniya was born directly, but he had no sooner come into the world than his mother died from the anguish she had endured. Lakhmaniya was placed upon the throne, and he ruled for eighty years. It is said by trustworthy persons that no one, great or small, ever suffered injustice at his hands. He used to give a lac to every person that asked him for charity; as was also the custom of the generous Sultán, the Hátim of the time, Kutbu-d dín. In that country the current money is *kaudas* (kauris) instead of *chítals*,[1] and the smallest present he made was a lac of *kaudas*.

Let us return to the history of Muhammad Bakhtiyár. When he came back from his visit to Sultán Kutbu-d dín and conquered Behár, his fame reached the ears of Rái Lakhmaniya and spread throughout all parts of the Rái's dominions. A body of astrologers, Brahmans, and wise men of the kingdom, came to the Rái and represented to him that in their books the old Brahmans had written that the country would eventually fall into the hands of the Turks. The time appointed was approaching; the Turks had already taken Behár, and next year they would also attack his country, it was therefore advisable that the Rái should make peace with them, so that all the people might emigrate from the territory, and save themselves from contention with the Turks. The Rái asked whether the man who was to conquer the country was described as having any peculiarity in his person. They replied, Yes; the peculiarity is, that in standing upright both his hands hang down below the knees, so that his fingers touch his shins.[2] The Rái observed that it was best for him to send some confidential agents to make enquiry about that peculiarity. Accordingly confidential agents were despatched, an examination was made, and the peculiarity was found in the person of Muhammad Bakhtiyár. When this was ascertained to be the fact, most of the Brahmans and many chiefs (*sdhdn*) went away to the country of Sanknát,[3] and to the cities of Bang and Kámrúp, but Rái Lakhmaniya did not like to leave his territory.

Next year Muhammad Bakhtiyár prepared an army, and marched from Behár. He suddenly appeared before the city of Núdiya with only eighteen horsemen, the remainder of his army

---

[1] [See Thomas, Jour. R. A. S. New Series II. 165.]
[2] [An old Hindú idea of the figure of a hero.]
[3] [Var. "Sankát" and "Saknát;" query "Jagganáth." See below.]

was left to follow. Muhammad Bakhtiyár did not molest any man, but went on peaceably and without ostentation, so that no one could suspect who he was. The people rather thought that he was a merchant, who had brought horses for sale. In this manner he reached the gate of Rái Lakhmaniya's palace, when he drew his sword and commenced the attack. At this time the Rái was at his dinner, and golden and silver dishes filled with food were placed before him according to the usual custom. All of a sudden a cry was raised at the gate of his palace and in the city. Before he had ascertained what had occurred, Muhammad Bakhtiyár had rushed into the palace and put a number of men to the sword. The Rái fled barefooted by the rear of the palace, and his whole treasure, and all his wives, maid servants, attendants, and women fell into the hands of the invader. Numerous elephants were taken, and such booty was obtained by the Muhammadans as is beyond all compute. When his army arrived, the whole city was brought under subjection, and he fixed his head quarters there.

Rái Lakhmaniya went towards Sanknát[1] and Bengal, where he died. His sons are to this day rulers in the territory of Bengal. When Muhammad Bakhtiyár had taken possession of the Rái's territory, he destroyed the city of Núdiya and established the seat of his government at Lakhnautí. He brought the surrounding places into his possession, and caused his name to be read in the Khutba and struck on the coins. Mosques, colleges, and monasteries were raised everywhere by the generous efforts of him and his officers, and he sent a great portion of the spoil to Sultán Kutbu-d dín.

When several years had elapsed, he received information about the territories of Turkistán and Tibet, to the east of Lakhnautí, and he began to entertain a desire of taking Tibet and Turkistán. For this purpose he prepared an army of about ten thousand horse. Among the hills which lie between Tibet and the territory of Lakhnautí, there are three races of people.

[1] [Stewart in his History of Bengal says *Jagganáth*.]

The one is called Kúch (Kúch Behár), the second Mich, and the third, Tiháru.[1] They all have Turkí features and speak different languages, something between the language of Hind and that of Tibet. One of the chiefs of the tribes of Kúch and Mich, who was called 'Alí Mich, had been converted to Muhammadanism by Muhammad Bakhtiyár, and this man agreed to conduct him into the hills. He led him to a place where there was a city called Mardhan-kot.[2] It is said that in the ancient times when Gurshásp Sháh returned from China, he came to Kámrúd (Kámrúp) and built this city. Before the town there runs a stream which is exceedingly large. It is called Bangamatí.[3] When it enters the country of Hindustan it receives in the Hindí language the name of Samundar. In length, breadth, and depth, it is three times greater than the Ganges. Muhammad Bakhtiyár came to the banks of this river, and 'Alí Mich went before the Muhammadan army. For ten days they marched on until he led them along the upper course of the river into the hills, to a place where from old times a bridge had stood over the water having about twenty (*bíst o and*) arches of stone. When the army reached the bridge, Bakhtiyár posted there two officers, one a Turk, and the other a Khiljí, with a large force to secure the place till his return. With the remainder of the army he then went over the bridge. The Rái of Kámrúp, on receiving intelligence of the passage of the Muhammadans, sent some confidential officers to warn Bakhtiyár against invading the country of Tibet, and to assure him that he had better return and make more suitable preparations. He also added that he, the Rái of Kámrúp, had determined that next year he also would muster his forces and precede the Muhammadan army to secure the country. Muhammad Bakhtiyár paid no heed to these representations, but marched on towards the hills of Tibet.

One night in the year 641 (1243 A.D.) he halted at a place

[1] [Stewart gives these names "Koomeh, Mikeh, (or Mickh) and Neharu."—*History of Bengal*, p. 46.]
[2] [Var. "Bardhan, Dardhan." Stewart has "Burdchan or Murdchan."]
[3] [The Brahmaputra. It is so called in this part of its course.]

between Deo-kot and Bangáwan, and stayed as a guest in the house of Mu'atamadu-d daula, who had formerly been an equerry in the service of Muhammad Bakhtiyár and had lived in the town of Lakhnautí. From this man he heard that after passing over the bridge, the road lay for fifteen stages through the defiles and passes of the mountains, and at the sixteenth stage level land was reached. The whole of that land was well populated, and the villages were flourishing. The village which was first reached had a fort, and when the Muhammadan army made an attack upon it, the people in the fort and the surrounding places came to oppose them, and a battle ensued. The fight raged from morning till the time of afternoon prayer, and large numbers of the Muhammadans were slain and wounded. The only weapons of the enemy were bamboo spears; and their armour, shields and helmets, consisted only of raw silk strongly fastened and sewed together. They all carried long bows and arrows. When night came on, the prisoners who had been taken were brought forward and questioned, and it was then ascertained that at five parasangs from that place there was a city called Karambatan,[1] and in it there was about three hundred and fifty thousand brave Turks armed with bows. The moment the horsemen of the Muhammadans arrived, messengers went to report their approach, and these messengers would reach their destination next morning. When the author was at Lakhnautí, he made enquiries about that place, and learnt that it was a pretty large city. The ramparts of it are built of stone. The inhabitants of it are Brahmans and Núnís,[2] and the city is under the sway of the chief of these people. They profess the Buddhist[3] religion. Every morning in the market of that city, about fifteen hundred horses are sold. All the saddle horses[4] which come into the

---

[1] [Var. "Karam-bain," "Laram-bain." Stewart has "Kármputtan."]
[2] ["Núníyán," var. "Túníyán."]
[3] ["Dín-i Tarsáí," which according to the dictionaries, means Christianity, or Fire-worship. It is not likely that either can be intended here, though Stewart in his *Hist. of Bengal* says, "their prince was a Christian." The term is probably applied to any established religion other than Muhammadanism.]
[4] ["Asp-i tang-bastah." Stewart reads "Tingkan," which is probably right.]

territory of Lakhnantí are brought from that country. Their roads pass through the ravines of the mountains, as is quite common in that part of the country. Between Kámrúp and Tibet there are thirty-five mountain passes through which horses are brought to Lakhnautí.

In short, when Muhammad Bakhtiyár became aware of the nature of the country, and saw that his men were tired and exhausted, and that many had been slain and disabled in the first day's march, he consulted with his nobles, and they resolved that it was advisable to retreat, that in the following year they might return to the country in a state of greater preparation. On their way back there was not left on all the road a single blade of grass or a bit of wood. All had been set on fire and burnt. The inhabitants of the valleys and passes had all removed far away from the road, and for the space of fifteen days not a sir of food nor a blade of grass or fodder was to be found, and they were compelled to kill and eat their horses.

When, after descending the hills of the land of Kámrúp, they reached the bridge, they found that the arches of it had been demolished. The two officers who had been left to guard it had quarrelled, and in their animosity to each other had neglected to take care of the bridge and the road, so the Hindús of Kámrúp had come there and destroyed the bridge. When Muhammad Bakhtiyár with his army reached the place, he found no means of crossing. Neither was there a boat to be found, so he was greatly troubled and perplexed. They resolved to fix on some place where to encamp, and prepare rafts and boats to enable them to cross the river.

In the vicinity of this place was perceived a temple, very lofty and strong, and of beautiful structure. In it there were numerous idols of gold and silver, and one very large golden idol, which exceeded two or three thousand miskáls in weight. Muhammad Bakhtiyár and the remnant of his army sought refuge in that temple, and set about procuring wood and ropes for constructing rafts to cross the stream. The Rái of Kámrúp was informed of the distress and weakness of the Muhammadans, and he issued orders to all the Hindús of his territory to come up, levy after levy, and all around the temple they were to stick their bamboo spears in the ground and to plait them together so as to form a kind of wall. When the soldiers of Islám saw this they told Muhammad Bakhtiyár that if they remained passive they would all be taken in the trap of the infidels and be made prisoners; some way of escape must be sought out. By common consent they made a simultaneous sally, and directing their efforts to one spot, they cleared for themselves a way through the dangerous obstacle to the open ground. The Hindús pursued them to the banks of the river and halted there. Every one exerted his ingenuity to devise some means of passing over the river. One of the soldiers urged his horse into the water, and it was found fordable to the distance of a bow-shot. A cry arose in the army that a fordable passage was found, and all threw themselves into the stream. The Hindús in their rear took possession of the banks. When the Muhammadans reached the middle of the stream, the water was found to be very deep, and they nearly all perished. Muhammad Bakhtiyár with some horse, to the number of about a hundred, more or less, crossed the river with the greatest difficulty, but all the rest were drowned.

When Muhammad Bakhtiyár escaped from this watery grave, the intelligence of it reached the people of Kúch and Mích. 'Alí Mích, the guide, sent his relatives forward on the road to meet him, and received him with much kindness and hospitality. When Bakhtiyár reached Deokot he was seized by sickness, occasioned by excess of grief. He would never go out, because he felt ashamed to look on the wives and children of those who had perished. If ever he did ride out, all people, women and children, from their housetops and the streets, cried out cursing and abusing him. In this position the remark often fell from his tongue, "Has any misfortune befallen Sultán Ghází Mu'izzu-d dín Muhammad Sám, that my fortune has turned so bad?" It was even so, for Sultán Ghází was killed about that time. Muhammad Bakhtiyár grew worse under his trouble, took to his bed, and died. Some writers say that there was a chief under Muhammad Bakhtiyár, of the same tribe as himself, 'Alí Mardán Khiljí by name. He was a very bold and dauntless man, and the district of Kúní had been assigned to him. When he heard of Bakhtiyár's sickness he came to Deokot, where Bakhtiyár was lying ill. Three days had elapsed since anyone had been admitted to see him, but 'Alí Mardán by some means got in to him, drew aside the sheet with which he was covered, and killed him with a knife. His death took place in A.H. 602 (1205 A.D.)

6. *Malik 'Izzu-d dín Muhammad Shírán Khiljí.*

It is related that Muhammad Shírán and Ahmad Írán were two brothers, sons of a noble Khiljí. They were in the service of Muhammad Bakhtiyár, and when this chief started on his campaign in Kámrúp and Tibet, he sent Shírán and his brother Ahmad with detachments of his troops to Lakhnautí and Jájnagar. On the arrival of the news of the defeat and death of Bakhtiyár, they returned from their stations, and came dutifully to Deokot. From that place he (Muhammad Shírán) went to Nárkotí, which belonged to 'Alí Mardán, and seizing him in punishment of the crime he had committed, put him in prison under the charge of the Kotwál of the place, whose name was Bábá Kotwál Isfahání. He then came back to Deokot and collected all the nobles. This Muhammad Shírán was a very active and high principled man.

When Muhammad Bakhtiyár sacked the city of Núdiya and defeated Rái Lakhmaniya, the soldiers, followers, and elephants of the Rái were dispersed, and the Muhammadans pursued and plundered them. Muhammad Shírán was three days absent from the camp on this pursuit, so that all the officers began to be apprehensive about him. After the third day, news was brought that Muhammad Shírán had captured eighteen or more elephants in a certain jungle, with their drivers, and alone by himself he was keeping them there. Horsemen were sent out to his assistance and all the elephants were brought in. In short, Muhammad Shírán was an energetic man, ready and full of expedients. When he returned, after taking 'Alí Mardán prisoner, as he was the chief of all the Khiljí nobles, they all rendered him homage, but each noble continued to rule over the districts which belonged to himself. 'Alí Mardán contrived to ingratiate himself with the Kotwál, and, escaping from prison, he went to the Court of Delhi. Upon his representations Sultán Kutbu-d dín sent Káimáz[1] Rúmí from Oude towards Lakhnautí, and in execution of the royal orders the Khiljí chiefs were quieted. Hisámu-d dín 'Auz Khiljí, who had received the districts of Gangatori[2] from Muhammad Bakhtiyár, came to receive Káimáz Rúmí, and went with him to Deokot. Here Káimáz transferred to him the district of Deokot, and then returned. Muhammad Shírán and other Khiljí chiefs having assembled, determined to attack Deokot, so Káimáz came back from the middle of his journey and fought a battle with the Khiljí chiefs, and Muhammad Shírán and the other Khiljís were defeated. Quarrels afterwards broke out among these chiefs in the neighbourhood of Makida[3] and Mautús, and Muhammad Shírán was slain. His tomb is in that country.

7. *Malik 'Aláu-d dín 'Alí Mardán Khiljí.*

'Alí Mardán was very resolute, bold, and fearless. When he escaped from the prison at Nárkotí, he came to Sultán Kutbu-d dín, and with him went to Ghaznín, where he fell into the hands of the Turks of that place. It is related that one day as he was going to a hunting-ground with Sultán Táju-d dín Yalduz, he said to one of the Khiljí nobles, who was called Sálár-i Zafar (victorious general), "What would you say if I were to kill

---

[1] [Var. "Kásmáz," "Kimár."] [2] [Var. "Kankori."]
[3] [Var: Sakananda.]

Táju-d dín Yalduz with one arrow, and to make you king on the spot." Zafar Khilj was a wise man, and he prevented him from committing the (crime). When he returned from the hunt Zafar gave him two horses and sent him away. On reaching Hindustan, he waited upon Sultán Kutbu-d dín and received much honour and favour. The province of Lakhnautí was conferred on him and he went to that place. When he had crossed the Koal river, Hisámu-d dín 'Auz Khiljí came from Deo-kot to meet him. He then entered Deo-kot, assumed the reins of government, and brought all the territories under his rule. When Sultán Kutbu-d dín died, 'Alí Mardán assumed royal state, and ordered his name to be read in the Khutba, under the title of Sultán 'Aláu-d dín. He was a cruel and sanguinary man. He sent his army in different directions and slew many Khiljí chiefs. The Ráis of the surrounding places grew apprehensive of him, and sent him presents and tribute. He began to issue orders to various parts of Hindustan, and to utter most extravagant vaunts before the assembly, and in open court he talked about the kings of Khurásán, Ghazní, and Ghor, and uttered the most useless absurdities. He even talked of sending his mandates to Ghaznín Khurásán, and 'Irák, requiring them to submit to his rule.

It is related that there was a merchant in that country who was reduced to poverty and had lost all his wealth. He requested a donation from 'Álí Mardán, and the king enquired what place he was a native of. He replied, Safáhán (Ispahán). The king then ordered a farmán to be written, granting to him Safáhán as his jágír. Through dread of his great severity and harshness, no one dared to say that Safáhán was not in his possession. If any person told him, when he made such grant, that the place was not his, he replied, "I shall take it." So he granted Safáhán to that merchant, who was indigent and miserable. The great and wise persons of the place represented in behalf of the poor fellow, that he required money for the expences of the journey and for the fitting out of an army to take possession of his grant of Ispahán. A large sum of money was accordingly ordered to be given to the merchant. To such a degree was the haughtiness and severity and false pride of 'Alí Mardán excited. Besides all this, he was a cruel man and a tyrant. The poor people, the peasants, and the army were all tired of his tyranny and cruelty. They had no way of escape but in rebellion. A number of Khiljí chiefs combined against him and killed him. They then placed Hisámu-d dín 'Auz upon the throne. The length of 'Alí Mardán's reign was two years, more or less.

8. *Malik Hisámu-d dín 'Auz Khiljí.*

Hisámu-d dín 'Auz was a man of kindly disposition. He was a Khilj of Ghor. It is said that once upon a time he was driving a laden mule along the skirts of the hills of Ghor to a certain village, on his journey from the country of Záwulistán to the highlands called Pasha-afroz. Two fakírs in religious garb came to him and asked him whether he carried any food on his mule. 'Auz Khiljí replied that he did. He had with him some traveller's bread, which he took from a bag on the back of the mule and spread it before the darweshes. When they had eaten the food, he produced some water and held it in a vessel before them. The fakírs partook of the food and drank of the water which he presented; they began to talk with each other saying, "This man has rendered us a service, we must not let him lose by it." They turned their faces towards 'Auz Khiljí and said, "O chief, go towards Hindustan; we give you the country as far as Muhammadanism has spread."

At this direction of the fakírs he returned from that spot, and placed his wife upon his mule, and took his way towards Hindustán. He joined Muhammad Bakhtiyár; and his fortune reached such a degree of success that his name was read in the Khutba and struck upon the coin throughout the territory of Lakhnautí. To him the title of Sultán Ghiyásu-d dín was given. He made the city of Lakhnautí the seat of his government, and built a fort for his residence. People flocked to him from all quarters, for he was exceedingly good, and possessed solid endowments, both external and internal. He was polite, brave, just and generous. During his reign, the army and the people in general lived in tranquillity and comfort. All his nobles were greatly benefitted by his gifts and bounty, and obtained immense wealth. He left many fine monuments of his goodness behind him in the country. He raised public buildings and mosques. He gave stipends to learned men and to shaikhs and saiyids; he also bestowed property and goods upon other classes of the people. For instance, there was a descendant of the Imám of Fíroz-koh, who was called Jalálu-d dín, son of Jamálu-d dín Ghazuawí. He came with a body of men from his native country to Hindustán in A.H. 608 (1211 A.D.) After some years he went back to Fíroz-koh, taking immense wealth with him. On being asked how he obtained those riches, he said, that when he reached Hindustan, he went to Dehli, and from thence he determined to proceed to Lakhnautí. When he reached that place the Almighty so favoured him that his name was mentioned in the Court of Ghiyásu-d dín. That kind-hearted king awarded him from his treasure a large dishfull of gold and silver *tankas*, worth about ten thousand silver *tankas*. He also ordered the chiefs, nobles and ministers to give something, and accordingly each one gave him some present, amounting in the whole to about three thousand pieces more, and at the time of his departure, five thousand pieces were added to what he had formerly received; so that the Imám-záda obtained eighteen thousand *tankas* through the favour of that Ghiyásu-d dín Khiljí, king of Lakhnautí.

When the writer of this book reached the territory of Lakhnautí in A.H. 641 (1243 A.D.), he witnessed the charity of this king with his own eyes.

The territory of Lakhnautí consists of two parts, on opposite banks of the Ganges. That to the west is called Dál,[1] the city of Lakhnautí is on this side. The eastern side is called Barbanda,[2] and the city of Deo-kot is on that side. From Lakh-

---
[1] [Var. "Azál."]   [2] [Var. "Baránd."]

nautí to the gates of Lakhnaur,[1] and on the other side of the river as far as the city of Deo-kot, embankments (*pul*) have been raised, which extend for ten days' journey. The reason for this is that during the rains all that country is inundated and if there were no embankments people would have to go to different parts and places in boats. In his reign, the roads by means of these embankments became passable by all men. It is also said that when, after the death of Malik Násiru-d dín Mahmúd, Sultán Sa'id Shamsu-d dín came to the territory of Lakhnautí to repress the rebellion of Ikhtiyáru-d dín, he noticed the charity of Ghiyásu-d dín. Whenever afterwards he mentioned his name he used to call him Sultán, and it pleased him to say that, considering his great charity, no one ought to hesitate about giving him that title. Indeed he was a generous, just, and good-natured man. All the territories of Lakhnautí, such as Jájnagar and the provinces of Bengal, Kámrúp, and Tirhut, used to send him offerings. The district of Lakhnaur submitted to him, and brought him elephants, furniture, and treasures in abundance, and he established his officers there.

Sultán Sa'id Shamsu-d dín sent armies several times from Dehli, and having conquered the province of Behár he stationed his officers there. In 622 (1225 A.D.) he invaded Lakhnautí and Ghiyásu-d dín advanced his boats up the stream to oppose him, but peace was made between them. Shamsu-d dín accepted thirty-eight elephants, and treasure to the amount of eighty lacs. He ordered the Khutba to be read in his name. On his departure he gave Behár to Malik 'Aláu-d dín Júní. Ghiyásu-d dín 'Auz came to Behár from Lakhnautí, and took it, and acted tyrannically. At last in the year 624 (1227 A.D.), Malik Shahíd Násiru-d dín Mahmúd, son of Sultán Shamsu-d dín, having collected an army in Hindustán, and accompanied by 'Izzu-l Malik Jání, marched from Oude to Lakhnautí. At this time Ghiyásu-d dín 'Auz had gone on an expedition to Bengal and Kámrúp, and had left Lakhnautí stripped of defenders. Malik Násiru-d dín

[1] [Stewart reads "Nagor (in Dirhhám);" but Nagor is right away from the river.]

Mahmúd captured the place, and when Ghiyásu-d dín heard of its fall, he returned and fought a battle with the conqueror, but he and all his officers were made prisoners. He was then killed, after a reign of twelve years.

TABAKAT XXI.

HISTORY OF THE SHAMSIYA KINGS OF HINDUSTÁN.

[Page 164 to page 225 of the Text.]

1.—*Sultán Shamsu-d dunyá wau-d dín Abú-l Muzaffar Altamsh.*

It was destined from all eternity by the most high and holy God that the country of Hindustan should be placed under the protection of the great king, the light of the world and religion, Sultán Abú-l Muzaffar Altamsh. [*The exordium goes on at some length in a similar inflated style of eulogy of the monarch and of Dehli his capital.*]

It is related by credible persons that Sultán Shamsu-d dín was chosen by the destiny of Providence in his early age from the tribes of Albarí[1] in Turkistan for the sovereignty of Islám and of the dominions of Hindustan. His father, whose name was Yalam Khán, had numerous dependents, relatives, and followers in his employ. The future monarch was from his childhood remarkable for beauty, intelligence, and grace, such as excited jealousy in the hearts of his brothers, so they enticed him away from his father and mother with the pretence of going to see a drove of horses. His case was like that of Joseph: "They said, father, why dost thou not trust Joseph with us, for we are sincere friends to him ? Send him with us in the morning, that he may amuse himself and sport, and we will take care of him." When they brought him to the drove of horses, they sold him to the dealer. Some say that his sellers were his cousins. The horse-dealers took him to Bukhárá, and sold him to one of the

[1] [قبائل البري]

relations of the chief judge of that city. For some time he remained with that great and noble family, the chiefs of which nourished and educated him like a son.

A credible person has related, that he heard in the gracious words of the king himself, that on a certain occasion one of the members of the family gave him a piece of money and ordered him to go to the bázár and buy some grapes. He went to the bázár, and on the way lost the piece of money. Being of tender age, he began to cry for fear; and while he was weeping and crying, a fakír came to him, took his hand, purchased some grapes, and gave them to him, saying: "When you obtain wealth and dominion, take care that you show respect to fakírs and pious men, and maintain their rights." He gave his promise to the fakír, and whatever fortune and power he obtained he always ascribed to the favour shewn him by that fakír. It is firmly believed that no king so benevolent, so sympathising, and so respectful to the learned and to elders as he was, ever rose by his native energy to the cradle of empire.

From that noble and distinguished family, he was purchased by a merchant whose name was Hájí Bukhári, and he sold him to another merchant named Jamálu-d dín Chast Kabá, who brought him to Ghazní. No Turk equal to him in beauty, virtue, intelligence, and nobleness, had at that time been brought to that city. Mention of him was made before his majesty Sultán Mu'izzu-d dín Muhammad Sám, who ordered that a price should be named for him. He was coupled with another Turk named Aibak, and a thousand dínárs in refined gold was fixed as the price of each, but Jamálu-d dín Chast Kabá demurred to sell him for this price, so the Sultán gave orders that nobody should purchase him. After this, Jamálu-d dín Chast Kabá stayed one year in Ghazní, and then went to Bukhárá, carrying the future Sultán with him. After staying there three years, he again brought him back to Ghazní; but no one, for fear of the king's orders, ventured to purchase. He had been there one year, when

Kutbu-d dín[1] returned to Ghazuín with Malik Nasíru-d dín Husain, after the invasion of Nahrwálá and the conquest of Guzerát. He heard an account of Shamsu-d dín, and asked the permission of Sultán Mu'izzu-d dín to purchase him. The Sultán said that orders had been passed that he should not be purchased in Ghazní, but he might take him to Dehli and buy him there. Kutbu-d dín consigned to Nizámu-d dín Muhammad the management of the business, and ordered him to take Jamálu-d dín Chast Kabá with him to Hindustán that he might purchase Shamsu-d dín there. According to these directions, Nizámu-d dín brought them to Dehli, and Kutbu-d dín purchased him and the other slave for one lac of *chítals*. The other slave was a Turk, whose name was Aibak, but this was changed to Tamgháj,[2] and he became chief of Tabarhindh. He was slain in the battle fought between Táju-d dín Yalduz and Kutbu-d dín. Altamsh was made chief of the guards. Kutbu-d dín called him his son and kept him near his person. His rank and honour increased every day. Marks of intelligence were evident in all his actions, so he was elevated to the rank of *Amír-shikár* (chief huntsman). When Gwálior was taken he became amír of that place. After that he obtained the district and town of Baran and its dependencies. Some time after this, when the proofs of his energy, bravery, and heroism were fully displayed, and had been witnessed by Kutbu-d dín, the country of Badáún was entrusted to him. When Sultán Mu'izzu-d dín Muhammad Sám returned from Khwárizm, after being defeated in the battle of Andkhod by the armies of Khítá, the Kokhar (Gakkar) tribes broke out in rebellion, and the Sultán marched against them from Ghazní. Kutbu-d dín, according to his orders, brought up an army from Hindustán, and Shamsu-d dín accompanied him with the forces of Badáún. In the height of the battle, Shamsu-d dín rode into the stream of

[1] [The author constantly prefixes by anticipation the title of Sultán to the names of Kutbu-d dín, Shamsu-d dín, and others who eventually became kings; but, to avoid confusion, this title has been omitted in passages relating to times anterior to their attainment of the regal dignity].   [2] ["Toghan" in Firishta.]

the Jailam, where that wretched rabble had taken refuge, and exhibited great bravery, galling the enemy so with his arrows that he overcame their resistance, and sent them from the tops of the waves into the depths of hell: "they drowned and entered the fires."

The Sultán in the midst of the battle observed his feats of daring and courage, and enquired who he was. When his majesty was enlightened upon this point he called him into his presence and honoured him with especial notice. Kutbu-d dín was ordered to treat Altamsh well, as he was destined for great works. His majesty then ordered the deed of his freedom to be written out and graciously granted him his liberty.

When Sultán Kutbu-d dín expired at Lahore,[1] the commander-in-chief, 'Alí Isma'íl, who had charge of Dehli, joined with some other nobles and principal men, and sent letters to Badáún inviting Shamsu-d dín. When he arrived he mounted the throne of Dehli in A.H. 607 (1210 A.D.) and established his authority. The Turks and the Mu'izzí chiefs assembled from all quarters in Dehli, but the Turks and Mu'izzí chiefs of that city did not join them. They resolved to try the effect of resistance, so they went out of Dehli, collected in the environs and raised the standard of revolt. Sultán Shamsu-d dín marched out of Dehli with a body of horse and his own personal followers, defeated them in the plains of the Jumna and put most of their horsemen to the sword. Afterwards Sultán Tâju-d dín made a treaty with him from Lahore and Ghazní and sent him some insignia of royalty. Quarrels arose several times between Sultán Shamsu-d dín Altamsh and Malik Násiru-d dín Kubácha about Lahore, Tabarhindh, and Kahrám; and in the year 614 (1217 A.D.) he defeated Kubácha. Hostilities also broke out at different times between him and the chiefs of various parts of Hindustán and the Turks, but as he was assisted by Divine favour, every one who resisted him or rebelled was subdued. Heaven still con-

---

[1] [The name is here invariably spelt "Lohor."]

tinued to favour him, and all the territories belonging to Dehli, Dadáún, Oudh, Benares, and the Siwálik hills came into his possession.

Sultán Táju-d dín Yalduz having fled before the army of Khwárizm came to Lahore. A dispute arose between him and Sultán Shamsu-d dín regarding the limits of their possessions, and a battle was fought between them at Náráin in A.H. 612 (A.D. 1215) in which the Sultán achieved the victory, and Táju-d dín Yalduz was taken prisoner. He was brought, according to orders, to Dehli and was sent to Badáún, where he was buried.[1]

After this another battle was fought in the year 614 H. (1217 A.D.) with Malik Násiru-d dín Kubácha, and he was again defeated.

Great events now occurred in Khurásán through the appearance of the Moghal Changíz Khán. In A.H. 615 (1218 A.D.) Jalálu-d dín, king of Khwárizm, having fled from the army of the infidels came towards Hindustán, and some fighting followed on the frontiers of Lahore. Shamsu-d dín led his forces out of Dehli towards Lahore, and Khwárizm Sháh fled before the army of Hindustán and went towards Sind and Siwistán.

After this, in 622 H. (1225 A.D.), Sultán Shamsu-d dín carried his arms towards Lakhnautí, and Ghiyásu-d dín 'Auz Khiljí placed the yoke of servitude on the neck of submission and presented thirty elephants and eighty lacs of the current coin. He also ordered the Khutba to be read and the coin to be struck in the name of Shamsu-d dín.

In A.H. 623 (1226 A.D.) he marched to conquer the fort of Ranthambhor[2] which is celebrated in all parts of Hindustán for its great strength and security. It is related in the Hindu histories that it had been invaded by more than seventy (haftád o

---

[1] [The author is silent here as to his death, but in the memoir of Táju-d dín he says that he was killed.]

[2] [This name is spelt in many different ways. Here in the text we have "Rantampor." It also occurs as "Biothambor," "Rustamboor," etc. Colebrooke derives the name from the Sanskrit *Rana-stambha-bhavantra*, "the base of the pillar of war."—Trans. R. As. Soc. I. 143.]

and) kings, and no one had been able to take it. In the space of a few months in the year 623, through the favour of God, the fort fell into the hands of Shamsu-d dín. One year after this, A.H. 624, he attacked the fort of Mandúr in the Siwálik hills[1] there also God bestowed victory on him, and much plunder fell into the hands of his followers. After another year, in A.H. 625 (122 A.D.), an army was sent from Dehli towards the cities of Uch and Multán. The author of this book, Minháj Siráj, had come from Ghor and Khurásán to Sind, Uch, and Multán, in the month of Rajab, A.H. 624. On the first of Rabi'u-l awwal, A.H. 625 (Feb. 1228), Sultán Sa'íd Shamsu-d dín reached the foot of the fort of Uch. Malik Násiru-d dín Kubácha had pitched his camp at the gate of the fort of Amrawat[2] and all his followers and baggage were in ships and boats moored in front of the camp.

On Friday, after the time of prayer, some swift runners came from the direction of Multán and reported that Malik Násiru-d dín Aitamur had been detached from Lahore and had come to the fort of Multán; also that Sultán Shamsu-d dín himself was marching towards Uch viâ Tabarhindh. Malik Násiru-d dín Kubácha fled with all his army in boats to Bhakkar, and ordered his minister, 'Ainu-l Mulk Husain Ashghari, to remove all the treasure from the fort of Uch to Bhakkar.

Sultán Shamsu-d dín sent two of his principal generals in advance with an army to the walls of Uch. One of these was Malik 'Izzu-d dín Muhammad Sálár, lord chamberlain, and the other was Kazlak Khán Sanjar Sultáni, chief of Tabarhindh. Four days after, the Sultán himself arrived at Uch with all his elephants and baggage, and pitched his tents there. He sent his minister, Nizámu-d dín Muhammad Junaidí, with other nobles, in pursuit of Malik Násiru-d dín to the fort of Bhakkar. Fight-

---

[1] [Briggs in the translation of Firishta says, " Mando and the country of Malwa;" and this statement has been adopted by Elphinstone. It is manifestly wrong, and there is no warrant for it in the text of Firishta, which fully agrees with the statement of our author. The true version of Firishta's words is " He marched to the fort of Mandúr, which fort, with all the Siwálik hills, he reduced."]

[2] [Var. "Amrút, Ahrút."]

ing continued for one month under the walls of Uch, and on Tuesday, the 29th of Jumáda-l Ákhir A.H. 625 (May, 1228), the place capitulated. In the same month Malik Násiru-d dín Kubácha drowned himself at the fort of Bhakkar in the waters of the Indus, having a few days before sent his son, Malik 'Aláu-d dín Bahrám Sháh to wait upon Sultán Shamsu-d dín. After a few days the treasures were taken possession of, and the remaining forces of Malik Násiru-d dín entered into the service of the conqueror. All that country down to the sea shore was subdued. Malik Sinánu-d dín Habsh, chief of Dewal and Sind, came and did homage to the Sultán. When the noble mind of the king was satisfied with the conquest of the country, he returned to Dehli.

The writer of this book had obtained an audience at the Court of that great and religious king on the first day his camp was pitched at Uch (may God preserve it!), and was received with favour. When his majesty returned from that fort, the compiler also came to Dehli (may God glorify it!) with the victorious army of that invincible king, and reached the city in the month of Ramazán A.H. 625 (August 1228). At this time messengers bringing splendid robes from the seat of the Khiláfat reached the frontiers of Nágore, and on Monday, the 2nd of Rabi'u-l awwal A.H. 626, they arrived at the capital, and the city was adorned by their presence. The king and his chief nobles and his sons and the other nobility and servants were all honoured with robes sent from the metropolis of Islám.

After great revelling and rejoicing, news arrived in Jumáda-l awwal, 626 (April, 1229), of the death of Prince Sa'íd Násiru-d dín Mahmúd. Balká[1] Malik Khiljí had broken out in rebellion in the territories of Lakhnautí, and Sultán Shamsu-d dín led thither the armies of Hindustán, and having captured the rebel, he, in A.H. 627, gave the throne of Lakhnautí to Malik 'Aláu-d dín Jání, and returned to his capital in the month of Rajab of the same year.

[1] [Var. "Malká."]

In A.H. 629 he marched for the conquest of Gwalior, and when his royal tents were pitched under the walls of the fort, Mīlak Deo,[1] the accursed son of Basīl the accursed, began the war. For eleven months the camp remained under the fort. In the month of Sha'bān of the same year the author of this book came to the Court from Dehli and obtained audience. He was ordered to preach in turn at the door of the royal tent. Discourses were appointed to be delivered three times every week, and during the month of Ramazán on every day. But in other months the rule of three times was observed. Ninety-five times religious assemblies were convened at the royal tents. On both 'Íds, viz. 'Íd-i fitr and 'Íd-i azha', the appropriate prayers were read at three different places in the army of Islám. At one of these, at the fort of Gwalior on the northern side, this well-wisher of the government, Minháj Siráj, was ordered on the Id-i azha' to read the Khutba and the prayers, and was honoured with the reward of a costly khil'at. The same rule was observed until the fort was conquered, on Tuesday, the 20th of Safar A.H. 630 (November, 1232).

The accursed Mīlak Deo went out of the fort in the night time and fled. About seven hundred persons were ordered to receive punishment at the door of the royal tent.[2] After this, promotions were made in the ranks of the nobles and great officers. Malik Ziáu-d dín Muhammad Junaidí was appointed chief justice, and the commander-in-chief Rashídu-d dín (peace be to him!) was made kotwal, and Minháj Siráj, the well-wisher of this government, was made law officer, and was entrusted with the supervision of the preaching, and of all religious, moral, and judicial affairs. Rich khil'ats and valuable largesses were distributed. May the Almighty aid the pure soul and generous heart of that most beneficent, heroic, and kind king! His majesty started on his return from the fort on the 2nd of Rabi'u-l awwal in the same

---

[1] [Firishta has the more likely name of "Drobal."]
[2] [Firishta says three hundred were put to death. *Siyāsat*, the word here employed, signifies punishment inflicted at the discretion of a judge in cases not provided for by law, and there is no doubt that the punishment of death is intended.]

year, and pitched his tents that day at about one parasang towards Dehli from the walls of the fort. A halt of five days was made there. After he had reached the capital he sent, in A.H. 632[1] (1234 A.D.), the army of Islám towards Málwa and took the fort and city of Bhilsá.[2] There was a temple there which was three hundred years in building. It was about one hundred and five *gaz* high. He demolished it. From thence he proceeded to Ujjain, where there was a temple of Mahá-kál, which he destroyed as well as the image of Bikramájít, who was king of Ujjain, and reigned 1316 years before this time. The Hindu era dates from his reign. Some other images cast in copper were carried with the stone image of Mahá-kál to Dehli.

In A.H. 636, he led the armies of Hindustán towards Banyán.[3] In this journey his majesty fell sick and was obliged by his severe illness to return home. Wednesday morning, the 1st of Sha'bán, was fixed by the astrologers for his entrance into Dehli, the seat of his government, and he entered the city in a howda on the back of an elephant. His illness increased, and nineteen days after, on the 20th of Sha'bán, 633 H. (end of April, 1235), he departed from this perishable to the eternal world. The period of his reign was twenty-six years. [*Lists of his judges, generals, relations, and victories, follow.*]

2. *Malik Sa'íd Násiru-d dunyá wau-d dín Mahmúd.*

Malik Násiru-d dín Mahmúd was the elder son of Sultán Shamsu-d dín. He was an intelligent, learned, and wise prince, and was possessed of exceeding bravery, courage, generosity, and benevolence. The first charge which the Sultán confided to him was that of Hánsí. Some time after, in 623 H. (1226 A.D.), Oudh was entrusted to him. In that country the prince ex-

---

[1] ["631" in some copies.]
[2] [In one copy the name is written "Bhilsán," and in another "Dilistán." This is probably the same as the "Bhaylsán" or "Mahábalastán" of Bírúní. See Vol. I. p. 59.]
[3] Var. "Badhyán" and "Bayána." Firishta, the Tárikh-i Badáúní, and the Tabakát-i Akbarí agree in saying "Multán."

hibited many estimable qualities. He fought several battles, and by his boldness and bravery he made his name famous in the annals of Hindustán. He overthrew and sent to hell the accursed Bartúh (?) under whose hands and sword more than one hundred and twenty thousand Musulmans had received martyrdom. He overthrew the rebel infidels of Oudh and brought a body of them into submission.

From Oudh he determined to march against Lakhnautí, and the king placed the armies of Hindustán under his command. Several well-known chiefs, as Bolán (?) and Malik 'Aláu-d dín Jání, went with him to Lakhnautí. Sultán Ghiyásu-d dín 'Auz Khiljí had marched from Lakhnautí to invade the territory of Bang (Bengal), and had left no force at his centre of government. Malik Sa'íd Násiru-d dín, on arriving there with his army, took peaceable possession of the fort of Basankot and of the city. Ghiyásu-d dín 'Auz Khiljí, on receiving this intelligence, returned to Lakhnautí, and Malik Nasiru-d dín with his army met him and defeated him. Ghiyásu-d dín, with all his relations and chiefs of Khilj, the treasures and the elephants, fell into his hands. He put Ghiyásu-d dín to death and confiscated all his treasures. From thence he sent presents and offerings to all the saiyids and the learned and religious men of Dehli and all towns.

When Shamsu-d dín received the khil'ats from the reigning Khalífa, he sent one of the most valuable with a red canopy to Lakhnautí, and Malik Násiru-d dín thus received great honour and distinction. All the nobles and great men turned their eyes towards him as the heir of his father's kingdom, but the decrees of fate did not accord with the wishes of the people. One year and a-half afterwards he fell sick and died. When the news of his death reached Dehli all people were greatly distressed.

Sultán Ruknu-d dín Fíroz Sháh.

Sultán Ruknu-d dín Fíroz Sháh was a generous and handsome king, full of kindness and humanity. In liberality he was a second Hátim. His mother, the queen of the world, Sháh Turkán, was originally a Turkí handmaid, but had become the chief wife of Sultán Shamsu-d dín Altamsh. She lavished many offerings and much charity on learned men, *saiyids*, and devotees.

In the year 625 H. (1228 A.D.) Sultán Ruknu-d dín received a grant of Badáún with a green umbrella. 'Aínu-l Mulk Husain Ash'arí, who had been the wazír of Násiru-d dín Kubácha, then became wazír of Ruknu-d dín. When Shamsu-d dín returned from the conquest of Gwalior to Dehli, he conferred the territories of Lahore, which had been the capital of Khusrú Malik, on Ruknu-d dín ; and on his return from his last campaign, from the Indus and Banyán, he took Ruknu-d dín with him to Dehli, for the eyes of all men were on him, as the eldest of the king's sons since the death of Násiru-d dín Mahmud. On the death of Sultán Shamsu-d dín Altamsh, the princes and nobles placed Ruknu-d dín upon the throne on Tuesday, 29th of Sha'bán 633 H. (beginning of of May, 1236), and the crown and throne were graced by his accession. The nobles were gratified and received robes of honour. When they returned home from the capital, the new monarch opened the doors of his treasury and gave himself up to pleasure, squandering the public wealth in improper places. So devoted was he to licentiousness and debauchery that the business of the State was neglected and fell into confusion.

His mother, Sháh Turkán, began to interfere in the government of the country. During the life of her husband his other women had looked upon her with envy and disdain. She now seized the opportunity of punishing them, and in blind fury and vindictiveness she put several of them to death. This state of things began to trouble the minds of public men. In addition to her other cruel acts she caused the young prince Kutbu-d dín, son of the late king, and a very excellent youth, to be blinded and afterwards to be put to death. These acts aroused an inimical feeling in the hearts of the great men in all directions. Malik Ghiyásu-d dín Muhammad Sháh, son of the late Sultán, and younger than Ruknu-d dín, commenced hostilities in Oudh. He seized upon the treasure of Lakhnautí in its passage to the capital, and plundered several towns of Hindustán. Malik 'Izzu-d dín Muhammad Sálárí governor of Badáún revolted. Malik 'Izzu-d dín Kabír Khán, governor of Multán, Malik Saifu-d dín Kochí, governor of Hánsí, and Malik 'Aláu-d dín, governor of Lahore, conspired and broke out into rebellion. Sultán Ruknu-d dín led his army from Dehli to repress these malcontents, but his wazír, Nizámu-l mulk Muhammad Junaidí, took the alarm and deserted him at Kílú-gharí. He then went off towards Kol and joined 'Izzu-d dín Muhammad Sálárí of Badáún. These two afterwards joined Malik Jání and Kochí. Sultán Ruknu-d dín marched on to Kahrám. The Turkí nobles and the royal attendants who were about the person of the Sultán leagued together, and, in the neighbourhood of Mansúrpúr and Náráín, Táju-d dín Muhammad, secretary and controller, Baháu-l Mulk Husain Asha'rí, Karímu-d dín Záhid, Zíáu-l Mulk son of Nizámu-l Mulk Junaidí, Nizámu-d dín Sharkání, Khwája Rashídu-d dín Málkání, Amír Fakhru-d dín, and other confederate officials, killed the Tázík.¹ In the month of Rabí'u-l awwal 634 H. (November, 1236 A.D.), Raziya, eldest daughter of the late Sultán, quarrelled with the mother of Sultán Ruknu-d dín, and the Sultán was constrained to return to Delhi. His mother had attempted to capture and kill Sultán Raziya, but the people rose, and the latter seized upon the royal palace and made the mother of the Sultán prisoner.

When Ruknu-dín arrived at Kílú-gharí he found that rebellion had broken out, and that his mother had been made prisoner. The guards and Turkish nobles came into the city, and joining Raziya, proffered their allegiance to her, and raised her to the throne. Being thus elevated to the throne, she sent an army of Turks and nobles to Kílú-gharí and they brought Sultán

¹ و دیگر جماعت کارداران تازیک را شهید کردند. Firishta, more intelligibly, says they deserted Ruknu-d dín.]

Ruknu-d dín prisoner to Dehli, where he was kept in confinement and died. His death happened on Sunday, the 18th of Rabi'u-l awwal A.H. 634 (November, 1236 A.D.) He reigned for six months and twenty-eight days. He was very generous; no king in any reign had ever scattered gifts, robes of honour, and grants in the way he did, but all his lavishness sprang from his inordinate addiction to sensuality, pleasure, and conviviality. He was so entirely devoted to riot and debauchery, that he often bestowed his honours and rewards on bands of singers, buffoons, and catamites. He scattered his riches to such a heedless extent, that he would ride out drunk upon an elephant through the streets and bázárs, throwing *tankas* of red gold around him for the people to pick up and rejoice over. He was very fond of playing with and riding upon elephants, and all the elephant drivers were much benefited by his bounty. His nature was averse to hurting any creature, and his tenderness was the cause of his downfall.

Kings should possess all virtues that their people may live at ease. They should be generous, that the army may live satisfied; but sensuality, gaiety, and the society of the base and unworthy bring an empire to ruin. May God pardon him!

Sultán[1] Raziya, Daughter of the Sultán.

Sultán Raziya was a great monarch. She was wise, just, and generous, a benefactor to her kingdom, a dispenser of justice, the protector of her subjects, and the leader of her armies. She was endowed with all the qualities befitting a king, but she was not born of the right sex, and so in the estimation of men all these virtues were worthless. (May God have mercy on her!) In the time of her father, Sultán Sa'íd Shamsu-d dín, she had exercised authority with great dignity. Her mother was the

---

[1] [The queen is always called "Sultán" and "Bádsháh," not Sultána, as by Briggs and Elphinstone. Sultán signifies "ruler," and although, from Musalmán aversion to female rulers, it is practically confined to the male sex, yet it is exceptionally used for queens regnant, as in this case. "Sultána" is not complimentary, for it signifies a *avid*.]

chief wife of his majesty, and she resided in the chief royal palace in the Kushk-firozí. The Sultán discerned in her countenance the signs of power and bravery, and, although she was a girl and lived in retirement, yet when the Sultán returned from the conquest of Gwalior, he directed his secretary, Táju-l Malik Mahmúd, who was director of the government, to put her name in writing as heir of the kingdom, and successor to the throne. Before this farmán was executed, the servants of the State, who were in close intimacy with his majesty, represented that, seeing the king had grown up sons who were worthy of the dignity, what wisdom could there be in making a woman the heir to a Muhammadan throne, and what advantage could accrue from it? They besought him to set their minds at ease, for the course that he proposed seemed very inexpedient. The king replied, My sons are devoted to the pleasures of youth, and no one of them is qualified to be king. They are unfit to rule the country, and after my death you will find that there is no one more competent to guide the State than my daughter. It was afterwards agreed by common consent that the king had judged wisely.

When Sultán Raziya succeeded to the throne, all things reverted to their old order. But the wazir of the State, Nizámu-l Mulk Junaidí did not give in his adhesion. He, together with Malik Jání, Malik Kochí, Malik Kabír Khán, and Malik 'Izzu-d dín Muhammad Sálárí, assembling from different parts of the country at the gates of Dehli, made war against Sultán Raziya, and hostilities were carried on for a long time. After a while, Malik Nasíru-d dín Tábashí Mu'izzí, who was governor of Oudh, brought up his forces to Dehli to the assistance of Sultán Raziya. When he had crossed the Ganges, the generals, who were fighting against Dehli, met him unexpectedly and took him prisoner. He then fell sick and died.

The stay of the insurgents at the gates of Dehli was protracted. Sultán Raziya, favoured by fortune, went out from the city and ordered her tents to be pitched at a place on the banks of the

Jumna. Several engagements took place between the Turkish nobles who were on the side of the Sultán, and the insurgent chiefs. At last peace was effected, with great adroitness and judicious management. Malik 'Izzu-d dín Muhammad Sálár and Malik 'Izzu-d dín Kabír Khán Ayyáz secretly joined the Sultán and came at night to her majesty's tents, upon the understanding that Malik Jání, Malik Kochí, and Nizámu-l Mulk Junaidí were to be summoned and closely imprisoned, so that the rebellion might subside. When these chiefs were informed of this matter they fled from their camps, and some horsemen of the Sultán pursued them. Malik Kochí and his brother Fakhru-d dín were captured, and were afterwards killed in prison. Malik Jání was slain in the neighbourhood of Bábul and Nakwán. Nizámu-l Mulk Junaidí went into the mountains of Dardár,[1] and died there after a while.

When the affairs of Raziya were thus settled, she conferred the office of wazír on an upright officer who had been the deputy of Nizámu-l Mulk, and he likewise received the title of Nizámu-l Mulk. The command of the army was given to Malik Saifu-d dín Aibak Bahtú, with the title of Katlagh Khán. To Kabír Khán was assigned the province of Láhore. The country now enjoyed peace, and the power of the State became manifest. Throughout its territories from Lakhnautí to Dewal all the princes and nobles made their submission.

Shortly after Malik Aibak Bahtú died, and Malik Kutbu-d dín Hasan Ghorí was appointed to his office, and was ordered to march against the fort of Rantambhor. The Hindús laid siege to this fort after the death of Shamsu-d dín, and had been before it some time, but when Kutbu-d dín arrived, he drew the Musulmán forces out of the fort and destroyed it. He then returned to Dehli.

About this time Malik Ikhtiyáru-d dín I'tigín was appointed lord chamberlain, and Amír Jamálu-d dín Yákút, the superintendent of the stables, was made a personal attendant of her

[1] [Var. "Sarmand-bardár." Firishta says "Sirmor."]

majesty. This created jealousy among the Turkish generals and nobles. The Sultán Raziya now threw off the dress and veil of women. She put on a coat (*kabá*) and cap, and showed herself among the people. When she rode on an elephant all men clearly saw her. She now ordered an army to march to Gwalior, and sent with it large gifts. There being no possibility of resistance, this well-wisher of the victorious government, Minháj Siráj, together with Majdu-l Umará Zía'u-d dín Junaidí, chief justice of Gwalior, and with other principal officers, came out of the fort of Gwalior on the 1st of Sha'bán, A.H. 635 (Feb. 1238), and proceeded to the Court of Dehli. In the month of Sha'bán of the same year, Sultán Raziya (may peace be to her!), appointed this well-wisher to the Násiriya college[1] and to the office of Kázi of Gwalior. In A.H. 637 (1239 A.D.) Malik 'Izzu-d dín Kabír Khán, governor of Lahore, broke out in revolt. The Sultán led her army from Dehli in that direction and pursued him. After a time he made peace and did homage. The province of Multán, which was held by Malik Karákash, was given to Malik 'Izzu-d dín Kabír Khán.

On Thursday, the 19th of Ramazán A.H. 637 (April, 1240), Sultán Raziya returned to the capital. Malik Altúniya, who was governor of Tabarhindh,[2] revolted, and some of the officers of the Court on the frontier supported him. On Wednesday, the 9th of the same month and year she marched with a numerous army towards Tabarhindh to put down these rebels. When she arrived there she was attacked by the Turks, who put Amír Jalálu-d dín Yákút, the Abyssinian, to death. They then seized the Sultán Raziya and sent her a prisoner to the fort of Tabarhindh.

Among the incidents which occurred at the beginning of the reign of Sultán Raziya, this was the most remarkable, that the Karmatians and heretics of Hindustán, being seduced by a person with some pretensions to learning, who was called Núr

[1] [مدرسهٔ ناصریه در حضرت منضم]
[2] [The *Habíbu-s Siyer* says distinctly *Sarhind*. Firishta has "Bhatinda."]

Turk, flocked to him in large numbers from all parts of Hindustán: such as Guzerát, Sind, the environs of the capital, and the banks of the Jumna and Ganges. They assembled in Dehli, and making a compact of fidelity to each other, they, at the instigation of this Núr Turk, declared open hostility against the people of Islám. When Núr preached, the rabble used to gather round him. He used to say that the learned Sunnis and their flocks were *násibís*, and to call them *marjís*.[1] He endeavoured also to inflame the minds of the common people against the wise men who followed the doctrines of Abú Hanífa and Sháfi'í. On a day appointed, on Friday, the 6th of the month of Rajab. A.H. 634 (March, 1237), the whole body of heretics and Karmatians, to the number of about one thousand men, armed with swords, shields, arrows, and other weapons, came in two parties to the Jáma' masjid of Dehli. One division came from the northern side and passed by the fort of Núr to the gate of the masjid. The other proceeded from the clothes bázár, and entered the gate of the Mu'izzí, under the impression that it was the masjid. On both sides they attacked the Musulmáns. Many of the faithful were slain by the sword and many were trampled to death by the crowd. When a cry arose from the people in consequence of this outrage, the brave officers of the government, such as Nasíru-d dín Aitamur Balarámi, Amír Imám Násir Shá'ir and others, fully armed with mail, cuirass, and helmet, with spears, shields, and other weapons, gathered on all sides and rode into the masjid. They plied their swords on the heretics and Karmatians; and the Musulmáns who had gone (for refuge) to the top of the mosque hurled down stones and bricks till every heretic and Karmatian was sent to hell, and the riot was quelled.[2] Thanks be to God for the favour and glory he has given to the faith.

---

[1] [*Násibís* are the enemies of 'Alí, and the *marjís* or "procrastinators" are a sect who think faith sufficient and works unnecessary.]

[2] This curious anecdote is omitted by almost all the general historians, but is quoted nearly *verbatim* by Núru-l Hakk in the Zubdatu-t Tawáríkh.—See note in Appendix "Karmatians."

When Sultán Raziya was taken prisoner to Tabarhindh, Malik Altúniya espoused her and led her army towards Dehli to regain possession of the kingdom. Malik 'Izzu-d dín Muhammad Sálárí and Malik Karákash left the capital and went to join them. Meanwhile, Mu'izzu-d dín had ascended the throne, Ikhtiyáru-d dín Yúgín, lord chamberlain, had been slain, and Badru-d dín Sankar Rúmí had been appointed his successor. In the month of Rabí'u-l awwal A.H. 638 (Sept. 1240), the Sultán marched his army from Dehli to repel his opponents, and Sultán Raziya and Malik Altúniya were defeated. When in their flight they reached Kaithal, their remaining forces abandoned them, and they both fell into the hands of the Hindús and were killed. The date of this defeat was the 24th of Rabí'u-l awwal A.H. 638 (Oct. 1240), and the Sultán Raziya was killed on the day following. She had reigned three years and six days.

5. *Mu'izzu-d dín Bahrám Shah.*

Sultán Mu'izzu-d dín Bahrám Sháh was a victorious king; a fearless, intrepid, and sanguinary man. Still he had some virtues. He was shy and unceremonious, and had no taste for the gorgeous attire which kings love to wear, nor for the belts, accoutrements, banners, and other insignia of royalty. When Sultán Raziya was sent to prison at Tabarhindh, the nobles and the generals agreed to send him to Dehli, and on Monday the 27th of Ramazán 637 (April, 1240) they raised him to the throne. After all the nobles and the generals and the army had returned to Dehli, on Sunday the 11th Shawwál of the same year, they assembled at the palace and made a general agreement to uphold him as king on condition of Ikhtiyáru-d dín Yúgín being made deputy. On that day the author of this work was present and composed the following gratulatory lines.

* * * * *

Ikhtiyáru-d dín, having been appointed deputy, he in virtue of his office assumed the direction of all affairs of State, and with the acquiescence of the wazír Nizámu-l mulk Mahzabu-d dín Muhammad 'Auz Mustaufí the duties of administration also came under his control. After a month or two this state of affairs became very irksome to the Sultán. The Sultán's sister had been married to Kází Násiru-d dín, but being divorced, the deputy took her to wife. Music played three times a day at his gate, an elephant was always there in waiting,[1] and he maintained great state. On Monday, the 8th of Muharram 638 H. (July, 1240), there was a sermon in the Palace of the White-roof, and after the sermon the Sultán sent two inebriated Turks from the top of the palace as assassins, who killed Ikhtiyáru-d dín in front of the royal seat in the White Palace. The wazír Mahzabu-d dín also received two wounds in his side, but his time was not come, and he rushed out away from them. Malik Badru-d dín Sankar became lord chamberlain and assumed the management of the State.

When Raziya and Altúniya marched from Tabarhindh upon Dehli, they were baffled in their enterprise and were defeated. Both were killed by the Hindús as we have already related. Badru-d dín Sankar now assumed a very imperious position; he issued orders and carried on the government without consulting the Sultán, and sought to domineer over the wazír Nizámu-l Mulk Mahzabu-d dín. The wazír complained to the Sultán and succeeded in setting him against Badru-d dín. When the latter perceived this he was afraid of the Sultán, and sought to set him aside and to raise one of his brothers to the throne in his stead.

On Monday, the 8th of Safar, 639 H. (Aug. 1241) Badru-d dín convoked a meeting of nobles and chiefs at the house of Sadru-l Mulk Táju-d dín 'Alí Músawí, *mushrif* of the State. There were present the chief Kází Jalálu-d dín Káshání, Kází Kabíru-d dín, Shaikh Muhammad Shámí, and others. When they had met and were deliberating about the removal of the Sultán, they determined to send Sadru-l mulk to the wazír Nizámu-l mulk Mahzabu-d dín to invite his attendance, and to

[1] [Regal privileges.]

finally settle the matter in concurrence with him. It so happened that when Sadru-l mulk came to the house of the wazír, one of the confidential attendants of the king was present. When the wazír heard of the arrival of Sadru-l mulk, he concealed this trusty servant in a place where he could hear the conversation. Sadru-l mulk entered and proceeded to talk about the removal of the king and to ask the co-operation of the wazír. The minister desired his visitor to return and say that he would wait upon the gentlemen as soon as he had performed his ablutions. Sadru-l mulk had no sooner departed than the wazír released the Sultán's man and asked him if he had heard what had passed. He then directed him to go quickly and tell his master that the best thing he could do would be to take horse and to proceed against the conspirators and scatter them.

The facts being reported to the Sultán by his faithful adherent, he instantly mounted and dispersed the plotters. Badru-d dín Sankar joined the king's party, and the Sultán returned to his palace, where he held a darbar. Badru-d dín was ordered to depart instantly to Badáún and assume the management of that province; Kází Jalálu-d dín Káshání was dismissed from his post of Kází, and Kází Kabíru-d dín and Shaikh Muhammad Shámí took the alarm and fled the city. After four months, Badru-d dín Sankar returned to the capital, but the Sultán's heart was entirely alienated from him, so he ordered him to be imprisoned. The king also directed Jalálu-d dín Músawi to be apprehended, and he had them both slain in prison.

These proceedings set the hearts of the nobles against the Sultán; they were alarmed and had no longer any confidence in him. The wazír also longed to exact vengeance for the wounds he had received. The nobles, generals, and Turks all became disaffected, while on his side the Sultán was alarmed by their proceedings. In the end this uneasy feeling spread like an epidemic, and was the cause of the fall of the Sultán and of rebellion among his people.

One of the most important events in the reign of Mu'izzu-d

dín was that which happened to the city of Lahore. An army of infidel Mughals came from Khurásán and Ghazní to the gates of that city and waged war for some time. Malik Karákash, governor of Lahore, was a brave, energetic, and intrepid man, but the people of the city did not support him, and were backward in keeping watch and in fighting. When Karákash perceived this lukewarmness, he one night left the city with his own soldiers and went off towards Dehli. The infidels pursued him, but the Almighty watched over him and gave him safe deliverance. When the city was left without a ruler the infidels captured it on Monday, 18th of Jumáda-l ákhir, 639 H. (December 1241), slaughtered the Muhammadans and made their dependants captives.

As soon as this dreadful intelligence reached Dehli, the Sultán assembled the people of the city at the White Palace, and the writer of this book received orders to preach and induce the people to support the Sultán.

There was a Turkoman darwesh named Ayúb, a devout man, clad in the hairy garment of a recluse. He had lived for some time quietly in the Sultán's water palace, and was brought into the society of the Sultán, who conceived a liking for him. This darwesh began to take a part in the business of the state. He had formerly lived in the town of Mihrpúr, where he had been imprisoned by Kází Shamsu-d dín Mihr. When the Sultán had become accustomed to listen to his advice, the darwesh exerted himself so that he induced the king to have Kází Shamsu-d dín Mihr cast under the feet of an elephant. On this fact becoming known the people conceived a great dread of the Sultán. The Sultán now sent Kutbu-d dín Husain and his wazír, with nobles, generals, and soldiers, to oppose the Mughals who were at Lahore, and to guard his frontier.

On Saturday, 10th Jumáda-l awwal, 639 H. (November, 1241), his majesty Mu'izzu-d dín conferred upon the author of this work the office of Kází of the capital and of all his territories, accompanied with many honours and costly presents.

The army which had been sent against the Mughals reached the banks of the Diyáh. There the minister Mahzabu-d dín Nizámu-l mulk, who cherished hopes of vengeance and of removing the Sultán from the throne, wrote a letter secretly to him. In this letter he represented that the generals and Turks in the army were never likely to become loyal, and that the best course for the king to adopt would be to send orders for him (the wazír) and Kutbu-d dín to kill all the generals and Turks in any way they could, and so free the kingdom of them.

When this letter arrived, the Sultán hastily and rashly, without thought or consideration, wrote the desired order, and sent it off. On its reaching the wazír he showed it to the generals and Turks, and told them how the king wished to deal with them. They all at once revolted, and at the suggestion of Khwája Mahzabu-d dín they formed a plot for the removal and deposition of the king.

On the Sultán's receiving intelligence of this revolt of his generals and army, he sent the Shaikhu-l Islám Saiyid Kutbu-d dín to endeavour to allay the outbreak. He accordingly went to the army, but exerted himself to increase the strife.[1] He returned with the army at his heels, and hostilities commenced under the walls of the capital. The author, Minháj Siráj, and some of the chief men of the city, endeavoured in vain to allay the strife and make peace.

The army reached the city on Saturday, the 19th Sha'bán, 639, and the siege went on until the month of Zí-l ka'da. Many were killed on both sides, and the suburbs of the city were laid waste. The reason of these protracted hostilities was that there was in the king's service a man named Fakhru-d dín Mubárak Sháh Farkhí, who was chief of the carpet spreaders (*mihtar-farrásh*). This man had gained the favour of the king, and had great ascendancy over him. Whatever he advised the king performed, and the counsels of the *farrásh* were not for peace.

[1] [در انارت آن فتنه میالفت نمود]

On Friday, the 7th Zí-l ka'da, the followers of Khwája Mahzab distributed three thousand *chítals* among a lot of foolish men, and excited inimical feelings among some even of this author's kindred (God forgive them!). They made a riot in the Jámi' masjid, after prayers, and drew their swords upon him. By God's mercy the author had a knife and a staff, which he seized, and with the help of some armed slaves whom he had with him he made his way through the crowd.

The generals and Turks took the fort, and next day, on Saturday, the 8th Zí-l ka'da, 639 H. (May, 1242), they obtained possession of the whole city. The Sultán was made prisoner. Mubárak Shah, *farrásh*, who had embittered the strife, was also taken and was killed. In the night of Tuesday, the 17th of Zí-l ka'da, the Sultán was slain. He had reigned two years one month and a-half.

0.—*Sultán 'Aláu-d dín Mas'úd Sháh bin Fíroz Sháh.*

Sultán 'Aláu-d dín Mas'úd Sháh was son of Sultán Ruknu-d dín Fíroz Sháh. He was a generous and good-natured prince, possessed of many estimable qualities. On Saturday, the 8th of Zí-l ka'da, 639 H. (May, 1242), when the city of Dehli was wrested from the hands of Mu'izzu-d dín, the generals and nobles by common consent released from prison the three princes Násiru-d dín, Malik Jalálu-d dín, and 'Aláu-d dín. They conveyed them from the White Palace to the public hall of the palace of Fíroz, and there they agreed to make 'Aláu-d dín king, although Malik 'Izzu-d dín Dalban had previously seated himself upon the throne. This Balban had caused his name to be proclaimed as king through the city, but it was not accepted. 'Aláu-d dín was raised to the throne, and the people gave a general acquiescence. Kutbu-d dín Husain Ghori was made deputy of the kingdom, and Nizámu-l Mulk wazír, and Malik Karékash lord chamberlain. The districts of Nágor, Mandawar, and Ajmír were assigned to Malik 'Izzu-d dín Dalban, and the country of Badáún was given to Malik Téju-d dín Saujar Katlak.

On the fourth day after the capture of Dehli the writer of these pages begged to be relieved of his office of Kází, and the post remained vacant for twenty-six days, till the fourth of Zí-l hijja, when Kází 'Imádu-d dín Muhammad Shakúrkání was appointed.

Nizámu-l Mulk Mahzabu-d dín exercised unbounded power over the country, and he took the district of Kol as his appanage. Previous to this he had caused music to play, and an elephant to wait at the door of his mansion. Everything was taken out of the hands of the Turkí nobles, so that they became embittered against him. They conspired together, and on Wednesday, 2nd Jumáda-l awwal, 640 H. (30th Oct., 1242 A.D.), they killed him in the camp before the city, in the plain of Hauz-ráni.

The author of this work resolved at this time to make a journey to Lakhnautí, and he started from Dehli on Friday, the 9th Rajab, 640 H. Táju-d dín Katlak paid him great attention in Badáún, and so also did Kamru-d dín Kairán in Oudh (May God immerse them in his mercy!). Tughán Khán 'Izzu-d dín Tughril had come with his army and boats to the confines of Karra. The author joined him from Oudh, and went with him to Lakhnautí. On Sunday, the 7th Zí-l hijja, 640 H., the author arrived at that place, having left his children and wives all in Oudh. Subsequently he sent some trustworthy persons who brought them to Lakhnautí. Tughán Khán showed him great kindness, and bestowed upon him boundless favours. The writer stayed at Lakhnautí two years.

In the course of these two years 'Aláu-d dín achieved many victories in different parts of his dominions. After the death of Khwája Mahzab, the post of wazír was given to Sadru-l Mulk Najmu-d dín Abú Bakr, and the office of lord chamberlain was given to Dáru-l Mulk Báligh Khán, together with the district of Hánsí. At this time there was much fighting going on.

When Tughán Khán returned from Karra to Lakhnautí he deputed Sharfu-l Mulk Ash'ari to the presence of 'Aláu-d dín, and he was named governor of Lakhnautí, receiving the honour of the red umbrella through Kází Jalálu-d dín, who was kází of Oudh. On Sunday, 11th of Rab'u-l ákhir, 641 H., the bearers of these honours arrived at Lakhnautí and Tughán Khán was invested.

One of the good things done by 'Aláu-d dín was that about this time, he, with the assent of the nobles and officers, released his two uncles. On the 'Íd-i azha' they left their confinement. Malik Jalálu-d dín received the district of Kanauj, and Násiru-d dín the district of Baliráich. Each one in his province devoted himself to peaceful pursuits and the improvement of the condition of his subjects.

In Shawwál 642 H. (March 1245), the infidels of Changíz Khán came to the gates of Lakhnautí. On the 1st Zí-l ka'da, Tamar Khán Kairán arrived at Lakhnautí with an army and generals under orders received from Sultán 'Aláu-d dín. Jealousy sprung up between Tamar Khán and Tughán Khán. On Wednesday, 3rd Zí-l ka'da of the same year, peace was made: Lakhnautí was given to Kairán Khán, and Tughán Khán proceeded to Dehli, The author of this work accompanied him and arrived at Dehli on Monday, 14th Safar, 1243. Here the author was granted the honour of an interview with the sovereign, and on Thursday the 17th Safar, at the suggestion of Ulugh Khán, he was appointed principal of the Násiriya college, and superintendent of its endowments. He was also made kází of Gwálior and preacher in the Jámi' masjid: all his old offices being again entrusted to him. He also received the royal grant of a horse with proper ornamental trappings: honours which none of his family had ever before attained.

In the month of Rajab news arrived from the upper parts (taraf-i bálá) that an army of infidel Mughals had arrived at Uchh. This army was under the command of the accursed Mankúta[1] (Mangú Khán). Sultán 'Aláu-d dín gathered his forces from all sides to drive back the Mughal invaders. When he arrived on the banks of the Biyáh tho' infidels raised the siege

[1] [Var. "Mankúna."]

of Uchh. The author accompanied his majesty in this campaign, and it was universally admitted by all men of knowledge and intelligence that such an army as was then under the orders of the Sultán had never before been seen. When the infidels heard of its strength and perfection they retreated towards Khurásán.

In this army there was a party of good-for-nothing fellows who had gradually made their way into the society of the Sultán, and were the means of leading him into unworthy habits and practices. It was thus that he acquired the habit of seizing and killing his nobles. He became confirmed in his cruelty; all his excellent qualities were perverted, and he gave himself up to unbounded licentiousness, pleasure, and hunting. Disaffection began to spread through the kingdom, and all the business of the State fell into disorder. The princes and nobles agreed to send envoys with letters inviting Násiru-d dín, and the result will be hereafter related. On Sunday, 23rd Muharram 644 H. (June, 1246) Sultán 'Aláu-d dín was put into prison and died. He reigned four years, one month, and one day.

7. *Sultán-i Mu'azzam Násiru-d dunyá wau-d dín Mahmúd.*

This prince, son of Sultán Sa'íd Shamsu-d dunyá wau-d dín (Altamsh) was born after the death of his eldest brother, whose name and titles were conferred upon him by his father. His mother was sent to a palace in the town of Loní,[1] where he was brought up and educated as a prince. Under the blessing of God he acquired every pleasing virtue.[2]

First Year of the Reign—Hijra 644 (1246 A.D.)

Sultán-i Mu'azzam Násiru-d dunyá wau-d dín ascended the throne in the Green Palace at Delhi with the most favourable auspices on Sunday, 23rd Muharram 644 H. (10th June, 1246).

[1] [Var. "Tolí," "Bolí."]
[2] [The author goes on in a strain of eulogy, and inserts specimens of two poems which he wrote on the accession of this king. A list of the king's nobles and relations is given, and the period of his reign is said to be "twenty-two years." The real period was twenty years. Our author's annals cease with the 15th year].

Princes and nobles, chiefs and great men, saiyids and learned men, all hastened with joy to express their devotion, and every one, according to his rank, offered congratulations upon his accession. On Tuesday, the 25th, he held a public court in the Fírozí palace, and the people with one acclaim approved of the elevation of this generous, virtuous, and noble looking prince. The great rejoiced at this renewal of the sovereignty, and all parts of Hindustan were happy under his equitable rule. (May his reign endure to the extreme limits of possibility!)

When (in the course of the last reign) the prince left Dehli for Ilahráich, his mother Malika-i Jahán Jalálu-d dunyá wau-d dín accompanied him. In that country and in the hills he fought many battles against the infidels. Under his kind rule Ilahráich attained great prosperity. The fame of his victorious and successful government spread in all parts of Hindustan, and when the princes and nobles were disgusted with the rule of 'Aláu-d dín, they sent letters secretly to him pressing him to come to the capital. The princess, his mother, prudently gave out that he was going to Dehli for medical attendance. He was placed in a litter, and started from Ilahráich attended by the princess, and by some careful men on horse and foot. When night came on they covered the prince's face with a woman's veil, mounted him on horseback, and making all speed they soon reached Dehli. No one knew of his arrival until the day he ascended the throne, and his occupation of the seat of royalty shed honour and splendour upon it.

In the month of Rajab, 644 H., he brought forth the royal standards, and led his army to the banks of the Indus and to Multán, in order to repulse the infidels of Chín. On Sunday, the 1st of Zí-l ka'da he crossed the river of Lahore, from whence he sent a force to ravage the hills of Júd, and the provinces on the Indus.[1] Ulugh Khán-i A'zam,[2] who now held the office of

---

[1] [The text has *áb áwí nowdaa*, but this evidently a mistake for *áwí* "Sindh," or the river Indus, which agrees with what follows, and with Firishta's statement.]

[2] [The titles *Kháu-i a'zam*, *Khán-i ma'azam*, and *Ulugh Khán*, are synonymous,

lord chamberlain, was placed in command of this army. The Sultán with the baggage and elephants encamped on the river Sodra.[1] Ulugh Khán, with the help of God, ravaged the hills of Júd and the Jailam, and sent many of the Kokhars (Gakkars) and rebellious infidels to hell. He then advanced to the banks of the Indus, and laid waste all the neighbourhood, but he was obliged to return for want of provender and other necessaries. He returned victorious to the royal camp on the Sodra with great renown, and on Thursday, 5th Zi-l ka'da of the same year his majesty started for Dehli. On the 'Íd-i azha' he offered up his prayers on the hills of Jálandar, and from thence proceeded to the capital. Minháj Siráj, the writer of this work, received under his majesty's orders the gift of a coat and turban, and of a horse with princely trappings.

Second Year of the Reign—Hijra 645 (1247 A.D.)

His Majesty reached Dehli on Thursday, 2nd Muharram, 645 (9th May, 1247) and was detained there for six months by heavy rains. In Jumáda-l ákhir the royal army marched to Panípat, but in Sha'bán it returned and proceeded towards Hindustán through the Doáb. In the neighbourhood of Kanauj there is a fortified village called Nandana,[2] where there is a very strong fort vying with the wall of Alexander. A body of infidel Hindús shut themselves up in this place, resolved to fight to the last extremity. For two days the royal army carried on a murderous conflict at this village, but at length the rebels were sent to hell, and the place was subdued.

The author of this work celebrated the victory and all the events of the campaign in verse. The slaughter of the rebellious

---

and signify "great Khán." They designate the same person, best known as Sultán Ghiyásu-d din Dalban, successor to Sultán Násiru-d din. I have employed the name Ulugh Khán as being most distinctive.] [1] [The Chináb.]

[2] [Var. "Talanda," and in another place, "Talanda." Briggs says "Bitunda" which place he identifies with Bulandshahr. But Bitunda or Bhatinda is in Patiala almost in a line between Dehli and Lahore. Neither this nor Bulandshahr can be the place here intended.]

infidels, the capture of their fortifications, and the success of Ulugh Khán-i Mu'azzam in killing and taking prisoner Dalakí wa Malakí,[1] these and all the other incidents are celebrated fully in the poem to which the author gave the name of his gracious master, and called it "Násirí-náma." For this poem the author received from the Sultán the grant of a fine annual allowance, and from Ulugh Khán he received the grant in *in'ám* of a village near Hánsí. (May God long maintain the seats of their empire and rule!) But I return to the thread of my history.

On Thursday, 24th Shawwál, 645 (February, 1248), the fort was captured after much fighting and bloodshed. Subsequently, on Monday, 12th Zi-l ka'da, 645, the army marched to Karra. Three days before Ulugh Khán had been sent on before with all the generals and princes of the army. The exploits and successes of this brave and skilful warrior, his victories in the field, his conquests of forts, fortified places, and jungles, his slaughter of rebellious infidels, his taking of booty and captives, and his capture of the dependants of great Ránas cannot here be recounted, but they are celebrated in the *Násiri-náma*,

There was in this neighbourhood a Rána[2] who (*ord*) was called Dalakí wa Malakí. He had many dependants, countless fighting men, great dominions and wealth, fortified places, and hills and defiles extremely difficult of access. All these he (Ulugh Khán) ravaged. He took prisoners the wives, sons, and dependants of that accursed one, and secured great booty. He secured 1500 horses of a peculiar breed, which he brought in for the use of the army. His other booty may be inferred from this. When he returned and waited on his sovereign all his brother nobles congratulated him on his victories.[3] On Thursday, 11th

---

[1] [قتل و اسر دلكي و ملكي] Our author in a following paragraph and elsewhere distinctly treats the two names as belonging to one person. Briggs, in his translation of *Firishta* says, "the Rájas Dulky and Mulky," and "these two rajas," but the text has "Dalakí Malakí," and adds, "this Dalakí Malakí was a raja."]

[2] [رانه بود]

[3] [The scene of this victory is not named, but Firishta tells us it was Kálinjar.]

Zí-l ka'da, 645, the Sultán started on his return from that country, and during his progress he was waited upon by Malik Jalálu-d dín Mas'úd, governor of Kanauj, who had the honour of an interview and went home. The Sultán then continued his journey to the capital.

Third Year of the Reign—Hijra 646 (1248 A.D.).

On Wednesday, 24th Muharram, 646 (20th May, 1248), the Sultán reached Dehli, and took his seat upon the throne with great state. When Malik Jalálu-d dín waited upon the king as he was returning, he was appointed governor of Sambal and Badáún, but he all at once took alarm about these two districts and came to the capital. The Sultán stayed at Dehli seven months, until the 6th Sha'bán. He then marched out on a campaign towards the hills and deserts; but he sent on his generals, and then returned to the capital, not finding occasion to proceed in person. He reached Dehli on Wednesday, 9th Zí-l ka'da. The royal army continued its march to the mountains of Rantambhor. Two important events occurred during this campaign. First—Kází 'Imádu-d dín Shakúrkání incurred suspicion, and on Friday, 9th Zí-l hijja he was dismissed from office in the White Palace, and by royal command proceeded to Badáún. On Monday, 12th Zí-l hijja, he was killed by 'Imadu-d dín Ríhán. Second—Malik Ikhtiáu-d dín Aibak was killed by the infidel Hindus near the fort of Rantambhor, on the 11th Zí-l hijja.

Fourth Year of the Reign—Hijra 647 (1249 A.D.).

On Monday, 3rd Safar, 647 (May, 1249), Ulugh Khán returned with his army to the capital. Being held in high estimation as a great supporter of the State, and the mainstay of the army, the Sultán, with the concurrence of the princes and nobles, gave his daughter in marriage to the son of the Khán. The marriage took place on Monday, 20th Rabí'u-l ákhir. On Monday, 10th Jumáda-l ákhir, Kází Jalálu-d dín Káshání came from Oudh and was made Kází of the State. On Monday, 22nd Sha'bán, the Sultán marched from Dehli. On Sunday, 4th Shawwál, he crossed the Jumna, intending to war against the Hindus in those parts. The author now received letters from his sister in Khurásán, and the Sultán being informed of the fact, he was graciously pleased, on the suggestion of Ulugh Khán, to give her one hundred beasts of burden,[1] and one hundred ass-loads of presents. The Sultán returned to Dehli on Wednesday. On Monday, the 29th Zí-l hijja, the author left Dehli for Multán, with the object of forwarding the presents to Khurásán. When he reached Hánsí, he, with the permission of Ulugh Khán took possession of his *in'ám*, village. He then proceeded towards Multán by way of Abúhar.

Fifth Year of the Reign—Hijra 648 (1250 A.D.)

On Sunday, 11th Safar (the author) had an interview with Sher Khán on the banks of the river Sind and Biyáh.[2] He proceeded from thence to Multán where he arrived on Wednesday 6th Rabí'u-l awwal. On the same day, Malik 'Izzu-d dín Lashkar Khán came from Uchh to take Multán, and the author had an interview with him. He encamped there until the 26th of Rabí'u-l ákhir, but was unable to conquer Multán, which was in the possession of the followers of Sher Khán. The author started for the capital and Malik 'Izzu-d dín Balban went off to Uchh. The author, passing by the fort of Marút (Mírat?) to Sarsuti and Hánsí, arrived at Dehli on the 22nd Jumáda-l awwal. In this year Ikhtiyáru-d dín Gurez made many of the infidel Mughals prisoners at Multán and sent them to Dehli, where their arrival

[1] [The word used is بردى for which the dictionaries give the meaning of "captive, slave, servant." It can hardly bear this meaning here, and in other places it is connected with *asp* (horse), so I have translated it "beast of burden," from the verb *burdan*, to carry.]

[2] [Firishta's account is somewhat different. He says that the Sultán was joined on the Biyáh by Sher Khán, and marched to Multán. Our text has no nominative in this sentence, but the words used "*muláḳát-i Sher Khán hásil shud*" show that the person who had the interview was not superior in rank to Sher Khán.]

caused much triumph. On Friday, 17 Zi-l ka'da, Kází Jalálu-d dín Kásbání died.

Sixth Year of the Reign—Hijra 649 (1251 A.D.).

Malik 'Izzu-d dín broke into revolt at Nágor, and the Sultán marched forth with his army to crush the outbreak, but 'Izzu-d dín came forward and made his submission. The Sultán then returned to the capital. After this Sher Khán marched from Multán to take Uchh, and Malik 'Izzu-d dín returned thither from Nágor, but he was captured in his encounter with Sher Khán and quietly surrendered the fort of Uchh to him, after which he went to Dehli, where he arrived on Sunday, 17th Rabí'u-l ákhir and was appointed governor of Badáún.

On Sunday, 10th Jumáda-l awwal, the writer Minháj Siráj was for the second time appointed Kází of the State and magistrate of the capital.

On Tuesday, 25th Sha'bán, his Majesty marched towards Gwálior, Chanderi, Bazawál (?) and Málwa. He advanced nearly as far as Málwa. Jáhir Deo[1] was the greatest of all the Ránas of that country and neighbourhood. He had five thousand horse and two hundred thousand infantry, but he was defeated. The fort of Balwar[2] which he had built was taken and plundered. Ulugh Khán exhibited great energy in this campaign, and great plunder and many captives fell into the hands of the victors. The Sultán returned in safety and with honour to Dehli.

Seventh Year of the Reign—Hijra 650 (1252 A.D.)

His Majesty reached Dehli on Monday, 23rd Rabí'u-l awwal 650 (2nd June, 1252) and dwelt for seven months at the capital

---

[1] [The text has "Jahírájár" with the variants "Jáhírájád" and "Jáhawárjár." Firishta and other writers say, "Jahír Deo." The name is doubtless the same as the "Chhhar Deo," found on a local coin bearing the name of Altamsh as sovereign. —See Thomas' Coins of Patan Sultans, page 15.]

[2] [Var. "Bagor or Begwar," and "Bazor or Bazawar." It is probably the same name as "Bazawál" a few lines above. Briggs in his translation of Firishta says "Narwar," which is perhaps right, though his text has "Tarwar."—See post, page 369.]

in great comfort and splendour, engaged in works of benevolence, and in strengthening the administration of justice. On Monday, 22nd Shawwál, he proceeded towards Lahore and Ghazni on the way to Uchh and Multán. When the author took leave of him near Kaithal he was honoured with the gift of a horse with trappings of gold and a saddle. In the course of this journey all the princes and Kháns near the king's route came in to wait upon him. Katlagh Khán from Dayána, and Lashkar Khán 'Izzu-d dín from Badáún, with their followers, attended the Sultán to the banks of the Diyáh. 'Imádu-d dín Rihán secretly set the feelings of the Sultán and of the princes against Ulugh Khán and perverted their minds.

Eighth Year of the Reign—Hijra 651 (1253 A.D.).

At the beginning of the new year, on Saturday, the 1st Muharram, Ulugh Khán received orders to go to his estates in the Siwálik hills and Hánsí. When the Khán under these orders proceeded from Rohtak towards Hánsí, the Sultán returned to Dehli, and directed his attention to the nobles and public affairs. In Jumáda-l awwal the post of wazír was given to 'Ainu-l mulk Muhammad Nizám Junaidí. Malik Kishlí Khán was made lord chamberlain. Ulugh Mubárak Aibak, brother of the Khán-i mu'azzam (Ulugh Khán) was granted the fief of Karra, and was sent thither. In the same year 'Imádu-d dín Rihán became prime minister (*wakíldar*).[1]

The royal army then marched from Dehli towards Hánsí, with the design of ousting Ulugh Khán. 'Imád Khán now brought forward Kází Shamsu-d dín Bahrálchí, and on the 27th Rajab he made him Kází of the state. Ulugh Khán went from Hánsí to Nágor, and his fief of Hánsí was,

---

[1] [Briggs, in Firishta (I. 281), reads it as *Wakíl-i dar*, officer of the door, one "who superintended the ceremonies of presentation." A very reasonable explanation; and Vullers explains it "Procurator palatii regii, i.q. vicarius." Still there is no doubt that 'Imádu-d dín was in reality minister, whatever the literal meaning of his title. In other places where it is used it would also appear to bear the meaning here given to it.]

through the interest of the lord chamberlain, bestowed upon Prince Ruknu-d dín. In Sha'bán the king returned with the army to Dehli. In the beginning of Shawwál he again set forth, with the intention of subduing Uchh, Multán, and Tabarhindh. When he approached the river Biyáh, a force was despatched to Tabarhindh. Previous to this Sher Khán, through the attacks of the infidels had crossed the river Sindh, and had gone towards Turkistán. Uchh, Multán, and Tabarhindh were left in charge of his officers. On Monday, 22nd Zi-l hijja, (the country) was conquered, and placed under the charge of Arslán Khán. The royal army then returned from the Biyáh.

Ninth Year of the Reign—Hijra 652 (1254 A.D.).

At the beginning of this year victories and spoils were gained in the vicinity of the mountains of Bardár[1] and Pinjor. The army then crossed the Jumna. On Wednesday, 16th Muharram, it passed over the Ganges at Miyápúr, and continued its march along the base of the hills to the banks of the Rahab.[2] In the course of these hostilities, 'Izzu-d dín Daramshí was killed at Tankala-báli.[3] In revenge for his death the Sultán ordered an attack to be made on Káithar (Kaithal), on Monday, 16th Safar, such that the inhabitants might not forget for the rest of their lives. He then marched to Badáún, and arrived there with great pomp and display. After a stay of nine days he started for Dehli.

On Sunday, 6th Rabi'u-l awwal, Sadru-l mulk Najmu-d dín Abú Bakr was made minister for the second time, and on Sunday, 20th of the same month, the author was honoured with the title of Sadr-i Johán (Chancellor of the World), in the neighbourhood of Kol. On Tuesday, 26th Rabi'u-awwal, the Sultán arrived at Dehli, and remained there six months, until news was brought of the confederacy of the nobles with Malik Jalálu-d dín. His Majesty left Dehli in Sha'bán, and proceeded towards Sanám and Tabarhindh. He passed the 'Id-i fitr in Sanám.

[1] [Sirmor?] [2] [See Vol. I. p. 49.] [3] [Var. Takiya-mbui.]

The forces of the confederate nobles, of Arslán Khán of Tabarhindh, Sanján Aibak, and Ulugh Khán, were assembled with Jalálu-d dín in the neighbourhood of Tabarhindh. His Majesty advanced from Sanám to Hánsí, and the nobles retired to Kahrám and Kaithal. The royal army marched thither, and then the confederates made propositions of peace. 'Imádu-d dín Ríhán was the cause of all the contention, so on Wednesday, 22nd Shawwál, the Sultán directed him to proceed to Badáún, which was given to him as his fief. Peace was thus made. On Tuesday, 17th Zi-l ka'da, after oaths had been taken and agreements concluded, all the nobles and officers waited on the king, and paid their allegiance. Lahore was given to Jalálu-d dín. On Tuesday, 9th Zi-l hijja, the king returned with pomp and splendour to Dehli.

Tenth Year of the Reign—Hijra 653 (1255 A.D.)

At the beginning of the new year an extraordinary event occurred. Under the behests of fate the mind of his Majesty was turned against his mother, the Malika-i Jahán, who was married to Katlagh Khán. Oudh was now granted to them, and they were ordered to proceed thither, which command they obeyed. This happened on Tuesday, 6th Muharram. On Sunday, 23rd Rabi'u-l awwal, his Majesty conferred the office of Kázi of the State and magistrate of the capital, as he had done before, on the writer of this work, Minháj Siráj. In Rabi'-l ákhir, Malik Kutbu-d dín, who was deputy of the State, uttered something which was offensive to the Sultán, and on the 23rd of that month he was arrested and placed in prison, where he was killed.

On Monday, 7th Jumáda-l awwal, the fief of Mírat was conferred on Malik Kishli Khán Ulugh A'zzam Bárbak-sultání, upon his coming from Karra to pay his respects to the Sultán. On Tuesday, 16th Rajab, Jamálu-d dín Bastámí was made Shaikhu-l Islám. In the same month Malik Táju-d dín Síwistání proceeded from Oudh, and expelled 'Imádu-d dín Ríhán from Bahráich, and he died.

In the month of Shawwál the royal army marched from the capital to Hindustán. On Sunday, 17th Zí-l ka'da, Ulugh Khán Mu'azzam went to Hánsí to superintend the military organization of the Siwálik hills, which having arranged he returned to Dehli. At the end of the year, on Wednesday, 9th Zí-l hijja, he proceeded to the royal camp. Previous to this, Katlagh Khán had been directed to leave Oudh, and go to the fief of Bahráich. He resented this, so the Sultán sent a force under Malik Baktam Rukní to put him down. The two armies met near Badáún, and Baktam was killed. The royal army then marched to Oudh to retrieve this disaster, but Katlagh Khán retreated to Kálinjar. Thither Ulugh Khán pursued him, but failing to overtake him, he returned to the royal camp with great booty.

Eleventh Year of the Reign—Hijra 654 (1256 A.D.)

At the beginning of the new year, in the month of Muharram, the royal army having achieved victory, marched triumphant towards Dehli under the protection of the Almighty, and reached the city on the 4th Rabíu'-l awwal. When Katlagh Khán heard of the Sultán's homeward march he began to interfere in the districts of Karra and Mánikpur. A battle followed between him and Arslán Khán Sanjar Chist, in which the latter was victorious. Katlagh Khán could no longer remain in Hindustán, so he proceeded into Mawás,[1] with the intention of proceeding to the highlands. He reached Santur,[1] and there took refuge among the hills and the tribes of those parts. The royal army marched out to quell this disturbance on Tuesday, 20th Zí-l hijja, and at the beginning of the following year the army went to Santúr, and fought a battle with the Hindus of the mountains. Katlagh Khán was with those mountaineers, and a

---

[1] [These two names are written مواسی and سنتور. (Var. سُتور) The former is probably Mewár, and the hills the Arávallí mountains. Briggs says there is a town called Santpúr, near Abú. Thornton has a "Santoo," 84 miles S.S.W. from Jodhpur.]

party of nobles in the royal army, who had suspicions fears, went and joined him. They were unable to withstand the troops of the Sultán, so they turned their backs. Ulugh Khán ravaged the whole of the hills with the sword, and penetrated as far as the town of Salmúr, in the defiles and fastnesses of the mountains. No king had ever laid hold upon Salmúr, nor had any Musulman army reached it. He now plundered it, and carried on a devastating warfare. So many of the rebellious Hindus were killed that the numbers cannot be computed or described.

Twelfth Year of the Reign—Hijra 655 (1257 A.D.).

After the return from the campaign, on Sunday, 6th Rabiu'-l awwal, Malik Sanján Aibak, of Khitá, fell from his horse and died. On Sunday, 26th Rabí'u-l ákhir, the Sultán reached the capital with his army.

When the army returned victorious, 'Izzu-d dín Kishlu Khán Balban advanced to the borders of the river Biyáh, with the forces of Uchh and Multán. Malik Katlagh Khán and the nobles who were with him proceeded to join this new revolter in the neighbourhood of Sámána.

When intelligence of this rebellion reached the Sultán, he placed Ulugh Khán at the head of an army, with which he marched from Dehli on Thursday, 15th Jumáda-l awwal. He approached the enemy, and there was only ten kos between the opposing forces, when he discovered that a party of conspirators in the capital, such as the Shaikhu-l Islám, Kutbu-d dín, and Kází Shamsu-d dín Bahráichí, had secretly addressed letters to to Katlagh Khán and Malik Kishlú Khán Balban, inviting them to come to Dehli, where they would find the gates open and every one in the city ready to assist and support these proceedings. Some faithful reporters in the capital conveyed intelligence of this conspiracy to Ulugh Khán, who sent the letters back to his sovereign in Dehli, informing him of the plot of the nobles, and advising him to order such of them as had fiefs in the neighbourhood of Dehli to proceed to those estates. When the storm had blown over, and they returned to the capital, the Sultán might make an end of them.

On Sunday, 2nd Jumáda-l ákhir, an order was issued directing Saiyid Kutbu-d dín and Kází Shamsu-d dín Dahráichí to proceed to their estates.

When the letters which the conspirators sent from the city reached Malik Katlagh Khán and Malik Kishlú Khán, they instantly started with all their forces to Dehli, and in two days and a-half they accomplished the distance, one hundred *kos*. On Thursday, 6th Jumáda-l ákhir, they alighted at their gardens (outside the city), and in the morning, after prayers, they came to the gate of the city and made the circuit of the walls. At night they pitched their camp within sight of Dehli, between the Jumna,[1] Kilu-gharí and the city. By the mercy of God it so happened that two days before these nobles came to their gardens on the Jumna, in reliance upon the promises held out in the letters, a number of the conspirators had gone out of the city. When the nobles heard of this they became very cautious in their proceedings.

The Sultán ordered the gates of the city to be closed, and as as the army was absent every preparation was made for war. 'Aláu-d dín Ayyáz Zanjání, lord chamberlain, the deputy of the lord chamberlain, Ulugh Kotwal Beg Jamálu-d dín Naishapúrí, and the *diwán i'arz i mamálik*, exerted themselves most laudably in making the city secure and in arming the fighting men. At night the nobles, officers, and chief men were posted on the walls of the city. On the following morning, a Friday, the Almighty showed the inhabitants a pleasant sight. Kishlú Khán had made up his mind to retire, and sundry other nobles and the mother of the Sultán, when they perceived this, all made up their minds to retreat. The greater part of their forces, however, would not consent to retreat with them, but encamped near the city. Many of the chief men and officers asked forgiveness, and

---

[1] [The text has "*Júd*," which I take to be a mistake for *Jún* = Jumna.]

joined the royal service, and those nobles returned disappointed to the Siwálik hills.

When the news of this enterprise reached Ulugh Khán and the officers of the royal army, they returned towards Dehli, and as they approached the result became known to them. On Tuesday, 11th Jumáda-l ákhir, Ulugh Khán entered the city safely and triumphantly. After this, on Wednesday, 8th Ramzán, Ziyáu-l mulk Táju-d dín was raised to the dignity of wazír.

At the close of this year the infidel Mughals approached from Khurásán, and advanced into the territories of Uchh and Multán. Kishlú Khán entered into a treaty with them, and joined them at the camp of Sálín-nawín.

Thirteenth Year of the Reign—Hijra 656 (1258 A.D.)

At the beginning of the new year, on Sunday, the 6th Muharram, the Sultán marched with his army from Dehli to oppose the infidel Mughals. Trustworthy writers have recorded that on Wednesday, 4th of the same month, Hulákú, chief of the Mughals, was defeated before the gates of Baghdád, by the forces of the Khalífa M'utasim Bi-llah.[1]

When the royal army left the city nobles and generals were appointed to the command of forces in different parts. The main body returned to the capital on the 1st Ramazán, and remained there five months. On the 18th Zí-l ka'da the country of Lakhnauti was given to Malik Jalálu-d dín Mas'úd Malik Jání.

Fourteenth Year of the Reign—Hijra 657 (1259 A.D.).

On the 10th Muharram the royal army marched from the the capital on a campaign against the infidels. On Sunday, 21st Safar, the districts of Dayána, Kol, Balá-rám, and Gwalior were assigned to Malik Sher Khán. Maliku-n nawwáb Aibak was appointed to command an army sent against the infidels of Rantambhor, and the Sultán returned to Dehli. On Wednesday,

[1] [A note in the printed text says that all the four MSS. used agree in this statement, so contrary to the truth. Baghdád fell, and the Khalífa was put to death.]

4th Jumáda-l ákhir, two elephants with treasure came to the court from Lakhnauti. On the 6th of the same month, the Shaikhu-l Islám Jamálu-d dín Bastámí died, and on the 24th Kází Kabíru-d dín also departed. (May God have mercy on them!) By the favour of the Sultán their *manasbs* were continued to their sons. In Rajab Malik Kishlí Khán-i a'zam Darbak Aibak died, and the office of lord chamberlain was given to his son, Malik 'Aláu-d dín Muhammad. On the 1st Ramazán, Imám Hamídu-d dín Máríkala died, and the Sultán graciously continued his *in'áms* to his sons.

After all this trouble the State enjoyed repose; troubles were appeased and wounds were healed. All things went on prosperously. On the 29th Ramazán the Almighty in his bounty gave the Sultán a son. The gifts and honours which were showered on the rich and poor exceeded all powers of description. At the end of Shawwál, Malik Tamar Khán Saujar under the royal orders returned to Dehli with his army.

Fifteenth Year of the Reign—Hijra 658 (1260 A.D.)

The new year opened auspiciously. On the 16th Ramazán Ulugh Khán was sent into the hills of Dehli, to chastise the rebel inhabitants of Mewát, and to intimidate their Deo. Ten thousand horsemen in armour, and a large army of brave and warlike soldiers were under his command. Great booty was gained, and many cattle captured. Defiles and passes were cleared, strong forts were taken, and numberless Hindús perished under the merciless swords of the soldiers of Islám.

I have resolved, upon reflection, to close my history at this place and with this victory. If life and opportunity are given to me, I may hereafter record any remarkable events that may happen. I beg the indulgent reader to forgive my errors, faults, and omissions. I pray that God may preserve in continued prosperity my gracious Sultán, and I hope that my composition of this work may be deemed meritorious both in this world and the next.[1]

[1] [I have here greatly compressed the author's flourishes.]

TABAKAT XXII.

[Page 281 to 324 of the printed text.]

No. 25. *Al Khákánu-i Mu'azzam Bahàu-l hakk wau-d dín Ulugh Khán Balbanu-s Sultání* [*otherwise called Ghiyásu-d dín Balban*].

The Khákán-i Mu'azzam Ulugh Khán-i 'azam belonged to the stock of the Khákáns of Albarí.[1] His father and the father of Sher Khán were born of the same father and mother, the father being of the race of the Khákáns of Albarí. He was *khán* over ten thousand houses (*kháná*), and the family was well known in Albarí of Turkistán, among the Turkí tribes. At the present time the sons of his (Ulugh Khán's) paternal uncles rule over these tribes with great distinction. I was informed of these facts by Kurbat Khán Sanjar. The Almighty desired to grant a support to the power of Islám and to the strength of the Muhammadan faith, to extend his glorious shadow over it, and to preserve Hindustán within the range of his favour and protection. He therefore removed Ulugh Khán in his youth from Turkistán, and separated him from his race and kindred, from his tribe and relations, and conveyed him to the country (of Hindustán), for the purpose of curbing the Mughals. God conducted him to Baghdád, and from that city to Guzerat. Khwája Jamálu-d dín Basrí, a man remarkable for piety and integrity, ability and worth, bought him, and brought him up carefully like a son. Intelligence and ability shone out clearly in his countenance, so his patron looked upon him with an eye of kindness and treated him with especial consideration.

In the year 630 H. (1232 A.D.) he brought him to Dehli when Sultán Sá'id Shamsu-d dunyá wau-d dín adorned the throne. With several other Turks he was brought into the presence of the Sultán. When the monarch observed him he bought all the lot of Turks and appointed them to attend before his throne.

[از تخمهٔ خاقان البری با نام بود] [1]

Ulugh was seen to be a youth of great promise, so the king made him his personal attendant, placing, as one might say, the hawk of fortune on his hand. So that in after times, in the reigns of this monarch's children, it might come to pass that this youth should save the kingdom from the violence and machinations of its foes, and raise it to a high pitch of glory and honour.

At this period, while he was discharging his duties, by the decree of fate, he recovered his brother Kishlí Khán (afterwards) lord chamberlain, at which he rejoiced greatly. His power became conspicuous. When Sultán Ruknu-d dín came to the throne, he went off along with the Turks from Dehli to Hindustán, and when the Turks were brought back he returned to Dehli in their army. He was imprisoned for some days and subjected to some indignity. The design in this may have been (God knows!) that he should taste the sufferings of the miserable, so that when he attained to the sovereign dignity he might have compassion on them, and be thankful for his own exaltation. [*A story is introduced here.*]

Let us return to our history. When Sultán Raziya ascended the throne Ulugh Khán continued to be one of the royal attendants (*Khása-dár*) till fortune favoured him, and he became chief huntsman (*Amír shikár*). Fate proclaimed that the earth was to be the prey of his fortune and the world the game of his sovereignty. He held this office and discharged its duties for some time, till the sun of the supremacy of Raziya set and that of Mu'izzu-d dín Bahrám Sháh shone forth. Fortune still befriended him. After remaining some time in his position of chief huntsman, performing his service, and exhibiting marks of ability, he was made master of the horse. The steed of sovereignty and empire thus came under his bridle and control. When Badru-d dín Sankar became lord chamberlain, he showed a paternal interest in Ulugh Khán, and took such care of his advancement that he was raised to a higher position, and received a grant of the lands of Riwárí. He went to that place, and by his vigour and bravery punished the hill chiefs[1] and brought the district under his rule.

When the power of the Mu'izzí dynasty was declining, the nobles conspired together and came to the gates of the city (Dehli). The princes and nobles all agreed as to the course to be pursued. Ulugh Khán,[2] grantee of Ríwárí, displayed such energy and exhibited such remarkable resolution in securing the submission of the provinces, that no one of the princes and nobles, Turks and Táziks, was worth the hundredth part of him. All the confederates admitted that in vigour, courage, and activity he surpassed them all. When the city was conquered he received a grant of Hánsí. On taking possession of the territory he applied himself to its improvement, and through his justice and generosity all the inhabitants were happy and content. His success was so great that other nobles began to look upon it with jealousy, and the thorn of envy began to rankle in their hearts. But it was the will of God that he should excel them all, so that the more the fire of their envy burnt, the stronger did the incense of his fortune rise from the censer of the times. "They seek to extinguish the light of God with their mouths, but God willeth only to perfect his light." [*The author continues in a high strain of benediction and eulogy.*]

To return to our history. In the year 640 H. (1242 A.D.) this humble individual (the author) had to travel to Lakhnautí with his family and dependants. In this journey he spent two years. Trustworthy persons have recorded that in the year 641 Ulugh Khán was appointed lord chamberlain. When the royal army marched from the capital he inflicted a severe chastisement on the rebels of Jalálí and Dewalí, and the Mawás in the *doab* between the Ganges and Jumna. He fought much against the

---

[1] مواسات کوه را مالش تمام داد] The word *mawás* signifies protection, dependence; but it appears to have some other technical meaning. Further on we read of the *Mawását* of the Doab, and "the *Mawását* and *Ráneysán*."]

[2] [The text says "the Sultán (may God prolong his reign);" plainly showing that this part of the work was written in the reign of Balban].

infidels and cleared the roads and neighbouring country from insurgents.

In the year 643 the author under the imperial orders, left Lakhnoutí with his family and returned to the capital in company with Tughán Khán Tughril. In this year the accursed Mankútí (Mangú-Khán), who was one of the generals of the Mughals and a prince of Turkistán, marched from the neighbourhood of Tálikán and Kunduz into Sindh. He laid siege to Uchh, one of the most renowned fortresses of Sindh, and equal to Mansúra.[1] There was a eunuch in (command of) the fort who belonged to the household of Táju-d dín. Abú Bakr-Kabír Khán Aksunkar was chief justice, and Mukhlisu-d dín was kotwal. When intelligence of this inroad reached the Court, Ulogh Khán made known his views to the Sultán and prepared an army to oppose the Mughals. The princes and nobles were opposed to this expedition,[2] but Malik Ulugh Khán was very earnest about it.

When the royal army marched towards the seat of warfare, the Khákán-i Mu'azzam[3] Ulugh Khán (may his reign endure!) appointed guides to lead the way, so that the marches might be made with the greatest celerity. In ordinary cases eight *kos* would be one day's march, but under his arrangements, twelve *kos* or even more were accomplished. The army arrived on the banks of the Biyáh, made the transit of that river, and reached Lahore on the banks of the Rávi. He there showed great energy and bravery in pushing forward the expedition, and incited the Sultán and the nobles to be earnest for the repulse of the infidel Mughals.

On Monday, 25th Shabán, 643 H. (Nov. 1245), intelligence

[1] زحصن أچه را كه در قلع نامدار بلاد سند است و ارض منصوره لس] بند ان داد The words are not very precise, but the mention of Mansúra is curious.]

[2] [استنكاري مي آورد]

[3] [In this memoir the title "Khákán-i Mu'azzam" is generally employed, but for for the sake of uniformity and simplicity I have substituted "Ulugh Khán."]

was brought to the royal camp that the infidel Mughals had raised the siege of Uchh. The reason of their retreat was that Ulugh Khán (when he reached the Biyáh) had sent forward messengers bearing letters from the Sultán addressed to the garrison of the fort, announcing the approach of the royal army, and dilating upon the vast numbers of the soldiers and elephants and the great valour and spirit of the forces which followed the royal standards. He also sent forward an advance force to reconnoitre. When the messengers came near Uchh, some of the letters fell into the hands of the accursed warriors, and some reached the garrison of the fort. The drums were beaten in the fort to announce the joy of the besieged. The contents of the letters and the approach of the army of Islám became fully known to the accursed foe, and the horsemen of the advanced force were in the vicinity of Sindh on the banks of the Biyáh of Lahore. Fear and dismay fell upon the hearts of the accursed, and the goodness of God lent its aid (to the forces of Islam). Trusty men record that when Mankútí heard of the approach of the army of Islám under the royal standard, that it had proceeded by the river Biyáh, near the skirts of the hills, and that it was advancing along the banks of the river,[1] he made enquiry of a party (of prisoners) why the army of Islám marched along the bases of the mountains, for that route was long, and the way by Sarsutí and Marút (Mírat!) was nearer? He was answered that the numerous fissures on the banks of the river rendered the way impassable for the army.[2]

This answer convinced Mankútí that he had not sufficient strength to withstand the approaching army, and that he must retreat. Panic obtained mastery over him and his forces, so that they could no longer retain their position. He divided his

[1] [بر كنار آب می آید]

[2] [از كثرت جر بر كنار آب راه نباشد] The text is far from intelligible, and is apparently contradictory. The royal forces are said to have marched along the banks of the river, although that route is declared to have been impracticable. The whole passage is omitted from Sir H. Elliot's MS.]

army into three bodies and fled. Many Musulmán and Hindú prisoners obtained their freedom. This victory is attributable to the activity, bravery, and strategy of Ulugh Khán; but for him the victory would not have been gained (may the Almighty keep him safe under his protection!)

After the achievement of this victory Ulugh Khán advised that the royal army should march towards the river Sodra[1] in order to impress the minds of the enemy with the great power, bravery, and numbers of the army of Islám. So the army proceeded to the banks of the Sodra, and from thence, on the 27th Shawwal, 643 H., it returned to Dehli, which city it reached on Monday 12th Zí-l-hijja 643 H. (May 1246).

For some time past the mind of Sultán 'Aláu-d dín had been alienated from the nobles, he was seldom visible to the army, and besides this he was given up to depravity. The nobles all agreed to write secretly from Dehli to Násiru-d dunyá wau-d dín, inviting him to set up his pretensions to the throne. On Sunday, 23rd Muharram, 644 (June 1246) he came to Dehli and sat upon the seat of empire. The Khutba was read and the coin of the realm was struck in the auspicious name of Násir. So Ulugh Khán represented how the accursed foe had in the previous year fled before the armies of Islám, and had gone to the upper parts (*taraf-i bálá*). It now seemed advisable that the royal army should proceed in that direction. This advice was approved and orders were given for the march. On Monday, the 1st Rajab, 644 H., the army set forth and proceeded to the river Sodra. Here Ulugh Khán was detached with several nobles and generals to make an incursion into the hills of Júd. The Rána of these hills had acted as guide to the infidel Mughals, and it was now determined to take vengeance. Ulugh Khán accordingly attacked the hills of Júd, and the countries on the Jailam, and led his forces as far as the banks of the Indus. All the women and dependants of the infidels which were in those parts were obliged to flee, and a party of the Mughal army

[1] [The Chináb.]

crossed over the Jailam, and saw the forces which were arrayed under the command of Ulugh Khán. The manifold lines of the army, the numbers of the horse, the armour and the arms, filled the observers with wonder and dismay. The bravery and generalship which Ulugh Khán displayed in scaling the mountains, breaking through defiles, capturing fortified places, and crossing jungles, cannot be described in writing. The fame of this campaign extended to Turkistán. There was no husbandry or agriculture in this country, and fodder became unobtainable. Hence he was compelled to retire, and he returned victorious and triumphant to the royal camp, bringing back all his officers and troops in safety.

On Thursday, 6th Zí-l ka'da, his majesty returned to the capital, which he reached on Thursday, 2nd Muharram, 645 H. The perseverance and resolution of Ulugh Khán had been the means of showing to the army of Turkistán and the Mughals such bravery and generalship that in the course of this year no one came from the upper parts towards Sindh. So Ulugh Khán represented to his Majesty, in the month of Sha'bán, that the opportunity was favourable for making an expedition into Hindustán. The Mawás and Ránas[1] had not been pinched for several years, but some coercion might now be exercised on them, by which spoil would fall into the hands of the soldiers of Islám, and wealth would be gained to strengthen the hands of the State in resisting the Mughals. The royal armies accordingly marched to Hindustán, passing down the Doab between the Ganges and Jumna. After some fighting, the fort of Nandann[2] was captured, and Ulugh Khán was sent with some other generals and a Muhammadan force to oppose Dalaki wa Malaki. This was a Rána in the vicinity of the Jumna, between Kálinjar and Karra, over whom the Ráís of Kálinjar and Málwa had no authority. He had numerous followers and ample wealth; he ruled wisely; his fortresses were strong and secure; in his territories

[1] [موانات و رایگان]
[2] [Var. "Talanda" and "Talanda." See supra, page 347.]

the defiles were arduous, the mountains rugged, and the jungles many. No Muhammadan army had ever penetrated to his dwelling place. When Ulugh Khán reached his abode, the Rána took such care for the safety of himself and his family, that he kept quiet from the dawn till the time of evening prayer, and when it grew dark he fled to some more secure place. At daybreak, the Muhammadan army entered his abode, and then pursued him, but the accursed infidel had escaped into the lofty mountains, to an inaccessible spot impossible to reach except by stratagem, and the use of ropes and ladders. Ulugh Khán incited his soldiers to the attempt, and, under his able direction, they succeeded in taking the place. All the infidel's wives, dependants, and children fell into the hands of the victors with much cattle, many horses and slaves. Indeed, the spoil that was secured exceeded all computation. At the beginning of Shawwál 645 H. (Feb. 1248), the force returned to the royal camp with their booty, and after the I'd-i azha', the whole army marched towards the capital, which it reached on the 4th Muharram, 646 H. (April 1248). A full poetical account of this campaign, in which the several victories are recounted, has been composed; the book is called *Násiri náma*.[1]

In Sha'bán, 646 H. (Nov. 1248), the royal army marched through the upper country to the neighbourhood of the Biyáh, and then returned to the capital. Ulugh Khán with several nobles under him, was sent with an ample force towards Rantambhor, to overrun the mountains of Mewát and the country of Báhar-deo, who was the greatest of the Ráís of Hindustán. He ravaged the whole of those territories and gained a large booty. Malik Bahán-d dín Aibak was slain under the fort of Rantambhor, on Sunday in the month of Zí-l hijja 646, while Ulugh Khán was engaged fighting in another quarter. The Khán's soldiers showed great courage and fought well; they sent many of the infidels to hell, and secured great spoil; after which they returned to the capital.

[1] [See *supra*, page 348.]

On Monday, 3rd Safar, 647 H. (May, 1249), they arrived at Dehli. In the course of this year his majesty was pleased to recognize the great ability and distinguished services of his general.[1] He therefore promoted him from the rank of a Malik and the office of lord chamberlain to the dignity of a *Khán*, and on Tuesday, 3rd Rajab, 647 H., he named him lieutenant of the government, army, and royal fortune (*bakhtiyárí*), with the title of Ulugh Khán. The truth of the adage that "the worth of titles is revealed by heaven," was proved in this case, for from that day forth the services of Ulugh Khán to the house of Násir became still more conspicuous. When he was thus promoted, his brother Kishli Khán Aibak, master of the horse, became lord chamberlain. He was a nobleman of kind and generous character, and endowed with many virtues. Malik Táju-d dín Sanjar Tabar Khán became deputy of the lord chamberlain, and my excellent dear son 'Alau-d dín Ayyáz Tabar Khán Zanjání,[2] who was Amíru-l hujjáb (superintendant of the royal doorkeepers), was made deputy *wakíldar*. These appointments were made on Friday, 6th Rajab 647, and Ikhtiyáru-d dín I'tigin, the long-haired, who had been deputy, now became master of the horse.

On Monday, 9th Sha'bán, 647 H. (Nov. 1249), the royal army left the capital and took the field. Passing over the Jumna it encamped and engaged in operations against the Mawás. [*Matters personal of the author, see page* 350.]

On Tuesday, 25th Sha'bán, 649 H. (Nov. 1251), the royal army marched towards Málwa and Kálinjar. When Ulugh Khán arrived there with the army of Islám, he defeated Jáhir of Ijárí, a great *rána*, who had a large army and many adherents, and destroyed both him and his kingdom. This Jáhir, *rána* of Ijárí, was an active and able man. In the reign of Sa'íd Shamsu-d dín, in the year 632 H. (1234), the army of Islám was sent from Hayána Sultán-kot, Kanauj, Mahr, Maháwan and Gwalior,

---

[1] [Many lines of eulogy are here compressed into this short but adequate statement.]
[2] [Var. "Ribání."]

against Kálinjar and Jamú, under the command of Malik Nusratu-d dín Tábasí, who was distinguished above all the generals of the time for courage, boldness, ability, and generalship. The army marched on fifty days from Gwalior, and great booty fell into its hands, so much that the imperial fifth amounted to nearly twenty-two lacs. When they returned from Kálinjar they were encountered by this Rána of Ijárí, who seized upon the defiles on the river Sindí in the road of the returning army. The author heard Nusratu-d dín Tábasí say, " No enemy in Hindustán had ever seen my back, but this Hindú fellow of Ijárí attacked me as a wolf falls upon a flock of sheep. I was obliged to retire before him until I reached a position where I turned upon him and drove him back." I tell this story so that my readers may clearly perceive what courage and generalship Ulugh Khán exhibited when he defeated and put to flight such a foe. He further took from him the fortress of Bazor,[1] and his conduct and feats in this campaign will stand as a lasting memorial of him.

On Monday, 23rd Rabí'u-l awwal, 650 H. (June, 1252), the army returned to Dehli and remained there for six months. On the 12th Shawwal of the same year, it marched through the upper country to the banks of the Biyáh. At this time Malik Balban held the fief of Badáún, and Katlagh Khán that of Bayána. They were both summoned to the Royal presence, and both attended with all the generals of the army at the royal abode. When the army reached the banks of the Biyáh, 'Imádu-d dín Ríhán conspired with other chiefs, and excited envy and enmity against Ulugh Khán. The envious found their own importance dimmed by his glory, and they resolved to do some hurt and injury to his august person, either in hunting, in passing through mountain defiles, or in crossing rivers. Ulugh Khán's good fortune preserved him, and his adversaries were unable to do him any harm. When the conspirators found that their plans were ineffectual, they agreed upon another course,

[1] [Var. " Bazol," " Barole." See note, page 351, supra.]

and presenting themselves at the doors of the royal tent, urged upon his majesty that Ulugh Khán ought to be sent to his estates. The result of all this was that the order was given to him indirectly.[1]

On Saturday, the new moon of Muharram, 651 H., Ulugh Khán proceeded to Hánsí with his followers and family. When the Sultán reached Dehli, the thorn of envy, which still festered in the malicious heart of Ríhán, impelled him to recommend his majesty to send Ulugh Khán to Nágor, and to give the country of Hánsí to one of the royal princes. His majesty accordingly went to Hánsí, and the Khán removed to Nágor. This happened in Jumáda-l ákhir 651 H. On his departure for Hánsí, 'Imádu-d dín Ríhán became *wakíldar*,[2] and the administration of the royal orders passed into his hands.

Through the envy and malignity of the new minister, the office of Kází of the State was taken from the author, Minháj Siráj, in Rajab, 651, and given to Kází Shamsu-d dín Dahráíchí. On returning to the capital, on the 17th Shawwál, Malik Saifu-d dín Kishlí Khán, brother of Ulugh Khán, was sent to his estate of Karra, and 'Izzu-d dín Balban, son-in-law of Katlagh Khán, was appointed to the charge of the office of lord chamberlain. All the officers who had been appointed through the interest of Ulugh Khán were removed, and the business and quietude of the State were disturbed, all through the machinations of 'Imádu-d dín.

At this period, when Ulugh Khán (May God prolong his reign!) went to Nágor, he led a Muhammadan force in the direction of Rantambhor, Hindí, and Chitror. Báhar Deo, Rái of Rantambhor, the greatest of the Ráis, and the most noble and illustrious of all the princes of Hindustán, assembled an army to inflict a blow on Ulugh Khán. But it was the will of God that the name of the Khán should be celebrated for his victories in the annals of the time, and although the Rái's army was large and well appointed with arms and horses, it was put to flight,

[1] [براين جمله رسانيد از منزل ميسره] "all this was brought about in a left-handed way."]
[2] [See note page 352, *supra*.]

and many of its valiant fighting men were sent to hell. The Musulmáns obtained great spoil and captured many horses and prisoners (*burda*). They then returned safe with their booty to Nágor, which, in consequence of Ulugh Khán's presence, had become a place of great importance.

At the opening of the year 651 H., the numerous people who had suffered oppression and hardship through the disgrace of Ulugh Khán retired to their closets, and like fish out of water, and sick men without slumber, from night till morn, and from morn till night, they offered up their prayers to the Creator, supplicating him to let the dawn of Ulugh Khán's prosperity break forth in splendour, and dispel with its brilliant light the gloom occasioned by his rival Ribán. The Almighty graciously gave ear to the prayers of the wretched, and the cries of the distressed. The victorious banners of Ulugh Khán were borne from Nágor, and he went to the capital. The reason of his return was this. The nobles and servants of the State were all Turks of pure origin and Tázíks of good stock, but 'Imádu-d dín was an eunuch and impotent; he, moreover, belonged to one of the tribes of Hindustán. Notwithstanding all this he exercised authority over the heads of all these chiefs. They were disgusted with this state of affairs and could no longer endure it. They suffered so much from the hands of the bullies who were retained by 'Imádu-d dín, that for six months they could not leave their houses, nor could they even go to prayers on Fridays. How was it possible for Turks and Maliks, accustomed to power, rule, and warfare, to remain quiet under such ignominy? The chiefs of Hindustán, of Karra, Mánikpúr, Oudh and the upper country to Badáún, of Tabarhindh, Sanám, Samána, and the Siwálik Hills, sent to Ulugh Khán inviting him to return. Arslán Khán led an army out of Tabarhindh, Dan Khán came forth from Sanám and Mansúrpúr, and Ulugh Khán collected his forces in Nágor and the Siwálik hills. Malik Jalálu-d dín Mas'úd Sháh bin Sultán joined them from Lahore, and they marched upon the capital.

'Imádu-d dín advised his majesty to go forth and repress the malcontents, and accordingly he led his army towards Sanám. Ulugh Khán was in the neighbourhood of Tabarhindh with several other chiefs. The author of this book started from the capital for the royal camp, which was stationed in the city near the royal residence. On Monday, 26th Ramazán, 652 H. he arrived, and on the "Night of Power" he read prayers in the king's abode. On the next day, 27th Ramazán, the opposing armies drew near to each other, the outposts met, and great disquietude arose. The 'Íd-i fitr was passed at Sanám, and on Saturday, 8th Shawwál, the royal army fell back to Hánsí. Malik Jalálu-d dín, Ulugh Khán, and the nobles with them proceeded to Kaithal. The chiefs and nobles on both sides deemed it desirable to hold a parley. General Karra Jamák, a personal attendant of Ulugh Khán, and well-known for his integrity, acted on the part of the insurgents; and the noble of the black banner, Hisámu-d dín Katlagh, well-known for his great age, a man of conciliatory character and great probity, was deputed to meet him. He exerted himself to the utmost with General Karra Jamák and Malik-i Islám Kutbu-d dín Hasan 'Alí.

The discontented nobles represented to his majesty that they were all willing to obey his commands, but that they had no security against the machinations and outrageous conduct of 'Imádu-d dín Ríhán. If he were banished from the Court they would all submit and willingly obey the orders of the Sultán. The royal army marched from Hánsí to Jínd, and on Saturday, 22nd Shawwál 652 H., 'Imádu-d dín was dismissed from his office of minister (thanks to God for it!) and the privileges attaching to the government of Badáún were given to him.

'Izzu-d dín Balban, deputy of the lord chamberlain, repaired to the camp of Ulugh Khán, and on Tuesday, 3rd Zí-l ka'da, Dáo Khán Aibak Khitái came to the royal camp to finally arrange the terms of peace. An extraordinary plot was now formed, with which the author of this book became acquainted. 'Imádu-d dín Khán with a number of Turks of low degree, and inimical to

Ulugh Khán, resolved upon cutting down Ban Khán Aibak Khitáí at the entrance of the royal tent, in order that Ulugh Khán, on hearing of the assassination, might (in retaliation) slay 'Izzu-d dín Balban. The peace would thus be prevented, 'Imádu-dín would retain his position in safety, and Ulugh Khán would be unable to come to Court. Kutbu-d dín Hasan heard of the conspiracy, and sent one of the chief attendants of the chamberlain, Sharfu-l mulk Rashídu-d dín Hanafí, to Ban Khán, advising him not to go to the royal tent in the morning, but to remain at his own lodging. Ban Khán acted on this advice, and so the plot failed. The facts became known to the great men, and under the command of the Sultan, 'Imádu-d dín was sent off to Badáún.

On Tuesday, 17th Zí-l k'ada, his majesty, with the desire of making peace, directed the author, Minháj Siráj, to offer terms of agreement to all. Next day, Ulugh Khán, with the other nobles, came to Court, and had the honour of kissing hands. The Sultán then turned homewards, accompanied by Ulugh Khán, and reached the capital on Wednesday, 9th Zí-l hijja. The kindness of the Almighty now became manifest. For a long time there had been no rain, but upon the approach of Ulugh Khán the Almighty displayed his mercy, and the rain, which is the life of herbs and plants, of men and animals, fell upon the earth. No wonder, then, that people looked upon the return of Ulugh Khán as a happy omen, that his compeers rejoiced over it, and that all were grateful to the Almighty for his bounty.

The year 653 H. opened. Something happened in the royal harem of which no one had accurate knowledge, but Katlagh Khán[1] was directed to take charge of the government of Oudh, and thither he proceeded. At the same time the government of Bahráich was given to 'Imádu-d dín Ríhán. The success of Ulugh Khán shone forth with brilliant radiance, the garden of the world began to put forth leaf, and the key of divine mercy opened the doors of the hearts of men who had been driven into

[1] [Step-father of the Sultán, see page 364.]

seclusion. Among these was the well-wisher of the State, and the partisan of Ulugh Khán, the writer of this book, Minháj Siráj Júzjáni. The censure of his adversaries, and the injustice of his foes, had forced him into retirement and had subjected him to distress and trouble; but now the kind influence of Ulugh Khán was exerted with the Sultán, and on Sunday, 5th Rabi'u-awwal, 653 H., the office of Kází of the State and the seat of justice were given for the third time to the faithful and grateful writer of this history.

Katlagh Khán had gone to Oudh, and some time passed, but circumstances so occurred that he became disaffected. Imperative orders were several times sent to him from Court, but to these he paid no heed. 'Imádu-d dín Ríhán busied himself in stirring up strife, and endeavoured by intrigue and deceit to throw the dirt of his wretched selfish plots on the prosperity of Ulugh Khán, and to cloud the glory of that Khákán with the emanations of his malice. But "Divine mercy is for ever sufficient," and it prevented the success of these schemes. Malik Táju-d dín Sanjar had been confined in prison by Katlagh Khán. The government of Bahráich had been granted to Sanjar, and this was the reason of his imprisonment. By a bold contrivance he escaped from Oudh out of the hands of his oppressors, and crossing the river Sarú[1] in a boat, he proceeded with a few horsemen to Bahráich. Under the decrees of fate the fortune of the Turks now triumphed, and the power of the Hindús was levelled with the dust. 'Imádu-d dín was defeated and taken prisoner, and put to death in Bahráich, in the month of Rajab, 653 H. With him Katlagh Khán's fortunes declined.

When these disturbances arose in Hindustán, several of the chief nobles of the Court were drawn away from their allegiance, and it became necessary to put down the insurrection and to punish the disaffected nobles. The army accordingly left Dehli, on the new moon of Shawwál, 653 H. (December, 1255), and marching towards Hindustán it reached Tilibhát[2] (Pilibhit?).

[1] [The Sarjú or Gogra.]   [2] [Var. "Talpat."]

Delay had occurred in assembling the forces of the Siwálik hills. These mountains were included in the government of Ulugh Khán, so he hastened to Hánsí. He arrived there on the 17th Zí-l ka'da, and so exerted himself that in fourteen days the soldiers of the Siwálik, of Hánsí, Sarsútí, Jínd, Barwála, and all those parts were collected, and marched to Dehli in great force, and well equipped, where they arrived on the 3rd Zí-l hijja. Ulugh Khán remained in Dehli eighteen days, recruiting and refitting the army of Mowát and the Koh-páya (hills). On the 19th Zí-l hijja he marched with a brave and well-equipped army to the royal camp, and reached Oudh in the month of Muharram, 654 H. Katlagh Khán and the nobles who were leagued with him were all subjects of the Sultán, but adverse circumstances had led them to revolt. From Oudh they retreated over the river Sarú, and by royal command Ulugh Khán pursued them with a strong force. They had, however, got a good start, the jungles were dense, the ways difficult, and the trees numerous, so he could not come up with them. He advanced as far as Bishanpur, on the confines of Tirhut, plundering all the Mawás and Ránas, and returned with great spoil to the royal camp. When Ulugh Khán crossed the Sarú from Oudh on his return from the pursuit, his Majesty marched towards the capital, and Ulugh Khán joined the royal army at Kasmandí. On Tuesday, 6th Rabi'u-l awwal, 654 H., they arrived at Dehli.

Katlagh Khán had found no place in Hindustán where he could make a stand, so in the midst of the campaign he proceeded towards Santúr, and strengthened himself in the hills of that country. The chiefs paid him every respect, for he was a noble of high rank, a grandee of the Court, and one of the principal Turks. He had, therefore, strong claims upon his compeers, and wherever he went he was treated with great consideration.

He made himself secure in the hills of Santár, and there he was joined by the Rána Debál [Deopál] Hindí, who held a prominent rank among the Hindus, and the custom of whose tribe was to afford a refuge to the fugitive. When intelligence of this junction reached the royal camp, the army marched towards Santúr, at the beginning of Rabí'u-l awwal, 655 H. Ulugh Khán, with the royal army and some officers of the court, by great exertions made his way into the hills with much fighting, and seized upon the passes and defiles. He penetrated as far as Salmúr, a fort and district belonging to that great Rái. All the Ránas of these parts recognized the Rái as their superior and paid him respect. He fled before Ulugh Khán, and the city and markets of Salmúr all fell into the hands of the army of Islám. By the favour of God the soldiers of Ulugh Khán thus subdued a place which the armies of Islám had never before reached, and they returned laden with plunder to the capital, where they arrived on the 5th Rabí'u-l ákhir, 655 H.

When the royal army had returned to Dehli, Katlagh Khán issued from the mountains of Salmúr, and Malik Kishlú Khán Balban came from Sindh to the banks of the Biyáh, where the two chiefs joined their forces,[1] and marched towards Sámána and Kahrám, taking possession of the country. To put down this confederacy and revolt the Sultán sent Ulugh Khán, Kishlí Khán, and several other nobles. Ulugh Khán left Dehli on Thursday, 15th Jumáda-l awwal, 655 (May, 1257), and hastened with all speed to Kaithal. Katlagh Khán was in the vicinity, and the two armies approached each other. Here they were all brothers and friends—two armies of one government.[2] Such an extraordinary state of affairs had never occurred. The antagonists were like coins from one purse, or salt from one cup, and yet the accursed devil had produced such dissension among them. * * * Ulugh Khán deemed it expedient to detach the household troops from the main army, and he placed them under the command of Sher Khán, his cousin. The main body with the elephants he put under the command of his own brother, Kishlí Khán, lord chamberlain. Two distinct divisions were thus formed.

---

[1] [This line, given in Sir H. Elliot's MS., is absent from the printed text.]
[2] [The author here exhibits his eloquence by repeating the statement four times, and using different words for *army* and *government*.]

The opposing armies drew near to each other in the vicinity of Sámána and Kaithal, and their lines were within view on either side. Just at this juncture some meddlesome servants of the Court at Dehli wrote letters to Malik Dalban and Malik Katlagh Khán, inviting them to come to the capital. The city they said was empty of soldiers, and the gates were in their own hands, while the nobles whom they addressed were servants of the State, and no strangers. They ought to come at once and resume their service of the Sultán. Ulugh Khán with his army would remain outside, and everything would turn out as they wished. All that had been represented might be easily accomplished. Some faithful adherents of the throne and partizans of Ulugh Khán got notice of this plot, and they sent off intelligence with all speed to Ulugh Khán. He advised the Sultán to turn all the conspirators out of the city. A full account of this conspiracy has been given in the history of the reign of Násiru-d dín. (God forgive them and lead them to repent of their wickedness!)

While the two armies were confronting each other, a person[1] came over as a spy from the camp of Malik Dalban Kishlú Khan, representing that he came on behalf of the chiefs and nobles who were with Malik Balban, and who were desirious of joining Ulugh Khán. If a promise of immunity and fair treatment were given to them, and a grant made for the support of the bearer of these overtures, he would bring over all the chiefs and nobles who were with Balban, and would arrange matters in respect of other officers.

Ulugh Khán, on perceiving the intentions of this person, gave orders that the whole of the army should be shown to him. Accordingly all the troops and munitions and implements of war, with the elephants and horses, were displayed before his eyes. The Khán then directed a letter to be written to the chiefs and nobles in the following terms: "Your letter has reached me and its import has been understood. I have no doubt that if you make your

[1] [The author here deals in irony, and says "a person called so and so, the son of so and so." The man was evidently well-known.]

submission grants will be made to you all, and your maintenance will be most amply provided for; but if you take a different course, then, on this very day, the world shall learn how your pretensions will be settled by the wounds of the trenchant sword and the flaming spear, and how you will be carried, fettered with the bonds of fate, to the foot of the royal standard." This letter, half sweet half bitter, half venom half lotion, half courtesy half severity, was written and delivered to that man and he returned.

When the letter was delivered to the officers of Balban, the wise among them perceived its drift, and knew that the dissensions between the nobles and generals would be settled elsewhere (*yakjá*). Fresh letters now arrived from Dehli, and Malik Balban and Katlagh Khán set forth in that direction and showed no intention of returning. Two days afterwards Ulugh Khán became aware of their design, and his mind was troubled as to what might happen to the throne and capital. After this extraordinary incident letters reached him (from Dohli), and he turned thither, safe under the protection of the Almighty, and reached the city on Monday, 10th Jumáda-l awwal, 653.

For seven months Ulugh Khán remained tranquil in the capital, when intelligence arrived that the army of the infidel Mughals had made a descent upon Sindh, under the command of Salin Nawín. When their general brought in this army, Malik Balban went to them of necessity, and the forces[1] of the fort of Multán fell back. When the news reached the capital, Ulugh Khán advised his Majesty to set the royal army in motion, and accordingly it marched forth on the 2nd Muharram, 656 H. (9th January, 1259), and encamped within sight of the city. Orders were sent to all parts of the kingdom, directing the nobles and officers to collect all the forces they could, and to

---

[1] [Sir H. Elliot's MS. has "*dashdarád*," but the printed text has "*kungurád*, battlements," which makes the passage to say that "the battlements of the fort of Multán fell down." The whole of it is obscure. شعبه و ملک بلبن چون اجتماعت آورده بود بضرورت نزدیک ایشان رفت وکنگرهای ملتان فرو رفتند]

join the army. On the 10th Muharram, the author received orders in the royal tent to compose an ode, to stir up the feelings of the Muhammadans and to excite in them a warlike fervour for the defence of their religion and the throne.

Ulugh Khán, with a numerous and well-appointed army, marched in company with his majesty and all the nobles, attended by their followers. When the infidel Mughal heard of this host on the frontier he had assailed, he advanced no further and showed no spirit. It seemed expedient, therefore, for the royal army to remain within sight of the city (of Delhi), and it remained encamped for four months or longer, while horsemen went in all directions, making war upon the Mawás. At length the news came that the accursed foe had retreated, and all disquietude on his account was at an end.

The reporters now informed Ulugh Khán that Arslán Khán Sanjar in Oudh, and Kalij Khán Mas'úd Kháni had taken alarm at the orders which they had received to join the royal camp, and were meditating revolt. Ulugh Khán advised his Majesty to nip this project in the bud, and to smother their intentions before they had time to form and gather strength. The advice was approved, although it was the hot season and the army had undergone fatigue through the inroad of the Mughals. On Tuesday, 6th Jumáda-l ákhir, the royal forces marched towards Hindustán, and came to the neighbourhood of Karra and Mánikpúr. Ulugh Khán exerted himself most strenuously in punishing the rebellious Hindus and Ránas.

Upon the arrival of Ulugh Khán, the two confederates, Arslán Khán and Kalij Khán, parted, and were obliged to send their families and dependants among the Mawás. They also deputed some trusty persons to wait on Ulugh Khán, and prevail upon him to inform the Sultán that they had been obliged to disperse their followers, and that they were ready to promise that they would both repair to the capital, and do homage as soon as the royal army was withdrawn. Upon this representation the forces were re-called, and reached the capital on Monday, 2nd Ramazán,

650. Arslán Khán aud Kalij Khán repaired to Court, and Ulugh Khán exerted himself so generously and strenuously in their behalf,[1] that their rebellion was forgiven, and in the course of two months Kalij Khán was appointed to the government of Lakhnautí, and Arslán Khán to Karra.

On the 13th Muharram, at the beginning of the new year, 657 (January, 1259), the royal forces again marched from Dehli. Ulugh Khán now very properly used his influence in favour of his nephew, Sher Khán, and on Sunday, 21st Safar, all the territories of Bayána, Kol, Jalesar, and Gwalior were consigned to him. There was nothing to require the action of the army during the rest of the year. On Wednesday, 4th Jumáda-l ákhir, treasure, wealth, and many valuables, with two elephants, were brought to Court from Lakhnautí. These presents were sent by 'Izzu-d dín Balban Uzbek, who was grantee of Lakhnautí, and by the influence of Ulugh Khán the grant was confirmed, and honours were bestowed upon him.

At the beginning of 658 H. (December, 1259), Ulugh Khán resolved upon a campaign in the hills near the capital. These hills were inhabited by a turbulent people, who committed depredations on the roads, plundered the goods of Musulmáns, drove away the cultivators, and ravaged the villages in the districts of Harriána, the Siwálik hills, and Bayána. Three years before they had carried off from Hánsí a drove of camels and a number of the people of Ulugh Khán. Their chief was a Hindu named Malká, a fierce and desperate fellow. It was he who carried off the camels, and he fomented disturbances among the Hindus from the hills to Rantambhor. But when he did these things the army was otherwise engaged, and the soldiers and followers of Ulugh Khán had not the means of transporting their baggage and implements. Ulugh Khán and all the princes and nobles were sorely vexed, but it was then impossible to do anything, as the army was fully employed in repelling the Mughal forces, which had attacked the frontiers of Islám in Sindh, at Lahore,

[1] [Translation greatly compressed.]

and in the vicinity of the river Biyáh. At length ambassadors to the Sultán came to Khurásán from 'Irák, on the part of Huláků Mughal, son of Tolí, son of Changíz Khán, and orders were given that the embassy was to halt at Márúta.[1]

Ulugh Khán and other nobles, with the royal troops and their own followers, suddenly resolved upon a campaign in the hills, and made the first march in advance on Monday, 4th Safar, 658. In their first forced march (*kashish*) they accomplished nearly fifty *kos*, and fell unexpectedly upon the rebels. These retreated to the summits of the mountains, to the defiles, to deep gorges and narrow valleys, but they were all taken and put to the sword. For twenty days the troops traversed the hills in all directions. The villages and habitations of the mountaineers were on the summits of the loftiest hills and rocks, and were of great strength, but they were all taken and ravaged by order of Ulugh Khán, and the inhabitants who were thieves, robbers, and highwaymen were all slain. A silver *tanka* was offered for every head, and two *tankas* for every man brought in alive. Eager for these rewards the soldiers climbed the highest hills, and penetrated the ravines and deepest gorges, and brought in heads and captives; especially the Afgháns, a body of whom, amounting to three thousand horse and foot, was in the service of Ulugh Khán. These men were very bold and daring, and in fact the whole army, nobles and chiefs, Turks and Tázíks, exhibited great bravery, and their feats will remain recorded in history. Fortune now so favoured Ulugh Khán that he was able to penetrate to a fastness which no Musulmán army had ever reached, and that Hindu rebel who had carried off the camels was taken prisoner with his children and dependants. Two hundred and fifty of the chiefs of the rebels were captured. One hundred and forty-two horses were led away to the royal stables, and six bags of *tankas*, amounting to thirty thousand tankas, were taken from the Ránas of the hills and the Ráís of Sind, and sent to the royal treasury.

[1] [Variants "Nárúya, Bárúta, Barúna."]

In the course of twenty days this great work was accomplished, and the army returned to the capital on the 24th Rabí'u-l awwal, 658. His Majesty, with a great retinue of chiefs and nobles, came forth to the plain of Hauz-ráni to meet him, and a grand Court was held in which many honours and rewards were bestowed.[1] After a stay of two days in the capital the Court went forth again to Hauz-ráni on a mission of revenge. The elephants were prepared, and the Turks made ready their trenchant swords. By royal command many of the rebels were cast under the feet of elephants, and the fierce Turks cut the bodies of the Hindus in two. About a hundred met their death at the hands of the flayers, being skinned from head to foot; their skins were all stuffed with straw, and some of them were hung over every gate of the city. The plain of Hauz-ráni and the gates of Dehli remembered no punishment like this, nor had any one ever heard such a tale of horror.

Ulugh Khán now represented to the Sultán that the Mughal ambassador in Khurásán should be brought to Court and be granted an interview. On Wednesday, 7th Rabí'u-l awwal, the Court proceeded to the Kushk-i sabz (green palace), and Ulugh Khán gave orders for armed men to be collected from all quarters round Dehli to the number of two hundred thousand foot and fifty thousand horse, with banners and accoutrements. Great numbers of armed men of all ranks went out of the city, and assembled in the new city of Kilu-gharí, at the royal residence, where they were drawn up shoulder to shoulder in twenty lines. * * * When the ambassadors arrived, and their eyes fell on this vast multitude, they were stricken with fear, * * * * * and it is certain that on seeing the elephants some of them fell from their horses. On the ambassadors entering the city they were received with the greatest honour, and were conducted before the throne with the highest possible ceremony. The palace was decked out in the most splendid array, and all the princes and

[1] [The author here becomes very diffuse in his descriptions and praises, which are not worth translation.]

nobles and officers attended in gorgeous dresses. A poem written by the author of this work was recited before the throne. I here insert it. * * * * After the reception the ambassadors were conducted in great state to the place appointed for their abode.¹

Let us return to the thread of our history. The last event which I have to record is this. When Ulugh Khán carried war into the hills, and punished the rebels in the way we have related, a number of them escaped by flight. They now again took to plundering on the highways, and murdering Musulmáns, so that the roads became dangerous. This being reported to the Khán, he sent emissaries and spies to find out the places where the rebels had taken refuge, and to make a full report of their state and condition. On Monday, 24th Rajab, 658 (July, 1260), he marched from Dehli with his own forces, the main army, and the forces of several chiefs. He hastened towards the hills, and, accomplishing more than fifty *kos* in one day's journey (!),² he fell upon the insurgents unawares, and captured them all, to the number of twelve thousand—men, women, and children—whom he put to the sword. All their valleys and strongholds were overrun and cleared, and great booty captured. Thanks be to God for this victory of Islám!

¹ [Here follows a long digression of no interest.]
² [یکمنزل بقدر پنجاه کروه زیادت برفت]

IX.

TÁRÍKH-I JAHÁN-KUSHÁ

OF

'ALÁU-D DÍN JUWAINÍ.[1]

[The *Táríkh-i Jahán-Kushá*, or *Jahán-Kushái*, "the History of the Conquest of the World," is the work of 'Aláu-d dín Malik, son of Bahául-d dín Muhammad Juwainí, but the author is better known to Europeans by the name of 'Atá Malik Juwainí. He was a native of Juwain, in Khurásán, near Naishápur. The date of his birth is unknown, but he was twenty-seven years of age when he began to write his history.

Bahául-d dín was one of the principal revenue officers of Persia under the Mongol governor Arghún; and his son 'Aláu-d dín, disregarding his father's advice to adopt literature as his profession, entered into public employ in his father's office before he had completed his twentieth year. When Mangú Khán was elected emperor, Arghún went to Tartary in 650, to pay his respects to the new sovereign, and Bahául-d dín with his son, our author, proceeded thither in his suite. Arghún was confirmed in his office, and he made Bahául-d dín chief superintendant of the revenues of his province. Shortly after his return in 651 (1253 A.D.), Bahául-d dín died at the age of sixty. When Huláku Khán arrived in Persia, in 654 H., the viceroy Arghún was called to court; and on his departure he left 'Aláu-d dín at court of the Emperor as one of his representatives. While thus situated our author followed in the suite of Huláku during his

[1] [This article has been drawn from M. Quatremère's notice in the *Mines de l'Orient*, and Baron D'Ohsson's account of the work in the Preface to his *Hist. des Mongols*.]

campaign against the Ismáʼílians. His brother, Shamsu-d dín, became wazír of Huláku in 662 (1263-4 A.D.), and ʼAláu-d dín was appointed governor of Baghdád.

ʼAláu-d dín had made himself conspicuous by his zeal against the Ismáʼílians, which incited three men of that sect to attempt his assassination. He escaped this danger, but only to endure great reverses and ignominy. Intrigues were formed against him, he was dismissed from office, fined heavily, tortured, and paraded naked all round Baghdád. He remained for some time afterwards in confinement at Hamadán, but his innocence being proved, the fine exacted from him was returned, and he was restored to his office, which he retained until his death in 681.

In character he was naturally mild and just, but he was so blinded by the power and success of his masters that he could see nothing but good in them and their doings. "Placed as he was," says M. D'Ohsson, "it is manifest that he could not write freely; but he of his own accord made himself the panegyrist of those barbarians who had utterly ruined his country, and who continued to waste and oppress the dominions of the Muhammadans. He speaks with a profound veneration of Changíz Khán and his descendants, he lauds Mangú to the skies, and in his honour he exhausts his stock of the most exaggerated hyperbole. More than this, he strives to prove in his preface that the ruin of so many Musulmán countries by the Mughal armies was a necessary evil, from which arose two benefits—one spiritual, the other temporal. He does not blush to boast of the gentleness of the Mughals towards those who submitted to them, and he praises with better reason their tolerance of all religions."

His occupations he tells us left him little leisure for the acquisition of useful knowledge up to the age of twenty-seven, and he expresses his regret that he had not adopted the course of life advised by his father; but years had matured his reason, and he was resolved to make up for lost time. He had several times travelled over Transoxiana and Turkistán, as well as the more western regions. He had been a witness of many events, and he had besides obtained information from well-informed and trustworthy persons, so in the year 650, during his stay at the court of Mangú, at the request of his friends he began to write his history, the chief object of which was to perpetuate the memory of the great actions of the Emperor Mangú. The style of the work is much admired by Orientals, "but a European may be allowed to pronounce it inflated, and to wish that the author had used more truth in his colouring, and more method in his narrative." The history stops at the year 655 (1257 A.D.), although the author lived up to the year 681 (1282 A.D.).

The MS. used by M. Quatremère and Baron D'Ohsson is an incomplete one belonging to the Imperial Library at Paris. "The *Jahán Kushái*," says Sir H. Elliot, "though not uncommon in Europe, is very rare in India. All my research has only procured for me one copy, and that belongs to Munshi 'Abdu-r Razzák, Sarrishtadár of the Civil Court of Farrukhábád. It is very clean, and well written in Nasta'lík, but contains many errors. Its extent is 275 folios of nineteen lines in each page." There is no copy of the work in Sir H. Elliot's library.]

Extracts.[1]

Punishment of Criminals.

It is a custom amongst the Mughals that when any one has committed a crime worthy of death, should he not be sentenced to that penalty, they send him to the wars, remarking that if he was destined to be slain, he may as well be slain in fight; or they send him on a message or embassy to rebellious chiefs, from whom they think it most probable he will never be allowed to return; or they send him to some hot place where a pestilent wind blows; and it was for such a reason they sent Baláktigín[2] on an embassy to Egypt and Syria.

* * * * *

[1] [All these extracts were translated by Sir H. Elliot.]
[2] [The same name probably as we have elsewhere found as "Bilkátigín."]

The Mughal Conquests.—The Kings of Hind.

In the space of twelve years the Mughals conquered every country, and nowhere were rebellion and turbulence left unrepressed. Having reached a place where they saw men with the limbs of beasts, and knew that there could be no habitation beyond it, they returned to their own country, bringing the kings of various countries with them, who presented their offerings of allegiance. Búkú Khán honoured all of them according to their respective ranks, and sent them back to their own countries; but he would not allow the king of Hind to come on account of his filth and ugliness.

* * * * *

Changíz Khán in Bokhárá.

Next day, the Imáms and elders of the city of Bokhárá went to do homage to Changíz Khán,[1] and he came within in order to see the town and fort. He entered the Jámi' Masjid and stood before the archways. His son, Túlí Khán, was on foot, and ascended the pulpit. Changíz Khán enquired, "Is this the palace of the Sultán?" They replied, "It is the house of God." He then dismounted, and ascended two or three steps of the pulpit, and exclaimed, "The country is denuded of forage, fill my horses' bellies." They opened the granaries which were in the city, and brought the corn. They brought forth the chests which contained the Kuráns into the area of the mosque, and scattered the books about, converting the chests into horse-troughs. They circulated their flagons, and the courtezans of the city were sent for to dance and sing, and the Mughals raised their own voices in response.[2] The Imáms, doctors, Saiyids,

---

[1] The usual way of pronouncing his name in India is Changez Khán, but perhaps Chingiz is more correct, for D'Ohsson, who spells the name "Tchinguiz," says it is derived from "Chink," strong, and "gaiz," the plural particle.—*Histoire des Mongols*, Tome I. p. 99. On his coins, moreover, the last syllable is not prolonged.—See *Journ. R. A. S. Soc.*, Vol. IX. p. 385.

[2] European travellers of this period are not complimentary to their musical talents.

scholars, and priests, were appointed to take charge of the quadrupeds, being singled out for that special duty. After one or two hours, Changíz Khán arose to return to his camp, and the others also departed, after the leaves of the Kurán had been kicked about in the midst of impurities.[1] * * *

One of the inhabitants fled to Khurásán after these transactions. They enquired of him the state of Bokhárá. He replied "The Mughals came, dug, burnt, slaughtered, plundered, and departed." A knot of learned men who heard him unanimously declared that it would be impossible to express any sentence more concisely in Pársí. The cream and essence of whatever is written in this volume might be represented in these few words.

* * * * *

Changís Khán's Pursuit and Defeat of Sultán Jalálu-d dín.

Changíz Khán detached a portion of his army, fully equipped, from Tálikán, against Sultán Jalálu-d dín, and when he heard of his still further successes, he himself marched with such expedition that there was no difference between night and day, and no time for cooking food. On his reaching Ghazna, he ascertained that the Sultán had left it fifteen days previous, for the purpose of crossing the river Sindh, so he appointed Yelwáj with his contingent to the charge of Ghazna,[2] and himself hastened like a cloud-impelling wind in pursuit of him.

He came up with the Sultán on the bank of the Sind, and hemmed him completely in with his army, several curves extending one behind another like a bow, of which the river was the

---

Simon de Saint-Quentin says, "Cantibus vel potius ululatibus." The Dominican, Vincent de Beauvais, says, "Tartari, modo interrogativo, clamoroso, loquuntur, gutture rabido et horribile. Cantantes mugiunt ut tauri, vel ululant ut lupi, vocem inarticulatas in cantando proferunt."—Vincentius, *Speculum Historiale*, lib. xxxi. p. 54, and lib. xxix. c. 71, ap. D'Ohsson.

[1] Compare D'Ohsson, *Histoire des Mongols*, Tom. I. p. 230; Price, *Mahomedan History*, Vol. II. p. 401; *Modern Univ. Hist.*, Vol. IV. p. 125; De la Croix, *Hist. Genghis Can*, p. 212.

[2] The *Rauzatu-s safa* says he was appointed Dárogha. *Felwdj* means an ambassador in Turki. Respecting him see D'Ohsson, Vol. II. p. 192.

string. Changíz Khán ordered his troops to advance, and enjoined that every attempt should be made to take the Sultán alive. Chagtái and Ogtái[1] also arrived to his support from Khwárizm.

When the Sultán saw that it was a time for exertion and action, he prepared for fight with the few men he had under him; galloping from the right to the left wing, from the left to the centre, and making furious onslaughts. But the army of the Mughals made good their advance by degrees, narrowing the field of battle and the opportunity of escape, while the Sultán was fighting like an angry lion.

> In every direction that he urged his steed
> He raised dust commingled with blood.

Orders were again issued that they should take him prisoner, and the army refrained from wounding with spear and arrow, in their anxiety to carry the commands of Changíz Khán into effect. Jalálu-d dín himself maintained his ground, and, mounting a fresh horse that was brought to him, made one more charge, and then retreated like the wind and like a flash of lightning upon water.[2]

When Changíz Khán saw that the Sultán had dashed into the river, and that the Mughals were anxious to follow him, he prevented them, and placing his hand in his mouth through excess of astonishment, exclaimed to his sons:—

> This is one whom you may indeed call a man!
> A true fighting elephant to tooth and marrow!"
> This he said, and looked in that direction
> Where the Sultán went like a Rustam on his way.

All his followers who were not drowned in the river were put to the sword,[3] and the ladies of his household and his children were brought to Changíz Khán. He ordered with respect to all

---

[1] "Ogtái," in the Mongol language, signifies ascent or exaltation.
[2] The Mod. Univ. History says that Changíz Khán lost twenty thousand men in this action.
[3] Or, "trunk and branch."
[4] D'Ohsson attributes these words to Juwaini—"Persons who were witnesses of this event have told me that so many Khawárizmians were slain, that the waters were red for the distance of a bow-shot." I cannot find the passage.

the males, even down to those who were sucklings, that the nipple of death should be placed in the mouth of their life, and that their bodies should be left to be devoured by crows.[1]

As all the property and wealth of the Sultán had been thrown that day into the river by his orders, Changíz Khán directed divers to search for it, and bring out what they could. This transaction, which was one of the wonders of the time, took place in Rajab, of the year 618 H., in accordance with the proverb, "Wonders occur in Rajab." Changíz Khán, after the battle marched to the banks of the Jihún (Indus), and sent Ogtái to Ghazna. On his arrival they proffered their submission. He ordered all the inhabitants to be brought out into the plain and counted, and, after selecting artizans from among them, he ordered all the rest to be slain. He also destroyed the city, and Ogtái returned towards Hirát, after burying the slain.

The Mughals winter in Hindustán, and return.

Chaghtái was left on the borders of Kirmán. He went in pursuit of the Sultán, and as he could not find him, he fixed his winter quarters in the plains of Hindustán.[2] The governor of the country in which he cantoned himself was Sálár Ahmad, who bound the girdle of obedience round his waist, and provided all the supplies he could for the use of the army. On account of the pestilential air most of the army fell sick and lost their strength, and as they had many slaves with them, having added to their number while encamped there (insomuch that to every tent there were as many as ten or twenty, who were engaged in preparing rice and other things for the use of their masters), and as the climate of the country agreed well with their constitutions,

---

[1] Mohammad of Nesa says that the Sultán was beseeched by his ladies to slay them, and preserve them from captivity, and that he drowned them. D'Ohsson observes that no other author mentions this.

[2] The name of the place mentioned in the original cannot be identified. It bears most resemblance to "the hills of Lahór, which is a city." It will be observed from the corresponding passage from the *Rauzatu-s safá*, hereafter given in a note, that it is there called "Kálinjar on the Sind." That it was somewhere in the plains is evident.—[See note in the Appendix on Sultán Jalálu-d dín.]

Changíz Khán[1] gave orders that in every tent every captive should prepare and clean five hundred *mans* of rice. All expedition was made, and within one week they ceased from that labour. He then issued orders that every prisoner in camp should be slain, and the next morning not a trace of captives or Hindús remained. He sent ambassadors to all the princes of that country, and they submitted. One was despatched to the Ráná, and he was at first well received, but was afterwards crucified; upon which an army was sent against the Ráná, and he was taken. An army was also sent to besiege Aghrák, in the fort in which he had taken refuge.

When the army had recovered its health, thoughts of return were entertained, in order that by way of Hindustán they might reach the country of Tangút.[2] They advanced some marches, and when they found there was no road, they came back again, and went to Fersháwar (Pesháwar), and employed themselves in returning by the same road which they came. * * * The reason of their expediting their return was that intelligence was received that Khitá and Tangút had exhibited signs of disaffection, in consequence of Changíz Khán's prolonged absence.

* * * * *

Capture of Bhera, and retreat from Multán.

When Chaghtái returned without finding the Sultán, Changíz Khán despatched Túrtái[3] with two túmáns of Mughals, to

---

[1] It would appear, therefore, that Changíz Khán entered India, unless he issued these orders from some other spot; but it is not easy to tell precisely what were his own proceedings immediately after the battle on the Indus.

[2] Some say "Tibet." The *Bahru-l Buldán* also says "Tangút." "Several thousand horsemen crossed the Sind in pursuit of Jaláu-d dín, and went thence to Multán and ravaged that country and Lobáwar, but as they could not remain there on account of the unhealthiness of the climate, they returned to Changíz Khán by way of Ghazna. Changíz took up his quarters at Mata Kulbor, but not being able to remain there on account of the badness of the air, he attempted to reach Tangút by way of Hindustán; but after going two or three marches, and finding no road, he went by way of Bámián to Samarkand."

[3] D'Ohsson says "Bela and Tourtái," and that the places plundered were Lahore, Multán, Pesháwar, and Malikpúr. Miles says, "Dowmur, Bakshi, and Bala

pursue the Sultán beyond the Sind, which he passed over, and then reached the banks of the Bhat,[1] which is a country of Hindustán, then held by Kamru-d dín Kirmání, one of the Sultán's nobles. Túrtál conquered that country, and took the strong fort of Bhera, and after ravaging that neighbourhood, he went towards Multán, but as there were no stones there, he ordered that the population of Dhera should be turned out to make floats of wood, and load them with stones for the manjaníks. So they floated them down the river, and when they arrived at Multán, the manjaníks were set to work, and throw down many of the ramparts of the fort, which was nearly taken, when the excessive heat of the weather put a stop to their operations. The Mughals contented themselves with plundering and massacreing all the country of Multán and Loháwar, and returned thence across the Sind to Ghaznín.

* * * * *

A Large Dragon.

Abú-l Fazl Baihakí has related in his Táríkh-i Násirí, that one of the soldiers of Sultán Mahmúd on the return from Somnát, killed a large dragon, and when they flayed it, the skin was found to be thirty yards long and four cubits broad. My object in mentioning this is, that Abú-l Fazl says, let any who doubts this fact go to Ghaznín, and see the skin, which is spread out like a curtain, and is suspended at one of the gates. Now the writer of this history says he is entitled to the same credit, when he asserts a thing which may seem impossible.

Noyana." He also says the Mughals "continued their pursuit to Mulkapoor and the sea-side."—*Shajrat-ul Atrak*, p. 179.

[1] There is a difficulty here. "Bhat" is here called a river and a country, and "Bhera" reads more like "Banda.' D'Ohsson (I. 309) reads "Biah,"for "Bhat," and "Bhera ;" but stones could not have been floated down the Biyáh to Multán. I prefer the reading adopted in the text, not only for this reason, but because there never was a fort of Biah, and because Bhera was a place of importance on the Bhat, or Jailam, having direct communication with Multán, and inexhaustible supplies of stones from the salt range in its vicinity. The *Rauzatu-s safá* gives no name to the fort.

Death of Muhammad Ghori.

In the year 602 H. (1205 A.D.), Muhammad Ghori determined on prosecuting a holy war in Hind, in order to repair the fortunes of his servants and armies; for within the last few years Khurásán, on account of the disasters it had sustained, yielded neither men nor money. When he arrived in Hind, God gave him such a victory that his treasures were replenished, and his armies renewed. On his return, after crossing the Jailam, he was encamped on the banks of the Jihún (Indus), so that one-half of the royal enclosure, where the private apartments were, was in the water. In consequence of which no precaution had been taken to ensure their protection. About the time of the mid-day siesta, two or three Hindús came through the water, and falling like fire upon the royal tent, slew the Sultán, who was entirely unprepared for such a treacherous attack.

* * * * *

Sultán Jalálu-d dín in Hindustán.[1]

When the Sultán had survived the double danger of water and fire, namely, the whirlpools of the Sind and the flame of Changíz Khán's persecution, he was joined by six or seven of his followers, who had escaped from drowning, and whom the fiery blast of evil had not sent to the dust of corruption; but, as no other course except retreat and concealment among the forests was left to him, he remained two or three days longer in his covert,[2] until he was joined by fifty more men. The spies whom he had sent out to watch the proceedings of Changíz Khán, returned, and brought him intelligence that a body [3] of

---

[1] In the highly flattering notice which M. Quatremère has taken of my first volume in the *Journal des Savants*, for September, 1850, and January, 1851, he has made some comments upon the extract from the *Jámi'u-l tawáríkh*, which corresponds with the passage here translated from the *Jahán Kushái*. I do not concur in all the corrections of the learned reviewer, but thankfully avail myself of some of them.—[See note in the Appendix on Jalálu-d dín.]

[2] Miles says, "he struck into the Chorí, or desert of Chart."—*Shajratu-l Atrák*, p. 178.

[3] The *Táríkh-i Alfí* says " nearly two hundred."

Hindu rascals,[1] horse and foot, were lying only two parasangs distance from the Sultán, occupied in rioting and debauchery. The Sultán ordered his followers to arm themselves each with a club, and then making a night attack upon this party, he slew most of them, capturing their animals and arms.

He was then joined by other parties, mounted on horses and mules,[2] and soon after certain intelligence was brought to him that two or three thousand men of the armies of Hind were encamped in the neighbourhood. The Sultán attacked them with a hundred and twenty men, and slew many of those Hindús with the Hindí sword, and set up his own troops with the plunder he obtained.[3]

Arabic Verse.

Whoever requires anything from me, let him live by his sword,
Whoever requires anything from other men, let him solicit them.

When the news spread throughout Hindustán of the Sultán's fame and courage, five or six thousand mounted men assembled from the hills of Balála and Mankála, for the purpose of attacking him. On his gaining intelligence of this movement, he set upon them with five hundred cavalry which he had under him, and routed and slew the Hindú armies.[4] The effect of this success was that he was joined by several more adherents from all quarters, so that his force amounted to three thousand men.

When the world-conquering Changiz Khán, who was then in the neighbourhood of Ghazní, heard of these new levies, he

---

[1] Price says "a banditti." It is probable that they were a gang of those dakoits who have only lately been extirpated from India.

[2] The original has "long-tailed animals," or horned cattle. The *Rauzatu-s safá*, the *Táríkh-i Alfí*, and other authorities, have "long-eared animals," mules or donkeys, which is a more probable reading. In another passage D'Ohsson considers "long-tailed animals" to indicate a species of sheep.—*Hist. Mong.*, Tom. III. p. 118.—[The *Jámi'u-t tawáríkh* says, "*Shutur sawár wa pae-sawár*—camel-riders and bullock-riders."]

[3] Firishta adds "a large quantity of money."

[4] D'Ohsson (I. 308), on the authority of Muhammad of Nesam, says that the prince of Jódí had one thousand cavalry and five thousand infantry, and that the Sultán, at the head of four thousand cavalry, put the Indians to flight, killed their chief with an arrow, and secured a considerable booty. He also says (III. 4) that many generals of 'Irák, dissatisfied with his brother Ghiyásu-d dín, joined his standards in India.

despatched a Mughal army, under Túrtái, to expel him, and as the Sultán was not able to oppose him, he went towards Dehli, when Túrtái crossed the river. The Mughals, when they heard of his flight, returned and pillaged the country round Malikpúr.

The Sultán, when he was two or three days distant from Dehli, deputed a messenger named 'Aiuu-l mulk to Sultán Shamsu-d dín, saying—"The great have opportunies of showing mercy, since it is evident in our relations with each other, that I have come to claim your protection and favour, and the chances are rare of meeting with a person of my rank on whom to bestow a kind reception. If the road of friendship should be made clear, and the ear of brotherhood should listen in our communications with each other, and if, in joy and affliction, aid and support be mutually afforded, and if our object and desires should be accomplished, when our enemies witness our alliance, the teeth of their enmity will be blunted." He then solicited that some spot[1] might be indicated in which he might reside for a few days.

As the courage and determination of the Sultán were noised abroad, and his exceeding power and predominance were celebrated throughout the world, Sultán Shamsu-d dín, after receiving the message, was engaged for some time in deliberation, reflecting upon the importance of the result, alarmed at his proceedings, and apprehensive of his attacks. It is said that he entertained a design against the life of 'Ainu-l mulk, so that he died;[2] but Sultán Shamsu-d dín sent an envoy of his own, with presents suited to such a distinguished guest, and offered the following subterfuge for not according to him the place of residence he desired, namely, "that the climate of these parts is not favourable, and there is no tract suited to the Sultán; but that, if he wished, Shamsu-d dín would fix upon some place near Dehli where the Sultán might take up his abode, and that it would be made over to him as soon as it was cleared of rebels and enemies."

[1] The *Basátín-i safá* uses the Mughal word "*yúrt*," or private domain.
[2] This gentle insinuation is more boldly expressed by others, who declare that he was murdered by the Sultán, but with what object it is impossible to say.

When the Sultán heard this reply he returned, and reached the borders of Halála and Mankála, where from several quarters he was joined by his soldiers who had escaped, and by entire bands of those who had been wounded by the sword, insomuch that his troops amounted to ten thousand men.

He sent Táju-d dín Malik Khilj to the mountains of Júd, who plundered that tract, and obtained much booty. He sent an emissary, also, to ask Rái Kokár Saknín's[1] daughter in marriage. The Rái consented, and despatched his son with a force to serve under the Sultán, who bestowed upon him the title of Katlagh Khán.[2]

There was a chief, by name Kubácha, who had the country of Sind under his government, and aspired to independence. There was enmity between him and Rái Saknín Kokár. The Sultán despatched an army against Kubácha, and appointed Uzbek Pái to command it. Kubácha was encamped with twenty thousand men on the banks of the Sind, at the distance of a *parasang* from Uchh. Uzbek Pái, at the head of seven thousand men, suddenly falling upon them by night, routed and dispersed them. Kubácha embarked on a boat, and fled to Akar and Bakkar,[3] two forts on an island, while Uzbek Pái took up his quarters in Kubácha's camp, captured all those whom he found within its precincts, and sent tidings of the victory to the Sultán, who, marching onwards, arrived at the camp in which the tent of Kubácha was pitched.

Kubácha afterwards, flying from Akar and Bakkar, proceeded

---

[1] The name is also spelt "Sangín" by some of the authors who treat of this period. Hammer calls him Kukarsengín. He appears on the stage eighteen years previous in the *Táju-l ma-ásir*, where the reading is "Sarkh." He must have been a Gakhhar, not a Kokar. As these tribes reside close to each other, the names are frequently confused.—(See *supra*, page 233.)

[2] This title, which signifies in Turkí "the fortunate Khán," was a favourite one about this period. We find Ogtái bestowing it upon the Atábak Abú Bakr, and upon Barák Hájib. The latter received from the Khalíf the title of "Katlagh Sultán," which Ogtái subsequently bestowed upon Barák's son.—Compare D'Ohsson's *Hist. de Mong.*, Tom. I. pp. 222, 439; Tom. III. 131, 132; and Price, *Mahammadan History*, Vol. II. pp. 427, 433. [See also *supra*, page 364.]

[3] [See Note in the Appendix on Jalálu-d dín.]

to Multán. The Sultán sent an ambassador to him, requiring the surrender of Amír Khán's son and daughter, who had fled from the battle of the Sind, and had taken shelter at Multán. Money was also demanded. Kubácha complied with the requisition, delivered up the son and daughter of Amír Khán, and sent a large sum of money for the use of the Sultán, soliciting that his territory might not be injured.

When the weather became hot, the Sultán left Uchh with the intention of proceeding through Balála and Mankála, to take up his summer-quarters in the mountains of Júd, and on his way laid siege to the fort of Parsrúr,[1] where he was wounded in the head by an arrow. When the fort was captured, the whole garrison was put to the sword. He returned from that place, when he received intelligence of the advance of the Mughal armies in pursuit of him, and as his way led him near Multán, he sent an envoy to Kubácha to intimate that the Sultán was passing in that direction, and to demand tribute. Kubácha refused, and assuming an attitude of defiance, advanced to fight him. The standards of the Sultán halted but for a moment, and then departed, returning towards Uchh, which also had revolted against him. The Sultán remained before it two days, and after setting fire to the city, went towards Sadúsán.[2]

Sultán Jalálu-d dín in Sind

Fakhru-d dín Sálárí was governor of Sadúsán on the part of Kubácha, and Láchín of Khitá, who was in command of the army, went out against Amír Khán,[3] the leader of the Sultán's advance guard. Láchín was slain in the action, and Uzbek Khán

[1] The original has "Pasrawar." Both the *Jámi'u-t tawáríkh* and the *Rauzatu-s safá* read "Dúrúm." The *Táríkh-i Alfí* has "Bas," and Firishta cautiously gives no name. Hammer has "Besrum." The position, antiquity, and importance of Parsrúr seem to indicate that as the correct reading.

[2] The *Táríkh-i Alfí* adds, "which is now called Siwistán." It is at present known as Sihwán.—See Vol. I. page 401.

[3] This name is in some copies read "Awar Khán," or "Anwar Khán," and in some "Anír Khán." Amír Khán is probably the right reading, and we may consider him to be the same person who was repulsed just before the action on the Sind, whom D'Ohsson calls "Orkhán," and whose daughter had fled to the Sultán for protection. We find the same Orkhán acting a conspicuous part in the subsequent events in Persia.

invested the city of Sadúsán. When the Sultán himself arrived, Fakhru-d dín Sálári presented himself before him in an humble posture, with his sword (round his neck), and clothed in a shroud.[1] The Sultán entered the city, and after staying there for one month, he conferred an honorary dress upon Fakhru-d dín Sálárí, and restored to him the governorship of Sadúsán.

The Sultán then went towards Dewal and Darbela, and Jaisí;[2] the ruler of that country, fled away on a ship, and went in the direction of the sea. The Sultán remained near Dewal and Damrila, and sent Khás Khán with an army to pillage Nahrwála, whence he brought back many captives.

The Sultán raised a jámi' masjid at Dewal, on the spot where an idol temple stood. While he was engaged in these operations, intelligence was received from 'Irák, that Sultán Ghiyásu-d dín had established himself in that province, and that most of the troops who were quartered there were attached to the interests of Sultán Jalálu-d dín, and were anxiously expecting his return. It was also represented, that Burák Hájib was in Kirmán, and had fortified himself in the city of Bardasír. It was also given out that the Mughal army was still in pursuit of the Sultán. He accordingly departed from Dewal and Damrila, and went by way of Makrán, but the climate was so very insalubrious that he lost the greater part of his army.[3]

---

[1] This was a common mode in the East to imply that one's life was in another's power. On the Sultán's return to Persia, we find his repentant generals going through the same emblematic form of contrition.—See also Briggs' Ferishta, Vol. III, p. 317.

[2] This name is spelt differently by different authors. It is not improbable that Jaisí was considered a mere title, and that it was ascribed to the ruler of Debal, because, at the time of the Arab invasion, Jaisiya, the son of Dáhir, was governor of that town, through the same kind of ignorance which induced Hátifí to call the ruler of the Panjab in Tímúr's time, "Pitháurá," two hundred years after his decease, and Rashídu-d dín and Bínákatí to call Bárí the capital of Oude, three hundred years after it had ceased to be so. Be it remembered these are all errors of foreign, not local writers.

[3] D'Ohsson (III. 5) adds that he left Uzbek to govern his possessions in India, and Wafa Malik those in Ghor and Ghazna. De Guignes (II. 281) says he left "Pehlevan Uzbek and Hussan Carme, surnamed Ouzpk Moult." The latter in the end expelled Uzbek, in the year 627, and seized all the possessions which he had in India.

When Durák Hájib heard of the approach of the Sultán, he sent him many presents, with the expression of his hearty congratulations, and, on the Sultán's arrival, Durák Hájib solicited that he would accept his daughter in marriage. The Sultán acceded to the request, and the marriage was celebrated. The Kotwál also came forth, and presented the keys of his fort, upon which the Sultán entered it, and remained during the night.

* * * * *

Sultán Jalálu-d dín's Allies.

After the lapse of a week, Sultán Jalálu-d dín arrived at Ghazna, where he was joined by many bodies of his adherents, and assumed the pomp and circumstance of a monarch. When Yamín Malik heard, in Hindustán, of the Sultán's arrival at Ghazna, he hastened to meet him. Aghrák Malik, also, with an army of Khiljís and Turkománs, came from Peshawar to do him homage, and A'zam Malik[1] brought a large force of Ghorians to serve under him. In all the troops now at his disposal amounted to twenty thousand cavalry.

The Sultán went with these large reinforcements to Parwán, on the borders of Bámián, where many roads converge. There he received intelligence that a body of ten or twelve thousand Mughal cavalry had gone in pursuit of him to Ghazna, where, as there was no army to oppose them, they had entered the city before the inhabitants had received intelligence of their approach, had burned several mosques, massacred all the people they found in the lanes and streets, and then continued their pursuit after the Sultán to Parwán, by way of Kaláwaz, staying at Ghazna only one day.[2]

Their Fate, after deserting the Sultán.

In the action which ensued the Sultán was victorious, and the

---

[1] *Malik* was at that time a title between that of *Amír* and *Khán*, for we find *Amírs* promoted to the rank of *Malik*, and *Maliks* to that of *Khán*.

[2] This relates to what occurred previous to the action on the Sind, but the author has deferred the narrative till he could accompany it by a statement of the fate of the Sultán's allies.

defeated Mughals returned to Changíz Khán in Tálikán; but after the victory strife arose in the Sultán's army, between the Khiljís, Turkománs, and Ghorians on one side, and the Khwárizmians on the other, respecting the division of the horses which had been taken as booty. Aghrák Malik and A'zam Malik went off by way of Peshawar, with all the Khiljís, Turkománs, and Ghorians. The Sultán returned to Ghazna with the Turks and Khwárzimians, who all remained true to him.[1] Aghrák Malik, A'zam Malik, and the other Khilj, Turkomán, and Ghorian chiefs, went, after first leaving the Sultán, to Nangnchár, which was in the fief of A'zam Malik. He entertained them all nobly, and treated them with great kindness, until disgust and hatred arose between Aghrák Malik and Koh Jándár, one of the Khilj chiefs, who had five or six thousand families under him.

Aghrák Malik turned his face towards Peshawar, at the head of twenty thousand men, and Koh Jándár cantoned himself at Nangnchár.[2] When Saifu-d dín Malik had encamped only one march distant from Nangnchár, he sent a messenger to A'zam Malik to say:—"Between us and you there exist the relations of father and son. I am father and you are son. If you desire to gratify me, do not allow Koh Jándár to remain in your territory, nor bestow upon him any tract of land." A'zam Malik said:—"In this matter it is not expedient that there should be any misunderstanding or wrangling between Musulmáns," so he went forth with fifty horsemen of his bodyguard to Saifu-d dín Aghrák, in order to effect a reconciliation. Saifu-d dín Aghrák advanced to meet him, and they sat down together to drink. A'zam Malik spoke on the subject of Koh Jándár, and Aghrák Malik pretended to listen to his persuasions. Saifu-d dín Aghrák then rose up suddenly in a state of inebriety, and went towards the camp of Koh Jándár, with a few horse-

[1] D'Ohsson says that before the battle of the Sind, the Sultán wrote urgently to his dissatisfied allies to join him, to which they consented when it was too late. The *Mod. Univ. Hist.* has the same statement.   [2] D'Ohsson reads "Bekerbar."

men. Koh Jándár, under the impression that he had come on a friendly visit, went out with his sons to meet him, and give him an honourable reception, when Aghrák Malik in his drunkenness drew his sword, with the intention of killing Koh, whose attendants seized the assailant and cut him in pieces.

When the news of this event reached the camp of Aghrák Malik, his troops suspected that he had been the victim of a plot between Koh and A'zam Malik. In consequence of which, they seized A'zam Malik and slew him. They then attacked the camp of Koh, and killed him and his sons. Many were slain on both sides, and even the women took part in the fray, and lost their lives.

About this time Pakchak and 'Aláu-l mulk Sadr were despatched by order of Changíz Khán to punish these drunkards. Pakchak was the commandant of these Mughals, and 'Aláu-l mulk of the infantry, and the residue of those armies of Khiljís, Turkománs, and Ghorians were all put to the sword and dispersed, within two or three months after they had deserted Sultán Jalálu-d dín, either in squabbles amongst themselves, or by the armies of Changíz Khán, so that not a vestige of them remained.

* * * * *

Burák Hájib.[1]

Burák Hájib having had some dispute with Táju-d dín Karímu-s shark, marched away with his army towards Hindustán. In the year 619 H., Ghiyásu-d dín designed to go to Fárs. * * * * When news was received of the arrival of the Mughal army, under Túlúí[2] Khán, Burák Hájib requested Ghiyásu-d dín to allow him to go to Ispahán, but he went with

---

[1] The previous history of this adventurer is given by Rampoldi, *Annali Musulmani*, Vol. VIII. note 69. See also pp. 267, 298, and 855 of the same volume. Hammer spells the name Borrak, in the *Gemäldesaal*.

[2] *Túlúí* signifies in the Mongol language "a mirror," and after his death it was forbidden that any other word should be used in this sense, except the Turkí one of *gurungu*.—D'Ohsson's *Hist. Mong.*, Tom. II. p. 60.

his tribe (Karákhitái) to Hindustán, by the road of Kirmán.[1] When he arrived at Júraft and Daryái, the garrison of the fort of Kawáchír urged Shujá'u-d dín Abú-l na'ím to follow after him, so Shujá'u-d dín plundered his camp, and brought back many Khitái slaves.

[1] Hindustán appears to have been a favorite retreat of the Kárákhitáis of Kirmán. A few years subsequent to this event, we find one of the successors of Burák Hájib fleeing to Hindustán. "On attaining to years of discretion, Hijjáj Sultán proceeded to treat his mother with indignity, and in one of his carousals proposing to her to dance before him, the insulted princess justly took offence, and withdrew to the court of Abáká. The Sultán, not a little terrified on his part, fled shortly afterwards into Hindustán. At the expiration of ten years, followed by a considerable army, raised for his assistance by the princes of India, he was returning to recover his inheritance, when he died on the march, in the month of Zi-l hijja, 679 H."—Price's *Mahommedan History*, Vol. II., p. 434. D'Ohsson says (IV. 92) that he fled to Dehli, and that Sultán Jalálu-d dín Khilji supplied him with an army to recover his possessions.

APPENDIX.

NOTE A.

The Hindú Kings of Kábul.

Abú Ríhán al Bírúní has the following statement respecting this dynasty in his lately discovered Arabic work, entitled *Táríkhu-l Hind*:—

"Kábul was formerly governed by princes of Turk lineage. It is said that they were originally from Tibet. The first of them was named Barhtigín, ° ° ° ° and the kingdom continued with his children for sixty generations. ° ° ° ° ° The last of them was a Katormán, and his minister was Kalar, a Bráhman. This minister was favoured by fortune, and he found in the earth treasures which augmented his power. Fortune at the same time turned her back upon his master. The Katormán's thoughts and actions were evil, so that many complaints reached the minister, who loaded him with chains, and imprisoned him for his correction. In the end the minister yielded to the temptation of becoming sole master, and he had wealth sufficient to remove all obstacles. So he established himself on the throne. After him reigned the Bráhman(a) Samand, then Kamlúa, then Bhím, then Jaipál, then Anandpál, then Nardajanpál, who was killed in A.H. 412. His son, Bhímpál, succeeded him, after the lapse of five years, and under him the sovereignty of Hind became extinct, and no descendant remained to light a fire on the hearth. These princes, notwithstanding the extent of their dominions, were endowed with excellent qualities, faithful to their engagements, and gracious towards their inferiors. The letter which Anandpál wrote to Amír Mahmúd, at the time enmity existed between them, is much to be admired. 'I have heard that the

[The *Fragments, Arabes et Persans*, were published in 1845; and this note must have been written by Sir H. Elliot soon after.]

Turks have invaded your dominions, and have spread over Khurásán; if you desire it, I will join you with 5,000 cavalry, 10,000 infantry, and 100 elephants, but if you prefer it, I will send my son with twice the number. In making this proposal, I do not wish to ingratiate myself with you. Though I have vanquished you, I do not desire that any one else but myself should obtain the ascendancy.' This prince was a determined enemy of the Musulmáns from the time that his son, Nardajanpál, was taken prisoner; but his son was, on the contrary, well-disposed towards them."

The publication of this extract by M. Reinaud has excited considerable discussion, and has given rise to some ingenious remarks and comments by those interested in this period of history, in which we have a series of names recorded, which add nearly a century to the barren annals of India previous to the Muhammadan conquest. A paper by Mr. E. Thomas, of the Bengal Civil Service, published in the Journal of the Royal Asiatic Society, Vol. IX. p. 177, is especially valuable, as in it he has endeavoured to trace the names of these particular kings upon a series of coins denominated Rájpút, of the bull and horseman type, and hitherto doubtfully ascribed to periods extending from A.D. 1000 to 1200. I shall avail myself freely of his remarks, though I am not prepared to coincide in his conclusions, for taking into consideration the difficulty of identifying Hindí names in Arabic manuscripts, in which ignorance and carelessness give rise to every imaginable kind of error, he has endeavoured to correct the Arabic from the unquestionable record of the coins themselves, which have hitherto existed without the ascription of a kingdom and a date, and "instead of applying coins to kings, to apply the kings to their own coins." It may easily be supposed that this principle gives too great a license to speculation, and it will appear in the sequel that very few of the attempted identifications can be admitted without question.

Before we examine these names in detail, it will be necessary to make a few general remarks on the subject of these Turks, and especially respecting Kanak, the most celebrated of them.

First of all, it admits of great question what particular position in the series of Kábul Turkish kings this Kanak occupied. M. Reinaud both in his translation of Al Bírúní in *Fragments Arabes*, and his

APPENDIX. 405

Mémoire sur l'Inde, considers him to be the great Kanika or Kanishka of the Buddhists, and it is respecting this Kanak that the anecdote is related which will be found in this work, Vol. II. p. 10. Mr. Thomas, trusting to translations or abstracts of Al Bírúní, makes Kanak the last of the Turkish kings, and the immediate predecessor of the Brahmin Samand; but as the existence of the great Kanak who opposed the Rái of Kanauj is not to be disputed, he must consider that the last of the Turks was a second Kanak.

This point requires further consideration, and we must consider what our several authorities say concerning it. The passage in the first line of the extract which I have translated thus, "The last of them was a Katormán," is in the original Arabic of Al Birúní—

و كان اخرهم لكتوزمان

which M. Reinaud translates, "The last of them (the Turks) was Laktouzemán," which is certainly correct, provided the reading is admitted to be so; but Mr. Thomas, after examining various copies of the *Jámi'u-t tawáríkh* and *Bindkítí*—the former of which is a translation, and the latter an abridgement of Al Birúní's account, finds great reason to dispute it, and leans altogether to another interpretation. He finds the following in an excellent Arabic version of the *Jámi'*, in the library of the Royal Asiatic Society—

و رجع كنك الى ولايته و هو آخر ملوك كتورمان

"and Kanak returned to his country, and he was the last of the Katormán kings."

The corresponding passage in the Persian *Jámi'* in the British Museum is—

و كنك بلولايت خود معاودت كرد و آخرين بادشاهان كتورمان بود

Bindkítí has the following—

و بعد از و كنك و او اخرين بادشاهان كتورمان بود

"and after him was Kanak, and he was the last of the Katormán kings."

All the copies of *Bindkítí* which I have seen concur in this reading, and of three several copies of the Persian *Jámi'u-t tawáríkh* which I have examined, two are in conformity with the extract given above, with the exception of reading Katoriyán for Katormán, and a third has—

بعد از باسديو از جمله ملوک ايشان يكي كنك بوده و ان آخرين بادشاهان كيورمان بوده است

"after Básdeo from among their rulers (i.e., of the Indians), one was Kanak, and he was the last of the Kayormón kings."

The omission of all notice of the Kábul Turkish dynasty, and the making Kanak succeed Básdoo, and the Brahmans succeed Kanak, without any notice or allusion to there being intermediate kings, is a culpable omission on the part of Rashídu-d dín and Bináķití. The making Kanak the last of the Turkish dynasty does not seem authorized by the only original of Al Birúní's *Táríkhu-l Hind* which we possess, and Rashídu-d dín must have had other copies or other works to have authorized him to make this statement. M. Reinaud (*Mem.* 30) considers that he has used some other work of Al Birúní's which has not come down to us, but this may reasonably be doubted.

M. Reinaud altogether ignores these readings of the manuscripts consulted by Mr. Thomas, and merely observes upon them, "On a vu ci-devant, que le vizir de Perse Raschid-eddin, avait, dans son Histoire des Mongols, mis à contribution un écrit d'Albyrouny autre que celui-ci, et que ne nous est point parvenu. Malheureusement, les manuscripts de l'ouvrage de Raschid-ed din different entre eux : au lieu de *Laktouzeman*, ils portent *Katourman*, et on ne distingue pas bien s'il s'agit là d'un prince ou d'un pays." Notwithstanding this, I have been given to understand by those who have seen the original manuscript of the *Táríkhu-l Hind*, that even that bears a closer resemblance to *Katourman* than *Laktouzeman*.[1] Taking all circumstances into consideration, I am disposed to get rid of the name of Laktouzeman from the *Táríkhu-l Hind*, and to substitute for it, by two slight changes in the original, al Katormán, which repre-

---

[1] [The name occurs only twice in Reinaud's printed extract. In the first instance, it is given as quoted above, but in the second it is لكتوزرمان *Laktúrzamán*. See *Fragments*, p. 135.]

sents the name of a tribe, or prince of that tribe, as well as the name of the country in which that tribe resided. I have therefore translated the disputed line, "The last of them was a Katormán."

Let us now enter upon some of the considerations which this name suggests.

The Katormáns, or Kators, have hitherto been better known to modern than ancient history. We are informed that it was the name of one of the tribes of Káfiristán,[1] and that the ruler of Chitral to this day bears the title of Sháh Kator,[2] and I have heard the same designation given to the chief of Gilgit. The country of Kator is also spoken of by Sádik Isfaháni, as being the country of the Siyáh-poshes, or black-vested, on the borders of Kábul.[3]

These Kators boast still of their Grecian lineage, and their claim to this honour is by no means, as many have supposed, of modern origin, attributable to our own enquiries after the descendants of the followers of the Macedonian conqueror.[4]

We find at the period of Timur's invasion of India, the Katorians making themselves conspicuous for their opposition to that monarch. After leaving Inderáb he entered their difficult country by way of Kháwah, and after an expedition of eighteen days reduced them to submission. As we thus have proof that this country and people were called by the name of Kator at so early a period, it seems probable that the Kators whom we read of in Abú-l Fazl Baihakí are no other than the descendants of the dynasty we have been considering, and that the Ghaznivide sovereigns organized them among their troops, as we know from the *Táríkh-i Yamíní* that Mahmúd was in the practice of doing with conquered nations, as exemplified in his treatment of the Khiljís, Afgháns, and Indians. It is evident from the extracts given in this work from the *Tabakát-i Akbarí* and the *Táríkh-i Mas'údí*, that a body of Kator troops was kept in pay, and that the Tilak mentioned therein was the commander of these foreign troops,

---

[1] Elphinstone's *Kabul*, vol. ii. pp. 376, 387.
[2] Burne's *Bokhara*, vol. ii. p. 209; and *Journal A. S. Bengal*, vol. vii. p. 331.
[3] *Takwimu-l-buldán*, p. 127.
[4] [For other references to the Kators, see Thomas's *Prinsep*, I. 314. Lassen, *Ind. Alt.* III. 890, 1176. Masson's *Narratives*, I. 193. Vigne, *Ghazni*, etc., p. 235. Trumpp, in *Journ. R. A. S.* xix. 1. *Jour. des Sav.* Vol. V., 1856, where M. Viv. de St. Martin attempts to identify them with the Cadrusii of Pliny VI. xxiii.]

which were rated as Indian, he being in one passage spoken of as commander of the Indians, in another of the Kator troops. It opens a very interesting subject of investigation to enquire if these Kators have no memorials of themselves in India. The identity of name and the period of the establishment of the Kators in Kumáún appear to render it probable that we have in them the descendants of those Kators who fought under the banners of the first Muhammadan conquerors.

A curious coincidence of names seems worth noticing in this place. It will be observed that Al Birúni makes the Turk kings of Kábul come from the mountains of Tibet, and Grecian and Chinese authors concur in saying that in the first years of the Christian era the valley of the Indus and some of the neighbouring countries were occupied by a race from Tartary. Ptolemy, Dionysius, and the author of the Periplus of the Erythrean Sea, give to the country watered by the Lower Indus the name of Indo-Scythia, and Ptolemy applies the same name to a country at the bottom of the Gulf of Cambay. The Chinese writers inform us that a people of Tatar race named Yue-chi or Yue-tchi crossed the Hindú-kush, and established themselves in Afghánistán. Fa-Hian speaks of these barbarians having occupied, long before his visit to India, the province of Peshawar.

De Guignes has informed us, after Chinese authors, that the nomade race of Yue-tchi, being driven about the year 160 before Christ from its original seat in the western provinces of China, by another race called Hioung-nou, established themselves in Transoxiana, and spread over the countries in that neighbourhood. Abel-Rémusat and Klaproth have also furnished us with further particulars from the same sources. We learn that the Yue-tchi took part in the struggle which took place between the Greek princes of Bactria and the Arsacidan monarchs of Persia, and that they contributed to the downfall of the former. A few years before Christ, the Yue-tchi chief, named Khieou-tsieou-hy, after subjugating the other independent rulers of his own tribe, proclaimed himself king, and conquered the countries situated between the Oxus, Hindú-kush and Little Tibet. His successor, Yan-kao-tchin, penetrated as far as India.

Some time after, the monarch of the Yue-tchi, whom the Chinese call Ki-to-lo, which Klaproth has converted into Ghidor, descended to the south of the Hindú-kush "in following the valley of the Indus" (?), and invaded India on the north. Among other regions he reduced the province of Pesháwar; but being himself compelled to return westward, left the government of the conquered country to his son.[1] M. Reinaud is of opinion[2] that it is to this Ki-to-lo that Fa-Hian alludes, when he says, "Formerly the king of the Yue-tchi, levied a powerful army, and came to attack the country he was anxious to obtain."

The conquerors, who remained in the valley of Kábul, received the name of the "Little Yue-tchi," while the mass of the nation was designated the "Great Yue-tchi." In these Little Yue-tchi we have the ancestors of our modern Játs, a subject which I may, perhaps, discuss at further length hereafter.

It is impossible not to be struck here with the coincidence of the name of Ki-to-lo with Kitor or Kator, the *l* and the *r* being as usual convertible. Here we seem to have the origin of the name Kitor, the establishment of a prince of that name between Kábul and the Hindú-kush, on the very site of the modern Káfiristán, or land of Siyáh-poshes and the country of Kitor, according to the authorities given above. It is probable that we are to look to one of his descendants for the Katormán, who was the last of the Turkish dynasty; and these united considerations have combined to induce me to adopt the readings to which I have given the preference above.

It is to be observed that Al Birúni asserts the Turkish dynasty of Kábul to have lasted for sixty generations; but we are not to suppose that the crown continued in the same family or tribe, but that they were members of the great Turkish stem of nations, which conveys no more definite notion than the Scythians of the ancients, or the Tartars of the moderns. There may have been Turks of other tribes who ruled in the kingdom, who, whether Sakas, Turushkas, Duráris, Yue-tchis, or Kators, would still be classed under the generic designation of Turks, as the last of the Turks appears to have reigned about A.D. 850. If we allow fourteen years as the

---

[1] *Nouveaux Mélanges Asiatiques*. Tom. I. p. 223. Laidlay's *Translation of Fa-Hian*. Fer-ivas-ki, p. 81. *Tableaux Historiques d'Asie*. p. 134.
[2] *Mémoire sur l'Inde*, p. 83, from which work the preceding abstract of Yue-tchi history is taken.

average duration of their reigns, we shall find the period of the conquest occurring about the first year of the era of Our Saviour; and if we allow sixteen years as the average duration, we shall exactly bring it to the period of the downfall of the Græco-Bactrian Empire in 126 before Christ.

Here, then, there is reason to suppose that the first monarch of the Turkish dynasty must have been the subverter of the Grecian Empire in the East. He is called by Al Bírúní "Barhtigín;" tigín being a common Turkish affix, signifying "the bravo," as Alp-tigín, Subuk-tigín. M. Reinaud conjectures that Barh or Barha answers, probably, to the word *pharahatara*, which Lassen and Wilson have read on certain Græco-Barbarian coins, and to be the same name which the Greeks have converted into Phraates and Phraoiles.[1] Al Bírúní informs us that the names of these princes were recorded on a piece of silk, which was found in the fort of Nagarkot, when it was taken by the Muhammadans; but that circumstances prevented his fulfilling his anxious desire to examine it.

Al Bírúní mentions that Kanak was of the number of these kings, and that he founded the Vihár, or Buddhist monastery at Peshawar, called after his name even in Al Bírúní's time, and which, probably, occupied the site of the present conspicuous building, called the Gor-khattrí, at the eastern entrance of that town. The romantic anecdote which he relates of him, and which, probably, has little foundation in truth, will be found among the extracts translated from the *Táríkhu-l Hind*, in this volume.

M. Reinaud considers this Kanak to have reigned a little prior to the commencement of our era, and to be the same as the Kanika or Nika of Fa-Hian; the Kanishka of Hiuen-thsang and the Rájátaranginí and the Kanerkes of the Græco-Barbarian coins; and General A. Cunningham has formed the same opinion independently with reference to the two first identifications, considering the same monarch to be the Kanika of the Chinese, and the Kanaksen from whom many Rájpút families trace their lineage.[2]

According to Hiuen-thsang, Kanika or Kanishka reigned over

---

[1] *Mémoire sur l'Inde*, p. 78.
[2] *Mém. sur l'Inde*, p. 73; Thomas' Prinsep, Index "Kanishka;" *Jour. Beng. As. Soc.*, Vol. xxiii.

the whole valley of Kábul, the province of Peshāwar, the Panjáb, and Kashmir. He crossed the Hindú-kush and Himalaya, and subjected Tukháristán and Little Tibet. He received the title of the Lord of Jambu-dwípa, which is equivalent to "The Paramount of all India." He was a long time a stranger to the dogmas of Buddhism, and despised the law; until, by chance, he was converted to that faith, and became one of its most zealous disciples and promoters.

The same Chinese author states that he reigned four hundred years after the death of Buddha, which, as it occurred 544 years before our era, would bring it to more than a century before Christ; but as he expresses his dates in round numbers, we cannot rely much upon his precision. We may with more probability look for it a century later, if, at least, he be the same as Kanerkes, for among the coins and other objects bearing his name, which were found in the tope of Manikyála, and which would appear to indicate that that monument was constructed under the reign of that prince, certain Roman medals were also found of the period of Octavius and Antony extending to as low as 33 B.C.[1]

The Yue-tchi evidently established themselves in Kábul subsequent to the reign of Kanishka, and probably not long after, for Fa-Hian, about the year 400 A.D., speaks of their occupation of that valley, as if it were a transaction of no recent date. If we assign to Ki-to-lo the date of A.D. 200, we shall have nearly seven hundred years from the first to the last of the Katormán dynasty, during which, probably, other families and other tribes may have intermediately occupied the throne, without entirely subverting the right of the Yue-tchi conquerors of the valley.

The statement of Al Bírúní, respecting the occupation of Kábul by the Turks, is in strict conformity with Bíládurí and Tabarí, and with the brief notices which the other early Arabic historians and geographers have given us respecting that city. They couple it, however, with the curious announcement of an occupation divided between the dominant Turks and subject Hindús. Mr. F. Thomas

---

[1] M. Raoul-Rochette, *Journal des Savants*, ann. 1836, p. 70. [Thomas' *Prinsep*. I. 150, and Index, v. Manikyála.]

has considered this subject at considerable length in another excellent paper by him, on the Coins of the Ghaznivides.[1]

The first in order is Mas'údí, who visited the valley of the Indus in 303 A.H. = 915 A.D. He says nothing of the political and religious revolution which we have been considering, by which Brahmans had been substituted for Buddhist Turks. On the contrary, he designates the prince who reigned at Kábul by the same title as he held when the Arabs penetrated for the first time into those regions.

Istahkrí, who wrote within six years after Mas'údí travelled in India, says:—

وكابل لها تهندز موصوف باتحصن واليه طريق واحد وفيها المسلمون و لها الربض بها الكفار من الهند

"Kábul has a castle celebrated for its strength, accessible only by one road. In it there are Musulmáns, and it has a town, in which are infidels from Hind."

Ibn Haukal began his travels in 331 A.H. = 942 A.D., and wrote an account of them thirty-five years later. He follows his predecessor implicitly in the main points, but respecting the occupants of the town, the Bodleian copy varies[2] from the Lucknow one, which bears the name of *Ashkálu-l Bildá*. In the former, "Hindú Infidels" is converted into "Infidels and Jews." The latter reads:—

وليس في هذه المدن التي في نواحي بلخ اكثر مالا وتجارةً من غزنة و انها فرضة الهند و كابل لها قلعة حصينة و اليه طريق واحد فيها المسلمون و لها ربض به الكفار من الهنود

The statement of Al Bírúní, in his *K'dnún-i Mo'súdí*, written less than a century after this, is:—

قلعه كابل مستقر ملوكهم الاتراك كانوا ثم البراهمه

Here there is no specification respecting the different occupancy of the castle and town, but nothing to impugn the correctness of what is asserted by Istakhrí and Ibn Haukal. There is no occasion to

[1] *Journal of the Royal Asiatic Society*, vol. ix, p. 267.   [2] *Ibid*, p. 286.

quote any of the later geographers, who add nothing to our information, and are careless as well as confused in their statements.

Before concluding this subject of the Turkish occupation of Kábul, the statement of Ibn Khallikán should be noticed, who states in his article on "Ya'kúb bin Lais," that Kábul, in the times of that prince, was inhabited by a Turkish race who appertained to a tribe called *Dardrí*. This name is new, and the assertion would authorise us to conclude that in his time the Turks were still predominant, though that fact would scarcely seem consistent with what we shall have to advance under *Kamlúa*. It is possible that the term Dnrárí may have connection with Darra, a hill pass, and that allusion may be to the country to the north of Kábul, just in the same way as in modern times the inhabitants of those same tracts are styled in Kábul "Kohistánís," or hill-men.

It does not appear when the city was either first or finally subdued by the Muhammadans. It is evident, however, that the first inroads were not followed by permanent occupation, and that there was no entire subversion of the native dynasty till the Ghaznivide dynasty rose to power.

The first invasion we read of was in the time of 'Abdu-llah, governor of 'Irák, on the part of the Khalif 'Usmán. He was directed by the Khalif to send an emissary to explore the provinces of Hind; and notwithstanding a discouraging report, 'Abdu-lla ordered the country of Sijistán to be invaded by one of his cousins, 'Abdu-r Rahman, son of Samra. 'Abdu-r Rahmán advanced to the city of Zaranj, and besieged the Marzabán, or Persian governor, in his palace, on the festival of the 'Id. The governor solicited peace, and submitted to pay a tribute of two millions of dirhams and two thousand slaves. After that, 'Abdu-r Rahmán subdued the country between Zaranj and Kish, which was then styled Indian territory, and the tract between Ar-Rukhaj (Arachosia) and the province of Dáwar—in which latter country he attacked the idolaters in the mountain of Zúr, who sued for peace; and though he had with him 8,000 men, the booty acquired during this incursion was so great, that each man received four thousand pieces of silver as his share. Their idol of Zúr was of gold, and its eyes were two rubies. The zealous Musulmáns cut off its hand and plucked out its eyes, and then remarked to the Marzabán how powerless was his idol "to do either good or evil." In the same expedition, Bust was taken. After this, 'Abdu-r Rahmán advanced to Zábul, and afterwards, in the time of Mu'áwiya, to Kábul.[1] The year in which this inroad was made is not mentioned, but as 'Abd-ulla was removed from his government in 36 A.H., we may consider it to have taken place about the year 35.

In the year 44 A.H. Muhallab ibn Abú Sufra, whose army chiefly consisted of the tribe of Azd, which was very powerful in Khurásán, and contributed largely to the downfall of the Ummayides—advanced on the Indian frontier as far as Danna (Danó) and Alahwás [or "Alahwár"=Lahore?] two places situated between Kábul and Multán. Firishta makes him penetrate as far as Multán, and opens his history by saying he was the first chieftain who spread the banners of the true faith on the plains of Hind. He says he plundered the country and brought back to the head-quarters of the army at Khurásán many prisoners who were compelled to become converts to the faith. Muhallab had been detached from the main army which had invaded

---

[1] Bilázurí, quoted in *Memoirs*, p. 173, and in *Geschichten der Chalifen*, vol. I. Anhang, p. 2. *Tarjima-i Futúhát* of Ahmad bin 'Asmi Kufí.—[I have found two Persian extracts from the *Futúhát* of Ahmad among the papers. They are short and important, so I give translations.—ED.]

Conquest of Sijistán by 'Abdu-r Rahmán Samrat under the Khalíf 'Urmán.—'Abdu-llah, son of 'Amir, wrote for his nephew on the father's side, 'Abdu-r Rahmán Samrat bin Jandab bin 'Abd Shamah bin 'Abd Sháfí, and having fitted out an army for him, sent him to Sijistán. 'Abdu-r Rahmán led his forces to Zaranj. The people of the city offered battle, and a fierce fight ensued between the opposing parties. The city was taken, and the Musulmáns obtained great spoil, carrying off many captives from Sijistán, and incalculable wealth. 'Abdu-r Rahmán then marched to subdue Kábul.

Conquest of Kábul.—When 'Abdu-r Rahmán came in sight of Kábul, the ruler of the place (Kábul Sháh), who was lame, was in the city. He came out and fought several engagements with the Musulmáns, but retreated into the city, and came forth no more. 'Abdu-r Rahmán besieged it, and remained seated before it, fighting with the garrison for a whole year. He and his soldiers had to endure many hardships during the siego, but at length they carried the place by assault; and when they entered it, they put the fighting men to the sword, and made the women and children prisoners. Kábul Sháh was taken captive, and brought before 'Abdu-r Rahmán; but when he was ordered to be beheaded he turned Muhammadan, and repeated the creed. 'Abdu-r Rahmán treated him with honour and kindness. The plunder and the captives which had been taken in Kábul, Zaranj, and Sijistán, was collected, and a fifth portion was set apart and sent to 'Abdu-llah bin 'Amir, with a report of the conquest of Sijistán and Kábul.]

Kábul from Merv, under 'Abdu-r Rahmán bin Shimar, and had made converts of twelve thousand persons. Muhallab subsequently made himself conspicuous as governor of Alahwár, and exterminator of the Azrakian insurgents, and as a traitor to his master, 'Abdu-llah ibn Zubair, the Khalif of Mecca. He was the ancestor of those chiefs, who, under the name of Muhallabís, often occur in the history of the later members of the Ummaya family, until they were nearly exterminated at Kandábil in 101 H.[1] Gildemeister doubts the truth of this expedition, as Sijistán had not yet been conquered; but he forgets that the Musulmáns did not penetrate to India through Sijistán, but through Kábul.

In Biládurí's account of this interesting expedition, there is a curious relation which must not be altogether omitted. He informs us that in the country of Kíkán, Muhallab encountered eighteen Turks, mounted on horses with their tails cut. As they were all killed fighting, Muhallab attributed the activity and valour of "the barbarians" to the fact of their horses' tails being cut. "Upon which he ordered his own horses' tails to be docked; and he was the first amongst the Musulmáns who adopted the practice."[2]

About the same time, 'Abbád, the son of Ziyád, made an incursion on the frontier of India, by way of Sijistán. He went through Rúdbár to the Hindmand (Helmand), and after staying at Kish, he crossed the desert, and reached Kandahár. Although the country was conquered, many Musulmáns lost their lives in this expedition.[3]

Biládurí informs us that under the Khiláfat of Mu'áwiya, 'Abdu-r Rahmán, son of Samrah, penetrated to the city of Kábul, and obtained possession of it after a month's siege. He conquered also the circumjacent countries, especially Ar-Rukhaj (Arachosia). The king of Kábul made an appeal to the warriors of India, and the Musulmáns were driven out of Kábul. He recovered all the other conquered countries, and advanced as far as Bust, but on the approach of another

---

[1] *Bryenii Elemerin Historia Saracenica*, ann. 101.
[2] Biládurí, see Vol. I. p. 116. Briggs, *Firishta*, vol. I. p. 4. The Chinese authorities seem to allude to this expedition. *Mémoires concernant les Chinois*, Tom. XV. p. 174. See also Tom. XVI. p. 372–5. Hammer, *Gemäldesaal der Lebensbeschreibungen*, vol. II. p. 9.
[3] Biládurí, ut suprà. Weil, *Geschichte der Chalifen*, vol. I. p. 292.

Musulmán army, he submitted, and engaged to pay an annual tribute.[1]

The Kábulís subsequently profited by the contests which distracted the Khiláfat, and the tribute was withheld; but in 64 A.H. = 683-4 A.D. 'Abdu-l 'aziz, the governor of Sistán, declared war against the king of Kábul, and in the combat which took place, that king was defeated and killed. The war continued under his successor, and he was compelled to submit to the payment of tribute, but whenever opportunity offered, renewed efforts were made by the Kábulís to recover their lost independence.[2]

Amongst the earliest attempts against Kábul may be noticed that of 'Abdu-llah, governor of Sistán, in 78 A.H.=697-8 A.D., or according to some, in the following year. When he arrived at Nímroz, Hajjáj desired him not to linger in Sistán, but to march without delay towards Kábul to enforce the payment of the tribute from Banbal, to which that chief had agreed; and ordered him peremptorily not to return until he had subjugated the whole province. Ranbal retiring before his assailant, detached troops to their rear and blocking up the defiles, entirely intercepted their retreat, and in this situation exposed to the danger of perishing by famine, 'Abdu-llah was compelled to purchase the liberation of himself and followers for a ransom of seven hundred thousand dirhams.[3]

To wipe out the disgrace which the Muhammadan arms had sustained, 'Abdu-r Rahmán bin Muhammad bin Asha's, was despatched to Kábul by the famous Hajjáj in 81 A.H.—700-1 A.D.;[4] or in the preceding year, according to some authors, he was sent at the head of forty thousand men into Sistán, and having there united to his own troops the troops of the province, marched without delay against the prince of Kábul. 'Abdu-r Rahmán returned to Sistán laden with booty, but incurred the displeasure of Hajjáj by not remaining to secure his conquest. Exasperated by a threat of supersession, he determined to carry his arms against his master, and, in order to strengthen his power, concluded a treaty with the enemies of his faith, in which it was

[1] *Mémoire sur l'Inde*, p. 179. [2] *Mémoire sur l'Inde*, p. 178.
[3] *Tarikh-i-Alfi*, Ann. 68, p.m. Muhammad. See the extracts from that work in a subsequent volume of this compilation. Price's *Mahommedan Hist.*, Vol. I., p. 464.
[4] *Mém. sur l'Inde*, p. 179; Weil, *Geschichte der Chalifen*, Tom. I. p. 449; Ockley's *History of the Saracens*. [82 A.H.] Bohn's Edit. p. 490.

APPENDIX. 417

stipulated that if his expedition should be attended with success, Ranbal should be absolved from every species of tribute, provided the latter should agree to afford him an asylum in the event of failure. After many vicissitudes of fortune, 'Abdu-r Rahmán was at last compelled to seek the protection of his ally, who, after treating him for some time with kindness and hospitality, was at last seduced by the promises or by the threats of Hajjáj to deliver up his guest. 'Abdu-r Rahmán frustrated the vindictive designs of his enemy by throwing himself down from a precipice while he was on his way.—A.H. 84.[1]

The interest which this contest excited throughout the Khiláfat seems to have invested the Prince of Kábul with a fictitious celebrity, insomuch that he is the hero of many Arab stories of the holy wars on the frontiers of Hind. Nevertheless there is no certainty as to the proper mode of spelling the name. The various readings of the European authors who have noticed him show how little the orthography is settled. Ockley[2] calls him "Zentil;" Weil,[3] "Zenbil;" Roinaud,[4] "Ratbyl" and "Zenbyl." Wilson,[5] "Rateil, Ratpeil, Ratbal, Rantal, Zantíl—variations easily accounted for by the nature of the Persian letters." E. Thomas,[6] "Ratpíl;" Price,[7] "Reteil," "Ratteil," or "Retpeil."[8]

Price observes that the name bespeaks him to be either a Tartar or Hindú, and that the real name might perhaps have been Vittel, still common among the Hindus. Wilson considers it as a genuine Indian appellation; Ratná-pála or Rutun-pál.[9]

---

[1] Price's *Mahommedan History*, Vol. I, pp. 456-463.
[2] *History of the Saracens*, Bohn's Edit., p. 490.
[3] *Geschichte der Chalifen*, I. pp. 449, 461.
[4] *Mémoire sur l'Inde*, pp. 71, 72, and 178.   [5] *Ariana Antiqua*, p. 133.
[6] *Journal of the Royal Asiatic Society*, Vol. xii. p. 344.
[7] *Retrospect of Mahommedan History*, Vol. i., pp. 454-5.
[8] [The Mujmalu-t Tawáríkh (Paris MS. p. 274), says:—

و پادشاهان زمین کابل و سندرا رتبیل گویند

"The kings of Kábul and Sind are called Ratbíl." Ibn Khurdádba (Oxford MS. p. 26), has ملکت سمرتند طرخان مکستان رتـل, which M. Barbier de Meynard (*Journ. Asiatique*, 1865, p. 251), renders "*Le roi de Sistan Retbíl*." Mas'údí (Paris Ed. II. p. 67), has "Zenbíl qui est resté commun jusqu' à ce jour." The various readings of the *Jámi'u-l Hikáyát* have been noticed in a previous page, *supra*, p. 178.]

[9] *Ariana Ant.* p. 133.

Mas'údí, in his chapter in the *Murúj*, which is consecrated to the kings of Syria, makes mention of a prince who reigned in the valley of the Indus, and who after having subjugated Eastern Persia, advanced to the banks of the Tigris and Euphrates. The name of this prince was Ranbal, under one of its various modifications, and he adds that the name formed in his time the designation of the indigenous princes of the country, and he calls the Buddhist princes of Kábul by this epithet, which he makes common to all. In this he is borne out by Tabarí, and M. Reinaud is induced therefore to consider the word significative.[1] But it is not improbable that this assertion arises from the ignorance of the Muhammadans, and that they were ready to apply all the stories relating to the border chiefs of India to that one who had obtained the greatest notoriety with historians by his transactions with the generals of the Khilafat, just as the *Hadíka Sanáí* speaks of Jaipál being the king of India in the time of Bahrám, and Hátifí speaks of Rái Pithaurá as the same even in the time of Tímúr.

The *Jámi'u-l Hikáyát* ascribes the name to a contemporary of Ya'kúb Lais, which would make him one hundred and sixty years later than the invader of Syria, a long time for a title to have remained attached to a succession of petty chiefs. Moreover, at one time we find him ruler in Sind, at another in Kábul, though at the period spoken of those countries were not united under one dominion.

Khákí Shírází says:—"In the year twenty-two the province of Sijistán was conquered for 'Umar-bin Khattáb, by the hands of 'Amru bin al Tamímí; and in the same year Makrán was subdued by Abdu-llah bin 'Abdu-llah Anán, who marched against it from Kirmán. The ruler of that province, whose name in the language of the country was Zambil, was also ruler of Sind, and was killed."

In the opening of the history of Mas'úd the Ghaznivide, by Abú-l Fazl Baihakí, reference is made to the Palace of Ranbal, where it certainly seems to apply to an individual rather than a class.[2]

The Ranbal of whom we have been speaking as the opponent,

---

[1] *Mém. sur l'Inde*, p. 178.

[2] [Tabarí, the Majmal, and Mas'údí are all clear as to the import of the name, and its use as a dynastic royal title. Weil says it is "a general name for the king of the Turkomans, but more especially for the prince of Kábul and the territories between Hirát and Kábul.—*Geschichte*, p. 449."]

ally, protector, and betrayer of 'Abdu-r Rahmán, must have been one of the Turkish dynasty of Kábul, of the Buddhist persuasion. We find, from the Arabic histories of the period, that some of his relatives still held dominion in Transoxiana, though the relationship was probably rather that of tribe than family. If the family had been Hindú rather than Turkish, Ran-bal, "strong in battle," would have been sufficiently significative to render that the most likely reading of this disputed name. The probable prevalence, however, of the language of the Hindús in those parts might still have encouraged the use of the terms, notwithstanding that the Brahmans had not yet attained their supremacy.

In 107 A.H.=725-6 A.D., under the Khiláfat of Hashám, part of the dominions of Kábul was taken, but the capture of the town itself is not noticed.[1]

The lieutenants of the Khalifs Al Mahdí and Ar Rashíd took tribute from the Ranbal of Sijistán, proportioned to the strength or weakness of that prince, and named governors to the countries where Islám prevailed—A.H. 158-193=A.D. 775-809. When Al Mámún was made governor of Khurásán, he demanded double tribute. He took Kábul, and the king submitted, and professed Islám. An agent on the part of Mámún resided in that city, and a post was established which enabled Al Mámún to procure from it fresh myrobalans.[2]

After this we read nothing of Kábul till the time of the Saffárides—A.H. 256=A.D. 868-9.[3] In the succeeding year[4] Ya'kúb Lais took Kábul, and made its prince a prisoner. The king of Ar Rukhaj was put to death, and its inhabitants forced to embrace Islám. Ya'kúb returned to his capital loaded with booty, and carrying with him the heads of three kings; and many statues of Indian divinities, which were amongst the booty, were sent to Baghdád for presentation to the Khalif.[5]

This Muhammadan conquest appears to have been more durable

---

[1] Gladwin's *Ayin Akberi*, Vol. ii. p. 209. Price's *Mahommedan History*, Vol. I, p. 567.   [2] Biládurí, quoted in the *Mém. sur l'Inde*, p. 195-7.
[3] *Historia priorum regum Persarum*, etc., p. 19.   [4] *Tabakát-i Násirí*.
[5] Ibn Asír, *Kitábu-l Ahrísí*, and Ibn Khallikán, quoted in *Mém. sur l'Inde*. p. 209.

than the preceding ones, for we find coins of Ya'kúb struck at Panjshír, to the north-east of Kábul, in the years 260 and 261 H.[1]

By referring to the passages given above from the geographers, we shall learn the state of the occupancy of Kábul from the time of the Saffárides to that of the Ghaznivides, which commenced as early as the time of Alptigín, according to the statement of Abú-l Fazl, and it is probably to his time that the story related by Al-Birúní refers, where he states that when the *Espehbed*, or general-in-chief, had the gates of Kábul opened to him, the inhabitants imposed upon him the condition not to eat cow's flesh or indulge in unnatural crimes.[2] Neither condition is strictly observed by the modern occupants.

We will now proceed to examine more particularly the attempted identification of the several names of this series of Kábul kings:—

Turks.	
Barhtigín.	Kamlú.
Kanak.	Bhím.
Katormán.	Jaipál I.
○ ○ ○	Anandpál.
Brahmans.	Jaipál II.
Kalar.	Bhímpál.
Sámand.	○ ○ ○

Barhtigín has been already sufficiently remarked upon.

Kanak—Katormán.—Both these names have also been the subject of extended remarks. It will be observed that all the authorities quoted above from the original, make Kanak the last of the Turks, excepting only the *Táríkhu-l Hind*, which makes him only one, and the most famous one of the middle series of the Turkish kings for sixty generations. Allowing that Kanak is Kanishka, for which ample ground has already been advanced, this becomes impossible, and we must fall back upon the better authority of the *Táríkhu-l Hind*, and consider the Katormán or Laktúzamán as the last. In the more modern narratives of Rashídu-d dín and Bináḳiti we must place a full stop after "Kanak returned to his country." Then proceed, "the last of the kings was the Katormán." This requires

[1] Fraehn *Summarische Uebersicht*, etc., and *Bulletin de l'Académie*, Tom. I. p. 81.
[2] *Mémoire sur l'Inde*, p. 246.

no violent alteration of the text. Indeed the mere omission of مِن from the Arabic, and اِل from the Persian reconciles everything, and this last omission is actually made in the British Museum MS.

The writers themselves knew little of the state of the case, and wished merely to translate Al Bírúní, who knew well enough what he was writing. For instance, Binákiti wishing to reduce the narrative of the Jású, makes it appear that Ujen was the predecessor of Kanak. Haidar Rází, again, among the names of the illustrious kings of India who succeeded Basdeo (here meant not for him of Kananj, but the great Krishna) mentions Arjun and Jasand (the former being manifestly the famous hero of the Mahá-bhárata, and the latter Jarásandha), and "after him came Kanak, Chand." This, thorough indifference to correct chronology, enables us to see that by Ujen is meant Arjun, the senior of Kanak by several centuries. Mr. Thomas is persuaded that to this Kanak, the last of the Turks, are to be ascribed the coins which bear the name of Sri Vanka Deva "of the elephant-and-lion type of coin, which preceded the bull-and-horseman money introduced by the Brahmans. The similitude of names and the needful correspondence of all available evidence are surely sufficient to authorise our indicating Vanka Deva" as the Kanak above mentioned. This is by no means admissible, and he has himself since found that the real reading on the coin is "Varka," and has, consequently, altogether abandoned this speculation.[1]

Kalar " is, we have little doubt, the Syálapati of our coins. There is less difference in sound between Syála and Kalar than would at first be imagined ; so that if our translator, Al Bírúní, wrote his Arabic version from oral tradition, this slight change in the initial pronunciation of the name would be fairly probable." This is carrying speculation to an extreme, and there is no warrant whatever for the presumed identification.

[1] [Mr. Thomas, who might naturally desire to reply to these early criticisms on his confessedly initiatory essay on the coins in question, agrees with me in thinking that Sir H. Elliot's text should be preserved intact in the present publication, without comment or controversy on his part. This kind of knowledge is happily progressive, and many valid advances may be admitted to have been made between the theories of 1847 and 1868, without compromising the original author, or his censor of days gone by. Many of the objections here advanced have already been answered, in anticipation, by Mr. Thomas, in his edition of *Prinsep's Essays* (London, 1858), an extract from which will be found below (p. 426).]

It is to be observed that the *Jámi'u-t Tawdríkh* and its followers omit all notice of Kalar, making Sámand the immediate successor of Kanak.

The Syála or Syál-pati (ποτις in Greek), of whom so many coins are found in Afghánistán, was probably a leader, and, perhaps, even the progenitor of the Syál Játs of Jhang Syál and other localities in the Panjáb.

Samand.—Coins of Samanta, or Samanta Deva, are found in great profusion not only in Afghánistán, but throughout the Panjáb and the whole of Northern India, and one has even been found in the province of Posen.[1] Mr. Thomas is of opinion that this is owing to his having called in the coins of his Buddhist predecessors, in order to give prevalence to his own creed of Brahmanism by the substitution of the bull-and-horseman type for that of the elephant-and-lion, which is considered emblematic of Buddhism;[2] but this supposition seems defeated by the fact of our finding Samanta coins with the elephant also upon them. The name of this reviver of the old faith became so celebrated, that we find it upon the coins of his successors, extending even down to the Muhammadan conquest of Dehli, in 1192 A.D., and the coins of Rái Pitháurá.

Professor Wilson attributed these coins to a Rájpút prince, who lived many years afterwards. M. Reinaud never hesitated to recognize in these medals the name of the king of Kábul, and his opinion was confirmed by the examination which M. Adrien de Longpérier made of them.[3]

It may be considered presumption to oppose such an array of authority in favour of this identification, but, nevertheless, I hesitate to concur in it without more cogent arguments than those that have yet been adduced. Putting aside the improbability that one man's name should be stamped on a series of coins, extending through more than two centuries, sometimes in supercession, and sometimes in conjunction with, that of the reigning monarch—and that, too, even in the case of the later Ghaznivides—there seems so obvious a solution

[1] M. Longpérier in *Fragments Arabes et Persans*, p. 223.
[2] *Journal Royal Asiatic Society*, vol. ix. p. 181.
[3] *Mémoire sur l'Inde*, p. 212. *Journal Asiatique*, Feb. 1843, p. 102, and *Fragments Arabes et Persans*, p. 219.

of this continuance of a single name, that it requires far less boldness to adopt this simple explanation, than to seek grounds for establishing a position which, from its many improbabilities, is always open to question. It may, perhaps, be admitted that the coins which bear the simple name of Sri Samant Deva are to be referred to the Sámand of Abú Ríhán; but even that admission is open to objection, there being a double mis-spelling in the name, for in the former we have a short *a* instead of a broad one, and a *t* instead of a *d*.[1]

It appears to me, then, that Samanta, whenever it is found with another name, is throughout merely a title, meaning the warrior, the hero, the *preux chevalier*, the leader of an army, the Amír; and that after being used concurrently with Sri Hamír on the later Ghaznivide coins, it was by the early Ghorian monarchs altogether displaced by that more appropriate title.

At this latter period the prevalence of the title of Samant is obvious from its frequent use by the bard Chand, who has celebrated the exploits of Rái Pithaurá, and his three hundred Samants, or stalwart knights.

Kamlúa.—Mr. Thomas wishes to appropriate to this monarch a medal bearing the legend of *K'hradarayaka* or *K'hadarayaka*, while he confesses that even to liberal ears these names are not quite accordant in sound. He then seeks to justify the appropriation by mutations, blots, or intermixture of letters.[2] We must reject this, it being not worthy of the least credit; and the discovery of the name of Kamlúa in another history sets the question at rest, and establishes the correctness of Al Birúní.

This discovery is in other respects important, as enabling us to fix a synchronism by which we may conjecture the periods of the other monarchs of this dynasty. In one of the stories translated from the *Jámi'u-l Hikáyát*,[3] it will be found that he was a contemporary of 'Amrú Lais, who reigned between 265-287 A.H. = 878-900 A.D. Kamlúa is there called the Rái of Hindústán, and he must have ruled sometime within this period.

If we admit that these names represent a continuous series of

---

[1] [Longpérier reads the name with a long *d—Sámanta*, See *Fragments Arabes et Persans*, 221-223.]

[2] *Jour. R. A. S.*, ix. p. 180.   [3] See *supra*, p. 172.

successive monarchs, and not rather those who alone were conspicuous, we shall have to place the commencement of Kamlúa's reign as late as possible within the twenty-two years above-named. For we must connect it with another synchronism which we obtain from the same *Jámi'u-l Hikáyát*, wherein we learn that Mahmúd was only fourteen years old when the defeat of Jaipál occurred near the miraculous fountain, which—as he died in A.H. 421,[1] when he was sixty-three years old—reduces that date to 372 A.H., or 982-3 A.D., fifteen years before the death of Subuktigín.

Jaipál died in 1002 A.D., and it is evident from the statement in the *Táríkh-i Yamíní*, that he was then a very old man. He had opposed Subuktigín, while yet that warrior was only general of Alptigín, and therefore before 976 A.D., making his reign at least a quarter of a century. If we assume that Kamlúa's reign commenced in 890 A.D., being about the middle of that of 'Amrú Lais, we shall have to divide the period extending from 890 to 1002 A.D., between the reigns of Kamlúa, Bhím and Jaipál, being an average of thirty-seven years for each, which seems much too long. But as there is no disputing the dates, we must admit the long duration of 112 years for only three reigns, or admit that the names of unimportant monarchs have been omitted; just as in the case of the Turkish series, of which only Kanak is mentioned, between the first and last of the dynasty.

In the same way, between Kalar and Sámand, and Sámand and Kamlúa—there may have been other omissions, and even long interregna of Muhammadan supremacy; and we may thus throw back the period of the Brahmanical revolution to an earlier date than has yet been conjectured. It must be confessed this would relieve us of some difficulties, and enable us to dispose of other names of this series, of which we have incidental notice elsewhere: as, for instance, in the *Seiru-l Mulúk*, where we meet with the name of Lomak.

Syála, Khedavayaka, Varka, and even Ranbal may have been individuals of the Kábul series, either Turk or Hindú, though not honoured with distinct mention by Abú Ríhán. Numismatists,

[1] April, 1030. See the inscription on his tomb in Thornton's *Gazetteer of the Countries adjacent to India*, vol. I. p. 300, [and *Journ. R. A. S.*, xvii. p. 161.]

indeed, are now so certain that these coins do belong to the Kábul series, and trace with such confidence the relative antiquity of each extant model from the difference in devices and execution, that we may readily concede the point to such able and experienced enquirers. All that is required is that there should be no unnatural forcing to suit preconceived theories.

Mr. Thomas has conjectured on other grounds that the accession of Sámand occurred in 935 A.D.,[1] but his computation does not rest on any such specific dates as the two mentioned above, and he considers that, under any circumstances, it is imperfect, and that "the utmost the materials at our command enable us to assert with any degree of certainty is that Syála's usurpation took place early in the tenth century;" but even this certainty is dispelled by the establishment of the fact that Kamlúa was, unquestionably, a contemporary of 'Amrú Lais. Altogether, we may consider the subversion of the Turk by the Brahman dynasty to have occurred about 850 A.D., shortly before its capture by Ya'kub Lais; and as it appears from the Arab geographers that Musulmáns held the castle, it is evident that the Brahmans were only occasionally dominant, and did not hold their power without long and frequent interruptions.

BHÍM.—The coins of Bhím are found in Kábulistán, but are seldom, if ever, met with in India. There is no reason to doubt that this is the same Bhím as the Sri Bhím Deva of the bull-and-horseman series, and this is the only one of which the identification can be admitted without question.

M. Reinaud considers that this Bhím is the one mentioned by 'Utbi and Firishta as the founder of Nagarkot;[2] but there is more reason to believe the hero of the *Mahá-bhárata* to be the one indicated.

Jaipál I.—It is strange that no coins of Jaipál are found. Firishta calls him the son of Ishtpál,[3] and distinctly avers that he was a Brahman, and Bírúní also includes him in that dynasty; but the introduction of the term Pál, which is now continued to the close of the dynasty, might incline us to suppose that a new family had com-

---

[1] *Journal Royal Asiatic Society*, vol. ix. p. 179.
[2] *Mémoire sur l'Inde*, p. 257.
[3] [Briggs' translation says "Hatpál," but the lithographed text has "Ishtpál."]

menced. This seems in other respects not improbable, for in the opening of the *Táríkh-i Yamíní* we find Jaipál's western border extended no further than Lamghán, Kábul being already in possession of Subuktigín. It seems probable, therefore, that the succession of the real Kábul sovereigns ceased with Bhím, and that the king of Northern India succeeded to the paramount sovereignty which, as far as the Muhammadans were concerned, had hitherto been held by the ruler of Kábul. It is a mistake to suppose that Jaipál was king of Dehli. It does not appear that any such place existed in his time, and Abú-l Fidá's determination of its latitude and longitude on the authority of the *Kánún-i Mas'údí* is a misquotation, which it is of importance to correct, for there is nowhere mention of Dehli either in that work or in the *Táríkhu-l Hind*. The principal places of his residence appear to have been Lahore, Bhera, and Waihind; and it may be doubted if any of these places, except perhaps the last, had been held by the kings of Kábul.

The assertion that he was a Brahman probably arises from ignorance on the part of Firishta. Al Bírúní is not specific in his statement that he was a Brahman, but merely includes him in the dynasty which commenced with a Brahman, and he may no more have been really of that caste than were the Bahmaní sovereigns of the Dekhin, though they were called after one. The term Brahman, in the conception of a Musulmán, might merely imply that he maintained the doctrines of that faith, and from his position was its staunchest defender and champion. There seems ground to suppose he must have been a Rájpút, and some reasons have been assigned in the note on Mahmúd's invasion for considering him a Bhattí.

Anandpál.—Mr. Thomas observes[1] that the coins of Anandpál are common, and are plentiful in the Panjáb and the northern parts of the Ganges Dúáb. But these are evidently to be referred to the monarch of Dehli, who lived a century and a half later, and we have to deal with Anandpál not Anangpál. 'Utbi calls him Andpál.

Jaipál II.—This is not the name given by Al Bírúní, where it appears more like Tardijanbál, and in the other authors who mention him it goes through various forms. Tadan Jaipál, Nanduwa

[1] *Jour. R. A. S.*, ix. p. 121, (and later, *Prinsep's Essays*, l. 330.)

Jaipál, Taru Jaipál, Parou Jaipál, Nardajanpála, Niranjanpál, Tasdar Jaipál, and many more.¹ The latest reading proposed by M. Reinaud is Trilochan Pál, after the "three-eyed" Siva. Persian authors generally call him Nabíra Jaipál, or the grandson of Jaipál, and in that relationship no doubt he stood to the first Jaipál. Hence Dow calls him "Pitterugopál." The real name was, perhaps, Púr Jaipál, or Jaipál junior, Jaipál the son or grandson. Al Bírúní tells us that his father Anandpál was an inveterate enemy of the Musulmáns from the time that Púr Jaipál was taken prisoner, but Púr Jaipál himself was well disposed towards them.

According to 'Utbí we find him holding dominion as far eastward as Kanauj and the Ráhib, respecting which the note on the ninth and twelfth expeditions of Mahmúd may be consulted. The same author mentions another son of Anandpál, by the name of Brahman Pál, who is probably a different one.

Abú Ríhán informs us that he was killed in 412 A.H.=1021-2 A.D. It does not appear exactly when he began to reign, but he certainly opposed Mahmúd during the Kanauj campaign in 409 H.

Bhím Pál.—In him we have the last of the dynasty of Kábul and Northern India. As he is mentioned by Abú Ríhán, he must have succeeded to some remnant of his father's domains; but it does not appear that in his time he contested the advance of the Muhammadans, though before he ascended the throne we find him taking an active part in defending his father's dominions, under the name of Nidar Bhím, "Bhím the Dauntless."²

From his letter to Chand Rái, which is recorded by 'Utbí, it would appear that he was inclined to peaceful counsels, and that bitter experience had taught him the hopelessness of contending with his relentless and sanguinary rivals.³

From a statement in the *Táríkhu-l Hind*, we may infer that his capital was Bárí, to the east of Kanauj.

Neither of Bhím Pál, nor of any other of the Pál family, are any coins extant.

Bhím Pál survived his father five years, and died, therefore, in 417 A.H., the eventful year of the capture and plunder of Somnát. Haidar Rází gives nine years as the period of his reign.

¹ [See *supra*, pp. 46-47.] ² [*Supra*, p. 36.] ³ [*Supra*, p. 46.]

NOTE D.

Extract of Mr. Thomas' Edition of Prinsep's Essays, (1858. Vol. I. p. 331), referred to in page 9 suprà.

"Before I leave the subject, I may be permitted to make some observations in reference to an original suggestion of my own, that the Srí Hamírah, on the reverse of the immediately succeeding Moslem coins, was designed to convey the title of the spiritual representative of the Arabian Prophet on earth, embodied for the time being in the Khalíf of Baghdád. Sir H. M. Elliot, placing himself under the guidance of Capt. Cunningham, has contested this inference. I am not only prepared to concede the fact that Muhammad bin Sám uses this term in connection with his own name on the lower Kanauj coins, but I can supply further independent evidence, that my opponents could not then cite against me, in the association of this title with the name of the early Sultáns of Dehli in the Pálam Inscription (1339 Vikramáditya); but, on the other hand, I can claim a still more definite support in an item of testimony contributed by the consecutive suite of the selfsame fabric of coins, where the श्रीहर: (*hamírah*) is replaced by the word श्रीख (*khalífa*). As far as I have yet been able to ascertain, this transition *first* takes place on the money of 'Aláu-d dín Mas'úd (639-644 A.H.); and here, again, I can afford, in all frankness, to cite further data that may eventually bear against myself, in recording that this reverse of *Srí K'halífa* is combined in other cases with a broken obverse legend of ... श्रीरिषम ... which, being interpreted to stand for the *Amíru-l Múminín* of the Arabic system, may either be accepted as the Sanskrit counterpart legend of Altamsh's anonymous coins in the Persian character,"[1] or be converted into a possible argument against my theory, if supposed to represent the independent spiritual supremacy claimed by subsequent Sultáns of Dehli; which last assignment, however, will scarcely carry weight in the present state of our knowledge. As regards the difficulty raised respecting the conventional acceptance of the *Srí Samanta Deva* of the coins as an historical, rather than an individually titular, impress, I have always been fully prepared to recognize the linguistic value of the

[1] Pathán Sultáns of Dihli, by Ed. Thomas. London, Werthimer, 1847; p. 17.

word *Samanta*, and yet claim to retain the *Sri Samanta Dera*—which comes down to us, in numismatic sequence, in the place of honour on so many mint issues—as an independent name or title, to which some special prestige attached, rather than to look upon it as an ordinary prefix to the designation of each potentate on whose money it appears. And such a decision, in parallel apposition to the succession of the titles of *Sri Hamira* and *Khalfa*, just noticed, would seem to be strikingly confirmed by the replacement of this same legend of *Sri Samanta Dera* on the local coins of Cháhad Dova, by the style and title of the Moslem suzerain, to whom that rája had eventually to concede allegiance.

The two classes of coins to which I allude may, for the moment, be exemplified, the one in the type given in 'Ariana Antiqua,' xix. 16; the other in pl. xxvi. fig. 31, Vol. i. *(Prinsep)*.

The former, when corrected up and amplified from more perfect specimens, will be found to bear the legends: Obv. जयावरी श्री समस्त देव. Rev. श्री वाहर देव—while the latter will be seen to display an obverse epigraph of जयावरी श्री समसीरस देव, with a reverse similar to the last.

I understand this obverse legend to convey, in imperfect orthography, the name of Shamsu-d dín Altamsh—whose other coins, of but little varied type, have a similarly outlined name, with the Moslem *Sri Hamirah* on the reverse.

NOTE C.

The Historians of the Ghaznivides.

The contents of this volume relate more especially to the history of the Ghaznivides. It therefore seems expedient to take a general review of the authors who have particularly treated of that dynasty.

First in order comes 'Utbí, who has already been sufficiently noticed. It may be remarked generally that he is deficient in dates, and, though the chief and earliest authority on all which relates to the early invasions of India, he evidently had no personal knowledge of that country, a circumstance which of course greatly detracts from his value. He is fuller in the reign of Subuktigín and the transactions in Turkistán than any of his successors.

Thirty years later comes Abú-l Fazl Baihakí, of whose voluminous and important work only a portion has come down to us.

After an interval of more than two centuries follows the *Nizámu-t Tawáríkh*, composed in 674 H., about a century after the extinction of the dynasty. The short notice which this work devotes to the Ghaznivides has been translated as an extract from that work, but it is of little authority, and confuses dates irremediably towards the close of the dynasty, in which the transactions were carried on too far eastward to be within the foreign ken of the author. Indeed he confesses that he knows nothing of their successors, the Ghorians, beyond the names of three of their kings.

The next, but after a period of two hundred years from 'Utbí is the *Tabakát-i Násiri*, the chief value of which is that it quotes the lost volumes of Abú-l Fazl Baihakí. It is for this reason, however, greatly to be regretted, especially as he is one of the earliest Muhammadan authors who wrote in India, that his notice of Mahmúd's reign is so very curt; for it is that in which we most feel the want of Baihakí's familiar gossiping narrative. It is true he is quoted in the *Jámi'u-l Hikáyát*, *Táríkh-i Guzída*, *Rauzatu-s Safá*, and *Firishta*; yet it may be doubted if any except the author of the first ever saw his *Táríkh-i Násiri*, which is mentioned by name in the *Tabakát*. In some of the other Ghaznivide reigns, this work differs from others, as will be seen from the passages which are extracted in the article TABAKÁT-I NÁSIRI in this volume.

The great copyist and extractor, Rashídu-d dín, follows after the lapse of about twenty years. In his *Jámi'u-t Tawáríkh*, he follows 'Utbí implicitly, as far as the *Yamíní* extends, taking out not only his facts, but giving a literal translation of that work, even to the images and similes. So little does he attempt to improve upon the *Yamíní*, that he even leaves out the important expedition to Somnát, which was undertaken after the close of that work. This resource fails him altogether in the later reigns, which are consequently very unsatisfactorily disposed of in the *Jámi'u-t Tawáríkh*.[1]

About twenty years later follows the *Táríkh-i Guzída* of Hamdu-lla

[1] [See an article by Major Lees, in *Jour. R. A. S.*, Vol. III. N.S., 1868.]

Mustaufí—although he mentions the *Maḳámát* of Abú Naṣr Miská'ti, and the *Mujalladát* of Abú-l Faẓl Baihakí, he does not appear to have read them: at least he gives no information derived from them, and altogether his account of Mahmúd's reign is very meagre. He mentions the names of the towns taken by him, omitting, however, all notice of Somnát, and without stating the dates of their capture. He is so often quoted by Mírkhond, Khondamír, and Firishta, that he has had more credit than he deserves in this portion of his universal history.

After a long interval of about a century, we have Mírkhond, who in his *Rauẓatu-s Ṣafá* has given us the first detailed account of the history of the Ghaznivides. It is founded in the early portion upon the *Yamíní*, but in later reigns rests upon some other authorities which are not quoted. Those which are mentioned, as the *Náṣirí* and *Guzída*, are too meagre to have furnished the fuller information found in the *Rauẓatu-s Ṣafá*. This portion has been translated by F. Wilken into Latin, and published with the original text at Berlin in 1832, under the title of *Historia Gasnevidarum*. He has added in footnotes passages from Firishta and Haidar Rází, where the details are more complete than in the *Rauẓatu-s Ṣafá*. Haidar Rází, however, is no original authority. I have found all the passages, except two, quoted by Wilken to be word for word the same as the *Táríkh-i Alfí*, even where other authorities are quoted, as Ibn Aṣír, Ibn Kaṣír, and Ḥáfiẓ Abrú. The chief omission to be noted in Mírkhond's account is that of the expeditions to India intervening between those of Kanauj and Somnát, and the attack upon the Játs of Júd after Mahmúd's return from Somnát.

Mírkhond is followed by his nephew Khondamír in the *Khuláṣatu-l Akhbár* and the *Ḥabíbu-s Siyar*. The former has been translated by Price with additions from Firishta, and from the latter a translation will be found in a later volume of this work. He follows the *Rauẓatu-s Ṣafá* closely, and has no new authorities, omitting some passages, but dealing more copiously with the biographies of cotemporary poets and ministers. Altogether, Mírkhond's narrative is preferable, and in this, as well as in many other portions of his history Khondamír might have saved himself the trouble of attempting to rival his uncle.

The next authority of any value is the *Táríkh-i Alfí*. Like as in other portions of that work, it is, in the history of the Ghaznivides, also somewhat deficient in connexion, and troublesome, from adopting a new era; but altogether, it is copious and correct. 'Utbí and Mírkhond are the chief authorities of the *Táríkh-i Alfí*, but something is added from the less known histories, which have already been mentioned as being quoted at second hand by Haidar Rází. It is to be regretted that Abú-l Fazl Baihakí is not amongst them. Here also we have no detailed account of the Indian expeditions between those of Kanauj and Somnát, and that to Thánesar is not mentioned.

Nizámu-d dín Ahmad, in his *Tabakát-i Akbarí*, gives a succinct account of the history of the Ghaznivides, and is particular in mentioning his dates. He notices very cursorily the events in Turkistán, Sistán, and 'Irák, confining his attention principally to what related to India. In his work we, for the first time, find mention of several expeditions to India, which are passed over by his predecessors; and it is, therefore, to be regretted that he does not signify on what authority he relates them. The only probable source, among those mentioned as his general authorities, is the *Zainu-l Akhbár*. Nizámu-d dín is followed closely by Firishta.

'Abdu-l Kádir, in his *Táríkh-i Badáúní*, follows Nizámu-d dín implicitly; but, in order to show the variations, he occasionally quotes the *Nizámu-t Tawáríkh*, and the *Lubbu-t Tawáríkh*. He adds, also, some verses of poets who were contemporary with the Ghaznivides.

The *Muntakhabu-t Tawáríkh* of Khákí Shírází is very brief, and scarcely deserves notice. It chiefly follows the *Habíbu-s Siyar*.

We next come to the history of Firishta, which gives the most complete and detailed account which we have of the Ghaznivides. Dr. Bird complains of the author's ignorance of the geography of Upper India; but he has exhibited no more than his predecessors, and in one or two instances attempts corrections. His chief resource is the *Tabakát-i Akbarí*, but he has also used the *Táríkh-i Yamíní*, the *Táríkh-i Guzída*, the *Rauzatu-s Safá*, and the *Habíbu-s Siyar*. Some of the other works which he quotes there is reason to believe he never saw. The translation by Briggs is generally correct and faithful in this portion, and there are no omissions in it of any great consequence.

APPENDIX. 433

The *Khuláṣatu-t Tawáríkh* discusses this history in a peculiar fashion of its own. It omits all notice of transactions on the frontiers of Persia and Turkistán, and confines itself solely to India, insomuch that it leaves out whole reigns in which the sovereign had no connection with India: and, in consequence, preposterously confines the whole number of reigns to seven only. There is no other novelty in this chapter, except that it substitutes two new readings of places, which if they are derived from the history of Mahmúd by 'Unsurí, which is quoted in the preface, may be considered authentic.

These are all the authorities which it seems necessary to notice, as all the subsequent ones follow in the wake of Firishta. Abú-l Fidá, Ibn Shuhna, Ibn Asír, Ibn Kasír, Nikbi, and Lárí, have had all that is valuable in them extracted by the diligence of European authors, who have translated, abridged, or commented on the reigns of the Ghaznivides. The Turkish histories of the period, such as the *Nakhbatu-t Tawáríkh*, and the work of Munajjim Báshí, we may fairly presume to have been exhausted by the industry of Hammer-Purgstall amongst the fourteen different histories which he quotes as authorities upon Mahmúd's reign—so that the only hope now left us for ascertaining any new fact with respect to the history of the Ghaznivides is in the recovery of the missing volumes of Memoirs, which we know to have been written by contemporary writers, and to have been in existence less than two centuries ago—such as those of Abú-l Fazl Baihakí, Abú Nasr Mishkání, and Mulla Muhammad Ghaznawí. The Makámát of Abú Nasr Mishkátí¹ (Mishkúní) is mentioned by Firishta (Briggs I. 32 and 97), and the same author is referred to in Wilken (Gasnevidarum, p. 189). Firishta quotes from him the anecdote about Mas'úd, which has been given from the *Tabakát-i Násirí* (*supra*, p. 271), and which is there also attributed to Abú Nasr Mishkán. The *Táríkh-i Mulla Muhammad Ghaznawí* is mentioned by 'Abdu-r Rahmán, who wrote the *Mir-átu-l Asrár* and *Mir-át-i Mas'údí*, in Jahángír's time. The author was contemporary with Sultán Mahmúd, of whom his work is said to give an ample account.

¹ [In Briggs' translation, the name is written "Mukutty."]

NOTE D.

Mahmúd's Expeditions to India.

The times, places, and numbers of Mahmúd's expeditions to India have offered great difficulties to those who have dealt with the history of that ferocious and insatiable conqueror. We look in vain for any enquiry on the subject from the native historians of this period, who, in their ignorance of Upper India, enter names and years without the scruples and hesitations which a better knowledge or a more critical spirit, would have induced.

It is only when European authors begin to discuss the matter that we are taught how many difficulties there are to solve, how many places to identify, how many names to restore. Those who have added most to our knowledge of this period, and have occasionally interspersed their narratives or notes with illustrative comments, and who will be quoted in the course of this Note, may be thus named in the order of their publications:—D'Herbelot,[1] De Guignes,[2] Hunt (?),[3] Dow,[4] De Sacy,[5] Mill,[6] Wilson,[7] Audiffret,[8] Rampoldi,[9] Briggs,[10] Wilken,[11] Ritter,[12] Bird,[13] Hammer-Purgstall,[14] Elphinstone,[15] and Reinaud.[16] It is needless to mention Gibbon, Malcolm, Conder, Gleig, Murray, and others, whose works, however useful, are mere copies and abstracts of others, and add nothing to our previous information.

It has been usual to consider the number of Mahmúd's expeditions

---

[1] *Bibliothèque Orientale*, Art. "Mahmoud." Paris, 1697.
[2] *Histoire Générale des Huns*, Tom. II. Paris, 1756.
[3] *Modern Universal History*, Vols. II. and III. London, 1759.
[4] *History of Hindustan*, Vol. I. London, 1768.
[5] *Notices et Extraits des Manuscrits*, Tom. IV. Paris, 1798-9.
[6] *History of British India*, Vol. II. London, 1818. [7] *Ibid*, 1840.
[8] *Biographie Universelle*, Art. "Mahmoud." Tom. XXVI. Paris, 1820.
[9] *Annali Musulmani*, Vol. VI. Milan, 1825.
[10] *History of the Mahom. Power in India*, Vol. I. London, 1829.
[11] *Historia Gasnevidarum*. Berolini, 1832.
[12] *Die Erdkunde von Asien*, Vol. IV. Part I. Berlin, 1835.
[13] *History of Gujarát*. London, 1835.
[14] *Jahrbücher der Literatur*, No. 73. Wien, and *Gemäldesaal der Lebensbeschreibungen*, Vol. IV. Leipzig, 1837.
[15] *History of India*, Vol. I. London, 1842.
[16] *Mémoire sur l'Inde* in the *Mémoires de l'Institut*, Tom. XVIII. Paris, 1849.

to India to be twelve. The first authority for this number is Nizámu-d dín Ahmad in the *Tabakát-i Akbarí*; and as Dow has also numbered them as twelve, most English authors following him as the standard, have entertained the same persuasion. But it is curious to observe that, while Nizámu-d dín mentions that there were altogether twelve, in recording them *seriatim*, he enumerates no less than sixteen; and Dow, while he marginally notes twelve, records no less than fifteen different invasions. Even Elphinstone, though he notes twelve, records more. The *Khuláṣatu-t Tawáríkh* gives twelve, and confines itself to that number, or in reality only to eleven, as by some mistake an expedition to Kashmír and Kálinjar are placed in one year, and the tenth expedition is omitted. The *Akhbár-i Muhabbat* follows it in both errors. I will not attempt to maintain this established number of expeditions, but will consider them in the actual order of their occurrence.

First Expedition.—Frontier Towns. A.H. 390 (1000 A.D.)—Nizámu-d dín Ahmad and Firishta mention that about the year 390 H. Mahmúd marched in the direction of India, and, after taking many forts and provinces, and establishing his own governors in them, he returned to Ghazní. This rests solely on the authority of these two authors, and is not supported by the *Táríkh Yamíní*; but there is no improbability in the statement.

It was to have been expected that Mahmúd, after establishing himself on the throne of Ghazní, would have embraced the first opportunity of invading India; for, while yet a prince, he had seen how easily the hardy warriors of Zábulistán had overcome the more effeminate sons of India. His father Subuktigín is described in the *Yamíní* as making several attacks upon the country of Hind, independent of the three which are more specifically mentioned, the scene of which was Kusdár and Lamghán. Even during the fifteen years of Alptigín's reign, Subuktigín is represented by Firishta in an untranslated passage to have made frequent attacks upon India, and even to have penetrated as far as Sodra on the Chináb, where he demolished idols in celebration of Mahmúd's birth, which, as it occurred on the date of the prophet's birth, Subuktigín was anxious that it should be illustrated by an event similar to the destruction of the idols in the palace of the Persian king by an earthquake, on the day of the prophet's birth. In the words of the *Bostān* :—

چو منیش در انواه عالم فتاد   تزلزل در ایوان کسری فتاد

Near the Lamghán valley two actions were fought, or more probably in the valley of Jalálabád, for as the plural, Lamghánát, is frequently used, there seems reason to believe that the valley to the south as well as the north of the Kábul river was included in that province. The first action fought in this neighbourhood was brought to a conclusion by the effect of the miraculous fountain or stream in the hill of Ghúzak, which emitted storms, thunder, and cold, whenever some impurity was cast into it. A more particular account of this will be found in the extracts from the *Yamíní* and the *Jámi'u-l Hikáyát*.[1]

What could have given rise to this extraordinary story is not easy to conceive, and no one has attempted an explanation. The most probable solution seems to be that a snow-storm came on, and not only harassed but alarmed the Hindús, who had never witnessed such a thing before; for it is quite compatible with probability that although the Lamghánát were then included in the country of Hind, yet that the soldiers, who, for the most part, came from the more eastern provinces, might never have seen a fall of snow. It is to be observed that the *Tabakát-i Akbarí* expressly says that Jaipál and the Hindús were unaccustomed to the *cold*, and that was the reason why they suffered more than the Musulmáns. It may fairly be surmised, then, that the snow and frost totally paralysed the Hindú warriors, and were felt as grievously by them as, nine centuries afterwards, by Indian and British troops combined, when they sustained the most grievous disaster that has ever befallen our nation. It is an extraordinary coincidence that the very scene of this first and last defeat of an Indian army was the same—what wonder if the cause also did not differ?

The minds of the natives of India would naturally have tried to account for such a supernatural phenomenon as a fall of snow, and superstition was at hand to render her assistance.

[1] [Supra, pp. 20 and 162.]

There was a stone, celebrated amongst the Turkish nations, which had the peculiar property of causing rain, and hail, and snow, and excessive cold, and violent tempests, if the possessor, after repeating the name of God, and breathing upon it, threw it into the water. This stone is called the "Yedeh," or "Jedeh." The first stone of the kind was said to have been given to Japhet by Noah, to whom the secret was disclosed by Gabriel. The stone came into the possession of Turk, the eldest son of Japhet, and in an action which was fought between him and his nephew, for the possession of the stone, the latter was killed; and, as he was the father of the Turkománs, this stone is said to be the cause of the unceasing enmity between that tribe and the Turks. Subsequently, the art of using this stone was more generally disseminated, and occasioned magicians to be generally called "yedehehis;" and we have frequent mention of its use in Mongol history for purposes similar to those for which we suppose it to have been applied on the present occasion. As early as the year 2634 before our era, we find the following statement in a quotation by M. Klaproth, to prove the antiquity of the compass among the Chinese: "Tchi-yeou raised a thick fog, in order that by means of the darkness he might spread confusion in the enemy's army. But Hiuan-yuan constructed a chariot for indicating the south, in order to distinguish the four cardinal points."[1]

In an action between the Mongols and Chinese, with respect to the latter, Rashídu-d dín says: "In consequence of the arts of the magician, the Chinese felt, in the middle of summer, a temperature which they had never experienced, even in winter, and were paralysed." Bergman says that the stone used at present among the nomadic nations is the Bezoar. Marco Polo, also, speaking of a country not far from the confines of India, says:—"When the Carannas wish to overrun the country and rob it, they, by their enchantment and diabolical agency, cause the day to become dark, so that you can see to little or no distance." In the mountains between Kashmír and Tibet, there is a lake, into which, if animal flesh is thrown, we are informed by Abú-l Fazl, that a storm of snow or rain will arise. There is said to be a similar one at Dámaghán, in

[1] *Lettre d M. A. Humboldt sur l'invention de la Boussole.* Paris, 1836; and Mr. Davies, in the *British Annual* for 1837.

Tabaristán, and Zakaríya Kazwíní mentions one near Ghazní, which is, no doubt, the one alluded to in Subuktigín's battle with Jaipál. Altogether, we may consider Jaipál's army to have been surprised and paralyzed by a snow-storm, and that superstition ascribed the unusual visitation to the "Yedeh" stone.¹

Second Expedition.—Peshāwar—Waihind. A.H. 391-2.—Mahmúd left Ghazní in Shawwál, 391 H., and a severe action took place on the 8th of Muharram, 392, at Peshāwar, in which he was completely victorious, and Jaipál and fifteen of his principal chiefs and relations were taken prisoners, after the loss of 5000 men.

He is then represented by all the later authorities to have marched from Peshāwar to Batinda, and invested it. Elphinstone observes that Batinda is beyond the Sutlej, "and seems formerly to have been a place of more consequence than its situation in a sort of desert would promise. It is said by Colonel Tod to have been the residence of the Rájá of Láhore, alternately with the capital, from which he took this name. As the battle of Peshāwar was on the 27th of November, Mahmúd would reach Batinda towards the end of the cold season, when the rivers of the Panjáb, though not all fordable, would offer little obstruction to cavalry." Dr. Bird also speaks of Batinda as being in the most easterly and inaccessible part of the Panjáb kingdom, and following the *Tabakát-i Akbarí* and Firishta, says that Jaipál used to reside there. The latter indeed says he resided there for the convenience of opposing the Muhammadans—which is an absurdity, if we are to understand the most eastern city of his dominions. Rampoldi, with his usual confusion of names and places, makes his residence Multán.

All these difficulties about Mahmúd's movements are at once obviated by correcting the reading, and rejecting Batinda altogether. The real name is Bihand or Waihind, as is plainly indicated in the *Yamíní*.² It was a place of considerable importance, on the western

¹ Respecting this stone and these fountains, further information may be obtained by referring to Bergman, *Nomadische Streifereien unter den Kalmüken*, Th. iii. p. 183. Miles, *Shajrat al Atrak*, pp. 24, 26, 56. Gladwin's *Ayeen Akberee*, Vol. II. p. 134. Marco Polo, Murray's Ed., p. 221. *Modern Universal History*, Vol. IV. p. 417. D'Ohsson, *Histoire des Mongols*, Tom. II. p. 615. *Khulásatu-t Tawáríkh*, Art. "Humáyún." *Mír-átu-l Istiláh*, Art. "Yedeh." *Asáru-l Bilád* and *Bahru-l Buldán*, Art. "Ghazní."

² [Ibn Asír gives the name of the place correctly as "Waihand."]

bank of the Indus, about fifteen miles above Attock, on the old high road from Láhore to Peshāwar, and only three marches from the latter. It was the capital of Eastern Kandahár, and is noticed by Birúní, Baihakí, and Abú-l Fidá, from which latter author we learn that its foundation is attributed to Alexander the Great. The name is now Húnd, and while I was in the neighbourhood I could not find that even any first syllable was ever added to it, either by natives or strangers.

By the capture of Waihind, Mahmúd's progress becomes easy and natural, and instead of having to cross and recross several foaming streams and marching through a hostile and difficult country, he has not yet crossed even the Indus.

Third Expedition.—Bhera (Bhátiá). A.H. 395 (1004–5 A.D.)—After a rest of three years, during which attention was occupied by affairs in the west, we find Mahmúd returning to India to take the city of Bhatees (Briggs), Battea (Dow), Bhatia (Elphinstone), Bhátnah (Bird), Bahadiyah *(Univ. Hist.)*, Bhadiyah (Rampoldi), Bahatia (S. de Sacy), Hebath (D'Herbelot),[1] Bihatia (Hammer-Purgstall). Briggs says he has failed in fixing the position of this place. Elphinstone says, "a dependency of Láhore, at the southern side of Multán." Bird says it is now called Bhatnír, situated on the northern extremity of the Dikanír desert. Reinaud says it is to the south-east of Multán, and in the middle of an arid country, apparently on the testimony of 'Utbi, but he makes no such assertion. Hammer-Purgstall conceives it to be the present Baháwalpúr. But how could a dependency of Láhore be on the southern side of Multán, itself independent? How could Mahmúd advance over all the Panjáb rivers to attack a city in a desert? Or Baháwalpúr, leaving a country full of hostile and martial populations in his rear? How could Bijí Rái, deserting his fort, "take post in a wood on the Indus," as Firishta says, if Bhátia were on the other side of the Sutlej? or how could he "take refuge on the top of some hills," as 'Utbí says, when there are no hills within a hundred and twenty miles from either place?

Here again we must correct the reading, and all becomes explicable and easy. The real name of the place is Bhera. It lies on the

[1] D'Herbelot in one part of his article on Mahmúd speaks of his deriving immense plunder from Baarea, the strongest fort in India.

left bank of the Jailam, under the Salt range. It bears evident marks of great antiquity, and has on the opposite side of the river the extensive ruins of Duraria, above Ahmadábád, which strike every beholder with astonishment. The only works which read Bhera are the *Khulásatu-t Tawáríkh* and its followers the *Akbár-i Muhabbat*, etc. That Dow's copy of Firishta must have been very near it, is evident, for, although Mahmúd advances against the city of "Batteea," he is made by a strange inadvertence to take the city of "Tahera." 'Utbí [and Ibn Asír] certainly read Bhátía, and Al Bírúní mentions Bhátía and not Bhera, but his Bhátía scarcely seems the one we are dealing with.

Whether Bhátía is written by mistake, or whether Bhátía is an old name of Bhera, is difficult to say. The latter is very probable, for the Bhatí or Bhattí Rájpúts still point to this tract as the place of their residence before their advance to the eastward, and their name is still preserved in the large town of Pindí Bhattián, on the Chináb. It is worthy of remark, as observed by Mr. E. Thomas,[1] that of the list of Hindú kings given by Al Bírúní, the four last beginning with Jaipál I. add the designation of Pál to that of Deva, borne by their Brahman predecessors. This would imply the succession of a new tribe, which he considers to be Bhattí Rájpút. There is no improbability in this, for there is no authority except that of Firishta for declaring Jaipál to be a Brahman, and Bhátía therefore may have been the local title of the capital of the tribe. Firishta[2] makes the Rájá of Bhátía to be a different personage from the Rájá of Láhore; but he afterwards tells us that the Láhore dominions extended from Kashmír to Multán—which, as has been shown, includes Bhátía.

It is to be observed, moreover, that Mahmúd does not pass through Multán, or the province of Multán, to get there, but passes "by the borders of Multán," as Firishta says, or "crosses the Indus in the neighbourhood of Multán," as 'Utbí says. Now, as Multán must have extended, as it always has, even down to the days of Mulráj, nearly up to the Salt range, it is probable that Mahmúd came from Ghazní by the valley of Banú, and following the course of the

---

[1] *Jour. A. S.*, ix. 184.   [2] Briggs i. 9.

Khuram, crossed the Indus near Isákhel and the old town of Rori, and so, passing the Sind-Ságar Doáb through Mitta Tiwána, reached Bhera by way of Khusháb and Sháhpúr.

A subsequent campaign also indicates the position of Bhera, as will be noticed more particularly hereafter. Meanwhile it is to be observed that Mahmúd annexed Bhera to his dominions, which, had it been any place trans-Sutlej, would have been out of the question.

Fourth Expedition.—Multán. A.H. 396.—[Ibn Asír and] the *Habíbu-s Siyar* place the expedition to Bhátía and Multán in the same year, but it is quite evident from the *Yamíní* that special preparations were made for this new campaign. Dr. Bird considers that Firishta has misplaced this campaign, and that it should be deferred till after the defeat of Ilak Khán. I see no reason whatever to doubt that it is correctly ascribed to the year 396 H., and that it has nothing whatever to do with the invasion which took place after Ilak Khán's defeat.

We find the governor or ruler of Multán with a Muhammadan name, "Abú-l Futúh, or "Abú-l Fath," and he is not an infidel but a heretic, one "who introduced his neologies into religion." There can be little doubt, therefore, that he was a follower of the Karmatian heresy, which we know, from Al Birúní, to have prevailed extensively at Multán, and for a long period previous to this invasion. "He says: "When the Karmatians became masters of Multán, their chief broke the idol in pieces, and massacred its ministers; and the temple, which was built of brick, and situated on an elevated spot, became the grand mosque in place of the old one, which was closed on account of the hatred borne against the Ummayide Khalífas, under whose rule it was constructed. Sultán Mahmúd, after subduing the Karmatians, reopened the old mosque, so that the old one was abandoned; and now it is as a plain, destined to vulgar uses."

The authors which treat of this period do not,—except in a few instances, as the *Tabakát-i Akbarí*, and the *Khulásatu-t Tawáríkh*—expressly say that Multán was held by Karmatians, but by "Muláhida," a more generic term, which, though it might include Karmatians, was more generally, at a subsequent period, used to designate the Isma'ílians.¹ For more on the subject of the occupation of Multán at this period, the passages mentioned in the note may be consulted.²

Abú-l Fath Dáúd was the grandson of Shaikh Hamíd Lodí, who is represented to have done homage to Subuktigín. The word "tribute," used by Briggs, is not authorized. Elphinstone says that Hamíd Khán had joined the enemies of his faith for a cession of the provinces of Multán and Laghmán, and submitted to Subuktigín after his victory over the Hindús. This statement is made on the authority of Firishta.³ Dáúd invited the co-operation of Anandpál, who, being defeated at Pesháwar, was pursued as far as Sodra,⁴ on the Chináb. From Sodra Mahmúd goes, by way of Batinda, to Multán, which is so circuitous a route as to be absurd. Here, again, Bhera should be read, which is in the direct line between Sodra and Multán.

Ibn Asír, Mírkhond, and Haidar Rází make Dáúd flee away to Sarandíp, but 'Utbí says a fine was levied from the inhabitants of 20,000,000 dirhams. Firishta says an annual tribute was fixed on Dáúd of 20,000 golden dirhams, or dínárs, with promise of implicit obedience and abstinence from heresy for the future.

The *Biographie Universelle* contains a curious statement, respecting this expedition: "La révolte du gouverneur qu'il avait laissé à Moultan et le débordement des fleuves qui semblait la favoriser, obligèrent Mahmoud de demander passage à Andbal. Sur son refus, il le poursuivit à travers le Candahar et le Kaboulistan jusqu' à Kaschmyre."⁵ What Kandahár and Kábulistán have to do with the pursuit is not easy to say. Authors agree in saying Mahmúd wished to march through Anandpál's territory, but it is very difficult to discern the reason of the request, as he had already crossed the

¹ Deféremery, *Histoire des Seldjoukides*, pp. 59, 86, 136-9.
² Reinaud, *Fragments Arabes et Persans*, p. 142. Ritter, *Erdkunde von Asien*, Vol. V. p. 6. Renaudot, *Anciennes Relations*, p. 172. Núru-l Hakk, *Zubdatu-t Tawáríkh*, fol. 366. Mír Ma'súm, *Táríkh-i Sind*, Ch. 2 and 3. *Khulásatu-t Tawáríkh*, v. "Baber." *Mír-átu-l Álam*, v. "Bahá-d dín Muhammad Zakariyá." *Tuhfatu-l Kirám*, Vol. III. v. "Multán." *Hadíkatu-l Akálím*, v. "Dipálpúr."
³ Briggs I. 9.
⁴ Hammer-Purgstall identifies Sodra with Weirabad (Wazírábád), but they are two different towns.
⁵ [This statement is generally supported by Ibn Asír. See *supra*, p. 24.]

Indus, beyond the borders of his territory, and by a route which would lead him more directly towards his object.

'Unsurí informs us that Mahmúd took two hundred forts on his way to Multán.

Fifth Expedition.[1]—*Defeat of Nawása Sháh,* A.H. 398.—When Mahmúd was called away from Multán by Ílak Khán's invasion of his territory, he left his Indian possessions in charge of Sewakpál, or "Sukhpál, a son of one of the Rájás of India,"[2] and who, having been formerly made a prisoner in Peshawar by Abú 'Alí Sanjarí, had become a convert to Islám. Sukhpál was taken prisoner by Mahmúd's advance cavalry, and was compelled to pay the sum of 400,000 dirhams; and being made over, as Firishta informs us, to Tigín the Treasurer, was kept in confinement during the rest of his life.[3]

Dr. Bird says that there was no such expedition as this, and that Firishta has confounded it with the previous expedition to Multán; but as it is mentioned by 'Utbí, Mírkhond, and Khondamír, as well as by Firishta, there is no reason whatever to discredit it.

Dr. Bird adduces, as an additional proof of confusion, that the name Nawása, "a grandson," belonged to Abú-l Fath Dáúd, because he was a grandson of Sheikh Hamíd Lodí; but there is no ground for saying that Dáúd was so called, as the name might have belonged just as well to the grandson of Jaipál, as of Sheikh Hamíd. He apostatised to idolatry, after being converted, whereas Dáúd could only have apostatised to the Karmatian heresy, and not to idolatry and plural worship. The designation of Nawása is considered doubtful. His name was Sewakpál or Sukhpál; Bitter says Samukkel. Dow reads "Shoekpal, who, on conversion to Islám,

---

[1] [Under the year 397 H. Ibn Asír gives the following brief account of this expedition:—"When Yamínu-d daula had finished (his differences) with the Turks he went on a campaign to India. The cause of this was that one of the sons of the sovereign of India named Nawása Sháh had become a Musulmán under the hands of Mahmúd, and had then been appointed ruler over part of Mahmúd's conquests in that country. After Mahmúd had retired he apostatised from Islám and assisted the infidels and rebels. When Mahmúd approached, the Hindu fled before him, so he again occupied the country, brought it once more under the rule of Islám, appointed one of his officers over it, and then returned to Ghazní."]

[2] [These are the words of Firishta according to the lithographed edition of the text.]

[3] Haidar Rází says that Mahmúd came to Naubár, in pursuit of the rebel, who fled to the remote parts of Ílíad, on learning his approach.

assumed the name Zab Sais." D'Herbelot has "Nevescha;" S. de Sacy, "Nawaschteh;" Wilken, "Nuvasch Shah." The *Tabakát-i Akbari* says, "Súkpál, the grandson of the Rájá of Hind." The readings in Firishta are by no means uniform. They are *Ab sabári*, *Abeár*, *Ab bashácr* and *Záb sá*. The *Tárikh-i Alfí*, and some other authorities, make it Záb Sais or Záb Sháh. Hammer-Purgstall says, "Sesbas, or Schiwekpal." All these are changes rung upon the word "nawása," or "grandson," especially "a daughter's child." Bird says, Price is mistaken in calling him Nawása Sháh; but 'Utbí gives this name, and there is no reason why we should reject it. It may have been bestowed upon him by Mahmúd as a mark of endearment, and Shah, "king," may have been added as a term of aggrandizement, or it might have been Sáh, a common title of respect. But what is more probable than all is that he was the grandchild (by a daughter) of Jaipál, because, in 'Utbí's account of the expedition to Kanauj, we find Bhím Pál, the great-grandson, complaining that his uncle had been forcibly converted to Islám. *Sukh Pál*, therefore, was the name, *Nawása* the relationship to Jaipál, and *Sáh* the honorific title. He was probably one of the relations of Jaipál, made over by him as hostage to Mahmúd; and that, perhaps, was the period of conversion.

The movement by which his seizure was effected was so rapid, and a new invasion of India was entered upon so soon after, that it is probable the scene of the transaction was the valley of Peshawar.

Sixth Expedition.— Waihind, Nagarkot.[1] A.H. 399 (1008–9 A.D.).— It will be observed that the account of the commencement of this expedition is described very differently in the *Yamíni*, the *Habíbu-s Siyar* and Firishta. I prefer, as on former occasions, the former, the river of Waihind, or the Indus, being a more probable place of action than Peshawar, which was then within the Muhammadan border. That the Gakkhars may have performed the part assigned to them is probable enough, whether the action was fought at one place or the

[1] [Ibn Asír places this campaign in the year 368, and says that Mahmúd encountered Brahman-pál on "the banks of the river Waihand (which is changed in some MSS. to Handmand). Many men were lost in the waters, and the Hindús were near gaining a victory, when God made the Musulmáns to triumph. Mahmúd pursued the foe to Bhím-nughur (Bhím-nagar), which he took, and gained immense plunder."]

other; but that the Gakkhars are the ancestors of the modern Játs, as Dr. Bird asserts, is altogether a mistake, and likely to lead to serious errors.

About the proceedings at Nagarkot all accounts agree, and that Nagarkot is the same as Kot Kángrá can admit of no doubt, for the name of Nagarkot is still used. Its position is well described, and corresponds with present circumstances. The impassable waters which surround it are the Bán-ganga and the Biyáh. The town of Bhím, which is about a mile from the fort, is now on the spot called Bhawan, which means a temple raised to a Sakti, or female deity, and Bhím is probably a mistake arising from its presumed foundation by the heroic Bhím. M. Reinaud considers that it was called Bhím-nagar from Sri Bhíma deva, of the Kábul dynasty. The different forms which the name assumes in different authors are shown at p. 34. Elphinstone is mistaken in saying that Nagarkot derived peculiar sanctity from a natural flame which issued from the ground within its precincts. This flame is at Jwálá-mukhí, fifteen miles distant, where carburetted hydrogen issues from the sandstone rocks, and fills the superstitious pilgrim with awe and veneration. These jets of gas are made to burn with increased vigour by the removal of plugs, whenever a distinguished visitor is likely to pay well for this recognition of his superior sanctity.

Dr. Bird, who has given a most critical examination of these invasions, says that the capture of Nagarkot and the previous action beyond the Indus occurred in two different years. He observes: "If we might trust Firishta, Mahmúd at this time (after the battle of Peshawar) marching into the mountains captured the celebrated fortress of Nagarkot. It was not, however, till the following year, A.H. 400, according to the *Tabakát-i Akbarí* and *Habíbu-s Siyar*, that this expedition was undertaken; and as the hostile armies prior to the last battle had consumed three or four months in operations west of the Indus, it is not probable that Mahmúd could have marched into India at the commencement of the rainy season. The Hijra year 399 given for the march to Peshawar, or the previous year A.D. commenced the 5th September, A.D., 1008; and as the spring season, when he left Ghazní, would not commence till A.D. 1009, he must have spent the summer in Kábul, and set out for Hindústán about October."

I cannot trace in the *Tabakát-i Akbari* and the *Habíbu-s Siyar* the assertion attributed to them; but let us leave these inferior authorities and refer to the *Yamini*. There we find that it is in pursuit (of the flying enemy) that Mahmúd went as far as the fort called Bhímnagar." The campaign, therefore, must have been continuous, and there was no break between the action trans-Indus and the capture of Nagarkot. He has already traversed the same road as far as Sodra on the Chináb, and he would only have had ten or twelve marches over a new line of country.

In these enquiries we must be very cautious how we deal with the word "spring." Both Dird and Elphinstone speak of the conquerors setting out in the spring of a Christian year, but the spring of a Ghaznivide invader is the autumn of the Christian year. It is the period when the breaking up of the rains admits of warlike operations. It is the *Dasahra* of the Hindús, and the season of the commencement of their campaigns. So, in the first decisive action against Jaipál, we find Mahmúd leaving Ghazní in August, and fighting the action at Peshawar in November. And so here we find him leaving Ghazní on the last day of Rabí'u-l ákhir, or the end of December, which, though unusually late in the season—so late, indeed, as to render marching in the uplands almost impossible—would still have enabled him to fight his action on the Indus at the beginning of February. He might then have completed his operations at Kángrá before the end of March, and have left India again before the severe heat commenced. The only difficulty about the whole campaign is his leaving Ghazní in the heart of winter; but that the action on the Indus and the one at Nagarkot occurred in the fair weather of the same year, there is no sufficient reason to doubt.

The opening part of the expedition is mentioned in more detail by Firishta, than by 'Utbí and Khondamír. His account is as follows:—

"In the year 399 H., Mahmúd having collected his forces, determined again to invade Hindústan, and punish Anandpál, who had shewn much insolence during the late invasion of Multán. Anandpál hearing of his intentions, sent ambassadors on all sides, inviting the assistance of the other princes of Hindústán, who now considered the expulsion of the Muhammadans from India as a sacred duty.

APPENDIX. 447

Accordingly, the Rájas of Ujjain, Gwáliár, Kálinjar, Kanauj, Dehlí, and Ajmír entered into a confederacy, and, collecting their forces, advanced towards the Panjáb with a greater army than had ever taken the field against Amír Subuktigín. Anandpál himself took the command, and advanced to meet the invader. The Indians and Muhammadans arrived in sight of each other on the plain of Peshāwar, where they remained encamped forty days, neither side shewing any eagerness to come to action. The troops of the idolators daily increased in number, and aid came to them from all sides. The infidel Gakkhars also joined them in great strength, and made extraordinary exertions to resist the Musulmáns. The Hindú females, on this occasion, sold their jewels, and sent the proceeds from distant parts to their husbands, so that they, being supplied with all necessaries for the march, might be in earnest in the war. Those who were poor contributed from their earnings by spinning cotton, and other labour. The Sultán perceived that on this occasion the idolaters behaved most devotedly, and that it was necessary to be very circumspect in striking the first blow. He therefore entrenched his camp, that the infidels might not be able to penetrate therein.

Mahmúd, having thus secured himself, ordered six thousand archers to the front to attack, and endeavour to draw the enemy near to his entrenchments, where the Musulmáns were prepared to receive them. In spite of the Sultán's precautions, during the heat of the battle, 30,000 infidel Gakkhars, with their heads and feet bare, and armed with spears and other weapons, penetrated on two sides into the Muhammadan lines, and forcing their way into the midst of the cavalry, they cut down men and horse with their swords, daggers, and spears, so that, in a few minutes, they slaughtered three or four thousand Muhammadans. They carried their success so far that the Sultán, observing the fury of these Gakkhar footmen, withdrew himself from the thick of the fight, that he might stop the battle for that day. But it so happened that the elephant upon which Anandpál rode, becoming unruly from the effects of the naphtha-balls and the flights of arrows, turned and fled. The Hindús, deeming this to be the signal for flight on the part of their general, all gave way, and fled. 'Abdu-llah Táí, with five or six thousand Arab horse, and Arslán Jázib, with 10,000 Turks, Afgháns, and Khiljís, pursued the enemy for two days and nights, so that 5,000 Hindús were killed in the retreat. Thirty elephants and enormous booty fell into the hands of the pursuers, with which they returned to the Sultán."[1]

Seventh Expedition.—Nárdín. A.H. 400.—The *Tabakát-i Akbarí* and Firishta do not mention this expedition at all; but it is recorded in the *Yamíní, Rauzatu-s Safá* and the *Habíbu-s Siyar*. The latter gives no name, but mentions an invasion of Hind in A.H. 400, between the transactions at Nagarkot and Ghor.

It is not easy to identify the place. 'Utbí speaks of it as in the middle of Hind, where chiefs were reduced who up to that time had obeyed no master. Mírkhond calls it "Nárín;" S. de Sacy has "Nardín," which he thinks there is reason to believe was situated in a part of India to the west of the Indus. This would be probable enough had it not been declared by 'Utbí to be in the heart of India, and a country of hill and valley. Hammer-Purgstall speaks of the "Mahárájá of Nardín." Reinaud confounds the campaigns of Náráin and Nardín.

On his return to Ghazní, after this expedition, Mahmúd received an embassy from the ruler of Hind (Jaipál), offering an annual tribute of fifty elephants, laden with rarities, and an Indian force of two thousand men—a curious stipulation, proving how early Indians became mercenary soldiers, even under their most bitter persecutors. This shows that this particular expedition must have made a great impression on Jaipál, and induced him to sue for humiliating terms.

It is barely possible that the Nárín,[2] between Inderáb and Kúndúz, may be indicated. It is the same longitude as Kábul, which we know to have been then comprised in India; and, with reference to Balkh and Ghazni, it might have been considered so far to the eastward and so difficult of access, as to deserve being spoken of as in the heart of Hind. In Istakhrí's map of Khurásán, the position is almost included within "Bilád Hind," and its neighbourhood to

---

[1] [This and the other passages from Firishta, are taken from Briggs' translation, but I have compared them with the text, and have made the translations more literal and exact.—ED.]

[2] This town is not mentioned by the Arab geographers, but it was passed by Lieut. Wood. See his *Journey to the Oxus*, p. 409.

Káfiristán gives colour to the mention of the "chief of the infidels." What militates greatly against this supposition is, that elephants formed part of the booty; and there are many other considerations also which compel us to look out for Náráin elsewhere.

Under all the circumstances mentioned, I am disposed to look upon Náráin as meant for Anhalwára, the capital of Gujarát, which Abú Ríhán tells us was called Nárána or Náráin in his time. It is to be observed that Mahmúd merely proceeded *towards*, not *to*, Náráin, and the country in the direction of Ajmír and Rájpútána was open to his incursions by the previous conquests of Bhátia and Multán. This was, perhaps, merely a preparative to his expedition to Somnát, and the reports he received of its wealth may, on this occasion, have sharpened his appetite for plundering that temple. This expedition would have been sufficient to instil alarm into Jaipál. Náráin was "in the middle of Hind," and Mahmúd would have advanced towards it "over ground hard and soft," and there "the friends of God might have committed slaughter in every hill and valley." It is evident from the statements in the *Mir-át-i Mas'údí*, that the Musulmáns had some relations with Ajmír previous to 401 H.; and it was, probably, on this particular occasion that it was visited by Mahmúd. The visit which that work makes him pay at a later period, just previous to the conquest of Kanauj, seems highly improbable.[1]

Eighth Expedition.—Multán. A.H. 401.—In the year 401, after the conquest of Ghor, Mahmúd marched to Multán, where he maimed and imprisoned the Karmatians and other heretics, and brought Dáúd prisoner to Ghazní, and confined him in the fort of Ghúrak for life. The *Tabakát-i Badúúní* says Ghori, and as Mahmúd had just conquered Ghor, it is not improbable that he may have confined his prisoner there.

The authorities for this expedition are the reverse of those for the last. It is mentioned in the *Tabakát-i Akbari* and Firishta, and it is not mentioned in the *Yamíní*, *Rauzatu-s Safá* and *Habíbu-s Siyar*. This would give reason to surmise that these two were in reality but one expedition, but the circumstances of the two are so different, not

[1] [I have allowed this notice of the Seventh Expedition to remain as it was written by Sir H. Elliot, but were he alive, he would probably change or greatly modify his opinions after a perusal of the note upon Nárána by Gen. Cunningham, printed at p. 393, vol. I. of this work.—ED.]

admitting in any way of the same construction; and they are so
consonant with the vow made by Mahmúd, that he would engage in
a religious war every year, that there is no reason to reject either as
improbable. The omission by 'Utbí is important, but others of a
similar kind will have to be noticed; and while I am prepared to
admit that we must not impugn what he actually states; yet he may,
perhaps, have omitted, through ignorance or negligence, some transactions which actually took place. The *Mir-át-i Mas'údí* says that
after this second capture and plunder of Multán, it was deserted, and
that Anandpál, who is there called "the Zamíndár of Multán," had
fled to Uch, where he resided.

Ninth Expedition.—Nindúna [or *Nárdín*.][1] A.H. 404 (1013 A.D.)—
Firishta inserts the expedition to Tháncsar in A.H. 402, but I am
disposed to follow the *Yamíní*, and place that expedition subsequent.
The long delay which occurred between this and the eighth expedition
may have been owing to the league which was entered into between
Anandpál and Mahmúd, and this invasion may have been occasioned
by the death of Anandpál, which according to Firishta occurred at this
time. A very full account of the preparations for this expedition will
be found among the extracts from the *Yamíní*, where it is stated that it
was entered upon in the year 404—a year to which all the other
authors ascribe it. Here we find the invader starting before the
winter set in, and his progress arrested by a heavy fall of snow—so
he could not have left the highlands till the commencement of
spring; and as the year began on the 13th of July, 1013, he could
scarcely have entered Hindústán before February, 1014, leaving himself but a short time for operations in that country.

Consequently, we find him proceeding no farther than the hill of
Bálnát,[2] a conspicuous mountain overhanging the Jailam, and now
generally called Tilla, which means a hill. It is still occasionally called
Bálnát, and there is a famous Jogí establishment on its highest
summit of great repute, and resorted to by members of that fra-
ternity from the most distant parts of India.

[1] [The *Yamíní* calls the place Nárdín (*supra*, p. 87), and so does Ibn Asír. The *Habíbu-s Siyar* also has Núrdín. The two former place the conquest in 404 H., but the latter in 406 H. The expeditions to Nárain and Nárdin are confounded by some writers, both Oriental and European.]

[2] [In the text of Firishta the name is "Bálnát," not "Bulnát," as in the translation. Sanskrit, "Bála-náth.]

APPENDIX. 451

The action which preceded the capture of Ninduna appears to have been fought at the Márgala pass, which answers well to the description given of it by 'Utbí. The subsequent operations are described more fully by Nizámu-d dín Ahmad:—

"In A.H. 404, the Sultán marched his army against the fort of Ninduna, situated on the mountain of Bálnáth. Púr¹ Jaipál left veteran troops for its protection, while he himself passed into one of the mountain valleys *(darra)* of Kashmír. The Sultán having reached Ninduna, invested it, and by mining and other modes of attack, put the garrison under the necessity of capitulating. Sultán Mahmúd with a few of his personal attendants entered it, and took all the property he found there. Having left Sárogh as governor of the fort,² he himself proceeded to the Kashmír valley, where Púr Jaipál had taken up his position. This chief, however, did not await his arrival, but fled, and when the Sultán reached the pass he obtained great spoil and a large number of slaves. He also converted many infidels to Muhammadanism, and having spread Islám in that country, returned to Ghazní."—*Tabakát-i Akbarí.*

It will be observed that 'Utbí calls the chief "Nidar Bhím," and Nizámu-d dín Ahmad calls him Purú Jaipál, but the difference is reconciled by considering Nidar Bhím as the governor, whom Jaipál left in the garrison when he fled towards Kashmír; and as we know from the *Yamíní* that Purú Jaipál's son was called Bhím-pál, we may consider this governor to have been the identical Bhím-pál, with the epithet of Nidar, "the dauntless."

The name of Ninduna cannot be restored. It is evidently the same place as is mentioned in Wassáf as being a noted town in the Júd hills, and by 'Abbas Shírwání in his *Shír-sháhí.* D'Herbelot calls it "Marvin," in which he is followed by Rampoldi, who confounds it with the capture of Thánesar. Dow calls it Nindoona, S. de Sacy, "Nazin" and "Nazdin." Briggs, "Nindoona." Mírkhond speaks of the victory, but does not name the place. Ritter places it near Muzaffarábád, because one stage to the west of it lies a place called "Dunni."

¹ ["Taro" in the MS. I have used.]
² At the beginning of Mas'úd's reign we still find this chief occupying the same post, according to Abú-l Fazl Baihakí.

The pass to which the Rájá fled was doubtless that of Bhímbar, or it might have been near where the Jailam debouches into the plains. Either way, Mahmúd would not have had far to go before his return to Ghazní. Briggs is wrong in representing him as plundering Kashmír. The original mentions nothing but a pass leading into Kashmír.

Tenth Expedition.—Thánesar. A.H. 405.—The *Habíbu-s Siyar* makes this expedition occur in the same year as the one to Bálnát. The *Rauzatu-s Safá* ascribes it to the following year. The *Yamíní* makes it occur subsequent to the Bálnát campaign, but says nothing about Mahmúd's returning intermediately to Ghazní. We have seen, however, that the season was so late as not to admit of his proceeding to Thánesar direct from Bálnát, unless he passed the season of the rains in India, which is not probable. The *Táríkh-i Alfí* omits all notice of this expedition.

Supposing Thánesar to have been the place visited, it is difficult to reconcile 'Utbí's narrative with the geographical features of the country. If Mahmúd had reached Thánesar by crossing the upper part of the desert of Rájpútána, he could have come to no stream with large stone or precipitous banks, or one flowing through a hill-pass. If, again, he had come to any stream with such characteristics he would nowhere have had anything like a desert to pass. Chandiol on the Chináb would alone answer the description, but that would be only halfway to Thánesar.

Firishta's account is as follows :—

"In the year 402 Mahmúd resolved on the conquest of Thánesar,[1] in the kingdom of Hindústán. It had reached the ears of the king that Thánesar was held in the same veneration by idolaters, as Mecca by the faithful ; that there was an old temple there, in which they had set up a number of idols, the principal of which was called Jagsom, and was believed to have existed ever since the creation of the world. When Mahmúd reached the Panjáb, he was desirous that, in accordance with the subsisting treaty with Anandpál, no injury should be sustained by that prince's country, in consequence

---

[1] Briggs and Hammer-Purgstall represent this place as thirty miles west from Dehli, but it is one hundred and twenty miles north of it.

of the Muhammadan army passing through it. An embassy was accordingly sent to inform the Rája of his design against Thánesar, and desiring him to depute his officers to remain with the army, in order that the villages and towns which belonged to him might be protected from the camp followers.

"Anandpál, agreeing to this proposal, prepared an entertainment for the reception of the king, at the same time issuing orders for all his subjects to supply the camp with every necessary of life.

"The Rája's brother, with two thousand horse, was also sent to meet the army, and to deliver the following message:[1]—'My brother is the subject and tributary of the king, but he begs permission to acquaint his majesty that the temple of Thánesar is the principal place of worship of the inhabitants of the country; that, although the religion of the king makes it an important and meritorious duty to destroy idols, still the king has already acquitted himself of this duty, in the destruction of the idols in the fort of Nagarkot. If he should be pleased to alter his resolution regarding Thánesar, and to fix a tribute to be paid by the country, Anandpál promises that the amount of it shall be annually paid to Mahmúd; besides which, on his own part, he will present him with fifty elephants, and jewels to a considerable amount.'

"Mahmúd replied: The religion of the faithful inculcates the following tenet: 'That in proportion as the tenets of the Prophet are diffused, and his followers exert themselves in the subversion of idolatry, so shall be their reward in heaven;' that, therefore, it behoved him, with the assistance of God, to root out the worship of idols from the face of all India. How, then, should he spare Thánesar.

"This answer was communicated to the Rája of Dehli, who, resolving to oppose the invaders, sent messengers throughout Hindústán to acquaint the other Rájas that Mahmúd, without provocation, was marching with a vast army to destroy Thánesar, now under his immediate protection. He observed that if a barrier was not expeditiously raised against this roaring torrent, the country of Hindústán would be soon overwhelmed, and every state, small and great,

---

[1] Hammer-Purgstall says that Anandpál, the Rája of Multán, sent his brother Muhammad to deliver this message. The confusion of names is surprising in such an author.

would be entirely subverted. It, therefore, behoved them to unite their forces at Thánesar, to avert the impending calamity.

"Mahmúd having reached Thánesar before the Hindús had time to assemble for its defence, the city was plundered, the idols broken, and the idol Jagsom was sent to Ghaznín, to be trodden under foot in the street, and decapitated. Immense wealth was found in the temples. According to Hájí Muhammad Kandahárí, a ruby was found in one of them, weighing 450 miskáls, the equal of which no one had ever seen or heard of.

"Mahmúd, after the capture of Thánesar, was desirous of proceeding to reduce Dehlí; but his nobles told him that it would be impossible to keep possession of it, till he had rendered the Panjáb a province of his own government, and had secured himself from all apprehension of Anandpál (Rája of Láhore). The king resolved, therefore, for the present, to proceed no further, till he had accomplished these objects. Anandpál, however, conducted himself with so much policy and hospitality towards Mahmúd,[1] that the Sultán returned peaceably to Ghaznín. On this occasion, the Muhammadan army brought to Ghaznín 200,000 captives, so that the capital appeared like an Indian city, for every soldier of the army had several slaves and slave girls."—*Firishta*.

There is nothing in the *Yamíní* to warrant this mention of Dehlí, the existence of which is nowhere alluded to by contemporary writers. The frequent mention therefore by Firishta of Dehlí and its Rájá, in the transactions with the Ghaznivides, seems not to rest on any solid foundation.

Mírkhond makes no mention of Thánesar by name, but speaks of the "Moslem" elephants. 'Utbí and Khondamír make mention of these elephants in connection with Thánesar. Though Firishta leaves no doubt that he considered the holy Thánesar to be meant, it is probable some other place may be alluded to; yet I know no place in India where he could, immediately after crossing a desert, have come upon a stream flowing through a hill-pass, except it be Kach Gandáva in Sindh, which is obviously out of the direction.

Dr. Bird considers Nárdín to have been in Káfiristán, and

---

[1] [This sentence is not in the printed text.]

Thánesar to be Panjshír, which is the name of a river joining that of Ghorband, and giving name to a pass which leads through Hindú Kush from Kábul to Turkistán, but here we should want both the desert and the elephants.

The term "Moslem" elephants is curious. The *Universal History* endeavours to explain the word thus :—

"Mahmúd Ibn Subuktigín now undertook another expedition into India, and reduced the kingdom of Marwin, which had a capital of the same name. Here he was informed that an Indian idolatrous prince occupied a province, which produced a race of elephants, called Moslem, or faithful elephants. This information excited him to attempt the conquest of that province; which having effected, he brought off with him a vast quantity of spoil, and a great number of those elephants. They were termed Moslem, or faithful elephants, because they sometimes performed a sort of genuflexion and prostration not unlike those of the Moslems or Muhammedans; which induced many of the latter to believe that they were religious animals."

Dr. Bird calls them "elephants of Sulaiman." S. de Sacy, "Sailèman." Wilken, "Moslem." With regard to their being Moslems and their adoration and genuflexions, see D'Herbelot, Art. "Fil." The *Jámi'u-t Tawáríkh* and D'Herbelot designate them as Musulmán. The reading of the *Yamíní* and of Ibn Asír is "Sailamán,"[1] which no doubt is related to the word Sailán and like "Sailání," signifies merely "Ceylonese elephants."

Eleventh Expedition.—Lohkot.[2] A.H. 406.—This was an attempt to penetrate into Kashmir, which was entirely unsuccessful, for Mahmúd advanced no further than Lohkot, and then returned. There is no allusion to it in the *Yamíní*,[3] the *Rauzatu-s Safá*, or the *Habíbu-s Siyar*,

[1] [The name is written with *sadd*, not with *sín*, which is fatal to the supposed connection with "Moslem."]

[2] [This place appears again in the "Fourteenth Expedition" of the year 413 H. (page 461 *infra*), where also the siege was unsuccessful. The circumstances of the two accounts are so similar as to make it probable that they relate to the same event. There is no record of the siege in the *Yamíní*, the inference to be drawn from which fact is that it occurred after the close of that work in 413 H.]

[3] There is an allusion to an attempt in Kashmir at the opening of the Kanauj Expedition, but this seems only to imply that he marched under the Lower Kashmir hills. Hammer-Purgstall actually represents Mahmúd as plundering the *capital* of Kashmir.

but it is mentioned in the *Tárikh-i Alfí*, the *Tabakát-i Akbarí*, and Firishta.¹ The *Tabakát-i Akbarí* ascribes it to the year 407, and calls the place simply Kot. Reinaud² considers that this attack was made during the expedition to Kanauj, but this is highly improbable; for though the governor of the passes leading into Kashmír came to pay his respects on that occasion, Mahmúd did not penetrate even the lower hills.

The position of Lohkot is difficult to fix. It is perhaps the same strong place which Al Bírúní and Rashídu-d dín speak of as Lohúr or Loháwar, in the hills of Kashmír³; and as they describe it as not far from Rájáwar, one of the boundaries of Hind, on the north, I think we may look for an identification in the present Kotta, where there is a lofty fort of evident antiquity. If so, he must have returned by the bed of the Panjál river, and the waters from which he could not extricate his army must have been those of the Jailam, expanding over the plain so accurately described by Quintus Curtius, and so faithful to present appearances.

Firishta thus speaks of this campaign:—

"Mahmúd, in the year 406, again marched with the design of entering Kashmír, and besieged the fort of Loh-kot, which was remarkable on account of its height and strength. After a while, when the snow began to fall, and the season became intensely cold, and the enemy received reinforcements from Kashmír, the Sultán was obliged to abandon his design, and return to Ghaznín. On his route, having lost his way, he came upon a place where the whole plain was covered with water—wherever they went they saw nothing but water. Many of his troops perished. This was the first disaster that the Sultán suffered in his campaigns against India. After some days he extricated himself with great difficulty from his peril, and reached Ghaznín without having achieved any success."

Twelfth Expedition.—Kanauj, Mathura. A.H. 409.—A full account has been given of this celebrated invasion by 'Utbi and Khondamír. As the statement of Nizámu-d dín differs from Firishta in some

¹ [The Asír makes a brief reference to it under the year 406, recording only Mahmúd's great losses from the waters. He does not name the place.]
² *Fragments, Arabes et Persans*, p. 118.   ³ [Vol. I. pp. 62–65.]

respects, it is given below. It is to be observed that all the authors, except Mirkhond, concur in representing that 409 H. was the year of this invasion, and most of them mention that he set out in the spring. This gives occasion to Dr. Bird to observe:—"As the spring season is mentioned, and as Hijra 409 commenced on the 20th May, A.D. 1018, Mahmúd must have left Ghazní in the end of the preceding year, 408, which would correspond with the spring of A.D. 1018. Muhammadan historians, not attending to the fact of the seasons west of the Indus being the same as those in Europe, and forgetting the particular commencement of the Hijra years, are constantly committing such blunders." Consequently he makes six or seven months to elapse before Mahmúd reaches Kanauj.

Here, with all due deference be it said, Dr. Bird seems to have fallen into the very error which he condemns; for it is abundantly evident that here, as has already been observed respecting the sixth expedition,[1] that the Indian spring after the close of the rains is meant. That spring occurs in Afghánistán much about the same time as our own in Europe is admitted. Indeed, it is observed in Afghánistán with the same kind of joyous festivities as it was in Europe, before more utilitarian notions prevailed; but in this instance, where the months are mentioned, we can be left in no manner of doubt. Starting in the spring, we find from 'Utbi that Mahmúd crossed the Jumna on the 20th of Rajab, 409=December 1018, and reached Kanauj on the 8th of Sha'bán, 409=January, 1019, and as this is declared to be a three months' journey, he must have started in October, so that he might have the whole of the six months of the cold season before him. The spring therefore alluded to was evidently not in accordance with the European season.

Elphinstone has been led into the same error by following the guidance of Dr. Bird, and observes:—"The whole of this expedition is indistinctly related by Firishta. He copies the Persian writers, who, adverting to the season in their own country, make Mahmúd begin his march in spring. Had he done so he need not have gone so high in search of fords, but he would have reached Kanauj at the beginning of the periodical rains, and carried on all his subsequent movements in the midst of rivers during that season. It is probable

[1] Supra, p. 445.

he would go to Peshawar before the snow set in above the passes, and would cross the Indus early in November."

In this last passage he acutely suggests as Mahmúd's probable movement, that which actually occurred, except that he must have crossed the Indus in October. There is, therefore, no correction necessary, and the native authorities have been wrongly censured.

He continues:—"His marches are still worse detailed. He goes first to Kanauj; then back to Mírat, and then back again to Mattra. There is no clue to his route, advancing or retiring. He probably came down by Mírat, but it is quite uncertain how he returned." Dr. Bird also remarks upon Firishta's ignorance of geography, upon the army moving about in all directions, without any obvious reason.

All this arises from following Firishta too implicitly, without referring to more original and authentic sources. The statement in the *Yamíni* is clear enough, and it does not appear why Firishta should have departed from it.

The *Yamíni* says that, after passing by the borders of Kashmír, that is, close under the sub-Himalayan range, and crossing the Jumna, Mahmúd takes Baran, which is the ancient name of the present Bulandshahr, for which more modern authors, not knowing what "Baran" was, substitute "Mírat"—then Kulchand's fort, which is the Mahában of the other—then crossing the Jumna he takes Mathura—and then recrossing the Jumna, he proceeds to Kanauj, and takes that and its seven detached forts, of which the ruins of some may still be traced. He then goes to Munj, " a city of Bráhmans," or, as Briggs says, " of Rájpúts," for which there is no authority—his original being merely "fighting men." This place must be the same as the old town of Manjháwan, or Majháwan, the ruins of which are still visible on the Pandú river, ten miles south of Kánhpúr. It is in the heart of the country of the Kanauji Bráhmans. He then proceeds to Chandálbhor's fort of Asní, lower down on the banks of the Ganges, ten miles N.E. from Fathpúr, where at a later period we find Jaichand depositing his treasure. It is a very old town, founded, it is said, by Aswaní Kumára, the son of Súraj, who held a sacrifice there, and founded a city called after his own name. On the 25th of Sha'bán, after capturing Sharwa or Sarúa,—which I conceive to be either Seunra on the Ken, between Kálinjar and Banda, or Sriswagarh on the Pahonj, not far from Kánch,—he reaches the retreat of Chand Rái in the hills. These hills must be those of Bundelkhand, for there are no others which he could have reached before the close of Sha'bán, seeing he only arrived at Kanauj on the 8th. There is to be sure no mention of his crossing or recrossing the Jumna, but this is no valid objection, for neither is there any mention of his crossing the Panjáb on his return to Ghazní. Of the two places mentioned above, in the plains of Bundelkhand, Sriswa-garh or Sriswa-garh, appears the most probable; for we know it to have been a place of considerable importance in the annals of the Bundelkhand Rájas; for about two centuries after this, the bard Chand informs us, that several chiefs were slain in defending it against Pirthí Rái of Dehli, who for the purpose of capturing it, had crossed the river Sind, which was the boundary between his dominions and those of Parmál Chandel, the Rája of Mahoba. It is to be observed that no other author except 'Utbí mentions the name of Sharwa— later authors not being able to identify it. Mahmúd's progress under the explanation now given appears to have been regular and consistent.

The *Rauzatu-s Safá* observes the same order, with the omission of some of the names. First, the fort of a converted Hindú (Baran); then the fort of Kulchand (Mahában); then the holy city not mentioned by name (Mathura); then Kanauj; then Munj; then the fort of Chandpál; and lastly, the pursuit of Chand Rája. The *Habíbu-s Siyar* follows this statement, omitting all occurrences after the capture of Kanauj. Nizámu-d dín and Firishta have reversed this order, and make Mahmúd proceed direct to Kanauj, then back to Mírat or Barun, then to Mahában, then to Mathura, then to the seven forts on the banks of a river, which the *Táríkh-i Alfí* adds were under the Dehli Rája; then to Munj, then to the fort of Chandpál, then in pursuit of Chandrái.

The following is extracted from Nizámu-d dín Ahmad. The number of troops which accompanied the Sultán is not mentioned. 'Utbí says he had 20,000 volunteers from Transoxiana. Mirkhond says these were in addition to his own troops. Firishta says he had 100,000 chosen horse and 20,000 northern foot.

"In A.H. 409, Sultán Mahmúd marched at the head of his army with the resolution of conquering the kingdom of Kanauj. When, having crossed seven dreadful rivers, he reached the confines of that kingdom, the governor of the place, whose name was Kora, submitted to him, sought his protection, and sent him presents.[1]

"The Sultán then arrived at the fort of Barna. The governor, whose name was Hardat, left the fort under the care of his tribe and relations,[2] and sought to conceal himself elsewhere. The garrison, finding themselves unable to defend the fort, capitulated in a few days, agreeing to pay a thousand times a thousand (1,000,000) dirhams, which is equal to 2,50,000 rupees, and also to present him with thirty elephants.

"The Sultán marched thence to the fort of Maháwan, on the banks of the river Jumna. The chief of the place, whose name was Kulchandar, mounted his elephant with the intention of crossing over the stream and flying away, but the Sultán's army pursued, and when they approached him he killed himself with his dagger.

"To live in the power of an enemy
Is much worse than to die."

The fort was captured, and eighty-five elephants, besides much other booty, fell into the hands of the victors.

"Proceeding from this place, the king arrived at Mathura,[3] which was a very large city full of magnificent temples. It is the birth-place of Krishn (or) Básdeo, whom the Hindús venerate as an incarnation of God. When the Sultán reached the city no one came out to oppose him.[4] The Sultán's army plundered the whole city and set fire to the temples. They took immense booty, and by the Sultán's order they broke up a golden image which was ninety-eight

---

[1] In the *Yamíní* this conversion is ascribed to the ruler of Baran, and in the *Habíbu-s Siyar* also, which Firishta by some mistake has quoted as his own authority. Firishta makes Mahmúd stay three days in Kanauj.

[2] [" *Kaum o khweshán.*"]   [3] [مـتـورا]

[4] Firishta says it belonged to the Rája of Dehli, for which there is no authority. He also says the Sultán remained twenty days at Mathura.

thousand three hundred miskáls in weight; and there was also found a sapphire weighing four hundred and fifty miskáls.

"It is said that Chandar Ráí, who was one of the Rájas of Hindústán, possessed a very powerful and famous elephant. The Sultán desired to purchase it at a very large price, but could not get it.[1] When the Sultán was returning from Kanauj, this elephant one night broke away from the other elephants, and went without any driver to the Sultán's camp, who took it, and being much pleased, he called it Khudádád (the gift of God).

"When he returned to Ghaznín, he had the value of the spoil counted. It was found to consist of 20,000,000 dirhams, 53,000 captives, and 350 elephants."—*Tabakát-i Akbarí*.

There are not fewer difficulties to contend with when we come to consider the names of the Hindú chiefs. 'Utbí calls the ruler of Kanauj Ráí Jaipál and Purú Jaipál, meaning the same Jaipál who has already been spoken of as the Rájá of Lahore. Mírkhond and Khondamír also call him Jaipál. He is the same as the Nardajanpál of Al Bírúní, of which none of his commentators are able to restore the correct reading. Nizámu-d dín Ahmad and Firishta call him Kora, or, according to Briggs, Koowur-Ray. We are at a loss what grounds these later authors have for this statement. It may, perhaps, be equivalent to Purú, and be meant for Kunwar, "a rája's son," a term of common use in the present day. Bird says he was called Kora from the appellation of his tribe; but there is no such tribe, unless Gaur be meant, which would be spelt in nearly a similar form. However this may be, we must, improbable as it may seem, follow the statement of 'Utbí, and conceive that the Rájá of Lahore was at this time in possession of Kanauj. There are certain details given which favour this notion. The son of this Purú Jaipál is, according to the *Yamíní*, Bhím-pál, who writes to Chand Ráí, respecting the Musulmáns, as if he had long been in communication with them. This Bhím-pál speaks of his uncle having been forcibly converted, which uncle, as we have already seen, seems evidently to be the same as Nawása Sháh. We also find Purú Jaipál holding

[1] Previous to this Firishta makes the Sultán attack Rája Chandpál, who evacuates his fort, and sends his treasure to the hills. He makes Chand Ráí also fly to the hills.

dominions on the other side of the Ganges during the next campaign on the Ráhib. We may suppose, therefore, that, without being *de facto* ruler throughout these broad domains, he may have held a sort of suzerainty or paramount rule, and was then in the eastern portion of his dominions, engaged in settling the nuptials of his son, Bhím-pál, or had altogether transferred his residence to those parts, to avoid the frequent incursions of his Muhammadan persecutors, who, in their late expedition to Thánesar, had shown that it was impossible for him to maintain independence in Lahore. Like as the reigning family was driven from Kábul to Dhera, and from Dhera to Lahore, so it seems now to have been driven from Lahore to Kanauj.

The Chandálbhor Phúr, or Púr, in some copies of the *Yamíni*, the ruler of Asi, may, perhaps, indicate that the Rájá was a Chandel Rájpút, for Asi is close to the spot where we find that clan now established. The name Phúr may have some connection with the legendary Fúr, or Porus, who opposed Alexander; for, be it observed, his capital is represented by Indian geographers to have been in the neighbourhood of Allahabad; and the Rájás of Kumáún, who are themselves Chandels, represent themselves to be descended from this Fúr, the ruler of Kanauj and Prayág. So addicted are the Asiatics to ascribe this name to Indian potentates that some Arabic authors name even Rái Pithaurá as Puras. On this name and the analogies which it suggests, much might be added, but it would lead us beyond the immediate purport of this Note to discuss them.[1]

Chand Rái, perhaps, also indicates the same lineage, for his dominions must have adjoined Bundelkhand, in which province are included Mahoba and Chanderi, the original seats from which the Chandels emigrated.

Thirteenth Expedition.—Battle of the Rdhib. A.H. 412.—'Utbí mentions no year for this expedition. Nizámu-d dín Ahmad attributes it to 410; Firishta to 412. The latter is the most probable. Mírkhond and Khondamir make no mention of it. 'Utbí places the scene on the Ráhib, which we know from Al Dírúní to be on the

---

[1] Compare Ritter, *Erdkunde von Asien*, Vol. IV. Part 1. p. 453. Elphinstone, *History of India*, Vol. I. p. 467. Lassen, *Pentapotamia Indica*, p. 16. Bohlen, *Das alte Indien*, Vol. I. p. 91. Lassen, *Indische Alterthumskunde*, Vol. II. pp. 147, 195. *Hadikatu-l Akdlím*, v. "Allahábád." *Yádgár-i Bahádari*, v. "Kanauj." Bird's *History of Gujarat*, p. 138. *Maipátu-l Haiwán*, by Shaikh Abu-l Fath Damarí.

other side of the Ganges, and is either the Rámgangá, or the Sye—apparently the latter in the present instance.

The other authors place the scene on the Jumna, and we might consider their account to refer to some other expedition, were not Purú Jaipál mentioned in both, as well as the circumstance of the surprise by eight men swimming over the river. It is also worthy of remark that Al Birúni gives the death of Púr Jaipál in 412 A.H., which makes it highly probable that he was slain in this very action, though that fact is not expressly mentioned in the *Tarīkh Yamīnī*.

Dr. Bird doubts this expedition altogether, because another expedition occurs against Kálinjar, and the two appear to have been in reality one. But here not even Firishta represents that Mahmúd went to Kálinjar, though he was engaged with the Rája of that place. 'Utbi's statement must be received as conclusive respecting a movement as far as the Ráhib; though he mentions nothing about Kálinjar or Nandá Rájá. Indeed, in that author we nowhere find mention of that submission to the Sultán, on account of which the Rái of Kanauj was sacrificed to the vengeance of the Hindú confederacy.

That Purú Jaipál should be found on the other side of the Ráhib, as 'Utbi says, or come to the aid of Nandá Rájá, according to Nizámu-d dín and Firishta, is confirmative of the probability previously noticed, that he had then established himself far to the eastward of Lahore.

The following is the statement of Nizámu-d dín:—

"It is said that when Sultán Mahmúd heard that a Rája named Nandá[1] had slain the Rái of Kanauj, for having recognized and submitted to the Sultán, he resolved to invade his territory. So, in A.H. 410, he marched again towards Hindústán. When he reached the banks of the Jumna, Púr Jaipál,[2] who had so often fled before his troops, and who had now come to assist Nandá, encamped in face of the Sultán; but there was a deep river between them, and no one passed over without the Sultán's permission. But it so happened

[1] Firishta adds that many of the neighbouring princes had joined in league with Nandá, whom he calls Rájá of Kálinjar.
[2] Firishta says the Rájá of the Panjáb, the grandson of Jaipál. [Sir H. Elliot's MS. gives the name as "Tarú Jaibál."]

that eight of the royal guards of Mahmúd's army having crossed the river together, they threw the whole army of Púr Jaipál into confusion, and defeated it. Púr Jaipál, with a few infidels, escaped. The eight men[1] not returning to the Sultán, advanced against the city of Bári,[2] which lay in the vicinity. Having found it defenceless, they plundered it, and pulled down the heathen temples.

The Sultán advanced from hence to the territory of Nandá, who, resolving on battle, collected a large army, which is said to have consisted of thirty-six thousand horse, one hundred and five thousand foot,[3] and six hundred and forty elephants. When the Sultán approached his camp, he first sent an ambassador, calling upon him to acknowledge fealty, and embrace the Muhammadan faith. Nandá refused these conditions, and prepared to fight. Upon this, the Sultán reconnoitred Nandá's army from an eminence, and observing its vast numbers, he regretted his having come thither. Prostrating himself before God, he prayed for success and victory. When night came on, great fear and alarm entered the mind of Nandá, and he fled with some of his personal attendants, leaving all his baggage and equipments. The next day the Sultán, being apprized of this, rode out on horseback without any escort, and carefully examined the ground. When he was satisfied that there was no ambush or strategical device, he stretched out his hands for plunder and devastation. Immense booty fell into the hands of the Musulmáns, and five hundred and eighty of Nandá's elephants, which were in the neighbouring woods, were taken. The Sultán, loaded with victory and success, returned to Ghaznín."[4]—*Tabakát-i Akbarí.*

Fourteenth Expedition.—Kirdi, Núr, Lohkot, and Láhore.[5] A.H. 413. We now lose the guidance of 'Utbí, and are compelled to follow the more uncertain authority of later writers. It has been questioned

[1] Firishta says that these eight must, of course, have been officers, each followed by his own corps. He gives no name to the city which was plundered.

[2] Nizámu-d dín is the only author who states this. His account is fully confirmed by the statement of Abú Ríhán, that Bári became the Hindú capital, after the loss of Kanauj.

[3] Forty-five thousand, in Firishta.

[4] Because, as Firishta adds, he was apprehensive about what might occur in the Panjáb and other countries in his rear, and was satisfied with what he had done that year.

[5] [Compare with this General Cunningham's Note, Vol. I. p. 395.]

whether this expedition ever took place. Elphinstone and Reinaud take no notice of it, and Bird says that it is a mere repetition of the previous one to Bálnát; and "the narratives evidently refer to the same places and transactions." Even if they did refer to the same places, there is no reason why the transactions should not have been different. As Firishta asserts that Kuriat[1] and Nardein lie apparently between Turkistán and Hindústán, it is evident that he thought he was dealing with places which had not yet been mentioned. His authority for assigning this position to the tract is not the *Tabakát-i Akbarí*, in which it is merely stated that the country has mountain passes, is very cold, abounds with fruit, and that its inhabitants worship lions. This latter, no doubt, alludes to the worship of Sákya Sinha (lion) the Buddha. But, though Firishta had little authority for his assertion, it is evident that he was correct in making it Kuriat. First, we must restore the true reading of Nardein. The latter, in the *Tabakát-i Akbarí* and *Khazv-l Makpár* is correctly given as "Núr;" and "Kuriat" in the same works, in the original of Firishta, is correctly given as "Kírát." Now, the position of Kírát and Núr is ascertained by referring to Al Bírúni's account of the Kábul river, which is thus described by him: "This body of water—the Kábul river—passes through the country of Lamghán, near the fort of Dirúna, and is then joined by *the waters of Núr and Kírát*.[2] When it reaches opposite Pesháwar, it forms a considerable stream," etc. Here, then, we must look for the waters of Núr and Kírát, between the towns of Jalálábád and Pesháwar, and we shall find that the country alluded to is that drained by the Kuner and Landye rivers—that is, Swát, Bajaur, and part of Káfiristán. This tract exactly corresponds with the description given in the *Tabakát-i Akbarí;* and plenty of Buddhist remains survive to explain the allusion to the worship of lions.

[1] Dow reads "Kiberat;" Briggs, "Kuriat" in the translation, but "Kairát" in the text; Wilken, "Ferath;" and "Kabrath." The real reading being Kírát, which same may be the same as that of the mountaineers of Sanskrit geography.

[2] [In page 47, Vol. I., my translation of the Persian version of this passage differs:—"uniting near the fort of Dirúna (the waters) fall into the Nárokirát;" and this is correct according to the Persian text, "..... *mamlik-i kala'i Dirúna waytann' mi-shawad wa dar áb-i Nurokirát mi-uftad.*" Sir H. Elliot follows Reinaud's translation of the text of Bírúni, which certainly seems more accurate than the Persian version. See *Mém. sur l'Inde*, 276.—ED.]

On the supposition that Núr and Kirát were in the neighbourhood of Bajaur, there is no difficulty in tracing the progress of the conqueror during this invasion. On his way from Ghaznín, he makes an incursion across the Kábul river, and while his general is engaged in capturing Núr and building the fort, to overawe the wild inhabitants, he himself proceeds to the impregnable Lohkot, by the same road which he had previously travelled; and then returned to Ghaznín after visiting Lahore.

As the *Habíbu-s Siyar* gives no account of this expedition, the following narrative is taken from Nizámu-d dín Ahmad. Firishta adds to it that the king of Lahore fled to Ajmír, and that Mahmúd, before returning to Ghazní, nominated commanders to the conquered provinces of Hindustán, and left troops for their protection. This author is mistaken in speaking of the stone which was found at Nárdín, and was represented to be four thousand years old. He has in this respect, from similarity of name, confounded this expedition with that against Nindúna or Nárdín, in the Bálnát hills.

"About this time, the king learned that the inhabitants of the two mountainous tracts *(darra)* of Kirát and Núr, were all worshippers of idols, and possessed some very strong positions. The Sultán immediately gave orders that his forces should be collected; and having taken many blacksmiths, carpenters, and stone-cutters with him, he proceeded towards those places. When he approached the country, he first attacked Kirát. This place was very cold, and abounded with fruit; and its inhabitants were worshippers of lions. The chief of that forest, however, made submission, and accepted Islám. All the other people also followed his example. Sáhib 'Alí[1] ibn Flár, a Muhammadan, was sent to reduce Núr, which he accomplished. He founded a fort at this place, and left 'Alí bin Kadr Júk[2] as governor of it. Islám spread in this part of the country by the consent of the people and by the influence of force.

"In A.H. 412,[3] the king advanced toward Kashmír, and invested

[1] Firishta says son of Arslán Jázíb.
[2] Firishta says Saljúkí, and it is not improbable that some of that enterprising race were in Mahmúd's service.
[3] Firishta gives no year, but it may be implied that he alludes to 413 A.H., as he has a separate expedition for both 412 and 414.

the stronghold of Lohkot.¹ He stayed before it one month, but finding the fort, on account of its strength and loftiness, altogether impregnable, he decamped and proceeded towards Lahore and Bágnr. He directed his followers to plunder the hill country, and immense booty was collected. The Sultán returned in the commencement of spring to Ghaznín."—*Tabakdt-i Akbarí.*

Fifteenth Expedition.—Gwálidr and Kálinjár. A.H. 414.—This is another expedition resting only on the same authorities, and respecting which also doubts have been entertained, but there seems no reason to suppose that the restless bigotry of Mahmúd did not undertake this new expedition. It does not appear that he had yet visited Kálinjár, though he had been twice in the neighbourhood. The mention of Gwáliár in connection with it seems to separate this altogether from the other expeditions towards Bundelkhand and the Lower Doáb.

The following is from the *Tabakdt-i-Akbarí* :—

"In A.H. 413 (1021 A.D.) Mahmúd again undertook an expedition against the territory of Nandá. Having reached the fort of Gwáliár, he besieged it. Four days after, the chief of the place sent messengers promising thirty-five elephants, and solicited protection. The Sultán agreed to the terms, and from thence proceeded to Kálinjár. This is a fort unparalleled in the whole country of Hindústán for its strength. He invested this fort also, and, after a while, Nandá, its chief, presented three hundred elephants, and sued for peace. As these animals were sent out of the fort without riders,² the Sultán ordered the Turks to seize and mount them. The enemy perceiving this, was much surprised, and Nandá sent a copy of Hindí verses in praise of the Sultán, who gave it to the learned men of Hind and other poets who were at his court, who all bestowed their admiration upon them. He was much pleased with the compliment, and in return conferred on him the government of fifteen forts,³ besides some other presents. Nandá acknowledged

¹ [See note in p. 456 *supra.*]
² Firishta says that in order to put the bravery of the Sultán's troops to the test, the Rája had intoxicated these elephants with drugs, and that Mahmúd ordered a select body of horse to seize or kill them or drive them away from the camp.
³ Among which, adds Firishta, was Kálinjár itself.

this favour by sending immense riches and jewels to the Sultán, who then victoriously and triumphantly returned to Ghazní.

"In A.H. 414, Mahmúd mustered all his forces, and found them, besides those which were employed on duty in the different parts of his kingdom, to consist of fifty-four thousand horse and one thousand three hundred elephants."—*Tabakát-i Akbarí.*

Sixteenth Expedition.—Somnát. A.H. 416-7.—The accounts of this celebrated expedition are given in great detail by most authors. Those who follow [Ibn Asír and] Mírkhond make it commence with 416 H. Those who follow Firishta with 415 H. Dr. Bird has given good reason for preferring the former year, where he shows the necessity of paying attention to the Indian seasons in examining these expeditions. A few additional circumstances, not to be found in the *Habíbu-s Siyar*, are mentioned by other authors, and are shown in the following extracts.

Though the position of Somnát is well-known in the district of the Guzerát peninsula, now called Bhábrewár, yet by some extraordinary mistake, in which he has been followed by Rampoldi, D'Herbelot considers it to be the same as Viziapur in the Dekhin.

[From the *Kámilu-t Tawáríkh* of Ibn Asír[1]:—

"In the year 414 H. Mahmúd captured several forts and cities in Hind, and he also took the idol called Somnát. This idol was the greatest of all the idols of Hind. Every night that there was an eclipse the Hindús went on pilgrimage to the temple, and there congregated to the number of a hundred thousand persons. They believed that the souls of men after separation from the body used to meet there, according to their doctrine of transmigration, and that the ebb and flow of the tide was the worship paid to the idol by the sea, to the best of its power. Everything of the most precious was brought there; its attendants received the most valuable presents, and the temple was endowed with more than 10,000 vil-

[1] [The account given of this expedition by Ibn Asír is the oldest one extant, and has been largely drawn upon by later writers. Firishta must have used it, Karwíní copied his account of the temple from it (see Vol. 1. of this work, p. 97), and the extracts which follow this show how much other authors are indebted to it. The whole account is more specific in its details than those of its copyists. For these reasons the Editor has inserted it here in full.]

lagos. In the temple were amassed jewels of the most exquisite quality and incalculable value. The people of India have a great river called Gang, to which they pay the highest honour, and into which they cast the bones of their great men, in the belief that the deceased will thus secure an entrance to heaven. Between this river and Somnát there is a distance of about 200 parasangs, but water was daily brought from it with which the idol was washed. One thousand Bráhmans attended every day to perform the worship of the idol, and to introduce the visitors. Three hundred persons were employed in shaving the heads and beards of the pilgrims. Three hundred and fifty persons sang and danced at the gate of the temple. Every one of these received a settled allowance daily. When Mahmúd was gaining victories and demolishing idols in India, the Hindús said that Somnát was displeased with these idols, and that if he had been satisfied with them no one could have destroyed or injured them. When Mahmúd heard this he resolved upon making a campaign to destroy this idol, believing that when the Hindús saw their prayers and imprecations to be false and futile, they would embrace the faith.

"So he prayed to the Almighty for aid, and left Ghazní on the 10th Sha'bán, 414 H., with 30,000 horse besides volunteers, and took the road to Multán, which place he reached in the middle of Ramazán. The road from thence to India was through a barren desert, where there were neither inhabitants nor food. So he collected provisions for the passage, and loading 30,000 camels with water and corn, he started for Anhalwára. After he had crossed the desert, he perceived on one side a fort full of people, in which place there were wells. People came down to conciliate him, but he invested the place, and God gave him victory over it, for the hearts of the inhabitants failed them through fear. So he brought the place under the sway of Islám, killed the inhabitants, and broke in pieces their images. His men carried water away with them from thence and marched for Anhalwára, where they arrived at the beginning of Zí-l Ka'da.

"The chief of Anhalwára, called Bhím, fled hastily, and abandoning his city, he went to a certain fort for safety and to prepare himself for war. Yamínu-d daula again started for Somnát, and on his march he came to several forts in which were many images serving as chamberlains or heralds of Somnát, and accordingly he (Mahmúd) called them Shaitán. He killed the people who were in these places, destroyed the fortifications, broke in pieces the idols, and continued his march to Somnát through a desert where there was little water. There he met 20,000 fighting men, inhabitants of that country, whose chiefs would not submit. So he sent some forces against them, who defeated them, put them to flight, and plundered their possessions. From thence they marched to Dabalwárah, which is two days' journey from Somnát. The people of this place stayed resolutely in it, believing that Somnát would utter his prohibition and drive back the invaders; but Mahmúd took the place, slew the men, plundered their property, and marched on to Somnát.

"He reached Somnát on a Thursday in the middle of Zí-l Ka'da, and there he beheld a strong fortress built upon the sea shore, so that it was washed by the waves. The people of the fort were on the walls amusing themselves at the expense of the confident Musulmáns, telling them that their deity would cut off the last man of them, and destroy them all. On the morrow, which was Friday, the assailants advanced to the assault, and when the Hindús beheld the Muhammadáns fighting, they abandoned their posts, and left the walls. The Musulmáns planted their ladders against the walls and gained the summit: then they proclaimed their success with their religious war-cry, and exhibited the prowess of Islám. Then followed a fearful slaughter, and matters wore a serious aspect. A body of Hindús hurried to Somnát, cast themselves on the ground before him, and besought him to grant them victory. Night came on, and the fight was suspended.

"Next morning, early, the Muhammadans renewed the battle, and made greater havoc among the Hindús, till they drove them from the town to the house of their idol, Somnát. A dreadful slaughter followed at the gate of the temple. Band after band of the defenders entered the temple to Somnát, and with their hands clasped round their necks, wept and passionately entreated him. Then again they issued forth to fight until they were slain, and but few were left alive. These took to the sea in boats to make their escape, but the Musulmáns overtook them, and some were killed and some were drowned.

"This temple of Somnát was built upon fifty-six pillars of teak wood covered with lead. The idol itself was in a chamber; its height was five cubits and its girth three cubits. This was what appeared to the eye, but two cubits were (hidden) in the basement. It had no appearance of having been sculptured. Yamínu-d daula seized it, part of it he burnt, and part of it he carried away with him to Ghazní, where he made it a step at the entrance of the Jámi'-masjid. The shrine of the idol was dark, but it was lighted by most exquisitely jewelled chandeliers. Near the idol was a chain of gold to which bells were attached. The weight of it was 200 mans. When a certain portion of the night had passed, this chain was shaken to ring the bells, and so rouse a fresh party of Bráhmans to carry on the worship. The treasury was near, and in it there were many idols of gold and silver. Over it there were veils hanging, set with jewels, every one of which was of immense value. The worth of what was found in the temple exceeded two millions of dínárs, all of which was taken. The number of the slain exceeded fifty thousand."[1]—*Ibn Asír.*]

The following is from the *Táríkh-i Alfí :—*

"It is said that the temple of Somnát was built by one of the greatest Rájas of India. The idol was cut out of solid stone, about five yards in height, of which two were buried in the earth. Mahmúd, as soon as his eye fell on this idol, lifted up his battle-axe with much anger, and struck it with such force that the idol broke into pieces. The fragments of it were ordered to be taken to Ghazní, and were cast "down at the threshold of the Jámi' Masjid,' where they are lying to this day. It is a well-authenticated fact that when Mahmúd was about to destroy the idol, a crowd of Bráhmans represented (to his nobles) that if he would desist from the mutilation they would pay several crores of gold coins into his treasury. This was agreed to by many of the nobles, who pointed out to the Sultán that he could not obtain so much treasure by

[1] [The continuation of this chapter, relating to Mahmúd's return, will be found, *supra* page 249.]

breaking the image, and that the proffered money would be very serviceable. Mahmúd replied, "I know this, but I desire that on the day of resurrection I should be summoned with the words, 'Where is that Mahmúd who broke the greatest of the heathen idols?' rather than by these: 'Where is that Mahmúd who sold the greatest of the idols to the infidels for gold?'" When Mahmúd demolished the image, he found in it so many superb jewels and rubies, that they amounted to, and even exceeded an hundred times the value of the ransom which had been offered to him by the Bráhmans.

"According to the belief of the Hindús, all the other idols in India held the position of attendants and deputies of Somnát. Every night this idol was washed with "fresh" water brought from the Ganges, although that river must be more than two hundred parasangs distant. This river flows through the eastern part of India, and is held very sacred by the Hindus. They throw the bones of their dead into it.

"It is related in many authentic historical works that the revenue of ten thousand populated villages was set apart as an endowment for the expenses of the temple of Somnát, and more than one thousand Bráhmans were always engaged in the worship of that idol. There hung in this temple a golden chain which weighed two hundred Indian mans. To this were attached numerous bells, and several persons were appointed whose duty it was to shake it at stated times during day and night, and summon the Bráhmans to worship. Amongst the other attendants of this temple there were three hundred barbers appointed to shave the heads of the pilgrims. There were also three hundred musicians and five hundred dancing-girls attached to it; and it was customary even for the kings and rájas of India to send their daughters for the service of the temple. A salary was fixed for every one of the attendants, and it was duly and punctually paid. On the occurrence of an eclipse multitudes of Hindús came to visit this temple from all parts of Hindústán. We are told by many historians that at every occurrence of this phenomenon there assembled more than two hundred thousand persons, bringing offerings. It is said in the history of Ibn Asír and in that of Háfiz A'brú[1] that the room in which the idol of Somnát was

[1] In Firishta this is related on the authority of the *Zainu-l Ma-ásir*.

placed was entirely dark, and that it was illumined by the refulgence of the jewels that adorned the candelabra. In the treasury of this temple there were also found numberless small idols of gold and silver. In short, besides what fell into the hands of his army from the plunder of the city, Mahmúd obtained so much wealth in gold, jewels, and other valuables from this temple, that no other king possessed anything equal to it.

"When Mahmúd had concluded his expedition against Somnát, it was reported to him that Rája Bhím, chief of Nahrwára, who at the time of the late invasion had fled away, had now taken refuge in the fort of Kandama,[1] which was by land forty parasangs distant from Somnát. Mahmúd immediately advanced towards that place,[2] and when his victorious flags drew near the fort, it was found to be surrounded by much water, and there appeared no way of approaching it. The Sultán ordered some divers to sound the depth of the water, and they pointed him out a place where it was fordable. But at the same time they said that if the water (the tide) should rise at the time of their passing it would drown them all. Mahmúd, having taken the advice of religious persons, and depending upon the protection of the Almighty God, proceeded with his army, and plunged with his horse into the water. He crossed over it in safety, and the chief of the fort having witnessed his intrepidity, fled away. His whole property, with numerous prisoners, fell into the hands of the army of Islám. All men who were found in the fort were put to the sword.[3]

"After this conquest, Mahmúd proceeded to invade the territory of the Bhátís, whose chief, being apprised of his intentions, proffered his obedience and submission.[4] The king left him in possession of his dominions, and returned to his own capital of Ghaznín."— *Táríkh i-Alfí.*

From the *Tabakát-i Akbarí*:—

"When Mahmúd resolved upon returning home from Somnát, he

---

[1] Firishta says Gandaha, which Briggs conceives to be Gandavi. Some copies read Khadába or Khandáva. [Ibn Asír has Kandahat, *supra* p. 249. It is probably Khandadár in Káthiwár. See Vol. i. p. 445.]

[2] [The MS. I have used breaks off abruptly here.—ED.]

[3] The statements in this paragraph are taken from the *Rauzatu-s Safá*.

[4] This is also mentioned in the *Rauzatu-s Safá*, but is not noticed by Firishta.

learned that Param Dev, one of the greatest Rájas of Hindústán, was preparing to intercept him. The Sultán, not deeming it advisable at the time to contend with this chief, went towards Multán, through Sind. In this journey his men suffered much in some places from scarcity of water, and in others from want of forage. After enduring great difficulties, he arrived at Ghaznín in A.H. 417.

"In this year, Al Kádir Bi-llah wrote a letter to him, accompanied with standards (signalising him as sovereign¹) of Khurásán, Hindústán, Nímroz, and Khwárizm, and granted titles to the Sultán, his sons and brothers. To the Sultán he gave the title of Kahfu-d daulat wau-l Islám (Guardian of the State and of the Faith); to Amír Mas'úd that of Shahábu-d daulat and Jamálu-l Millat (Lustre of the State and Ornament of the Faith); to Amír Muhammad of Jalálu-d daulat and Jamálu-l Millat (Glory of the State and Ornament of the Faith); and to Amír Yúsuf, of Azdu-d daulat and Muwaiyidu-l Millat (Support of the State and Maintainer of the Faith). He at the same time assured Mahmúd that he would recognise the person whom he should nominate as his successor. This letter reached the Sultán in Balkh."²—*Tabakát-i Akbarí.*

The difficulties experienced in the desert are thus related by Minháju-s Siráj Júzjání. From the mention of Sind and Mansúra, it is evident that Mahmúd returned by a much more westerly course than he pursued in coming; and if we compare this narrative with the one given in the *Jámi'u-l Hikáyát* (v. sup. p. 192), we shall be confirmed in this view, for the river there mentioned can be no other than the Sind or Panjnad.

From the *Tabakát-i Násirí:*—

"On his return from Somnát through the territory of Sind and Mansúria, he resolved to take his army by way of the desert. On his demand for guides, a Hindú came forward and promised to lead the way. When the army of Islám had for some time³ marched

---

¹ [These words are not in the text but seem to be implied.]

² This letter must have been written in reply to one addressed to him by Mahmúd after his capture of Somnát, from which there is an extract given in Yáfi'í's history.

³ [The text says "yakshabí." In the *Jámi'u-l Hikáyát* the period is said to have been three days—*supra*, p. 192.]

behind him, and it became time to call a halt, people went in search of water, but it was nowhere found. The Sultán summoned the guide to his presence, and asked him where water was procurable. He replied, "I have devoted my life for the sake of my deity Somnát, and have brought thee and thy army into this desert, where no water is, in order that all may perish." The Sultán ordered the guide to be killed, and the army to encamp. He rested patiently until night came on, and then the Sultán went aside from the camp, and prostrating himself on the earth, entreated with the deepest supplication Almighty God for aid in this extremity. When about a quarter of the night had elapsed, a light shone to the north of the camp. The Sultán ordered his army to march in that direction, and when day broke the Omnipotent led them to a place where there was a supply of water. Thus did all the Musulmáns escape from this imminent danger."[1]—*Tabakát-i Násirí*.

From the *Rauzatu-s Safá* :—

"It is related that when Sultan Mahmúd had achieved the conquest of Somnát, he wished to fix his residence there for some years, because the country was very extensive, possessed many unusual advantages, as well as several mines which produced pure gold. Indian rubies were brought there from Sarandíp, one of the dependencies of the kingdom of Guzerát. His ministers represented to him that to forsake Khurásán, which had been taken from his enemies after so many battles, and to make Somnát the seat of government was very improper. In short, the King made up his mind to return, and ordered that some man should be appointed to hold and carry on the administration of the country. The ministers observed that it was impossible for a stranger to maintain possession, and therefore he should assign it to one of the native chiefs. The Sultán accordingly held a council to settle the nomination, in concurrence with such of the inhabitants as were well disposed towards him. Some of them represented to him that amongst the ancient royal families no house was so noble as that of the Dábshilíms, of whom only one member survived, and he had

[1] Firishta adds that many of the troops died raging mad from the intolerable heat and thirst.

assumed the habit of a Brahman, and was devoted to philosophical pursuits and austerity.¹—*Rauzatu-s Safá*.²

With respect to the name of Somnát, Firishta observes "that Soma was the name of a prince, after whom the idol Nát was called—Nát signifying among the Hindús lord or chief—and is rendered applicable to idols. Thus we have Jagnát, the lord of the creation." Bird, in one part of his work, says that it is derived from the Sanskrit *Swayambhú Náth*, "self-existing lord;" but in another part, more correctly, from Soma Náth, "the moon-lord," or "regent of the moon," which was one of the names under which Mahádeva was worshipped. It is evident from the statement of Al Bírúní that Somnát was no idol, but the lingam or phallic emblem of that deity. The embellishments of the story have been commented on by Wilson. "The earlier Muhammadan writers say nothing of the mutilation of its features, for, in fact, it had none; nothing of the treasures it contained, which, as it was solid, could not have been within it. * * * Firishta invents the hidden treasure of rubies and pearls with quite as little warrant. Somnáth was in fact a linga, a náth, or deity ascribed to Soma, the moon, as having been erected by him in honour of Siva. It was one of the twelve principal types of that deity, which were celebrated in India at the time of the first Muhammadan invasion." That there were, however, precious stones upon this lingam we know from the account of Al Bírúní, who tells us that the top was garnished with them and with gold. He also informs us that the name of "moon-lord" was derived from the fact of the stone being washed with more particular ceremony twice during the month, at the full and new moon.

The resemblance which the Muhammadan authors wish to establish between this lingam and the Arabian Lát seems to be a mere fancy; for though there was doubtless at one time considerable connection between these parts of India and Arabia, it does not appear to have been exemplified in this particular instance.

There is one other matter which seems to require a passing notice in this place, as of late years it has engaged some attention. I allude to the removal of the Somnát gates.

¹ See *infra*, extracts from *Majma'-i Wasáyá*.] ² [Lith. Ed., Vol. iv. p. 48.]

Seventeenth Expedition.—Játs of Júd. (A.H. 417.—This expedition is also recorded only by the later authorities, but the attack upon the Játs is not in itself improbable, though some of its attendant circumstances are. It is probable that, on the dissolution of the kingdom of Láhore, the Játs of the Júd hills acquired considerable power, and by predatory incursions were able to harry their neighbours. Their advance so far from their own country to attack the Muhammadan army, and the strength of the force with which they opposed it, show that they possessed no inconsiderable power. From a passage quoted by M. Reinaud from the *Kámiln-i Tawáríkh*, (416 H.), it appears that they "had invaded the principality of Mansúra and had forced the Musulmán Amír to abjure his religion.[1] It does not quite appear what particular portion of the hilly country is here meant, but most probably the Salt range, on the part nearest to Multán. The Játs have now moved further to the north and east, but some of their clans point to the Salt range as their original seats.

The chief improbability, and it is almost insurmountable, consists in Mahmúd's being able to organise a powerful fleet of fourteen hundred boats at Multán, and in being opposed by at least four thousand boats manned by mountaineers. Even in a time of the briskest trade, fourteen hundred boats could not be collected in all the rivers of the Panjáb. It is also remarkable that Mahmúd should choose to fight at all on the river, when his veteran troops would have been so much more effective on land than on water. If he could have equipped so large a fleet on a sudden emergency, it adds to the surprise which Elphinstone invites us to entertain, that Mahmúd, neither in going to or returning from Somnát availed himself of the Indus. On his return, however, he does seem to have come for some way on the banks of the Indus.

As the year 417 H. began on the 22nd Feb., 1026, there was ample time for Mahmúd to have returned to Ghazní in order to escape the heats and rains of Hindústán, and return again to Multán before the Ghazní winter, all within the same year.

The following account is taken from Nizámu-d dín Ahmad:—

"In the same year (417 H.), the Sultán, with a view to punish the Játs, who had molested his army on his return from Somnát, led a

[1] *Mémoire sur l'Inde*, p. 272.

large force towards Multán, and when he arrived there he ordered fourteen hundred boats to be built, each of which was armed with three firm iron spikes, projecting one from the prow and two from the sides, so that anything which came in contact with them would infallibly be destroyed.[1] In each boat were twenty archers, with bows and arrows, grenades,[2] and naphtha; and in this way they proceeded to attack the Játs, who having intelligence of the armament, sent their families into the islands and prepared themselves for the conflict. They launched, according to some, four, and according to others, eight thousand boats, manned and armed, ready to engage the Muhammadans. Both fleets met, and a desperate conflict ensued. Every boat of the Játs that approached the Moslem fleet, when it received the shock of the projecting spikes, was broken and overturned. Thus most of the Játs were drowned, and those who were not so destroyed were put to the sword.[3] The Sultán's army proceeded to the places where their families were concealed, and took them all prisoners. The Sultán then returned victorious to Ghaznín."—*Tabakát-i Akbarí.*

NOTE E.

Coins of the Ghaznivides and Ghorians.

["The Coins of the Kings of Ghazní" form the subject of two valuable papers by Mr. Thomas in the *Journal of the Royal Asiatic Society*,[4] the last of which is followed by a supplement on the Coins of the Ghorí dynasty. The same writer has also published two papers on the Coins of the "Patán Sultáns of Hindústán," beginning with Muhammad Ghorí (1193 A.D.), and extending to Sikandar Sháh (1554 A.D.) These articles contain so much that is useful by way of correction and illustration, that a few extracts and a general summary of the results so far as they relate to the reigns noticed in the present volume are here given.

[1] For a similar mode of armament about the same period, see *Chronicles of the Crusades,* p. 199.

[2] [ناروج. Apparently some explosive or inflammable missile.]

[3] Firishta adds that some of the Ját boats were set on fire.

[4] [Vol. ix. p. 267, and Vol. xvii. p. 138.]

Among the coins noticed by Mr. Thomas is an important one described by M. Dorn in the *Bulletin de l'Académie Impériale des Sciences de Saint Petersbourg*, Tom. xii., 1855. This is a coin struck at Ghazní in 359 A.H., bearing the name of the Sámání suzerain Mansúr bin Núh and of Bilkátigín as ruler in Ghazní. The succession of Bilkátigín after the death of Alptigín has been passed unnoticed by almost all historians, but the *Jámi'u-l Hikáyát* has two stories (pp. 180-181 *supra*) in which he is spoken of as ruler, and the *Tabakát-i Násirí* (p. 267 *supra*), on the authority of Baihakí, states that Bilkátigín was raised to the throne on the death of Alptigín's son, Abú Is'hák (in 367 A.H.), and that he reigned two years.

Firishta's version is that Alptigín conquered Ghazní in 351, and died in 365, when he was succeeded by his son, Abú Is'hák, who dying two years afterwards, was followed by Subuktigín. This account is consistent in itself, but it is not reconcilable with the fact of Bilkátigín's coin bearing the date of 359. It can hardly be supposed that the name of Bilkátigín would be found upon a coin struck at Ghazní in the life time of Alptigín, although indeed there are coins extant bearing the same name Bilkátigín which were struck at Balkh twenty-five years earlier in A.H. 324.

The *Tabakát-i Násirí* (page 267 *supra*) states that Alptigín died eight years after the conquest of Ghazní, which is placed by Firishta in 351 (962 A.D.) This would make the year of his death to be 359 (969 A.D.), the date of Bilkátigín's coin. Mr. Thomas, therefore, places the death of Alptigín in 359, leaving the interval between that year and 366, the date of Subuktigín's accession, to be filled up by Abú Is'hák and Bilkátigín.

"The opinion advanced by many Muhammadan authors that Subuktigín should be looked upon as the first monarch of the Ghaznaví race, is not borne out by the record on his money: on the contrary, however powerful and virtually independent they may have been, Subuktigín, Ismá'il, and Mahmúd himself in the early days of his rise, all acknowledged the supremacy of the Sámání emperors, and duly inscribed on the currency struck by themselves as local governors, the name of the Lord Paramount, under whom they held dominion. It was not until the year 389 A.H. (999 A.D.)

that the house of Ghazní assumed independence as sovereign princes, which event is duly marked on Mahmúd's medals of the period, in the rejection of the name of the Suzerain Sámání, and the addition of the prefix Amír to his own titles.

"The numerous coins of Mahmúd, in their varied titular superscriptions, mark most distinctly the progressive epochs of his eventful career, commencing with the comparatively humble prænomen of Saifu-d daula, bestowed on him by Núh bin Mansúr in 384 A.H., proceeding onwards to the then usual Sámání titles of sovereignty, Al amír, As Saiyíd, conjoined with the epithets Yamínu-d daula and Amínu-l millat conferred on him by the Khalíf Al Kádir-bi-llah, advancing next to the appellation Nizámu-d dín, and the occasional prefix of the pompous designations of Maliku-l Mamálik and Maliku-l mulúk, and finally ending in the disuse of all titular adjuncts, and the simple inscription of the now truly celebrated name he had received at his birth.

"The absence of any numismatic record of the title of Ghází, said to have been adopted by Mahmúd on his return from some of his early expeditions into India, leads to an inference, not altogether unsupported by other negative evidence, that the term in question was not introduced into current use, in the full sense of its more modern acceptance, till a somewhat later period.

* * * * * *

"Mahmúd is related to have assumed the title of 'Sultán,' and to have been the first Oriental potentate who appropriated this term.[1] A reference to the coins of this prince, however, leads to some doubt on the subject, and although their testimony in no wise militates against the generally received account of the origin of the designation, yet it inferentially controverts the assertion of its immediate adoption and use by Mahmúd himself. * * * * Had Mahmúd assumed this prænomen, or had he received it from any competent authority, he would most probably have inscribed the appellation on his coins, whereon it will be seen he at one time much rejoiced to record his greatness. Moreover, had this title been adopted and employed by Mahmúd in the sense in which it was subsequently used, it is but reasonable to infer that it would have been continued

---

[1] *Khuláṣatu-l Akhbár* (Price), ii. 282; *Elphinstone's India*, i. 538.

by his immediate successors, and, as such, would have appeared on their money; whereas, the first Ghaznaví sovereign who stamps his coinage with the term is Ibráhím. 451 A.H. During the interval, the designation had already been appropriated by another dynasty, the Saljúk Tughril Beg having entitled himself Sultán so early as 437 A.H., if not before that date.

      °   °   °   °

"The coins of Mahmúd also afford evidence on the non-recognition of the Khalíf Al Kádir-bi-llah in the province of Khurásán, until about eight years subsequent to his virtual accession. It is necessary to premise that in the year 381 A.H. the Khalíf Al Taia'li-llah was dethroned by the Buwaihide Bahá-u-daula, the then Amíru-l umará of the Court of Baghdád, and his place supplied by Ahmad bin Is'hák, who was elevated to the Khiláfat under the denomination of Al Kádir-bi-llah. The author of the *Táríkh-i Guzída* relates that 'the people of the province of Khurásán objecting to this supersession, which was justified by no offence on the part of the late pontiff, continued to recite the public prayers in his name; and it was not until Mahmúd of Ghazní, in disavowing his allegiance to the Sámánís, became supreme in that country, that any alteration in the practice was effected, when Mahmúd, between whom and the now Imám there existed a friendly understanding, directed the *Khutbah* to be read in the name of Al Kádir.'

"The accuracy of this relation is fully borne out by the archæological evidence furnished by the collection under notice. Mahmúd's coins invariably bearing the designation of the superseded Khalíf Al Taia' in conjunction with his own early title of Saifu-d daula, up to the year 387 H., while his money of a closely subsequent period is marked by the simultaneous appearance of the name of Al Kádir in association with his own newly-received titles of Yamínu-d daula and Amínu-l millat.[1] Another medal bears unusually explicit testimony to this self-imposed submission, in the addition made to Mahmúd's detailed honorary denominations which are here seen to

[1] [These passages are very suggestive. The honours and high sounding titles conferred upon Mahmúd as a champion of the Faith had been well earned, but his merits might perhaps have passed unrewarded, but for the personal service rendered to the usurping Khalíf.]

conclude with the novel designation of *Wali Amíru-l muminín*—Servant of the Commander of the Faithful."

The coins of Alptigín bear the name of the Sámání sovereign 'Abdu-l malik, followed by "Alptigín." That of Bilkátigín has the name of Mansúr bin Núh, and below it "Bilkátigín." Those of Subuktigín are of similar character. They bear the names of Núh bin Mansúr and Subuktigín, as also that of the Khalíf At Taia'-li-llah.

The various legends on the coins of Mahmúd have been already noticed.

MUHAMMAD.—The legend is, "*Jálalu-d daulat wa jamalu-l millat*, Muhammad bin Mahmúd;—the glory of the State and the beauty of the Faith, Muhammad son of Mahmúd."

Another coin bears his father's titles, "*Yamínu-d daulat wa Amínu-l Millat, Nizámu-d dín Abú-l Kásim Muhammad bin Mahmúd.*" The name of the Khalífa Al Kádir bi-llah also appears.

MAS'ÚD.—The coins of this sovereign differ considerably in their legends. Some have the simple legend "*Mas'úd*" or "*Mas'úd bin Mahmúd*." Others have the titles "*Sultánu-l mu'azzam, Maliku-l 'álam;* the great Sultán, king of the world." Another legend is equally high sounding, but of a religious character. "*Násir dínu 'llah Háfiz 'ibádu-llah, Zahír Khalífu-llah;* defender of the religion of God, protector of the servants of God, supporter of the Khalífa of God." In others this is contracted into "*Násiru-d dínu-llah Abú Sa'íd Mas'úd bin Mahmúd,*" and in others changed into "*Násiru-d dínu-llah Háfiz 'ibádu-llah;* defender of the religion of God, protector of the servants of God." On the earlier coins the name of the Khalífa Al Kádir bi-llah appears, on later ones the name of Al Káim bi Amru-llah, his son and successor designate is added, and after the death of Al Kádir the name of Al Káim appears alone.

MAUDÚD.—"*Shahábu-d daulat wa Kutbu-l millat;* the meteor of the State and the pole-star of Religion." In some coins " *Abú-l fath;* father of victory" is added; and in others it is substituted for *Kutbu-l Millat*. Another variety in the legend is "*Fakhru-l imlat*, the glory of the faith."

The name of the Khalífa, Al Káim bi Amru-llah.

'Abdu-r Rashíd.—"*Izzu-d daulat, Zainu-l millat, Sharafu-llah;* the glory of the State, the ornament of Religion, the honoured of God."

Khalífa's name, Al Káim bi Amru-llah.

Farrucku-zád.—On some coins the simple name "*Farrukh-zád*" or "*Farrukh-zád bin Ma'súd.*" On others the titles "*Jamálu-d daulat wa Kamálu-l millat;* the ornament of the State and the Perfection of Religion." He is also called in some "*Abú Shujá',* father of courage."

Name of the Khalífa, Al Káim bi Amru-llah.

Ibráhím.—The legends of the coins issued in the long reign are very various. The simplest is "*Ibráhím bin Mas'úd.*" Another is "*Abú Muzaffar Ibráhím.*" Others are "*Sultánu-l 'azam,* the great Sultán;" "*Zahíru-d daulat,* the protector of the State;" "*Nasíru-d daulat,* "*Zahíru-l millat,* defender of the State and protector of the Faith;" *Káhiru-l mulúk, Saiyidu-s Salátín,* conqueror of kings and chief of monarchs."

The Khalífa's name Al Káim bi Amru-llah.

Mas'úd II.—"*Abú Sa'd,* the happy;" "*Sultánu-l 'azam,* the great king; "*Sultánu-l 'ádil,* the just king;" "*Alá'u-d daulat wa Sanáu-l millat,* supreme in the State, pre-eminent in Religion;" "*Zahíru-l ímán,* defender of the Faith;" "*Nizámu-d dín,* administrator of Religion;" "*Maulána-s Salátín,* king of kings." All these various titles were used, and sometimes two or more of them on one coin.

The Khalífa's name, Al Mustazhar bi-llah.

Arslán.—"*As Sultánu-l 'azam, Sultánu-d daulat, Malik Arslán bin Mas'úd.*"

The Khalífa, Al Mustazhar bi-llah.

Bahrám.—"*Bahrám Sháh, Sultánu-l 'azam, Yamínu-d daulat.*"

Khalífa, Al Mustarshad bi-llah.

Khusrú Sháh.—"*As Sultánu-l 'azam, Mu'izzu-d daulat,* The Great Sultan, Glory of the State."

Khalífa, Al Muktafí l-Amru-llah.

Khusrú Malik.—"*Sultánu-l 'azam; Táju-d daulat,* Crown of the State; *Sirráju-d daulat,* Lamp of the State."

Khalífas, Muktafí and Mustanjid.

Muhammad Ghorí.—This conqueror is called by many historians

Shaháb-u-d dín, a name which the *Rauzatu-s Safá* tells us was changed to Mu'izzu-d dín when his brother Ghiyásu-d dín became king. He is also commonly known as Muhammad Sám or Muhammad bin Sám, a name which the coins show him to have borne in common with his brother. The superscription on his coins is "*As Sultánu-l 'azam Mu'izzu-d dunyá wau-d dín Abú-l Muzaffar Muhammad bin Sám.*" On some coins this is contracted into "*Sultánu-l 'azam Abú-l Muzaffar Muhammad bin Sám,*" and on others to "*Sultánu-l 'azam Muhammad bin Sám.*"

The most interesting coins, however, of this monarch are those described by Mr. Thomas (*J. R. A. S.*, xvii. p. 194) as struck in honor of his "Martyred Lord" by *Táju-d dín Yaldaz*, at Ghazní, after the death of *Muhammad bin Sám*. Local coins are also extant of the closely succeeding kings: *Kubáchah* of Sind, *'Aláu-d dín Muhammad Khwárizmí, Jalálu-d dín Mankburín*; *Changíz Khán* and *Saifu-d dín al Hasan Karlugh* of Ghazní and Multán.

KUTBU-D DÍN AIBAK.—Coins unknown.

ÁRÁM SHÁH.—"*Abú-l Muzaffar Áram Sháh Sultán.*"

ALTAMSH.—"*As Sultánu-l 'azam Shamsu-d dunyá wau-d dín Abú-l Muzaffar Altamsh as Sultán.*" Some of the copper coins have only the name "*Shams*," and others "*Altamsh*."

RUKNU-D DÍN.—"*As Sultánu-l mu'azam Ruknu-d dín binu-s Sultán.*"

SULTÁN RAZIYA (QUEEN.)—"*As Sultánu-l 'azam Jalálatu-d dunyá wau-d dín Malikatu-l bint Altamsh-s Sultán Mihrat Amíru-l muminín*, the great Sultán, the glory of the world and the Faith, the Queen, the daughter of the Sultán Altamsh, the beloved of the Commander of the Faithful."

MU'IZZU-D DÍN BAHRÁM SHÁH.—"*As Sultánu-l 'azam 'Aláu dunyá wau-d dín.*"

'ALÁU-D DÍN.—"*As Sultánu-l 'azam 'Aláu-d dunyá wau-d dín Abú-l Muzaffar Mas'úd Sháh.*"

NÁSIRU-D DÍN.—"*As Sultánu-l 'azam Násiru-d dunyá wau-d dín Abú-l Muzaffar Mahmúd ibnu-s Sultán.*"

The last two superscriptions are shortened on the smaller coins by stopping at the word *dín*.

APPENDIX E.

The following extracts are taken from three works resembling the *Jámi'u-l Hikáyát*. Like the *Jámi'*, these works are of a general character, but the stories selected from them were intended by Sir H. Elliot to illustrate the reigns of the Ghaznivides, and the extracts relate almost exclusively to that dynasty. The Appendix to this volume therefore seems the most appropriate place for their appearance. If introduced in chronological sequence, two of the extracts would come in much later and be far removed from the other works on the Ghaznivide dynasty.

EXTRACTS FROM THE *Majma'-i Wasáyá*.

[The following stories are taken from a work which the Munshí who translated them calls *Majma'-i Nasáyah*. In the list of works prefixed to Sir H. Elliot's original volume it is entered "No. LXXIX. Wasaaya, Nizámu-l Mulk." No copy of the work is to be found in Sir H. Elliot's library, nor have I been able to obtain access to one. There is no doubt, however, that the extracts are derived from the work of Nizámu-l Mulk Túsí, the celebrated wazír of Malik Sháh Saljúk. This work was largely used by Hammer in his *History of the Assassins*, and he refers to it as the "*Wasaya*, or Political Institutes of Nizámu-l Mulk." The title of the work then is *Majma'-i Wasáyá*; but it is possible that the copy used by the Munshí bore the title *Majma'í Nasáih*, which is almost identical in signification. The work consists of a series of counsels addressed to the author's own sons.

Malik Sháh Saljúk reigned from 1072 to 1092 A.D., and Nizámu-l Mulk fell by the dagger of an assassin one month before the death of his master. The work, then, was written in the decline of the Ghaznivide dynasty; and a few stories relating to them and to India have been selected. One passage concerning Nizámu-l Mulk himself, and Hasan Sabáh the founder of the sect of the Assassins, has no direct reference to India, but it is interesting, and it enables us to identify the work as being the same as that used by Hammer. (See *History of the Assassins*, Transl. p. 44.)

The wording of the Extracts has been revised in part by Sir H. Elliot and in part by some unknown hand, but the translation seems not to have been tested; it must therefore rest upon the authority of the Munshí.¹]

Khwája 'Alí Khesháwand.

In the beginning of Sultán Subuktigín's reign the office of Wazír was conferred on Khwája Abú-l 'Abbás Isfaráíní, but Amír 'Alí Kheshawand, who was the head of the Hájibs and one of the greatest and most trustworthy officers of the Sultán, entertained hostility against him. The Khwája had informed the King of this, and therefore his Majesty was never angry with him. Although complaints were brought against him from different parts of the country, and his every action was immediately reported, yet the King saw no occasion to call him to account. If any person represented to the King any irregularity or misconduct on the part of the Khwája, he considered the man had been instructed by 'Alí Kheshawand; who at last, seeing his endeavours useless, abandoned the pursuit, but only waited for a suitable opportunity. At last the star of the Khwája's fortune began to decline, and the country under his rule fell into disorder. He appointed unjust governors in the provinces, who exercised tyranny over the subjects, so that a large portion of the country became desolate. In Khurásán and the bordering countries, more especially, such a dreadful famine prevailed, that it is recorded in history, and an account of it is given in many historical works. In short, the government assessment upon the lands was not at all realised, and the majority of the people emigrated from the country. Khwája Abú-l 'Abbás' only resource on seeing these circumstances, was to throw himself upon the King's mercy, and solicit remission. Reports were sent to his Majesty from all quarters, and the Khwája being greatly troubled and alarmed, sent in his resignation of the office of Wazír. The Sultán said he should suffer no punishment or injury if he paid into the treasury all the money which he had realized from the country, and which had been entered in his own accounts. On doing this he should be acquitted. The office of Diwán was, however, conferred on Khwája Abú-l Hakk Muhammad, son of Husain of Balkh. In this matter Shamsu-l

¹ [See Hammer, *History of the Assassins*; D'Herbelot, *Mahd-arbah*; Vullet's *Gesch. der Seldschuken*, 102, 160; Defrémery, *Histoire des Seldjoukides*.]

Káh Khwája Ahmad Hasan was made mediator between the Sultán and Khwája Abú-l 'Abbás, and he took the messages from the one to the other. After much correspondence, it was settled that the Khwája should pay one hundred thousand dinárs into the royal treasury. The Khwája accordingly engaged to satisfy the demand, and he delivered all the property, movable and immovable, which he had amassed during his former employments of deputy of the *amíds*, superintendent of the post-office at Khurásán, and minister of the Sultán. After he had given over everything that he possessed, he represented his indigence and poverty to the King, who compassionated his case, and having called him to his presence, said, if you swear by my soul and head to your pauperism, nobody shall hurt you. He answered, I will not swear till I again enquire of my wives, children, and dependents, and if I find anything remaining with them, I will send it to the King, and then take the oath. Having said this, he returned, and on administering very binding oaths and using all kinds of threats, he found that some small things belonging to his son were in the possession of a merchant. He took them also, and sent them to the royal treasury, and after this he swore to his indigence by the King's soul and head. 'Alí Kheshawand, however, was still seeking cause to disgrace him and make him feel the result of his animosity, although at the same time he was aware of the oath that Khwája Abú-l 'Abbás had taken.

At this juncture the Sultán undertook an expedition to Hindústán, and one day 'Alí Kheshawand, having gone to him while he was sitting alone, told him how he had long since known the deceitful conduct of Abú-l 'Abbás, and that he had several times determined to bring it before his Majesty's notice, but he had hesitated lest the representation of it might be put down to some selfish motive. Your Majesty, said he, has discovered his other faults and embezzlements without my help, and now he has sworn to his indigence falsely, because he has still in his possession some rarities of such value that few kings can boast of in their stores. The Sultán was much surprised on hearing these words, and said, If it is true, Abú-l 'Abbás deserves great punishment. 'Alí Kheshawand observed, If the King order me, I can prove my assertion. The King remarked that in case he failed to prove it he should suffer death.

This was agreed to, and 'Alí Khesháwand departed from the King's presence.

At this time Khwája Abú-l 'Abbás was in confinement in one of the forts. 'Alí Khesháwand, among the plunder from one of the kings of Hindustán, had obtained a dagger from his treasury, the handle of which was adorned with a large ruby of Yemen, sixty miskáls in weight. He had also taken from the store of the Sámání kings a jar which contained a sír of syrup. He had concealed these from every person that the King might not know of them. He now took both those rarities to the fort, and placed Khwája Abú-l 'Abbás in charge of his own men. After a few days he returned to the court, and having brought the dagger and the jar with him, he reported to the King that after many difficulties, and menaces and threats, he had discovered them; that one of them had belonged to the sovereigns of India, and was sent as a present to the throne, but that the Khwája had concealed it; and that the other he had stolen at the time when the treasury of the Sámání kings was taken possession of. Now, said he to the Sultán, what are your orders? Shall we take strong measures against him to realize the arrears or not? The King, in great rage, replied, I give you both those things, and you may exact from him the remainder of the government demands by any means you like. After this the Sultán proceeded to India, and 'Alí Khesháwand delivered the poor minister to his enemies, by whose severities he met the mercy of God.

Troubles of a Minister.

The object of relating this story here is to show that to be at enmity with great and powerful men is very dangerous, and is sure to bring evil. May God protect and help us!

Certain classes of men are particularly deserving of patronage and encouragement, such as the literati, the judicial and revenue officers, secretaries, ambassadors, and envoys. In all political and revenue matters their advice should be taken, because by this much benefit is derived and great advantage obtained. The aid of these people is indispensably necessary. It is impossible to manage the affairs of a kingdom without their instrumentality, and a minister can do nothing without their assistance. The difficult point is, that the minister's life, not to mention his property and wealth, is endangered. If a man, then, must choose the profession of a minister, he should obtain the help and co-operation of those men, and conciliate them by affability and kindness. He should raise them by his bounty and favour from indigence and poverty to opulence and abundance, from insignificance and meanness to dignity and importance, so that if any person should be envious of him, they may through gratitude give him assistance, and remain loyal and devoted to his cause, neither opposing nor revolting from him, but preventing others by their examples from quarrelling with him. For when one person shows a rebellious spirit, others join with him either secretly or openly, particularly those who may have suffered any hurt from the minister, or are jealous of his preferment. But perhaps you think, that if relations and confidants and trustworthy men be appointed to all offices, no mismanagement can take place or loss be sustained. You must know that this is a great mistake. Because, on the contrary, it is very dangerous for a minister to entrust his relations with the government duties. Don't you know that from the great confidence and implicit reliance which I place in your brothers, I have appointed them to conduct the affairs of the kingdom and have made them superintendents of all the officers of the different divisions of the country, and have entrusted one of them with the privilege of exercising a general control over all, and of reporting all matters, good or bad, to me. I am sure that they will strive to the utmost of their power to uphold their character and preserve my fame. Now-a-days, however, the chief lady is displeased with me because she wishes that the Sultán should appoint her son his heir-apparent; but her object is not realised, because he sees the marks of greater intelligence, wisdom, and prudence, as well as the symptoms of greatness and royalty in Barkiyáruk; while she considers him of no worth, and thinks that I have persuaded the King to entertain the opinion. At all events, she is disgusted with me, and seeks on all sides to find some one whom she may persuade to rise against me and make the Sultán angry with me. She is in search of my enemies and adversaries, but finds none, and therefore can only complain to the King that the Khwája has sent his people to different parts of the kingdom. This is known to nobody else but himself, but it has made an impression upon the King's mind. Still, if God please, the end will be good and no evil will ensue. I mean to say that if we entrust our relations and kinsmen with offices it creates suspicions against us, and is considered incompatible with honesty and justice; but if we employ strangers, may God protect us from their rebellion and quarrels! You know well what injuries I have received, am receiving, and must receive, from these people. The origin of my quarrel with him (Hasan Sabáh) was through Imám Muwáfik Naishápúri (may the Almighty cause his soul to enjoy peace!) who was one of the most learned and holy men of Khurásán. His age had advanced beyond seventy-five, and he was known to be a very successful teacher. Every lad that read the Kurán and religious books with him obtained a great degree of proficiency in that branch of learning. For this reason my father sent me with the Saint 'Abdu-s Samad from Tús to Naishápúr, and I became his scholar. He showed me much kindness and favour, and I felt great love and affection towards him. I was his scholar for four years, and he taught me with great attention and care. I was associated with four other students who were of equal age with me, and possessed great quickness of perception and solidity of judgment. After leaving the Imám they always came to me, and we sat together and repeated our past lessons. Hakím 'Umar of Naishápúr did not change his ancestor's abode. He was born in Naishápúr and continued to reside in it. The father of Makhzúl Ibn Sabáh 'Ali Bin Muhammad Bin Ja'far was a very pious man, and bigoted in his religion. He generally resided in Re, and Abú Muslim Rází, the ruler of the country, placed great confidence and faith in him, so that he referred to him all questions which arose regarding the Sunní persuasion, and also consulted with him in all matters of dispute. He always spoke oracular words; but to lower himself in the estimation of Abú Muslim he committed absurd and unlawful deeds.

As Imám Muwáfik Naishápúrí was the head of the people who followed the doctrines of the Sunní religion, that artful man, to clear himself of the charge of being a Ráfizí, brought his son to Naishápúr and placed him under the care of the said Imám, and himself, like a saint, chose a solitary life. At times he ascribed his descent to an infidel family of Ghazal, and said that he was a descendant of Sabáh Khamírí, that his father came from Yemen to Kúfa, from that place to Kúm, and from thence to Re. But the citizens of Re, particularly the people of the country of Tús, denied the fact, and affirmed that his forefathers were natives of their country. In short, one day 'Umar Khayám (one of my schoolfellows) said to me, it is well-known that the pupils of Imám Muwáfik are sure to become men of fortune. There is no doubt of this, but let us make some agreement of union, to be fulfilled on one of the party becoming wealthy? I replied, you may propose any you like. He observed, I propose that if any one of us become rich, he shall divide his wealth equally with the other, and not consider it his own property. I agreed, and this was the promise made between us. It so happened that I went to Khurásán, Mawárán-n nahr, Ghaznín, and Kábul, as I have shortly related before. When I returned from these places I was entrusted with the office of minister; and in the reign of Alp Arslán, Hakím 'Umar Khayám came to me, and I entirely fulfilled my promise. First, I received him with great honour and respect, and gave him presents, and then I told him, you are a clever and qualified man, worthy of being the head of all the King's officers, and by virtue of being a scholar of Imám Muwáfik, you shall be blessed in this office. I will bring you to the notice of the Sultán, and speak to him of your intelligence and honesty, in such terms that he will place confidence in you in the same degree that he does in me. On this, Hakím 'Umar observed, "you are of noble birth, and possess a generous disposition and excellent morals, and these induce you to do me this favour. Otherwise how could such an insignificant man as I am expect this kindness and hospitality from the minister of a kingdom which extends from east to west. I value your favour the more because it is shown with sincerity, and not out of compliment. Such conduct will enable you to obtain much higher dignity and rank. The favour and kindness which you have shown to me is undeniable, and if I were to devote my whole life to you I should still be unable to express my thanks for this single act of kindness. My sole desire is that I may always remain with you. To aspire to the rank which you advise me to obtain is not becoming, as it would evidently be very ungrateful on my part. May

God keep me from doing such a thing! I therefore propose, through your assistance, to seek some retirement where I may apply myself to scientific studies, and pray for the increase of your life."—He persisted in this request; and when I saw that he had openly told me the secret of his heart, I wrote an order for an allowance of one thousand golden miskáls to be annually given to him out of the income of my estates at Naishápúr for his maintenance. After this he left me, and engaged in the study of sciences, particularly Astronomy, and made very great progress in it. In the reign of Malik Sháh he came to Merv and was greatly respected and rewarded there for his knowledge of Natural Philosophy. The King showed him much favour, and raised him to one of the highest ranks that were given to philosophers and learned men. But that irreligious man (Hasan Sabáh) was not so famous in the days of Alp Arslán as he was in Khurásán. He was born in the reign of Malik Sháh. In the year when the Sultán achieved the conquest over Kádir, and completely quelled the disturbances which he had raised, this man came to me in Naishápúr. As much regard and favour was shown to him in consideration of his old friendship, as any faithful and righteous person might show to the extent of his power. He was treated with fresh hospitality and kindness every day. One day he said to me, "Khwája, you are a lover of truth and possessed of excellent virtues. You know that this world is a worthless thing. Is it proper that for the wealth and pomp of this world you should break an agreement, and enrol yourself among those to whom the passage in the Kúran about the violators of promises refers." I observed, "May it never be!" He said, "Yes, you are exceedingly kind and affable, but you know yourself that this was not the agreement between us." I replied, "I acknowledge and admit that we have promised to be partners not only in our titles and ranks, but also in all the estates which we may acquire." After this (conversation took place between us), I took him to the King's court, and at a suitable opportunity I recommended him, and informed the King of the promise which we had made between ourselves. I praised him so much for the great wisdom and excellence of his disposition and character, that the King put confidence in him. As he was a very cunning and artful man, he put on the appearance of honesty, and gained much influence over the King's mind. He obtained such a degree of confidence, that in all important affairs and great undertakings, in which integrity and faithfulness in the agents were needed, the King engaged his assistance and acted according to his advice. In short, I assisted him in obtaining this rank; but at last, by his bad behaviour, many difficulties arose, and I was about to lose all the credit which I had acquired in the course of so many years. In the end he fully shewed the wickedness of his disposition; and marks of bitter animosity and malevolence displayed themselves in his every word and action. If any slight mismanagement took place in the ministerial office, he multiplied and magnified it and reported it to the King, and if the King consulted him about it, he represented the evil of it with some apparently specious arguments.

In Halab (Aleppo) there is a kind of white stone of which pots of all sorts are made. On one occasion it passed the Sultán's tongue that he wished he had some of this kind of stone in Isfahán, and he spoke about it again. One of the camp followers, hearing of the King's wish, after his Majesty had returned (to the capital), said to two merchants of Arabia that if they sent five hundred mans of that stone he would pay them double hire. Accordingly they agreed to carry the 500 mans of stone with their other commodities, each man having 500 mans weight of goods of his own. One of them had six camels and the other four. They divided the stones between them so that they had equal loads upon all their camels. When they reached Isfahán the camp follower came to me, and I took the stone to the King, who was much pleased, and ordered him to be invested with rich apparel, and gave a reward of one thousand dirhams to the merchants, which was to be divided among them by me. I gave six hundred dínárs to him who had six camels, and four hundred to the other. That ungrateful person (Hasan Sabáh) having heard of this, said that I had made a mistake in the division, and had apportioned the money unjustly; that the due of one was still left for the King to pay, and that I should have given eight hundred dínárs to the master of six camels, and two hundred to the other. These words were told the same day to the King, who called me; and when I went to him, that wretch was also standing there. The Sultán looked at me and smiled, and asked me what was the matter. He, then, throwing aside all disguise, said, "The King's money has been divided unjustly, and the due of one has not been given to him." I and the courtiers asked him how? He observed, "The whole load of ten camels consists of three divisions each of five hundred mans, and ten multiplied by three makes thirty. Again, four, the number of one person's camels, into three, makes twelve; and six, the number of the other person's camels, into three, makes eighteen. Now if ten be subtracted from each product, eight, the remainder of the latter product, was due to him who had six camels; and two, the remainder of the other product, to him who had four: and therefore eight hundred dínárs should have been given to the former and two hundred to the latter." In short, when, in spite of me and to puzzle the others, he had given this solution of the question, the King asked him if he could give a plainer statement so that he might understand. He said: "There were ten camels, and the whole load was 1500 mans; therefore each camel had a weight of 150 mans; hence, four camels of one person carried 600 mans; (*i.e.*,) five hundred mans of his own commodities and one hundred mans of the stone for the King. In the same manner, the six camels of the other person carried nine hundred mans, of which five hundred mans were of his own goods and four hundred mans of the Sultan's stone. Thus out of 1000 dínárs for five hundred mans weight of stone two hundred are due upon every hundred mans weight, and consequently eight hundred should be given to the one and two hundred to the other. This was the proper division according to a just calculation; but if it was only a reward without any regard being paid to the weight, then it was all right."[1] When that ungrateful person had spoken all this, the Sultán sided with me, and passed the matter by as a jest. But I saw that it had a great effect upon the king's mind. He (Hasan Sabáh) had several times made those kind of complaints. His grand object was to examine and rectify the accounts of the receipts and disbursements of the revenue of the country. Indeed he got through a great amount of work in the short space of time I was on leave. He

[1] Stories of arithmetical ingenuity are very common in the East. A decision on a similar knotty question is attributed to 'Alí. See Richardson's *Dissertation, Pref. to Persian Dict.*, p. lxiii.

completed this great task in a very short time. But as all the nobles and government officers were aware of his excessive malevolence and jealousy, as well as of his acting contrary to the promises which we had made between us, he obtained praise from no one; and when he submitted the accounts, he suffered such disgrace that he had no courage left to stop at the court.[1] Had not this ungrateful person (whom may God protect!) been so disgraced, there was no remedy for me but that which he at last took.

My object in relating this is to show that one day's trouble of examining the records and accounts and reporting them is not considered equivalent to thirty years' official service, and hence you may judge of other concerns and troubles. May God guide and help! I have said all this to make you desist from seeking the office of wazír; and if it has made no effect upon you, it is necessary that I should mention in detail the rules and precepts which you must observe, and which will be of great advantage and use to you, if God pleases.

º   º   º   º

The Value of Petticoat Influence.

When the kingdom of Khwárizm fell into the possession of Sultán Mahmúd, he ordered the ministers of his court to appoint some qualified person to the management of it. They were for some days consulting with each other. The greatest noble of the court, Altúntásh, contrived to have the appointment conferred upon himself; but when the offer was made to him, he outwardly showed great reluctance in accepting it. Khwája Ahmad Hasan, who was not well disposed towards him, and was anxious to get him out of the way, used his best exertions to get the patent of the appointment drawn up and signed. But as Altúntásh was the greatest pillar of the state, every one thought that the King would not like to send him away from the court. However, as Khwárizm was a very great kingdom, the Sultán agreed to the appointment, and ordered him to proceed to his new government.

---

[1] (The accounts which he rendered had been mutilated or falsified. See Hammer, *Assassins*, p. 46.)

Altúntásh was a great friend of Imám Násiru-d-dín Girámí, who was one of the chiefs of Ghaznín. As he had no time to pay him a farewell visit, he despatched a man with a letter, in which, after expressing his anxiety to see him, he stated that he would not return again to Ghaznín, and expressed his hopes that the Imám, observing the obligations of friendship, would come over to Khwárizm. The Imám, who was desirous of seeing that country as well as Altúntásh, of whom he was an old and intimate friend, went to Khwárizm, where, on his arrival, Altúntásh showed him a thousand kinds of hospitality and favour.

My object in relating this story is to say, that one day the Imám observed that while Altúntásh was at court all the world came to his threshold to pay their respects; such a position in consideration of fame and honour, as well as pecuniary advantage, was an hundred times better than the governorship of Khwárizm. What made him prefer it to a rank in which he exercised influence over the whole kingdom? Altúntásh replied, "O Imám! I have not told this secret even to my dearest relations or sons, but I will not conceal the truth from you. I have resigned that power on account of Jamíla Kandahárí. For years I had the management of all the government affairs in my hands, and during that time she thwarted me in everything. For this reason there was darkness before my eyes, and I could use no remedy against the evil. Now I have sought retirement, and have procured release from all such troubles. If God please, I shall escape her machinations in this distant province."

Now from what I have said, the disadvantages of the ladies of the royal household being against us may be learnt, but the advantages of their being in our favour are equally numerous, and no one's patronage is more efficacious than theirs, for by no one is so much influence and power exercised over the royal mind as by them, as the following story of Khwája Ahmad Hasan illustrates.

The Power of Female Intrigue.

Sultan Mahmúd towards the latter part of his reign was frequently dissatisfied with Khwája Ahmad, and during this time his enemies were assailing him with their calumnies and opposition. Khwája

APPENDIX.   497

Hasnak Mishkáti[1] had been many years watching to find a suitable opportunity of injuring him, and every day it was rumoured that Khwája Ahmad Hasan's place was to be bestowed on him, but as the King's new bride, the daughter of the Khán of Turkistán,[2] was in Ahmad's favour, nothing could be done against him. This lady was called in Ghaznín Mahd-i Chigil, and Jamila Kandahárí was one of her favourite attendants. Under the protection of this lady the Khwája was safe from all dangers. Even such a person as Altúntásh, who was viewed as vicegerent of Subuktigín, could never succeed in any hostile design against him.

On one occasion, when the tents of the Sultán were pitched in the vicinity of Kábul, Khwája Ahmad came on some government business to Ghaznín, and it was reported to him that some merchants were going to Turkistán, who were to return to Ghaznín in the beginning of winter. The Khwája remembered that he required a certain number of *postíns* (great coats) every year for himself and sons, and thought it advisable that some agent should go with the merchants to effect the purchase. To this man's care he committed many valuable and rare commodities of Ghaznín to sell. The same day this news was conveyed to Khwája Hasnak by his spies, and he informed Altúntásh of it. This noble was much rejoiced on receiving the intelligence, and he told Khwája Hasnak that they "could not have found a better opportunity for disgracing him, since he always boasted that he never looked to his own advantage, but to that of the Sultán alone; whereas he is now sending merchants to trade in foreign countries. But we must ascertain this with certainty first, lest the disgrace recoil upon us." Khwája Hasnak said, "the report is perfectly true, and there is no doubt about its correctness; and verily if this fact were disclosed, the Khwája must suffer irremediable ruin."

The Khwája being apprised of their intentions, informed Jamíla Kandahárí of the matter. There was such friendly communication between the Khwája and Jamila, that although it often happened that during a whole year they never had an opportunity of seeing each other, yet one could send messages to the other ten times a day,

---

[1] [He is called Hasnak Mikál in the *Dastúru-l wuzrá*, and Manktí in the *Zínatu-l majális*.]   [2] [Ilak Khán.]

and in such a manner that, excepting the person employed on their mission, nobody knew anything of the matter. In short, Jamíla sent to tell him not to be afraid, because the remedy was very simple. At the same time she repaired to Mahd-i Chigil, and represented the matter to her, suggesting that the Queen should write letters to her mother and brothers, with a detail of the articles which the Khwája had given to the merchant, and add others that were suitable as presents to her royal relatives, mentioning that they were sent as presents on her part, and requesting that they also would send in return some articles of such kinds as were adapted to a female toilette. Jamíla recommended that these letters should be taken to the merchant as soon as possible by some unfrequented road, so that they might be given to him that very night, with the injunction that if the servants of Altúntásh should seize and carry him back, he should say nothing to them, but when conducted to the royal court, he should then declare that he was sent by Mahd-i Chigil, and show the letters and presents which he was commissioned to deliver.

In short, at the instigation of Khwája Hasnak, Altúntásh represented the case to the Sultán, who asked him whether it was a true report. Altúntásh replied that he had ascertained it for certain, and that it was all correct. The King then asked him how he knew that it was true? Altúntásh replied, "If you order me, I can bring the merchant with all the articles which are consigned to him." The King consented. On this Altúntásh immediately despatched his people after the caravan, and they brought the merchant back. According to the instructions, the merchant said nothing to his detainers on the way, but when he entered the court he cried out, that he was sent by Mahd-i Chigil, and then showed the letters under her seal, with the presents which had been despatched, such as scarfs, necklaces, etc. The informers were much chagrined and ashamed, and could advance no excuse for what they had done. On the other hand, Mahd-i Chigil complained to the King that, when after so long a period she had sent from the court of such a great king some trifling presents to her relations, her messenger had been intercepted, and the scarfs and necklaces exposed in open court. By such words she produced great effect upon the King's mind, and with much indignation he ordered the accusers to be put to death; but as Mahd-i Chigil knew that they were innocent, she was unwilling that the blood of so many persons should be shed through her false representations, and begged that their lives might be spared. In short, Altúntásh and Hasnak received a complete defeat, and were covered with ignominy and shame; while the merchant, after being much honoured, was again despatched to Turkistán.

* * * * * * * * * *

Sultán Mas'úd and Khwája Hasnak.

Sultán Mahmúd was always on bad terms with his eldest son Mas'úd; and Khwája Ahmad, although he was unable completely to reconcile them, yet on all occasions he greatly appeased the King's anger. Though he never met the prince except about once a year in the King's presence, he nevertheless did not cease to exert his friendly offices.

When Khwája Ahmad was dismissed, Khwája Hasnak Mishkáti was appointed in his place. This person was a youth of no experience, and but little acquainted with the vicissitudes of the world. His chief attractions were the sincerity of his heart, the affability of his manner, and the readiness with which he served a friend or chastised an enemy. Though the Sultán was in reality disgusted with Mas'úd, yet this secret sentiment remained concealed till the time that he declared his son Muhammad his heir. Hasnak was not in favour with Mas'úd, since, in accordance with the custom of Diwána, he interfered greatly with the rights and privileges of his princely appanage. Mas'úd was so angry with him in consequence, that when one of the rulers of India sent a sword as a present to him, the person who brought it, expatiating on its value, observed that it was so sharp and well-tempered, that even iron could not resist it. When the assembly was broken up, the prince asked his intimate companions what particular use it was adapted for? Some said it was to cut off infidels' heads, and others observed that it was to destroy his Majesty's enemies. In this manner every one expressed his own opinion; but Mas'úd observed, that he would like to fasten it to his side, and when, on the morrow, Hasnak came to pay his respects to him, to cleave his head with it down to his breast. If I were to do this, the King would never demand my blood in retaliation for his murder. He said this in a determined tone, but those who were present dissuaded him, and remarked that a great disturbance would ensue, and the Sultán would be very angry. When the Khwája was informed of what the prince had resolved, he thanked God for his narrow escape.'

A short time after this, Sultán Mahmúd expired, and Sultán Muhammad occupied the throne of sovereignty in Ghaznín. Sultán Mas'úd at this time was in Isfahán, whence he returned with all speed. Sultán Muhammad advanced to oppose him, but the ministers of Mahmúd's court, considering that Mas'úd was much better adapted to wield the sceptre of the kingdom, seized Sultán Muhammad, and kept him prisoner in a fort. They then proceeded as far as Hirát to welcome Mas'úd. At the meeting, when Hasnak dismounted from his horse, the attendants of the prince seized him, and suspended him from a gibbet. They then summoned Khwája Ahmad Hasan, and having entrusted him with the office of wazír, bestowed all kinds of honour on him. Although his ministry was not of long duration, yet it was very successful in its results. He was often heard to say, "Thank God, affairs have reached this conclusion ; my friends are exalted, and my enemies crushed."¹

o   o   o   o   o

The Story of Dábshilím.²

When Sultán Mahmúd had achieved the conquest of Somnát, he wished to stay there for a year because the country was very extensive and abounded with curiosities. There were numerous mines which also produced gold; and the rubies of Sarandip (which was one of its dependencies) were carried to all countries. But his ministers persuaded him that it was highly impolitic to leave

---

¹ [This story is given in the *Ziaatu-l Majális*, but Abú-l 'Abbás is the minister it is told of, not Khwája Ahmad.]

² [This story is given by Firishta (I. p. 75) ; it is also repeated in the *Nigáristán*. Dábshilím is the name of the King of Hind to whom the bráhman Bidpáí (Pilpay) related his fables,—*Anwár-i Suhailí*. See also *Useful Tables* in Thomas' *Prinsep*, No. xxvii.]

Khurásán, which had been conquered, after battling with so many powerful enemies, and to make Somnát the seat of government. In short, the King determined to return; and he ordered that some person should be appointed to govern and retain possession of the country. They represented that no more power or glory could be gained in that country, and therefore they proposed to him to entrust some native with the office. The Sultán consulted in the matter with such people of the country as were of a friendly disposition to him. Some of them told him that no chiefs of the country were equal to the family of Dábshilím, and that at that time only one person of that house was surviving, and he was engaged in worshipping God in the habit of a saint. He ought to have the governorship of the country. Others, however, objected to this, alleging that he was a man of a bad disposition, and had fallen under the wrath of God. He had not willingly taken retirement and devoted himself to worship, but he had been several times seized by his brothers, and in order to save his life he had taken refuge in a place of sanctity; but there was another Dábshilím, who was one of his relations, and who was a very wise, learned, and intelligent man, whom all respected for his philosophical acquirements. He was also at this time the chief of the principality. If the Sultán would appoint him governor and send a farmán to him, he might come and take upon him the management of the country. That he was also very honest and faithful in observing his promises; so that, notwithstanding the great distance which intervened, if he agreed to pay tribute, he would send it every year to Ghaznín. The King said if he presented himself before him the proposal might be accepted, but why should he give such a large kingdom to a person who had already borne the title of king in India, and had not yet come to meet him nor had proffered submission. In short, the devoted Dábshilím was called, and placed in charge of the kingdom. He agreed to pay a tribute, and promised never to act contrary to the King's orders as long as he lived, and also to forward all the gold and rubies which might be extracted from the mines to Ghaznín. But he said there was another Dábshilím among his relations, who was his bitter enemy, and on one occasion some bloodshed had even taken place between them. That he had no doubt this Dábahilím would come against him after hearing of the King's departure; and as he was not possessed of sufficient power, he must of course be overcome and lose the dominions. But if the King would now march against this enemy and remove the ground of fear, he would send annually a tribute to the treasury of Ghaznín equal to all the revenues of Khurásán, Zábulistán, and Kábulistán. The Sultán observed that he had come with the intention of making conquests, and since he had not returned to Ghaznín, he might as well therefore remain six months more. With this resolution he marched towards that Dábahilím's dominions. The people of the country, however, remarked to the pious Dábahilím that it was not proper for him to excite the King to invade his territory, because the person whom the Almighty had made great and powerful could not be subdued by his endeavours. This was also told to the King, who first hesitated, but as he had already marched his troops, he did not like to abandon his resolution. So he proceeded towards the enemy, and having conquered his country, took him prisoner, and gave him over to the pious Dábahilím, who represented that in his country it was considered a very great sin to kill a ruler, and if any king did commit the crime, all his army revolted against him. It was a custom among the kings of the country that when any of them prevailed over another and captured him, a dark room was made under the victor's throne, in which the captive ruler was placed on a cushion, and the doors of the room were shut. But a hole was made in one of them, and through it a dish of food was given to him, and then that also was shut. As long as the victorious king occupied the throne, it was his duty to send a dish of food every day to the subterranean abode, even if the captive died after only a few days' confinement. It happened that the prisoner lived many days. The pious Dábahilím said that as he could not keep him prisoner in this manner, he wished the Sultán would take the prisoner to Ghaznín, and that after he (the new ruler) had established his authority in the country, the captive might be sent back to be confined in the usual way. The King agreed to this, and returned. The pious Dábahilím mounted the throne of Somnát, and began to send successively to the Sultán the presents and rarities of the country; and he also ingratiated himself with all the ministers of his court by sending them presents. When he had confirmed himself in the governorship, he sent tribute, with some jewels, to the King, and asked him to send back his enemy to him. The Sultán at first hesitated in complying with his request, and was unwilling to render him up into the hands of his enemy; but as the devout Dábshilím had gained the favour of the ministers of the throne by his munificence, they all taxed the King with showing mercy to an infidel, and said that it was very improper for a king to act contrary to his promise. It was also to be apprehended that the pious Dábshilím might rebel, and the country be lost. At last the young prince was made over to the people of the pious Dábshilím, and farmáns were sent to the authorities in India to conduct him to the confines of Somnát. When he was taken to that country the pious Dábshilím ordered a dwelling to be made under the throne on which he used to sit. It was the custom among these people that when their enemy was brought near the metropolis of the kingdom, the ruler was to advance one march to receive him. He was also to put a dish and a vessel of water over his head, and make him go on foot before his horse till he arrived at court.[1] After this the King sat on the throne, and his enemy was taken to the subterraneous house, and there seated on a cushion. According to this custom Dábshilím went out; but it happened that the captive had not yet arrived. Dábshilím went out hunting, and exerted himself greatly in the field. When the hot wind began to blow, the soldiers and all the people sought shelter where they might rest, and Dábshilím also alighted and went to sleep under the shade of a tree, covering his face with a red handkerchief. In India there are plenty of birds of prey with hard claws and sharp bills. One of these birds came flying towards him, and when it saw the red handkerchief, it mistook it for a piece of flesh, and pouncing down on Dábshilíms' face, it tore out his eyes with his beak. This created great confusion among his people, and in the meantime the young captive was brought in. The pious Dábshilím was now blind and useless, and, since no other person beside this young man had a right to the

[1] This mode of receiving the banished monarch on his return seems to resemble the present practice of Hindu women forming a procession to meet a stranger with brass pots upon their heads in token of welcome.

governorship, all the people saluted him as their king, and the few persons who held aloof were seized. In short the same dish and vessel of water which were brought for this young chief were placed on the head of the pious Dábshilím, and he was forced to run to the court, where he was placed in the prison he had prepared.

The moral of this story is, the person who really deserves honour and respect cannot be disgraced by the endeavours of his enemy. If for a season he be degraded, he soon recovers his rank. But the envious person brings on himself ignominy and shame.

2.—*Nigáristán*.

[This "Picture-gallery" is a collection of anecdotes and stories relating to various dynasties. It was compiled by Ahmad bin Muhammad bin 'Abdu-l Ghafúr al Ghaffárí al Kazwíní, commonly known as Kází Ahmad al Ghaffárí. *Nigáristán*, the name of the work, expresses by the *abjad* the date of its compilation, A.H. 959 (A.D. 1552). Twenty-eight standard works are mentioned in the Preface of the work as the sources from which the stories have been extracted.[1] There is a copy of the work in Sir H. Elliot's library, and also some miscellaneous extracts from other copies. There are other works which bear the same name.]

Mahmúd and Ahmad Hasan Maimandí.

It is related of Sultán Mahmúd of Ghazní that one day in his youth he went to take a walk in the gardens, and was accompanied by Ahmad Hasan Maimandí, who was one of his most favoured servants. As he passed by a rivulet, his eye fell upon a person who was loitering there, and he asked his companion who the man was? "A carpenter," he replied. The Sultán again asked him what his name was, and he replied, "Ahmad." "You seem to be acquainted with the man," says the Sultán. "No," answered he, "I never saw him before." "Then, how is it," observed the Sultán, "that you came to know his profession and name?" "I knew his name," he replied, "by his readiness to answer your Majesty when your

---

[1] [See Morley's *Catalogue*, p. 50; Hammer-Purgstall *Redekünste Persiens*, pp. 307-9; Krafft's *Catalogus der Handschriften der K.K. Orientalischer Akademie zu Wien*.]

Majesty called me by my name; and as to his profession, I saw him walk round that dry old tree, and look carefully at it." The Sultán, on hearing these words, said, "You would indeed be a most sagacious fellow if you could tell me what that man has eaten to-day." "Honey, or the juice of some fruit," said Ahmad. The Sultán then called the man and asked him, first, "Do you know this boy (Ahmad Hasan)?" The reply was that he had never seen him before. Mahmúd then enquired of the man who he was, what was his name, and what he had eaten that day? The answer was exactly what Ahmad had already given. Greatly wondering, the Sultán turned towards Ahmad and asked him how he knew that the man had eaten honey? to which he thus replied: "I know it because he kept wiping his mouth, and the bees were swarming around him."

Treasures of Bhím-nagar.[2]

It is recorded in many authentic histories that when the Sultán succeeded in capturing the fort of Bhím-nagar, on the confines of India, which was believed to be of incomparable strength, and commonly reported to contain immense wealth, he obtained as booty no less than seventy thousand millions of dirhams, seven hundred thousand and four hundred mans of gold and silver vessels, rare vestments of different kinds, the exact value of which appraisers found it impossible to calculate; and vast quantities of precious stones and pearls, beyond all computation. An edifice (*khána*) fell into the Sultán's hands, which measured 30 cubits by 15, the sides and covering of which were entirely made of pure silver.

A Splendid Comet.

In 330 A.H. (941-2 A.D.), a comet made its appearance, the tail of which reached from the eastern to the western horizon. It remained in the heavens eighteen days, and its blighting influence caused so severe a famine, that wheat, the produce of one jaríb of land, was sold for three hundred and twenty miskáls of gold. "When the value of a spike of corn was esteemed as high as the Pleiades, conceive what must have been the value of wheat."

The famine in the land was so sore that man was driven to feed

---
[2] [Nagarkot or Kangra. See *supra*, p. 85, and Briggs' *Firishta*, I. p. 48.]

on his own species, and a pestilence prevailed with such virulence that it was impossible to bury the dead who fell victims to it.[1]

3.—*Zínatu-l Majális.*

[This is another collection of anecdotes and stories, which have been drawn, as the writer tells us in his Preface, from a great variety of histories and other works, from the *Jámi'u-l Hikáyát* down to the *Nigáristán*. The work was compiled in 1004 Hijra (1595 A.D.), by Majdu-d dín Muhammadu-l Husna, commonly known as Majdí. There is a new and well-written copy of part of the work in Sir H. Elliot's collection, besides some extracts from a copy belonging to R. H. Cust, Esq.]

EXTRACTS.

Destruction of Robbers by Poison.

It is related that in the reign of Sultán Mahmúd of Ghazní a number of Kúch and Balúch robbers having taken possession of a strong place on the road to Hurmuz, plundered all the caravans that passed that way. On one occasion they robbed a body of merchants and killed a young man of Khurásán, who was of their number. His old mother preferred her complaint to Mahmúd, who observed that such accidents occurred in that part of the country because it was too far from his capital. The old woman replied, "Keep no

---

[1] The magnificent comet here noticed was splendid enough, even allowing for Oriental exaggeration, to have attracted attention in Europe; and it may, therefore, probably be noticed in the collection of Lubienietski. It would be one of particular interest if we could establish it as an early visit of Halley's comet; but astronomers date its probable appearance as occurring in A.D. 930. It is to be remembered, however, that the known and recorded intervals of that comet are August 1531, October 1607, September 1682, March 1759, and November 1835; and that between the perihelion passages of the first and second, and of the second and third, of these recorded appearances, there is no less a difference than fifteen months; and again a difference of eighteen months in the perihelion passage of the third and fourth re-appearance, arising from the disturbing action of the planets; so that if we allow during the several centuries which have intervened, a period of eleven years for the perturbations arising from that source, we may perhaps be permitted to recognise an old visitor in the comet of A.H. 330. It must be confessed, however, that the probabilities in favour of this surmise would have been greater had the recurring intervals been prolonged, instead of being abbreviated; but it is difficult for the mind to forego a hypothesis when once assumed, however weakly it may be supported by probable antecedents.

more territory than you can manage." The Sultán was impressed by the truth of these words, and ordered proclamation to be issued that whoever wanted to go to Hurmuz should get ready, and the Sultán would furnish a guard.

When the travellers were ready, the King ordered three hundred of his guards (*ghuldm*) to accompany them. But the merchants said that if there were a thousand horsemen they would be too few. The Sultán replied, that whatever property of theirs should be lost he would make good from his treasury. He then called an old man from amongst the guards, and gave him some instructions, which will be shortly mentioned. When the caravans reached Isfahán, the leader ordered some panniers of apples and other choice fruits to be loaded on camels, and these fruits were charged with poison. At every stage the fruit was taken out and examined, and if any was found rotten it was thrown away. In this manner, when they arrived at the abode of the thieves, they brought out the fruits and spread them on the ground as if to air them. The robbers fell on them, and the guards mounted their horses and took to flight. The merchants were in utter despair respecting the safety of their property and lives. The robbers fell upon the caravan, and bound the merchants, and then they began to eat the fruits which were spread out, and such as no individual had ever seen before in that country. After a short time the poison took effect upon them, insomuch that their hands and feet were quite paralysed. The guards then turned their horses' heads, set upon the half-dead robbers, and finished them with their sharp swords. In this manner the roads were made clear, and security established for travellers.[1]

Mahmúd's Distrust of his Uncle 'Abdu-r rahmán.

It is related in the *Tárikh-i Násiri* that when Sultán Mahmúd of Ghaznín came to Hirát, 'Abdu-r rahmán Khán, who was one of the ministers of state, lodged in a very comfortable dwelling belonging to a learned man of great renown. One day, 'Abdu-r rahmán represented to the King that the house in which he had put up

[1] [This is the same story as the one taken from the *Jámi'u-l Hikáyát* (*supra* p. 194), but it is very differently told. It is also given in the *Tárikh-i Guzída*. See Reinaud, *Mém. sur l' Inde*, p. 171.]

belonged to an old man, who was considered by the people to be very wise and learned. He had a private room, in which he always used to sit, and not come out again for a long time. I asked the people what he did there? They answered that he used to perform worship and say his prayers. "One night," said 'Abdu-r rahmán, "I suddenly went into the room, and saw a large vessel full of wine, and a brazen idol placed before him. After drinking, he prostrated himself before the image. I have brought the idol and the vessel here, in order that your Majesty may give any order you like about that deceitful old man." The Sultán, after a moment's consideration, ordered the man to be brought into his presence, that full enquiry might be made into his case. He then told 'Abdu-r rahmán to place his hands over the Sultán's head and swear that what he had said was true. 'Abdu-r rahmán exclaimed, "Upon your soul and head, all that I have said is a lie." "O coward!" said the King, "what caused you to bring such a charge against that old Fakír?" He replied, "the man had an excellent house, and I thought that your Majesty would punish him and give the house to me." The Sultán thanked Almighty God for having guarded him against an improper act which he might have committed in haste. As it was his habit to think and ponder on every subject, he discovered the truth in this matter, and he never trusted 'Abdu-r rahmán again. Be it not concealed from wise men that the advantages of deliberation are numerous, but that haste and inconsiderateness in affairs of state produce shame without end.

Mas'úd Repents of his Avarice.

It is related in the *Táríkh-i Násirí* that, after the death of Sultán Mahmúd of Ghaznín, his heir, Sultán Muhammad ascended the throne. Enmity then arose between him and his brother, Sultán Mas'úd, governor of 'Irák, who resided at Hamadán. Mas'úd led his army against his brother, who on receiving the intelligence came out to oppose him at the head of the armies of Khurásán and Ghaznín. One day, without any apparent cause, the cap of the King fell from his head, and this was regarded as a bad omen. The same day, at evening, 'Ali Kheshávand and a body of the King's own slaves, espousing the cause of Sultán Mas'úd, surrounded and seized Muhammad and deprived him of sight. Mas'úd then proceeded to Ghaznin and sat upon the throne.

At the same time, Abú Suhal Zaurnki,[1] the 'Ariz, represented that Sultán Muhammad had distributed from the public treasury a large sum among his nobles, army, attendants, and courtiers, but as he was not the real sovereign, the King ought to order these people to refund the money; then, if he liked, he might after a few days give the large fees himself, in order that to him only their obligations might be due.

Sultán Mas'úd having liberated Hasan Maimandi, his father's minister, who had been imprisoned in the fort, raised him to the post of wazir, and consulted him upon these suggestions. The Khwája said, the King might do what he liked, but he should consider this matter well, and see the good and evil of it before adopting any resolution. Sultán Mas'úd, however, would not listen to his advice, and maintained his own determination. The Khwája then summoned Abú Nasr Miskúni,[2] and said: "These cowardly people have been making such and such representations to the King. I wish you to go to him and tell him on my part that such an act was never done by any of the former kings, and it will make people disgusted with him." Abú Nasr said, "Here is what Sultán Muhammad gave me," and he refunded it to the royal treasury. Abú Suhal observed to the King that if all persons would follow the example of Abú Nasr, the money would be soon realised. The Sultán went out hunting, and ordered Abú Suhal to collect it. Abú Suhal appointed officers for that purpose, and inflicted torture and punishment on those who had spent what they had received. People were greatly disgusted with the government, and much confusion ensued in the affairs of the kingdom. Sultán Mas'úd became ashamed of what he had done, and was so much displeased with Abú Suhal, that he removed him from the office he held. He was often heard to say, "May such base servants never find their way into the court of a king."[3]

[1] [The Bú Suhal Zauzani of Baihaki, *supra* p. 68.] *Zauzan* is the name of a town and district between Naishapur and Hirát.

[2] [The "*Mishkán*" of Baihaki, and the *Jámi'u-l Hikáyát*. See *supra* p. 106, 190.]

[3] [This story explains Baihaki's unintelligible allusion about Abú Suhal, *supra* page 88.]

Ibráhím's Lack of Qualified Officials.

It is narrated that one day Sultán Ibráhím of Ghaznín[1] held a public court, and all his nobles and officers were present; but he sat very pensive and spoke not to any one, till the time of mid-day prayers. His ministers were afraid, and had no courage to ask him the cause of his anxiety, till at last one of his courtiers who was most familiar with the King, advanced to the throne and begged to know the reason of his Majesty's being so thoughtful. The King told him that his chief chamberlain had become old, and the boat of his life had reached the brink of death. "To-day," said he, "having looked at all my courtiers, I do not find any one worthy to succeed him. I was therefore thinking that if he should die, his work will still have to be done, and I must of necessity appoint some unqualified person to fill his place." The courtier observed, in reply, "My lord, your eye is as bright as the sun, and has a powerful effect. It turns stones to rubies, and dust to gold. If you instruct some one, he will then be able to do everything." The Sultán said, "It is true; but still the sun, though he be the great luminary, cannot at once make a ruby out of a stone; and although an alchemist may be acquainted with the art of making gold, yet he cannot effect his purpose without obtaining all the requisite ingredients."

Ibráhím maintains a body of Trained Officials.

Sultán Ibráhím[2] of Ghaznín having mounted the throne, determined to establish his government on a strong and secure foundation. Through the invasions of the Saljúks and the weakness of his predecessors, 'Abdu-r Rashíd and Farrukh-zád, the affairs of the kingdom were in a state of embarrassment, and the management of the country had been left to worthless characters. With this view, he called Khwája Abú-l Kásim Hasírí, who was an old man, and had been one of the confidential officers of Yamínu-d daula Mahmúd, and who excelled all his contemporaries in wisdom and in the purity of his mind. He consulted with him, and Abú-l Kásim observed that, one day when he was deputed by the King's grandfather,

[1] [Apparently Ibráhím II.]   [2] [Ibráhím II.]

Sultán Mahmúd, on a mission to Ilak Khán, the ruler of Máwaráu-n nahr and Turkistán, he heard from the Khán, who was the wisest man of the time, that a kingdom might be compared to a garden, and the king to a gardener, who, if he wishes to make a good garden, must have three kinds of trees in it—firstly, fruit-bearing trees from which fruit may be gathered at once; secondly, trees from which fruit may soon be expected, which, though they do not yield fruit, yet by their blossoms and verdure, add beauty to the garden; and thirdly, young trees which some time afterwards will produce fruit. When the trees are old and withered, the gardener uses them for fuel; and young trees being planted in succession, they in their turn bear flowers and fruit, so that the garden is never without fruit, or wanting in flowery beauty.

Sultán Ibráhím, on hearing these words, determined on observing them in his government. He always trained up a body of men qualified to conduct the important duties of the government; and in doing this, he took especial care that his officers should not think that the King could not do without them, and that there were no people able to fill their offices. He also wished them to feel that there were other persons equal to them, and qualified to perform their duties; and that as it was by his favour only that they had held office, they ought always to endeavour to please him.

The Punishment of Túmán.[1]

It is related in the Táríkh-i Násiri, that when 'Abdu-r Rashíd succeeded to the throne of Ghazní, he showed great favour to one of his slaves named Túmán, and so advanced him from day to day, that at last the direction of all affairs came under his control. This Túmán was a low-minded, ill-bred tyrannical fellow, who did his best to bring down the great and noble, and to get low and bad men appointed to their places. Among these he patronised and sup-

---

[1] [This is the same story as that given in page 196 from the Jámi'u-l Hikáyát, and which I could not find in the MSS. of that work. Search was also made for the story in Sir H. Elliot's imperfect copy of the Zínatu-l Majális, but without success. The text has since been discovered among some miscellaneous extracts from this work, and as it shows that there are several differences in the story or errors in the translation, I have here introduced a new version after the text of the Zínat.—ED.]

ported Abú Suhal Ráziki,¹ whom he pitted against the good Khwája 'Abdu-r Razzák, son of Hasan Maimandí. Abú Suhal employed all kinds of deceit and calumny against the Khwája; Túmán also added his slander. 'Abdu-r Rashíd was young, simple, and inexperienced. He dismissed his minister 'Abdu-r Razzák, and ordered him to be fined.

Túmán had favoured with his notice a fellow named Khatíb Lút, a base and harsh man; and he now advanced him to the dignity of Díwán of the State (Chancellor of the Exchequer). Khwája Abú Táhir Hasan, who was one of the old officials of the state of Ghazní, under the orders of 'Abdu-r Rashíd, proceeded at this time to Hindustán, in order to bring the revenues of that country to the capital. When he arrived in Hindustán he found agents of Túmán in every city and town, who by their oppressive conduct were irritating the people. The Khwája made a report of the facts, which he addressed to Abú-l Fazl, the financial minister (*sáhib-i díwán-i rasálat*). Abú-l Fazl communicated the account to 'Abdu-r Rashíd, who called for Túmán and reproached him. This caused Túmán to conceive a hatred against Abú-l Fazl, and to calumniate him. 'Abdu-r Rashíd, in his simplicity, ordered Abú-l Fazl to be fined and imprisoned. After this dismissal Túmán exercised unlimited power, and he appointed Khatíb Lút to the management of the country of Parshawar. This man there raised the standard of oppression, and reduced the people to great distress.

When Khwája Abú Táhir reached that country (on his return from Hindustán) the people complained of Khatíb Lút, so the Khwája called for him and admonished him. Khatíb gave insolent replies and was abusive, so the Khwája, to maintain his own dignity, directed him to be turned out of court, and afterwards he ordered him into confinement. Khatíb's people communicated the circumstances to Túmán, who showed the letters to the King, and said that Khatíb knew what sums of money had been exacted improperly from the people, and the Khwája had therefore confined him. 'Abdu-r Rashíd, without any investigation, and merely upon these absurd statements of Túmán, directed him to seize the Khwája and bring him a prisoner to court along with Khatíb.

¹ [*Erzeroi*, see pp. 68 and 609.]

APPENDIX.   513

Túmán proceeded to Parshawar with three hundred horse, and having captured Abú Táhir, put him in chains. He then released Khatíb Lút from confinement, and returned. When they were one day's journey from Ghazní, they received the unexpected intelligence that the infidel Tughril had slain 'Abdu-r Rashíd and usurped his place. The horsemen who had come with Túmán then went to Khwája Abú Hasan (Táhir), and with many apologies, said, "The power is now in your hands; whatever you order we will execute." The Khwája directed them to remove the fetters from his feet and place them on Túmán. The soldiers then pulled him roughly from his horse and placed the chains on his feet. Khatíb Lút and his dependents were also seized, placed upon camels, and carried to Ghaznín. All this calamity fell upon 'Abdu-r Rashíd because he was a simpleton,[1] and listened to the reports of sycophants.

NOTE G.

Mir-át-i Mas'údí.

[This is professedly a life of Mas'úd the Ghaznivide, and finds an appropriate place here after the story books. The author of this extraordinary work was by name 'Abdu-r Rahmán Chishtí. He explains the motives which impelled him to its composition, and the sources of his information after the following manner: "The history of the King of Martyrs, Sálár Mas'úd, the facts of his birth, of his coming to Hindustan, and of his martyrdom, are told by different men in various ways, which have not found a place in any historical work of repute. The writer had long endeavoured to ascertain the real facts; and, after much research he obtained possession of an old book written by Mulla Muhammad Ghaznawí. This man was servant of Sultán Mahmúd Subuktigín. He was also in the service of Sálár Sáhú, and of the Prince of Martyrs, whom he survived. The writer perused this old book from beginning to end with the greatest pleasure, and the doubts which he had entertained were dispelled. The book was very long, it entered into details about the wars of Sultán Mahmúd, and Sálár Sáhú, mentioning incidentally here and there the King of Martyrs, and closing with an account of his

[1] [*Lauh-i sáda*; lit., *tabula rasa.*]

VOL. II.   33

martyrdom. Several of the beloved friends and attendants of the Martyr Sultán, in the abodes of the blessed, have urged the writer to the task which he has undertaken; but no one has made the same demand on behalf of Sultán Mahmúd. It therefore seemed expedient to him that he should select and commit to writing all that related to the Martyr King. He would not, however, have been able to succeed, even in this, without the directions he graciously received from the spirit of the departed. When he had set about his selection, and had engaged earnestly in the work, one night the spirit of the deceased martyr appeared to the writer in a vision, and most condescendingly expressed, with his blessed tongue, his approval of the work. Being thus graciously honoured, the author humbly replied that he had begun the work, and begged for assistance wherever his narration might be too high, or too low, too short, or too long. The spirit, with great affability, directed the author to write, and that he would attend to him and assist him. The present work is the result, to which the author has given the name *Mir-át-i Mas'údí*. May the reader of it also be (*mas'úd*) blessed. This is the author's prayer. The biography of the King of Martyrs having been derived from the aforesaid history, is here related in five chapters (*dástáns*). Sundry incidents, and miraculous statements, which have been found in trustworthy books, have been selected, and, after being verified by oral communications with the author's spiritual visitors, have been inserted in the present work."

The book may then be called a historical romance. In it fact and fiction are freely mingled, and the great actions and exploits of other men are appropriated, without scruple, to the hero of the tale. The author quotes the *Rauzatu-s Safá*, the *Táríkh-i Fíroz Sháhí*, of Shams-i Siráj, and the *Muntakhabu-t Tawáríkh*; but he professes, as we have seen, to base his work mainly on the lost *Tawárikh-i Mahmúdí* of Mulla Muhammad Ghaznawí. It is much to be regretted that he has quoted so little of that work; for his quotations from the *Rauzatu-s Safá* are fair, though somewhat abridged, and stripped of redundant ornament. Putting his hero Mas'úd aside, the accounts which he gives of the Musulmán conflicts with the Hindus agree in many respects with what we gather from other sources; his incidents seem to be borrowed rather than invented, and, as he used a contemporary work which is not known to us, it may be that some of his novel statements may be true, or may serve to explain, or elucidate other writers, though no reliance can be placed on them when unsupported.

The work bears no date; but the author tells us that he wrote in the time of Jahángír, a time far too distant for him to have had any personal knowledge of the scenes he depicts. Sir H. Elliot accredits him with another work, the *Mir-át-i Asrár*. The MS. is a duodecimo of 214 pages, 165 of which were translated by Mr. R. D. Chapman, B.C.S., by request of Sir H. Elliot. The editor regrets that the nature of the book has compelled him to reject a full half of the translation. It may be that even now too much has been printed; but the book is unknown to the European reader, and the extracts given will probably satisfy, rather than excite further curiosity.]

CHAPTER 1.

Of the expedition of Sálár Sáhú, general (pahlawán) of the army, into Hindustán, by order of Sultán Mahmúd of Ghazní, to the assistance of Muzaffar Khán; and of the birth of Mas'úd at Ajmír.

Sultán Mahmúd of Ghazní (God make the light of his tomb to shine!) having subdued the kingdom of Rúm and the whole of the countries of Túrán and Irán, spreading everywhere the religion of Muhammad, was seated on his throne awaiting an occasion of further executing the purposes of Allah, when suddenly one day, four men mounted on camels, appeared from the direction of Hindustán, making loud lamentations. The officers of state and the attendants brought word immediately to the Sultán, and they were summoned to the presence.

Bowing to the ground, they spake as follows:—"Sultán Abú-l Hasan attacked us with his army, and slew Hurmuz, the servant of Muzaffar Khán; he also very nearly succeeded in putting to death Muzaffar Khán himself, his wife and children, and all those about him, so that he was obliged to evacuate the place with all his dependants, and escape towards the desert. He has now been living for some years in Ajmír. At the present time Rái Bhírún and Rái Súm-giriyá, with four and forty other Hindu princes, have assembled from all sides to attack Muzaffar Khan and destroy the Musulmáns. The infidels surround us on all sides, and we have no hope but in thee, Oh Asylum of the World! For God's sake, give a thought to these poor followers of Islám." "Be of good courage," said the Sultán, "I will protect the Musulmáns." Khwája Hasan Maimandí, the wazír of the Sultán, asked them in whose name they worded their *khutba*. "Hitherto," they answered, "in addition to the one sole God Almighty and the glorious Asylum of Prophecy (Muhammad), we have repeated in our *khutba* the names of the Faithful Khalífas. Now that the Sultán has promised us his assistance, we shall word our *khutba* in the name of the Sultán Mahmúd of Ghazní." The Sultán was delighted with this reply, and ordered Khwája Hasan Maimandí to select one of the generals and bring him quickly, that he might be sent with an army.

After a long consultation the command was given to Sálár Sáhú, general of the army, and several officers of importance, and 700,000 (*haft lak*) veteran cavalry were appointed to the duty, and started off. The Sultán bestowed his own scimitar, girdle, and dagger, together with an Arab charger, upon the general, and the other officers were all honoured with dresses and horses, and were addressed by their lord as follows:—" If you wish to please me, please my brother, Sálár Sáhú ; serve him with all your power and do his pleasure. My brother Sálár Sáhú is a careful, just, discriminating man ; he will do nothing that is not loyal, considerate, and right."

It was on the fifth of the month of Zíhijja, in the year 401 (1011 A.D.) that Sálár Sáhú left Kandahár for Ajmír with his army (the Sultán having at that time quitted Ghazní, and taken up his residence at Kandahár).

Making the four camel-riders who had been sent as messengers by Muzaffar Khán their guides, they took the way to Ajmír by way of Thatta. Having traversed the intervening desert, they arrived within three days' march of Ajmír. The General then sent forward the camel-riders to give notice to Muzaffar Khán, while he remained himself encamped by the side of the road. On that night spirits addressed him in mysterious voices, and revealed to him that two pieces of good fortune would befal him during the expedition : in the first place he should be victorious over the unbelievers ; and

secondly, a male child should be born to him. At this time many
spirits appeared to Sálár Sáhú, pouring such like glad tidings into
his ears, as is fully related in the *Tawáríkh-i Mahmúdí*. From that
time he perceived a supernatural influence at work within him. * *

When the news of the arrival of the General reached Muzaffar
Khán he was overjoyed, and caused music to be played. The unbelievers who had assembled to besiege Ajmír were struck with a
panic, and agreed together that since Mahmúd's army had come up
on one side, and Muzaffar Khán, taking courage, was preparing to
sally out on the other, it would be imprudent to attempt an engagement with two separate armies. Therefore they had better retreat
for the present, and determine on some approved plan of fighting
after the two forces had coalesced. So they raised the siege of
Ajmír, and retiring to a distance of seven kos, encamped near the
Koh-pukhar.

Muzaffar Khán then went to meet the General, and, conducting
him into Ajmír, besought him that he would permit him to remove
his people from the fort and lodge the General there. But Sálár
Sáhú would not consent, saying, he had come to his assistance, and
it would be very unseemly to turn him and his children out of his
fort, and to take up his quarters there himself. So he pitched his
tents on the banks of the tank Pukhar,[1] sacred among the unbelievers; and, having taken a few days rest, again put himself in
motion by Muzaffar Khán's advice. The enemy also drew up their
forces in line, and the flower of both armies joined in battle. The
field raged with the conflict for three days; but on the third the
breeze of victory began to blow on the side of the General, and the
unbelievers yielded and fled. The Faithful pursued them to a
distance of several parasangs, slew a great number of their officers,
took a few prisoners, and then returned. The General took possession of the enemy's camp that day, and, having interred such of
the Faithful as had been blessed with the honour of martyrdom,
and distributed the whole spoil of the unbelievers among the
soldiers of his army, he returned the next day towards Ajmír.

He then built a mosque at the gate of the fort of Ajmír, and

---

[1] [Hind., *pokhar*; Sans., *pushkara*, a lake.]

having performed a religious service in honour of Mahmúd of Ghazní, he sent an account of all that had happened, together with congratulations on the victory, to the Sultán.

After this he appointed officers to many places in the neighbourhood of Ajmír, which had never been under the sway of Muzaffar Khán, and brought them so under control that the collectors settled down, and revenue began to flow in on all sides.

The rebels, who fled, took refuge with Rái Ajípál¹ at Kanauj. When the letter of Sálár Sáhú reached the Sultán, he was overjoyed at the good tidings, and bestowed a special dress of honour, with several Arab horses upon him, and was graciously pleased to order the government of the country to be given to his faithful brother, Sálár Sáhú. He also wrote as follows: "If the Rái Ajípál (Jaipál), Prince of Kanauj will adopt the Musulmán faith, well; but if not, we ourselves will proceed towards that country with our all-conquering army." The Sitr Mu'alla' (dignified veiled one) also was ordered to join her husband (Sálár Sáhú).

When Sitr Mu'alla' reached Ajmír with the dress of honour and the farmán, Sálár Sáhú gave himself up entirely to pleasure and rejoicing; and, through the power of Almighty God, on that very night—*i.e.*, on the ninth of the month Shawwál, in the year 404—Sálár Mas'úd left the loins of his father and entered the womb of his mother. Nine months passed in ease and pleasure; and in the tenth month, on the twenty-first of the month of Sha'bán, in the year 405, on Sunday, at the pure time of dawn in the first hour, the world-enlightening son was born. The beauty of Yúsuf, the grace of Abraham, and the light of Muhammad shone upon his brow.

○   ○   ○

The Sultán was also extremely delighted at the birth of his sister's son, and had rich dresses of honour prepared for the father, mother, and the infant Mas'úd. He also, in the most gracious manner, issued a mandate under his own hand to this effect: "Let the Government of the Kingdom of Hindustán be bestowed upon our brother and his son; and if the Rái Ajípál give in his submission, well and good; if not, let him know that we ourselves will

¹ [The Jaipál of other writers.]

make an expedition into Hindustán, and on the same occasion will see our nephew Sálár Mas'úd."

Khwája Hasan Maimandí, who had an hereditary feud with the General of the army, was jealous of the honours and favours bestowed on him by the Sultán; but to what purpose?

Meanwhile, although Sálár Sáhú sought to lead Rái Ajípál in the right way, he would not cast his lot into the scale of truth; and from excess of worldly-mindedness he did not even desire peace. On the contrary, he encouraged the rebels of the surrounding country, who had taken refuge with him after their flight from Ajmír, to attack the dominions of the Sultán. The General, troubled by anxiety arising from his infatuation, communicated the state of affairs to the Sultán, and, after a few days, Mahmúd took the road to Hindustán with his army. The General Sálár Sáhú, and Muzaffar Khán, went to meet the Sultán with their armies, and conducting him first to Ajmír, displayed Sálár Mas'úd to the fortunate gaze of their royal master, and then presented offerings of money and all kinds of property.

The Sultán bestowed the whole on Sálár Mas'úd, and, during the several days that he remained at Ajmír, he would not let him (Mas'úd) go out of his sight. He then turned towards Kanauj with his army, in rage and indignation, appointing Sálár Sáhú and Muzaffar Khán to the van of the army.

He first came to Mathura, and plundered that nest of idolatry which was a very holy spot among the people of India. After subduing and plundering all the chiefs of the neighbourhood who were reported to be rebellious and factious, he next proceeded against Rái Ajípál, the King of Kanauj, who did not venture to resist him, but fled, as is detailed in the history called the *Rauzatu-s Safá*, as follows:— ○ ○ ○ ○

The author of the *Tawárikh-i Mahmúdí* relates that when the Sultán returned to Ghazní after the Indian expedition, Sálár Sáhú, the general, petitioned to be allowed to attend him, but the Sultán said, "The subjugation of this country of Kanauj is your work, my brother, and I have therefore appointed you its governor." When they had reached the neighbourhood of Lahore he presented the General with a dress of honour and sixteen Arab horses, and dismissed him; nor did he neglect Sálár Mas'úd, but bestowed upon him costly gifts. He also honoured Muzaffar Khán with presents of dresses and chargers, and sent him away with the General, ordering him to serve him in every way in his power.

So the General returned to Ajmír, and immediately appointed officers throughout the districts of his province, whether now or old, for the protection of the people and the redress of the oppressed. He then fixed an annual tribute to be paid by the Rái Ajípál, and left him at Kanauj on condition of service, whilst he himself remained at Ajmír, enjoying all happiness and peace, governing India as deputy of the Sultán.

He was exceedingly fond of his son, and when Mas'úd was four years four months and four days old, he sent him to a tutor, Mír Saiyid Ibráhím, to be instructed in the creed of Islám. ⁰ ⁰ ⁰ ⁰ The Almighty had endued him with a great aptitude for learning, so that by the time he was nine years old he had acquired most sciences, practical and abstract, and at ten years of age he was so given up to devotion that he passed the whole night in deep study, and never left his chamber before a watch of the day had passed. ⁰ ⁰ ⁰ In short, he excelled in everything, small and great, and was skilled in whatever came before him. ⁰ ⁰ ⁰

The Prince of Martyrs was most spotless in body and mind. His pure soul was occupied always in meditating on God, and he was free from sin, external and internal. ⁰ ⁰ ⁰

Chapter 2.

Of the return of Sálár Sáhú and the Prince of Martyrs to Ghazní, and of the feud of Hasan Maimandí, the wazír of Sultán Mahmúd of Ghazní, with Sálár Mas'úd, on account of the destruction of the image of Somnát.

In the course of the next ten years the General subdued many of the countries of India, and lost all fear of the efforts of the unbelievers. The revenue, too, began to flow in regularly and without trouble.

The Sultán Mahmúd was in Khurásán, when some rebels, inhabiting the skirts of the mountain, banded together for the purpose of attacking Kábuliz, and Malik Chhachú, Governor of

Kábulíz, reported the matter to the Sultán. As soon as the intelligence reached him, a farmán was issued in the name of the General, ordering him to leave half his forces for the protection of the country of Ajmír, and to proceed himself with the other half to Kábulíz, and so to punish the unbelievers, as to make them careful not to rebel again, adding, that he (the Sultán) would go himself, but that he was occupied with important matters.

Kábulíz is situated in the vicinity of Kashmír. It was an important place, and had a very lofty fort. The town was originally in the hands of Rái Kalíchand Fir'auní.[1] He had grown presumptuous on account of the abundance of his wealth and forces, and the extent of his kingdom; therefore, when Sultán Mahmúd went on the Kanauj expedition in the year 407, upon his arrival in Kashmír, he took the fort of Rái Kalíchand with the greatest difficulty, and appointed civil officers of his own. The particulars of the siege of the fort, and of the death of Rái Kalíchand with 50,000 of his companions, are related in the *Rauzatu-s Safá*, but cannot be told in a brief work like the present.

The General of the army having left Mír Saiyid Ibráhím, Muzaffar Khán, and other confidential nobles of his province, to attend upon Sálár Mas'úd, proceeded with his train by successive marches to Kábulíz.

The unbelievers assembled in such numbers that the very ground round Kábulíz was black with them. Malik Chhachú, not being strong enough for an open fight, had shut himself up in the fort of Kábulíz, and the unbelievers, having ravaged the province, were on their way home when the General met them, and, offering them battle, fought for three hours. The army of the Faithful was victorious. Innumerable unbelievers were slain, and their army put to flight. Forty officers were taken prisoners, and several thousand men bit the dust. It was a great victory. Sálár Súhú wrote his dispatch of victory to the Sultán as soon as he had entered Kábulíz. The Sultán was greatly pleased, and that instant issued a farmán under his own hand to this effect, "We bestow the province of Kábulíz, as an iná'm upon our victorious brother, in addition to his jágír; let him make the land his own."

[1] ["Kulchand."—The addition of "Fir'aúní" is a blunder. See *supra*, p. 43, and 458.]

APPENDIX.

As soon as it was determined that the General should live at Kábullz, he sent messengers to Ajmír to fetch Sálár Mas'úd, and to tell that light of his eyes to come quickly to him, along with his mother, leaving the officers whom he had appointed at Ajmír each at his post. When the messengers reached Ajmír, Sálár Mas'úd was delighted, and the next day started off for Kábullz with his mother, accompanied by several thousand horsemen, who were like stars shining round that peerless moon. Engaging in the chase as he went, stage by stage, he reached the town of Rawál. The zamíndár of that place, Satúgan, was father-in-law of Khwája Hasan Maimandí's son. He came out to meet Sálár Mas'úd, and insisted that he should do him the favour of staying that day at his house, that so he might get honour, as he said, among the other zamíndárs. But as the star of Hasan Maimandí's bad faith shone in the forehead of Satúgan, Sálár Mas'úd would by no means consent to alight at the abode of such a treacherous unbeliever. According to his usual habit he had the tents pitched outside the town.

Again Satúgan besought him to eat the food that he had prepared for his party, but the Prince of Martyrs answered him, "The Prophets" (the delight of Allah be upon them and on us all!) "never eat food prepared in the house of a Hindu, nor will I." Satúgan then entreated him to take sugar, rice, and all things necessary, and have his food prepared by his own cooks. But as evil was in the heart of Satúgan, neither was this agreed to. In the morning, as they were starting, Satúgan brought 200 mans of sweetmeats, prepared in various ways, some of the choicest kind for Sálár Mas'úd; but he had caused the whole to be poisoned. Sálár Mas'úd, with divine perception, suspecting the truth, put it all with the baggage, and gave special orders that none should touch it. He then gave Satúgan a dress of honour, and dismissed him.

When he had marched one stage, he ordered Malik Nekbakht to bring the sweetmeats presented by Satúgan. As soon as he had given of the choicest kind to some dogs, they all fell down dead from the poison the moment they tasted it. The Prince of Martyrs, turning towards those present, said with his pure tongue, "The wretched infidel thought me, too, one of the undiscerning." His attendants were astonished at this proof of his ability, and bowing to the ground, began to extol him. When they told his mother what had taken place, she wept bitterly to think what a terrible misfortune might have happened, and declared that the unbelievers had attempted to commit this treachery at the instigation of the deceitful Hasan Maimandí. Then calling Sálár Mas'úd into her presence, she clasped him to her bosom, and gave large alms to the poor and wretched as a thank-offering.

The night was passed at that place. In the morning, when it was marching time, Mas'úd besought his mother to stay there that day, as it was a good hunting-ground, and he wanted to enjoy some sport. So they did so.

Sálár Mas'úd, taking with him some thousands of the flower of his young men—angels in form, and reckless in courage—took the road to the town of Rawáil,[1] hunting as he went, and sent forward spies to learn what Satúgan was doing. When he had nearly reached the town, the spies brought him word that Satúgan had just completed his ablutions, and was worshipping his idols. Upon hearing which they turned their horses straight towards the town. At the same time, the unbelievers got warning, and turned out to oppose them. But the brave youths, flourishing their swords, hovered on all sides, like moths round a flame; and the unbelievers, unable to withstand them, were routed, and the Faithful scattered their heads in every street.

Having put a great many of them to the sword, they took the reprobate Satúgan alive, and brought him before the prince, who addressed him thus: "Oh, Satúgan, did you not know us, that, in the blackness of your heart, you should try such a vile plot on us." He then ordered that he, with his wife and children, should be bound and carried to the army. He then gave the whole place over to plunder. So they brought Satúgan, with his wife and children, to the camp.

This was the first exploit, and maiden victory, of Sálár Mas'úd. His mother caused pæans of joy to be sung, distributed bountiful alms, and gave horses, dresses of honour, and money to all the soldiers of the prince. At that time Mas'úd was twelve years old.

[1] [Here written "Zawál."]

The next day he wrote an account of the affair to the Sultán Mahmúd, and, starting off the couriers, proceeded himself, march by march, with great splendour to Kábulís. Before the messengers of the Prince of Martyrs reached the Sultán, Náráyan, brother of Salúgán, had brought a complaint through Hasan Maimandí that Sálár Mas'úd had carried off his brother, with his wife and little ones as prisoners, and had plundered the town of Rawál. The Sultán was in perplexity at this intelligence, when Mas'úd's account of the perfidy of Salúgan reached him. The Sultán then issued a farmán, signed with his own hand, to Sálár Mas'úd, informing him that Náriyan had brought an accusation before the arrival of his account, and ordering him to keep the guilty man with good care, as he would himself make inquiries and punish him. The Prince of Martyrs was filled with joy on the receipt of this farmán; but mourning fell on the house of Hasan Maimandí, and his hidden treachery was made manifest.

When they had arrived within one kos of Kábulís, the General received intelligence of their approach, and, smitten with a longing desire to behold his son, who was like a second Joseph, he started off himself, like Jacob, regardless of ceremony, to meet him.

    o   o   o   o

It happened that Mahmúd had long been planning an expedition into Bhardána, and Gujerat, to destroy the idol temple of Somnát, a place of great sanctity to all Hindus. So as soon as he had returned to Ghazní from his Khurásán business, he issued a farmán to the General of the army, ordering him to leave a confidential officer in charge of the fort of Kábulís, and himself to join the court with his son Sálár Mas'úd. Accordingly, they presented themselves before the Sultán, who received them with special marks of favour, and showed such great kindness to Mas'úd that his wazír became jealous.

Afterwards he invited Sálár Sáhú to a private audience, and asked his advice about leading an army against Somnát. "Through the favour of Allah," said that officer, "the power and grandeur of your Majesty have struck such terror into the hearts of the unbelievers, that not one of them has the daring to oppose you. The best plan is at once to commence the enterprise." This advice was most pleasing to the Sultán, though Khwája Hasan Maimandí dissented from it. After some conversation, it was settled that the General of the army should return to Káhulíz, and guard that province against the rebellious unbelievers, leaving Sálár Mas'úd, with his victorious army, in attendance upon the Sultán. As soon as he had dismissed Sálár Súhú, the Sultán set out for Somnát with his victorious host, Mas'úd serving under him in the enterprize with several thousand youths in the flower of their age. They performed many illustrious deeds, and the Sultán showed them increasing favour and kindness.

They first reached Multán, and, when everything was fully prepared, took the road for Somnát. The details of the expedition are thus given in the history called the *Rauzatu-s Safá*. * * * * *

God bestowed great grace on this king, and his perfections may be understood from the following relation of the author of the *Nafahát*.

When the Sultán Mahmúd Subuktigín had gone on the expedition to Somnát, they suggested to Khwája Abú Muhammad of Chisht, that he ought to go and help him. The Khwája, though he was seventy years old, set out with some darweshes, and when he arrived made war upon the pagans and idolaters with all his sacred soul. One day the idolaters made a successful assault, and the army of the Faithful, nearly overwhelmed, fled to the Shaikh for protection. Khwája Abú Muhammad had a disciple in the town of Chisht, Muhammad Kálú by name. He called out "Look, Kálú!" At that moment Kálú was seen fighting with such fury, that the army of the Faithful proved victorious. The unbelievers were routed. At that very time Muhammad Kálú was seen in Chisht, striking upon the wall with a pestle, and when he was asked the reason, he said, "When the Almighty commanded a man of Abú Muhammad of Chisht's exalted piety to go to the assistance of the Sultán, who could stand before him?"

It is related in the *Táríkh-i Mahmúdí* that the Sultán shortly after reached Ghazní, and laid down the image of Somnát at the threshold of the Mosque of Ghazní, so that the Musulmáns might tread upon the breast of the idol on their way to and from their devotions. As soon as the unbelievers heard of this, they sent an embassy to

Khwája Hasan Maimandí, stating that the idol was of stone and useless to the Musulmáns, and offered to give twice its weight in gold as a ransom, if it might be returned to them. Khwája Hasan Maimandí represented to the Sultán that the unbelievers had offered twice the weight of the idol in gold, and had agreed to be subject to him. He added, that the best policy would be to take the gold and restore the image, thereby attaching the people to his Government. The Sultán yielded to the advice of the Khwája, and the unbelievers paid the gold into the treasury.

One day, when the Sultán was seated on his throne, the ambassadors of the unbelievers came, and humbly petitioned thus: "Oh, Lord of the world! we have paid the gold to your Government in ransom, but have not yet received our purchase, the idol Somnát." The Sultán was wroth at their words, and, falling into reflection, broke up the assembly and retired, with his dear Sálár Mas'úd, into his private apartments. He then asked his opinion as to whether the image ought to be restored, or not? Sálár Mas'úd, who was perfect in goodness, said quickly, "In the day of the resurrection, when the Almighty shall call for Ázar, the idol-destroyer, and Mahmúd, the idol-seller, Sire! what will you say?" This speech deeply affected the Sultán, he was full of grief, and answered, "I have given my word; it will be a breach of promise." Sálár Mas'úd begged him to make over the idol to him, and tell the unbelievers to get it from him. The Sultán agreed; and Sálár Mas'úd took it to his house, and, breaking off its nose and ears, ground them to powder.

When Khwája Hasan introduced the unbelievers, and asked the Sultán to give orders to restore the image to them, his majesty replied that Sálár Mas'úd had carried it off to his house, and that he might send them to get it from him. Khwája Hasan, bowing his head, repeated these words in Arabic, "No easy matter is it to recover anything which has fallen into the hands of a lion." He then told the unbelievers that the idol was with Sálár Mas'úd, and that they were at liberty to go and fetch it. So they went to Mas'úd's door and demanded their god.

That prince commanded Malik Nokhakht to treat them courteously, and make them be seated; then to mix the dust of the nose and ears of the idols with sandal and the lime eaten with betel nut, and present it to them. The unbelievers were delighted, and smeared themselves with sandal, and eat the betel leaf. After a while they asked for the idol, when Sálár Mas'úd said he had given it to them. They inquired, with astonishment, what he meant by saying that they had received the idol? And Malik Nekbakht explained that it was mixed with the sandal and betel-lime. Some began to vomit, while others went weeping and lamenting to Khwája Hasan Maimandí and told him what had occurred.

The Khwája writhed like a snake, and said, "Verily, the king is demented, since he follows the counsel of a boy of yesterday! I will leave the service of the Sultán for your sakes, and do you also go and attack his country. We will open his Majesty's eyes." Accordingly the unbelievers returned with the news to the Hindu princes. And Khwája Hasan, from that day, resigned the office of Wazír, became disaffected, and left off attending to the duties of his office.

Afterwards the image of Somnát was divided into four parts, as is described in the *Tawárikh-i Mahmúdí*. Mahmúd's first exploit is said to have been conquering the Hindu rebels, destroying the forts and the idol temples of the Rái Ajipál (Jaipál), and subduing the country of India. His second, the expedition into Harradawá[1] and Guzerát, the carrying off the idol of Somnát, and dividing it into four pieces, one of which he is reported to have placed on the threshold of the Imperial Palace, while he sent two others to Mecca and Medina respectively. Both these exploits were performed at the suggestion, and by the advice, of the General and Sálár Mas'úd; but India was conquered by the efforts of Sálar Mas'úd alone, and the idol of Somnát was broken in pieces by his sole advice, as has been related, Sálár Sáhú was Sultán of the army and General of the forces in I'rán. Many of the most illustrious nobles and bravest Turks were of his kindred; and wherever the Sultán led his army and conquered kingdoms, the victory was owing to the exertions and courage of him and his relatives.

The author of the *Tawárikh-i Mahmúdí* has narrated at length the quarrel between Sálár Mas'úd and Hasan Maimandí, and the valour,

[1] ["Dhardána," *supra*, page 524.]

success, and good conduct of the Commander-in-chief and Sálár Mas'úd. To relate it all here would make this work too long; therefore I have only briefly mentioned them. Also, these exploits of Sultán Mahmúd, and Sálár Mas'úd, I have related only so far as they concern that Prince of Martyrs, and insomuch as he was personally mixed up with them, otherwise I had not indulged in such prolixity. "God knows the truth."

Chapter 3.

Departure of the Prince of Martyrs from the court of Sultán Mahmúd.—His expedition into Hindustán.—He reaches Multán; occupies Dehli, and, passing the Ganges, takes up his residence in Sutrakh, from whence he sends out armies on all sides.

Khwája Hasan Maimandí had been long versed in all the affairs of the administration, so that a great many of the factions, from different parts of the empire, were ready to obey his word. Thus, owing to his disaffection, there was ground for the apprehension of disturbances on all sides. The Sultán, being informed of this, took every means in his power to conciliate Khwája Hasan Maimandí, but without success. For whenever that individual saw Sálár Mas'úd at court, and beheld the favours the Sultán bestowed upon him, he writhed within himself like a snake, and fell into grief and rage, declaring that he could not endure to set eyes upon Mas'úd.

The Sultán, perplexed at this state of things, one day called Sálár Mas'úd apart, and, addressing him kindly, said that Hasan Maimandí was a man of evil disposition, and that, through excessive insolence, he had taken a violent antipathy to him (Mas'úd), which so engrossed him that he had left off attending to business. "I am determined," continued the Sultán, "by degrees to deprive him of the wazírship, and to promote Amír Jang Mikáíl to the post. But till this is accomplished, do you go tó Kábuliz and employ yourself in the chase, and in attendance upon your parents. In a short time I will dismiss him and recal you; rest assured, meanwhile, that my affection for you is greater than you can imagine."

Sálár Mas'úd, perceiving the drift of the Sultán's discourse, replied, "Oh, sire! what have I to do at my parents' house? With your permission, I will make an expedition into Hindustán, and, wresting the kingdoms, now in the hands of pagans, out of their hands, will spread the true faith, and cause the khutba to be read in your majesty's name." The Sultán replied, "It is no pleasure to me to deprive myself of you, my child, that I should thus separate myself from you—no; go for a short time to your father, I will send for you ere long." [*Mas'úd departs with his followers.*]

The author of the *Tawáríkh-i Mahmúdí* relates that there were, with his own followers and those who joined him, 1,100,000 (*yas-dak lak*) men in Mas'úd's army, the home and family of each of whom was at Ghazní.

As soon as the General of the army heard of all that had happened, he went with Sitr Mu'allá' in terrible distress from Kábulís to the camp of Sálár Mas'úd, and, after embracing him, entreated him with tears to remain with them; but he would by no means consent. Seeing that their child was not to be prevailed upon, they became desirous to go with him. But Mas'úd said, that if they came with him, Hasan Maimandí would certainly persuade the Sultán that they had rebelled, and therefore they had better remain behind. "I have already," said he, "petitioned the Sultán, and now I beseech it of you, to be allowed to travel for one year, after which I will return." At length his parents were obliged to submit. They however sent, with Sálár Mas'úd, a fine army and councillors, many of whom were of his own age, and had been his companions, and they selected the bravest of their kindred among the Tatars of Sálár Sáhú to accompany him. They also bestowed upon him treasure, horses, and gifts of all kinds. So the General of the army returned towards Kábulís with his consort, weeping and lamenting.

*   *   *   *

To resume our history. The Prince of Martyrs, adorned with all dignity of body and mind, reached the banks of the river Indus, and immediately ordered boats to be collected. These were brought, after some search, and he commanded Mír Husain 'Arab, and Amír Bázid Ja'far to cross over the river with 50,000 horse, and attack Sahúr.[1] They did so; and Rái Arjun, the zamíndár of that place,

[1] Shore?

having already taken refuge in the hills, they demolished his house, where they found 500,000 gold pieces. Taking these, and a good deal of other plunder, the two Amírs rejoined Mas'úd. Having thus effected his first conquest in India, Mas'úd crossed the river himself with his army, and encamped on the opposite bank, and, as it was a good sporting country, he enjoyed the pleasures of the chase.

After a short time, Mas'úd marched onward and arrived at Multán. That city was deserted; for, since Sultán Mahmúd, the faithful, had plundered it for the second time, it had never been restored, and the Ráís Arjun and Anangpál, lords of the place, had gone to reside in the province of Uch. From thence they sent ambassadors to Mas'úd to inquire if he thought it right thus to overrun a foreign country, adding, "Perhaps you will have cause to repent it." Mas'úd replied, "The country is God's; his slave has no kingdom; but he to whom God gives it will be the possessor. This has been the principle of my ancestors from the time of Asadu-lla Ghálib until now; to convert unbelievers to the one God and the Musulmán faith. If they adopt our creed, well and good. If not, we put them to the sword." He then bestowed honorary dresses upon the ambassadors, and dismissed them with a caution to prepare for war, as he would shortly follow.

As soon as the ambassadors had departed, he sent six Amírs, viz., Mír Husain 'Arab, Amír Bázíd Ja'far, Amír Tarkán, Amír Nakí, Amír Fíroz, and 'Umr Mulk Ahmad, with several hundred thousand horse to attack the Ráí Anangpál. That prince came out of his stronghold to meet them with his forces drawn out in battle array. The combat raged for three hours; many noble Turks were made martyrs, while countless unbelievers were slain, and the Ráí Anangpál was at length obliged to yield. The army of Islám entered the city and plundered it, carrying off an immense amount of property. They then rejoined Mas'úd, who bestowed honorary dresses and horses on each of the six Amírs.

The rainy season had now set in, so they remained at Multán the next four months. After the rains, Mas'úd led his army against Ajúdhan.¹ Although, in those days, that place and its vicinity was

¹ [Ajúdha or Ayodyha is the old form of the name Oudh. The scene of Mas'úd's later exploits is laid in the neighbourhood of Oudh.]

thickly peopled, it was subdued without a struggle. Mas'úd was delighted with the climate of Ajúdhan, and as, moreover, it was a good sporting country, he remained there till the end of the following rains, when he set off for Dehli. Rái Mahípál was then king of the city. He had an immense army, and many war elephants, and was, in consequence, overflowing with pride. Sultán Mahmúd and Sálár Sáhú, when they came into Hindustán, conquered Lahore, and made it a city of Islám; but they were unable to attack Dehli, and retired without even attempting it. But now Sálár Mas'úd, lion-like, marched on by successive stages till he reached that city.

The Rái Mahípál led out his army to oppose him. The two forces lay several miles apart; but the young warriors, on either side, used to meet daily and skirmish from morning till night. Thus a month and some days passed away, till Mas'úd, becoming apprehensive of the result, sought help from God. As soon as he had done so, he received the unexpected intelligence that Sálár Saifu-d dín, the Sultánu-s Salátín, Mír Bakhtiyár, Mír Saiyid 'Azízu-d dín, and Malik Wahíu-d dín, five Amírs, were coming from Ghazni to join him with a numerous force. On their arrival joy and delight filled Mas'úd's army. These men, likewise, had left Ghazni on account of the evil conduct of Hasan Maimandí. Saifu-d dín was a younger brother of Mas'úd's father, Mír Bakhtiyár and 'Azízu-d dín were also related to him. Malik Daulat was a servant of Sultán Mahmúd, and Miyán Rajab had been a confidential slave of Sálár Sáhú, who reposed such confidence in him, that he gave him to Mas'úd; and he, as a mark of his favour, had bestowed a jágír upon him. But no sooner had Sálár Mas'úd started on his expedition, than Hasan Maimandí deprived him of it, without informing the Sultán. Miyán Rajab, therefore, followed Mas'úd, who considered him so trustworthy as to appoint him adjutant (Kotwál) of the army.

Khwája Hasan, from his enmity against Mas'úd, had quarrelled with all connected with him, and forced them to leave the country. The fact was, Sultán Mahmúd had become old, and spent his whole time in the society of Malik Ayáz, neglecting the business of the state. So Hasan tyrannized on all sides. However, it is related in the history called Rauzatu-s Safá, that Mahmúd became at length dissatisfied with his conduct, and, removing him from the office of wazír, imprisoned him in one of the forts of Hindustán, where he was put to death, and that Mír Jang Múkíl was appointed in his place. Certain it is, that he was doomed to destruction, who unjustly persecuted one favoured of 'Alí, and blessed with divine grace.

To resume: Rai Mahípál was alarmed at this accession to the forces of his enemy. Four days after the two armies joined in battle. Mas'úd was engaged in conversation with Sharfu-l Mulk, when Gopál, son of Mahípál, charged him, and, aiming with his mace at his head, wounded him on the nose, and struck out two of his teeth. Sharfu-l Mulk drew his sword, and with one blow sent Gopál to hell: Mas'úd bound up his wounded nose with a handkerchief, and continued on the field of battle. All praise to the courage and valour of Mas'úd, who took no notice of his wound, but continued fighting until evening prayers, and even at night remained on the field. Many brave Turks were martyred, and countless unbelievers slain.

In the morning they again beat the drums of war, and the young men of courage came forth to battle. Mír Saiyid 'Azízu-d dín was fighting in the foremost rank, where he was suddenly struck with a spear on the head, and became a martyr. Unable to contain himself, on hearing of the Mír's death, Mas'úd himself charged the enemy, followed by the Turkish Amírs, careless of their lives as moths round a flame. The unbelievers were unable to withstand the shock, and fled. The Ráis Mahípál and Sirípál alone, with a few others, remained upon the field. Although all their friends entreated them to fly and try the fortune of war another time, they constantly refused, asking where they could go if they left the field. At last they were both slain; a great victory was won, and the throne of Dehlí fell into the hands of the conqueror.

Mas'úd, however, did not ascend the throne, still affirming that he was only fighting for the glory of God. He buried 'Azízu-d dín at Dehlí, and, erecting a lofty tomb over his grave, appointed men to keep and provide lamps nightly for it. Amír Bázid Ja'far was placed in command of the garrison of Dehlí, consisting of 3,000 picked horse. He was besides ordered to raise 5,000 or 6,000 fresh troops from among the people of the country; Mas'úd at the same time telling him, in the most gracious manner, that he was responsible for the happiness of the inhabitants, and must take every precaution to preserve them from oppression.

He left Dehli on the 16th of the month Azar, having remained there six months, and led his army against Mírat. The Princes of Mírat had already heard that no one could hope to stand before Mas'úd; that in whatsoever direction he or his troops turned, they gained the victory. So they were afraid, and sent ambassadors with valuable presents to Mas'úd, acknowledging his supremacy, and offering to be the servants of his slaves; in fact, submitting entirely to him. Mas'úd was much pleased, and bestowing the kingdom of Mírat upon them, proceeded with all his train towards Kanauj.

When Sultán Mahmúd had ejected Rái Ajípal from Kanauj, Mas'úd had procured his pardon and re-establishment; remembering this service, he had already sent an embassy to Mas'úd with most valuable presents. And when the latter had reached Kananj, and pitched his tents upon the banks of the Ganges, he sent his eldest son to welcome him with the usual gifts. Mas'úd received the son of Ajípál with great respect, and in order to allay all apprehension on the part of his host, determined to accept the gifts. He then presented the prince with a charger and a dress of honour, dismissed him, and ordered his servants to get all things ready as quickly as possible, as he intended to cross the river and enjoy some sport. When they had prepared the boats they came and informed him, and he immediately commanded the army to pass over and encamp on the opposite bank, which they did, Mas'úd accompanying them. Presently came Rái Ajípal with ten horses to pay his respects. Mas'úd received him with marks of great affection, and, seating him near himself, reassured him in every way. He then presented him with a special dress of honour and those ten horses, and allowed him to depart, requesting him to send supplies for his army, and advising him to take every care of his country, so as to improve his subjects daily.

After that, he marched on in the direction of Satrakh; and, on the tenth day, reached that city. At that time Satrakh was the most flourishing of all the towns and cities of India; it lies in the centre of that country, and abounds in good hunting ground. Moreover, it was a sacred shrine of the Hindus; so Mas'úd fixed his head quarters there, and sent out armies on every side to conquer the surrounding country. Sálár Saifu-d dín and Miyán Rajab he despatched against Bahráích, appointing the son of Miyán Rajab kotwal of the army in his father's stead; for, although but young, he was possessed of great ability and courage.

As soon as Saifu-d dín and Miyán Rajab reached Bahráích, they sent back word that there were no supplies to be obtained there, and that their army stood in danger of perishing, unless help was afforded them. Mas'úd ordered the chaudharís and mukaddims of the pargannahs to be brought before him, and those of seven or eight of the pargannahs were brought. He then called to his presence Bípás, Chaudharí of Saddabur, and Narharí, Chaudharí of Amíthí, and encouraged them in every way, exhorting them to encourage the cultivation of the lands, which would be advantageous both to them and to their ryots. He also proposed to them to take money in advance, and bring him in supplies. They petitioned to be allowed to deliver the supplies before they received the money; but he insisted on paying in advance. So depositing ready money with the chaudharís and mukaddims, he presented each one of them with a dress and betel-nut, and sent men with them to bring in the supplies as quickly as possible, while Malik Fíroz 'Umar was appointed to have the necessary quantities conveyed to Saifu-d dín at Bahráích, as soon as they arrived.

Mas'úd next commanded Sultánu-s Salátín and Mír Bakhtiyár to proceed against the Lower Country (*mulk-i faro-dast*), saying, "We commit you to the care of God. Wherever you go, first try gentle measures. If the unbelievers accept the Muhammadan faith, show them kindness; if not, put them to the sword." He then embraced Mír Bakhtiyár, saying, "We part to-day; whether we shall ever meet again is uncertain." Both the brothers wept at this sorrowful thought, and remained long clasped in each others' arms. Then Mír Bakhtiyár departed. Wonderful time! Wonderful friendship! and wonderful firmness of faith, to cast themselves thus into the sea of unbelievers, purely for the sake of witnessing to the truth of the one God. It is said that Mír Bakhtiyár subdued the Lower country, and advanced as far as Kánúr, where he drank the wine of martyrdom. His holy sepulchre is well known in that place.

Mas'úd then dispatched Amír Hasan 'Arab against Mahúna; Mír Saiyid 'Azízu-d dín, celebrated now as the Lál Pír, against Gopamú and its vicinity; and Malik Fazl against Benares and its neighbourhood. Each of these went away in the direction of their several commands, while Mas'úd himself continued to reside with great magnificence at Satrakh, enjoying the pleasures of the chase.

One day ambassadors arrived from the Princes of Karra and Mánikpúr, bringing two saddles, bridles, and other rare presents, with this message, "This kingdom has belonged to us and our fathers from time immemorial. No Musulmán has ever dwelt here. Our annals relate that the Emperor Alexander, Zú-l karnain, made an expedition against this country, and reached Kanauj; but there he made peace with Rái Kaid, and returned without having crossed the Ganges. Sultán Mahmúd, also, with your father, came as far as Ajmír, Guzerát, and Kanauj, but spared our country. But you, without any respect for the rights of property, establish yourself in a country that does not belong to you. The action is unworthy of a great mind like yours. It is an infinite sorrow to us that you should be the only child in the house of your father, and that he should have no other descendants. Consider, we pray you, the right. Satrakh is a pleasant place; but it is not fitting that you should remain there. We have 90,000 picked soldiers; the princes of the country of Bahráích and other places will come to our help on every side, and you will find yourself in great difficulties. You had better take the prudent course of retiring of your own free will."

Mas'úd raged at this like a fierce lion, and, compressing his lips, addressed the ambassador thus, "Well is it for thee that thou comest as an ambassador; had any one else addressed such an insolent speech to us, we would have had him torn in pieces. Go, tell thy princes their country belongs to the all-powerful God, who gives it to whom he wills. Think not that we are come only to take a journey. We intend to make our abode here, and, by the command of God, will uproot unbelief and unbelievers from the land." o o o

So saying, he dismissed the ambassador, who went and told his master all that had passed, adding "This cub, in truth, fears no one. Do you use your best endeavours, for he cares nought for your 90,000 picked men." The unbelievers were greatly alarmed. At length a barber, who was present, said, he would settle the business if authorised to do so. The Rái ordered him to make the attempt [*to poison Mas'úd, in which he succeeded, but the intended victim recovered.*]

At that time Mas'úd was eighteen years of age. God had lavished upon him o o o every excellence of body and mind. * o o This slave once, in the beginning of life, looked upon the Sultán in a vision. From that hour his heart grew cold to the business of the world, and for three or four years he lost all thoughts of self in the pain of separation from him.

To continue our history. Mas'úd immediately ordered those about him to write letters to the governors of the provinces under his sway, informing them of the attempt of the unbelievers, and how God had turned it to good; for he feared lest short-sighted, ill-disposed persons should adopt a wrong idea; and thus, by their distortion of facts, evil might arise. He also sent a letter to his honoured father at Kábulis. They soon wrote out all the dispatches and brought them to him, and he signed them himself, and started them off by the hands of special messengers.

[*Mas'úd's mother dies from grief, and Sálár Sáhú then proceeds to join his son.*]

Chapter 4.

Sálár Sáhú arrives at Satrakh.—Mas'úd marches against Dahrdích. —Death of Sálár Sáhú at Satrakh.—Mas'úd wages war with the unbelievers, and tastes the wine of martyrdom at Bahráích.

When Sálár Sáhú reached the neighbourhood of Satrakh, Mas'úd went out to meet him, and, conducting him home, held great rejoicings for three days and nights with social feasts. All men took fresh courage upon the arrival of the General of the army, while the unbelievers on every side were struck with dismay and apprehension.

A few days after, Malik Fíroz took three spies of the unbelievers at the passage of the river Saru (Sarjú), and sent them to Satrakh. The servants of Mas'úd recognized two of them as the Brahmans who had brought the saddle filled with sorceries and enchantments, as a present from the Ráis of Karra and Mánikpur to Mas'úd; and the third as the barber, who had presented the poisoned nail-cutter. Sálár Sáhú ordered them all to be put to death. But Mas'úd wished them to be released, saying, there was nothing to be gained by killing them. Sáhú consented, for his son's sake, to release the two Brahmans, but declared he would never let the barber go. So they immediately put him to death. They then found upon the Brahmans letters from the Ráis of Karra and Mánikpur to the Ráis of the neighbourhood of Bahráích, and read them. The contents were as follows:—"A foreign army is encamped between you and us. Do you draw out your army on your side, while we attack them on ours, and thus we shall destroy the Musulmáns."

Sálár Sáhú was enraged, and instantly sent off two spies to gather intelligence of the Ráis of Karra and Mánikpur. They brought word that the unbelievers were amusing themselves with their sons and daughters in fancied security. The General immediately beat to arms, and started off, leaving Mas'úd in Satrakh. He proceeded that night to the head-quarters of the ill-fated unbelievers, and, dividing his army into two bodies, sent one division against Karra, and the other against Mánikpur. The brave Musulmáns quickly surrounded each place, and the heathen came out to battle; but the forces of Islám prevailed, and, putting thousands of unbelievers to the sword, they took the two Ráis alive, and brought them before Sálár Sáhú, who put chains about their necks, and dispatched them to Satrakh, writing to Mas'úd that he had sent him some eaters of forbidden food, whom he was to keep with all care. Mas'úd sent them on to Sálár Saifu-d dín at Bahráích. Meanwhile, Sálár Sáhú reduced Karra and Mánikpur, and plunder and slaves to a great amount fell into the hands of the army. He then returned in triumph to Satrakh, leaving Malik 'Abdu-llah in the neighbourhood of Karra, and Mír Kutb Haidar at Mánikpur.

All the princes of Hindustan were alarmed at these doings; deeming it impossible to cope with the army of Islám, they began to retreat. Ere long, however, all united together, and prepared for war. Sálár Sáhú and Mas'úd one day went out hunting. [*And Mas'úd despatched a tiger with his sword.*]

A despatch reached Sálár Sáhú from Sálár Saifu-d dín, at Bahráich, praying for immediate assistance, as the unbelievers were assembling on all sides. Mas'úd begged to be allowed to go to Bahráich, and chastise their insolence; but Sáhú would not consent, saying, he could not bear to be separated from him, and entreating him not to leave him alone in his old age. Mas'úd then asked permission to proceed to Bahráich for a few days to enjoy the hunting, for which he said that place was famous. Sálár Sáhú was obliged to yield; but he wept bitterly at the thought. Mas'úd, when he came to take leave, was himself melted into tears. He left in great sorrow, and turned his face towards Bahráich.

His mere coming was sufficient to quiet the unbelievers, whose dimness of perception alone had caused the rising. Mas'úd hunted through the country around Bahráich, and whenever he passed by the idol temple of Súraj-kund, he was wont to say that he wanted that piece of ground for a dwelling-place. This Súraj-kund was a sacred shrine of all the unbelievers of India. They had carved an image of the sun in stone on the banks of the tank there. This image they called Bálárukh, and through its fame Bahráich had attained its flourishing condition. When there was an eclipse of the sun, the unbelievers would come from east and west to worship it, and every Sunday the heathen of Bahráich and its environs, male and female, used to assemble in thousands to rub their heads under that stone, and do it reverence as an object of peculiar sanctity. Mas'úd was distressed at this idolatry, and often said that, with God's will and assistance, he would destroy that mine of unbelief, and set up a chamber for the worship of the Nourisher of the Universe in its place, rooting out unbelief from those parts. The Almighty was pleased to prosper the undertaking, and the light of the true faith there is now brighter than the sun, and clearer than the moon.

Mas'úd came to Bahráich from Satrakh on the 17th of the month of Sha'bán, in the year 423. In the second month a letter came from 'Abdu-l Malik Firoz from Satrakh.   *   *   *   *   *

The contents were as follows: "On the 15th of the month of Shawwál, of the year 423, Sálár Sáhú was taken with a pain in the head. He said, 'My time is come at last;' and ordered us to bury him in Satrakh. And on the 25th of the same month he went his last journey, obeying the will of the Almighty." Mas'úd wept bitterly at this heartrending intelligence. He was quite beside himself, and, uttering loud lamentations, covered his garments with earth. After a time, recovering some degree of composure, he called to mind Hasan Maimandí, accusing him as the cause of all his misfortunes. "My honoured mother," said he, "died at Kábulíz; and my honoured father has met his death at Satrakh. Now I know what it is to be an orphan." ○ ○ ○

An ambassador arrived at the court of Mas'úd from the Ráís of the country round Bahráich, Malik Haidar introduced him to the presence, and he presented the despatch that he had brought. The unbelievers, in their pride, had written as follows: "You come from the Upper Country (*mulk-i bálá dast*), and know nothing of these parts. This is the land of nobles; never shall inhabitants of the Upper Country remain here. Think more wisely on this matter." Mas'úd demanded of the ambassador how many Ráís were banded together, and what were their names? He detailed the names of each one as follows: "Rái Ráíb, Rái Sáib, Rái Arjun, Rái Bhikan, Rái Kanak, Rái Kalyán, Rái Makrú, Rai Sakrú, Rái Karan, Rái Bírbal, Rái Jalpál, Rái Sripál, Rái Harpál, Rái Harkú, Rái Prabhú, Deb Nárayan, and Narsing, are there with 2,000,000 cavalry, and 3,000,000 infantry."[1] Mas'úd would not send a written answer; but dismissing the messenger, dispatched with him Malik Nekdil, with seven attendants, to answer the Ráís in person, his real object being to discover the actual amount of their force.

When Malik Nekdil arrived, one went in and told the chiefs, who assembled together, and, calling Malik before them, inquired what message he had brought from Sálár Mas'úd. Malik Nekdil replied, "My master bids me say, hearing of the nature of this country, I came to enjoy the pleasures of the chase. It is a waste, a barren wilderness. Do you agree upon conditions with me? Let us settle the matter like brothers, and I will settle the country."

[1] [*Sic.*]

The unbelievers answered, "Until we have fought with you once, it does not befit us to talk of peace. You have come here violently, and we have left you alone; but now, till one party or the other be subdued, what peace can be looked for, or what concord be expected?" Rái Karan said, "You do not yet know the nature of the climate of these parts. The water will settle our business for us. You had better leave this river Saru and go northwards again, otherwise we must fight." Rái Kalyán, one of the most able of those chiefs, said, "Oh, princes, you are unwise to think that Sálár Mas'úd has proposed peace through fear. He intends to strike an unexpected blow. Only consider that the Sálár is a man of such honour that he used to stand in the presence of Sultán Mahmúd, and had a feud with the wazír of the Sultán. Leaving his father and mother, he conquered the whole country of India, and his father died in Satrakh. He has not yet visited his tomb. He has only acted thus to deceive us, and means to say, Let him who feels inclined drive me out, and I will fight him. But you do not understand. What objection is there to peace, if he will indeed agree to it?" The unbelievers all began to talk like fools; so Malik Nekdil, seeing that the assembly had no leader, rose up, and, departing, returned to the prince, and told him all that had happened. The unbelievers on their side advanced and encamped in the jungle on the banks of the river Kasahla.

As soon as Mas'úd heard of this, he called a council of the great nobles and asked their advice as to whether he should await their attack, or himself take the initiative. All the most experienced chiefs counselled him to attack them, and this agreeing with his own opinion, he set out after evening prayers, and, marching all night, reached the camp of the unbelievers by dawn. Drawing out his army, Mas'úd confided the van to Sálár Saifu-d dín, and, distributing the other chiefs in the two wings, the rear, and the van, he himself took the command of the centre, and in this order advanced to the charge. The enemy were prepared and gave them battle. Till midday Sálár Saifu-d dín had to endure the brunt of the conflict. At last Miyán Rajab and Amír Nasru-lla attacked his opponents with a body of cavalry from the right wing, whilst Amír Tarkán and Amír Bázid did the same from the left; and the prince himself charged from the centre. Several thousand unbelievers were killed, and the soldiers of Islám, too, tasted the wine of martyrdom. But at length the unbelievers were driven to the last extremity and fled. Two chiefs were taken prisoners, and the victory was complete. The Musulmáns pursued their foes for several kos, and took much plunder in horses and baggage.

Mas'úd remained encamped on the spot for a week, burying the soldiers who had attained martyrdom, and reading the *fátiha* for their pure souls. On the eighth day he returned towards Bahráich. As the weather was warm, and he had come a long journey, he rested for some time under a mahúá tree on the bank of Súraj-kund, at which time he said, "The shade of this tree is very refreshing; and this spot is pleasing to me. It would be well to plant a garden here like those found in our own country. Here will I often come, till the crowds of unbelievers, and the darkness of unbelief, be removed from hence. Until this place be cleansed from idolatry, it is impossible for the faith of Islám to spread in the land of India. If it please God, I will, through the power of the spiritual Sun, destroy the worship of the material." He passed orders then and there that the ground should be levelled, and all the old trees cut down and removed quickly, with the exception of the mahúá tree under which he was standing. He left Miyán Rajab Kotwal to perform this service, and departed with his train for Bahráich by regular stages. From that time he was frequent in religious duties; occasionally, only to satisfy his chiefs and ministers, he would go into the council-chamber, and sometimes into his ladies' apartments.

In three or four days Miyán Rajab rooted up all the old trees, and cleared about an hundred bighas or more of ground around Súraj-kund. He then reported his proceedings to Sálár Mas'úd, and besought further orders. The Prince made an excursion that way, and, summoning the pioneers who had accompanied his troops from his own country, ordered them to lay out the grounds in parterres and walks after the manner of their native land. He also commanded Miyán Rajab to send people in all directions to collect all manner of trees, one of each kind, for the garden. Such diligence was used, that in a very short time it was completed. He them ordered them to build a platform of masonry under the shade of the mahúá tree, to serve him for a seat, as he said he had taken a great fancy to that place. After that, he himself arranged the plan upon which he wished the garden to be made, and, leaving Miyán Rajab there, returned with his train to Bahráich. Miyan Rajab knew the disposition of his lord, and employed himself day and night upon that work.

The next day an ambassador arrived with many costly presents from Rái Jogi Dás from the Hindu Koh. Malik Haidar introduced him to the presence. The ambassador made many protestations of friendship on the part of the Rái his master. After a short time, the ambassador, Govind Dás, presented his gifts, and expressed the desire his sovereign felt to kiss the feet of the prince. Sálár Mas'úd received them with great courtesy, and bestowing gold embroidered dresses of honour on both ambassadors, replied, that if they would adopt the faith of Islám, they might enjoy their own country without fear.

Several other chiefs also came to visit him, though they did not relinquish their opposition. After their defeat they wrote to all the Báis round, saying, "This is the land of our fathers and ancestors, which this boy wants to take from us by force. You had better come speedily to our assistance, or we shall lose our country." The Báis answered that they would come immediately, and told them to prepare the munitions of war. Sahar Dev from Shabhún, and Har Dev from Halúna, joined the army of the unbelievers with large forces, and addressed them as follows, "You do not know the tactics of war. Order the blacksmiths to prepare 5,000 balls each, with five poisoned prongs. Before the battle we will fix them firmly in the ground. When the Musulmáns charge with their cavalry, the prongs will enter into the horses' feet; they will fall, and we will finish their business. Prepare besides plenty of fireworks." They did so. In two months all the Ráis of the Hindu Koh and the countries round assembled with innumerable forces, and, encamping on the bank of the river Kahsala, sent one to tell Mas'úd, "that if he wished to save his life, he had better leave that country and go elsewhere, as the land belonged to their fathers and ancestors, and they were determined to drive him from it." The

APPENDIX.

Prince boldly replied, "Through the grace of God, my steps have not yet turned back, and by His assistance, they shall not do so now. The country is God's, and the property of him on whom He bestows it. Who gave it to your fathers and ancestors?" The messengers, returning, informed the Ráís of all that had passed, which caused them to exclaim, "Truly this boy answers boldly; he knows not fear."

The Prince of Martyrs told Malik Haidar to summon Sálár Saifu-d dín, Amír Nasru-lla, Amír Khizr, Amír Saiyid Ibráhím, Najmu-l mulk, Zahíru-l mulk, 'Umdatu-l mulk, and Miyán Rajab. He did so; and after Mas'úd had consulted with them it was agreed that, rather than allow the unbelievers to attack them, they had better take the offensive, and thus, with God's help, they might hope to conquer.

The next day they were preparing, when news arrived that the enemy were driving off the cattle. The Prince sprang up like an angry lion, and beat to arms; buckling on his armour and mounting his horse, he himself put his troops into battle array, and advanced to the attack. The enemy also made ready, and, fixing the prongs in the earth, stood with their fireworks ready for use. The noble Turks rode fearlessly to the attack, and numbers of them were put to death by means of the prongs and fireworks. Still the fight waxed hotter, and many of the unbelievers were put to the sword. When Mas'úd heard what had happened, he left the vanguard to attack the enemy on another side, while he himself took them in flank. They fought courageously, and great numbers were killed on both sides. At length the unbelievers were forced to fly. Mas'úd remained on the field of battle, while some of the nobles led the pursuit, and, after plundering the army of the unbelievers, returned to the presence. The Prince then left the field, and, encamping on the banks of the Kahanla, ordered them to number the army, and report to him how many were missing. They found that but two-thirds remained, one-third having tasted the wine of martyrdom. * *

When he went to visit his garden, he would sit under the mahúá tree where they had built a fine large platform. The tree was close to the Súraj-kund, with the idol Báláruk'h on its banks, and in its waters the unbelievers were wont to bathe before offering it their worship. Mas'úd grew angry whenever his eyes fell upon that tank and idol. Miyán Rajab, who knew well his lord's thoughts, one day presented the following petition: "My lord, now that your lordship has completed this garden, and made it your constant place of worship and resort, the spot has become sacred to the faith of Islám. If you give the command, I will remove this idol and its temple." The Prince replied, "You do not consider that God is without equal, as shall appear. In a short time the angels shall, by order of the Preserver of the Universe, remove the darkness of the unbelievers, and sprinkle upon them the true light of Islám, which is like the waters of life." ○ ○ ○

After the death of Miyán Rajab, many erroneous reports were circulated concerning him. Some ignorant persons say, that he was sister's son to Mas'úd. This is quite a mistake. What connection has a slave with his lord? Others, again, have changed his name, saying, that Rajab was the name of the father of Sultán Firoz.[1] This is also false. He was one of Mas'úd's oldest servants. It is also reported that he was of a cruel and hard disposition; but those who search the truth will find nothing of the kind on record.

To resume the history. After some days, Mas'úd's sorrow abated, and he departed by regular stages. ○ ○ ○ That loved one of the Lord of the Universe was then nineteen years of age. ○ ○ ○

Meanwhile, the Hindu unbelievers assembled from all quarters with one accord, and gathered together an army in numbers like a swarm of ants or locusts, to attack Bahráich. Mas'úd, hearing of their proceedings, came into the council chamber and commanded his ministers to have his whole army, small and great, collected before him. They did so. And when all his followers were drawn out in line, Mas'úd advanced and addressed them as follows:— ○ ○ ○ The Prince continued, "Oh friends, hitherto, when we have fought the unbelievers, the Almighty has granted us victory; now all the armies of India are assembled. It is the custom of my ancestors never to leave fighting, I must follow their example, and, for the love of the truth, yield up my life, which is but the covering

[1] [The father of Sultán Firoz was called Sipáh-sálár Rajab, according to Shams-i Siráj. His tomb stands in Bahráich.]

APPENDIX. 545

of that which is hidden. You I commit to God. Do you take the road to the Upper Country and depart. If any one desires martyrdom, purely for the love of the Almighty, let him remain with me; but, God knows that, with perfect free will, I give you leave to depart." Having spoken thus, he wept. Who could be so stonyhearted and ill-starred, as to leave him at such a time? The people wept with one voice, and began to say, "If we had a thousand lives we would spend them for thee. What is one life worth, that for its sake we should deprive ourselves of thy presence?" Praise be to God! It was like the day of judgment, or even more solemn.

       °   °   °   °

It was on the 18th day of the month Rajabu-l murajjab, in the year 424, at early dawn, that the army of the unbelievers approached the advanced guard. ° ° ° Mas'úd marched towards the army of the unbelievers; as soon as he reached the outskirts of the city, he drew up his forces in order of battle, and disposing them on the two wings and before and behind him, he continued his march. ° ° ° The Prince of Martyrs, according to his usual custom, went and stood under his favourite tree, while his forces prepared for the fight, which raged furiously from morning till the time of evening prayer. Thousands upon thousands fell on both sides, but victory declared for neither.

All night the two armies remained on the field; and at dawn of day the drums again beat to arms. The Musulmán youth advanced fearlessly to the charge, desiring nothing so much as martyrdom; such was their longing for union with God. Perfect is the love of the moth; it cares for nothing but to burn.

The army of the enemy was innumerable, like mountains on every side; so that although numerous forces fought in the army of Islám, they were mown down like so much grass. Many of the greatest nobles met their deaths. In the course of that day, from morning till evening prayer, two-thirds of the army were slain, leaving but one-third to mourn their loss. Still, through the power of the love of God, none thought of flight. When the Prince heard that Sálár Saifu-d dín had sealed his faith with his blood, and that such a noble or general had been slain, he rejoiced and praised God that they had attained their chief desire, declaring that he would not desert them, but would speedily follow. He then gave orders for burying Sálár Saifu-d dín, which they by some means or other contrived to do; and they reported that the unbelievers had been victorious, and that the whole army of Islám was slain, requesting to know whether they were to continue the fight, or to occupy themselves with burying those that had suffered martyrdom.

Mas'úd ordered them to bring the bodies of the Faithful slain and cast them into the Súraj-kund, in the hope that through the odour of their martyrdom the darkness of unbelief might be dispelled from that spot. They did so, and as soon as the tank was filled, he made them throw the rest into holes and pits. The Prince then dismounted, and performing fresh ablutions, paid his evening devotions with all attention, and went through the burial prayers over the innumerable corpses of the Faithful, with which the tank, the pits and holes were filled, reading the *fátiha* for their pure souls. He then remounted his mare of sacred blood, and, collecting the remnant of his forces, rushed upon the enemy. Although their army appeared like a mountain, yet it was entirely destroyed, as masses of ice are melted by the heat of the sun. Sálár Saifu-d dín had put many of the chief princes to the sword; the remainder the Prince of Martyrs destroyed. The unbelievers who, in the pride of victory, had advanced, fled back. The Prince remained standing on his side of the field; whichever way he looked, nothing met his eye but the bodies of the slain—some wounded, some in the agonies of death, others already defunct, while the survivors were occupied with the dying and the dead. He beheld this heart-rending spectacle without emotion; indeed so strong within him was the desire for martyrdom, that he actually rejoiced. * * *

Meanwhile, the Ráí Sahar Deo and Har Deo, with several other chiefs, who had kept their troops in reserve, seeing that the army of Islám was reduced to nothing, unitedly attacked the body-guard of the Prince. The few forces that remained to that loved one of the Lord of the Universe were ranged round him in the garden. The unbelievers, surrounding them in dense numbers, showered arrows upon them. It was then, on Sunday, the 14th of the month Rajab, in the aforesaid year 424 (14th June, 1033), as the time of evening prayer came on, that a chance arrow pierced the main artery in the arm of the Prince of the Faithful. His sun-like countenance became pale as the new moon. Repeating the text in praise of martyrdom, he dismounted. Sikandar Díwání, and the other servants of that loved-one of God, carried him to the shade of the mahúá tree, and laid him down upon a couch. Sikandar Díwání, taking his honoured head upon his lap, sat looking towards Mecca, weeping bitterly. The Prince of Martyrs opened his eyes but once, then drew a sigh, and committed his soul to God. ○ ○ ○ ●

A sound of woe and lamentation broke from the people; they wept aloud, and, brandishing their swords, rushed upon the army of the unbelievers, and gave up their lives, while the enemy kept their ranks and showered their arrows. By the time of evening prayer not one was left. All the servants of Mas'úd lay scattered like stars around that moon. Sikandar Díwání, who sat holding the honoured head of the Prince of Martyrs upon his lap, received several wounds in the breast; but such was the love he bore to that loved-one of the Lord of the Universe, that he never moved his knees from under his head, and yielded his life in his service.

○ ○ ○ ●

Before the author of this work had read the history of which he has spoken, he used often, by order of the Emperor Náru-d dín Muhammad Jahángir, to go into the north country at the foot of the mountains. Achárj Mall Bhadar, who was the representative of the Rája of the Hills, once came that way to meet me, and we chanced to speak of the Prince of Martyrs. That Brahman, who was perfectly versed in the works of Hindu historians, related to me, at length, from his own histories, the account of Mas'úd's expedition, from the time he came into India till his death; and all the wars he waged with the unbelievers. Moreover, he told me, that after Rái Sahar Deo had slain the Prince of Martyrs, he returned to his tent, where the Prince appeared to him in a vision, saying, "Thou hast slain me—dost think to escape? This is not manly." Stung by this reproach, Sahar Deo came to the field of battle the following morning and was killed, as has been related. Some years after, the Tawáríkh of Mulla Muhammad of Ghazni fell into my hands. I found all that the Brahman had related to me from the Indian histories corroborated there. The Brahman affirms that the family of the present Rája of the Hills is descended from Rái Sahar Deo, and that he had seen the Indian histories in their library. Thus much detail have I entered into for the sake of my ordinary readers. What I have related in the preface will suffice for those who read with a spiritual object.

After the death of Mas'úd, Muzaffar Khán died also. The unbelievers drove his descendants from Ajmír, and re-established their idols; and idolatry again reigned over the land of India. Things remained in this state for 200 years; but after that time that chief of holy men, the venerable Khwája Mu'ínu-d dín, of Chisht, was walking round the Ka'ba, when a voice reached him from the other world, directing him to go to Medina. Upon his arrival there, the Prophet (the peace of God, and rest be upon him!) appeared to him, and said, "The Almighty has entrusted the country of India to thee. Go thither and settle in Ajmír. By God's help, the faith of Islám shall, by thy piety and that of thy followers, be spread in that land." That holy man reached Ajmír in the reign of Rái Pithaura. Through the power of his religious faith, he persuaded Ajípal Jogí, who was Pithaura's spiritual guide, to become his disciple. But the darkness of unbelief did not rise from the heart of Pithaura, who was a second Abú Jahl; on the contrary, he even encouraged the followers of the holy Khwája to evil practices, till the holy man uttered a curse against that unbeliever.

After some years, Sultán Mu'izzu-d dín, otherwise called Shahábu-d dín Ghorí, made a second expedition from Ghazní, slew Pithaura before Dehli, and placing Kutbu-d dín Aibak on the throne of Dehli, returned himself to Ghazní. Khwája Mu'ínu-d dín, of Chisht, through the powerful assistance of his prayers, brought the whole country of India into the hands of Kutbu-d dín Aibak. ° ° ° The Mír died in Ajmír, and was buried in the old fort there. His sepulchre is a celebrated place of pilgrimage.

Since that time, no unbeliever has ruled in the land of India.

° ° ° °

Some people say that the Prince of Martyrs came into India in the time of that Khwája. This is quite erroneous. I have examined trustworthy works, and find that the Prince lived in the time of Khwája Abú Muhammad of Chisht, ages before the time that that chief of holy men, Mu'ínu-d dín of Chisht, came into India, and became a martyr. Rather more than two centuries intervened between the two. The date of Mas'úd's death has been mentioned already; Khwája Mu'ínu-d dín died on the 6th of the month of Rajab, in the year 632. He lived 170 years. God knows the truth.

[NOTE.—The following identifications of places mentioned in the foregoing Extract have been kindly supplied by General Cunningham, who visited the locality on his Archæological Survey in 1862-3. Satrakh, which is placed at ten days' march on the opposite side of the Ganges from Kanauj, is probably the same as Vasákh or Basákh, a name of Sáhet or Ayodhya (Oudh), Saddhór and Amethí must be Bhadór and Amethí, two towns between Karra-Mánikpur. The Súraj-kund, with the idol temple and mahdá tree, is probably at Asokpur, between Ayodhya and Goada (or Ganda). Acordiug to local report, Mas'úd's sister's son Hátila was killed at Asokpur, and a small tomb there is said to mark the spot, though he was buried a few miles E. S. E. of Bahráich. At Asokpur there is a mound which has a mahdá tree upon it, and a tank at its foot, which is probably the Súraj-kund. The name of Sáhar Deo, who is represented as the chief of Mas'úd's antagonists, still survives in the varying forms of Suhal Dhav, Sohíl Dal, and Sohíl Deo. According to Buchanan Hamilton (ii. 380), this neighbourhood was selected by the Nawab Wazír of Oudh as a favourable spot for a garden.—See *Archæological Report* for 1862-3.]

NOTE H.
Sultán Jalálu-d dín Mankbarní.

As the expedition of Jalálu-d dín Mankbarní[1], the Sultán of Khwárizm, into Hindustán is among the most interesting of the many romantic adventures of his remarkable reign, I will add below various extracts from Oriental authors, who have treated of it in a manner somewhat different from the *Jahán-kushá*.

The European reader may obtain full information on the subject of this expedition from consulting Abú-l Fedá, *Annales Muslemici*, Vol. iv. p. 382; Abú-l Faraj, 293; M. Petit de la Croix, *Histoire de Genghizcan*, ch. xxxiv.; D'Herbelot, *Bibliothèque Orientale*, Art. "Gelaleddin;" De Guignes, *Histoire Générale des Huns*, Tom. ii. p. 280-1; Hammer, *Gemäldesaal der Lebensbeschreibungen*, Vol. vi. pp. 188-193; Col. Miles, *Shajrat-ul Atrák*, pp. 166-180; Price, *Retrospect of Mahom-*

[1] So Hammer distinctly enjoins that we should write the word, and not either Mankberni or Minkberni; and yet the inscription on this potentate's coins transposes the two last letters, making the word Mankbarín. See *Gemäldesaal*, Pref. p. xiv., and Vol. vi. p. 187, and E. Thomas, *Journal R. A. S.*, No. xviii. p. 363.

medan *History*, Vol. ii. pp. 410–413 and 520; D'Ohsson, *Histoire des Mongols*, Vol. i. pp. 300–18, Vol. iii. pp. 3–5; *The Modern Universal History*, Vol. iii. pp. 272–282, Vol. iv. 154–164; Rampoldi, *Annali Musulmani*, Vol. viii. 256–77. From the last two a few extracts have been copied into this Note. The four French authorities, which are all good, are chiefly founded upon the *Sírat-í Jaldíu-d dín Mankharní* by Muhammad bin Ahmad of Nessa, the friend of the Sultán and the companion of his journeys and expeditions. This work is in the National Library of Paris, No. 845. It is in eight chapters, and the history is brought down to Jalálu-d-dín's death, A.D. 1231. It was composed only ten years subsequent to this event.[1]

It is needless to quote Wassáf, for his account is a poor abridgement of the *Jahán-kushá*.

The following extracts are taken from the history of the Saljúkians in the *Jámi'u-t Tawáríkh* of Rashídu-d dín. The Sultán's proceedings in Hindustán are recorded in almost precisely the same words as the *Jahán-kushá* uses. The following passages were written by Rashídu-d dín's continuator, but he himself has treated of the same subject in his history of Changíz Khán:—

"At[2] nightfall every one retired to his tent, and in the morning both armies were again drawn up in battle array. This day also Sultan Jalálu-d dín marched on foot at the head of his army, and all at once made a charge upon the Moghals, and put them to flight. The kettle-drums were beaten in triumph by order of the Sultán, and his whole army pursued the Moghals on horseback. The Sultán rushed upon them like a fierce lion or crocodile upon its prey, and put many to death. Changíz Khán shortly afterwards, being reinforced with a small body of men, moved like destructive lightning or a rapid torrent against the Sultán. In the meantime, a dispute arising between Saifu-d dín Aghrák and Amín Malik, Governor of Hirát, on account of the division of the booty, and especially respect-

---

[1] See Rémusat, *Nouv. Mél. Asiat.*, Tom. i. p. 435

[2] [This extract appeared in Sir H. Elliot's original volume, published in 1849. The translation has since been compared with the text of the MS. in the E. I. Library, and many emendations introduced. Quatremère's criticisms in the *Journal des Savants* for 1851 have also been considered, and several admitted.]

ing the right to a particular horse,[1] the latter struck Aghrák on the head with a whip.[2] The king called upon Amín Malik to give an explanation of his conduct, but he replied that Kankali[3] troops would not submit to be questioned. Upon learning this, Saifu-d dín deserted the Sultán under cover of night, and went off with his troops to the hills of Kirmán and Sankúrán.[4] The desertion of Saifu-d dín Aghrák materially affected the power of the Sultán, and diminished his chance of success. He resolved to cross the Indus, and make towards Ghazní; and for that purpose he ordered boats to be got ready.

"This circumstance coming to the knowledge of Changíz Khán, he hastened in pursuit of the Sultán, and surrounded him. At daybreak, the Sultán found himself in a position between water and fire, the Indus on one side, and the fiery enemy on the other. He prepared to give battle, but was maimed like a fierce lion in the claws of a leopard. The victorious army of the Sovereign of the World (Changíz Khán) fell upon the right wing commanded by Amín Malik, and drove it back with great slaughter. Amín Malik being thus defeated, fled towards Persháwar; but the Moghal army had got possession of the road, and he was slain, in the midst of them. Changíz Khán compelled the left wing also to give way, but the Sultán firmly maintained his ground in the centre with seven hundred men, and opposed the enemy from the morning to mid-day, moving now to right now to left, sustaining every attack, and on each occasion slaying a number of the enemy. Meantime the army of Changíz Khán came pressing forward, and crowding upon the position occupied by the Sultán. At last Ajásh Malik, son of the king's maternal uncle, seeing all was lost, seized the bridle of the Sultán's charger, and led him from the field. The Sultán bade adieu to his sons and the ladies of his household with a burning heart, and

---

[1] Most of the authorities specify an Arab horse.

[2] The *Táríkh-i Alfí* concurs in this statement, and it is adopted by D'Ohsson, D'Herbelot, and Rampoldi.

[3] The Kankali was a Turkish tribe. The name signifies "invention," and the tribe is said to have been so designated from their ingenuity in constructing carriages upon a certain occasion.—*Shajrat-i Atrák*, p. 35. [The MS. of the E. I. Library reads "Kalmak."]

[4] The *Táríkh-i Alfí* mentions only Kirmán.

weeping eyes. He ordered his favourite horse to be brought,[1] and springing upon it, he rushed again into the torrent of conflict, like a crocodile into a river, charging the enemy with irresistible force. Having succeeded in driving them back, he turned his horse's head, threw off his coat of mail and shield, and urging his horse, plunged into the river, though the bank was upwards of thirty feet above the stream. He then swam across like a noble lion,[2] and reached the opposite bank in safety. Changíz Khán witnessed the gallant exploit, and hastening to the bank prohibited the Moghals from attempting to follow. The very heavens exclaimed in surprise 'They never saw in the world any man equal to him, nor did they ever hear of one like him among the celebrated heroes of antiquity.' Changíz Khán and all the Moghal nobles were astonished to find that the Sultán crossed the river in safety, and sat watching him as he drew his sword and wiped the water from his scabbard. The Khán, turning round to the Sultán's sons, addressed them in words expressive of his admiration. ○ ○ ○ ○

"After his escape, the Sultán was joined by about ten persons who had also succeeded in crossing the river. They all concealed themselves in the woods, where fifty other persons joined their number. When the Sultán received intelligence that a number of Hindús, consisting of cavalry and infantry, were lying within two parasangs of him, and had given themselves up to pleasure, he ordered his followers to provide themselves with clubs. Thus armed, they made a sudden night attack upon the Hindú force, put many to death, and plundered their cattle and weapons. Upon this, several other people, some on camels and some on horned cattle, came over, and declared for the Sultán. They brought information that there were in the neighbourhood two or three thousand men of the Hindú force.

[1] Muhammad of Nessa tells us that in recognition of the noble service performed by this horse the Sultán kept it till the capture of Tiflis in 1226, without ever riding it in action.

[2] [The words of the MS. of the E. I. Library would seem to differ slightly from those in the MS. used by Sir H. Elliot—

بر مثال شتر غیور از میدان جیحون عبور کرد

"He crossed over like a proud camel from the plains of the Jihán." This seems the preferable translation, though "the Jihán" may possibly signify "the river (Indus)".]

The Sultán attacked them with one hundred and twenty men, put a number of them to the sword, and equipped his followers with the arms taken from the vanquished. When the report of the strength and improved circumstances of the Sultán was spread throughout India, a number of men from the hills of Balála[1] and Nakála assembled, and in a body of about five or six thousand horse, attacked the Sultán, who, drawing up in array five hundred horse, dispersed them. The Sultán afterwards received aid from several individuals and bodies of men, so that there now flocked round his standard not less than three or four thousand men. Intelligence of this gathering came to the knowledge of the world-conquering king (i. e., Changiz Khán) while he was within the limits of the Ghaznín territory, and he sent troops to oppose him. When this force crossed the river, the Sultán was not able to cope with it, and he therefore passed on as a fugitive towards Dehli.

"The Moghals, on hearing that the Sultán had proceeded towards Dehli, returned, and pillaged the confines of Ghor. The Sultán, on reaching the vicinity of Dehli, deputed messengers to King Shamsu-d dín to communicate his arrival, and to prefer a request to reside temporarily in some village near Dehli. The King killed the ambassador, deputed a messenger on his part with presents to the Sultán, but objected to comply with his demand for a place of residence, on the pretext that the climate of the neighbourhood would not suit the constitution of the Sultán. On receiving this reply, the Sultán returned to Balála and Nakála. Those who had effected their escape joined him, and he had now about ten thousand men under him. He deputed Táju-d dín Malik Khilj, accompanied by a force, to Rái Kokár[2] Saknín, in the hills of Jádí, with a request for the hand of his daughter, which request Rái Kokár complied with, and sent his son with a number of troops to wait upon him. The Sultán gave the

---

[1] All who record these events concur in reading the first word as Balála. The second may be either Bankála or Mankála. The *Tárikh-i Alfí* adds "in the vicinity (*nawáhí*) of Lahore."

[2] Probably the same as the Rái Sarkí spoken of in the *Táju-l Ma-ásir* (*supra*, p. 233) twenty years before. Rái Kokar may mean something more than chief of the Gakkhars. S. Binning says "Khokar was formerly in possession of a Musulmán, whose descendants still retain the title of Rájá, and enjoy a small jágír. The district comprehends the large town of Pind Dádan Khán."

name of Kailagh Khán to the son, and sent an army under the command of Uzbek Páí against Násiru-d dín Kubácha, who was at enmity with Rái Kokár. Kubácha, though he was an Amír under the Ghorian Kings, and governor of the country of Sind, yet was presumptuous enough to aspire to independence. When Kubácha with twenty thousand of his followers were encamped on the banks of the Indus within one parasang of Uch, Uzbek Páí,¹ with seven thousand men, suddenly fell upon them at night, defeated, and dispersed them. Kubácha embarked in a boat for Akar and Bakar (two island forts in his possession),² while the Uzbek descended upon his camp, taking possession of whatever fell in his way. He sent the news of this victory to the Sultán, who marched out, and together with the army, which was under the command of the Uzbek, reached the palace of Kubácha. The latter fled from Akar and Bakar to Múltán, where

---

¹ The *Rauzatu-s Safá* also names him as the Sultán's general, owing apparently to some confusion of the names of contemporaries—for Uzbek, the son of Jahán Pahlawán the Atábak, was at that time ruler of Azurbáiján, where we find him, a short time subsequent, engaged in active opposition to Jalálu-d dín. It will be observed that Firishta speaks of him under a still more curious form.

²[The text of this passage as printed in Sir H. Elliot's original volume ran thus:—

در کشتی باکر و بکر دو قلعه داشت در جزیره رفت The MS. of the

East India Library has در کشتی باکر و بکر قلعه است در جزیره رفت

Quatremère, Jour. des Savants, Sep. 1850, p. 529, offers a correction, and says the text should be read as it is given by Rashídu-d dín in the *History of the Mongols*

باکر بکر در قلعه' که در جزیره است رفت and translated "il se rendit dans un canton d'Agronhgber à une forteresse située dans une île." If the learned reviewer had pointed out where Agronhgber is, or was, I would readily have altered my reading, but having found the passage in the *Jahán-kushái* expressed in the same words as in the *Jámi'u-t Tawáríkh*, I prefer retaining it. That the ascertainment of the right reading is difficult may be inferred from the name being left out altogether by most of the authorities subsequent to the *Jámi'u-t Tawáríkh*. The *Rauzatu-s Safá* says only "a fort." Translator says "fled to some place." Briggs (iv. 415) says "Nagaur," which is not supported by the original; but doubtless the proper reading of his copy was "Bakar." The *Taríkh-i Alfí* says plainly "he went towards the island of Bakar." Altogether, I make little doubt that the famous island-fort of Bhakkar is the one indicated. Bhakkar, indeed, does comprise two islands. But, when instituting inquiries on the spot, I could not find that the small island lying to the north was ever called "Akar." It now goes by the name of the shrine on it. But that it might once have been called so, is not improbable, as the tendency to the reduplication of the name of Bhakkar is even now shown by its being rarely mentioned, except when coupled with the name of one of the towns lying on either side of it,—as "Barí-Bhakkar," "Sakkar Bhakkar."

the Sultán sent an ambassador to him with a demand for money, and for the surrender of the son and daughter of Amír Khán, who had taken shelter at Múltán, having fled from the battle which took place on the banks of the Indus. Kubácha sent the son and daughter of Amír Khán with a large contribution in money, soliciting at the same time that his territories might not be despoiled. The weather, however, growing hot, the Sultán determined to proceed from Uch to the Júdí hills, to Balála and Nakála, and on his way besieged the fort of Disrám, where in an engagement he was wounded in the hand by an arrow. In the end, the Sultán captured the fort, and put all who were in it to the sword. At this place he received intelligence of the movement of the Moghal troops, who were endeavouring to effect his capture, so he turned back. When he was in sight of Múltán, he sent an ambassador to Kubácha to intimate his return, and to demand the tribute due by him. The advanced guard of the Sultán waited but for a short time, and as the inhabitants of Uch were hostile, he set fire to the city and marched upon Sadúsán, where Fakhru-d dín was governor on behalf of Kubácha. Láchín of Khitá was commander of the troops, and he led them forth to oppose Okhán, who was general of the Sultán's army, but he was slain in the conflict. Okhán then besieged Sadúsán, and when the Sultán arrived, Fakhru-d dín Sálárí with tears supplicated for pardon, and presented his sword and coffin[1] in token of submission. The Sultán remained there for one month, and showing favour to Fakhru-d dín, he made over to him the government of Sadúsán and marched towards Dowal (Debal) and Damrila. Hasar, who was the ruler of this territory, took to flight, and embarked in a boat. The Sultán, on reaching the borders of Dowal and Damrila, deputed Khás Khán with a force to Nahrwála, from which place he brought away much spoil and many prisoners. Shortly after, the Sultán entered Dowal and Damrila, and erected a Jámi' mosque in the former place, opposite the temple of an idol.[2] In the meantime,

[1] The *Jahán-kushá* has " winding sheet " instead of " coffin." They both imply the same sentiment, that Fakhru-d dín was fit only to die, and placed his life in the Sultán's hand. The *Táríkh-i Alfí* says " his coffin and his sword suspended from his neck." On the Sultán's return to Persia, we find the repentant generals going through the same emblematic form of contrition.

[2] Firishta says that the name of the chief of Daibal, or Thatta, was Jaishí, and

intelligence was received from 'Irák that Ghiyásu-d dín Sultán had settled himself in 'Irák; that most of the troops of that country professed their attachment to Sultán Jalálu-d dín, and felt anxious for his presence. Upon this the Sultán prepared to join them, but on learning that Durák Hájib was with hostile intentions fortifying the strong post of Durdsir in Kirmán, he determined on proceeding to 'Irák by way of Makrán."

Mírkhond's account of this expedition is very clear and explicit, and is chiefly derived from the *Jahán-kushái* and *Jámi'u-t Tawáríkh*. He is, in some respects, fuller than either of those authorities. The following extracts are taken from the history of the Kings of Khwárizm in the Fourth Book, and the history of Changíz Khán in the Fifth Book of the *Rauzatu-s Safá*:—

"When[1] the Sultán arrived at Ghaznín, which his father, Sultán Muhammad, had bestowed upon him as an appanage, he was joined by the armies of his father, which had been dispersed in different directions. Saifu-d dín Aghrák, with forty thousand Kankalís,[2] Turks, and Khiljs, and Yamín Malik, the governor of Hirát, with his valiant Kurds, were amongst those who joined his standard.

"When spring returned, the Sultán left Ghaznín with his army, and went to Báráni (Parwán) where he fixed his camp. There he learned that Pakchak and Yemghúr[3] were engaged in the siege of Wálián,[4] and they were nearly capturing it, when the Sultán, leaving his heavy baggage in the camp, attacked the Moghals, and put to the sword nearly one thousand men of the advance guard. As the Moghal force was smaller than that of their opponents, it retreated across the river, and after destroying the bridge, fled during the night. The Sultán returned to his camp with much booty, and remained encamped at Báráni.

that the Sultán demolished the temples of the idols at that place. This may probably have been a regal title, for some such name was borne by the son or brother of Dáhir, who was governor of Debal. [See Vol. I. pp. 197, 201.]

[1] [Translated by Sir H. Elliot.]
[2] The *Gensáldemsal* says Kanikli, and calls the governor of Herat "Tizín," but in the next page calls him "Emín."
[3] "Balghúr" in the *Táríkh-i Alfí*. Price reads "Begjek and Yemghúr." Milcs has "Begchuk and Tumkoor."
[4] [See Thomas, *Jour. R. A. S.*, ix. 315.]

APPENDIX. 557

"When Changíz Khán heard of this defeat, he despatched Kútúká[1] and another of the Núyáns, with thirty thousand men, against the Sultán, and himself followed in their rear. As soon as Kútúká reached Bárání, the Sultán prepared for action, and gave orders that his men should dismount and bind the reins of their horses round their waists, fighting only with swords and arrows from morn till evening. At the approach of night, both infidels and Musulmáns retired to their respective camps, and on the return of morn, the Sultán's army saw a double line of troops opposed to them, more than they had contended with the day before. The reason was, that Kútúká during the night had devised a stratagem, by ordering each of his troopers to make human figures with basket-work and felt, and place them in the rear. The Sultán's army, conceiving that reinforcements had reached the Moghals, became alarmed, and proposed to leave the field; but the Sultán making them take heart, prevented them carrying this foolish design into effect, and ordered them again to fight during that day also on foot. After a time, when they saw their own strength and the weakness of the Moghals, they suddenly mounted their horses, and charging the enemy, slew the greater part of these infidols, and the two Núyáns fled, with only a few followers, to Changíz Khán. * * *

"On the day of this victory,[2] a quarrel arose between Saifu-d dín Aghrák and the governor of Hirát respecting a horse, upon which occasion the latter struck Aghrák's horse on the head; and as the Sultán was not confident that any remonstrance of his would be listened to, he did not call the governor to account. The consequence was that during the night Saifu-d dín Aghrák left the camp in anger, and went off with his Kankalí, Turkoman, and Khilj troops towards the hills of Sankrák.[3] * * *

[1] "Sankghór Náyán" in the *Tárikh-i Alfí*, and "Kaikúr" in the original *Jahán-kushái*. D'Ohsson says, "Shiekí Coutoucou." The *Universal History* also has "Kútúká," and places him at the head of eighty thousand men." The *Gemäldesaal* says, "Schiki Kutuhu." Miles has "Kykocr."

[2] The *Modern Universal History*, on the authority of Muhammad of Nessa, says that Jalálu-d dín, after reproaching his prisoners with their cruelties, caused nails to be thrust into their ears, to revenge the miseries which his subjects had so long suffered from the Mongols and Tátárs.

[3] Price reads "Sekrank." Hammer, "Sinkrak." The *Jámi'u-t Tawárikh*, "Sankúrán." Rampoldi says, "Sangrak, non molto distante da Gazna." Miles reads "Sonkran."

"The right wing of the Sultán, which was commanded by Khán Malik, was first attacked by the enemy, and many of his personal attendants and the greater part of his troops were killed. The left wing was also destroyed, but the Sultán kept on fighting from morn till noon, supported by seven hundred men who were with him in the centre, and laid many low in the dust at every attack, performing incredible deeds of valour, of which Rustam and Isfandyár would have been envious. The army of Changíz Khán kept pressing on in increasing numbers, and constantly contracting the space of the Sultán's action, insomuch that they were nearly taking him prisoner. ○ ○ ○

"After his last charge, the Sultán turned his horse's head, and seizing his royal umbrella and throwing off his coat of mail, and lashing his horse, urged him into the river Sind, which was flowing more than thirty feet below the bank. Some of the cavalry followed his example. ○ ○ The Tátár soldiers drew their bows, and the waters of the Sind were red with the blood of the slain. When the Sultán escaped from that danger, he went along the bank of the river, and witnessed the enemy plundering his camp on the opposite side.

"Changíz Khán likewise stood on the bank of the river and watched the Sultán dismount from his horse, take off his saddle, spread his saddle-cloth, his arrows, and his tunic in the sun to dry them, empty the water out of his scabbard, fix his umbrella on the point of his spear, and then sit down under the shade. About the time of afternoon prayers he was joined by seven of his followers who had escaped the whirlpools of the river, and, accompanied by them, at sunset the Sultán went his way. When Changíz Khán saw all this, he seized the collar of his tunic between his teeth;

" 'He lauded him and said, from no father
Will such a son be produced throughout the world.
He is like a victorious lion in a forest,
And as courageous as a crocodile in a river.'

Turning round to his sons, he exclaimed—'Such a son, and no other, should be born to a father:'

" 'No one in the world has seen a man like this,
Nor heard of one amongst the heroes of antiquity.'
○   ○   ●   ○

"This event took place in Rajab, 620 H. (July, 1223 A.D.)

  * * * *

"The Sultán remained two years in Hindustán, * * The officer whom he deputed to Shamsu-d dín was poisoned by that king. When the Sultán left Bisrám, and was passing by Múltán, Kubácha offered opposition, and the Sultán, after defeating him, went to Uch. * * *

"After the Sultán had crossed the Sind, Changíz Khán detached Balá Núyán, with two tumáns, or twenty thousand men, in pursuit. After crossing the river, he arrived at a fort which was held by one of the Sultán's officers, and after the fort was captured, he ordered a general massacre of the inhabitants. Thence he went towards Multán, and the inhabitants closed the gates against him. The Núyán discharged stones from his manjáníks, and demolished some of the gates, and was near taking the fort; but as the Moghals were unable to withstand the excessive heat, the Multánís escaped that Balá (calamity); for Balá Núyán marched away from Multán, and after pillaging and devastating the whole of that province and Laháwar, he went to join Changíz Khán.

  * * * *

"After consulting with his sons and officers, it was finally resolved by Changíz Khán that a detachment of the army should be sent to Kíj and Makrán and the borders of Hind to watch the proceedings of Sultán Jalálu-d dín, and that another should be sent towards Ghaznín to destroy that capital, and the descendants of Subuktigín, so that all desire for the restoration of the Sultán might be extirpated, and should then return towards Túrán in the spring.

"In furtherance of these designs, Changíz Khán sent Chaghtáí with a large army towards the Makráns (Makránát), and Ogtáí was ordered to return to Ghaznín from the lowlands on the banks of the Sind. The chiefs and elders of that city felt themselves compelled to submit; but under the apprehension of further opposition on the part of Sultán Jalálu-d dín, the Moghals sent to Paradise all the inhabitants of that tract,—the old as well as the young, the weak as well as the strong,—and destroyed the colleges and schools, making them the abode of owls.

"After this massacre and pillage Ogtái Kaán, by order of Changíz Khán, went through Garmsír and Hirát towards Máwárán-n nahr and Turkistán. Chaghtái, who had gone to Makrán, after bringing the whole of that country and its borders under subjection, took up his winter-quarters at Kálinjar,[1] a country on the banks of the river Sind. The governor of that province entertained them hospitably, rendered all kinds of acceptable services, and provisioned the Moghals to the fullest extent of his power.

"The greater part of the army fell sick, owing to the badness of the climate. And since many prisoners had fallen into the hands of the Turks, insomuch that each soldier had as many as ten or twenty, ° ° ° orders[2] were issued, as a precautionary measure, to put them all to death. Ambassadors were despatched by Chaghtái to the chiefs[3] who were in the vicinity of his camp, and most of them proffered their allegiance; but against those who were at first submissive and afterwards offered opposition, armies were sent, and they were all put to the sword.[4]

"After the troops had recovered from their sickness, as no tidings of Jalálu-d dín reached them during the time they were in their winter-quarters, they returned with the grand army towards their native country, ° ° and Chaghtái and Ogtái went on a hunting expedition to Bokhárá."

[1] This is not the famous fort in Bundelkhand, nor the hill fort on the frontier of Kashmír mentioned by Firishta (I. 89, 99). The Tárikh-i Alfí says it was "within the confines of Multán." Col. Miles reads "Lanjoor;" but all the readings throughout the Shajratu-l Atrák are adopted without any consideration or authority, and carry no weight with them.

[2] In the corresponding passage in the Jahán-kushái, these orders are attributed to Changíz Khán, which would make it appear that he himself wintered in Hindustán—an improbable supposition.

[3] The Shajratu-l Atrák says, "to the countries of Koch, Kutch, Mukran, and the port of Surat."

[4] There is great confusion of names and places in respect to these winter-quarters. D'Ohsson's statement adds to the difficulty. He says "After the sack of Ghaznín, Ogtái asked leave to besiege Sístán, but Changíz Khán ordered his return on account of the great heat. He cantoned himself on the plain which the Mongols call Bérouan, and pillaged the whole surrounding country. Changíz Khán waited for the Nóyán Bela and Túrtái, and on their arrival he marched, and was joined by Ogtái near the fort of Counaoun Couryan. He wintered in the mountainous country of Bonya-ketver, near the sources (?) of the Sind, where an epidemic sickness broke out. In the spring of the year 1328, Changíz Khán resolved to return to Mongolia by India and Tahbet, after ordering the massacre of the prisoners."

APPENDIX.

A very curious statement respecting this expedition is found in the *Tazkira* of Daulat Sháh, Art., "Jamálu-d dín Muhammad 'Abdu-r Razzák Isfahání," who was a contemporary of the Sultán's. It differs from all other accounts; and much of it is nonsense, but part may be true:—

"Sultán Jalálu-d dín defeated the Moghals in the vicinity of Panjshír, one of the districts of Kábul. * * * When he dismounted from his horse after crossing the Sind, he fixed his spear in the ground, and sat down, drying his turban, clothes, and arms.

"The Khán came to the bank of the river, and praising the gallantry of his antagonist, called out to him on the opposite bank: 'Oh prince, I hear that you are of lofty stature: rise, and let me see you.' Jalálu-d dín rose, and again the Khán addressed him: 'Oh prince, sit down again, for all that I have heard respecting your stature and appearance is exceeded an hundredfold.' Jalálu-d dín sat down, when the Khán again said. 'It was my anxious desire that you should become my vassal; but now go your way in safety.' The Khán then retired from the bank of the river.

"Of the remnant of Jalálu-d dín's army, about seventy men managed to join him by some means or other; and they plundered in the neighbourhood of Lahore an Aughán (Afghán) caravan which was on its way to Multán. They thus set themselves up in arms and equipments, and four hundred of the Afgháns joined the Sultán. It was about that time that the Hazára Láchín, from which tribe Amír Khusrú of Dehli is descended, flying from the neighbourhood of Balkh before the Moghal army, joined the Sultán, to the number of seven hundred men. They took the fort of Kargishghál (?), and the King of Multán made peace with the Sultán. 'Aláu-d dín Kaikubád (Mas'úd (?), a legitimate son of the King of Hind, gave him his daughter in marriage,[1] and the Sultán maintained independent power in Hind during three years and seven months. When

---

[1] We have a sufficient proof that he was handsome, from the fact of the wife of Uzbek Jahán Pahlawán falling in love with him, and betraying her gallant husband's fort to him for the gratification of her passion.

[2] D'Ohsson (ii. 4) also says that, when the Sultán learnt that Shamsu-d dín Altamsh was advancing to render assistance to Kubácha, he went out to oppose him, but, instead of fighting, Altamsh proposed peace and the hand of his daughter, which were both accepted by the Sultán.

intelligence was received of the return of Changíz Khán towards the desert, Sultán Jalálu-d dín left Hind, and went to Kirmán, by way of Kij and Makrán."

The *Táríkh-i Alfí* contains (ann. mort., 609), the following particulars not noticed by the other authors; but in the general narrative it follows the *Jahán-kushá*, the *Jámi'u-t Tawáríkh*, and the *Rauzatu-s Safá* indifferently.

"When Sultán Jalálu-d dín reached Ghaznín, Malik Amín went out to do him honour with fifty Hazáras, and the whole army and peasantry were rejoiced at his arrival. The Sultán married the daughter of Malik Amín, and encamped during the whole winter on the plain of Ghaznín. * * * By reinforcements his army amounted to more than one hundred thousand men.

"Sanakghúr Núyán reached Birwán on the morning of the eighth day after the Sultán had arrived there. The Sultán advanced one parasang and prepared for action, and ordered all his men to dismount their horses, and devote themselves to death in the approaching fight with the infidels. * * The Moghals during the night made figures of men, and placed them in the rear on their spare horses. * * The archers of Malik Saifu-d dín Aghrák put the Moghals to flight and committed great havoc, and the Sultán making a charge with his whole army, completed the rout and slaughter. Sanakghúr Núyán, with another Amír, who commanded the advance, fled to Changíz Khán with only a few followers. * *

"On the retreat towards the Sind or Níláb, Amír Khán, who commanded the rear-guard, was defeated, and fled to the Sultán. * * Changíz Khán gave the strictest orders that every kind of precaution should be taken to prevent the Sultán's crossing the river. * * Amínu-d dín Malik, who commanded the right wing, fled to Peshawar, and falling into the hands of the Moghals, was slain there. * * When Changíz Khán witnessed the Sultán's exploit of swimming the river, he exclaimed, 'A wise man should be cautious in dealing with one who can save himself from such whirlpools and can perform such gallant actions.' * * *

"When the intelligence of the Sultán's successes came to the ears of the world-conquering Changíz Khán, he dispatched two sons of

Amírs, one named Túrtáí and the other Bákín, with an immense army to seize the Sultán, but as his troops were in great alarm at the Moghals, he went towards Dehlí before the enemy could reach him. ° ° Shamsu-d dín to all appearance received 'Ainu-l mulk with great distinction and kindness, but in his heart he entertained the greatest alarm: for like as the Khwárizmsháhís were afraid of the Moghals, so, but to a greater extent, were the soldiers of Hind afraid of those of the Sultán. ° ° The Sultán returned towards Laháwar after his unsuccessful advances to Shamsu-d dín. ° ° °

"Kubácha had collected a large army within the borders of Uch and Multán. Upon this occasion, when he heard of the approach of the Moghals, he foreswore his allegiance to the Sultán, and prepared to demand reparation for former injuries. ° ° °

"At that time the ruler of Tatta was a person called Jaisar, who, when he heard of the approach of the Sultán, placed his treasure and property in a boat, went toward the sea, and took refuge in some of his islands.

"The Sultán remained some time at Tatta, demolished the temples which were there, and built a large Masjid-i jámi'."

Firishta, in the account of this transaction, contained in the *History of Sind* (Vol. ii. pp. 610–5), has followed the *Rauzatu-s Safá* almost verbatim, adding only a few particulars which his greater local knowledge enabled him to supply:—

° ° °

"Sultán Jalálu-d dín, after applying to Shamsu-d dín for such aid as would enable him to return to his native country, where he learnt the sentiments of the Sháh towards him, returned by way of Lahore towards the abodes of the Khakkars, and after arriving in that country, he went to the hills of Balála and Dankála, and thence despatched Tájn-d dín Khilj to the hills of Júdí, to plunder that province. ° ° The Ráí of the Khakkars, Kokár Sanká, who had attained the honour of Islám in the time of Sultán Shahábu-d dín, solicited the Sultán that he would prevent Násiru-d dín Kubácha from harrying his country, as he was for ever doing. The Sultán gave the Ráí's son the title of Kalij Khán, and sent one of his nobles, who was known as Uzbek Báhí (he was Jahán Pahlawán Uzbek), with seven thousand men against Kubácha, the ruler of Uch and Multán, who was encamped with twenty thousand men on the bank of the river Sind, which is near Uch.

"As Uzbek Báshi found Kubácha unprepared, he made a night attack upon him, and so routed the whole camp, that Kubácha with the greatest difficulty was able to flee away on a boat to some other place. Uzbek Báshi remained in Kubácha's camp, and sent to communicate the tidings of his victory to the Sultán, who, when he heard of the advance of the army of Dehli, thinking it not expedient to remain where he was, left that hill-country and went to Uch. ° ° °

"When the weather became hot, the Sultán prepared to take up his summer quarters in the hills of Júd, and Dalála and Dankála. ° ° As soon as the Sultán heard that Chaghtái Khán was in pursuit of him, reflecting upon the fact that, at the commencement of their intercourse, Sháh Násiru-d dín Kubácha had been well affected to him, he went towards Multán, and asked for a contribution in money. Kubácha, hearing of the advance of the Moghal army, rejected the demand, and prepared to wreak vengeance on the Sultán, ° ° who marched on towards Daibal, which is now called Thatta, committing on his road massacre and pillage in every city and town which belonged to Sháh Kubácha. When he arrived at Thatta, the ruler of that place, whose name was Jashi, of the tribe of Súmra, placed his property and wealth on board a boat, and fled in haste with his children and relations to some islands. ° ° °

"Relinquishing the conquest of Sind and Gujerát, the Sultán in the year 620 H., went to 'Irák, by way of Kich and Makrán. ° ° Chaghtá Khán, who was in pursuit of him with the Moghal army, came to Multán and laid siege to that place, but Sháh Násiru-d dín Kubácha exhibited such determined courage, that the siege was raised after forty days, and Chaghtái, marching to Kich and Makrán, and having laid those countries waste, wintered at Kilinjar, a country situated on the banks of the Sind. While quartered there, he put to death nearly thirty or forty thousand Hindustánís who had been taken captive, on the ground that they made the air of the camp pestilential; but as, notwithstanding this butchery, the deaths in the camp still continued, and as the Moghals could obtain no intelligence of Sultán Jalálu-d dín, respecting where he was and what he was doing, Chaghtái Khán broke up his camp and marched towards Túrán. When Sálár Ahmad, the governor of Kálinjar, wrote to Kubácha, complaining of the ruin which had been brought upon his province, that prince was much grieved, and used his best endeavours to restore the country to its former prosperity."

The following extracts from the *Modern Universal History* present some new features. The account is chiefly taken from La Croix's life of Gengiz Can, which is founded upon the biography by Muhammad of Nessa, and the *Jámi'u-t Tawárikh*. Like as in most other portions of Oriental History, so in this, the *Universal History* is the best authority for the English reader to consult.

"The chief reason for the Sultan's quitting Gazna was to give his disunited troops time to rejoin him. He did all that was possible to bring the three Turkish commanders to listen to reason. He wrote and sent to them several times representing the ruin which must attend their separation, and the advantages which might arise from their union.

"They at length suffered themselves to be persuaded by the sense of danger, but it was too late; for Jenghiz Khán, informed of what was in agitation, sent sixty thousand horse to seize the passes, and prevent their joining the Sultan, who, finding himself deprived of this powerful aid, retired towards the river Sind, or Indus. There he halted, in a part where the stream was most rapid, and the place confined, with a view both to take from his soldiers a desire of flying, and prevent the Mungls from bringing up all their army to engage at once. Ever since his departure from Gazna, he had been tormented with a severe colic; yet, at a time when he suffered most, hearing that the enemy's vanguard was arrived at a place called Harder, he quitted his litter and mounted on horseback; then, marching in the night with his chosen troops, surprised the Mungls, and, having cut them almost all to pieces, returned to his camp with a considerable booty.

"Jenghiz Khán, finding by this event that he had to do with a vigilant enemy, proceeded with great circumspection. When he approached the Indus, he drew out his army in battalia: to Jagatay he gave the command of the right wing; the left to Oktay; and put himself in the centre, surrounded by six thousand of his guards. On the other side, Jaláloddín prepared for battle; he first sent the boats on the Indus farther off, reserving only one to carry over the Sultána his mother, the queen his wife, and his children; but unluckily the boat bulged when they were going to embark, so that they were forced to remain in the camp. The Sultán in person assumed the command of the main body. His left wing, drawn up under the shelter of a mountain, which prevented the whole left wing of the Mungls from engaging them at one time, was conducted by his chief wazir; and his right wing by Amín Málek. This lord began the battle, and forced the enemy's left wing to give ground, in spite of all the troops which sustained them. The right wing of the Mungls likewise wanting room to extend itself, the Sultán made use of his left as a body of reserve, detaching from thence squadrons to sustain the other troops. He himself, at the head of the main body, charged that of Jenghiz Khán with so much resolution and vigour, that he put it into disorder, and penetrated to the place where the Khán had at first taken his station; but that prince had retired from thence to give orders for all the troops to engage.

"This disadvantage had like to have lost the Mungls the battle; for the report being spread all over the army that the Sultán had broken through the main body, the troops were so discouraged, that if the Khán had not immediately rode from place to place to show himself, they would certainly have fled. In short, what gained him the battle, was the orders which he gave to Bela Novián to cross the mountain, if practicable, and attack the Sultán's left wing, which the Khán observed had been much weakened by the several detachments. Bela, accordingly, conducted by a guide, marched betwixt rocks and dreadful precipices, and, attacking that disabled wing behind, obliged it to give way. The Sultán's troops, which were in all but thirty thousand, much fatigued with having fought ten whole hours against more than three hundred thousand men, were seized with a panic, and fled. In this confusion his eldest son was taken prisoner. One part of the troops retired to the rocks on the banks of the Indus, where the enemy's horse could not follow them. Many others, closely pursued by the Mungls, threw themselves into the river, some of whom happily crossed over; while the rest placing themselves round their prince, continued the fight through despair.

  o   o   o   o   o

"When he was in the middle of the river, he stopped to insult Jenghiz Khán, who was come to the bank to admire his courage, and emptied his quiver of arrows against him. Some brave Mungl captains would have thrown themselves into the river to swim after Jaláloddín, but the grand Khán would not permit them, telling them this prince would defeat all their attempts.

o o o o o o o o o o o

"This prince as soon as he was landed safe in India, ascended a tree to pass the night secure from wild beasts. Next day, as he walked melancholy along the banks to see if any of his people appeared, he perceived a troop of soldiers with some officers, three of whom proved to be his particular friends. These, at the beginning of the defeat, had found a boat, in which they sailed all night with much danger from the rocks, shelves, and violence of the current. Soon after he was joined by three hundred horse, who informed him of four thousand more saved by swimming over two leagues from thence. The Sultán went to meet them, and promised to provide for their necessities. Mean time Jamálorrazad, an officer of his household, who was not at the battle, knowing that his master and many of his people had escaped, ventured to load a very large boat with arms, provisions, money, and stuff to clothe the soldiers, and cross over to him; for which eminent piece of service Jaláloddín appointed him great steward of his household, and surnamed him Ekteároddín; that is, *the chosen, or the glory of the faith.*

o o o o o o o o o

"On this intelligence, Jenghiz Khán sent orders to his brother Utakín, and marched with the troops that remained with him as far as Kandahar, which he took.

"Some time after the reduction of this fortress, Multán, a city of India, was subdued by Bela Nevián, who had orders to conquer Lahúr also; but, as he was informed there was in that place a stronger army than his own, he did not go thither. A Patán prince, named Kobádia, had sent those forces, thinking he had more reason to provide against the Mungls than against Jaláloddin; for, although the Sultán was then in arms on his frontiers, yet he had only a few troops with him, and could only make a slight irruption into the territories of a prince named Rána, whom he slew for having insulted him in his distress.

* * * * * * * *

"The defenders of Gazna made frequent sallies on the besiegers, several times destroyed their works, and broke above a hundred of their battering-rams; but one night, after an obstinate engagement in which Oktay fought in person to encourage his soldiers, who began to be intimidated, one side of the city walls fell down, and, filling up the ditch, a great number of Mungls easily entered sword in hand. The governor, seeing all lost, at the head of his bravest soldiers, charged among the thickest of his enemies, where he and his followers were slain. However, Gazna was not entirely ruined, nor did all the inhabitants perish; for after the pillage had lasted four or five hours, Oktay ordered it to cease, and taxed the people who were left alive at a certain rate to redeem themselves and the city. This prince continued here till the whole province was reduced, and then went to rejoin his father in Tartary.

"Meantime, Jagatay having entered Kermán, the ancient Karamania of Persia, took by degrees all the cities in that province. After he had reduced Tiz, one of the first cities, with some other places which he destroyed, he proceeded to Kalánjer, a country bordering on Hindustan, where, intending to pass the winter, the soldiers by the help of their slaves built houses, cultivated gardens, and kept flocks of sheep, as if they intended to make a settlement; but when the scorching winds began to blow, to which they were not accustomed, almost all of them fell sick, while the greater part of those who lived became so weak and languid that they were not fit for service. By this distemper the country of Fárs, or Párs, which is the proper Persia, and that part of Khúzestán which belonged to Kayssoddín, Sultán Jaláloddín's younger brother, escaped for this time the invasion of the Mungls. Jagatay, by removing his troops from one place to another, gradually restored them to health; and finding the slaves which the soldiers had taken were a burthen, ordered the throats of the greater part of them to be cut. Then having committed the care of the conquered countries to one of his lieutenants, he, pursuant to his father's orders, directed his course to Bálkh, where the general rendezvous was appointed."

The account of Rampoldi, in his *Annali Musulmani*, differs much from others, and contains many improbabilities, notwithstanding that he quotes Mirkhond and translates D'Herbelot; yet, as it is founded in some portions on independent Arabic sources, it presents some passages worthy of translation:—

* * * *

"In the tract of country between Kábul and the Indus, according to the account of Kara Tchelebi, the Tartars, after the manner of locusts, had spread desolation and extermination with ineffable rapidity, and inflicted such damage, that six centuries were not able to repair it. * * *

* * * *

"The Sultán was prevented making his last desperate charge by his nephew Malek Agiasch, who said, 'Beware how you precipitate yourself rashly upon those who so surpass you in numbers, lest you be accused of madness, as one who deals a blow upon the edge of a razor.' * * * The hundred thousand Tartars did not cease to discharge at him a million of arrows, but were not able to hit him. When he had passed the greatest current of the stream, he was obliged to go much further in order to find a ford, as the banks of the Indus were nearly everywhere very steep. He saved himself finally at the ford of Kaitoul. * * Only seven soldiers out of the three hundred¹ who had dared to follow, unwilling to abandon the unhappy prince, escaped to the opposite bank: the rest being either slain by arrows or drowned in the river. Among the latter was his nephew, Malek al Agiasch. * * *

"Oktay took Gazna by assault after a siege of four months. It was burnt and destroyed to the very foundation, after about two hundred thousand persons had been inhumanly massacred.

* * * * *

"The Sultán having composed an army out of these refugees, thought of obtaining for himself an asylum, and a principality at

¹ De Guignes says four thousand.

the same time, beyond the Ganges, because the whole country which extended on both banks of the Indus had been successively subdued by Jenghiz, who had made himself master of Multán, Lahor, Jenghapúr, Dehli, and Agra, compelling the freedmen of Scheab-o'ddin of Gaur, who had possessed themselves of those places within the last fifteen years, to flee from their abodes and abandon their estates, or at least to repair to some lofty castles, which by their situation were judged to be impregnable, at least for many years. ° ° °

"The troops of Jenghiz triumphantly overran in this year (1223) the whole country, from the Ganges and Indus to the Caspian Sea, and from the Sihoun to the Euphrates. ° ° Jenghiz returning from India, closed the warlike achievements of this year by taking Khandaar.

° ° ° ° . °

"Scarcely had Jelale'ddin Mankberni learnt that Jenghiz had crossed the Sihoun with the greater part of his Mongols, and had taken the road of Tartary, when he repassed the Indus and entered Persia, through the provinces of Kaboul, Gazna, and Kandaar, and immediately occupied Mekran, Sejestan, and Farsestan, expelling everywhere the few Mongols who had remained to protect those conquests. ° ° ° While the Sultán was engaged in recovering his dominions in Persia, his brother Tatar Shah was extending his conquests in Hindustan, where in a short time he conquered and expelled every Mongol who dared to show his face."

D'Ohsson observes that neither the date nor the place of action on the Sind is known. "'Aláu-d dín says it took place in the month of Rajab (August), but Muhammad of Nessa says the 22nd of Shawwál (9th December), which appears more exact. Nowhere do we find any precise indication of the place which was the theatre of this event."

Price says the action at Barwán took place probably in the spring of 618 A.H. (1221 A.D.), in which D'Ohsson concurs; and that the action on the Indus took place in Rajab of that year, or September, 1221, but he is disposed to place it a year later. But there is no reason to doubt that it took place in 1221 A.D., and as the action of

Parwán certainly occurred in the spring of that year. It would be much too late to defer the action on the Indus till December, for the retreat to the Sind was nearly instantaneous after the action at Parwán. Independent of which, the march from Ghazní to the Sind would have been impracticable in December, and the passage of the river would have been no such very gallant feat in that month, when the river was at its lowest. Besides, what becomes of the proverb which is said to have celebrated the occasion: "Marvels occur in Rajab." And although it is highly improbable that the event did give occasion to the proverb, inasmuch as it is in Arabic—a language spoken by no class of people concerned in the transaction—yet an old proverb may have been made applicable to the event, and as it is quoted by an author nearly contemporary, we may be sure that Rajab and no other was the month in which the achievement was performed.

The crossing of the Indus in the same fashion had been accomplished four years before by Shamsu-d dín Altamsh, when in pursuit of Násiru-d dín Kubácha, and though he succeeded in reaching the opposite bank with a few followers, many were drowned in the attempt. The credit which has been given in later years to Mahárájá Ranjít Sing for the same feat, was not so well earned, because he caused his cavalry and infantry to ford the Indus where the bottom is rocky and shingly, and where the stream was not more than knee deep, though the current was so rapid as to make the footing insecure. Many men and horses certainly were lost, but Ranjít Sing himself crossed on an elephant.

Respecting the place where the Sultán crossed the Indus there is much doubt. Hammer, however, sees no difficulty, reproving D'Ohsson for not knowing that it was at the ford of Kaitul, quoting for his authority D'Herbelot, who calls it Caitool, quoting for his authority Muhammad of Nessa. But the question is where is Kaitul or Caitool?

NOTE I.
Karmatians.

[The religion of Islám had no sooner become a power than divisions, feuds, and schisms broke out among its professors. Dissensions and heresies appear to be inseparable from all newly-established creeds, and the fervid Oriental temper, excited to the highest pitch by the worldly success and the intolerant fanatical doctrines of Islám, impelled professing Musulmáns to unparalleled excesses and most execrable crimes. The overthrown but uneradicated superstitions of the old religion, and the mystical theology and philosophy of nations with which the Muhammadans came in contact, had their share in the production and development of these heresies; but the acting moving spirit which gave them political importance was lust of personal distinction and temporal power. Thus the principal divisions turn upon the question of the rightful succession to the Prophet in the office of "Leader of the Faithful."

One of these heretical sects, the Karmatians, appear on the scene very frequently in the present volume. This sect is an offshoot of the Isma'ilian heresy, and is often confounded with it. There were some points of doctrinal difference, but the uninitiated were ignorant of them, and unable to distinguish them; so the two names came to be often used indifferently. Orthodox writers, hating and despising the heretics, were prone to speak of them by some general name; or if they attempted to be more specific, their ignorance frequently led to a confusion and misappropriation of terms. Thus the title Isma'ilian includes Karmatians, Assassins, and others, and for the Isma'ilians the wider term "*Mulāḥida*, heretics" is often used.

The Isma'ilians do not admit the rightful succession of the Imáms recognised by the orthodox. They acknowledge 'Alí, Hasan, and Husain, but maintain that the line closed with Isma'il, son of Ja'far Sádik, who was the seventh and last Imám. From him they take the name Isma'ilian, and from him also they are called "Seveners." The teaching of the Isma'ilians put a metaphorical interpretation on the Kurán, which tended to explain away and supersede its doctrines, leaving only a negative religion, and substituting license for morality. The doctrines of the Isma'ilians were embraced by a man named 'Abdu-llah, son of Maimún, a native of Persia, who devoted his powers not only to the overthrow of Arab ascendancy, but to the subversion of Islám and indeed of all religion. His mode of action was by secret influence and missionary exertion. The culminating doctrine of his teaching was the vanity of all

APPENDIX. 573

religions, and the indifference of men's actions, the good receiving
no recompense, the evil no chastisement, either in this world or
the next.

Among the followers of 'Abdu-llah was one named Ahmad, or,
as he was afterwards called, "Karmat." He rose about the year
278 н. (891 A.D.), and was the founder of the Karmatians. The
term *Karmata* or *Karmat* belongs to a kind of Arabic writing in
which the letters are very small and the lines very close. This style
being well suited for secret communications, was adopted by Ahmad,
and hence he was called Karmat, and his followers Karmati or
Karámata, *anglicè* Karmatians. Teaching the doctrine that everything desirable was allowable, he differed from his predecessors by
endeavouring to carry out his views by violence, and began an open
unrelenting war upon the ruling powers. In 290 н. (903 A.D.), the
Karmatians made a fearful inroad into Syria, and in 311 (923 A.D.),
they plundered Basra and Kúfa. In 319 н. (931 A.D.), under a
famous leader, Abú Táhir, they took the city of Mecca with terrible
slaughter, plundered the temple, and carried away the holy *hijra-l
aswad*, or black stone, which they retained for twenty years. Ar
Rází, the twentieth Khalíf, actually agreed to pay them an annual
subsidy to secure the safe passage of the pilgrims to Mecca.

The Fatimide throne of Egypt, founded by an Isma'ílian in 297 н.
(909-10 A.D.), in rivalry of the Arabian *Khiláfat*, grew rapidly in
power, and became a source of great jealousy and trouble to the
occupants of the throne of Baghdad. Political rivalry thus combined with religious hatred to make the war between the faithful
and the heretics most savage and unrelenting.

From the Isma'ílians sprang another sect which forced itself
upon the notice of the Crusaders and introduced a new word,
"*Assassin*,"[1] into the languages of Europe. This sect was founded
by a native of Re, named Hasan Sabáh, who was schoolfellow and

[1] [De Sacy insists, though his dictum has been disputed, that this term is derived from the term "*hashishin*," hemp eaters, because these fanatics probably infuriated themselves with this drug in preparation for their bloody work; but he acknowledges that there is no proof of such having been their practice. The fanatical fury of these murderers hardly needed any stimulus, and the craft as well as the boldness which they exhibited in the execution of their designs are hardly referrible to a state of frenzied inebriation. Does not the name of their founder *Hasan* or *Al Hasan* present sufficient materials for the formation of the word *Assassin* ?]

companion of Nizámu-l mulk, the well known wazír of the Saljúkí government, and author of the *Majma'u-l Wasáya*. An extract from that work, in page 490 of this volume, gives some account of this redoubtable character. The forcible removal of all foes and rivals by the dagger of the assassin, was the profession and the distinctive practice of this abominable sect. Nizámu-l mulk, above referred to, fell under their daggers, and the author of the *Jahán-kushá* had nearly become a victim to Isma'ílian assassins. In 483 H. Hasan Sabáh obtained possession of the strong fortress of Alah-amút, or Alamút (the eagle's nest), in the province of Rúdbár, about eleven parasangs north of Kazwín, and here he and his descendants maintained themselves for nearly two centuries,[1] when the fortress and many others fell under the iron tread of the Mongols. The excesses of the Assassins had impelled Mangú Khán to determine upon the extermination of the whole sect of Isma'ílians, and under him and his successor Hulákú their fortresses were taken, and many thousands of their men, women, children, and babes at the breast, were put to the sword.

The Karmatians appeared to have pushed themselves eastwards into the valley of the Indus at an early period. From Bírúní we learn that the Karmatians destroyed the great idol at Multán, and the heretical chief, whom Mahmúd of Ghazní drove away from that town, was no doubt a member of this sect, for the name of Karmatian is applied to him by one or two writers, although the more general name of *Mulihida* is more frequently used.

Mahmúd's wazír, Hasnak, was brought to the stake by Mas'úd upon the charge of being a Karmatian. The personal enmity of Mas'úd no doubt precipitated this act; but there is ample proof that the Khalíf was greatly incensed against the wazír for having received a *khil'at* from the Egyptian Khalíf, and that he had urged Mahmúd so strongly to execute him that the incensed monarch broke out in the indignant words recorded by Baihakí: "Tell the doting old Khalíf that out of regard to the 'Abbásides I have modelled

[1] [From this stronghold the Chief of the Assassins was called the *Shaikhu-l jabbal* or, as we have it in English, the "Old Man of the Mountain."]

[2] [The Assassins are the *Mulhidat-i Alamút*, who are stated to have been patronised by 'Aláu-d dín Ghorí. He is censured for the attention he paid to them by the author of the *Tabakát-i Násirí*, *supra* p. 289.]

with all the world. I am hunting for the Karmatians, and wherever one is found he is impaled. If it were proved that Hasnak is a Karmatian, the Commander of the Faithful should soon see what had happened to him. But I have brought him up, and he is to me as my sons and my brothers. If he is a Karmatian, so am I." When Mahmúd departed, and Hasnak's enemy succeeded, the Khalif's animosity was soon appeased.

Though Mahmúd expelled the Karmatian chief from Multán, the heresy was not suppressed, for in 571 (1175 A.D.). Muhammad Ghori once more "delivered Multán from the hands of the Karmatians."[1] In 634 (1237 A.D.) we find them in some force at Dehli, where they made a concerted assault upon the faithful in the great mosque, and slew a considerable number; but they were finally overpowered, "and every heretic and Karmatian was sent to hell."][2]

NOTE J.

Geographical Index.

[The following descriptive list of countries and places, more or less frequently referred to in the preceding pages, will probably be found useful, and may obviate the necessity of reference and enquiry. Some of the names are well known, and are marked on the maps; but others are only to be found in the works of the old geographers.

Bardasír.—A large town of Kirmán, on the road leading to Khurásán, lying north-east of the town of Kirmán. It is also called Kawáshír.

Bust.—A city of the district of Garmsír, in Sijistán. It is situated on the west of the river Helmand, and is noted for its great heat.

Dáwar.—Known in old times as the "Biládu-d dáwar," and by the modern inhabitants as Zamín-dáwar. A large province, con-

---

[1] [*Supra*, p. 293.]
[2] [See Vol. i. of this work, pp. 453, 481, and 491, and Vol. ii. pp. 93, 293, and 336; Hammer Purgstall, *History of the Assassins*; Defrémery, *Histoire des Séljoucides et des Ismaéliens*; D'Herbelot, v. *Carmath*; Price, *Mahommedan History*, Vol. ii. pp. 167, 333; Reinaud, *Fragments*, p. 142; *Mém. sur l'Inde*, p. 264; Rampoldi, v. 367; *Das Buch der Länder*, 2nd Index; Dorn, 89; Gibbon, chap. liv.]

tiguous to Rakhkhaj, Dust, and Ghor, and the opening of the latter to Sijistán. Elphinstone says: "On the right bank of the river (Helmand) lies the rich country of Zamín-dáwar, which has the Parapomisar mountains on the north, and some hills connected with that range are found within its limits. This fine country extends for forty or fifty miles to the west of the Helmand."—See Elphinstone's *Caubul.* 4to., p. 122; Reinand, *Mém. sur l'Inde*, 173.

Fáriyáb.—See Tálikán.

Garmsír.—The hot country, so called from the heat of the climate. A narrow tract of country in Sijistán, along the lower course of the Helmand.—See Thornton, *Garmschl.*

Ghor.—Also called Ghoristán. The mountainous country between Hirát and Ghazni. According to Istakhrí and Ibn Haukal it was a rugged mountainous country, bounded by the districts of Hirát, Farrah, Dáwar, Rabát, Kurwán, and Gharjistán back to Hirát, which were all Muhammadan countries. Ghor itself was a country of infidels, containing only a few Musulmáns, and the inhabitants spoke a language different from that of Khurásán.—See Elphinstone's *Caubul*, Vol. i., p. 244.

Gharjistán.—The correct orthography of this name according to Yákút and others is Gharjistán or Gharshistán. Yákút says it is bounded on the west by Hirát, east by Ghor, north by Merv, and south by Ghazní. The ruler of the country was called Shar, and from this title the land was also called Gharju-s Shar. The Mervrúd waters the country, and its chief towns are Bashín and Súrmín, but the Shar generally dwells at a town in the hills called Bilkan.[1]

Gílán.—(In Arabic, *Jílán.*) A country between the Caspian and Black Seas, in great part the same as Tabaristán.

Gilgit.—A small unexplored country on the southern declivity of the Hindu Kush, between Chitral on the west, and Baltistán (Little Tibet) on the east.—Burnes, *Bokhara II.*, 209.

Gurdes.—A country between Ghazni and India.

Júzján.—Also called Júzjánán. Júzján is the Arabic form of the native name Gúzgán. It must not be confounded with the country of Jurján or Gurgán, on the eastern shores of the Caspian. Yákút

[1] [Colonel Anderson's text of Ibn Haukal makes the name of this place to be "Kankán," or, as he transcribes it, "Ouagan."]

APPENDIX. 577

says the names Júzján or Júzjánín both designate a large district of the province of Balkh, between that city and Merv. The chief town was Yahúdíya, and Ibn Haukal mentions Shabúrkán, Andkhod, and Ambár among its principal places, adding that Ambár was the largest town.

Kazwín.—In Persian, *Kazbín* or *Kashwín.* A celebrated town of Persia, a little to the west of Teherán.

Khwárizm.—Choresmia. The country on the east of the Caspian Sea, the capital of which was Gurgánj,[1] The Arabs converted the name of the country into Jurján, and that of the capital to Jurjániyá. The Mongol form of the name was Orgánj. Noshtigín, a Turkí slave of Malíksháh Saljúk, was made governor of this province, and contrived to secure his independence. His son, Kutbu-d dín, extended his dominions, and acquired the title of Khwárizm Sháh, a name which had been borne by the rulers of the country before the Muhammadan rule. The empire of the Khwárizm Sháhs rose upon the ruins of the Saljúk dynasty, and their territories extended from Ázarbáíján and the Caspian Sea to the Indus, and from the Persian Gulf to above the Síhún or Jaxartes. A succession of nine princes reigned for 138 years from 491 to 628 Hijra (1097 to 1230 A.D.) : but in 618 H. the last of them, Jalálu-d dín Mankburní was driven by Changíz Khán beyond the Indus, and he was killed in Mesopotamia ten years afterwards, stripped of all his dominions.

Kum.—A town of 'Irák-'ajamí, between Teherán and Ispahán.

Máwaráu-n Nahr.—" (The country) which is beyond the river (Oxus);" Transoxiana, including Bokhárá and Samarkand.

Ra or Raiy.—An ancient city, the ruins of which are situated a little to the south of Teherán. All Oriental writers agree upon its antiquity, and it is called "the mother of cities." It was once a very large place, the capital of the Jabbál (the hills), and very rich and flourishing; but it was destroyed, and the inhabitants were put to the sword by the Tatars at the beginning of the seventh century of the Hijra.

Rakhaj.—Or more properly *Rukhkhaj*, from which, preceded by

[1] [The town of Khwárizm or Kás (Káth), on the east of the Jíhún, was for a time the capital. See Defrémery, *Hist. des Samanides*, p. 275; D'Ohsson, *Hist. des Mongols*, i. 138; Jaubert's *Édrisí*, ii. 192; Aboulfeda, 479.]

the article *al* (ar Rukhaj) comes the Arachosia of the ancient geographers. One of the dependencies of Sijistán, the chief town of which, bearing the same name, was situated on the Hindmand or Helmand.

Sabúrkán, Shabúrkán.—A city of Júzján, west of Balkh. The Shibbergán and Shuborgán of the Maps.

Sakáwand.—In the territory of Kábul, which belonged to Kumlu. It is mentioned by Istakhrí and Ibn Haukal as one of the dependencies of Bámián, along with Kábul, Ghazní, and Parwán. Idrísí gives it as being seven days' journey from Kábul, and the same distance from Khuuïab, for which I would read Hariab, حرياب, as I believe it to be the Iryáb or Irjáb of Sharífu-d dín and the Haryúb of the present day,—which is at the head of the Kuram valley, to the south-east of Kábul. Sakáwand would therefore be at or near Jalálábád;—and this position agrees with Idrísí's account of the warm climate of Sakáwand and Haríáb, at which places the palm tree did not grow, and snow did not fall. The Buddhist establishments mentioned by Fa Hian and Huen Thsang were no doubt still flourishing in the time of Kumlu.—*Gen. Cunningham.*

Sarakhs.—An ancient city of Khurásán, situated about mid-way or six days' journey, between Merv and Naishápúr,

Sijistán.—Same as *Sistán.* A province south of Hirát.

Takinábád.—A large city of Garmsír.—See *Tabakát-i Násirí*, supra, p. 293.

Tálikán.—A city of Tukháristán between Balkh and Merv, three days' journey from the latter. There is another town of the same name east of Kunduz. The Tálikán of Tukháristán is the one most frequently mentioned, and it is generally coupled with Fáriyáb, a city of Júzján west of the Oxus, three days' journey from Tálikán, three from Shabúrkán, and six from Balkh.—See Elphinstone's *Caubul*, ii., 221, 240.

Tukháristán, Tukhíristán.—A province of Balkh, lying east of the city of that name, and west of the Jihún. The chief town was Tálikán.

Tús.—An ancient city of Khurásán, two marches N.E. from Naishápúr, and a little to the north of the modern town of Meshhed. It consisted of two towns, Tabarán and Núkán, and was a place of considerable importance. The city was devastated by the Uzbeks in 996 H. (1588 A.D.), and its place has been taken by Meshhed.

Zábul, Zábulistán, Záwulistán.—A large province south of Balkh and Kábul, including Sistán, and having Ghazní for its capital. Rustam Zábulí, the hero of the Sháh-náma, is said to have been a native of this country.

Zaranj.—The chief town of Sijistán, from which the lake formed by the Helmand and the Farra is often called the Lake of Zaranj (the Zarrah of the Maps).

Zúr.—Name of a mountain in Dáwar, and of a celebrated idol which was there worshipped. According to Elphinstone, it is in the middle of the Lake Zaranj or Zarrah, which the natives call the Sea of Zúr. Conolly however says it is not in the lake, but in the vicinity of it.—See Elphinstone's *Caubul*, Book iv. chap. iv. ; Reinaud, *Mém. sur l'Inde*, p. 174.]

END OF VOL. II.

www.ingramcontent.com/pod-product-compliance
Lightning Source LLC
Chambersburg PA
CBHW031934290426
44108CB00011B/547